TWENTY LESSONS

IN ENVIRONMENTAL SOCIOLOGY

THIRD EDITION

Kenneth A. Gould

Brooklyn College of the City University of New York

Tammy L. Lewis

Brooklyn College of the City University of New York

New York   Oxford

OXFORD UNIVERSITY PRESS

Oxford University Press is a department of the University of Oxford.
It furthers the University's objective of excellence in research, scholarship,
and education by publishing worldwide. Oxford is a registered trade mark of
Oxford University Press in the UK and certain other countries.

Published in the United States of America by Oxford University Press
198 Madison Avenue, New York, NY 10016, United States of America.

Library of Congress Cataloging-in-Publication Data

Names: Gould, Kenneth Alan, author. | Lewis, Tammy L., author.
Title: Twenty lessons in environmental sociology / Kenneth A. Gould, Tammy
    L. Lewis.
Description: Third edition. | New York : Oxford University Press, 2021. |
    Includes bibliographical references and index. | Summary: "This is a
    textbook on environmental sociology"—Provided by publisher.
Identifiers: LCCN 2020017083 (print) | LCCN 2020017084 (ebook) | ISBN
    9780190088514 (paperback) | ISBN 9780190088521 (ebook)
Classification: LCC GE195 .G68 2021 (print) | LCC GE195 (ebook) | DDC
    304.2—dc23
LC record available at https://lccn.loc.gov/2020017083
LC ebook record available at https://lccn.loc.gov/2020017084

Printing number: 9 8 7 6 5 4 3 2
Printed by LSC Communications, Inc., United States of America

The First edition was dedicated to Anna and Isabel.
The Second edition was dedicated to Allan Schnaiberg.
The Third edition is dedicated to Rachel Carson.

Contents

This book was artisanally crafted in Brooklyn, NY under Covid-19 quarantine.

Annotated Table of Contents

Internet; and a person physically dismantling a computer that has been "thrown away" in the United States and exported to an "e-waste processing center" in another country. Although these snapshots are only three out of many possibilities, they offer an excellent opportunity to connect structures across time and space and to learn about the insights and creative uses of theory in environmental sociology.

Part 2   Systemic Causes of Environmental Disruption

of characterizing the dominant mode of state policymaking. Specifically, it argues that, in practice, the United States is generally less pluralist than one might hope. Offering a sampling of theories of environment–society relationships, social inequality, and state formation—it proposes that to better understand how contemporary US policies result in environmental racism and inequality, one must consider the historical, legal, economic, and cultural roots and evolution of the US nation-state itself. Such an exploration suggests that the United States remains an imperial presence in the Americas and globally, and this has dire consequences for any effort to produce social and environmental justice here or elsewhere. In this way, we might locate the deeper origins of the environmental state and, in turn, think through a different set of questions that might achieve reform or transformation of those practices. It concludes by offering thoughts for how individuals and groups might address these challenges, drawing on recent and ongoing cases in North America.

4. Labor Productivity and the Environment   76
Allan Schnaiberg and Kenneth A. Gould

Increasing labor productivity has come to be viewed by political, economic, and academic elites as a panacea for economic progress. Yet this perspective represents only one view of increasing production by workers. The mechanisms by which labor productivity is achieved typically include substantial labor reduction, involving downsizing and shifts of the benefits of productivity away from workers and consumers and toward investors and senior management. Moreover, because replacing human labor with mechanical, chemical, and electronic technologies often requires heightened use of energy and water and increased disposal of wastes into natural systems, ecological disruption is typically associated with growing labor productivity through changes in production technology.

5. Corporate Power: The Role of the Global Media in Shaping What We Know about the Environment   86
Elizabeth H. Campbell

Transnational corporations (TNCs) are the most dominant and powerful social actors in the global political economy. Their main goal is to access markets, cheap labor, and resources to maximize their profit margin and returns to shareholders. They have been successful in eroding or delaying local, national, regional, and global environmental and public health protection mechanisms through powerful special interest groups that lobby governments and global institutions. The largest TNCs have more political and economic power than many developing countries. In the absence of strong state regulations, TNCs' power in the 21st century has served to undermine social welfare benefits, job security, public health, and environmental standards. This has not been widely reported in the global news media since the media are increasingly controlled by these same TNCs. It is not in the interests of TNCs to critique the social and environmental consequences of their growing influence in the global economy. Corporate control over news and information strongly shapes what the public knows and does not know about key social and environmental issues. The control of news, media, and information is a critical form of power in environmental conflicts.

Environmental sociology is grounded in the recognition that all societies are part of ecosystems and that environmental problems stem from real conditions in the world. Thus, environmental sociologists engage with natural science to understand socioecological processes. However, it is important to examine how scientific research and the political and social uses of science can be manipulated by people in power, particularly leaders of corporations and politicians. Sociologists recognize that science is both a way of gaining knowledge of the world (the logic of science) and a set of social institutions (the establishment of science). The logic of science, which is based on a combination of empirical and rationalist philosophies, must be the foundation for sociological inquiry into human-environment interactions, but how the establishment of science is influenced by social context must also be studied.

A key factor in the way that societies establish their interactions with ecosystems is the choice of technologies they use and the ways they use them. Throughout human history, technological change has led to significant, sometimes dramatic, changes in the relationship between social systems and ecosystems. Because of the importance of technological change and technological choice in establishing patterns of social system–ecosystem relationships, we need to understand how technological innovation alters social systems and ecosystems and how and why societies develop and implement new technologies. This lesson looks back at major epochs in the technological transformation of society–environment dynamics and explores the interests of the social institutions that most affect the future direction of technological change.

must shift national and international policy discussions away from simply reducing carbon emissions to limiting the overall amount of energy that is available for consumption and actively suppressing fossil fuel production. The lesson concludes with some ideas for how to begin this change and invites the reader to think about ways that life could actually be improved if we were to reduce the amount of energy we were able to consume on a daily basis.

Part 3 Some Social Consequences of Environmental Disruption

United States are presumed to be safe before they go onto the market, and most have never been properly tested for their environmental health impacts. Without a strong regulatory system that prioritizes environmental health, individuals are on their own to determine if there are harmful substances in their water, air, soil, food, and consumer products. Women, by virtue of their physiology and their role as the primary shoppers and caregivers within the home, are now expected to protect their families from chemical exposures through a consumer practice called precautionary consumption. The lesson concludes by outlining new issues capturing sociologists' attention and reasons for optimism that improvements to our environmental health are possible in the future.

Most of the food people eat today arrives on their plates through a food and agriculture system that is globalized, corporatized, and industrialized. The first part of this lesson outlines how such a food and agriculture system came to be and what it means for food to be globalized, corporatized, and industrialized. The second part of the lesson examines the social and environmental implications of food and agriculture today. This includes the significant environmental degradation resulting from intensive resource use and high chemical use, the dangers of farm work, and the persistence of hunger and the rise of obesity. The effects of food and agriculture on development are also analyzed, including the depopulation of rural areas, the privatization and commodification of formerly public goods, and the rise of slums in the Global South. The last part of the lesson examines efforts to make food and agriculture more sustainable, just, and healthy. This includes efforts by both alternative food and agriculture movements and their use of market-based forms of activism, as well as food justice movements.

Farms do not leap to mind as significant polluters. Yet, pollution from agriculture and especially livestock operations may now be the largest contaminant of America's waterways. This lesson uses the transformation of eastern North Carolina's pork industry as a case study to explain how industrialized agriculture has become a leading polluter. The lesson describes the recent growth and restructuring of that industry and its widespread adoption of confined animal feeding operation technologies.

The concept of "externalities of scale" is introduced, which encompasses the various economic, social, and environmental harms associated with large-scale production and absent in smaller operations. The lesson then describes how this industry has negative impacts on the health, quality of life, and economic well-being of surrounding communities. Exploring the issue further, the authors describe how this industry has affected the ecology of eastern North Carolina, an environment particularly vulnerable to this form of production. They also detail the political struggle surrounding the industry, and highlight the roles of various stakeholders in both promoting and opposing these changes. The authors conclude that the transformation of hog production in eastern North Carolina and the associated negative consequences are illustrative of broader trends in how animals are being raised throughout industrialized nations.

While landscapes, storm events, built environments, and populations interact in different ways in every storm, less-privileged people are consistently hit the hardest by disasters. The impacts of floods and hurricanes in particular are not just a matter of the intensity of the wind or of the amount of rainfall that an area receives. Rather, these disasters are the result of a complex mix of natural and human causes that stem from of the intersection of various forms of vulnerability and social inequality. Physical vulnerability refers to the risk of being exposed to hazards that are specific to a particular location, such as tornadoes or earthquakes, while social vulnerability refers to the ways in which gender, race, class, age, and so forth serve to make someone more likely to be impacted by a disaster and to have difficulty accessing the resources they need to recover from it afterward. Mitigation efforts that attempt to prevent or reduce storm impacts, such as levees, better evacuation routes and communication networks, and flood insurance policies, are often helpful in the short term. However, they can make matters worse in the long term by encouraging populations to remain in flood-prone locations or by exacerbating preexisting social inequalities by helping middle- and upper-class home and business owners rebuild at the expense of low-income communities. Creating communities that are resilient to disasters is extremely difficult and involves making difficult choices about how to restrict or regulate land use in ways that are fair and equitable.

The purpose of this lesson is to provide a sociological approach for understanding global climate change, perhaps the most daunting crisis facing all of humanity. It provides a general overview of the causes and consequences of climate change and how incorporation of a sociological imagination augments our understanding of these topics. The lesson begins by treating the scientific basis of climate change dynamics, with particular focus on sociological theories surrounding the anthropogenic drivers and consequences of climate change. Applying the arsenal of sociological theories to the topic of climate change requires rigorous attention to the inequalities surrounding its causes and effects, which include disparities at the inter- and intranational levels. Using diverse theoretical perspectives, the lesson situates climate change within global political-economy and global inequality dynamics. We then shift focus to intranational inequalities and demonstrate the efficacy of applying an intersectionality framework to enhance understanding of the topics at hand. The chapter ends with a discussion of current efforts to address and deny climate change, the political landscapes that serve as backdrops to both, and possibilities for future alternatives.

Part 4   Some Social Responses to Environmental Disruption

16.   Normalizing the Unthinkable: Climate Denial and Everyday Life   295

Kari Marie Norgaard

Global warming is the most significant environmental issue of our time, yet public response in Western nations has been meager. Why have so few taken any action? This lesson draws on interviews and ethnographic data from a community in western Norway during an unusually warm winter to describe how knowledge of climate change is experienced in everyday life. That winter the first snowfall was two months later than usual; ice fishing was impossible; and the ski industry had to invest in artificial snowmaking. Stories in local and national newspapers linked the warm winter to global warming. Yet residents did not write letters to the editor, pressure politicians, or cut down on use of fossil fuels. This lesson describes the emotions of guilt, helplessness, and fear of the future that arose when people were confronted with the idea of climate change. The lesson presents a model of socially organized denial to describe how people normalized these disturbing emotions by deploying conversation norms and discourses that served as "tools of social order." Most studies of public response to climate change have focused on information deficit approaches. Many in the general public or environmental community have also presumed that the failure to engage is a function of lack of concern. Instead, this research describes how for the highly educated and politically savvy residents, global warming was both common knowledge and unimaginable. "The social organization of climate denial" is described through multiple levels, from emotions to cultural norms to political economy. The research from Norway is supplemented by comparisons to the United States, telling a larger story behind the public paralysis in the face of today's alarming predictions from climate scientists. The lesson describes the lack of response as an active process the author calls "socially organized denial." As a result, information about climate science is known in the abstract but disconnected from political, social, and private life.

17. Labor and the Environment   310

Brian K. Obach

Beliefs about the need for environmental protection are influenced by many factors, including one's economic position. Workers may feel that environmental policies either advance or threaten their economic interests. Many people are employed in fields related to environmental protection or otherwise benefit from environmental policies. Some political leaders have supported environmental regulation and financial assistance for "clean industries," arguing that this type of development will ensure a healthy and sustainable economy. But not everyone agrees that environmental measures are beneficial economically. Some sectors of the economy are threatened by environmental policies that could curtail their operations. Conservative political leaders often oppose pro-environmental policies on the grounds that such measures impose burdensome costs on employers and weaken the economy, resulting in job loss. Workers in these occupations, often encouraged by employers who see environmental regulation as a threat to profits, may mobilize politically to oppose policies supported by environmentalists, setting off so-called jobs versus the environment conflicts. Labor unions can play an important role in shaping how workers perceive environmental issues, and they are positioned to help build a broad movement for a just and sustainable economy. However, labor unions have been in decline for decades due to technological developments, economic globalization, and a general assault on organized labor by employers. The structure of the labor relations system and the history of unionism in the United States have yielded a mixed record on environmental issues. At times, unions have allied with environmental advocates and provided key support for environmental policies; but in other instances, unions have sided with employers in opposition to environmental measures. Increasingly, unions have joined with environmentalists in support of policies that promise both environmental and economic benefits. Environmental measures are not likely to succeed unless workers believe that their economic fate is tied to a healthy environment.

assessed. Finally, alternatives to development are discussed, including degrowth.

Conclusion: Unanswered Questions and the Future of Environmental Sociology 389
Kenneth A. Gould and Tammy L. Lewis

In the conclusion, interlinking themes from throughout the book are briefly highlighted and analyzed. Those themes are brought to bear on the question of how we can/should act on the socioenvironmental knowledge that we have, with reference to the frameworks provided by the founding thinkers in environmental sociology. The authors then suggest areas of research that need to be pursued by environmental sociologists in the future and address concerns about what can practically be accomplished in the present. Students are encouraged to continue both their study of environmental sociology and their participation in the contemporary social, political, and environmental worlds. The lesson concludes by suggesting that the subfield of environmental sociology would benefit from the creation of structures to increase North–South intellectual exchange.

Acknowledgments

We thank the people of Akwesasne for grounding us in the reality of what it means to be engaged in the struggle for physical, social, cultural, and environmental health.

Thanks also to our colleagues Jeff Broadbent, Stella Čapek, and Mike Mascarenhas for convincing us of the need for a book such as this. We thank our colleagues who used the first and second editions of the book, and especially those who provided us with suggestions for the third edition. A big thanks, too, to the contributors of all three editions for their commitment to clearly communicating environmental sociology to the next generation.

Over the years, our students at the University of California-Davis, Northwestern University, Denison University, Muhlenberg College, St. Lawrence University, and Brooklyn College of the City University of New York have inspired us to create effective means to communicate the importance of sociology in understanding environmental issues.

For ongoing encouragement, enthusiasm, and cheese, we thank our editor at Oxford University Press, Sherith Pankratz. Oxford University Press and the authors thank the following reviewers for their feedback:

Benjamin Clifford Brown, University of New Hampshire
Ryan Ceresola, Hartwick College
Robert Garot, John Jay College and CUNY Graduate Center
Erik Nelson, Pennsylvania State University
Hyung Sam Park, University of Central Florida
Kristen Shorette, SUNY Stony Brook
Elisabeth Wilder, Northeastern University
Chenyang Xiao, American University

Finally, for their ongoing support, we thank our family.

About the Contributors

Diane C. Bates is a Professor of Sociology at The College of New Jersey, where she teaches courses in environmental sociology, research methods, demography, and urban sociology. She has a BA from Humboldt State University and an MA and PhD from Rutgers University. Her research on the relationship between environmental change and human migration in the United States and Latin America has been published in multiple academic journals as well as *Superstorm Sandy: The Inevitable Destruction and Reconstruction of the Jersey Shore* (Rutgers University Press). Her most recent research explores the potential of community partnerships to improve scientific (including environmental) literacy among undergraduate students.

Shannon Elizabeth Bell is an Associate Professor of Sociology at Virginia Tech. Her research focuses on environmental injustices related to fossil-fuel extraction and energy production and spans a number of subdisciplines including environmental sociology, social movements, gender, and rural sociology. She is author of *Our Roots Run Deep as Ironweed: Appalachian Women and the Fight for Environmental Justice*, which received the Association for Humanist Sociology Book Award, and *Fighting King Coal: The Challenges to Micromobilization in Central Appalachia*, which won the Society for Human Ecology's Gerald L. Young Book Award and the Association of American Publishers PROSE Award. She is also the recipient of the Rural Sociological Society's Excellence in Research Award, the Environmental Sociology Practice & Outreach Award, and the Robert Boguslaw Award for Technology & Humanism.

Elizabeth H. Campbell is Director of the United Nations Relief and Works Agency's (UNRWA) Representative Office in Washington, DC. Prior to joining UNRWA, Campbell was the senior humanitarian policy advisor in the Bureau of International Organization Affairs at the Department of State, where she worked on refugee and humanitarian issues in the United Nations system. Campbell has also served as a senior advocate for Refugees International, where she focused on the humanitarian crises in East Africa and the Middle East. She was director of Refugee Council USA, an NGO consortium focused on refugee resettlement and protection. Campbell holds a BA from St. Lawrence University, and an MA and PhD in Sociology from the State

University of New York at Binghamton. She has published several articles and book chapters on refugee and humanitarian issues and has served as an adjunct professor at Georgetown University's School of Law, James Madison University, and the State University of New York at Binghamton. Her courses have focused on humanitarian affairs, refugees, environmental studies, and inequality and social justice.

Stella M. Čapek is the Elbert L. Fausett Emerita Distinguished Professor of Sociology in the Department of Sociology/Anthropology at Hendrix College. She has taught courses on Environmental Sociology; Social Change/Social Movements; Medical Sociology; Urban/Community Sociology; Images of the City; Gender and Family; Food, Culture, and Nature; Travel and Tourism; and Sociological Theory. She is especially interested in interdisciplinary environmental studies, environmental justice, ecological identity, social constructions of nature, and sustainable community design. She has published articles on environmental justice, tenants' rights, urban/community issues, local interactions with wildlife, green design, and health and environment. She has taught about sustainability and ecotourism in Costa Rica and in the US Southwest. She has coauthored two books, *Community Versus Commodity: Tenants and the American City* (1992) and *Come Lovely and Soothing Death: The Right To Die Movement in the United States* (1999). She has also published environmentally themed creative nonfiction.

Adam Driscoll is an assistant professor at the University of Wisconsin-La Crosse where he teaches courses in Environmental Sociology, Environmental Justice, and Sustainable Living. He received his PhD in sociology in 2014 from North Carolina State University in Raleigh. His research analyzes the direct and indirect relationships among political-economic structures, agricultural production, and environmental degradation. He also conducts research within the scholarship of teaching and learning, examining online pedagogy, the efficacy of online education, and gender bias in student evaluations of instruction. His work has appeared in *Teaching Sociology*, the *Journal of World-Systems Research*, the *International Journal for the Scholarship of Teaching and Learning*, and *Innovative Higher Education*.

Bob Edwards is a Professor of sociology at East Carolina University in Greenville, NC. He received his PhD in sociology in 1995 from The Catholic University of America in Washington, DC. A longstanding interest in understanding the social organization of inequalities integrates his research on social movements, organizations, social capital, and civil society with his work on environmentalism, environmental justice, and the social impact of natural disasters. He has published over 60 refereed articles and chapters appearing in *American Sociological Review*, *Annual Review of Sociology*, *Social Problems*, *Social Forces*, *Mobilization*, *Teaching Sociology*, *Journal of Democracy*, *Journal of Public Policy*, and *Natural Hazards Review*. He is co-editor of *Beyond Tocqueville: Civil Society and the Social Capital*

Debate in Comparative Perspective and of four thematic issues of *American Behavioral Scientist.*

Kenneth A. Gould is Dean of Humanities and Social Sciences and Professor of Sociology at Brooklyn College of the City University of New York; and Professor of Sociology, and Earth and Environmental Sciences at the CUNY Graduate Center. His work focuses on the political economy of environment, technology, and development and is best known for its contribution to the development of the "treadmill of production" model of socioenvironmental dynamics. Gould's research examines the responses of communities to environmental problems, technology and social change, the role of inequality in environmental conflicts, and the impacts of economic globalization on efforts to achieve ecologically and socially sustainable development trajectories. He is coauthor of *Environment and Society: The Enduring Conflict* (1994), *Local Environmental Struggles: Citizen Activism in the Treadmill of Production* (1996), *The Treadmill of Production: Injustice and Unsustainability in the Global Economy* (2008), and *Green Gentrification: Urban Sustainability and the Struggle for Environmental Justice* (2017); and co-editor, with Tammy L. Lewis, of *Thirty Readings in Introductory Sociology* (2013), and *Ten Lessons in Introductory Sociology* (2014).

Jill Lindsey Harrison is Associate Professor of Sociology at the University of Colorado Boulder. Her research focuses on environmental justice, environmental politics, workplace inequalities, and immigration politics. In her research, she identifies the narratives, other interactive dynamics, and broader political economic structures through which people come to define highly inequitable circumstances as reasonable and unproblematic. She also identifies the practices through which other groups push the state to remedy those inequalities. She has done so through research on political conflict over agricultural pesticide poisonings in California, immigration policing in rural Wisconsin, and government agencies' environmental justice efforts. Her first book, *Pesticide Drift and the Pursuit of Environmental Justice* (MIT Press, 2011), won book awards from the Rural Sociological Society and the Association of Humanist Sociology. Her second book, *From the Inside Out: The Fight for Environmental Justice within Government Agencies*, was published by MIT Press in 2019. She has also published articles in *Social Problems, Environmental Sociology, Environmental Politics, American Journal of Public Health, Political Geography, Geoforum, Antipode, Society and Natural Resources, Agriculture and Human Values,* and *New Labor Forum*, as well as numerous edited volumes.

Maki Hatanaka is an Associate Professor in the Department of Sociology at Sam Houston State University. Her recent research examines how changing forms of sustainability governance and new forms of supply chain management are affecting agrifood producers, communities, and the environment. Her work has been published in several edited volumes and numerous academic journals including *Science, Food Policy, World Development, Agriculture and Human Values, Journal of Rural Studies, Sociologia Ruralis,* and *The Local Environment.* She is also co-editor of *Twenty Lessons in the Sociology of Food and Agriculture* (Oxford University Press, 2019) and *Contested Sustainability Discourses in the Agrifood System* (London: Earthscan, 2018).

Jason Konefal is an Associate Professor in the Department of Sociology at Sam Houston State University. His research examines the relationship between political economic structures and practices and opportunities for social change. Specifically, he is interested the use of private governance to just sustainability transitions in food and agriculture. Dr. Konefal's publications have appeared in the *Journal of Rural Studies, Agriculture and Human Values,* and *Organization & Environment.* He is also co-editor of *Contested Sustainability Discourses in the Agrifood System* (London: Earthscan, 2018) and *Twenty Lessons in the Sociology of Food and Agriculture* (Oxford University Press, 2019).

Tammy L. Lewis is Professor of Sociology at Brooklyn College of the City University of New York; and Professor of Sociology and Earth and Environmental Sciences at the CUNY Graduate Center. She teaches courses on urban sustainability, transnational social movements, environmental sociology, and research methodology. She is the author of *Ecuador's Environmental Revolutions: Ecoimperialists, Ecodependents, and Ecoresisters* (2016, MIT Press); and *Green Gentrification: Urban Sustainability and the Struggle for Environmental* Justice (2017, Routledge, with Kenneth A. Gould). She is co-editor of *Ten Lessons in Introductory Sociology* (2018) and *Thirty Readings in Introductory Sociology* (2017). Her work has appeared in *Conservation Biology, Environmental Sociology, Mobilization, Social Science Quarterly,* and *Teaching Sociology,* among others. In 2017–2018, she was chair of the Environment Sociology of the American Sociological Association.

Michael Mascarenhas is a first-generation college graduate, person of color, anti-colonialist, antiracism comrade. Professor Mascarenhas's scholarship examines the interconnections between contemporary neoliberal reforms, environmental change, and environmental justice and racism. This interdisciplinary body of research brings together concepts from critical race theory and environmental studies to help cultivate knowledge that contributes to political activism and coalition politics. Michael Mascarenhas is an Associate Professor in the Department of Environmental Science, Policy and Management at the University of California, Berkeley. He is the author of *Where the Waters Divide Neoliberalism, White Privilege, and Environmental Racism in Canada* (2012); and *New Humanitarianism and the Crisis of Charity: Good Intentions on the Road to Help* (2107). Professor Mascarenhas was an expert witness at the Michigan Civil Rights Commission on the Flint Water Crisis and an invited speaker to the National Academes of Sciences, Engineering, and Medicine's Committee on Designing Citizen Science to Support Science Learning.

Justin Sean Myers is an Assistant Professor in the Department of Sociology at California State University, Fresno. He received his PhD in Sociology from The Graduate Center–The City University of New York, his MA in Sociology from San Diego State, and his BA in Sociology from Sonoma State. His research utilizes qualitative and historical methods to examine how marginalized communities are organizing against environmental and food inequities. His previous work has documented how the food justice movement in Brooklyn is challenging racial neoliberalism, Big Food, and the growth machine politics of municipal government. This scholarship has appeared in *Environmental Sociology* and *Geoforum*. Other work on food politics has appeared in *Agriculture & Human Values* and the book *Twenty Lessons in the Sociology of Food and Agriculture*. He is currently writing a book on the food justice movement in Brooklyn.

Norah MacKendrick is Associate Professor of Sociology at Rutgers University in New Brunswick, New Jersey. She studies gender, environmental health, risk, and consumer culture. MacKendrick is the author of *Better Safe Than Sorry: How Consumers Navigate Exposure to Everyday Toxics* (University of California Press). Her research has been published in *Gender & Society*, *Sociological Forum*, *Signs: The Journal of Women in Culture and Society*, *Journal of Consumer Culture*, and *Contexts*.

Laura McKinney is an Associate Professor of Sociology and Director of Environmental Studies at Tulane University in New Orleans, Louisiana. Her research focus lies at the intersection of international development, gender, and the environment. She received the Morton-Deutsch Award from the International Society for Justice Research for the best article published in *Social Justice Research* in 2015. She was a Weiss Award Finalist for Excellence in Undergraduate Teaching at Tulane University. She serves as an advisory member of *Sociological Perspectives* editorial board, and former managing editor of the *Journal of World-Systems Research*. In her role as council member of the Rural Sociological Society (RSS), she also chairs the Diversity Committee. She is past Chairperson of the International Development Research Interest Group for RSS and the Environment and Technology Division of the Society for the Study of Social Problems. Her work has been published by *Social Forces*, *Social Problems*, *Social Science Research*, *Population and Environment*, and *Agriculture and Human Values*, among other outlets.

Kari Marie Norgaard is Associate Professor of Sociology and Environmental Studies at the University of Oregon. Her research on climate denial, tribal environmental justice, and gender and risk has been published in *Sociological Forum; Gender and Society; Sociological Inquiry; Organization and Environment; Rural Sociology; Race, Gender & Class*; and other journals, as well as by the World Bank. Her research has also been featured in *The Washington Post, National Geographic*, and *High Country News*, and on National Public Radio's "All Things Considered." Her first book, *Living in Denial: Climate Change, Emotions* *and Everyday Life*, was published by MIT Press in 2011. Norgaard is the recipient of the Pacific Sociological Association's Distinguished Practice Award for 2005.

Brian K. Obach is a Professor of Sociology at the State University of New York at New Paltz. He specializes in the study of social movements, environmental sociology, and political economy. He is the author of *Organic Struggle: The Movement for Sustainable Agriculture in the United States* and *Labor and the Environmental Movement: The Quest for Common Ground*, in which he examines the promise and pitfalls of cross-movement alliance building between unions and environmental advocacy organizations.

David Naguib Pellow is Dehlsen Chair of Environmental Studies at the University of California, Santa Barbara. His teaching and research focus on ecological justice issues in the United States and globally. His books include *What is Critical Environmental Justice?*; *The Slums of Aspen: Immigrants vs. the Environment in America's Eden* (with Lisa Sun-Hee Park); *Resisting Global Toxics: Transnational Movements for Environmental Justice; The Silicon Valley of Dreams: Environmental Injustice, Immigrant Workers, and the High-Tech Global Economy* (with Lisa Sun-Hee Park); and *Garbage Wars: The Struggle for Environmental Justice in Chicago*. He has served on the Boards of Directors for the Center for Urban Transformation, Greenpeace USA, and International Rivers.

Allan Schnaiberg was Professor of Sociology at Northwestern University, Evanston, Illinois, from 1969 to 2009. His work in what later became known as "environmental sociology" (and still later "environmental justice") started in 1971. Trained as a demographer and earlier as a chemist and metallurgical engineer, he was able to mediate between the sociopolitical expressions by natural scientists in the 1970s and the later analyses by social scientists of the societal–environmental dialectic. His development of the "treadmill of production" model of socioenvironmental dynamics greatly influenced the field of environmental sociology. The treadmill model was further developed in his collaborations in later years with Kenneth Gould, Adam Weinberg, and David Pellow. The common thread in his research was the ways in which both environmental problems and environmental protections have been infused with social inequalities. He traced these inequalities through his analyses of sociology of science, energy crises, appropriate technology, sustainable development, recycling, and environmental impact assessment. He died in 2009.

Richard York is Professor of Sociology and Environmental Studies at the University of Oregon. His research focuses on the social structural forces that affect the natural environment and the philosophy, history, and sociology of science. He has published dozens of articles, including ones in *American Sociological Review, Ecological Economics, Conservation Biology, Nature Climate Change, Social Problems, Sociological Theory,* and *Theory and Society.*

He has published three books with Monthly Review Press: *The Critique of Intelligent Design* and *The Ecological Rift*, both with John Bellamy Foster and Brett Clark; and *The Science and Humanism of Stephen Jay Gould* with Brett Clark. He has received the Frederick H. Buttel Distinguished Contribution Award from the Environmental Sociology Section of the American Sociological Association for lifetime achievement.

Nicole Youngman received her PhD in sociology from Tulane University and is a sociology instructor at Southeastern Louisiana University, specializing in environmental sociology and sociology of disaster. Her research focuses on the historical relationship among municipal growth machines, canal development, and flood risk in New Orleans.

An Introduction to Environmental Sociology

Kenneth A. Gould and Tammy L. Lewis

THE ORIGIN AND PURPOSE OF THIS BOOK

The idea for this reader emerged from a discussion among a small group of environmental sociology professors en route to visiting Akwesasne, the St. Regis Mohawk reservation, to learn more about their environmental justice struggles with toxic contamination from nearby industrial plants. On the ride to Akwesasne, we started to talk about our environmental sociology courses and how dissatisfied we were with the undergraduate, introductory-level readers (edited books with chapters from various authors) in our subfield. The point of a reader is to bring together exemplary works in a given subfield to expose students to the range of ideas, concepts, theoretical approaches, and empirical research without requiring them to read a large number of individual books. For us, the problem with the traditional reader is that the chapters are usually drawn from professional journal articles, written by sociologists for sociologists. That is, the materials used to speak to undergraduate students, whom we don't expect to be familiar with the subfield, are the same materials that professional, trained sociologists use to speak to professional, trained sociologists, whom we rightly *do* expect to be quite familiar with the language, theories, data, and debates in the subfield. The result is that the audience for whom the initial materials were written is poorly matched to the audience for the collected reader. Granted, the versions of professional journal articles included in most readers have been edited to make them more accessible to undergraduates. But still, the bulk of each chapter originates in professor-to-professor communication rather than professor-to-student communication. And neither the professors nor the students are particularly happy with the outcomes.

As we drove in a university van to the Mohawk reservation, we were struck by how odd it was that sociology professors, who largely earn their living by finding ways to explain their field to undergraduate students, are stuck assigning readings that are clearly not designed for that purpose. Each of us in the van taught environmental sociology to undergraduates. We decided that it would be much more useful to have an undergraduate reader that was based on our most successful professor-to-student communications (our classes) rather than our most impressive professor-to-professor communications (our published professional journal articles).

It was at that point that two of us decided to launch the project that has resulted in this book. We made a list of what we thought were the most important topics to include in an undergraduate environmental sociology course. We then approached our environmental sociology colleagues whom we knew were enthusiastic teachers and had successfully taught undergraduate-level courses in environmental sociology. We asked them to choose among the topics and match them with their favorite class lectures, the ones both they and their students seemed to enjoy and get the most out of. Then, rather than asking them to give us their best professional research paper on that topic, we instead asked them to grab their lesson notes and write up the lesson as closely as they could to the way they actually teach it in class. We told them that what we wanted was the best approximation of a favorite class lecture in environmental sociology in written form.

To our knowledge, this is a completely new approach to creating an undergraduate reader, one that starts with the classroom experience rather than being forced to fit into that experience. As editors, a big part of our job was to remind our contributors that the audience for their writing is undergraduate students. After all, when professors write in their subfield, it is almost always for other professors. That is, we know how to talk to you about what we do and what we know, but we generally have less practice in writing to you about that.

Given our histories as US-based professors, our network of colleagues tends to be US-based, which resulted in a collection from a US perspective. We discuss this more in the concluding lesson of the book.

Oxford University Press is a not-for-profit publisher, and we think that is an important model in a time of high-cost, high-debt, high-profit higher education. Oxford has been enthusiastic about the project and committed to keeping the cost of the book as low as possible for students.

Oxford published the first edition of this book in 2009, and much to our delight, it was well received by students and professors taking and teaching environmental sociology courses. Also to our delight, the subfield of environmental sociology continued to expand, with many more sociology departments adding or expanding course offerings in environmental sociology. Less delightful has been the continuing deterioration of the global environment in the years since the book's first publication. When we were asked to create the updated second edition in 2014, we took stock of what had gotten better, what had gotten worse, and what the important developments in environmental sociology had been since 2009. Now, in 2020, we have updated again in the context of significant climate change impacts, the sixth mass extinction, and the Trump administration. In the years since the second edition, we have seen reason for hope and despair. On the climate change front, global carbon emissions are higher than ever; total atmospheric carbon is higher than at any time in human existence; massive hurricanes have devastated Puerto Rico, Barbuda, and other vulnerable areas; all while corporations and governments continue to build new fossil fuel infrastructure and expand exploration. At the same time, we are heartened by the attention to climate change manifest in the Paris climate agreement, Indigenous resistance to pipeline construction, and national policy proposals like the Green New Deal. While the extinction crisis threatens everything from koalas to pollinators, the emergence of movements like Extinction Rebellion and school strikes for climate remind us that awareness and concern are growing. Although the appointment of anti-environmentalists to key government positions in the United States and their reversal of major environmental protection policies are deeply troubling, we see environmental policy improvements in other countries.

In preparing a new edition that addresses these and other changes, we gathered feedback from students and faculty who have used the book and applied their insights to guide us through this new revision process. All of the lessons in the third edition have been updated or are new. In particular, the third edition expands our focus on climate change, arguably the most critical and contested socioenvironmental issue of our era. This edition of *Twenty Lessons in Environmental Sociology* includes an expanded glossary to help you more quickly and easily familiarize yourself with the key terms and concepts of the subfield. What all of us who have contributed to this new edition hope we have achieved is an even more user-friendly introduction to what we think is the most critical area of human inquiry in the 21st century.

Our hope is that you will find the lessons in this book accessible, interesting, and challenging and that the fact that each lesson was originally written specifically for undergraduate students will make the experience of taking a course in environmental sociology more enjoyable, engaging, and beneficial.

WHAT IS ENVIRONMENTAL SOCIOLOGY?

Put most succinctly, environmental sociology is the study of how **social systems** interact with **ecosystems**. Of course, since environmental sociology explores all of the ways that these two very complex systems affect each other, it is a very wide field of scientific investigation. Just trying to understand social systems or ecosystems alone is a daunting task. Trying to understand how the two affect each other is a monumental effort indeed. Ecosystems, their qualities and changing dynamics, affect social systems in many ways, from the way we organize language to the way we organize economic systems. Similarly, social systems and their qualities and shifting dynamics also affect ecosystems in numerous ways, from the organization of backyard gardens to the disorganization of global climate systems.

That social systems and ecosystems are deeply interconnected may seem obvious, but the intellectual history of sociology over the past 150 years or so provides little evidence that the depth and breadth of this dynamic interaction has been fully appreciated by sociologists. Similarly, the intellectual history of the science of ecology over roughly the same period also provides little evidence that the full scope of the impact of social systems on ecosystems had been well incorporated. Part of the reason for this lack of focus had to do with the need to first develop some fairly workable understandings of both social systems and ecosystems separately, before attempting to understand how they interact. However, since they do interact a lot, it is still surprising that our explanations of each developed with little reference to the other.

Another part of the explanation of this lack of synthesis has to do with the notion of bifurcation. That is, in Western tradition, nature and society tend to be thought of as separate domains. This has been referred to as the **nature–society dichotomy**. Society happens in some places and nature in others, and the two are examined separately by different groups of researchers. For example, it is common for people to think of the city as a place where society happens, and the "wild" frontier as a place where nature happens. Natural scientists didn't pay much attention to urban environments, and social scientists didn't pay much attention to the wild. Yet another part of the reason for the failure to treat the two systems as dynamically intertwined has to do with the nature of academic organization. This is especially true for sociology, which emerged as a discipline much later than the natural sciences.

In seeking to carve out a distinct intellectual and organizational niche for itself within the academy, and thus establish itself as a legitimate field of scholarly pursuit, sociologists put much effort into defining sociology as something distinct from the natural sciences. That is, sociologists intentionally tried to separate their field of study from the already established fields that studied physical nature, such as biology and chemistry. As a result, any attempt at incorporating the natural world within sociology was seen as ceding intellectual ground to natural science, and thus undermining the effort to establish sociology as a distinct field of study with a separate area of investigation.

Despite the social barriers to fully integrating the study of social systems and ecosystems, over time, the increasing confidence of sociology as a fully established and legitimate discipline created the social space for the emergence of environmental sociology. At the same time, both the increasing urgency of the negative impacts of social systems on ecosystems and the resulting negative impacts of ecosystem disorganization on human societies created the social need for the emergence of environmental sociology. Thus, as sociology matured, and as environmental problems became more and more prevalent and affected communities around the world, sociologists began to systematically examine nature–society connections.

All that said, it is important to note that environmental sociology is not equally rooted in sociology and ecology. Environmental sociology remains a subfield of sociology, one in which its practitioners are more open to including ecological variables within their analyses and have chosen to apply and develop sociological analysis precisely where social systems and ecosystems intersect. Environmental sociologists bring the sociological lens and apply their sociological imaginations to the ways in which social systems generate and respond to ecological change. They are not ecologists and are not prepared to address the deep complexity of ecosystems. Instead, their training is in the study of the deeply complex ways that social systems are organized and change. Their special focus is on how social systems are organized and change in response to the natural world, just as the changes they produce in the natural world force them to further respond and change.

A BRIEF HISTORY OF ENVIRONMENTAL SOCIOLOGY

One social response to environmental change has been the institutionaliza-tion of the study of social system–ecosystem interactions. The brief history we present here highlights the institutional trajectory of environmental so-ciology. We focus on the development of organizational structures intended to sustain the **subdiscipline**. In elaborating this history, we touch upon the key social forces that led to its emergence and how it fits into the broader context of sociology. The institutions are clearly tied to key individuals in the field. However, rather than focus on these individuals, we focus on the "real-world" events and intellectual concerns embedded in the era in which the subfield emerged.

Environmental sociology has been an officially recognized subfield within sociology only since around 1976, with its institutionalization as one of the American Sociological Association's topical sections. Prior to that time, "the environment" was not considered within the purview of sociology. Indeed, as noted earlier, in developing sociology as a discipline, the "founding fathers" sought to distance the study of "social facts" (Emile Durkheim) from studies of the biophysical world in order to legitimize the new "science of society," sociology (see Lesson 1). In the late 1800s, the environment was not part of sociology. When we consider that a key concern of classical sociology was to understand the broad-scale social changes brought about by industrializa-tion and modern state bureaucracies, the omission of "the environment" and examination of "environmental inequalities" seems impossible from our con-temporary perspective. Today, environmental sociologists study how social institutions interact with the environment and ask how industrial capitalism and modern state bureaucracies affect social and environmental inequalities and vice versa.

If we revisit the "classics" in sociology, searching to discover to what degree the founders may have looked at the environment, we do not see much in the analyses of Max Weber or Émile Durkheim. For example, we could stretch to see that Durkheim analyzed the effects of "cosmic factors"—season, temperature, etc.—on suicide rates (though he dismissed their causal relevance), but there really is not much there. Contemporary research by John Bellamy Foster and others suggests that Karl Marx was more attentive to the environment, though this was not a central focus and is certainly not Marx's legacy. In the 1970s, bringing the environment into sociological anal-ysis occurred consciously and deliberately.

The institutional history of environmental sociology coincides with the emergence of the modern "ecology movement." Both were born in the late

1960s and early 1970s. Within a relatively short span of time, the professional organizations of sociologists incorporated formal niches for environmental sociology. The Rural Sociological Society's Natural Resources Research Group formed in the mid-1960s (it has had numerous name changes). The Society for the Study of Social Problems started a group on environmental problems in 1973, and the American Sociological Association's Environmental Sociology section formed in 1976 (for a time it was called the section on "environment and technology").

The institutionalization of environmental sociology reflected the growing attention of society in general, and social scientists in particular, to issues of the environment. Intellectuals working in the fields of human ecology, rural sociology, and urban sociology and researching topics such as social movements found their intellectual interests intersecting with real-world events during this time period. This same era witnessed numerous environmental "crises," such as the energy crisis of the early 1970s, the Santa Barbara oil spill (1969), toxic wastes being discovered in the residential neighborhood of Love Canal (1978), and the accident at the nuclear power plant at Three Mile Island (1979).

Coupled with these crises was rising public concern regarding the environment and the resulting emergence of environmental organizations, including the Environmental Defense Fund (1967), Friends of the Earth (1969), and the Natural Resources Defense Council (NRDC, founded 1970). Political actions were also taking place. In 1969, Congress passed the National Environmental Policy Act, which President Nixon signed into law in 1970. The Environmental Protection Agency (EPA) was established in 1970, followed by the passage of key environmental laws: the Clean Air Act (1970), the Clean Water Act (1972), the Pesticide Control Act (1972), and the Resource Conservation and Recovery Act (1976). The year 1970 also marked the first Earth Day. Political attention was not just national but international, including the 1972 United Nations Conference on the Human Environment held in Stockholm. Environmental sociologists were not immune to their surroundings. They, too, responded to socioenvironmental changes and began researching the causes of environmental degradation, public opinion regarding the environment, and the social responses of the public and institutions to environmental changes.

Just as early sociology sought to distinguish itself from other sciences, early environmental sociology tried to distinguish itself from "mainstream sociology." Writing in the late 1970s, William Catton and Riley Dunlap, early environmental sociologists, wrote an oft-cited paper that argued that virtually all sociological theories were anthropocentric; that is, they view human society as the center of the natural world, with humans controlling and using the environment without regard for the natural resource-based limits to social growth. They termed this sociological worldview the "**human exemptionalism paradigm**" (HEP). By contrast, they argued for a competing worldview that would critique mainstream sociology's HEP worldview. They called their alternative the "**new ecological paradigm**" (NEP). The NEP started from the assumptions that humans are one of many interdependent species in the global ecosystem and part of a large web of nature, that humans depend on a finite biophysical environment, and that humans cannot stand above ecological laws. The HEP–NEP distinction provided environmental sociology with a way to differentiate itself from mainstream sociology. However, we have yet to see sociology as a discipline fully embrace the NEP worldview, though "the environment" and "environmental issues" have drawn the attention of researchers working in various other sociological subfields with greater frequency over time.

Environmental sociology has by now established itself as a recognized subfield in sociology. Increasing awareness of the environment as a social problem has reinforced this, giving environmental sociologists a relevant role to play in examining the potential paths toward environmental reform and synthesis of the social and ecological systems. On its website, the Environmental Sociology section of the American Sociological Association explains the role of environmental sociology in this way:

> Many of society's most pressing problems are no longer just "social." From the maintenance of genetic diversity to the disposal of radioactive wastes, from toxics in the groundwater below us to global warming of the atmosphere above, the challenges of the 21st century are increasingly coming to involve society's relationships with the environment and technologies upon which we all depend.... Facing the challenges of the 21st century requires more than sound scientific understanding and technological solutions. Too often missing from the debate is knowledge of the complex social, economic and political relationships that drive society in destructive directions. Environmental Sociology brings together the tools of social sciences and applies them to these key issues of our day. Examining environmental issues in turn is reshaping the field of sociology.

Many of our environmental sociology colleagues in other nations are not organized in the same manner as American sociologists are. Because of this, the interactions between North American environmental sociologists and sociologists throughout the rest of the world have been facilitated by the International Sociological Association's Research Committee on Environment and Society (RC24), which was formed in 1971 and has seen continued growth (in international meetings) and increased significance among environmental sociologists over time.

Finally, in looking to institutions, there is every reason to believe that environmental sociology will continue to thrive as a subdiscipline. The structures for the continued production of knowledge and dissemination of knowledge and the education of professionals are well established and growing. For instance, there are well-established journals in which environmental sociologists publish. Increasingly, research in environmental sociology is being published in "mainstream" sociological journals. Recent institutional growth in the field is evidenced by the growth in graduate programs dedicated specifically to environmental sociology (students interested in this should explore the Environmental Sociology section's website at http://envirosoc.org for the most up-to-date list). In fact, environmental sociology is one of the fastest-growing subfields in the discipline today, which is perhaps an indicator of the growing awareness that social system–ecosystem dynamics are severely out of balance. This book will introduce you to the work that environmental sociologists do.

THE LAYOUT OF THE BOOK

This book is divided into four parts as a way of broadly organizing your introduction to the ways in which environmental sociologists think about and study the relationships between social systems and ecosystems. The book begins with a brief introduction to socioenvironmental theory, followed by three sections addressing the social causes, consequences, and responses to environmental disruption. The book concludes by looking at where the sociological study of society–environment interactions might productively focus in coming years and suggests some important questions that remain incompletely answered.

Part 1 of the book introduces you to the variety of theoretical frameworks that environmental sociologists have developed to describe and explain the patterns they have uncovered in the ways that social systems and ecosystems interact. These patterns of interaction range from the micro-level, at which people as social beings encounter and comprehend the natural world, to the macro-level, at which the global economy shapes and is shaped by the constraints of the biosphere. By beginning with a broad overview of socioenvironmental theories, we hope to provide you with an opportunity to see how these theories both guide and emerge from the types of analyses you will read in the next three parts of the book.

Part 2 of the book explores the systemic causes of social disruption of ecosystems. The focus here is on the ways in which major social institutions such as governments, corporations, and labor generate and respond to environmental change and interact with each other in regard to environmental conditions. Since science and technology are primary mechanisms through which humans understand and mediate their relationships with ecosystems, an additional focus of Part 2 is the social institutions and processes that shape science and technological innovation. An examination of population dynamics and the ways in which human population change and distribution intersect with ecosystemic processes follows. Part 2 concludes with a look at the critical social and environmental arena of energy. Throughout Part 2, you will be asked to think critically about the social dynamics of power as environmental sociologists recognize that the capacity to determine the nature of social system–ecosystem interactions is not distributed equally throughout society.

In Part 3 of the book, the focus is on the consequences of environmental disruption for social systems. That is, where Part 2 looks at how and why society changes the environment, this next part of the book looks at how the environment changes society. The disorganization of ecosystems produced by social systems affects those social systems in a wide variety of ways. Those social impacts of human-induced environmental change do not affect all people equally or in the same ways. Therefore, you will find that a primary focus of Part 3 is on issues of social inequality in terms of who bears the costs of environmental disruption (and who reaps the benefits), from local through global levels of distribution. In particular, the concepts of "environmental justice" and "environmental health" are introduced and further explored through specific analyses of food production and consumption systems, "natural" disasters, and global climate change. Paralleling what you will have read in Part 2, your reading of Part 3 will help you to see that just as the power to determine the ways in which social systems and ecosystems interact is unevenly distributed throughout society, so is the power to avoid, deny, or deal with the results of these interactions.

Part 4, the final part of the book, examines the ways in which society has responded to human-induced environmental disruption. Much of the focus here is on how and why communities, social movements, and nongovernmental organizations have mobilized (or failed to) to address a wide variety of environmental concerns. This type of citizen mobilization has emerged all over the world—at the local, regional, national, and transnational levels—with great variation in the environmental issues focused on and the strategies employed. Part 4 exposes you to this rich variety of social response to problems arising from the ways that social system–ecosystem relations are currently organized. Part 4 also introduces you to "sustainable development," a concept intended to guide efforts toward reorganizing the relationships between social systems and ecosystems in ways that produce fewer environmental disruptions and greater social benefits. We conclude with a brief discussion of the future of environmental sociology; raise some questions that remain to be fully answered about the social causes, consequences, and responses to environmental problems; and suggest some areas of focus for the further sociological study of social system–ecosystem relations. In the spirit of engaging students in an area we find intellectually stimulating and vitally important to the future, we hope that you might take on researching and answering these questions to advance the state of the subdiscipline and improve the prospects for our collective socioenvironmental future.

CHANGES TO THE THIRD EDITION

The four-part layout of the book is identical to the second edition of the book. The main changes to the third edition are as follows:

- Completely new lessons on "Theories in Environmental Sociology" (Lesson 2), "The Sociology of Environmental Health" (Lesson 11), and "Environmental Social Movements" (Lesson 18) written by new contributors.

- A brand-new lesson has been added on "Climate Change" (Lesson 15), also written by a new contributor.
- Greater focus on issues of gender inequality and Indigenous peoples throughout.
- We invite students to post photos that represent the book's themes on social media using hashtags linked to the book.
- Finally, all of the authors updated the data and examples in their lessons. Many of the chapters are significantly revised. The main themes, however, remain the same.

We hope you find these changes to be useful. Instructors have indicated to us what has worked for them in the second edition and we have attempted to revise based on the needs of the subdiscipline. Instructors should also note that we have expanded and updated the instructors' resource guide (available for adoptors from Oxford) based on users' feedback.

Finally, we would like to thank the formal reviewers who provided many helpful suggestions regarding revisions for the third edition:

- Benjamin Clifford Brown, University of New Hampshire
- Ryan Ceresola, Harwick College
- Robert Garot, John Jay College and CUNY Graduate Center
- Erik Nielsen, Pennsylvania State University
- Hyung Sam Park, University of Central Florida
- Kristen Shorette, SUNY Stony Brook
- Chenyang Xiao, American University
- 2 anonymous reviewers

We are also grateful to our colleagues and students who have used the book and offered useful feedback, suggestions, and encouragement. We hope that *Twenty Lessons in Environmental Sociology* continues to be a valuable tool in supporting their efforts to teach and to learn.

SOURCES

Buttel, Frederick H. 2003. "Environmental Sociology and the Explanation of Environmental Reform." *Organization & Environment* 16:306–344.

Catton, William R., and Riley E. Dunlap. 1978. "Environmental Sociology: A New Paradigm." *American Sociologist* 13:41–49.

Foster, John Bellamy. 1999. "Marx's Theory of Metabolic Rift: Classical Foundations for Environmental Sociology." *American Journal of Sociology* 105 (2): 366–405.

Schnaiberg, Allan. 1980. *The Environment: From Surplus to Scarcity*. New York: Oxford University Press.

Part 1

THEORY

The Social Construction of Nature
Of Computers, Butterflies, Dogs, and Trucks

Stella M. Čapek

Student using public Wi-Fi in newly constructed urban greenspace, Brooklyn, New York
Post your photo on the social construction of nature to #TLESsocialnature.
Photo by Ken Gould.

Environmental sociology is a wide-ranging field that includes a variety of theories and methodological approaches. If you did this for a living, you might find yourself studying topics as seemingly different as the environmental movement (local and global), public opinion, natural resource use, social impacts of technology, inequality and environmental justice, and cultural ideas about nature and gender. Or you might study the economics and politics of environmental policy; sustainable community design; food and identity; or particular issues such as climate change, deforestation, and population—and that is only a partial list. But regardless of the topic, the job of theory in environmental sociology is to make social structure visible— that is, to identify the stable, persistent, often hidden patterns of social relationships that become established over time. And social relationships are only the beginning of the story, since *environmental* sociology is about understanding the two-way relationship between society and the environment.

Theory is like any other process that makes hidden things visible; just as ultraviolet light reveals striking color patterns that are there all along but invisible to the naked eye, sociological theories throw a certain kind of (analytical) light on society to illuminate social and environmental connections that are not immediately obvious.

One way to look at social structure is to see it as invisible "strings" that link individuals to social groups and to the environment in a patterned way. Why are these relationships so invisible in the first place? Some are taken for granted and are simply not thought about, while others are masked by power relationships. Still others are extremely complex, making it difficult to discern a pattern. Environmental sociology offers theoretical models that make key relationships more visible and allow us to understand better what holds them in place. By making structures visible, theories also offer us the opportunity to make more conscious choices about participating in or changing these patterns. Without understanding how they work, and who and what is attached to them (including ourselves), conscious choice is impossible.

In the following discussion, we will consider several snapshot images that will invite us to apply theories from environmental sociology. Because theory can often seem abstract, I want us to imagine actual bodies in actual places—our own bodies or those of others. In fact, whether we are considering the globalization of environmental problems or the background levels of chemicals in our bloodstreams, our research questions and theories always connect to real people in specific situations. The three scenes that I will ask us to consider are these: a person throwing a can out of the window of a speeding truck; a person sitting at the keyboard of a computer, making a fast connection on the Internet; and a person physically dismantling a computer that has been "thrown away" in the United States and exported to an "e-waste processing center" in another country. Although these snapshots are only three out of many possibilities, they offer an excellent opportunity to connect structures across time and space and to learn about the insights and creative uses of environmental sociology.

I will draw on several theories from environmental sociology. They are all related, even though they address very different scales of human action, from individual and small group (micro) behavior to "big picture" (macro) patterns like globalization and shifting ideas about time and space. First, I will discuss a micro-level concept, "naturework," that comes out of symbolic interactionist theory. Symbolic interactionism focuses on how human beings and social groups symbolically communicate and acquire a sense of identity through social interaction. Naturework, as we will see, refers to our culturally influenced interpretations of nature (in other words, it looks at how human beings construct ideas about nature and their relationship to it). Then, I will "zoom out" to theories of globalization and modernization that explore how space and time are being experienced in new ways by human beings. The context for these experiences is a fast-paced global capitalist system shaped by a "treadmill" logic, a social structure that continues to churn out ideas, material arrangements, and identities that have enormous implications for the environment. All of these theories shed light on the snap-shot scenes we will consider—the truck, the computer, the people who have a relationship to these technologies, and even creatures like butterflies and dogs. They will show how small, cumulative actions ripple outward into the global ecosystems of the planet, and how important it is to keep nature "in the picture" as we make social decisions.

NATUREWORK AND ITS USES: OF TRUCKS AND BUTTERFLIES

Scene One: A truck zooms down the freeway, the window rolls down, an arm appears, and fingers reach out to toss a can from the moving vehicle. The can sails through the air and lands along the edge of the highway with a small crash. Maybe it's a beer bottle or a cigarette butt. Or an entire ashtray full of cigarette butts. Whatever it is, it lands on the side of the road as the truck quickly disappears over the horizon. The object becomes part of a jagged mosaic of broken glass shards, cigarettes, cans, miscel-laneous objects considered trash, and—as I once learned doing a highway cleanup— wings from migrating butterflies that can't compete with the cars speeding down the highway. The delicately beautiful but damaged butterfly wings are a small, well-kept secret in a roadside "wasteland" that stretches for miles.

What can environmental sociologists do with this scene, and how can they use theory to create new angles of vision on it? I choose this particular act— often referred to as "littering"—because it seems to be a very simple, *un-thinking* act. But of course, this unthinking act would be *unthinkable* under a different set of social circumstances, perhaps in a place where the earth is seen as sacred, or where recycling is highly valued. Sociology in general, and environmental sociology in particular, suggests that the simplest act is not simple at all and is rarely individual or private—it is part of a network of actions and social relationships that have consequences for other people and for the environment.

Gary Alan Fine has coined a useful term, "**naturework**," that refers to how we constantly work to transform "nature" into culture, filtering it through the screen of social meanings that we have learned. Most of time we aren't aware that we're doing this, but **symbolic interactionists** point out that human beings are always working to figure out meanings and "constructing" reality as part of an ongoing interactional process. For example, when we look at a tree, if we even notice it at all, we notice some things about it and not others. While nature, or the tree, does in fact exist, what is more important is that we inevitably construct a culturally influenced image of what the tree is and behave toward it accordingly. I grew up loving a landscape of lakes and pine forests, and pine trees are precious to me. But I know someone who considers pine trees to be ugly and useless "weeds" (never mind that weeds are often very useful plants, if you have learned something about them). My friend doesn't mind seeing lots of pine trees cut down, but I do. Our cultural experience has shaped our "naturework." This is why Fine points out that "being 'in nature' implies being in culture." And when we transform nature into culture, we create consequences for individuals as well as social policy.

Let's consider a few examples. For example, we invent (or someone else invents) terms like "wilderness," "Mother Nature," "desert," "human being," "freeway," and "climate change." Some of these terms are more contested than others, but all represent a human interpretation of what "nature" is "doing." Likewise, we invent words for what animals are "saying" and teach them to children; for example, in English, a dog says "bow wow!" while in Czech, the same dog (according to human translators) says "haf haf!" Language is part of a broader task of classifying and making sense of things, and in fact, much of naturework has to do with creating and maintaining borders between categories. For example, where is the line drawn between humans and (other) animals? (If we didn't care about this line, we wouldn't insult people by calling them "animals.") Or between humans and the technologies that we invent? Between nature and "civilization"? What kind of nature is "good" or "bad," dangerous or safe? Do we include nature inside the boundaries of our skin, or do we see it as exclusively outside us?

Uncovering naturework leads to even more specific questions. For example, how do you (or I) feel about particular animals? Should they be hunted? Protected? Pets? Food? What about the human body? Should you shave the hair off of certain parts of your body? Should you mask the odors of nature? Should you apply cosmetics to distinguish yourself from or to signal your connection with nature? Do you think of nature as female (as in "Mother Nature")? Do you know the names of the trees, the birds, the rivers? Does the sight of a tree or a sunset make you glad? When you go camping (if you go camping), do you take many things with you? Do you carry a "smart" phone? Does your race, class, ethnicity, and/or gender shape your relationship with nature? When you walk or drive, are you plugged into your own private music system and personal theme music? Are you a "frequent flyer"? Do you try to travel sustainably? Do you pay attention to climate change? Do you have allergies and see nature as an attacker or a nuisance? Do you know where your trash goes?

All of these small, often unthinking decisions represent naturework and result in a particular relationship with the ecosystem and a specific set of outcomes. Although naturework might seem more obvious when we interpret big events like hurricanes (which used to have only female names!), most naturework happens on a daily basis and is enacted through the seemingly insignificant details of our lives. It doesn't *feel* like work because the categories that we use to understand the world appear normal to us and, in many cases, emotionally and morally reassuring.

Let's go back to the truck, the highway, the arm, and the flying can. How might the concept of naturework help us to interpret this situation? In fact, many things have to be in place for the can to be tossed out the window. First, one has to feel separated from the place where the can will fall. If this piece of earth is considered just "dirt" or empty space at the edge of a highway, not an alive organic material that interacts with us at every moment, it is easy to see it as a kind of trash receptacle or sponge to absorb waste. This is also not likely to be a place where one's loved ones live. Second, one has to assume that they are not accountable for the act of "trashing." Speeding down the highway, it is easy to leave behind any thought of consequence or accountability and to assume that no one will care, or at least no one will know who threw the can (notice that this also implies that we are accountable at most to another human being—perhaps a police officer—rather than the ecosystem or the Earth's biosphere). Third, in not giving this action much thought, one has to assume it is fairly trivial (as the word "littering" suggests). No thought is given to cumulative impacts because "nature" will clean it up, there is plenty of space in the trash can, or there are better things to worry about on a given day. All of these assumptions add up to one conclusion: *It doesn't matter*.

The idea that it doesn't matter is supported by social patterns that encourage a certain kind of naturework. Let's look at this more closely. A person driving down the highway in a fast-moving vehicle is likely to feel quite (unrealistically) separated from what is outside, including nature in the form of landscape and weather. US culture, or very specific groups in that culture, invented the idea that cars and trucks are a good way to get around, that their average replacement time should be about 3 years, that they are better than public transportation, that they are an important marker of status, that speed is to be valued, that the Earth is just material that we drive on and use for our own purposes, and that throwing a can out the window represents freedom. The common piece of naturework in all of these constructions is the view that we are separate from the natural world and have the power to control it or ignore it. William Catton and Riley Dunlap, in a classic article on the models, or paradigms, that we use to interpret our relationship to the ecosystem, call this view the "human exemptionalist paradigm" (HEP: see Introduction). Instead of seeing ourselves as part of the ecological system of the planet (or what they called NEP, a "new ecological paradigm"), we see ourselves as apart from it, in a controlling position that is enhanced by our technology. A banner that I saw displayed at a local Toyota dealer could be a poster for the HEP worldview: next to an image of a speeding car are the words "Hear the atmosphere scream as you tear it in half." The ad sells the idea that the domination of nature (especially through speed and technology) is an attractive and highly desirable experience. One need not look far to find many messages like this in contemporary societies like the United States.

But what if the Earth were considered sacred, or if, as scientist Donella Meadows and others have argued, we are in fact participants in a partnered dance with nature? What if invisible strings linked the hand to the can that is thrown and the strings lingered in place, reminding us of consequences? What if ecological thinking were so prevalent that it would be impossible to "litter"? Sociologists Michael Bell and Loka Ashwood point out that at present in the United States, if a person does not consciously go out of their way to take environmentally beneficial actions, by default the status quo results in environmental harm. A different set of default arrangements, a different design, could support ecological sustainability. Under those conditions—and this is Bell and Ashwood's point—even unthinking acts would be more likely to produce environmental benefits. For example, if more sustainable materials were designed into the front end of the manufacturing process, it would be far easier to recycle materials. "Green architect" William McDonough, for example, discusses a "cradle to cradle" concept, where a product reaches the end of its life cycle only to be "born" into a new use. Urban and environmental sociologist Harvey Molotch reminds us that "How we desire, produce, and discard the durables [i.e., the material objects] of existence helps form who we are, how we connect to one another, and what we do to the earth."

Let's explore the "desire" piece of the formula. A key point to remember is that while we are busy constructing the meaning of the world and our own identities through naturework, others are busily attempting to construct our identities *for* us. For example, the advertising industry, an essential feature of contemporary global capitalism, works around the clock to construct us primarily as "consumers" always in need of a newer, more "cutting-edge" product (see Lesson 5). The social psychology of capitalism depends on us experiencing a kind of "halo effect" around an item we desire, a halo that quickly begins to fade as soon as we possess the item and our attention moves to a new object (think about how this works in your own experience when you buy things). The social and economic (and political) relationships of capitalism depend on intense competition and a drive to increase profits. This pattern is built around a kind of "**treadmill**" logic, as Allan Schnaiberg and others have pointed out; individuals and corporations run in place faster and faster in an effort to keep up in the (now global) game of competition (see Lesson 2). The treadmill creates a voracious appetite for natural resources as people are persuaded to "toss" older products. This may include tossing a can out of the window or getting rid of a truck or a computer after a few years, to replace it with the latest model. It is not considered too important to know where things go after they leave our hands. What is important is the desire for the new object.

The advertising industry fuels our desires by specializing in a particular kind of naturework: It attracts buyers by invoking a love of nature but sells products that often disconnect us from nature. In the multibillion-dollar cosmetics industry, for example, the "natural look" not only carries a large price tag but sells a fabricated image of perfection. "Natural skin" enhanced by cosmetics is billed as fresh and flawless, while nature itself includes many flaws and irregularities (and much more variety). Similarly, local organic apples are likely to contain many more blemishes but more freshness and diversity (and significantly fewer dangerous pesticides) than their mass-produced relatives available at national grocery store chains and based on monoculture and industrialized agriculture (see Lesson 12). "Natural" cosmetics often contain unsafe products that arguably do some violence to the environment and to the body that wears them (see Lesson 11). From name-brand undergarments billed as the "natural woman's" look to cosmetics that disguise what nature has given, it is a simulacrum, or false imitation, of nature that is being sold, not nature itself. In fact, "real" nature is not considered particularly attractive. This should not be surprising since the advertising industry has to be interested only in what can be captured and converted into a commodity and sold, and nature "in the raw" eludes capture.

If we shift our attention from cosmetics to ads for vehicles, we also find nature in the picture. A desire for the pure, untouched, and wide-open landscape is a staple feature of most ads for cars, trucks, jeeps, sport utility vehicles, and off-road vehicles. But in this case, nature is seen as a place to "get away from it all" and/or a place that is waiting to be conquered by human technology. Nature is in fact a backdrop or a stage set for the enactment of key cultural fantasies about "freedom" and "domination" and "individualism." Since the vehicle conquers nature by representing the freedom to go anywhere, and since, if the vehicle and others like it truly do go anywhere, there will soon be no pristine environment, the ad is selling pure paradox. Just as importantly, it sells the idea that the purchase of an expensive product is the admission ticket to this ego-enhancing performance.

But suppose that one's own naturework leans in the direction of ecological sustainability (see Lesson 20), and one wishes to step off the "treadmill" by becoming disinterested in consuming new products. Sociologist Zygmunt Bauman argues that this person is the true outsider, the deviant in a consumption-based society. To be socially accepted or even understandable to one's neighbors, a person needs to revel in the seduction of ever-new and identity-expanding choices offered by consumer goods, whether these are the latest models of cars, adventure tourism "packages," cosmetics, or a multitude of other possibilities. How true is this? Bauman is right that this has been the mainstream script for many years in countries like the United States. But the acceptance or rejection of this notion depends on time, place, situation, awareness, and socioeconomic position. The theories of environmental sociology can help us consider under what conditions ecologically sustainable actions become more or less possible. They can also teach us about what stands in the way of sustainable actions and solutions—from naturework to the treadmill logic of global capitalism to what Bell and Ashwood call "technological somnambulism": the tendency to unquestioningly accept the use of and spread of new technologies.

Consider this example: because of a history of strong labor unions, Sweden passed a law that supports the right of workers to discuss the implications of a new technology before it is introduced into the workplace. But at my college, such decisions are administratively made at the top. A new photocopying machine undercut previously successful efforts to use recycled paper because the paper tended to jam in the new machine, causing extra work for administrative assistants. The paper was phased out, and no one had a chance to talk about it at all. "Nature" became a threat to efficiency and was removed. But as more colleges and institutions become interested in how they contribute to a sustainable "ecological footprint," the possibility arises for more democratic discussions, better research into design, and a clearer grasp of the cost–benefit balance that comes with any new technology.

Since technologies always have complex (and often unanticipated) impacts on society and the environment, environmental sociology can play a key role in identifying impacts that are not immediately obvious (see Lesson 7). For example, it can help us to identify the range of "stakeholders" who will be helped and/or harmed by a particular technology, and it can offer a systematic way to evaluate the "goods" and "bads" for social groups (and for nature, or the ecosystem, an often forgotten stakeholder). For example, I benefit from a feature on the newer photocopier that allows me to be a "remote user," printing two-sided (good for the environment!) copies from my office. That new possibility represents a positive and exciting aspect of innovation. But the machine doesn't use recycled paper, and if it breaks down, my colleagues and I can't fix it ourselves by undoing a paper jam, as we could with the previous model—we have to call our Information Technology division and hope that someone is "home." So when we look at a new technology (smartphones, for example), we always need to ask for whom it is beneficial and why. The difficult challenge is to arrive at an overall picture of costs and benefits. That would require many groups with different kinds of knowledge and experience to be part of a democratic discussion. The theories of environmental sociology produce models and research findings that contribute to a "big-picture" understanding of any technology, as well as the naturework through which we see it.

Today, we have growing evidence that the mainstream script based on "conquering" nature is fraying around the edges, under pressure from the realities of climate change and impending oil scarcity, as well as movements for social and environmental justice. When I find myself looking at yet another advertising banner at the local car dealer with a picture of a truck and the words "It's a big, tough truck. What's not to like?" I think about how many of my students and colleagues would make a list of "what's not to like" quite different from what they thought even a year ago. Certainly, Ford and General Motors have discovered that suddenly there is much "not to like" about their large, fuel-inefficient vehicles. Many of my students now find the image of the lone vehicle presented as a powerful object of desire conquering an empty landscape (is it Alaska? Montana? New Mexico?) to be laughable, even ridiculous. Many of them would like bike paths, public transportation, and fuel efficiency. But to arrive at critique and to construct fresh choices, a person needs to have thought about it and to become aware of the many uses of naturework.

OF TIME, SPACE, AND COMPUTERS

Scene Two: Somebody sits with their fingers on a computer keyboard, looking at an electronic screen offering the promise of instant global communication. Not long ago, Time *magazine celebrated this hypothetical person by selecting them as "Person of the Year." The magazine's cover contained the image of a partially reflective metal-like computer screen that "you" are invited to look into. The accompanying message is that you, the person with fingers on the keyboard, are Person of the Year because, in a world democratized and decentralized by the Internet, you have tremendous power and influence. Like the truck's passenger in Scene One—but even more so—"you" have the freedom to go anywhere, fast. But unlike the passenger in the truck, you aren't tossing anything out of the window. Or are you?*

Clearly, *Time* magazine's editors decided that in the United States, use of the Internet was so widespread that the computer (and its imagined connection to "you") deserved a place on the cover instead of the usual photographs of influential people. The accompanying article claims that the ability to use the Internet represents the end of top-down authority and the rise of democratic freedom to shape the world. It also celebrates "community and collaboration on a scale never seen before." A very empowered "you" sits in front of the screen, reveling in your historically new choices.

What would an environmental sociologist notice about this image and what it presupposes? First, this is an image aimed only at those who have access to this technology. Second, the sociologist would take a hard look at the idea that access to the Internet makes you free from top-down authority and constraint. On the one hand, smartphones and social media have contributed significantly to social change movements around the world (for example, what came to be known as the "Arab Spring," the #MeToo movement, the Youth Climate Strike, and more). On the other hand, while there are significant opportunities to gather and share information in ways previously unavailable (and unimaginable), spyware on many websites and restricted access to information in the wake of 9/11, and the Trump administration's "purging" of climate data from government websites, undermine the assumption that the Internet represents total freedom. And an *environmental* sociologist would inquire about connections to and disconnections from the environment experienced by the person sitting at the computer screen.

We could begin, once again, with the concept of naturework. Where is nature in this picture? Unless "you" are looking at a virtual image of nature on the screen, the environment seems to be conspicuous by its absence. The computer is most likely indoors—although a new technological advantage is ever-increasing portability, so you may have taken your laptop (or your smartphone, or some even newer technology, a great example of the "treadmill" of production!) to a park. You are probably looking intently at the screen for extended periods of time, and you are probably in a sedentary posture. Nature is present in the form of your body, and your actions are shaping that body (your eyes, your posture, your health). Nature is also present in the materials that make up the room you are sitting in (the built environment) or in trees in the park—but if you are looking at the computer screen, you are less apt to notice your surrounding environment. Chances are that you are also ignoring your *internal* environment that is sending signals about eye strain, hunger, brain overload, and bad posture. All of this adds up to a separation from your immediate environment, a version of what sociologist Anthony Giddens calls "disembedding." Let's consider how the ideas of Giddens and some other scholars of modernity might help us analyze the relationship between the computer, the person, and the natural environment.

Giddens claims that a new aspect of human experience in "late modern" societies is the way that time and space are rearranged to "connect presence and absence." Because of an increasingly globalized and interconnected world and because of the development of electronic communication and spaces (like cyberspace) that appear not to be connected to actual places, human beings experience what Giddens calls disembedding and "distanci-ation." **Disembedding** refers to social relations being "lifted out" of their local contexts and restructured across time and space. We no longer exclusively interact face to face with other people in the same physical location. Rather, global economies and electronic communication networks connect us to physically absent people in places that are geographically remote from us (a country halfway across the globe, or a friend in another city). This way of relating to people and places at a distance, or **distanciation**, comes to be a normal and expected part of our social organization and interactions.

New technologies harness the wonder of new understandings of nature, including how to make space and time work differently (up to a point). The problem is that these technologies are offered as if there were no strings attached—like the car sitting in a pristine landscape, the computer or iPhone suggests limitless freedom and no drawbacks. But there are limits of a very real kind. Giddens points out that relationships at a distance depend entirely on trust—trust that unseen people are who they claim to be and trust in "expert systems," such as those who set up and maintain the electronic networks (or the Information Technology experts who maintain the photocopier for me, the "remote user"). When these systems break down, social trust is damaged.

There are other kinds of limits that interfere with our ability to understand the bigger picture. Giddens argues, for example, that the new arrangement of space and time "tears space away from place." Notice the violence of the metaphor—this new development not only breaks the historical relationship between humans and physical places, but there is some roughness to the break. Giddens's metaphor suggests ragged edges and torn roots. And there is an additional twist—our local places are becoming harder to know and understand because they are, Giddens says, penetrated and reshaped by distant global influences. This makes it more difficult to clearly understand our relationship to the environment, since what is visible locally may be deceptive. Radiation and invisible toxic pollution affect us whether we see them or not and can be disguised in the most beautiful landscape.

Time is also experienced in a radically new way in modern societies. Social relationships are increasingly separated from a natural calendar of seasons and cycles of day and night. We produce materials such as nuclear waste and climate change effects whose impact reaches far into a future whose timescale we cannot even imagine. The expanding possibility of instantaneous global communication has reshaped expectations about how time "works." Speed is highly valued, from raising speed limits on highways to faster Internet connections and instant messaging. However, an environmental sociologist can easily make the argument that rising speeds make it more difficult to pay attention to one's local environment, whether a person is in a truck driving down a freeway or sitting at a computer keyboard, intently concentrating on the Internet "highway." Add an iPhone to this mix and lack of attention to the local environment may increase exponentially (as car accident statistics show quite clearly). Although many people pride themselves on their ability to multitask, studies show that it often doesn't work very well in terms of work quality, personal health, and consequences for social relationships. People report not having enough time to pay attention to everything from family to politics to their own mental health (think about how this works for you—do you have enough time?).

A feature of the new time–space structure described by Giddens and others is that it blurs the boundaries between many formerly separate categories of experience. Sociologist George Ritzer—best known for studying the global spread of "McDonaldization" and new forms of consumption—draws on sociologist Jean Baudrillard's concept of "implosion" to describe these new combinations of time and space. **Implosion** refers to one phenomenon collapsing, or contracting, into another. One example is the merging of the categories of home and shopping. In an electronically networked world, one does not need to leave one's home to go shopping; if one desires, one can shop in the middle of the night at an online "cyberstore." Who is minding the cyberstore, and where is this person located? We usually don't know. Even money is not required, just a credit card (with a promise of payment or growing debt in the future). Thus, home/store, local/global, and future/present collapse into one ambiguous category. Another example is the "pop-up" event—a local shopping opportunity (perhaps a food truck) that generates excitement by being temporarily located in a particular space for a limited time.

As Ritzer and others point out, such implosions represent ever-new opportunities for selling goods and promoting consumption, a feature that goes hand in hand with the expanding treadmill of global capitalism. Speeded-up experiences of time and access to new, disembedded spaces erase earlier limits to consumption. Ritzer calls this a "reenchantment of the world," a process that draws in new consumers through ever more "spectacular" opportunities to consume. Meanwhile, just as these implosions create new connections, they create disconnections, particularly from local people and natural environments. The fact that distant or virtual spaces appear more real and compelling than our immediate environment can create a disturbing gap in our understanding of the environmental consequences of our behavior. The seductive magic of a computer or a smartphone permits its user to leap across space and time, a thrilling possibility. But this possibility is "embedded" in a system that persuades consumers to use up resources even faster, producing more waste as they pursue the latest upgrade. Although we may *assume* that our key relationships are no longer with the physical places that surround us (including nature, in a local and specific way), we still have a relationship with our local environment. Even if—especially if—that relationship is neglected, there are ecological consequences.

THE TRUCK AND THE COMPUTER REVISITED: TOSSING NATURE OUT THE WINDOW?

Putting together some ideas from the theories we have considered, we can look at the similarities and differences between the truck and the computer. Both are, we could say, fast-moving vehicles, although the computer is connected to fast motion in cyberspace. The truck speeding through the landscape is already altering the human experience of time and space, leaving places behind and focusing attention inside the vehicle or on the road ahead. But the computer screen is a gateway into a virtual world where time and space are compressed and recombined, making the disconnection from the natural environment even more striking. Both vehicles are attractive because they allow the "driver" to rush toward certain things (freedom?) and away from others (boredom? stultifying locations and relationships? limits?). Both involve the consumption of items that enhance the identity of the consumer. The truck is connected to a certain lifestyle that is linked to other consumption items (some of which are used up and tossed out of the window on the way). The computer is likewise connected to a lifestyle that is attractive to its "driver." Does he or she also use things up and toss them away while speeding through cyberspace? If so, what are they, and where do they land?

To answer such questions, we need, once again, to look for nature and environment in the picture. Leaving aside the interesting debate about where nature ends and technology begins (a discussion well worth having but probably not now), we can see that the truck is driving through an actual place, even if the landscape is seen only through windows or in a rearview mirror. The computer seems to have nothing to do with nature at all. But a closer look at both scenes will reveal naturework that creates separation and (illusory) control. The natural environment is as physically real as ever but has become less visible because of social organization, socially constructed beliefs, and technology. So, for example, our computers connect us to the coal, oil and gas, and nuclear power industries that charge them and to large data centers that make our quick searches and downloads possible by emitting greenhouse gases. Invented cyber landscapes like "The Cloud" offer us "places" to store data beyond our individual laptops and devices. What could be wrong with a cloud, gently hovering over us, speeding up our searches, and keeping our data safe? (Google has bragged that "an 18-wheel truck could run over your laptop and all your data would still safely reside on the web, accessible from any Internet-connected computer, anywhere in the world.") A great idea, except that clouds of data add up to clouds of greenhouse gases. Typically, we know little about the landscapes that enable our technologies—including disputed landscapes like the Fukushima nuclear reactor disaster, the BP oil spill, the Tar Sands pipeline connecting the United States and Canada, and hydrofracking sites.

We said earlier that it is the job of social and environmental theory to make relationships visible. If we return to the image of the invisible strings connecting people to each other (and to their technological inventions), and if we follow the strings back to the hands that put together the computer and the hands that will someday dismantle it, it will be impossible to ignore the ecological impact of the production, distribution, consumption, and disposal of computers, especially when multiplied by the number of users. No matter how liberated from place or from nature a person feels, the reality is that the computer was manufactured from Earth elements and goes back to the Earth, and that there are tangible material consequences at each end of the production process (see Lesson 7). These include components that are poisonous to human beings and other life forms. There is a real cost—medical, social, and political—to ignoring these matters. Yet, quite often no more thought is given to throwing away an older model of a computer than is given to throwing the can out of the truck. With a growing mountain of obsolete equipment and the message that throwing things away is necessary and even pleasing, it is clear that something big is going out the window—the idea of nature as a visible or significant presence and an enormous amount of material that can do environmental harm. And so we arrive at our third and last snapshot.

Scene Three: People of all ages pick through a heap of discarded electronic equipment from the United States. The actual place may be southern China or Delhi, India (we know this because of research conducted by environmental sociologists). We can begin to imagine this low-tech "e-waste processing center," a place where people with few other choices manually harvest this highly toxic electronic waste for salvageable materials. The pay is low, and there are no protections in place for their bodies or for the surrounding environment.

We can only begin to imagine this scene because most computer users in the United States and in many other places have never seen it. It is disturbing to imagine it and to think that in some way we participate in it. Although from a distance, the computer production process appears to be a clean and "high-tech" operation, at both the assembling and disassembling ends, it is hazardous and farmed out to low-wage assembly-line-style factories in developing nations. Instead of a can being thrown to the edge of a US highway, electronic toxic waste is landing in places that are globally "at the edge of the highway" as nations of the Global North (and even more so multinational corporations) speed by in pursuit of economic growth and political power. The "tearing away" from place first evident in the truck scene now has global dimensions. The difference is that globalization extends the arc of the object being disposed of and expands its geographical reach. Like the butterfly wings at the edge of the highway, the export of toxic components has been a well-kept secret, although recently, China and countries of the Global South are refusing to become dumping grounds for the world's wealthier nations. A challenge for theorists in environmental sociology is to make these global structures plainly visible so that we can see and so that we can act.

CONCLUDING THOUGHTS: OF NATURE AND DOGS

Although this discussion has included only a small slice of what environmental sociologists do with theory, it reflects the wide range of interests and levels of analysis that are characteristic of the field. From naturework to shifting arrangements of time and space in the context of global capitalism, it offers tools for understanding the connection between our individual identities, nature, and broad patterns that are reshaping the context of our human experience and generating new kinds of relationships.

At the same time, we can notice that there is creative resistance to these patterns, some of which is also expressed through technology—for example, one might be using the computer to research social change and to connect with organizations working for ecological sustainability. There are many groups around the world working for environmental justice and for safeguards that would change Scene Three, for example, by making it more visible to the people in Scene Two, or by working to organize the people in Scene Three for better alternatives (see Lessons 10, 18, and 19). When environmental sociologists produce theories and research to document and analyze relationships between society and environment, they contribute to the possibility of real social change, including well-informed discussions about proposals like the Green New Deal, a comprehensive and long-range plan to address climate change.

Here is a closing thought and one last image. My friend and colleague Elaine lives in a rural area over in the next town, in a self-designed house that reflects her fondness for stained glass art and large dogs. On her way to work, some of the dogs run alongside her truck for a little while, then turn around and go home before she hits the main road. But one morning, after an ice storm, the story line changed. She had to drive very slowly on the slippery unpaved road leading from her house. Because the truck couldn't "outrun" her most enthusiastic dog, he jumped in the back of her truck, rode to the university, and entertained himself by barking at passersby for much of the day. We don't know whether he *really* said "bow wow!" or "haf haf!" but we know that he attracted a lot of attention as an element of "nature" out of place.

I remember this story for several reasons. I like to think about how that dog insisted on connecting time and space and refused to be left behind in the "home" space while my friend went to "work" (he didn't appreciate distanciation). He brings to mind the many things we think we can outrun, including our impacts on the environment. Like the barking dog, fossil fuel scarcity and climate change are reminders of ecological actualities that we cannot continue to outrun. In our speeded-up world, you could say that our road is getting slippery and there are plenty of signs that we need to slow down and take an immediate, careful, and radical look at our actions and at our connections to the environment.

I propose that it would be even more appropriate to see social theory as the barking dog in this picture, shaking up our usual routines and reminding us that we are engaged in a dialog with the environment, whether we want to see it or not. It is our social structures that are blocking our view of everything from tiny damaged butterfly wings to global flows of hazardous waste. If we accept the invitation from environmental sociology, we will be connecting the invisible strings that link our hands with the things that we throw away, looking to see where they land, questioning relationships of power and desire, and moving toward a better design for socioecological relationships.

SOURCES

Bauman, Zygmunt. 1997. *Postmodernity and Its Discontents*. New York: New York University Press.

Bell, Michael Mayerfeld, and Loka L. Ashwood. 2016. *An Invitation to Environmental Sociology*. Thousand Oaks, CA: Pine Forge.

Catton, William R., and Riley E. Dunlap. 1980. "A New Ecological Paradigm for Post-Exuberant Sociology." *American Behavioral Scientist* 24:15–47.

Fine, Gary Alan. 1998. *Morel Tales: The Culture of Mushrooming*. Cambridge, MA: Harvard University Press.

Giddens, Anthony. 1990. *The Consequences of Modernity*. Stanford, CA: Stanford University Press.

McDonough, William. 2002. *Cradle to Cradle: Remaking the Way We Make Things*. Minneapolis, MN: Sagebrush Educational Resources.

Meadows, Donella. 2004. "Dancing with Systems." *The Systems Thinker* 13(2):2–6.

Molotch, Harvey. 2003. *Where Stuff Comes From: How Toasters, Toilets, Cars, Computers, and Many Other Things Come to Be as They Are*. New York: Routledge.

Ritzer, George. 1999. *Enchanting a Disenchanted World: Revolutionizing the Means of Consumption*. Thousand Oaks, CA: Pine Forge.

Schnaiberg, Allan, and Kenneth Alan Gould. 1994. *Environment and Society: The Enduring Conflict*. New York: St. Martin's.

Smith, Ted, David A. Sonnenfeld, and David Naguib Pellow, eds. 2006. *Challenging the Chip: Labor Rights and Environmental Justice in the Global Electronics Industry*. Philadelphia, PA: Temple University Press.

Theories in Environmental Sociology

Justin Sean Myers

Discarded television on shore of Hudson River, Staatsburg, New York.

Post your photo on theory to #TLEStheory.

Photo by Ken Gould

If you are not reading this lesson on it, it is probably on the table or chair next to you or maybe it is in your bag or on your body. Yes, I am talking about your cell phone, and odds are it is an iPhone. Officially launched in June 2007, Apple sold over 2.2 billion of them by the end of 2018. It is a product that has revolutionized how people communicate, obtain information, and consume media content. We listen to music, watch movies, and take photos through it. With FaceTime, we can video chat with friends and family all over the world and even do a job interview in our living room (hopefully fully dressed). We can use it to track our finances, diets, and workout routines. Through apps like Instagram, Snapchat, and Venmo, we can share our lives and money with the world as well (sometimes we share too much). Let's be honest, without a cell phone and Google Maps, we wouldn't know how to get anywhere. And with cloud computing, streaming services, and unlimited data plans, we can watch Netflix and live TV almost wherever and whenever we want. The iPhone is no longer a luxury for most people: it is a necessity for modern living, it has become part of us. We're constantly on it, and if we forget it at home or leave it in the car, we feel like we're missing a part of us; and more importantly, we feel like we're missing out.

This ubiquitous object, which is so integral to everyday life, is also a rich example to use to introduce social theory. The analysis of the cell phone can illuminate the similarities and differences through which environmental sociologists study and explain socioenvironmental relations. While environmental sociologists seek to answer fundamental questions about why socioenvironmental problems and inequities exist, what produces them, and what needs to change to address them, not all theories approach these questions in the same way. Ecological modernization theorists might look at Apple's efforts to reduce the use of toxic materials and increase the use of recycled materials in the iPhone as an example of how socioenvironmental relations are improving and how capitalism is capable of greening itself. In contrast, treadmill of production theorists might look at the growth imperatives of Apple and its need to sell more iPhones every year as a prime example of how capitalism and its technological innovations are incapable of greening themselves and will continue to produce ecological destruction at an ever-escalating scale. Ecological Marxists might inquire into whether the energy consumption and carbon production needed to power the cloud is fueling a rift in the carbon cycle that amplifies climate destabilization. World system theorists might research which countries receive the most and the least profit from the production and sale of the iPhone and how this is connected to their position in the global capitalist economy. **Risk society** theorists might investigate how and why people are using the iPhone to monitor their air quality, find mercury free fish, and eat GMO free foods. Ecofeminists might focus on the gendered inequities that emerge from the mining of aluminum for the iPhone, the working conditions in factories making it, and the e-waste dumps where many broken cell phones go after we are done using them.

There is no one way to be an environmental sociologist, and there is no one way to study socioenvironmental relations. That is the task before this lesson, to explore the theoretical toolbox of an environmental sociologist and guide you through the frameworks you have at your disposal to investigate socioenvironmental relations. What links all these different frameworks together is that each is shaped by environmental sociology being a social science, which entails a commitment to linking theory to data and ensuring that the explanatory power of theory stands up to empirical verification over time. Thus, a theory is not just a theory of what could be going on but utilizes data to support the claims that the theory asserts about how the social world works and why it works that way. Very basic questions guiding theoretical frameworks include the following: What is happening? Who is it happening to? Who is directing what is happening? How it is happening? Why is it happening? How is this connected to what has already happened and what might happen in the future?

At the same time, these frameworks also differ because each has particular philosophical assumptions built into them that shape what is perceived as an issue or problem worthy of study, what questions are asked, how information is gathered to answer the questions posed, how the information collected is interpreted, and how that information is leveraged for social change. Certain frameworks might focus these questions through the lens of class, race, or gender, or approach such questions from the point of view of corporations and markets; while others will approach it through the lens of social movements and marginalized communities. The theorist could be a conflict theorist looking at struggles over access to environmental resources, while others might be symbolic interactionists investigating how people construct meanings about the environment that either prevent or facilitate ecological degradation (as discussed in Lesson 1). Frameworks can also differ based on whether they study socioenvironmental interactions at the micro, meso, or macro level. For instance, a framework may focus on how individuals explain the reasons for their political mobilization against mining companies extracting copper and gold for iPhones. This is the micro level, which focuses on the behaviors of and between individuals. Other researchers may focus on how the cultural, political, and economic structures of the Apple corporation play a role in pushing it to green its production practices. This is the meso level, which studies groups and institutions. Finally, an environmental sociologist might analyze the global carbon output of the iPhone commodity chain over time to see whether the iPhone is indeed requiring less resources to create it, consuming less energy during its lifespan, and producing less waste during its postconsumption phase. This is the macro level, which studies the society as a whole and the processes, institutions, and structures shaping it. Consequently, since theories orient the researcher toward asking particular questions at certain levels (over other questions at other levels), they differ in their explanations of what is happening, why, to whom, and how—all of which leads to different trajectories for social change.

We can think of theoretical frameworks as intellectually and methodologically guided narratives of how the world works; a **theory** is "a set of concepts and ideas and the proposed relationships among these, a structure that is intended to capture or model something about the world" (Maxwell 2013, 48). In short, they are frameworks for making sense of what you see and the data you are collecting, be it through interviews, archives, ethnography, or statistical analysis; data that will be able to support, refute, or modify your theoretical presumptions about what is happening. Through the concepts of a theoretical framework, you are able to draw connections between what is happening that might otherwise remain hidden or invisible. Consequently, theories are quite powerful and important components of being an environmental sociologist because they assist us in making visible the invisible relations, structures, and processes shaping everyday life and the organization of socioenvironmental relations. Yet, one theory is often not able to illuminate or make visible all aspects of life; based on their assumptions, questions asked, and methods used to answer the questions, theories will be able to tell a story about the world, but not the only story.

Theories can shine light onto certain issues while being unable to explain other problems or relations. Thus, we need to be aware of the strengths and limits of the theories we are using, of what the theory can make visible but also what may still remain invisible, what the theory can explain and what it cannot explain. We now turn toward our first theory, **ecological modernization theory**.

ECOLOGICAL MODERNIZATION THEORY

"Truly innovative products leave their mark on the world instead of the planet." This is the tag line on Apple's website asserting their environmental bona fides, an assertion followed by a wealth of information about how the company is working toward reducing their products' **ecological footprint**, the impact of the item on the environment based on its withdrawal of resources and addition of pollution and waste. Here is a short list for the iPhone X series: it is free of mercury, brominated flame retardant, PVC, beryllium, and has a glass display that is free of arsenic; its battery is free of cadmium and lead; the solder in the main logic board is assembled with 100 percent recycled tin; and 40 of its components contain recycled plastic, including the glass frame that is made with 32 percent bio-based plastic and the speaker enclosure that is made with 35 percent postconsumer recycled plastic. Plus, when you are done with your iPhone, there is the Apple Trade In program where it can be recycled free of charge, or you can exchange it for credit to be reused by another person.

These claims appear to be a win-win for us and Apple. We can continue to buy high-tech products, Apple can continue to make a profit, and we can consume less of the planet in the process. From these statistics, it looks like Apple is indeed shrinking our ecological footprints and dematerializing the economy (using less materials to produce the same or greater quantity of goods). If you approach the iPhone and Apple through ecological modernization theory, then you would come away with a fairly rosy picture. This is because ecological modernization theory is essentially a theory of environmental reform. It investigates how corporations and the state, the major economic and political institutions of today, are responding to the environmental crises that emerged in the 1970s by restructuring **commodity chains** (extraction, production, consumption, postconsumption) to make them more ecologically sustainable. Central to such efforts are efforts by companies to increase energy efficiency and restructure their production processes to incorporate more recycled materials and minimize the production of pollutants and waste. Through such efforts, ecological modernization theory proposes that the economic growth needs of capitalism can be reconciled with ecological principles in a win-win situation where future growth can be increasingly decoupled from resource extraction and the production of waste and pollutants.

By analyzing how the leading companies and industries are improving their ecological footprint, advocates for this theory contend that the processes of modernization and industrialization do not have to be abandoned. Instead they argue for the creation of more ecologically friendly technologies. By way of new technologies, destructive production practices can be restructured around **cradle-to-cradle design**. This is a process where products are designed with a closed-loop system in mind to minimize the extraction of raw materials, avoid toxic materials, and minimize the production of waste. This would occur through utilizing synthetic materials that can be reused without degradation and organic materials that when they degrade can be consumed (decomposed) by other lifeforms. The hope is that by having design processes and commodity chains mirror ecological processes—a concept known as **biomimicry**—environmental problems caused by modernization, including air and water pollution, deforestation, and climate destabilization will be addressed. Thus, technology, which was once the driver of ecological degradation, would now be harnessed toward environmental reform.

Central to this technological greening of capitalism, according to ecological modernization theorists, is the modernization of the economic as well as the political systems shaping capitalism. First, ecological modernization claims that the market structures are flexible enough to reconcile the existing tension between growth and the environment in ways that corporations center ecological values and practices within their operating procedures. Second, ecological modernization claims that government can also incorporate ecological values alongside of economic values within its operations and that it can and needs to push markets toward addressing environmental problems. Yet, if the state is going to realize this goal, ecological modernization theorists propose that it will have to jettison its top-down command and control model reliant on lawsuits, fines, and national-level regulations (e.g., Clean Water Act and the Clean Air Act). Instead, the state needs to adopt financial incentives, such as ecotaxes, and embrace public-private partnerships where the state works with companies to develop new technologies through publicly funding privately led research. Through adopting these more flexible and conciliatory pro-market practices, the state can fuel technological innovation within industry that facilitates growth but also reduces withdrawals and additions, thereby bringing together economic and ecological values.

Such a process, it is claimed, can sustain both capitalism and the environment in a mutually beneficial relationship. Examples of this would be the adoption by companies of environmental management systems (EMS), which lays out a series of processes to document and calculate the firm's impact on the environment and then what steps could by taken to reduce the firm's impact on the environment. Many of the leading technology companies have EMS's, including Apple, Panasonic, LG, Google, Microsoft, IBM, and Samsung. The incorporation of environmental agreements within multilateral trade agreements that historically focus only on economic matters, such as the North American Free Trade Agreement (NAFTA), also underscores the ascendancy of ecological issues alongside the traditional economic ones. So does the emergence of recycling within public utilities and private companies and environmental insurance policies that cover losses associated with pollution.

The use of ecotaxes (instead of income taxes) in Japan and Europe is also indicative of the shift away from top-down regulations toward market-based mechanisms. In Japan, taxes on sulfur dioxide (SO_2) lead to technological innovations, including the flue gas scrubber, which reduced air pollution in the country. Denmark, Germany, and the Netherlands implemented various carbon taxes on fossil fuel consumption that utilize market signals to push corporations toward reducing their carbon dioxide (CO_2) footprint by moving toward the use of renewable energy. One form of public–private partnerships is seen in Denmark where the Danish Environmental Protection Agency (EPA) worked with companies and financed and subsidized the creation of cleaner technologies in wood and furniture, graphic, electroplating, and fish-processing industries to reduce CO_2 and volatile organic compound (VOC) emissions.

In the United States, the automobile company Tesla would be an example of ecological modernization. Through market-led technological development, a product has been created that has significant consumer demand and is slowly pushing other automobile companies to adopt electric car production, the end result of which will be a significant reduction in fossil fuel consumption, air pollution levels, and CO_2 generation. Federal and state governments can then assist in both the adoption of this technology by other companies and its purchase by consumers through financial incentives in the form of tax credits. Right now these incentives, which range up to $7,500 at the federal level and vary in the thousands at the state level, help generate the effective demand for these vehicles at a time when the purchase price of electric vehicles is higher than comparable gasoline models (although electric cars cost less to own over their lifetime).

Besides government employing market-centric policies and creating public–private alliances to generate greener technology, consumers are an integral component for ecological modernists. As with the Tesla example, if consumers do not purchase cleaner, less polluting commodities, then capitalism will be unable to green itself. This is because if there is no demand for greener products, than the market will not generate them. One area where this is occurring is within organic food sales, which has grown from $3.4 billion in 1997 to $45.2 billion in 2017, a fifteenfold increase (Organic Trade Association 2018). As a result, organic food sales constituted 5.5 percent of total food sales by 2017. Driven largely by the price premium attached to organic food, this growth in organic production, and the conversion of conventional farmers to organic farming, should produce declines in pesticide usage that would be beneficial to the health and resiliency of ecosystems. These examples suggest that under some conditions, capitalism can indeed become greener.

TREADMILL OF PRODUCTION

While ecological modernization theorists might see Apple as an example of a company at the forefront of green capitalism, treadmill theorists would see Apple in a very different light because of their different conceptual approach. In 2008, the first full year it was available, iPhone sales were a mere 13.7 million; yet by 2018, Apple was selling 217.7 million iPhones a year. Even if each unit is less toxic, made of more recyclable components, and is itself more recyclable, the total environmental impact of its production, consumption, and postconsumption is still far greater in 2018 than what it was in 2008. And this process is bound to continue for the company, according to treadmill theorists, because if it wants to maintain its high stock price (around $220 per share in September 2019), as well as its status as a darling of Wall Street, it will have to sell more iPhones every year moving forward than it has in the preceding year. If Apple is unable to do so, then its stock price will decline, investors will seek out other more lucrative investments, and another company might step up to dominate the cell phone market. Additionally, with a lifespan of an iPhone being less than three years, treadmill theorists would ask how much waste is being produced with such a high rate of turnover? Given that Apple does not release statistics on its Trade In program, we do not know how many iPhone users trade in their phone nor how many are reused versus recycled; therefore, it is hard to know for certain whether Apple is successfully moving toward a closed-loop system that minimizes e-waste.

Then there is the issue that the 200 million plus iPhones, and the more than 2.5 billion smartphones globally, are a massive consumer of data as we use them to access digital music, movies, TV, maps, and social media. And while the iPhone might have combined a cell phone with digital cameras and digital music players, so we don't have to lug all three around with us anymore, we do not just have an iPhone but probably a laptop and possibly a tablet, a smart watch, a smart TV, and a smart car too—all of which are continually sucking down data from the sky. But this data, your data, doesn't merely float in a puffy cloud. It is materially rooted in some data center on the planet that is consuming a lot of energy and producing quite a bit of carbon to keep that data accessible to you 24/7. With ever wider swaths of the globe becoming hooked up to the cloud, global data traffic is doubling every four years and turning these data centers into the "factories of the digital age"; factories that produce as much CO_2 as the airline industry. For example, in 2010, global data center traffic was only 1.1 zettabytes (one billion terabytes); and cloud traffic accounted for under 12 percent of this data amount (Cisco 2011). By 2021, global data center traffic will have increased over twentyfold to 20.6 zettabytes, and cloud traffic will account for 95 percent of this data (Cisco 2018).

In looking at these numbers, it appears all is not that green with Apple. At the per unit level, each Apple product is greener than the previous model. But by volume, the environmental impact is far greater, and the cloud infrastructure that it is connected to consumes more and more resources every year. Apple is therefore a clear example of the anti-ecological structure of capitalism. This would be the take from a treadmill theorist. **Treadmill of production theory** aims to explain how the relations between capitalism, the state, labor, and the environment produces environmental degradation as a normal part of its operations with little hope for correction without structural transformation (Schnaiberg 1980). This framework has been popularized by Kenneth A. Gould, David N. Pellow, and Alan Schnaiberg and is influenced by both neo-Weberian sociology and Marxist political economy. Treadmill theory is a conflict theory that explains the social and ecological problems facing society as an outcome of how industrial capitalism privileges the needs of an economic system organized around profit maximization and continual economic growth. It focuses attention on the power that corporations and the economic and political elite wield within this system (see Lesson 5).

While ecological modernization theory sees liberal capitalist democracy as having the capacity to reform itself, treadmill theory sees its structural configuration as preventing environmental reform and the substantive re-structuring of society around ecological principles. This is because the state generally privileges the profit needs of corporations over and against the social and environmental needs of people and the planet (see Lessons 3, 9, and 13). On top of this, when the state does attempt to balance these often competing needs, it does so in ways that further degrades the social and en-vironmental needs of people and the planet (see Lesson 17). Treadmill theory refers to this conflict within the political system as one between exchange values and use values. For instance, the state tries to balance the demands of corporations and investors for economic growth and conditions that facilitate the private accumulation of socially produced wealth (exchange values) with the demands from the public for social amenities, services, and goods—such as public parks, public education, public transportation, affordable housing, and clean air and water (use values). Given that the public's demands often require regulations and taxes on corporations and the elite to fund such pro-grams, policies, and projects, regulations and taxes that diminish profit rates, the state is constantly trying to juggle the provision of social amenities and environmental protection with capital accumulation, a scenario that often pits it against one of these core constituencies. The state often tries to meet both demands by facilitating economic growth to grow the economic pie and create the tax revenue to meet the public's needs; however, this often works at cross purposes since the economic growth generated to fund such public desires often degrades the social and environmental amenities the public desires.

A prime example of this scenario is when efforts to improve the wages and benefits of automobile workers combine with attempts to reduce air pollu-tion through new environmental regulations on the fuel economy and emis-sions output of automobiles. Both of these initiatives impose new costs onto automobile companies. Auto companies may try and reduce the costs of new greener technology in their cars through selling more cars overall, since each car may have a smaller profit margin now. Automobile companies may also respond to these new labor costs through investments in labor-saving technology, which leads to workers becoming unemployed, and thus the need to sell even more automobiles to generate more jobs for those previously unemployed. Such layoffs also push the state to incentivize the growth of other industries to hire the newly unemployed workers, which means that more withdrawals and additions are produced to employ the same number of workers as before. Other tactics employed by auto companies to maximize earnings, given these new costs and increased competition from European and Asian automobile companies, include starting new workers at lower hourly wage rates and with reduced benefits packages compared to long-term workers while simultaneously speeding up production processes so that workers are more "productive" for the company (see Lesson 4). Both of these changes to the working conditions of employees harms their quality of life inside and outside of the jobsite, as they will be more exhausted at work and less able to buy a house, send their children to college, and save for retirement. The end result of these changes is that automobile companies extract more and more resources from the planet than before, consume more energy and chemicals to produce automobiles with automated processes, increase air pollution and the volume of waste through selling more automobiles, and employ less workers than before or employ workers whose quality of life is and will continue to be much lower than employees hired in previous decades. Thus, efforts to improve the social and environmental amenities within the treadmill of production (TOP) often exacerbate the very withdrawals and additions that they were trying to reduce based on how the treadmill operates.

Additionally, even when the state tries to balance the needs of economic growth, social welfare, and environmental sustainability, the capitalist class often rejects regulations and taxes as a threat to their power and profit maximization practices; thus, they generally attempt to gain either direct or indirect control over the state to ensure that use values are not prioritized over exchange values. Such a framing of the conflict-ridden politics of the liberal capitalist state helps to explain the anti-environmental shift in the 1980s after the passage of monumental environmental legislation in the 1970s (such as the creation of the EPA, the Clean Air Act, the Clean Water Act, and the Endangered Species Act). For soon after the passage of such legislation, Ronald Reagan was elected as president under the banner of rolling back such actions and creating a United States devoted to free market politics (Layzer 2012). Consequently, the state prioritized the demand for capital accumulation over clean air and water, disinvested in protecting the environment and the public's environmental health, sought to undo the Clean Air Act, and worked to make the EPA as ineffective in enforcing environmental regulations as possible. Another example of the state asserting exchange values over and against use values is the effort of the Trump administration to rollback the Corporate Average Fuel Economy (CAFE) standards, which are fleetwide averages designed to improve the fuel efficiency of cars and light trucks (Eisenstein 2019). In 2012, the Obama administration announced that CAFE standards would require an average of 54.5 mpg by 2025. The Trump administration has not only sought to reduce these requirements to 37 mpg, but to stop requirements on the production of hybrid and electric cars, and to eliminate the legal waiver enabling California to have stricter standards than those at the federal level given the state's long history of horrible air quality. Although the Obama administration's standards would have saved US consumers billions of dollars on gasoline and healthcare costs as well as reduced deaths linked to air pollution, the Trump administration has primarily pushed for these changes to protect the profits of oil, gasoline, and automobile companies. I live in California's San Joaquin Valley, which has the worst air quality in the country. Lowering the CAFE standards, eliminating requirements for electrification of the automotive fleet, and eliminating California's ability to set stricter air quality regulations will only intensify environmental inequities and increase air pollution and health inequities for the more than 4 million people who call it home, a region with some of the highest poverty rates in the country. From a treadmill perspective, the federal government is clearly choosing Big Oil, Big Gas, and Big Auto over the lives of San Joaquin Valley residents and the region's **carrying capacity**, precisely because this is how the TOP operates.

Since a main problem with the treadmill is how it organizes political and economic structures in an anti-environmental manner, treadmill theorists have long critiqued reform efforts such as recycling as a pathway to challenge overconsumption and endless economic growth. From the TOP perspective, the option of recycling within the treadmill enables us to go about our regular consumeristic ways, rather than reducing our level of consumption, because as long as we recycle, we can feel better about our impact on the planet. Such feel-good behaviors effectively keep the treadmill humming along even though the majority of recyclable items are either thrown directly into waste bins or are unrecyclable because they are contaminated (by mixed materials and food and liquids), existing municipal streams are unable to recycle them, or there is no profitable market for their resale—which means the potentially recyclable item ends up in the landfill too.

The central problem here is that the treadmill's push toward endless economic growth leads to single-use products, **planned obsolescence**, and the prioritization of disposability that fuels escalating levels of ecological degradation (see Lesson 7). Planned obsolescence is a design process where the product is created to have an "artificially" short lifespan to ensure that consumers will have to buy a new product in the future. Utilizing this design process, companies are able to increase demand for their newest products even through the older models are still functional. For instance, the rechargeable batteries in Apple's AirPods or AirPods Pro earbuds have a lifespan of around two years; after that, most people will throw them out and buy new ones even though all that needs to be replaced is the battery. This process will unfold precisely because the AirPods were not designed in a way to replace the battery, that is, they were designed to be obsolete. Sure, Apple might recycle the AirPods for you, but with 70 percent of the US economy tied to consumer spending, such processes are not going to change anytime soon. For these theorists, recycling our technological gadgets presents the illusion that we can have our cake and eat it too.

Consequently, treadmill theorists deny that the best hope for solving environmental problems is to embrace new technologies since technological development is driven by capitalist profit motives not ecological values, which means that new technologies often intensify ecological withdrawals (resource extraction) and additions (waste and pollution). This can be explained through the **Jevons paradox** in which increases in efficiency of resource consumption actually increases rather than decreases the demand for that resource (see Lessons 6 and 9). This can happen in two ways. First, given that newer commodities are more energy efficient, people tend to use them more and thus consume more of the resource that powers it. Second, while each commodity is more efficient than its predecessor, the total consumption of those items increases as more people buy them since they become more affordable; this increases overall consumption of that resource and the energy that powers it. For instance, the average gas mileage of cars and light trucks in 1975 was under 13 mpg; but in 2017, it was 25.2 mpg. However, vehicle miles per vehicle nearly tripled (from 1.2 trillion to over 3.2 trillion), and there are millions and millions of additional cars on the road today compared to the 1970s; as a result, overall gasoline consumption is much higher today than decades ago.

This process is interconnected with and fueled by the structural processes of the TOP. Returning to the previous example of how the automobile industry responded to labor organizing and environmental regulations, the improvement in the average mpg of cars and light trucks was undone at the national level for a number of reasons. One, the pursuit of growth by the automobile industry fueled the shift toward sport utility vehicles (SUVs) over cars because their profit margins are higher even though their gas mileage and emissions output are far worse than cars. Additionally, if we scale out beyond gas consumption and tailpipe emissions to the automobile industry's adoption of production technology that replaced workers (with good wages and benefits) with fossil fuels and chemicals (robotics), we see that the automobile industry consumes far more resources than it did in previous decades. Not to mention that the subsequent growth of an automobile-centric environment created growth and resource-consuming opportunities in industries that catered to the automobile, those that maintain and repair cars as well as those that supply fuel, parts, and insurance for cars. If we then include the housing industry, which has built an extremely resource intensive form of existence around the automobile—that of the suburban single-family home with its multicar garages, irrigated green lawns, and swimming pools—the ecological impacts are far worse. These impacts have been exacerbated by the shift in federal transportation dollars from public transportation toward roads, highways, and freeways for private automobiles. Factoring in the ecological withdrawals and additions of these transformations, the stand-alone increase in average mpg of cars and light trucks appears to be negligible if not a drop in the ocean. Overall, the shift away from public transit, biking, and walking as forms of transportation toward the automobile has degraded the environment while diminishing people's quality of life through higher transportation costs, worse air quality, longer commute times, and higher accident and fatality rates.

Another aspect of the TOP is its detrimental effect on workers, who are continually expected to work longer and harder and faster for less, an issue that is largely unaddressed within ecological modernization theory. This scenario has played out with Apple as it has contracted with suppliers in China, like Foxconn, to produce its iPhones even though the company has a long history of exploitative labor practices (Barbosa 2016; Hamilton 2019). In 2019, Foxconn's factories employed a workforce that was around 50 percent temporary. Chinese labor laws only allow temporary workers to constitute 10 percent of a company's workforce. Yet, such workers are utilized because they do not receive the benefits of full-time workers including paid sick leave; paid vacations; and medical, unemployment, and pension programs. The outcome is that workers often work illegal overtime of up to 100 hours per month, even though the government only allows 30 hours per month. In fact, workers at Foxconn need to get approval from managers to "not do overtime." On top of these issues, 10- to 12-hour workdays, 6 to 7 days a week, are the norm where they either sit or stand, repeating the same motions time and time again in very noisy and hot conditions with regular beratement by managers for not working fast enough. All of these conditions exist because the company is expected to pump out half a million iPhones per day at its Zhengzhou factory to keep up with the growth demands of Apple; and workers have very little in the way of labor rights and legal protections to change the working conditions at Foxconn, which is why the iPhone is produced there in the first place.

Thus, rather than seeing new technologies as saving the planet, treadmill theorists contend that reducing the ecological and social destruction of liberal capitalist democracies will require a restructuring of power relations between corporations, people, and the state as well as between marginalized communities and the economic and political elite. Since technology is driven by capitalists and the state in ways that amplify rather than address social, economic, and ecological inequities facing humanity, what is needed to create a more ecological and just society is procedural justice (equity in decision-making; see Lessons 4 and 7). This entails the democratization of voice in technological development and how and who will receive the benefits and burdens of technological change. Through the empowerment of marginalized communities and the general population by way of social movements, the state can be pushed to prioritize use values, environmental amenities, and social equity over capital accumulation. In this respect, ecological problems are not technical problems but political problems. Such an analysis has pushed treadmill theorists to critique ecological modernists for failing to focus on how the inequities wrapped up with ecological problems are raced, classed, and gendered. It has also driven treadmill theorists to study how marginalized communities are organizing and building power to contest the TOP and what strategies are successful or not in doing so, all in the hope of strengthening environmental justice movements and their attempts to halt the treadmill or at least force it to more equitably distribute the "goods" and "bads" it produces (see Lessons 10 and 18). Next, we turn toward another theory influenced by Marxist political economy, that of Ecological Marxism.

ECOLOGICAL MARXISM

Let us return to Apple's AirPods. There are indeed perks to having wireless headphones. No more time spent untangling cords, having to carry your phone with you or having your cord pulled out of your phone, not to mention your cord shredding or falling apart. With AirPods, not only is there no cord failure to worry about but your phone will never be damaged again through your headphone cord knocking over a drink of water or dragging your phone off the table and onto the floor. However, if ecological modernization theory contends that capitalism is greening itself and moving toward incorporating biomimicry within its production processes to reduce withdrawals and additions, then why has Apple long resisted efforts to create more cradle-to-cradle practices within its product design? The planned obsolescence of the AirPods is by design after all: they were created to become waste. And this design process occurred even though Apple has received a lot of criticism for having non-replaceable batteries in their iPhones, and most recently, for slowing down iPhones with older batteries. In fact, while in the 1990s many cell phones had replaceable batteries, today almost none do. And the iPhone battery has always been sealed within the product. The only way to replace it is to either do it yourself, which would void the warranty on the iPhone, or bring it to Apple and pay them to do it for you. Why is this occurring? Why are technological innovations moving toward more and more of a linear waste stream and creating ever higher levels of pollution and waste? **Ecological Marxism** contends that it has an answer.

Ecological Marxism, which is associated with theorists John Bellamy Foster, Richard York, Brett Clark, and Rebecca Clausen, among others, builds on the work of conflict theorist Karl Marx by linking the socially destructive tendencies of capitalism with the ecologically destructive tendencies of capitalism, emphasizing how they are interconnected. Capitalism's inherent need to expand (or suffer economic recessions and depressions) and increase its rate of profit (generally through increasing the productivity of labor) means that capitalism will expand and intensify its ecological degradation (see Lessons 4 and 9). From this perspective, capitalism alienates both humanity from itself but also from nonhuman nature.

To theorize the ecological degradation of capitalism on people and the planet and why this happens, ecological Marxism uses the concept of

metabolic rift. Karl Marx theorized that capitalism produces a rift in the metabolic relations between human and nonhuman nature based on capitalism's continual drive for endless accumulation of wealth. This happens because capitalism breaks up the ecological flow of nutrients within a circular loop of reuse (extraction, production, distribution, consumption, reuse) and shifts it toward a linear production line of waste (extraction, production, distribution, consumption, waste) with disastrous social, economic, and ecological consequences. Marx's example of this process focused on how the capitalization of agriculture degraded soil fertility because food waste and "nightsoil" (manure) was not being recycled back to the farm and the rural country from which it came but treated merely as a waste product to be dumped anywhere and everywhere within the city and broader urban environment. This shift from circularity to linearity robbed the soil of the nutrients it needed while making urban life toxic for communities and workers through food, human, and animal waste being dumped in the streets, waterways, and landfills. Thus, for Marx, "all progress in capitalist agriculture is a progress in the art, not only of robbing the worker, but of robbing the soil" (Marx 1976: 637–638). Moreover, with the growing division between town and country producing a metabolic rift, capitalist-led science and technology was called on to create synthetic, fossil-fuel-based fertilizers to ensure capitalist agriculture could continue growing food in spite of the loss of soil fertility. This invention, rather than solving the ecological crisis, actually intensified it by creating new ecological problems such as polluted waterways, eutrophication, and carbon dioxide emissions. Akin to treadmill theorists, ecological Marxists contend that capitalism's attempt to solve a metabolic rift through technological innovation, rather than reducing that metabolic rift, generally produces newer and ever larger metabolic rifts that threaten humanity, the planet, and capitalism.

Recent research has explored how this metabolic rift may be moving from industrial agriculture to certified organic farming too, as it turns toward relying on more off-farm agro-inputs (organic fertilizers and pesticides) with negative effects on water quality. The concept has also been applied to other social-ecological relations, including the carbon cycle, where the overproduction of carbon due to the burning of fossil fuels combined with deforestation has disrupted the carbon cycle. As a result, more carbon is produced with fewer places for this carbon to be absorbed, which generates carbon or biospheric rift that leads to climate and oceanic destabilization (see Lesson 15). Ecological Marxists have also applied the concept to the disruption of the oceanic ecosystem due to the capitalization of fishing, which has either fully exploited, overexploited, or depleted over 75 percent of global fisheries. The collapse of fish stocks globally has led to declines in predator fish and fish-eating birds, both of which also eat sea urchins. Consequently, sea urchin populations have exploded and devastated kelp forests, coral reefs, and seagrass beds that are vital to the healthy functioning of oceanic ecosystems. To address this metabolic crisis, capitalism has produced the **technofix** of aquaculture, aka fish farming, a solution that has actually intensified and amplified oceanic destabilization rather than reduced it. This has occurred because farmed fish are fed a diet rich in fishmeal and fish oil, which further depletes fish stocks. Additionally, farmed fish often disrupt marine ecosystems through their waste production, transmission of diseases to wild fish, and when nonnative fish escape their pens. Thus, for ecological Marxists, aquaculture is another example of how capitalism's new technology amplifies rather than reduces the metabolic rift as well as the alienation of humanity from nonhuman nature. Ecological modernists might look at this differently, however, seeing in aquaculture the promise of using greener technology to raise and harvest fish in more sustainable but less profitable ways. This could be done through decreasing the need for external inputs, particularly animal-based inputs, by utilizing ecosystem biodiversity to create closed-loop ecological flows between plants and animals within aquaculture systems or integrating the wastes of aquaculture systems into fertilizers for land-based agricultural practices. This would of course entail moving away from a monoculture aquaculture system where only one fish is grown toward one that reflects the biodiversity of healthy oceanic ecosystems. The question is whether aquaculture will move away from a linear waste stream to a system organized around biomimicry; time will tell.

Ecological Marxists also analyze the relationship between capitalism and the environment through a focus on the contradictions of capitalism; how the normal functioning of capitalism creates crises that threaten the system's viability. Historically, Marxists theorized crisis as systemic to capitalism based on several economic tendencies that threated the conditions for capital accumulation (e.g., not enough business opportunities to invest in for an adequate return, not enough effective demand to buy mass-produced commodities so companies can realize a profit, or markets that are too competitive and provide marginal and declining profit rates). These economic crises tied to capital-labor relations are called the first contradiction of capitalism. The work of ecological Marxists, most notably James O'Connor (1998), shifts the focus away from "pure" economic factors toward how capitalism's destruction of the environment actually threatens the system's long-term viability. This happens because the scale of ecological degradation today pushes capitalism to internalize environmental costs that were once externalized onto nature, communities, workers, the public, and the state (see Lesson 13). O'Connor named this capital-nature conflict the second contradiction of capitalism and saw it as problematic for capitalism because it reduced the profit rates for companies and at a large enough scale can threaten the long-term viability of businesses and industries. This problem is seen in many economic sectors today. The continued destruction of soil fertility and ecosystem diversity through industrial agriculture means that more and more money needs to be spent for synthetic fertilizers and pesticides, which increases the costs of production for farmers and reduces their rate of profit. Lumber companies in the United States are engaging in more expensive management of forests through long-term cutting and replanting practices instead of the prior practice of clear-cutting. Private insurance companies will face billions of dollars in claims due to sea-level rise and coastal flooding attributable to climate destabilization. And public and private insurers will face billions in losses for commodity crops destroyed through shifting climates and extreme weather events (droughts, floods, hurricanes), also attributable to climate destabilization. Apart from these costs, a growing problem will be the need to expend more and more money to ensure the work force is healthy enough to be productive for capitalists. With more and more pollution comes higher rates of respiratory issues, cancers, blood disorders, sterility, birth defects, and abnormalities in liver and kidney function, all of which increase healthcare costs for individuals, employers, insurance companies, healthcare providers, and the state.

Overall, while ecological Marxism is a conflict theory like treadmill of production, its focus is on theorizing how the economic conditions and structures within capitalism drive ecological degradation in ways that threaten the reproduction of capitalism. Although they agree with treadmill theorists that capitalism cannot be reformed to save the planet and that technological innovation within capitalism tends to exacerbate rather than address ecological problems, their analytical focus is primarily on studying the processes of capitalism and not the social movements emerging to oppose capitalism and restore the metabolic rifts destabilizing the planet. We now turn to the final theory influenced by Marxist political economy, **world systems theory**, which shifts focus from metabolic rifts and the contradictions of capitalism toward how power relations between nations structure international trade relations to favor certain countries over others.

WORLD SYSTEMS THEORY

When you wake up in the morning and check the news app on your cell phone, you might see headlines reading "Avocado Demand Threatens Mating Grounds for Monarch Butterflies"; "Coffee and Chocolate Consumption Driving Deforestation in Africa"; "Another Shipment of E-waste Arrives in India"; "Polluted Air from China Settles in Los Angeles." After reading such headlines, do you wonder why this is occurring? Do you stop and think, why are the things I am consuming both coming from and ending up back in low-income countries? World systems theory seeks to explain this relationship through looking at capitalism as a global economic system linking all countries into the pursuit of profit and a competition-based logic prioritizing economic growth as an end in itself. For these theorists, the world economy is one of unequal economic and ecological exchange affixed to a global division of labor that emerged from Western European colonialism beginning in the 1400s. In this global economy, a small number of "core" countries have political and economic power to dictate the division of labor and terms of trade to be favorable to themselves, specialize in high-value commodities, and receive a large share of global wealth. These countries now include Western Europe, the United States, Australia, New Zealand, and Japan. Then there are the "periphery" countries that were often either directly or indirectly colonies of Western Europe and the United States and specialize in low-value, raw material commodities and receive a small share of global wealth. These countries include many countries in Africa, Central and Southern America, and Southeastern Asia. Then there are "semiperiphery" countries that specialize in the export of both raw materials and manufactured goods and receive a medium sized share of global wealth and aspire to become a core country specializing in high-value services and goods. These countries include Mexico, Brazil, Argentina, Taiwan, South Korea, India, China, Saudi Arabia, Russia, and South Africa.

This global division of labor, and its winners and losers, becomes clear when looking at which countries benefit the most from the production of an iPhone. If I asked you who benefited the most from the iPhone, besides Apple, would you say China? Many Americans do, but this is not true. Raw materials for components, a low-value activity, comes from China, Chile, Rwanda, Congo, Turkey, and Peru, among others; while most of the technology, a higher-value activity, comes from Taiwan, Korea, Japan, and the United States. China's largest role is in supplying the raw materials, the battery, and the labor that assembles all these components together in factories owned and run by companies like Foxconn, which is actually a Taiwanese company. As a result, the majority of profit goes to the designer of the iPhone, Apple, while the core countries of the United States and Japan come in second, followed by the semiperipheries of Taiwan, South Korea, and China. The periphery countries that supply only the raw materials for the iPhone do not even show up on this list of the top five.

For world systems theorists, this global division of labor between core, semiperiphery, and periphery often goes back to the origin of capitalism that has permanently affected who benefits and who bears the burden from global trade. Given that many peripheral and semiperipheral countries were colonies or subordinate to the core countries, global trade has long been shaped to exploit the ecological wealth of these countries. This enabled the core countries to become very wealthy and invest in their own industrialization and urbanization while periphery countries became poorer and poorer through this export-led development model. This occurred because their economies were organized around meeting the needs of core countries rather than their own. In short, they were extraction zones (see Lesson 19). This meant that periphery countries were drained of their ecological wealth through the export of raw materials, and profits from such activities were not reinvested in the periphery country but traveled to Europe with the raw materials. Periphery countries were unable to create robust public infrastructures or investment in their people like Europe and the United States were able to, nor were the profits accumulated as nest egg for future national investment. Furthermore, export-led resource extraction meant less and less ecological wealth to tap into to jumpstart domestic-led development in the future and produced a range of ecological problems for the periphery, including deforestation, biodiversity loss, and air and water pollution.

Given the competitive structure of capitalist markets, such historical processes have been exacerbated over the last fifty years as periphery and semiperiphery countries try and play catch-up development with core countries. This often leads to the hyperextraction of resources with minimal environmental regulations to generate enough revenue to jumpstart industrialization, which means escalating rates of deforestation, soil erosion, water and soil mining, and air and water pollution due to strip mining, cattle ranching, clear-cutting, and industrial agriculture. Alongside these practices, periphery countries often engage in the hyperconsumption of the waste of core countries, such as plastics and electronics, as a way to generate revenue. Thus, extraction zones and waste dumps are increasingly concentrated within periphery and semiperiphery countries even though the consumption of such commodities occurs in and is organized by core countries.

This is exactly why those news headlines showed up on your phone. The increase in consumption of avocados, coffee, and chocolate in the United States and Europe is fueling deforestation throughout the world because the global economy is geared toward meeting the consumer needs of core countries with little thought to the social, economic, and ecological impacts on semiperiphery and periphery countries. In this regard, high-income countries are not framed as "environmental states" that are uniting growth and environmentalism, as ecological modernists claim, for they are only able to green the economy within their national borders by exporting the negatives of growth to semiperiphery and periphery countries. Thus, what appears to be a **dematerialization** of the economy, the decoupling of withdrawals and additions from economic growth, only appears so because ecological modernists look at the firm or nation state rather than the global economy. For instance, while industrial production is much cleaner in the United States today due to legal requirements and technological innovation—particularly in the Rust Belt regions of Michigan, Indiana, Illinois, and Ohio—so much so that Torontonians can breathe clean air again, much of this is due to the exportation of noxious industries to other countries with less stringent environmental regulations such as China and India. Thus, what first appears to be a great example of ecological modernization is less so. Particularly because many of the factories in China were powered with cheap and dirty coal, which has produced toxic level air quality in Beijing and other major Chinese cities, and due to wind patterns, this dirty air now blows over the Pacific Ocean to California.

Therefore, when the push toward profit maximization is faced with stricter environmental regulations, often passed by the state based on the public's demands for cleaner air and water, companies will export production and pollution overseas to countries organized as pollution zones. While core companies will develop and utilize more expensive and cleaner technologies in the core, as ecological modernization theory has shown, these same companies transfer the older and dirtier technology overseas. The end result is that Americans can continue to buy their goodies (at much cheaper prices, too) while having cleaner air and water because of the global division of labor within capitalism.

RISK SOCIETY

Are you worried about pesticides on your produce, pollutants in your tap water, toxins in the air you breathe? Do you use apps on your iPhone to avoid produce that contains the most pesticide residue, to find filtered water refill stations, to check the air quality outside? If so, you are not alone. Millions of people in the United States do the same to try and insulate themselves from these manufactured risks. But why do we engage in such practices and what are the psychological, social, and political effects of such practices? Ulrich Beck's (1995) theory of the **risk society** is helpful here, which claims that high-income Western countries are no longer industrial societies but risk societies; and that this change entails significant transformations in how societies are organized, particularly the anxieties and worries of its residents, how they are to be addressed, and by whom. In industrial societies, like the United States in the 1950s, there is an emphasis on class inequities and class solidarities, with the pivot of social relations and social struggle being around the politics of wealth distribution and how social movements within working-class and middle-class communities try to challenge how the state distributes wealth. This is very different compared to risk societies, like the United States today, where there is a focus on individualization and political consumerism, which shifts social struggle to the politics of risk distribution and how individuals need to buy products to protect themselves from toxins. In such a society, according to Beck, we are no longer worried about acquiring "social goods" but avoiding "social bads." This societal shift from a "logic of goods" to a "logic of bads" manifests in people being less worried about hunger or scarcity, the concerns of industrial society, and more worried about protecting themselves from unhealthy food and its associated problems of diet-related disease, being seen as lazy or gluttonous, or being seen as a failed body. This fear emerges because risk is much more equally distributed across the population in a risk society than goods distribution was in an industrial society. According to Beck, "poverty is hierarchic, smog is democratic (Beck 1992: 36)." Why is this so? First, the risks that haunt people today are clearly not "natural risks" that are temporary, locally specific, and outside of human control, for example, drought, plagues, or forest fires attributable to supernatural forces (nature, gods, or demons). Instead they are "manufactured risks" produced by human society continuously as a part of everyday life, often at a regional and global scale, and can last thousands of years. A chemical spill in one location at one point in time has the potential to travel hundreds if not thousands of miles away and can affect the communities depending on these ecosystems for generations. For instance, the testing of nuclear bombs by the United States in the Marshall Islands archipelago poisoned Marshallese residents hundreds of miles away and produced "jellyfish" babies born without skeletal structures and translucent skin. Another example is how millions of gallons of herbicides, including Agent Orange, were sprayed by the United States over 4 million acres during the Vietnam War to eradicate tree cover and agricultural crops for the North

Vietnamese and Viet Cong troops. The toxicity of such defoliants has produced hundreds of thousands of birth defects, cancers, rare illnesses, and deaths for the people of Vietnam, issues that are ongoing to this day.

A key aspect of risk society is that manufactured risks take on a scale and a threat that far outpaces the ability and willingness of contemporary political institutions to reduce or eliminate such risks. For instance, governments and regulatory agencies do not debate how to eliminate risk or prevent risk from being produced in the first place (the **precautionary principle**) but on how much risk (pollution) is allowed and how to distribute this risk across the population. Given this approach to risk management, what occurs is the slow and steady poisoning of people and the planet, a toxification that occurs alongside the shift from group membership (classes) to processes of individualization. This process of individualization forgoes collective solidarities in favor of prioritizing individual choice and creating your own unique life path unmoored by tradition, culture, class, and family. This is potentially freeing, as your biography is now yours to make and remake as you see fit; but it also involves a lot of risk management, as we now have to make endless decisions about our life. This "reflexive modernity" engulfs our entire existence: who am I, what high school sport defines me, what friends do I want, what partner(s) should I choose, what college should I go to, what major should I pick, where should I vacation? We have even named this anxiety: fear of missing out (FOMO). Risk management has even impacted our food practices, with people micromanaging each food purchase, scanning the list of ingredients for additives, chemicals, toxins, and allergens. This constant need to choose everything, and choose well, produces a lot of anxiety and stress for people, and they have turned toward the market to try and protect themselves from these manufactured risks. In such a society, people engage in what Andrew Szasz (2007) calls "inverted quarantine" where people buy products on the market to try and protect themselves from an increasingly toxic environment, such as the organic produce, bottled water, and air purifiers I mentioned earlier. However, none of these products addresses the structural relations creating toxicity in the first place; and, in fact, they can exacerbate pollution and waste through their production, consumption, and postconsumption. Szasz claims that such practices operate as a form of "political anesthesia" that pushes people away from the collective mobilization necessary to take on the actors creating the problems in the first place. Bottled water means not fighting for better funded municipal water systems. Purchasing organic food means not challenging the pesticide usage of industrial agriculture. Air purifiers can reduce attempts to pass stricter air quality regulations on automobiles, factory farms, and fossil fuel and petrochemical industries. These three market-based options all hold out the hope that they can provide a solution to the problem that they cannot. They offer the illusion of risk reduction when in fact they actually magnify risk production. For instance, in 1975, the average US resident consumed a gallon of bottled water per year; now it is over 30 gallons, a thirtyfold increase. A whole infrastructure is needed to extract the water from the ground, process it, and get it into your body.

Even if the bottle is recyclable or made from recycled plastic, plastic production is a polluting process, and a lot of these single-use bottles are not even recycled (their recycling rate ranges from 27 to 33 percent).

For risk theorists, society manufactures risks that we have to individually manage; as a result, one's social status is connected not merely to their wealth and income but to their ability to protect themselves from exposure to this risk. Culturally, this shifts political debate from an emphasis on creating equality to one of securing safety and from one of ensuring possession to one of realizing avoidance. It also produces a society that is no longer riveted by a class struggle over who gets what percentage of the economic pie but an individualized struggle over who can best insulate themselves from toxicity. At the same time, Beck's theory often ignores or overstates how much equalization of risk has actually occurred. Smog and poisoned water do not affect everyone equally, as the poisoning of Flint, Michigan underscored; and as environmental justice advocates have long stated, risk exposure is mapped over existing race, class, and gender inequities (see Lessons 10 and 11). While more and more people are subject to toxification, this is still an unequitable process of both who is exposed to it and who has the income and political power to protect themselves from such risks. Additionally, Beck's claims of the de-emphasizing of class mobilization by the working class and middle class in risk society might have rung true in the 1990s and 2000s; but since the Great Recession, it appears that class conflict is, once again, moving toward the center of political struggle in the United States.

ECOFEMINISM

You may not know Tian Yu, but she made international headlines in March 2010 when she was just a teenager. Like many others in China, she had moved from the agrarian countryside to the industrializing urban centers to find employment and a better life than working on a farm. She found herself working at Foxconn's Longhua factory over 12 hours a day, 6 to 7 days a week, having to skip meals and toilet breaks to do "mandatory" overtime and continually being berated and reprimanded by supervisors for not working fast enough: all to meet the production quotas that Apple, Samsung, Sony, and Dell had placed on Foxconn, which keeps its assembly line running 24/7. With little time to sleep or meet friends, dormitory life was equally alienating. Then Yu was not paid for a full month's work due to a bureaucratic error, an error that no one in the company helped her to solve. By this time, a little more than a month into her job, she was sleep deprived, isolated, out of money, without a paycheck, and unable to contact family because her cell phone was broken. This is when she went back to her dormitory on the fourth floor and jumped: she was only 17. In a coma for nearly two weeks, upon waking up she found herself paralyzed from the waist down, with three spinal fractures and four hip factures. For the rest of her life she will be in a wheelchair and by-and-large unable to work in factories or on farms. Yu was not alone either; 17 other workers attempted suicide that year at the factory, and 14 died. They were all 25 or younger. How did Foxconn respond to the suicides? The company installed safety nets on the roofs, windows were locked and surrounded by wires, and it tried to get workers to sign an "anti-suicide" pledge that absolved the company of responsibility if they killed themselves.

What is the relationship between gender and the environment? Are gendered inequities and environmental inequities interconnected? How do capitalism and patriarchy interconnect in ways that harm women and the planet? Such questions, among others, motivate **ecofeminism**, which combines ecological theory with feminist theory to explore how socioenvironmental relations are shaped not just by capitalism but patriarchy as well. The intersection of capitalist domination over labor and nature with patriarchal domination over women is capitalist patriarchy. Consequently, ecofeminists investigate how women's relationship to the environment is shaped by structural inequities, often drawing relations between the oppression and exploitation of nonhuman nature, which is gendered female, with the oppression and exploitation of women. These processes overlap in how capitalist patriarchy sees both nonhuman nature and women as property, commodifies both in the pursuit of profit, and exploits and appropriates the free labor of nonhuman nature and women. Such processes also shape the Western mindset that sees the physical environment and women (and care work and the home) as part of nature and men (and the political and economic realms) as part of culture, with the latter being more important and superior to the former.

Emerging from such a theoretical focus is an exploration of the contradictions and conflicts that emerge between the needs of capitalists for profit; the social needs of people for food, water, shelter, and healthcare; and the ecological needs of the planet. This has entailed studying how ecological degradation in South America, Africa, and Asia has negatively affected women's ability to care for their families by polluting water for drinking and cooking and clear-cutting trees that would be used to cook food and build homes (see Lesson 15). In the United States, this has involved studying how industrial pollutants have toxified women's bodies and produced miscarriages, birth defects, cancers, and rare illnesses. Such work underscores that the toxification of nonhuman nature is at the same time the toxification of people since both are part of the environment and interconnected (see Lesson 1).

In the book *Ecofeminism*, Maria Mies and Vandana Shiva contend that the ecological degradation of the planet is rooted in the scientific project of the enlightenment, which is not objective nor value-free but privileges the standpoint of Western men and devalues the knowledge and experience of women and Indigenous peoples. Examples include the devaluation of midwives within Western medicine through the medicalization of childbirth, which privileges the perspective of the doctor over the mother as well as organizes birth around efficiency for the doctor and hospital rather than the comfort of the mother. Another example are witch hunts, which occurred simultaneously with the rise of the enlightenment, capitalism, and the enclosure (privatization) of the commons, all of which operated to criminalize the existence of women who were working class, elderly, single, and widowed. Oftentimes these were women who sought to grow food, raise cattle, and hunt wildlife in the commons and had ecological knowledge of plants that were used to assist people with their ailments and help women regulate births. From this perspective, the witch hunts were about limiting women's social, political, and economic independence from a male-dominated, profit-oriented society based on their customary practices and ecological knowledge instead of capitalist techniques and modern science.

The **bioprospecting** of US and European companies is also indicative of these colonizing processes. In this process, northern companies go to Africa, Latin America, and Southern Asia to find genetic samples of plants that can be commodified, trademarked, and turned into a profit stream even though such plants and the knowledge of how to use them have been common knowledge within Indigenous communities for millennia. However, within Western property regimes, this Indigenous knowledge is not valued nor compensated since it is not seen as of value or of worth because it exists outside of "science." Thus, Western companies can engage in new forms of ecological colonialism in which they steal the ecological knowledge of peripheral countries in an attempt to create patents that can then be sold throughout the global economy for millions if not billions of dollars.

While risk society theorists claim that risk is equally distributed throughout society, an ecofeminist theorist might ask who exactly is expected to protect the family from the toxicity of modern life? Who is buying organic baby food, bed sheets free of toxic flame retardants, and scanning the ingredient list of toothpaste for harmful chemicals? Norah MacKendrick's work, *Better Safe Than Sorry: How Consumers Navigate Exposure to Everyday Toxics*, answers this question (see Lesson 11). MacKendrick finds that the practice of inverted quarantine is gendered and that the time and money spent on what she calls "precautionary consumption" falls on women. This practice, which is demanding in both time and money, falls on women based on cultural ideals of femininity and motherhood, one reproduced through environmental health advocacy groups, retailers, and the marketing campaigns of companies. At the same time, it is not a practice available to all women but principally upper- and middle-class households. More importantly, MacKendrick emphasizes that this burden to protect oneself and one's family from socially produced risk falls on women even though such activities are not effective in reducing the production of toxic risk in the first place. Precautionary consumption cannot protect the family from the socially produced risk of modern life and the failure of the state to protect citizens from pollution. MacKendrick's work builds on Szasz's argument by adding a strong intersectional analysis that brings together the overlapping privileges and oppressions connected to gender, race, and class. It showed how inverted quarantine is gendered, raced, and classed; how environmental health groups play a role in selling consumerism as the solution; and how such groups facilitate a political environment that enables the continuation of regulatory failure at the state level in which the government gets away with not regulating industry to protect all of us.

Much like treadmill theorists' focus on how environmental justice movements are trying to stop the treadmill, ecofeminists examine women's involvement in environmental movements, exploring how and why women become involved in environmental activism, and how women work to legitimate their knowledge, experience, and power in a male-dominated society that regularly disregards their experiences and voice (see Lesson 18). This scholarship has found that the gendered identities of women can be called on to legitimate their activism. Oftentimes this takes the form of "activist mothering," where a women's motherhood identity is invoked to justify their intervention into the public sphere based on protecting their children from environmental pollutants. Shannon Bell's work expands on this concept through exploring how Appalachian women in the environmental justice movement explain and legitimate their activism (see Lesson 10). In *Our Roots Run Deep as Ironweed*, Bell finds that women articulate something beyond a motherhood identity, what pushes them to oppose destructive mining practices in Appalachia is a "protector identity" where they have an obligation not merely to protect their children and grandchildren but their entire community. These women activists fight for the physical health and safety of their community; to protect community bonds, social networks, and kinship ties; to protect the "homeplace" that their family has lived on for generations; to protect the physical landscape of Appalachia from destruction; and to protect their cultural ties to land. Overall, Bell finds that the cultivation and maintenance of an "Appalachian identity" is central to the activism of these women.

However, Bell also learned that while gendered identities were a strength and asset for these women activists, they also faced gendered intimidations. Men continually challenged their right to speak in public and against mining company practices because a "woman's place was in the home." Men also tried to reassert a traditional patriarchal social order by calling these activists overly emotional when they did speak in public; they employed sexual harassment by referring to them as "bitches" and "whores" when they did speak up; and they threatened them with physical violence and death for speaking out. Gender therefore played a central role to both the empowerment of women in Appalachia as well as attempts to repress and oppress their activism. Such research also underscores the claim of ecofeminists that the capitalist exploitation of land is interconnected with the patriarchal oppression of women. In this instance, the male-dominated capitalist industries profiting off of the ecological destruction of Appalachia try to minimize the power of women activists to stop this destruction through asserting patriarchal beliefs and values about who should run the show, who has a right to speak, and who is the superior gender. Consequently, the capitalist destruction of Appalachia is supported and reinforced through patriarchal power structures.

While ecofeminism has found that nonpolitical women often become activists after encountering an environmental inequity, this raises the question of whether women's activism is only ever tied to or seen as legitimate if it is based on their role in the domestic sphere and the motherhood role. If this is the case, it shows how women's empowerment is still constrained by patriarchal values and beliefs. Tracy Perkin's research on women activists in the environmental justice movement in the central valley of California has found that this is not always the case. The women activists she interviewed were all politically engaged prior to joining the movement; and while some were directly affected by environmental inequities, many of them legitimated their activism through a social justice identity alongside of a motherhood identity, showing that the processes shaping women's activism is context specific and shaped by broader processes than just a motherhood identity.

Given the feminist praxis of ecofeminism, which aims to empower women and challenge capitalist patriarchy, it is a conflict theory akin to treadmill theory, ecological Marxism, and world systems theory. However, rather than prioritizing class relations, there is an intersectional approach that explores the relationship between gender, class, and race and the interconnected oppressions tied to patriarchy, capitalism, and white supremacy. In particular, there is emphasis on the intersection between gender and the environment with much of the research being qualitative in form and grounded in exploring the lives of women and how they construct and negotiate inequitable environmental relations.

WRAPPING UP

In October 2019, Apple released their latest product, the AirPods Pro. Marketed as the higher-end version of the AirPods, the product has a new in-ear design, features active noise cancellation technology, is water and sweat resistant, and contains the H1 chip with "Hey Siri" support: all for the low low price of $249. What the AirPods Pro do not have, unfortunately, are replaceable batteries. A month later, Apple released iOS 13, the latest operating system for iPhones. The OS is faster than previous versions, with app launch times being twice as fast, and includes a new systemwide Dark Mode feature; revamped apps for Maps, Photos, and Music; and a new Siri voice. All these updates must be wonderful; too bad my mother will not get to experience them, as she has an iPhone 5, which isn't supported by iOS 13. She will forever be stuck in iOS 12 unless she buys a new phone. It appears that technological obsolescence and the treadmill of production is still strong within Apple; maybe next year they will get around to better integrating cradle-to-cradle design within their products.

Theories within environmental sociology raise fundamental questions about why socioenvironmental problems exist, what and who is producing them, and who they effect and why. They also provide explanations of what needs to change and how to address the problems emerging from socioenvironmental relations. However, since each theory has its own philosophical assumptions and scale of analysis, their examination of the problems and the solutions to ecological degradation differ. Ecological modernization theory is one of gradualism, which contends that capitalism can green itself through technological innovation, and it supports such claims by looking at the leading industries and how they are moving toward cradle-to-cradle design. This is due, in part, to the theorist's beliefs that technological development, economic growth, and progress are good and beneficial. Treadmill of production theorists contest such claims because of the economic growth needs of capitalism and their belief that the state prioritizes capital accumulation over environmental protection. Additionally, treadmill theorists assert that ecological degradation is not a technical problem in need of more innovative technology but a political problem rooted in inequitable relations between the general public and the economic and political elite. Moreover, they contest ecological modernization's claim that the market is self-generating green technology, countering that most greener solutions emerge through government regulations and social movement demands, not market signals.

In fact, sampling differences, not just philosophical differences, explain why treadmill theorists, ecological Marxists, and world systems theorists all critique the arguments of ecological modernization theory. Ecological modernization theory has tended to focus on individual products or firms rather than the nation state or the global economy. From the level of the product or firm, what initially looks promising often becomes ecologically catastrophic once it is scaled up to the volume of national or global consumption. Additionally, ecological Marxism's concept of the metabolic rift shows how capitalism's quest for profit and its shaping of technological development toward this end continually produces ever greater levels of environmental destruction, while worlds system theory shows how the benefits and burdens of commodity chains are rooted in a global division of labor that reproduces economically and ecologically unequal exchange that privileges core countries (and their residents and consumers) over semiperiphery and periphery countries (and their residents and consumers). Merely greening a company or a nation-state will not rectify this unequal division of labor; only restructuring power between and within nations will, according to conflict theorists. Consequently, gradualism looks politically viable from the scale and philosophical assumptions of ecological modernization, while from the scale and philosophical assumptions of treadmill theorists, ecological Marxists, and world systems theorists, gradualism is increasingly insufficient to counter the ecological degradation of capitalism. For these theoretical frameworks, a wholesale transformation of the economic, cultural, and political structures of society are necessary to avoid planetary collapse. Such arguments also emerge from treadmill, ecological Marxism, and world system theories because they are critical approaches to the study of socioenvironmental relations that question how the dominant political and economic structures of society are organized; this is much less the case for ecological modernists who are "realists" focusing on how the dominant institutions can be reformed rather than transformed.

At the same time, another key variable that influences the outlooks of these opposing theoretical camps is where they emerged. Ecological modernization theory emerged from and is much more popular in Western Europe (e.g., Scandinavia, Germany, Switzerland, and the Netherlands) where the progress made in greening capitalism is more advanced but also better supported by the state. Thus, one could read ecological modernization theory as a prescription for where capitalism could go given particular state-corporation-citizen relations. Treadmill theory was born in the United States and is much more popular here because it has more explanatory power in why the United States has been less able to green capitalism and why efforts for environmental reform have faced so much resistance by corporations and the state. In a country with a conservative anti-statist and anti-environmental culture, and a federal government generally dominated by Republicans or pro-corporate Democrats, the state has long tried to roll back any and all environmental regulations while working to open up more land to mineral, gas, and oil exploration. In such a nation, ecological modernization theory has less analytic weight because it has less explanatory power.

Finally, it must be noted that all of these theories have been tied to the perspective and experiences of predominantly white males and have overwhelmingly focused on how class inequities and class conflict shapes socioenvironmental relations. Ecofeminists have emphasized how such analysis leaves out the question of gender as well as an intersectional approach that is important to understanding how people experience socioenvironmental relations and who bears the burdens of the toxicity of modern life. Most of these theories discussed in this lesson are either macro-level theories of socioenvironmental relations or meso-level theories of organizations as well. Ecofeminism tends to provide a different perspective on socioenvironmental relations through exploring micro- and meso-level theories of groups and communities. Ecofeminism brings us down to earth and flesh and blood people through qualitative methodologies that explore how people live socioenvironmental relations and how through their everyday practices people are trying to make the planet a more just and sustainable world.

Each of the theories discussed in this lesson are just that, theories, assumptions about the world that need to be verified, altered, and refined through engagement with data collected through interviews, archives, ethnography, or statistical analysis. No matter which of these theories you end up drawing on in your study of the world, it is important to remember that no theory provides absolute knowledge of socioenvironmental relations; each theory can be beneficial in particular ways while also creating its own limits or "blinders" based on the questions you want to ask, the philosophical assumptions guiding these questions, how you will collect data to answer your questions, and how you will interpret this data. Theories are critical to being an environmental sociologist because they guide your investigation of the world, but they must also be continually refined in light of changes within the world, which is constant; thus your theory toolbox should be a work in progress as you tweak it regularly to take into account the ongoing transformation of socioenvironmental relations in the 21st century.

SOURCES

Andersen, Mikael Skou and Ilmo Massa. 2000. "Ecological Modernization—Origins, Dilemmas and Future Directions." *Journal of Environmental Policy & Planning* 2 (4): 337–345.

Apple. 2019. "Environment." https://www.apple.com/environment/.

Barbosa, David. 2016. "How China Built 'iPhone City' with Billions in Perks for Apple's Partner." *New York Times*. https://www.nytimes.com/2016/12/29/technology/apple-iphone-china-foxconn.html.

Beck, Ulrich. 1995. *Ecological Politics in an Age of Risk*. Cambridge: Polity Press.

Beck, Ulrich. 1992. *Risk Society: Towards a New Modernity*. Thousand Oaks, CA: Sage.

Bell, Shannon Elizabeth. 2013. *Our Roots Run Deep as Ironweed: Appalachian Women and the Fight for Environmental Justice*. Urbana: University of Illinois Press.

Buttel, Frederick. 2000. "Ecological Modernization as Social Theory." *Geoforum* 31:57–65.

Chan, Jenny. 2013. "A suicide survivor: the life of a Chinese worker." *New Technology, Work and Employment* 28 (2): 84–99.

CISCO, 2011. *Cisco Global Cloud Index: Forecast and Methodology, 2010–2015*. San Jose, CA: Cisco Systems Inc.

CISCO, 2018. *Cisco Global Cloud Index: Forecast and Methodology, 2016–2021*. San Jose, CA: Cisco Systems Inc.

Dedrick, Jason, Greg Linden, and Kenneth L. Kraemer. 2018. "We Estimate China Only Makes $8.46 from an iPhone – and That's Why Trump's Trade War Is Futile." *The Conversation*. https://theconversation.com/we-estimate-china-only-makes-8-46-from-an-iphone-and-thats-why-trumps-trade-war-is-futile-99258

Eisenstein, Paul A. 2019. "Trump Axes California's Right to Set Own Auto Emissions Standards." *NBC News*. https://www.nbcnews.com/business/autos/trump-about-strip-california-its-right-overrule-emissions-regulations-n1055811.

Federici, Silvia. 2004. *Caliban and the Witch: Women, the Body and Primitive Accumulation*. Brooklyn: Autonomedia.

Foster, John Bellamy. 2000. *Marx's Ecology: Materialism and Nature*. New York: Monthly Review Press.

Frey, R. Scott, Paul K. Gellert, and Harry F. Dahms 2018. *Ecologically Unequal Exchange: Environmental Injustice in Comparative and Historical Perspective*. London: Palgrave-Macmillan.

Gould, Kenneth A., David N. Pellow, and Alan Schnaiberg. 2008. *The Treadmill of Production: Injustice and Unsustainability in the Global Economy*. New York: Routledge.

Gould, Kenneth A., Allan Schnaiberg, and Adam S. Weinberg. 1993. *Local Environmental Struggles: Citizen Activism in the Treadmill of Production*. Cambridge: Cambridge University Press.

Hamilton, Isobel Asher. 2019. "Apple and Foxconn Confirmed They Broke a Chinese Labor Law by Employing too Many Temporary Workers at the World's Biggest

iPhone Factory." *Business Insider*. September 9, 2019. https://www.businessinsider
.com/apple-foxconn-breaking-chinese-labor-law-2019-9.

ICF International. 2011. "Electronics Waste Management in the United States Through
2009." Washington, DC: US Environmental Protection Agency.

Layzer, Judith A. 2012. *Open for Business: Conservatives' Opposition to Environmental
Regulation*. Cambridge, MA: MIT Press.

Longo, Stefano B, Rebecca Clausen, and Brett Clark. 2015. *The Tragedy of the Commodity:
Oceans, Fisheries, and Aquaculture*. New Brunswick, NJ: Rutgers University Press.

Marx, Karl. 1976. *Capital*, Vol. 1. London: Penguin.

Maxwell, Joseph A. 2013. *Qualitative Research Design: An Interactive Approach*, 3rd ed.
Thousand Oaks, CA: Sage.

MacKendrick, Norah. 2018. *Better Safe Than Sorry: How Consumers Navigate Exposure to
Everyday Toxics*. Oakland: University of California Press.

McGee, Julius Alexander and Camila Alvarez. 2016. "Sustaining without Changing:
The Metabolic Rift of Certified Organic Farming." *Sustainability* 8 (2): 115.

Mies, Maria and Vandana Shiva. 1993. *Ecofeminism*. London: Zed Books.

Mol, Arthur P.J. 2001. *Globalization and Environmental Reform: The Ecological
Modernization of the Global Economy*. Cambridge, MA: MIT Press.

Organic Trade Association. 2018. "Maturing U.S. Organic Sector Sees Steady Growth
of 6.4 Percent in 2017." https://ota.com/news/press-releases/20236.

Pearce, Fred. 2018. "Energy Hogs: Can World's Huge Data Centers Be Made More
Efficient?" *Yale Environment 360*. https://e360.yale.edu/features/energy-hogs-can-
huge-data-centers-be-made-more-efficient.

Perkins, Tracy E. 2012. "Women's Pathways into Activism: Rethinking the Women's
Environmental Justice Narrative in California's San Joaquin Valley." *Organization
& Environment* 25 (1): 76–94.

O'Connor, James. 1998. *Natural Causes: Essays in Ecological Marxism*. New York:
Guilford Press.

Schnaiberg, Allan. 1980. *The Environment: From Surplus to Scarcity*. New York: Oxford
University Press.

Szasz, Andrew. 2007. *Shopping Our Way to Safety: How We Changed from Protecting the
Environment to Protecting Ourselves*. Minneapolis: University of Minnesota Press.

Part 2

SYSTEMIC CAUSES OF ENVIRONMENTAL DISRUPTION

3

The State and Policy

Imperialism, Exclusion, and Ecological Violence as State Policy

David Naguib Pellow

"No Dumping" sign on shore of New York Harbor, Brooklyn, New York.

Post your photo on imperialism, exclusion, and ecological violence to #TLESecologicalimperialism.
Photo by Ken Gould

When most people think of the state and policy in relation to the environment, specific environmental policies such as the Clean Air Act or the Endangered Species Act or the Environmental Protection Agency may come to mind. However, what I'd like to do in this lesson is to explore the role of the US nation-state as an institution that embraces and advances the institutional practices of **imperialism**, **settler colonialism**, **environmental racism**, and **ecological violence**. In other words, rather than looking at environmental policy as an add-on to the business of the state, this lesson considers the more fundamental orientation, role, function, ideology, and goals of the state as policymaker and how that leads to troubling environmental outcomes. Doing so allows us to make important connections across various dimensions of state practices and guards against narrow interpretations of environmental policy. Drawing on theories of the state, environment, and social inequality, the lesson explores how this dynamic emerged in history and then applies it to several cases. We therefore recast or reconsider state imperialist policy as environmental policy, rather than examining practices that are formally defined as environmental.

THE NATION-STATE AS AN ENGINE OF PROFIT AND ENVIRONMENTAL HARM

Perhaps the most enduring academic view of the state (i.e., the government and its various administrative arms, agencies, and structures) is that of **pluralism**. The concept of a pluralist state is closely associated with the writings of Alexis de Tocqueville and Robert Dahl. The pluralist idea is that politics in a democracy is a process in which various associations (for example trade unions, business groups, faith-based organizations, and activist organizations) engage in a competition for access to state resources and governmental influence. In contrast to a context in which the state is an autocratic authority, pluralism involves groups sharing power with the state, thus avoiding dominance by the government or by any single interest group. Interest groups and associations strive to influence state policymaking through this process, thus allowing citizens multiple venues for voicing their concerns and gaining access to the political system. In practice, however, the political process in the United States is often less pluralist than we might hope. The theoretical perspectives presented in this lesson reflect this more critical view of power and social change with a focus on environmental concerns.

The Treadmill of Production

Sociologists Allan Schnaiberg and Kenneth Gould developed a theoretical framework that captures the dynamics of how market forces and political institutions interact to produce ecological disorganization while creating wealth and power for a minority of persons and lower wages and considerably less power for the majority. This "treadmill of production" is a system in which we can observe the increasing accumulation of wealth and investments into capital-intensive technologies, rising social inequalities, and greater ecological "withdrawals" (extraction of ecosystem materials) and "additions" (pollution), all of which are encouraged and facilitated by the nation-state. The treadmill is a model that describes and explains how capitalist societies have become deeply anti-ecological and socially destructive (see Lesson 2).

While the litany of ecologically destructive practices associated with the treadmill is familiar (for example polluted air, land, and watersheds), the social costs are less apparent in the popular imagination. One of the best ways to increase profits is to not only ignore polluting processes but to reduce labor costs. Many businesses do this by introducing computer automation, cutting wages, downsizing employment rolls, and reducing workers' benefits. As a result, we witness increasing levels of economic inequality and instability nationally and globally. Some indicators include the following: the number of temporary workers has increased dramatically in the last two decades; the richest 85 people on the planet possess as much wealth (property, assets, stocks) as do the poorest 3.5 billion; 1 percent of the population of the United States possesses around 40 percent of the wealth in that country; 20 percent owns 80 percent of the wealth; and real wages have declined precipitously since the early 1970s. What all of this leads to is a workforce where a growing percentage of people are nonunionized, hold temporary jobs, receive low wages, and are at risk of experiencing high levels of under- and unemployment. By contrast, at the other end of the spectrum, we see a smaller elite class of white-collar "knowledge workers" with higher pay, higher education levels, higher social status, greater career mobility options, and safer jobs. Furthermore, we have greater pollution levels, social instability, social conflict, and pressures on the state to take up the slack for people who have been downsized and have little or no childcare or healthcare benefits. The state has, of course, been offering billions of dollars in subsidies to corporations in hopes of encouraging such organizations to remain within the national borders and therefore has fewer funds to pay out to citizens/consumers/workers in social benefits. Furthermore, as the ideology of economic growth at all costs remains a dominant theme in this nation, there is less political will or sympathy for downsized workers and declining public support for labor union demands for better working conditions (see Lesson 17).

According to Schnaiberg and Gould, the modern treadmill of production really grew in scope beginning in the post–World War II era. This was a time when wages were rising for most workers and a new era of prosperity was ushered in by an alliance among industry, labor unions, and the state. The post-1945 political economy was largely held together by an implicit contract. Private capital's need for a reliable labor force aided in the development of strong trade unions that could collectively bargain for wage increases and safer working conditions. Workers' need for jobs and their general satisfaction with unprecedented material gains led to a "no strike" pledge with management. The state played its part by strengthening public education in order to produce a higher-quality labor force while also expanding consumer credit to make sure that domestic demand for goods kept pace with the increase in production. Overall, these were good economic times.

But as economic globalization intensified, industry and government began to tighten their belts. As early as the 1960s in the United States, the treadmill had already begun to undergo significant changes from its post-1945 structure. With increasing international competition, investors and managers became concerned about the existing pact between management and labor, which ensured a relatively high wage for workers as employees accommodated the treadmill by maintaining the peace between unions and companies. As global economic competition heated up, industry felt the need to cut costs in order to remain solvent and/or to continue offering high rates of return to investors and shareholders. They did this by weakening the labor movement, reducing workers' wages, and downsizing many positions in firms. Those actions—combined with the movement of companies to lower-cost regions of the country or to other nations—created massive unemployment in urban areas and a national crisis in the form of chronic economic downturns during the 1970s–1990s (see Lesson 4). Before and during this time, we also saw an exponential increase in the use of chemicals and toxins in industrial production (combined with a weak environmental regulatory system), producing widespread ecological harm in many urban and rural areas across the nation. So in many urban areas, we now have extensive unemployment and underemployment, hundreds of square miles of abandoned factories, and a landscape marred by toxic waste sites. This massive hollowing out of US urban industrial landscapes has contributed significantly to the rise of economic insecurity that is fueled and amplified by racial anxieties among white workers and voters. One result was the creation of the "rust belt" of the Midwestern/Great Lakes region, a part of the country where support for Donald Trump's anti-immigrant, Islamophobic, sexist, and racist policymaking has been strong. A number of studies find that these cultural reactionary politics are robust in that region even among many voters who are not terribly concerned about the economy but are more focused on the threat of displacement by nonwhites. Ecological disruption and social disruption exist side by side and go hand in hand: these dynamics form the essence of the treadmill of production. The treadmill of production produces and reinforces social and economic inequalities locally, nationally, and globally.

Environmental Justice Studies

A related and growing field of scholarly inquiry—environmental justice studies—focuses on a subset of concerns associated with the impacts of the treadmill of production. Environmental justice studies emphasize the unequal outcomes of market-based and state economic and environmental policymaking on people of color, Indigenous populations, and the working class or poor. The major concern of scholars in this field is the problem of environmental inequality—that is, when a population suffers a high burden of environmental harm and is excluded from environmental decisions affecting its communities (see Lesson 10). More often than not, such populations include those groups on society's political, economic, and cultural margins. Research on environmental inequality dates back to the 1970s when scholars were reporting significant correlations between socioeconomic status and air pollution in US urban centers. Hence, for five decades, we have had quantitative and empirical evidence of social disparities in the distribution of pollution in the United States. Beginning in the 1980s, researchers focused more directly on the links between pollution and race via studies of the proximity of hazardous waste sites to communities of color. This research demonstrated that, in many cases, race was the best predictor of where hazardous waste sites would be located in the United States, prompting the use of the term **environmental racism** to characterize these disparities. Scholars and activists working on this problem frequently embrace the idea of environmental justice, which is a goal or a vision in which no community is unfairly burdened with environmental harms and where social justice and ecological sustainability prevail. Unfortunately, many societies are structured along intensely unequal social relations and heavily invested in toxic and chemical-intensive technologies; so environmental justice will likely remain an elusive goal for some time.

The Risk Society

Another theoretical framework I would like you to consider is German social scientist Ulrich Beck's idea of the **"risk society"** (see Lesson 2). The risk society is marked by a fundamental transformation in the relationship among industry, the state, civil society, and the environment. That is, at this point in history (which some scholars refer to as "late modernity"), we witness an exponential increase in the production and use of hazardous chemical substances. These actions emanate from the state and industry to civil society through production, consumption, and disposal practices, elevating the level of social and physical risk to scales never before imagined. The United States officially produces around 30 million tons of hazardous waste annually. But that figure only reflects the wastes regulated by the Resource Conservation and Recovery Act of 1976. It does not count the tons of hazardous waste that come from households, agricultural industries that return certain hazardous wastes to the ground, utility wastes from coal combustion, oil and natural gas exploration drilling waste, cement kiln wastes, and recycled hazardous wastes. This massive volume of hazards is toxic and poisonous to ecosystems and human health and has been a core part of the US economy and industrialization for generations. What this means is that the very existence of the modern US nation-state is made possible by the production of toxins—chemical poisons—that permeate every social institution, human body, and **nonhuman natures** (see Lesson 11). To be modern, then, is associated with a degree of manipulation of the human and nonhuman worlds that puts them both at great risk. To be modern also appears to require the subjugation and control over certain populations designated as "others," those less than fully deserving of citizenship, as a way of ameliorating the worst impacts of such a system on the privileged. These two tendencies—the manipulation of the human and more-than-human worlds—are linked through the benefits that toxic systems of production produce for the privileged and the imposition of the costs of that process on people and nonhuman natures deemed less valuable and therefore expendable. In a sense, then, Beck and Schnaiberg and Gould come together to offer a broader theory of environmental inequality

from which we can more effectively analyze the role of the state as a contributor to ecological and social violence.

In his classic book, *Imagined Communities: Reflections on the Origin and Spread of Nationalism*, Benedict Anderson proposes the following definition of a nation: "an imagined political community . . . and imagined as both inherently limited and sovereign." The nation is imagined because while members of this community cannot know or meet everyone inside its bor-
ders, in our minds, we each live in and share this community. The very idea of a nation-state is rooted in *sovereignty*—the ability of a nation's citizens to self-govern and to determine their own fate without interference from others. This is important because very often a powerful nation's practices prohibit another nation from self-governance, and this is frequently done in order to gain access to valuable ecological resources, in addition to consumer and labor markets.

While the US nation-state clearly embraces the agenda and logic of capitalism, this also has broader social impacts and roots. Ultimately, this is be-
cause states—as nations—are inherently exclusionary constructions; they write certain people and social categories out of power, belonging, and citizenship while including others. For example, states reflect historic and ongoing gender ideologies and interests. Consider Donald Trump's policy-
making infrastructure that is aggressively focused on excluding immigrants, Muslims, non-Christians, and LGBTQ persons from the nation and/or from consideration for full citizenship rights in the United States. Leading feminist legal theorist Catherine MacKinnon describes the state (for example, police, military, and legal institutions) as gendered insofar as it has a predominantly male orientation—meaning that not only do men constitute the majority of people in positions of authority within the state, but the state generally works to protect men's interests. The state as a gendered institution is revealed in its relationship to nonhuman natures as well. No doubt drawing from biblical roots that encourage humans to dominate the Earth and men to dominate women, the United States and European Union states engage nonhuman natures through ideologies and practices of domination. Specifically, in her groundbreaking book, *The Sexual Contract*, Carole Pateman contends that Western European nation-states were founded on a "sexual contract," which sought the exclusion of women from public spheres of power. Environmental historian Carolyn Merchant links that exclusion to the ways in which Western cultures imagine and behave toward nonhuman natures, in what Jim Mason (2005) calls "**dominionism**." Geographer David Harvey would agree. In his writings, he argues that the idea that people were meant to dominate nature—emerging from the Enlightenment period—is only half right. He con-
tends that the domination of nature thesis is not so much about dominating or controlling the environment or nonhuman nature as it is a means through which the domination of humans by other humans is accomplished. Thus, historically, the rich rule the poor, men control women, and powerful nations rule over weaker nations; and this is accomplished through the resources and power ultimately derived from human exploitation of ecosystems.

My point here is to locate the state's treatment of people in the same ideological, discursive, and structural space as the state's relationship to nonhuman nature. For example, the field of environmental justice studies maintains that the exploitation of people and the exploitation of the environment are linked. Thus, when the environmental integrity of working-class neighborhoods, Indigenous lands, and communities of color is harmed by state and corporate practices, this also results in harm done to public health and the social well-being of the persons living in these spaces (see Lesson 10).

Building on Carole Pateman's writings, Charles Mills argues that the US nation-state constitutes a "racial contract" in that it reflects the fact that European Americans founded this nation, at least partially, through acts of violently controlling and excluding Native Americans and Africans. Drawing on Hobbes's notion of the body politic as a leviathan, Mills asks if we take the nation as a body metaphor seriously, what about those parts of the national body that are viewed as surplus, as waste? His answer is that they can be discarded like any other form of waste. Mills argues that some populations—such as African Americans—constitute such waste, or "black trash," and are therefore viewed as socially and politically disposable. If these bodies and their communities are viewed as a form of social contamination, it might also make sense that society's physical waste would be co-located among these bodies, communities, and spaces. If the people themselves are viewed as dirty, filthy, and disposable, then environmental racism and injustice (via the location of polluting factories or waste dumps in these communities) are perfectly rational state practices. During his years in the White House, Donald J. Trump made repeated references to immigrants, Muslims, people of color, *and their communities* using demonizing language such as "rat and rodent infested," "dangerous," and "shithole countries." In a statement about Latin American migrants coming to the United States, he stated, "We have people coming into the country, or trying to come in—and we're stopping a lot of them—but we're taking people out of the country. *You wouldn't believe how bad these people are. These aren't people. These are animals.* And we're taking them out of the country at a level and at a rate that's never happened before." Thus, the state excludes certain populations from power and meaningful citizenship, and this practice intersects conveniently and reinforces the treadmill of production by placing the least desirable persons in the least desirable spaces. For example, sociologists Robert Bullard, Paul Mohai, Robin Saha, and Beverly Wright reported the following in a 2007 study titled "Toxic Waste and Race at Twenty, 1987–2007":

- In 2000, the majority of persons in neighborhoods hosting hazardous facilities are people of color (host neighborhoods are defined as communities within 1.8 miles of a facility). People of color are 56 percent of the population in these neighborhoods, as compared to non-host areas, where people of color are 30 percent.

- Those neighborhoods hosting clusters of several hazardous facilities have higher percentages of people of color than communities without such clusters (69 percent vs. 51 percent). Those areas containing clusters of facilities also contain populations experiencing high poverty rates.

• Not only do racial disparities in hazardous facility siting still exist, they have actually *intensified* over time, resulting in greater environmental inequalities today than reported in 1987. That is, in many parts of the nation, African Americans, Latinx folk, and Asian Americans/Pacific Islanders are more concentrated in neighborhoods hosting hazardous facilities than they were years earlier.

What much of this implies, then, is that the US state does not operate based on pluralist principles of governance. Rather, the US state (like any other state) largely exists to further the interests of some groups over others. This practice extends beyond the US border into other nations, producing unequal relations between the United States and peoples around the globe. Another way of thinking about this is to define it as imperialism. *Imperialism* is best characterized as a system of foreign power in which another culture, people, and way of life penetrate, transform, and come to define a colonized society. In the next sections, I discuss the role of US imperialism in relation to other peoples of the Americas and the world and how it produces environmental harm. The point here is to frame these practices as a key dimension of the de facto environmental policy regime of the US state.

US IMPERIALISM

The Monroe Doctrine is one of the most important factors in the development of US imperialism in the 19th century. On December 2, 1823, President James Monroe declared the Americas off limits to any new European colonization. Latin American leaders initially hailed this new policy as a protective mechanism until they realized that the United States would soon turn the doctrine into its opposite: Latin America, especially the Caribbean basin, was turned into a virtual US sphere of influence. Politicians and media leaders used the doctrine to develop the idea of "America for the Americans." Simón Bolívar, remembered by many people as the great liberator of many South American nations, would soon declare that the United States seemed destined to torment the Americas in the name of freedom. Many Latin American leaders and environmental activists (especially Indigenous leaders) argue that the United States pursues a similar agenda to this day, with continued proclamations of bringing democracy and freedom to nations around the world. This underscores an unresolved tension in US history and present-day politics: the contradiction between our ideals of freedom and our predilection for conquest. And that propensity for conquest is driven not only by a desire for consumer markets and cheap labor but also by a thirst for access to ecological wealth in the global South.

A short while later, a more powerful ideological proposition was put forth on the public agenda, which took the Monroe Doctrine much further. This was

Manifest Destiny, the ideology of racial and cultural superiority that guided the United States westward across the continent into Mexican territory, south into Central America and the Caribbean, across the Pacific, and beyond. There was a strong religious component to this concept, which embraced the domination of allegedly inferior peoples and the United States' right to do whatever it wished with their lands and ecosystems. Writing in support of the annexation of Texas during July 1845, politician John O'Sullivan coined the phrase "Manifest Destiny" to describe American expansionism:

> Yes, we are the nation of progress, of individual freedom, of universal enfranchisement. This is our high destiny, and in nature's eternal, inevitable decree of cause and effect we must accomplish it. All this will be our future history, to establish on earth the moral dignity and salvation of man—the immutable truth and beneficence of God. For this blessed mission to the nations of the world, which are shut out from the life-giving light of truth, has America been chosen; and her high example shall smite unto death the tyranny of kings, hierarchs, and oligarchs, and carry the glad tidings of peace and good will where myriads now endure an existence scarcely more enviable than that of beasts of the field.

O'Sullivan's phrase was adopted by Republican congressman Robert Winthrop and others in their work to mobilize for war against Mexico and the takeover of that nation's northern territories. Following O'Sullivan's ideas, God had entrusted the United States with "the development of the great experiment of liberty and federated self-government." Even the great poet Walt Whitman found the white man's burden appealing: "We want to see our country and its rule far-reaching only inasmuch as it will take off the shackles that prevent men the even chance of being happy and good." Before the decade ended, the United States had conquered the entire Southwest and forced Mexico to accede to the Treaty of Guadalupe Hidalgo, signed in 1848.

Some scholars contend that the expansionist tendencies we saw in the 1830s and 1840s continue through today with free-trade agreements and proxy wars the US military and corporations are waging in the Americas. For nearly two centuries, we have seen a massive and intensified transfer of ecological and economic wealth from south of the border north to the United States, from what Uruguayan author Eduardo Galeano calls "the open veins of Latin America." As a result, some observers and critics like Galeano believe the United States is the most economically privileged nation on the planet, in large part thanks to the extraction of copper from Chile; hardwoods from Brazil; oil from Mexico, Venezuela, and Ecuador; tin from Bolivia; bananas from Guatemala, Costa Rica, and Honduras; sugar from Cuba; and beef from Argentina. This arrangement—which some scholars call imperialist—has not alleviated poverty in Latin America, and the ecological toll from this resource extraction is extraordinary, including deforestation, oil spills, air pollution, soil erosion, species extinction, and the harm associated with countless tons of herbicides and pesticides that US-based agencies and corporations send to be sprayed on crops, watersheds, and agricultural workers' bodies in the region. Women, children, migrant farm workers, and poor populations suffer especially great burdens from pesticides (see Lesson 11). Not surprisingly, Indigenous peoples do as well. For example, Plan Colombia (a Colombian–US economic and military aid project designed to fight both anti-government Colombian rebels and the cocaine trade that included the aerial spraying of tons of pesticides on coca and poppy plants in Colombia) disproportionately impacts Indigenous people's land and health in that nation, violating their right to a clean environment as is customary under international law. The Foundation for Advancements in Science and Education recently concluded that US chemical manufacturers regularly sell tons of pesticides that are banned in the United States (because of their highly toxic content) to Latin American nations, where they are in widespread use in agriculture. Compounding these dynamics is the longstanding troubling relationship the United States has developed in support of brutal and repressive regimes in Latin America, with the goal of stemming the tide of communism during the Cold War, maintaining the region as a US sphere of influence, and securing access to ecological wealth, low wage labor markets, and consumers of American goods. Unfortunately, this was achieved by training tens of thousands of military personnel in the United States from Latin American countries in subjects like counterinsurgency, military intelligence, and counter-narcotics operations. This training occurred at the School of the Americas (SOA)—a US army school in Fort Benning, Georgia (since renamed the Western Hemisphere Institute for Security Cooperation). The list of nations where SOA graduates come from is long and includes Argentina, Bolivia, Brazil, Chile, Colombia, Costa Rica, the Dominican Republic, Ecuador, El Salvador, Guatemala, Honduras, Mexico, Panama, Paraguay, Peru, Uruguay, and Venezuela. The result was that ordinary Latin Americans and Indigenous peoples who desired land reform, better wages, improved health care, education, and the basic right of self-determination and democracy were labeled communists by US-backed regimes and murdered, tortured, and disappeared by paramilitary death squads and state security forces trained by the United States. Ironically, these US-supported policies and practices have led many people to flee violent repression as refugees who then seek asylum in the United States but are prevented from entering the country by the Trump regime, exacerbating a crisis that America played a large role in creating.

The process set into motion with the Monroe Doctrine and Manifest Destiny continued far beyond Latin America to Asia and elsewhere. At the same time the US empire was going global, there was a domestic expansion into Native American territories as well.

U.S. Federal Policies and Treaty Making

The same year the Monroe Doctrine came into being, another, much older ideology of domination was being refashioned. In 1823, Supreme Court Chief Justice John Marshall reinterpreted the "doctrine of discovery," an idea that European explorers and nations employed for centuries. The decision in the

US Supreme Court's *Johnson v. McIntosh* case resulted in what has been called the Marshall Doctrine, which concluded that the right of native peoples to their lands is diminished and that the sovereignty of the discoverers (read "Europeans") was inherently superior to that of Indigenous peoples. Some scholars argue that this was a creative interpretation of the original doctrine of discovery laid out in a series of papal bulls begun by Pope Innocent IV in the 13th century and evolving over the years, so that by the early 17th century, it had become a core part of international law, or what is referred to as the "law of nations." These legal norms allowed Europeans to acquire land in foreign places only if it was uninhabited or if native peoples gave or sold the land by consent. This meant that Europeans were thus expected to enter into treaty making with native peoples around the world, which recognized their sovereignty; and the British, for example, generally did so. So Justice Marshall's doctrine was important because it represented a major shift in policy that departed from what was considered international law at the time. Marshall pushed even further in what are called the "Cherokee opinions" of the early 1830s (the Supreme Court decisions in *Cherokee Nation v. Georgia*, 1831, and *Worcester v. Georgia*, 1832), seeking to strengthen the logic of the *McIntosh* decision, given that it was not likely to withstand international legal scrutiny. Thus, he developed the thesis that native peoples within North America constituted nations since they inhabited territories and were ruled by governments with the capacity to engage in commerce and treaty making. However, Marshall maintained—drawing on the ideas contained in the *McIntosh* decision—that native nations were a "peculiar type" of nation that were "domestic" to and "dependent upon" the United States. Hence, native nations were relegated to a subordinate sovereignty vis-à-vis the United States. In other words, this was nothing less than a relationship enjoyed by an empire with its colonies. The implication of these legal decisions was that ecological materials such as land, minerals, forests, fish, buffalo, and water within Native American territories were legally constructed as available for the taking if the US government deemed it necessary. One example of this policy was the Dawes Severalty Act of 1887, through which the federal government began "registering" Indians and forcing them to live on lands that were subdivided into small, individual private property lots. The aim was to "civilize" Native Americans by encouraging them to embrace the notion of private property while drastically reducing their land base, liberating "surplus" lands for white settlers, private companies, and the federal government. While much of this land was dedicated to homesteading (for white families who settled in the West), much of it was ultimately used to create the first national parks and national forests in the United States, which Ansel Adams became famous for photographing, often excluding evidence of native peoples from such vistas. Some estimates are that the Dawes Act resulted in the removal of two thirds of the land (around 150 million acres) that native peoples previously occupied. A 1928 congressional study—the Meriam Report—concluded that these policies left "an overwhelming majority of the Indians . . . poor, even extremely poor". Native peoples were relegated to lands that the federal government believed to be of little economic value, with few mineral and other natural resources.

Other native peoples challenged the Dawes Act in the courts, but in the 1903 *Lone Wolf v. Hitchcock* case, the Supreme Court extended federal power to argue that the US government possessed a right to selectively abide by treaties it had made with native nations. This was the final consolidation of the Marshall Doctrine and led to a formal disempowerment of native nations.

One of the great ironies of the Dawes Act was that much of the land base to which Native Americans were relegated eventually was determined to be among the most well-endowed, ecologically rich areas on the planet. It is estimated that two-thirds of all uranium deposits in the United States, one-fourth of the nation's sulfur coal, and one-fifth of oil and natural gas reserves are on (or beneath) Native American reservation lands. Moreover, reservation lands are also rich in metals and minerals such as gold, iron, molybdenum, copper, iron, zinc, nickel, and bauxite. Thus, the unequal relationship between the US government and tribal governments—as developed in the *McIntosh, Cherokee*, and *Lone Wolf* cases—made possible the transfer of such environmental wealth from Native America to the United States of America. The controversial Bureau of Indian Affairs was the agency that supervised this effort and, unfortunately, often failed to ensure the protection of ecosystems during and after extractive projects. One outcome of these state policies is that, particularly on reservations where uranium mining has occurred, the extent of radioactive contamination is considerable. Socially and economically, another more visible outcome of this history is that native communities are among the poorest in the hemisphere, with a range of public and mental health problems that have been at epidemic levels for many years. Native American Studies scholars such as Paula Gunn Allen, Ward Churchill, Andrea Smith, David Stannard, Haunani-Kay Trask, Waziyatawin, and others reveal that unemployment, alcoholism, domestic violence, rape, suicide, and numerous other social ills are abnormally high in many Native American communities; and each of these scholars attributes those outcomes to the effects of US imperialism.

More recently, scholars have deepened the analysis of the US empire to focus on the phenomenon of **settler colonialism**, which refers to the complex processes involved when one society permanently invades the terrestrial, aquatic, and aerial territories inhabited by another, Indigenous, society, thus occupying and controlling both human and nonhuman spaces and resources through violent means. What this means is that settler colonialism is an example of environmental injustice because the invading power directly undermines the ecological conditions that Indigenous peoples need to thrive politically, culturally, and economically. Settler colonialism is a framework that undergirds all environmental justice struggles in the United States, *whether directly involving Indigenous peoples or not*, because environmental justice conflicts always involve land and resources entangled with histories of conquest.

The Struggle Goes On

The practices of imperialism, environmental racism, settler colonialism, and ecological violence continue today, within and beyond US borders. The struggle against the Dakota Access Pipeline is a case in point. This pipeline will run more than 1,100 miles, carrying crude oil from the Bakken oil fields in the Dakotas to a refinery in Illinois. In 2016, thousands of people began mobilizing with the Standing Rock Sioux Reservation (in North and South Dakota) to block this pipeline (after it was to be rerouted around the majority white town of Bismarck, ND), which threatens sacred Indigenous sites and water quality in the Missouri and Cannonball rivers. This mobilization became the largest gathering of Native nations since at least 1876 and inspired people around the world to draw connections among issues of Indigenous sovereignty, environmental justice, and climate change (see Lesson 10). At the time of this writing, numerous Indigenous nations in North America are teaming up with environmentalists in the United States and Canada to oppose the extraction, processing, and transport of tar sands oil. There are at least three multibillion-dollar pipeline projects in various stages of development that companies like TransCanada Corporation (the company behind the Keystone XL pipeline), Enbridge Inc., and Kinder Morgan Energy Partners are championing. Indigenous peoples and their allies (among them scholar-activists like Bill McKibben) are concerned that tar sands extraction will enable the consumption of an enormous volume of fossil fuels, thus contributing massive amounts of carbon emissions to the Earth's atmosphere and accelerating climate change (see Lesson 15). The Alberta tar sands contain the second largest oil deposit in the world—something the Canadian and US governments and corporations are desperate to tap. Tar sands projects require the use of large amounts of water and dangerous chemicals and have already devastated the Athabasca River delta and watershed in Alberta, which includes deforestation of the boreal forests; open-pit mining; drainage of water systems; proliferation of toxic chemicals; habitat and biodiversity disruption; and damage to the Indigenous Dene, Cree, and Métis First Nations' cultural life ways. Activist groups like the Indigenous Environmental Network have mobilized people throughout North America to oppose these projects and to support Native peoples and environmental justice.

Native Hawaiians, or *Kanaka Maoli*, live in a state that hosts more federal hazardous waste sites than any other US state. Many of these sites were created through polluting activities carried out by the US military, which has compromised—and in some cases, destroyed—native land and fisheries. Between 1964 and 1973, the US Navy released 4.8 million gallons of radioactive waste into Pearl Harbor from its submarines. The Navy also dumped more than 2,000 55-gallon steel drums of solid radioactive waste off the shoreline, posing a major threat to ocean life. Similar dynamics characterize the Clark and Subic US military bases in the Philippines and many others elsewhere. The US military is one of the world's greatest sources of pollution; and, with more than 700 bases around the planet, one of the leading purveyors of institutional violence. These examples also suggest that US state practices often tend to steer clear of pluralism and remain largely anti-democratic and unilateralist. But the risk society thesis is useful for assisting us in realizing that although environmental and climate injustices abound, to some degree or another, we are all at risk. For example, the largely white and economically privileged town of Santa Barbara, California, has experienced two major oil industry disasters in the last half century—in 1969 and 2015. And the BP-Deep Water Horizon oil spill of 2010 in the Gulf of Mexico released 100 million gallons of fossil fuels into waterways and ecosystems that impacted a range of human and nonhuman populations.

What is to be done? One of the first things we should acknowledge is that many of us reap significant benefits from these policies, including the comforts of cheap gas, electronic gadgets, heating and air conditioning, and other material privileges that are unearned, yet they are the result of unfortunate state and corporate policies that harm people and ecosystems all around us. Perhaps that is one reason why we find it difficult or unappealing to confront these issues. But facing the fact that our way of life is linked to appalling conditions elsewhere can also be empowering because we can begin to build relationships of solidarity and cooperation for a better world with people whom we never knew we had a connection. In fact, this topic is closely related to the concept "environmental privilege," which a number of scholars have developed in recent years to describe the social problem whereby elite populations exert power in order to maintain exclusive or restricted access to coveted environmental amenities such as cleaner air, water, land, green space, national parks, recreational sites, and upscale residential neighborhoods. Kenneth Gould and Tammy Lewis analyze this process in great depth with respect to the phenomenon of green gentrification—wherein certain neighborhoods enjoy an environmental upgrade as socially privileged populations (the "sustainability class") displace marginalized communities who previously lived with a range of ecological and social disamenities in the same geographic space. Until this body of research emerged, few scholars raised the question about the harm of environmental privilege and how it is inescapably linked to environmental injustice. For example, while scholars have delved deeply into the problem of environmental racism and inequality and how it results in heavy burdens of pollution and other environmental risks in low-income communities and communities of color, there has been less attention paid to what is arguably a primary driving force behind that phenomenon: the unrelenting quest for environmental privilege among communities with greater social and political capital.

CONCLUSION

This lesson considers the historical and ongoing actions of the US nation-state as imperial practices that routinely produce environmental harm and social inequality. Offering a sampling of theories of environment–society relationships, social inequality, and state formation, I argue that in order to better understand how contemporary US policies result in environmental racism and inequality, one must consider the historical, legal, economic, and cultural roots and evolution of the US nation-state itself. Such an exploration suggests that the United States remains an imperial presence in the Americas and globally, and this has dire consequences for any effort to produce social and environmental justice here or elsewhere. In this way, we might locate the deeper origins of the environmental state and, in turn, think through a different set of questions that might achieve reform or transformation of those practices. For example, instead of seeking only to strengthen regulation of polluting industries in poor neighborhoods and communities of color, one might also push for a greater democratization of the state and industry. Specifically, communities struggling for environmental justice would likely benefit from a stronger civil society base that involves strengthening the capacity of nongovernmental organizations, neighborhood groups, and workers' organizations to negotiate more ecologically sustainable and socially progressive institutional policies domestically and abroad.

Today, environmental justice and human rights movements are merging as a global force for social change and democratization. Activists in Europe, the Americas, Africa, Asia, and the Pacific are collaborating to challenge socially and ecologically harmful state and corporate policies around hydroelectric power, incineration, and mineral extraction, for example, while offering alternatives for sustainability and social justice (see Lesson 18). Articulating a vision of global justice and human rights, the Principles of Environmental Justice—drafted at the First National People of Color Environmental Leadership Summit in Washington, DC, in 1991—contain a number of key demands along this vein (see Lesson 10). For example, the first principle calls for the "right to be free from ecological destruction"; the second principle calls for the right to be "free from any form of discrimination or bias"; the fourth principle invokes the "fundamental right to clean air, land, water, and food"; the fifth principle affirms the "fundamental right to political, economic, cultural and environmental self-determination of all peoples"; the eighth principle cites the right "to a safe and healthy work environment"; and the tenth principle contends that governmental acts of environmental injustice are violations of international law and of "the Universal Declaration On Human Rights, and the United Nations Convention on Genocide." Taken separately and together, these principles speak impressively to a body of international law and human rights that has been in development for several decades. More importantly, in order for these principles to become reality, states and corporations would have to undergo dramatic transformations that would embrace transparency, power sharing, and democracy as standard operating procedure. The work of activists in the environmental justice and human rights movements reveals sophisticated efforts at combating global environmental inequalities through the engagement of a range of institutions, thus developing an emerging form of global citizenship and, by extension, a burgeoning transnational public sphere that might ultimately lead to greater democratization of our global society.

And yet, troubling questions remain as to whether all of that effort will ever be enough. That is, what if, as some philosophers contend, the very essence of a modern nation-state is the embodiment of authoritarianism employed to define certain groups as unworthy or only partially worthy of inclusion and recognition as members of the polity? What if modern nation-states are built on a juridical/legal and cultural foundation of human dominance over nonhuman natures? In other words, according to this idea, integral to the modern nation-state are the ideologies and practices of racism, classism, heteropatriarchy, and dominionism. If that is so, then it would make sense that scholars begin thinking about solutions to social and environmental crises in ways that move beyond the state altogether. And scholars in settler colonial nations like the United States might begin to take seriously the challenge of decolonizing our scholarship by centering analyses of settler colonialism in much of our work. I believe this is a topic that environmental sociologists will be debating in the years ahead.

SOURCES

Allen, Paula Gunn. 1992. *The Sacred Hoop*. Boston, MA: Beacon Press.

Anderson, Benedict. 1991. *Imagined Communities: Reflections on the Origin and Spread of Nationalism*. New York: Verso.

Beck, Ulrich. 1992. *Risk Society: Towards a New Modernity*. Thousand Oaks, CA: Sage.

Bullard, Robert D., Paul Mohai, Robin Saha, and Beverly Wright. 2007. "Toxic Waste and Race at Twenty, 1987–2007." United Church of Christ.

Churchill, Ward. 2003. *Perversions of Justice: Indigenous Peoples and Anglo-American Law*. San Francisco: City Lights.

Dahl, Robert. 1961. *Who Governs? Democracy and Power in an American City*. New Haven, CT: Yale University Press.

Galeano, Eduardo. 1997. *Open Veins of Latin America: Five Centuries of the Pillage of a Continent*. New York: Monthly Review Press.

Gill, Lesley. 2004. *The School of the Americas: Military Training and Political Violence in the Americas*. Duke University Press.

Gould, Kenneth Alan and Tammy L. Lewis. 2017. *Green Gentrification*. London: Routledge.

Harvey, David. 1997. *Justice, Nature and the Geography of Difference*. Cambridge, MA: Blackwell Publishers.

Hirst, Paul Q., ed. 1994. *The Pluralist Theory of the State: Selected Writings of G. D. H. Cole, J. N. Figgis, and H. J. Laski*. London, UK: Routledge.

Hoover, Elizabeth. 2017. *The River is In Us: Fighting Toxics in a Mohawk Community*. Minneapolis: University of Minnesota Press.

MacKinnon, Catherine. 1982. "Feminism, Marxism, Method, and the State." *Signs* 7 (Spring): 515–544.

Mason, Jim. 2005. *An Unnatural Order: The Roots of Our Destruction of Nature*. San Francisco: City Lights.

Merchant, Carolyn. 1980. *The Death of Nature: Women, Ecology and the Scientific Revolution*. San Francisco: Harper.

Miller, Frank. 1928. *Meriam Report: The Problem of Indian Administration*. Washington, D.C.: Institute for Government Research.

Mills, Charles W. 1999. *The Racial Contract*. Ithaca, NY: Cornell University Press.

O'Sullivan, John. 1845. "The Great Nation of Futurity." *The United States Democratic Review* 6 (July): 426–430.

Pateman, Carole. 1988. *The Sexual Contract*. Palo Alto, CA: Stanford University Press.

Pulido, Laura. 2000. "Rethinking Environmental Racism: White Privilege and Urban Development in Southern California." *Annals of the American Association of Geographers* 90 (1): 12–40.

Qiu, Linda. 2018. "The Context Behind Trump's 'Animals' Comment." *New York Times*, May 18, 2018.

Schaffer, Brian, Matthew MacWilliams, and Tatishe Nteta. 2018. "Understanding White Polarization in the 2016 Vote for President: The Sobering Role of Racism and Sexism." *Political Science Quarterly* 133(1). https://doi.org/10.1002/polq.12737.

Schnaiberg, Allan, and Kenneth Gould. 2000. *Environment and Society: The Enduring Conflict*. Caldwell, NJ: Blackburn Press.

Smith, Andrea. 2005. *Conquest: Sexual Violence and American Indian Genocide*. Cambridge, MA: South End Press.

Smith, Mick. 2011. *Against Ecological Sovereignty: Ethics, Biopolitics, and Saving the Natural World*. Minneapolis: University of Minnesota Press.

Stannard, David. 1992. *American Holocaust: The Conquest of the New World*. New York: Oxford University Press.

Trask, Haunani-Kay. 1999. *From a Native Daughter: Colonialism and Sovereignty in Hawai'i*. Honolulu: University of Hawai'i Press.

Voyles, Traci Brynne. 2015. *Wastelanding: Legacies of Uranium Mining in Navajo Country*. Minneapolis: University of Minnesota Press.

Waziyatawin. 2008. *What Does Justice Look Like? The Struggle for Liberation in Dakota Homeland*. St. Paul, MN: Living Justice Press.

Whitman, Walt. 1920. *The Gathering of the Forces*. New York: G.P. Putnam's Sons.

Whyte, Kyle Powys. 2017. "The Dakota Access Pipeline, Environmental Injustice, and U.S. Colonialism." *RED INK: An International Journal of Indigenous Literature, Arts, & Humanities* 19 (1): 154–169.

Labor Productivity and the Environment

Allan Schnaiberg and Kenneth A. Gould

4 September 20, 2019, Global Climate Strike protest at Wall Street's Charging Bull sculpture, New York, NY.

Post your photo on labor productivity and the environment to #TLESproductivity.

Photo by Ken Gould

THE PROMISE VERSUS THE HISTORY OF PRODUCTIVITY

Conceptualizing Productivity

The essence of labor productivity is an increase in economic production for each worker employed. In many societies, the argument has been made that with increased labor productivity, social problems will be solved. In theory, it is argued that higher productivity and **profitability** *permit* more savings and investments in social and environmental programs. In recent decades, even more economic policy has been mobilized to argue that companies and economies without growing labor productivity are doomed to be displaced by firms and countries where productivity is higher. As international trade increased and manufacturing shifted to lower-wage societies, labor productivity has become labeled as the key component of "global economic competitiveness."

Yet in practice, the historical processes by which productivity gains have actually been achieved give the lie to this argument. Productivity tends to be a solution primarily for investors and some managers (many of them also become some of the downsized workers). For workers, their communities, and the natural world in which they are embedded, this has become one of the most egregious bait-and-switch social policies. The corporate strategy of constant increases in labor productivity is a central element of the treadmill of production (see Lesson 2).

The Perspective of Corporate Investors and Managers

The greater the productivity of an organization, the greater its profitability, according to modern economics. If I am able to raise the amount of production accomplished by each of my workers each day, my costs of production are reduced. I am then able to sell the commodity that my workers made at a somewhat lower price than my competitors and thereby increase my share of the market for this product.

When this happens over some time period, my profits tend to rise, for two reasons: (1) while I may lower my price somewhat, I generally do not lower it as much as my savings on workers' wages, so I increase my profit on every item I sell; (2) as I compete more effectively over my competitors, I make additional profits because of the increased number of items I am selling. The first of these effects is often defined as my *profit margin* per item I sell (revenue minus costs), and the second is my *profit ratio* (total revenue divided by total cost). These processes vary within countries and across the global economy. For the productive company, they are uniformly desirable outcomes; for the less productive, they are often fatal. In modern economic analysis and journalism, as well as modern politics, though, the focus is on the "winners" and not the "losers," in what can be seen as a kind of **economic Darwinism**.

Yet this is a very selective view of "productivity." Productivity typically has negative effects on the social fabric of a society and the ecological sustainability of its natural environment. To understand this, let's first look more realistically at how productivity is increased. Measurement of actual worker productivity is complex since it requires holding constant a variety of efficiency components in production, to separate out the effects of the workers themselves.

Generally, managers fall back on a simplified calculus: If I can do the same job with fewer workers, then workers' productivity has increased. Some of this is achieved by reorganizing production technologies. But it often generates greater pressure on workers to work harder, longer, and with more workplace tension than they faced previously. Managers can unilaterally decide to "downsize" a workforce—that is, to lay off some significant portion of their workers—and have been doing so in Western economies for decades now.

The Perspectives of Workers/Communities

In order for this to increase productivity, the remaining workers must be willing and/or able to compensate for the lost production of those who were downsized. Their *willingness* can be induced by coercive and/or seductive measures: "Work more or we'll fire you," and/or "Work harder and we'll pay you some additional bonus payments." The first is effective where workers have few better job opportunities. However, the coercive strategy carries with it new potential threats of slowdowns, sabotage, and higher worker turnover in response to the rising stress of the workplace (see Lesson 17). The seductive approach is more effective when the firm has more control of its other costs than its competitors. Its effectiveness dwindles when the total of new worker bonus payments begins to approximate the prior payroll levels of the larger workforce.

In addition to their willingness to increase their labor efforts, though, workers must have the *capacity* to do so. Reducing the labor force by only a modest proportion of workers may be designed to increase the workload of the remaining workers. From a managerial perspective, this creates more efficiency and enhances both productivity and profits. Contrary to the image of owners as job creators, the economy is structured to reward job eliminators.

Perspectives on the Environment

Most of the changes in 20th-century production systems after 1945 consisted of some combination of new energy applications and new chemical processes, generating much less labor-intensive forms of production. For instance, corn production changes, as noted in the next section, exemplify this process in agriculture. Rising chemical pollution emerged in both workplaces (including cornfields) and communities (rivers and streams near cornfields). Parallel changes occurred in much manufacturing, where the materials and processes by which products were formed moved away from the hands of workers and into mechanical and electronic machinery (see Lesson 7).

The modern environmental movement in the 1960s arose in great degree in response to new fears of chemical pollution, exemplified by Rachel Carson's book *Silent Spring*, which presented the widespread reproductive effects of DDT, an early and powerful pesticide (see Lesson 18). In the 1970s, some environmental movement attention moved to shortages of fossil fuels, due to changes in the concentration of oil production overseas and the decline of US production.

More recently, decades of scientific research has affirmed that the use of fossil fuels has increased carbon dioxide and other "greenhouse gases." These have been correlated with rising atmospheric and oceanic temperatures, altering climate and water distribution and threatening even more disruptions of social and economic life, as well as of ecosystems (see Lesson 15). Although the modern environmental movement was initiated in the United States, the aggregate pollution and depletion (of both energy sources and natural habitats) actually rose in the United States during the period of organized environmental movements, and much greater movement resistance has become embedded within the European Union and the Global South.

We now outline two major paths by which investors and managers attempt to increase the productivity of their workers.

RAISING PRODUCTIVITY BY CHANGING PRODUCTION TECHNOLOGIES

One major approach is investment in new production technologies, frequently involving more electronic and mechanical equipment, within existing workplaces. This was the essential strategy used by corn growers.

The Case of Corn

One of the most detailed examples is Michael Pollan's history of corn production. Maize was a very old plant in the Americas. It was generally harvested by hand; and even among early cultivators in Latin America, some manual pollination was done to create new varieties of corn. Corn became essentially an industrialized crop in the United States, especially after 1945. Ever-growing levels of fertilizers, pesticides, and herbicides were utilized to increase the yield of corn per acre.

Gradually, corn production has become essentially a plantation operation, with growing sizes of landholdings and replacement of the labor of planting, harvesting, and storing the grain with mechanized equipment. Likewise, with the large capital investments involved, planters wanted more predictable crops to cover their loans for the new equipment. Additional equipment was purchased to irrigate cornfields. And the demand for high-yield hybrid corn seeds rose as planters sought to further reduce their risks of pests and water shortages.

The scale of capital investment in corn production rose substantially, and the successful planters bought out the land of smaller and "less productive" farmers, resulting in fewer farms, fewer farmers, and more concentrated ownership by large producers. In addition, the debt burden for even large landholders became unsustainable, and many abandoned corn production. Overall, there were substantial increases in the levels of corn production. At first blush, this seemed to serve the economic interests of large landholders quite well. There were a number of social and ecological costs, however. As corn production was industrialized, rural labor forces were eliminated, communities contracted, and local enterprises collapsed because of a lack of wage income and consumer spending. As the dependence on rural labor decreased, so did rural populations, as economically displaced farmers and their children left rural areas in search of employment opportunities. Rural schools closed, services diminished, and the aging population that remained grew increasingly disenchanted.

Moreover, agricultural wastes from cornfields increasingly became toxic; and with growing irrigation, there was an increased runoff of chemical pesticides and herbicides into local streams and rivers. And the fossil fuel demands per bushel of corn produced rose substantially. From the standpoint of energy efficiency, the energy inputs involved in corn production vastly exceeded the caloric value of the corn produced. Labor efficiency increased, but energy efficiency declined, producing fewer jobs and more fossil fuel demand simultaneously. Production processes generated fewer social benefits and more ecological disruption.

Despite these social and ecological problems, corn production in the United States has increased substantially. While this seemed to reward "productive" corn planters, it also created new cross-pressures on them. The first problem with rising corn production was that there was too limited a market for all the corn produced. One of the hidden vulnerabilities of increased productivity is that more product must be sold. Productive organizations that lack sufficient markets will find their profits reduced eventually, and investors will move their capital elsewhere. Corn planters responded to this challenge in several ways. Paradoxically, as corn surpluses grew and prices fell, corn producers actually increased their acreage and planting, selling more corn at lower prices, to hold on to their equipment and land. This created still more corn surpluses, further dropping prices and threatening the revenues of corn planters.

Two additional strategies were developed. The first was to widen the use of corn, both in foodstuffs and as animal feed. Pollan outlines how grass-fed beef and other food animals became transformed into corn-fed animals. For livestock owners, this eventually led to enclosures for animals since there was no longer any necessity for grazing. The factory cornfield eventually led to the factory farm, with diminished freedom of movement for all livestock (see Lesson 13).

Because this enclosed corn-fed regimen raised the threat of communicable diseases among densely settled animals, corn feeds were reformulated to include antibiotics and other organic chemicals, designed to both reduce disease and hasten the growth of the animals. The end result of this has been an increase in the chemical levels of corn and meat of all kinds, eventually entering into the human food chain and the land and waters near both cornfields and factory farms.

As corn prices dropped further, research into the use of corn as a synthetic food component rose because the price of corn products was competitive with many other natural food sources. Yet even this expansion of the market did not sufficiently cushion the income of corn planters. They began an extensive and successful lobbying campaign to argue for federal price supports for corn. Part of the campaign was to portray corn producers as just "farmers" living in small towns who needed protection from the vagaries of weather and markets. In this way, those who drove the decline of rural America were able to capture the public revenues dedicated to supporting rural communities.

In the post-9/11 political climate, moreover, corn producers scored yet another victory. After the crisis of US terrorism, a new drive to increase "energy security" and "energy independence" in the United States was put on the national agenda. One of the most direct and least politicized strategies that emerged was federal support for the vastly expanded production of ethanol, produced from fermented corn. So successful had this been for corn planters that in the decade following federal support, the market for corn was no longer saturated, and corn prices began to rise. This means that corn, a "renewable" resource, has became a core element of both food and transportation. The fact that producing corn is energy inefficient in both domains has been essentially ignored by most analysts. Since that time, problems with ethanol production from corn have led some researchers to search for more energy-efficient (and cost-effective) feedstocks for ethanol, such as saw grasses. Corn prices have also fluctuated.

Is Corn's History Representative of Other Productivity Processes?

The details of productivity changes for corn overlap to a considerable extent with those for other commodities. While it is true that agricultural production entails more uncertainties than factory production, many of the historical processes just outlined hold for many industries. Where the role of human labor has been reduced in the production process, the alternative technology is often a mixture of increased fossil fuel energy and increased application of synthetic chemicals. Waste has always been a byproduct of all manufacturing processes. However, when machines replace human labor, they offer new capacities for managers and investors but also new challenges. Purchase of new equipment generally entails both capital outlays and debt, and the result is increased managerial pressure to recoup the investment with increased production and sales.

Just as water power replaced some human workers and steam replaced water power, fossil fuels and electricity replaced steam as a driving force of production (see Lesson 7). This was true not only in the actual production machinery but also in the materials used in products. Wood was replaced by metals and metals by plastics and other synthetic materials. Many of these new processes and products entail toxic chemicals in processing or products.

While some new forms of pollution control were added to production systems and some forms of energy efficiency were even achieved, aggregate production and its **ecological externalities** increased. Contemporary environmental regulation has required producers to negotiate some *qualitative* controls over their production systems. However, almost no governments sought to place *quantitative* limits on the volume of production and profits. Under the Trump administration, many of the qualitative controls have been reduced, eliminated, or have gone unenforced.

Some of this involved direct political struggles between "shareholders" (investors and managers) and "stakeholders" (workers and community residents). But much of this economic expansion was built into the logic of a newly capitalized production apparatus. Once an enterprise laid out financial capital for a new set of production machinery, there was an increasing motive to recoup this investment and raise profits by increasing the volume of production and net revenues. Workers could be downsized—but it was less economically and politically acceptable for managers to downsize newer capital equipment. Owners are committed to their equipment in a way that they are not to their workers. Indeed, in fields such as information technology, growing capital outlays were increasingly necessary to *sustain* profits, let alone increase them, in the face of growing technological competition.

In part because of this disparity between disinvesting in workers and investing in physical production equipment, ecological pressures on habitats were both directly and indirectly increased. The indirect pressures arose precisely because the ratio of physical capital to workers grew substantially and the capacity of managing physical capital to generate profits outstripped managerial controls of workers. In order for employment to remain stable, workers had to join in efforts to ensure that firms were encouraged to invest still more and expand production. This appeared to be the only way in which replacement jobs could be generated. Production had to constantly expand to produce more goods and services just in order to employ the same number of workers (see Lesson 2). Economic growth was made to appear necessary for workers.

An earlier form of pressure involved mobilizing the firm's workers to reject the government's environmental regulation (see Lesson 17). This sometimes meant that workers in industrial communities accepted living in a highly toxic environment because their employment seemed dependent on maintaining existing production forces. And government agencies likewise avoided threatening these sources of jobs. The Trump administration has encouraged workers to reject environmental regulation as a way to preserve or recover jobs that have been displaced or threatened by mechanization. Coal miners in West Virginia are a case in point (see Lesson 9).

However, the alliance for new investments and jobs was even more powerful in aligning workers with investors' and managers' interests. Despite this "common front" organized around growth, increases in the profits and wealth of the economic elite far outstripped the wages of workers, thus increasing economic inequality. Additionally, workers are encouraged to vote for tax reductions for corporations, as well as reduced environmental and public health protection, to help sustain business "competitiveness" in national and global markets. Freudenburg (1991) argued that, in reality, "good" business climate ratings—the classification for business areas in which there are limited environmental regulations and worker protections—actually correlate with worse economic outcomes: the states named as having "bad" business climates (in other words, having environmental regulations and safety protections for workers) actually had better economic performance (growth in jobs and incomes) over subsequent 5- and 10-year periods.

This coalition for labor productivity and competitiveness also leads to a disjuncture between the rising social needs of displaced and reduced-wage workers, on the one hand, and workers' support for lower taxation of corporations and investors, on the other hand. Moreover, there seems to be diminished community support for mainstream environmental movements. Environmental enforcement can raise the costs of corporations and often requires larger regulatory expenditures by government agencies. In effect, then, one benefit of choreographing rising labor productivity by investors and managers is that it mutes the voices raised in opposition to the negative social and environmental outcomes. Workers in rural and rust belt regions end up supporting policies that ultimately make them relatively poorer and reduce their health outcomes.

RELOCATION AND "OUTSOURCING"

Domestic Relocation

The concept of relocation is deceptively simple: If local workers cost too much, firms should find less expensive workers elsewhere. Relocating plants domestically, to areas with less expensive workers, is one major strategy. For some decades after the 1960s, US manufacturers shifted production out of rust belt communities (Eastern, Northern, and Midwestern), where workers were unionized. Plants were shifted to "sunbelt" communities (Southern and Western), where state laws, work shortages, and managerial threats and inducements inhibited worker unions from forming. Industries such as textiles were shifted almost completely from rust belt states.

Many of the sunbelt communities, in their quest for new employment and tax dollars, simultaneously offered little enforcement of environmental protection or worker safety. This afforded higher rates of productivity for employers since corporate expenses for some raw materials (including water), for much of their waste disposal, and for worker safeguards were lower than they had been in the somewhat more regulated rust belt communities.

Outsourcing: International Relocation

Outsourcing, or moving production away from Northern industrial economies and into less developed Southern ones, is an extension and substitute for relocation within the country. This has been the most common US pattern of recent decades. This shift has primarily been due to the search for higher productivity and profits, both for less expensive labor and for lowered waste disposal costs. Ironically, whereas some of the earlier movement of capital to less developed areas involved less sophisticated technologies, movement has been accelerated even in the production (and servicing) of high-technology products, such as electronics. While the labor component of total production costs is not small, a large portion of the costs of production involves larger energy and chemical applications to production.

The most notable of these shifts has been in the production of silicon computer chips, the ultimate in high-value products. Part of the movement of "silicon" from Silicon Valley in California appears to have been the highly toxic production processes and the growing concerns of local environmental groups and worker organizations.

Much of the investment in less developed countries—ranging from China to Mexico—involves heightened workplace pollution and local air and water pollution. In each case, the host government has colluded with foreign investors, trading these social and ecological costs to provide more job opportunities (often for displaced agricultural workers) and higher tax revenues. These interests coalesce with those of investors in countries like the United States who are seeking greater returns on their investments (directly tied in the modern economy to higher productivity and profits).

In the United States, domestic relocation meant moving away from unionized workers. As union membership declined in the United States, the very investment strategy that had lowered union resistance also permitted a global search for new production locations for investors. Historically, in addition to union resistance, this centrifugal tendency had been restrained by the friction of space, the complexities of communications, and the unpredictable systems of national control over foreign investors.

With the rise of electronic communications, rapid airplane travel, and the increasing global pressures to "free up markets," many of these frictions were reduced. A faster pace of technological research and development made previous investments in production technology depreciate much faster (and were often accelerated with **depreciation allowances** in taxes paid to the government). Indeed, the pace of increased capitalization of production and the rise of large profits and corporate mergers made many such costs relatively small in the face of new opportunities for investment and profits.

Ecologically, this search for less expensive workers and workplace locations expanded the range of habitats that were becoming disrupted to make room for factories, mines, and natural resource processing facilities. New workers often lived in the midst of corporate structures that seemed modern and communities that were among the most despoiled in modern human history.

Both China and Mexico exemplify such recent trends, although Mexico was far more directly pressured by foreign investors. The health and ecological costs are substantial in both countries. Acceptance of these conditions by both workers and their governments supports the productivity-based model of "competitiveness."

Among the most recent of these processes is the outsourcing of white-collar service work—built around the availability of both more powerful computers and advanced telecommunications systems. The direct effect of these new office systems on the environment is primarily in energy intensification of overseas service work. However, the rising toxic problems of both computer chip production and e-waste may also predict other health hazards for humans and habitats.

CONCLUSION

Increased labor productivity has become a standard economic indicator for the US economy. When productivity "falters," alarms are raised that the United States will no longer remain "competitive" with its global trading partners.

The harsh reality is that manufacturing is basically no longer carried out in the United States, and agriculture offers a limited range of jobs (and many of those are reserved for low-wage, undocumented workers). Labor unions have been largely downsized, along with their previous members. Major unions today have grown in the service sector because US investors have moved their capital abroad (see Lesson 17).

Yet communities and workers still fantasize about the return of the factory, and every domestic and foreign manufacturer is encouraged to relocate to a US community. Communities and their populations seeking jobs are willing to subsidize private producers and often to ignore local ecological degradation to attract new investors. Politicians exploit these nostalgic fantasies, ignoring the structural, technological, and historical changes that make a return to the economy of the past impossible.

Labor productivity has largely been achieved by investors and managers, and only a small group of workers has benefited from it. In the process, a substantial human and environmental toll has been paid. Despite the associated social and ecological costs, increasing labor productivity remains a central goal of corporations and a key strategy of states in pursuing economic growth and global competitiveness.

SOURCES

Bell, Shannon E. 2016. *Fighting King Coal: The Challenges to Micromobilization in Central Appalachia*. Cambridge, MA: MIT Press.

Carson, Rachel. 1962. *Silent Spring*. Greenwich, CT: Fawcett Publications, Inc.

Freudenburg, William R. 1991. "A 'Good Business Climate' as Bad Economic News?" *Society and Natural Resources* 3 (Spring): 313–331.

Gould, Kenneth A., David N. Pellow, and Allan Schnaiberg. 2008. *The Treadmill of Production: Injustice and Unsustainability in the Global Economy*. Boulder, CO: Paradigm Publishers.

Pellow, David N., and Lisa Sun-Hee Park. 2002. *The Silicon Valley of Dreams: Environmental Injustice, Immigrant Workers, and the High-Tech Global Economy*. New York: New York University Press.

Pollan, Michael. 2006. *The Omnivore's Dilemma: A Natural History of Four Meals*. New York: Penguin.

Smith, Ted, David A. Sonnenfeld, and David N. Pellow, eds. 2006. *Challenging the Chip: Labor Rights and Environmental Justice in the Global Electronics Industry*. Philadelphia, PA: Temple University Press.

5

Corporate Power
The Role of the Global Media in Shaping What We Know about the Environment

Elizabeth H. Campbell

Secretary of State and former ExxonMobil CEO, Rex Tillerson, called out at 2017 People's Climate March, Washington, DC.

Post your photo on corporate power and the environment to #TLEScorporatepower

Photo by Ken Gould

In pursuit of privileging corporate actors in the global market, **transnational corporation** (TNC) elites have been increasingly successful in lobbying international organizations, such as the World Trade Organization (WTO), for increased freedoms on the movement of capital, technology, and goods and services. The WTO, established in 1995, is the main governing organization of the multilateral trading system, staffed by unelected bureaucrats whose proceedings are held in secret, thereby denying public participation. TNCs, with the consent of global organizations and through binding regional and global trade agreements, undermine the efforts of individual governments to regulate TNCs within their borders. Take, for example, Chapter 11 of the 1994 North American Free Trade Agreement (NAFTA), negotiated to promote the free flow of goods and services among the United States, Canada, and Mexico. This provision was supposedly written to protect investors if foreign governments tried to seize their property, but corporations have stretched NAFTA's Chapter 11 to undermine environmental decisions and the decisions of local communities. In California, a billion-dollar case was filed against the United States because of a 1999 effort by the state government to protect the health of its citizens through the enactment of an environmental protection law that banned the chemical methyl tertiary-butyl ether (MTBE). This gasoline additive, found to cause cancer in laboratory animals, infiltrated 30 public water systems and another 10,000 groundwater sites. University of California scientists were commissioned to assess the problem, and their study warned that the state was placing its water resources at risk. California's governor ordered that MTBE be phased out of all gasoline sold in the state.

In response, Methanex, a Canadian company that is the world's largest producer of the key ingredient in MTBE, claimed under Chapter 11 of NAFTA that its market share, and therefore its *future* profits, were being expropriated by the governor's action. The company argued that it must be allowed to sell the product in California or be paid $970 million in compensation. While this claim did not prevail, some cases have, including one by the US company Ethyl that made MMT, a gasoline additive. Canada banned imports of MMT because of air pollution concerns. Ethyl launched a NAFTA Chapter 11 claim against Canada, forcing Canada to lift the ban, to pay Ethyl $13 million, and to formally apologize for damaging the company's reputation.

Since NAFTA's inception, Canada has been sued 41 times, more than either the United States or Mexico, and spent more than $95 million in legal costs defending itself—mainly against American companies—and has paid out over $219 million in damages and settlements. Canadian environmental protection laws are sometimes more stringent than those in the United States, making them a target of US corporations. When Canada lost or settled one of the disputes, the costs to pay out damages and finance legal fees came out of Canadian taxpayers' pockets. The only NAFTA country that has largely escaped the sting of Chapter 11 is the United States, as it has won all of its Chapter 11 challenges. While not yet binding law, the 2018 negotiated United States-Mexico-Canada (USMCA) Agreement, NAFTA's successor, provides some updates and changes to Chapter 11 that make it more difficult for TNC's to successfully sue governments.

For almost 25 years, however, NAFTA's Chapter 11 has provided profoundly special rights and privileges to transnational corporate actors to which no other actor is entitled. It does not protect ordinary people who may become ill from contaminated water or air pollution (see Lesson 11) or taxpayers who will pay the bill if the secret tribunal decides in favor of such companies, making it impossible for elected officials to advance environmental protections at the request of their voters for fear of facing these large financial risks. NAFTA sets no caps on the amount of damages that can be awarded a corporation. This is an example of a foreign corporation invoking regional trade agreements that trump federal and state laws aimed at protecting the health and environment of its people.

Motivated largely by profit, TNCs increasingly operate with little public accountability. How did this happen? Why did the American public agree to a shift in power from local people and states to unaccountable, unelected international institutions and TNCs? How did the public endorse job insecurity and outsourcing (see Lesson 17), lower wages, downsizing of the welfare state, decline in social services, and a rollback of environmental protection standards? Like all industries, the media industry is now both global in scope and largely owned by a handful of TNCs. This lesson examines the rise and influence of corporate power in the global media industry, including social media, and its impact in shaping what we know or don't know about social and environmental issues.

THE NEED FOR DIVERSITY OF VIEWS IN A DEMOCRACY

The largest media giants have achieved unprecedented success in writing the media laws and regulations in favor of their own corporations and against the interests of the public. Their concentrated power permits them to become one of the largest factors in socializing each generation about politics, the environment, and personal values. Today's media **conglomerates** have almost total power to set the agenda for what will and will not be discussed in mainstream newspapers and magazines and on TV and radio. As a result, environmental issues are often debated in such ways to ensure that corporations are never pointed out as a cause or source of environmental degradation. Social media plays a critical role in restricting its members to similar viewpoints and therefore establishing clusters of users who think and communicate similarly, significantly reducing diversity of opinions.

Debate on global warming is a classic example (see Lesson 15). For well over two decades, the debate about global warming, driven by corporate interests and crafted by powerful think tanks and public relations (PR) firms, has largely centered on whether or not it is a problem. People generally do not favor action on issues when arguments appear to be "balanced" on both sides and there is clear doubt, even if only among a small minority. Corporations and the institutions representing them play a key role in providing the media with "credible experts" who are normally not climate scientists but who nonetheless confidently dispute scientific claims of global warming. By disproportionately saturating the global media with these so-called experts, they offer enough manufactured doubt to ensure that governments take no initiative to act. The organization DeSmog offers an extensive database of individual climate deniers involved in the global warning denial industry. The group thoroughly investigates the academic and industry backgrounds of those involved in the PR spin campaigns that are stalling action and confusing the public. During the 2016 general election, not a single debate moderator from the corporate media asked a question about climate change or disruption, despite it being the greatest existential threat of our time. How is it possible that an issue that threatens the economy, national security and health, and one that exacerbates poverty and racism, was never raised? Powerful **think tanks** that have enormous influence in shaping the debate in Washington, DC, and across the globe—such as the CATO Institute, the Heritage Foundation, the Heartland Institute, and the Competitive Enterprise Institute—use scare tactics by asserting that cuts in energy consumption would hurt the world's workers, the struggling poor, and the elderly. Further, they argue that renewable energy sources like solar and wind are not only expensive but also environmentally damaging. These think tanks use emotive arguments and fear tactics to bash environmentalists and environmental issues rather than engaging with them on a more reasoned, substantive basis. For example, Stephen Moore, fellow for Project for Economic Growth at the Heritage Foundation, said on CNN in 2018 that the reason there is "manufactured hysteria" about the warming planet is due to the number of climate scientists who are getting really rich off the "climate-change industrial complex," citing the total amount of US federal funding for climate change research and implying climate change science is a hoax. Moreover, such think tanks promote the views of a few scientists who disagree with the vast majority of climate scientists that warming is a consequence of the increasing levels of greenhouse gases in the atmosphere, much of which stems from the burning of nonrenewable energy resources like coal, gas, and oil. Widespread public concern over this issue is not translating into government action, in part because the issue cannot be seriously debated and better understood in the mainstream media. The corporate media works hard to avoid larger questions of power and institutional reform by instead focusing on controversial scientific reports.

By reducing complex issues like climate change to simplistic special-interest-driven sound bites about whether or not it really exists, citizens consuming the media become incapable of understanding and acting on real debate and questioning and instead prefer easy answers, quick fixes, and easy-to-grasp phrases. Audiences thus grow apathetic, cynical, and quiescent about media presentations of environmental issues, which has resulted in an increasingly widespread lack of interest in engaging in them. Further, the issue has become so politically divisive that elected government officials are not able to effectively address the increasing frequency of storms and floods for affected communities. In the Spring of 2019, record-high flooding across Iowa, Illinois, Minnesota, Nebraska, South Dakota, and Wisconsin pummeled the Midwest and threatened to burst the levies in Louisiana. Mayor Frank Klipsch of Davenport, Iowa, a place devastated by floods, said that raising human-caused climate change was divisive and would politicize a conversation about preventing floods in the future. Instead, he said, "We know there's something going on, so how do we come together and deal with that?" Not being able to name the problem makes it incredibly difficult to find solutions.

At the same time, since 2011, George Mason and Yale universities have conducted a series of surveys about climate. Over that time, the share of

Americans who say they are concerned about climate change has risen. The number one reason that respondents cited was they were "directly experiencing climate change impacts," such as floods, hurricanes, and "super-storms." These include storms like Hurricane Sandy in 2012, which inflicted $70 billion in damage and was the second-costliest hurricane on record in the United States until surpassed by Hurricanes Harvey, Maria, and Irma in 2017. Democracy demands an informed, active, and involved citizenry in order to ensure that the majority of voices and interests are well represented. A well-informed citizenry that is exposed to all angles and interests in a substantive issue is more motivated and better equipped to engage in the political decision-making process. The consolidation of media by a few corporations who are not willing or able to have scientifically informed discussions about climate change and its dramatic impacts make it extremely difficult for those most impacted to have the tools necessary to make changes that could be life-saving.

THE RISE OF TRANSNATIONAL CORPORATIONS

Historically, the corporation was a public institution created by the government to serve public interests. Early American corporations could only be created through special charters granted by state legislatures. These charters limited what corporations could do, for how long, and how much they could accumulate. In legal theory, corporations were classified as concessions or grants of the government. They were political creations over which the state exerted great regulation and control. In the United States, corporations were required by law to serve the public interest. If corporate actions were found to violate the public interest, states reserved the right to revoke their charter and dissolve the corporation. The initial creation of private finance was to aid in the expansion of state colonial and imperial interest as well as to help in war efforts between empires. As corporations increased their wealth and therefore their political power, laws that initially tried to manage them were relaxed.

By the mid-19th century, corporations became increasingly privatized in both law and ideology. That is, they were beholden no longer to public officials but rather to private citizens who invested in them. As a result, their power and influence in the public greatly expanded. Many legal and cultural justifications for public accountability were stripped away. Corporations were reinvented as natural manifestations of free exchange among individuals, separate from the state. The public charter system basically collapsed, and the right of state legislatures to regulate corporations was eliminated.

Relying on the Fourteenth Amendment, added to the Constitution in 1868 to protect the rights of freed slaves following the Civil War, the US Supreme Court ruled in the 1886 *Santa Clara County v. Southern Pacific Railroad* decision that a private corporation is a "natural person" under the US Constitution.

That decision granted corporations the same rights and protection extended to persons by the Bill of Rights, including the right to free speech. Corporations were thus given the same "rights" to influence the government in their own interests as were extended to individual citizens, paving the way for corporations to use their wealth to dominate public thought and discourse. Corporations, as "persons," were thus free to lobby legislatures, use the mass media, and construct a public image that they believed would best serve their interests.

Prior to the 1886 Supreme Court ruling, only humans were "endowed by their creator with certain inalienable rights." Today, corporations can claim rights instead of just privileges. In terms of politics, it was once a felony for corporations to give money to politicians and political parties. By claiming the human right of free speech, corporations expanded that to mean the unlimited right to put corporate money into politics. This corporate right was reaffirmed and expanded by the Supreme Court in 2010 in its ruling in the *Citizens United v. Federal Election Commission* case. Today, corporations largely control the two main US political parties and individual politicians. In terms of business, state and local communities once had stronger laws that protected and encouraged local entrepreneurs and local businesses. Today, by invoking "discrimination" under the Fourteenth Amendment, many of these laws have been abolished. Local and regional economies are less able to protect themselves from predatory TNCs that have no long-term investment in the local communities. The Fourteenth Amendment has also been invoked by corporations to defend their right to privacy. In doing so, TNCs have been successful in ensuring that federal regulatory agencies do not investigate them for crimes and do not gain access to environmental information crucial to protecting public health. Finally, as natural persons, corporations successfully lobbied states to change corporate charter laws to eliminate "public good" provisions from charters, to allow for multiple purposes, and to exist forever.

DEFINING CHARACTERISTICS OF CORPORATIONS

From this "right" of the corporation, corporate interests have been increasingly equated with the human interest: Consumption is happiness. Through advertising, marketing, and control of information, corporations are able to create desires, invent needs, and foster traditions that encourage unquestioned consumption. Product advertisement is a multibillion-dollar industry. Corporations today spend over half as much per capita on advertising than the world spends on education. Those who control the mass media control the core culture.

Unlike that of other entities, corporate influence is better situated to penetrate all aspects of social, cultural, and political life through a wide variety of means. In addition to their power to influence the public through advertising and through the control and influence of the mainstream media, corporations have exceptional influence on public policy. This can range from financing large parts of elections to creating corporate-funded think tanks and "grass-roots" front groups to represent industry interests in the name of concerned citizens. PR firms, for-profit companies that develop and manage messaging through the media for clients with the intention of changing the public's views or actions by influencing their opinions, have become adept at creating the impression of grassroots support for corporate causes so as to convince politicians to oppose environmental reforms. The names of the corporate front groups are carefully chosen to mask the real interests behind them. For example, the chemical and pesticide industry has promoted a large number of front groups to promote its interests. These include the Alliance for Food and Farming, which is actually made up of farm and pesticide groups that have a history of promoting "conventionally grown" pesticide-laden crops and fighting government regulators. The Koch brothers, well known for supporting a variety of conservative politicians and issues, between 1997 and 2017 funneled more than $127 million to 92 organizations that attack climate change science while presenting themselves as experts (see Lesson 15). In the four weeks leading up to the 2018 midterm elections, the five major oil companies spent $2 million on targeted ads on Facebook and Instagram aimed at eroding support for environmental initiatives.

Today, there is a common set of shared beliefs, values, and assumptions of how corporations operate. Corporations are largely understood to be private, sovereign enterprises. There is a fundamental belief in the separation between the public and the private. Sustained economic growth is viewed as the sole path toward human progress. In order to maximize this growth, the preferred environment is the "free" market economy. The assumption is that privatization—or a corporate-controlled economy—removes inefficiencies in the public sector, allowing more goods to be brought to more people faster.

The largest TNCs penetrate every single country. They exceed most governments in size and power and define the policy agendas of states and international bodies. All TNCs are motivated by profit above and beyond any other interest, such as environmental integrity or social equity. TNCs are extremely mobile. They are able to transcend state boundaries with little difficulty. Detached from people and place, TNC owners are easily able to hire and fire employees at will. Employees of TNCs are therefore expendable, a trend that contributes to rising job insecurity (see Lesson 17). There is no longer a commitment to the local community since TNCs belong to the global marketplace. This is dangerous, as it is the local community that is best situated to detect and respond appropriately to environmental issues. Absentee ownership is a key defining feature of today's TNCs. Most are monopolistic and discourage competition. Fewer than 10 percent of the world's companies account for more than 80 percent of all profits. Ten years ago, banks and energy companies dominated the top ten. Today it is technology companies, with Apple holding the number one spot. More than 30 financial institutions have consolidated assets greater than $50 billion each—meaning each has more assets than two-thirds of the world's countries produce in annual GDP. There are fewer than five countries in the world whose GDP is larger than the more than $200 billion of liquid cash Apple holds in securities worldwide. Importantly, many of the world's largest and most powerful private companies are "stateless superpowers," from Microsoft to Facebook. With unmatched political and economic resources, the main goal for corporations today continues to be their struggle to wholly liberate themselves from the burden of public social and environmental accountability—yet, at the same time, lobby Congress for greater subsidies to pursue their interests (see Lessons 12 and 13).

CORPORATE WELFARE

Each year, the US Congress pays out tens of billions of dollars to American corporations in the form of direct subsidies and tax breaks (see Lesson 3). Corporate welfare costs more than four times as much as welfare to the poor. TNCs thus collect more government handouts than all of the nation's poor people combined. One of the largest recipients of corporate welfare are weapons contractors like General Electric (GE)—also a global media conglomerate that owned and operated NBC Universal until March 2013. One way contractors get subsidies is by mandating that military aid given to foreign countries be used to buy American weapons. Each year this program results in the transfer of tens of billions of US taxpayer dollars to US weapons merchants. The most successful US industries would not be competitive internationally if the federal government had not developed their basic technology with taxpayers' money through programs like the Advanced Technology Program and then given it away to private corporations (see Lesson 7).

In addition to providing jet engines for military aircraft, GE makes nuclear reactor missile propulsion systems and delivery vehicles for nuclear weapons. It has designed more than 90 nuclear power plants in over 10 countries. Between 1946 and 1965, GE made plutonium for the US military at Hanford Nuclear Reservation, a massive 570-square-mile facility in Washington. One of the worst incidents during GE's tenure at Hanford was a calculated experiment in which radioactive particles containing more than 500 times the radiation of the Three Mile Island accident, when nuclear reactors suffered a partial meltdown, were deliberately released into the air. The toxic and radioactive legacy left behind at Hanford is staggering. Thousands of citizens living downwind continue to suffer from cancer and other chronic illnesses. Today, GE continues to sell nuclear technology abroad, with no acknowledgment of the complex and persistent environmental damage caused by radioactive material. In addition to penetrating the global ecosystem and food chain, nuclear waste is a global problem with no sustainable solutions.

In 2018, GE spent more than $5 million on 12 lobbying firms to help press the US Congress to craft legislation that would benefit its company and garner contracts. GE's top issues included defense, taxes, trade, and finance, including support for the recently passed tax cut bill. In the 2018 election cycle, it shelled out over $3million in campaign contributions. This work paid off, as it continues to be among the top contractors of the US federal government, raking in several billions of dollars annually. GE has also garnered billions in subsidies over the years from federal, state, and local governments.GE garnered direct subsidies from the government despite multiple proven instances of fraud, waste, and abuse in handling government contracts. Some of this negligence includes violations of polychlorinated biphenyl (PCB) regulations, violations of California's pesticide registration requirements, emission violations, violations of Florida's and New York's hazardous waste laws, and violation of the Clean Air and Clean Water Acts. Indeed, GE is no friend of the environment. GE has lobbied hard to overturn the US Superfund Law of 1980, which allows the government to hold polluters responsible for cleaning up their toxic chemicals. GE argued instead that it was unconstitutional for the EPA to force the company to pay for the cleanup of the Hudson River in New York, where GE dumped carcinogenic PCBs for over three decades. Given GE's history and its historic control over the global media, it should be no surprise that complex environmental issues were not presented or thoroughly debated on NBC or its countless subsidiaries.

The powers to educate, jail, rehabilitate, care for the poor, and manage nature itself are all being entrusted to corporations, which have no accountability to the public. As these public functions are sold off to private corporations, the government itself is transformed, if not dismantled, into an institution of private enterprise, where ordinary citizens have no voice. TNCs are considered individual citizens under the law and are dependent on public money for their own growth and expansion, but they are not accountable to the public. As more public lands and institutions are privatized by TNCs, as TNC profit margins trump all other interests, and as the public is increasingly squeezed out of the decision-making arena, there has been comparatively little media attention directed at this seismic social change. The following sections thus examine more closely the role of the corporation in the global media and how it shapes our knowledge and decisions on a wide variety of issues.

THE HISTORY OF CORPORATE GLOBAL MEDIA

We are increasingly inundated with information, but what do we know? How do we know it? And what don't we know? We quickly tire of sound bites, sensationalized stories, and buzz words—but often before we even begin to understand the complexity behind the attention-grabbing headlines. Like all industries, the media are also becoming increasingly global in the age of the connected international corporate system. It currently serves two main functions. First, the global media plays a central economic role for non-media firms by facilitating their business interests. This is done by providing advertising outlets to facilitate corporate expansion into new markets, new countries, and new regions. Second, the global media's news and entertainment provide an informational and ideological environment that helps to sustain the political, economic, and moral basis for marketing goods and for having a dominant free-market agenda. The media are central to convincing us that American-style democracy and the free-market economy are the only paths toward "freedom."

The role of the media in our society can only be understood in a political and economic context. That is, who owns and controls the media, and for what purposes, has always been a political issue. Until the 20th century, media were largely local and national. Today, in the same way that corporations have become increasingly global in nature, so too have the media. The owners and producers of media no longer have only their national interests in mind but rather the interests of making profits on a global scale. As the global capitalist system continued to develop, communication was central to expanding commercial interests.

The first form of global media was wire-based international news agencies such as Reuters and eventually the Associated Press. These entities produced news and then sold it to local and national newspaper publishers. By the 1850s, there were about four main commercial news agencies that had established a cartel, dividing the entire world market for news production and distribution. These were European—Germans, French, British, and eventually Americans. Since the very beginning of global media, dating back to at least the mid-19th century, global news services have been oriented to the needs and interests of the wealthy nations that provide their revenue. These news agencies sold news content to their own nations as well as colonized nations, which could not support their own global news services.

The emergence and ascension of the TNC laid the groundwork for the rise of the global media. The film industry and then radio broadcasting were two of the first forms of global media. By 1914, 85 percent of the world film audience was watching American films. The experience with these media elevated the importance of control of media and telecommunications systems in general as a powerful political tool. By the end of World War II, through the use of global media, the United States was able to assert its global dominance as a hegemonic power or world leader.

Along with its policies of opening markets throughout the world for trade, the United States also advocated for the "free flow of information." In theory, the idea that news, information, ideas, and opinions have unrestricted movement across political boundaries is largely positive. In practice, however, the "free flow of information" has instead meant that US-based TNCs are able to operate globally, across borders, with minimal oversight, fewer checks and balances, and fewer contending voices. As we have seen in recent years, this lack of accountability is also a defining characteristic of social media. Federal regulators are determining whether to hold Mark Zuckerberg, the cofounder and CEO of Facebook, accountable for privacy lapses in how Facebook handles the data of its more than two billion users. While the American-dominated global media wanted free access to news and information markets, they were not necessarily interested in freedom of information and diversity of opinions and perspectives, critical aspects of a flourishing and sustainable democracy. The post-World War II era was thus characterized by a shift away from public-owned national and local media toward commercially owned global media. While public media are funded largely by public tax dollars, private media are funded by corporate advertisers selling increased consumption.

With the spread of English global news media came increased commercial marketing—that is, more commercials and advertising—and the consolidation of formerly distinct media industries such as film, music, publishing, and broadcasting. By the 1970s, the beginning of economic "free"-market rule on a global scale, the trajectory and nature of the global media system were clear: it was largely a profit-driven system dominated by TNCs based in highly industrialized capitalist nations, especially the United States. State deregulation of private industries, a decline in the social welfare state, and privatization of state-run companies and services—the defining characteristics of economic globalization—greatly facilitated the expansion of TNCs and hence the increasing growth and consolidation of global media.

Between 1941 and 1975, several laws that restricted channel ownership within radio and television were enacted in order to maintain unbiased and diverse media. Under the Reagan administration, Congress and the Federal Communications Commission began a concerted deregulation between 1981 and 1985. The number of television stations a single entity can own increased from seven to 12 stations. The industry continued to deregulate with enactment of the Telecommunications Act of 1996. Signed by President Bill Clinton on February 8, 1996, it was considered by the FCC to be the first major overhaul of telecommunications law in almost 62 years. In the radio industry, the 40-station ownership cap was lifted, leading to an unprecedented amount of consolidation. Further, large social media networks benefitted from this US law stating that internet content providers are not responsible for posts by their users, paving the way for foreign entities like Russia and its state-affiliated groups to use Facebook's advertising and events features to promote divisive material aimed at skewing the vote in swing states. Think tanks and congressional representatives alike argued that the cost of federal regulations to the economy totaled billions of dollars annually. These unsubstantiated concerns were manifested in several pieces of legislation that sought to override the mandates of the Clean Air Act, the Clean Water Act, the Safe Drinking Water Act, and the Endangered Species Act, among others.

Contrary to the fact that TNC interests are outwardly against governmental regulation, the TNC-dominated system of economic globalization has been a political choice that has nonetheless been aided by governments. After all, it is states that are signatories to various international trade agreements that facilitate the growth and expansion of TNC interests. Today, the system of free-market liberalism rests on the widespread acceptance of a global corporate ideology. This ideology has played an important role in rationalizing and sanctifying unequal relations of power. It helps explain why the Enron scandal—perhaps the largest corporate scandal in history—quickly disappeared, while Hollywood drama continues to receive ongoing prime-time coverage. It also helps to explain why the media has focused primarily on the drama of National Security Agency whistleblower Edward Snowden's asylum-seeking adventure and not on the complicity of communications TNCs like AT&T, Google, Microsoft, and Apple in giving the spy agency information about you without your knowledge and consent. The ideology that the free-market economy is actually free and that what is good for corporations is good for the people—acting through the global media—is today a powerful form of social control.

Today, social media like Facebook, Twitter, and Google do more than just host posts and advertisements. Their algorithms prioritize certain posts over others and target certain demographic groups while ignoring the rest. With an estimated quarter of the world's population active monthly on Facebook, accountability is more important than ever. As a monopoly, whose customers are advertisers, not users, social media giants have long grown under the veneer of objectivity and the assumption that what is prioritized reflects only the interests and actions of the users. For too long these corporations have easily evaded the accountability conversation as a "nontraditional" media source.

As a result of this growing evidence, in October 2019, Twitter CEO, Jack Dorsey, announced that Twitter would no longer take political ads, a stark contrast to how Facebook handles political advertising. Dorsey said that political ads, including manipulated videos and the viral spread of misleading information, presented challenges to civic discourse "all at increasing velocity, sophistication, and overwhelming scale." The CEO went on to say that he believed that such ads had "significant ramifications that today's democratic infrastructure may not be prepared to handle." Dorsey now believes that the reach of political messages "should be earned, not bought." Mark Zuckerberg, CEO of Facebook, continues to argue that Facebook serves as a platform of free expression and views political ads as newsworthy. Twitter ads make up a small fraction of what presidential candidates for 2020 have spent on digital advertising overall, as most of the money goes toward Facebook and Google ads. As disinformation continues to spread, Facebook and other platforms will continue to face pressure to revise their policies and practices.

CORE ELEMENTS OF THE GLOBAL MEDIA CORPORATE IDEOLOGY

There are two core elements of the new global media corporate ideology, including social media. The first element is the idea that markets allocate resources efficiently and should provide the means of organizing economic and perhaps all human life. It is dominated by a strong belief in privatization—reducing public control and increasing corporate control, thereby increasing profit margins. The second element is that freedom is often equated with the absence of any state business regulations. Political freedom is something different, and it is often subservient to economic freedom. In other words, the idea is that economic freedom leads to and guarantees political freedom. Media are, however, not free at all. Instead, it tends to regard corporate domination as natural and benevolent. The media preach both overtly and covertly the virtues of commercialism and the market. Today's global media have no social, moral, or political obligations beyond the pursuit of profit. This has been particularly striking in the ability of Russia to use social media to influence global democratic elections—from France, to the United Kingdom, to the European Union—with no accountability.

Concentrated wealth and power, on the one hand, and dire poverty, hunger, famine, and landlessness, on the other, cannot exist outside of systemic propaganda in modern democracies. There are several essential ingredients or news filters that constitute the propaganda model. These elements interact with and reinforce one another. The raw material of news must pass through these filters in order to be printed or aired. The elite domination of the media and the marginalization of competing voices that results from the operation of these filters occur so naturally that media employees believe they are interpreting the news "objectively." President Donald Trump's withdrawal of the United States from the Paris Climate Change Accord was well covered in the global media as "unconscionable" and "shameful," but those same global media elites have not engaged Trump on his climate agenda in any meaningful way. These media lament, in almost apocalyptic terms, Trump's withdraw from the Paris Accords, but when given the opportunity to press Trump on his climate change policies—or even broach the subject at all—they chose not to do so.

The media coverage of the 2019 Green New Deal resolution framework largely returned to opposing environmental concerns with the livelihoods of working-class people, a tried and true method for dividing people between the presumed choice of having clean air or a job. Commentators strongly pushed back on the idea that environmental sustainability and good jobs could be part of the same effort, that the two issues could be tied together, and that energy and jobs should be looked at comprehensively. For example, USA Today ran a piece from the Cato Institute warning that the Deal was a green-painted Trojan horse filled with the biggest single government expansion the United States has seen since the 1930s, scaring people into believing it would overwhelm taxpayers and create socialism.

The core challenge the Green New Deal faces is not so much on the merits of the concept or even its political feasibility, it is that many of its Democratic supporters have met an aggressive and one-sided onslaught from the right with very little by way of response. According to data from Navigator, a progressive polling project, 37 percent of Republican viewers of Fox News had heard a lot about the Green New Deal compared with 14 percent of all registered voters. Only 6 percent of non-Republican, non-Fox viewers had heard a lot about it; and 40 percent had heard nothing at all. In total, 74 percent of Fox-viewing Republicans oppose the deal. What this data reveals is that the corporate media failed to effectively address the substantive elements of the Deal, allowing right-wing propaganda to easily fill the void.

SIZE, OWNERSHIP, AND PROFIT ORIENTATION

In the United States, more than 90 percent of the news, commentary, and daily entertainment are controlled by only five firms that are among the world's largest corporations: Comcast/NBC Universal, the Walt Disney Company, AT&T/WarnerMedia, and CBS Corporation and Viacom (both are controlled by National Amusements). In comparison, in the mid-1980s, 90 percent of the US media was controlled by some 50 corporate owners. In addition Facebook, Google, Twitter, LinkedIn, and Yahoo are the biggest players in social media, with billions of global users and a combined market value of hundreds of billions of dollars. Like the other "traditional" media, social media is a business, and its primary goal is the accumulation of wealth.

The above five corporations own newspapers, magazines, book publishing houses, movie and TV production studios, Internet services, and record labels. They also own the national delivery systems for the programming they control or lease, such as broadcast networks and cable. Moreover, they increasingly own the delivery mechanisms into each American home or office as well, such as telephone company lines, cable systems, and satellite dishes.

The process of increased ownership over all aspects of media production and distribution is called vertical integration (see Lesson 13). Vertical integration is a defining characteristic of TNCs and is defined as the control over a total process—from the raw material (news) to fabrication (fashioning it into a newspaper or broadcast network) to sales. Vertical integration allows for price control and monopoly. If there are only five corporations controlling the bulk of the information, and these corporations are largely interested in selling their specific agenda and self-interest (free-market ideology), it means that, despite more information, there is less and less diversity in its content; hence, it becomes less democratic, negatively impacting society at large in a wide range of ways.

Like all media, the radio industry continues to follow the trends toward greater consolidation. The nationwide leader, Clear Channel Communications, owns about 1,200 of the 11,000 radio stations in the country. In the case of Minot, North Dakota, the concerns regarding media consolidation were realized on January 18, 2002, when a train containing hazardous chemicals derailed in the middle of the night, exposing countless Minot residents to toxic waste—suffocating anhydrous ammonia fertilizer. Upon trying to get out an emergency broadcast, the Minot police were unable to reach anyone by phone at the local radio stations, all six of which are owned by Clear Channel. Since Clear Channel seeks to ensure that each of its stations use the same programing largely produced outside of the locales where it is played, it relies on satellite feeds and no longer requires human presence at its stations throughout the day and evening.

These five media corporations constitute a private ministry of information and culture. Through their ascendance to power, they have successfully implemented a system of tiers. At the top are leading news sources such as the *New York Times* and CNN, from which the local papers and broadcast networks, situated at the bottom, get their national and international news; therefore, there is a single perspective being portrayed from the global to the national to the local level. While it is expressed in different media and by different actors, the message stems from the same source. The directors of these companies are usually businesspeople interested less in the quality of the product and more in the size of the profit margin. If, for example, information about the personal lives of Hollywood film stars attracts a large audience base, this will be the sole determining factor in shifting media resources to cover this information. Profit-driven media are further entrenched by the fact that it is banks and other institutional investors who are large owners of media stock. Again, profit margin is the single most defining factor in what constitutes news, not moral, political, or social obligations to keep the public informed of key issues relating to their health and well-being.

Since these companies are extremely diverse and own everything from radio to newspapers and from theme parks to online entertainment services, the corporate media owners have big stakes in policy decisions. In other words, it is less likely for these corporate owners to encourage their reporters to investigate environmental problems linked to corporations. Take, for example, the story that "the cloud," that magical place where we are now encouraged to store our digital music, photos, documents, and other data, is in reality a growing source of greenhouse gas emissions (see Lesson 1). Perhaps you have not been made aware of this issue by the corporations that own the data centers generating the emissions, as well as the news media you rely on for information. "The cloud" relies on an expanding series of enormous data centers that are in continuous operation and require a tremendous amount of electricity. Some of them draw as much power as 180,000 households and can be seen from space. The electricity that powers the data centers is most commonly generated from the burning of fossil fuels (see Lesson 9). Since the data centers cannot be allowed to fail in a power outage, they are often backed up by large diesel-fueled generators. What appears to you as a clean, efficient, and reliable **postindustrial**, dematerialized, data storage and retrieval system is actually a coal-powered collection of very material storage facilities warehoused in a variety of locations here on Earth. Storing data in "the cloud" increases greenhouse gas emissions and accelerates global climate change, but that story has not been widely told in the corporate media.

THE ROLE OF SOCIAL MEDIA IN SPREADING "FAKE NEWS" ABOUT THE ENVIRONMENT

Social media permit misinformation to be spread at a scale and scope unknown in history. With more than 200,000 scientific studies containing the word "climate" published every year, there has never been as much information on the topic as there is today; but with this wealth of information comes disinformation. Misinformation, conspiracy theories, and rumors abound on the social media, helping to support climate doubt and other forms of environmental and scientific skepticism. According to Climate Feedback, a site where scientists rate the accuracy of articles from mainstream media, approximately one big fake news story is shared millions of times in the English-speaking press each month. Most fake news, however, comes from climate sceptics who spread false claims on social media. For example, YouTube's recommended algorithm recently began promoting a video about climate change on dozens of popular YouTube channels. The video has been promoted almost two million times, with 250,000 views. The video is a July 2017 talk by author Steve Goreham purporting to prove that climate change has nothing to do with humans. The video was posted by "Friends of Science," a Canadian advocacy group that negates the conclusions of science on climate change.

During the last three months of the 2016 presidential campaign, the 20 top fake news stories on Facebook generated more engagement—shares, likes, and comments—than the 20 top stories from "real" news websites. These hoaxes are shared among all kinds of people, not only like-minded conspiracy theorists. A December 2016 survey by the Pew Research Center suggests that 23 percent of US adults have shared fake news, knowingly or unknowingly, with friends and others. Misinformation can be very difficult to correct and often has lasting effects, even after it is discredited. Social media helps to further the barrage of misinformation about climate change and its growing consequences, making it more difficult to implement solutions. Further, studies show that the ideological segregation reinforced by social media make it more difficult than ever to be exposed to alternative views. Instead, social media platforms excel at creating "echo chambers" where individuals and groups reinforce their existing thinking.

THE ROLE OF ADVERTISING

The media, including social media, are required to conform to advertisers' wishes. Facebook acknowledged recently that it had allowed businesses to target or exclude users for ads for housing, employment, and credit based on their ethnicity, in apparent violation of anti-discrimination laws. Political discrimination is therefore structured into advertising allocations. Only those with money can buy space. Those with the most money are TNCs, which also share the same ideology and agenda of the promotion of free-market capitalism. Advertisers choose selectively among programs on the basis of their own principles. Large corporate advertisers on television will rarely sponsor programs that engage in serious criticism of corporate activities. Other institutional voices, perspectives, and ideas are systemically denied opportunities to access the global media, as they do not bring to bear the same resources needed to purchase space to sell their ideas. Such examples include local organic farming cooperatives, environmental sustainability projects, alternative energy sources, endangered species issues, environmental justice issues, conservation issues, and anti-fracking initiatives.

In addition, the global media's attempt to attract larger audiences (in order to secure more profits) means that there is increased competition for advertising. Advertisers are also primarily interested in profit margins and thus wish to advertise their products in places where they can reach the largest audiences. Increasingly, this is on social media sites. In 2018, corporations spent 33 percent of advertising costs on digital platforms, up from 25 percent in 2014.

Social media has further accelerated the phenomenon best described as "infotainment" and "advertorials." These terms depict how "news" has become mostly entertainment information and how editorial commentary is largely driven by the special interests of advertising companies. Morning and evening news programs today largely consist of analyses of the previous evening's television shows, particularly the so-called reality-based TV programs. Guests largely include celebrities, design and fashion experts, pop culture specialists, and musicians. This has led to the deterioration of the quality of news, which has now been reorganized largely to serve corporate ambitions and no longer includes the independent, diverse public information on which democracy depends. Simply debating whether the news has a liberal or conservative bias is a distraction from corporate control and dominance of the global media. Moreover, online, citizens increasingly live in "filter bubbles" that expose users only to ideas with which they already agree. Algorithms increasingly determine what we see and don't see about the environment and how it shapes our lives.

GLOBAL MEDIA SOURCES

As the global media corporations continue to be concerned mostly with profit margins, there has been a dramatic reduction in the number of field reporters and overseas bureaus. Investing in sustained, in-depth, field-based investigation and reporting is expensive. Most of these positions and bureaus have been cut. Parts of American news production have been outsourced to countries like India with huge concentrations of inexpensive labor. Another cost-saving technique has been the increasing reliance on "official sources" for important political and economic information. The global media increasingly turns to information provided by the government, businesses, and other "experts" as the key source for important stories on a wide variety of issues. Institutions like the Pentagon, the US State Department, and corporate entities have the resources available to provide media organizations with information via press statements, speeches, forthcoming reports, scheduled press conferences, and photo opportunities.

These large bureaucracies of the powerful subsidize the mass media and gain special access by their contribution to reducing the media's costs of acquiring the raw materials necessary to produce the news. The large entities that provide this subsidy become "routine" and "authoritative" news sources with privileged access to the global media. Free speech is thus directly tied to one's wealth. Media power is political power, and only the wealthiest are able to fully access it. Those institutions or entities without entire departments dedicated to PR are often unable to access the global media to express their concerns or offer their own reports on key issues. This has contributed to a narrowness of the news, a lack of rich debate, and a general decline in the diversity of perspectives portrayed in the news. If most reporters turn to the same sources for authoritative positions on issues, there is little room for widespread debate; hence, it is easy to conclude that the news is objective. Moreover, as journalists increasingly rely on corporate and governmental entities as the sole source of their information, they often become more reluctant to challenge these sources so as not to damage their established relationships and ongoing access to these sources.

VIOLATING THE CORPORATE AGENDA

Since the media carries the free-market agenda, when it criticizes or diverges from the agenda, corporate-sponsored institutional monitors harass and put extreme pressure on the media to toe the line. Whenever the media does not adopt the official corporate or governmental position on an issue, these monitors will systemically attack the media for careless reporting, unfounded claims, and other violations. Global warming is a long-standing example, and a more recent one is the release of the Green New Deal. Instead of engaging this issue thoroughly to examine different options of addressing the root causes, each new scientific report or global treaty has been met by harsh, well-organized, PR-driven, corporate backlash that seeks to discredit the individual authors and the reports themselves (see Lesson 15).

These tactics reach back to the beginning of the modern environmental movement with the 1962 publication of Rachel Carson's book *Silent Spring*, which detailed the environmental destruction that DDT and other dangerous toxins caused and subsequently helped to raise awareness about environmental destruction (see Lesson 11). In response, the agrichemical industry doubled its PR budget and distributed thousands of book reviews trashing *Silent Spring*. The Monsanto chemical company published *The Desolate Year*, a parody in which failure to use pesticides causes an insect plague to devastate crops across the United States. Today, entire PR firms exist in part to help corporations distribute propaganda and lobby against environmental protection. Energy and Corporate trade associations spend $1.4 billion a year on the services of anti-environmental PR professionals who help wage their battles in the global media.

The threat of these attacks serves to condition the media to expect trouble—and cost increases—for violating the corporate agenda. In return, the media respects these power holders and rarely questions their ulterior motives. Self-censorship thus occurs without the need for an officially stated policy to deter the media from covering certain topics. When the Green New Deal was released, ABC, CBS, and NBC did not cover it on any of their broadcast shows. The *L.A. Times* and *Washington Post* relegated the news to AP's wire dispatch. Of the corporate media that covered it, the press played up the divergence between Speaker of the House Pelosi and Congresswoman Alexandria Ocasio-Cortez. Any conflict, however, was made moot by the widespread media assumption that the Green New Deal was politically dead on arrival, due to the Republican controlled Senate and the discomfort of centrist Democrats. An exception was CNN's all-day substantive coverage. Genuine political variety in the media is absent. One outlet may have a more conservative or liberal tilt, but their news sources, criteria for selection of issues, and corporate sponsors are largely the same.

GLOBAL MEDIA EVASION

While it is clear that the global media focuses largely on pursuing a free-market agenda that encourages consumption and acceptance of official positions on a wide variety of political, economic, environmental, and social issues, equally important is what the media fails to focus on. A great example is garbage, a key social and environmental issue of the 21st century. What happens to the household, corporate, chemical, restaurant, industrial, and toxic waste generated each and every day? Most of the public has absolutely no idea since it is largely ignored by the global media, yet it is a defining feature of modern industrial societies. Of course, the millions of metric tons of garbage and the long-term social and environmental impacts of landfills and incinerators are important issues currently affecting millions of people's lives—though not those of key power holders; thus, it becomes a nonissue.

Because it focuses on style and process over content, the media focuses its attention on things like a spokesperson's wardrobe, word choice, and presentation skills rather than the content of his or her argument or statement. Moreover, by offering "two sides of the story," the media fails to look at the multiple sides and angles to any story. In any given issue, there is not simply a "pro" and an "anti" position but rather a wide range of views and opinions. These voices are all shored up into either the "for" or the "against" camp. This is certainly clear with environmental issues: one must choose to be either an "environmentalist" or an "anti-environmentalist" when in fact some individuals and groups support some reforms and conservation efforts but have concerns about others.

For instance, the issue of hydraulic fracturing for natural gas extraction (fracking) is often simplified in the news media as those who are in favor or against it. A more complete examination might put the single issue into a broader framework that examines energy production and consumption and various priorities and goals of either reinforcing or changing these habits (see Lesson 9). Because the media isolates complex issues such as energy into a single issue of fracking in a specific region, the public fails to understand the relationships and connections between global energy production and consumption. In other words, "both sides of the story" are never the complete story.

In addition, complex issues like energy, while often reported on, are never explained by the media. Dependence on nonrenewable fossil fuels, corporate control over these resources, and the violence created by their withdrawal are rarely examined. News articles seek to "report" on real-time events but rarely provide a context in which the public might be better able to understand them. Extremely complex social, political, economic, and environmental processes are reduced to fragmented and unconnected factoids. This type of reporting fails to associate social and environmental problems with the socioeconomic forces that created them. Most of the public is thus left with the impression that energy consumption, corporate power, the war on terrorism, and toxic waste are completely distinct, unrelated issues. It is clear that the rise of global commercial media coincides with a decline in public-owned media and public affairs news stories. Crowd-sourced, Internet-based news sources suffer from low levels of social credibility and limited resources to support investigative journalism.

CONCLUSION: CORPORATE MEDIA POWER IN THE WIRELESS FUTURE

Today, the single most valuable piece of property worth owning are the radio frequencies of the electromagnetic spectrum over which an increasing amount of communication and commercial activity is broadcast in the era of wireless communications. Personal computers, tablets, wireless Internet, smartphones, radios, and television all rely on the radio frequencies of the spectrum to send and receive messages, pictures, audio, and other data. In an era where more and more of daily communications are in cyberspace, access to the airwaves is critical.

Those who can pay will, of course, be connected, but it is unclear about the millions of people who cannot afford access. If the flow of human communications is controlled by global media companies, and governments increasingly have little influence, to whom will citizens turn to ensure that a diversity of social, political, environmental, and economic views are expressed—especially when they may differ from those of the corporate owners? Moreover, when companies like Time Warner and Disney own the channels of communication as well as much of the content that flows through them, what mechanisms will be put in place to ensure that a diversity of voices and perspectives is nourished?

In addition, these companies control the channels of communication and have demonstrated a willingness to exploit the personal data of individuals floating through cyberspace. What safeguards will be put in place to protect citizens? When citizens' very right to communicate with one another is no longer ensured or secured by the government but is controlled by global media conglomerates, how will citizens access the important information, news, and analysis needed to make informed decisions about critical social and environmental issues? In cyberspace, you don't just watch the media TNCs; they watch you, and they report your activities to the government that could regulate them. The control of information is a critical issue in the attention given to, and the social response to, environmental problems.

SOURCES

Anderson, Sarah, Scott Klinger, and Javier Rojo. 2013. Fix the Debt: CEOs Enjoy Taxpayer-Subsidized Pay. May 2, 2013. https://ips-dc.org/ceo-tax-subsidized-pay/.

Anderson, Sarah and Sam Pizzigati. 2018. "Executive Excess 2018: How Taxpayers Subsidize Giant Corporate Pay Gaps." August 28, 2018. https://ips-dc.org/executive-excess-2018/

Bagdikian, Ben. 2004. *The New Media Monopoly*. Boston, MA: Beacon.

Beder, Sharon. 1998. *Global Spin*. White River Junction, VT: Chelsea Green.

Bernasconi-Osterwalder, Nathalie, Liesbeth Casier, Ashley Racine and Scott Vaughan. 2017, August. "Response to the United States Trade Representative's Stated Objectives on NAFTA Negotiations: an Environmental Perspective." https://www.iisd.org/library/response-united-states-trade-representative-s-stated-objectives-nafta-negotiations

Brummette, John, Marcia DiStaso, Michail Vafeiadis, and Marcus Messner. 2018, May 1. "Read All About It: The Politicization of 'Fake News' on Twitter." *Journalism & Mass Communication Quarterly*.

Carlock, Greg, Emily Mangan and Sean McElwee. 2018, September. A Green New Deal: A Progressive Vision for Environmental Sustainability and Economic Stability. https://www.dataforprogress.org/green-new-deal-report

Carson, Rachel. 1962. *Silent Spring*. Greenwich, CT: Fawcett Publications, Inc.

Cho, Joshua. 2019. "According to NYT 'Relentless Flooding' in Midwest Just Happens." June 11, 2019. https://fair.org/home/according-to-nyt-relentless-flooding-in-midwest-just-happens/

Collins, Chuck and Josh Hoxie. 2017. "Report: Billionaire Bonanza 2017: The Forbes 400 and the Rest of Us." November 8, 2017. https://ips-dc.org/report-billionaire-bonanza-2017/.

Cook, Gary. 2012. "How Clean Is Your Cloud?" April 17, 2012. https://www.greenpeace.org/international/publication/6986/how-clean-is-your-cloud/

Derber, Charles. 1998. *Corporation Nation*. New York: St. Martin's Griffin.

Gould, Kenneth A., David N. Pellow, and Allan Schnaiberg. 2008. *The Treadmill of Production: Injustice and Unsustainability in the Global Economy*. Boulder, CO: Paradigm.

Herman, Edward and Noam Chomsky. 2002. *Manufacturing Consent: The Political Economy of the Mass Media*. New York: Pantheon.

Herman, Edward and Robert McChesney. 1997. *The Global Media*. New York: Continuum.

Hocevar, John. 2017. "Climate Deniers are Failing the Victims of Harvey and Irma." September 13, 2017. https://www.greenpeace.org/usa/climate-deniers-failing-victims-harvey-irma/.

Hollar, Julie. 2019. "CNN Town Hall Went Deep on Climate Crisis—But Was Anyone Listening?" September 6, 2019. https://fair.org/home/cnn-town-hall-went-deep-on-climate-crisis-but-was-anyone-listening/.

Jackson, Janine. 2015. "Getting Media to Take Climate Threats Seriously? There's a Snowball's Chance." March 6, 2015. https://fair.org/home/getting-media-to-take-climate-threats-seriously-theres-a-snowballs-chance/.

Johnson, Adam. 2016, October 19. The Debates are Over, and No One Asked about Climate Change. Retrieved from https://fair.org/home/the-debates-are-over-and-no-one-asked-about-climate-change/.

Johnson, Adam. 2017. "In a Dozen Interviews, Media Never Bothered Asking President Trump about Climate Change." June 3, 2017. https://fair.org/home/in-a-dozen-interviews-media-never-bothered-asking-president-trump-about-climate-change/.

Korten, David. 2001. *When Corporations Rule the World*. Bloomfield, CT: Kumarian.

McChesney, Robert and Victor Pickard. 2011. *Will the Last Reporter Please Turn Out the Lights: The Collapse of Journalism and What Can Be Done to Fix It*. New York: The New Press.

McCright, Aaron M. and Riley Dunlap. 2000. "Challenging Global Warming as a Social Problem: An Analysis of the Conservative Movement's Counter-Claims." *Social Problems* 47 (4): 499–522.

McMichael, Philip. 2011. *Development and Social Change: A Global Perspective*. Thousand Oaks, CA: Sage Publications.

Moyers, Bill. 2002. "Trading Democracy." NOW, PBS, February 1, 2002.

Moore, Stephen. 2018. "Follow the (Climate Change) Money." Rasmussen Reports. December 18, 2018. https://www.rasmussenreports.com/public_content/political_commentary/commentary_by_stephen_moore/follow_the_climate_change_money

Reyes, Oscar and Orenstein, Karen. 2017. "Report: Green Climate Fund, a Performance Check." September 26, 2017. https://ips-dc.org/report-green-climate-fund-a-performance-check/.

Richardson, Reed. 2017. "With Climate Denial in the White House, Will Media Echo Official Know-Nothingism?" May 1, 2017. https://fair.org/home/with-climate-denial-in-the-white-house-will-media-echo-official-know-nothingism/

Sinclair, Scott. 2015. "NAFTA Chapter 11 Investor-State Disputes to January 1, 2015." January 14, 2015. https://www.policyalternatives.ca/publications/reports/nafta-chapter-11-investor-state-disputes-january-1-2015

Smith, Mitch and John Schwartz. 2019. "In Flood-Hit Midwest, Mayors See Climate Change as a Subject Best Avoided." May 15, 2019. https://www.nytimes.com/2019/05/15/us/midwest-flooding-climate-change.html

Spatz, Charlie. 2016. "Meet the Team of Racists and Climate Deniers Shaping Donald Trump's America." November 22, 2016. https://www.greenpeace.org/usa/meet-team-racists-climate-deniers-shaping-donald-trumps-america/.

Spencer, Miranda. 2019. "Establishment Media and the Green New Deal: New Wine in Old Bottle." May 1, 2019. https://fair.org/home/establishment-media-and-the-green-new-deal-new-wine-in-old-bottles/

Spinks, Sara. 2019. "Online Politics Needs to be Cleaned Up." November 18, 2019. https://www.oii.ox.ac.uk/blog/online-politics-needs-to-be-cleaned-up-but-not-just-by-facebook-and-twitter-say-oxford-academics/

Stauber, John and Sheldon Rampton. 1995. *Toxic Sludge Is Good for You*. Monroe, ME: Common Courage Press.

Vaughan, Scott. 2018. "USMCA Versus NAFTA on the Environment." October 3, 2018. https://www.iisd.org/library/usmca-nafta-environment

Wyatt, Vicky. 2016. "Exxon Hiding Behind Congressional Climate Deniers." June 2, 2016 https://www.greenpeace.org/usa/exxon-hiding-behind-congressional-climate-deniers/.

Zepezauer, Mark and Arthur Naiman. 1996. *Take the Rich Off Welfare*. Tucson, AZ: Odonian.

6

The Science of Nature and the Nature of Science

Richard York

In vitro orchid propagation, Santa Marianita, Ecuador.
Post your photo on science and nature to #TLESscience.
Photo by Tammy Lewis

On July 16, 1945, the detonation of the first atomic bomb—Trinity—lighted the skies near Alamogordo, New Mexico. It was the product of the Manhattan Project, which had started with a small group of researchers in 1939 but by 1945 had become the greatest scientific undertaking in history. How large the explosion would be was not known with certainty beforehand. Of course, there was the concern that it would be a dud and produce no explosion at all. However, some of the scientists on the project thought it might be big enough to incinerate the entire state of New Mexico. In fact, there was some concern that the explosion could ignite the atmosphere, thereby destroying virtually all life on Earth. In the actual event, it produced a 20-kiloton explosion, far greater than any bomb had ever produced before, but fortunately not sufficient to engulf the Earth. More than seven decades later, we still live with the dark legacy of this explosion and the many thousands—most much bigger—that followed it. Science had unlocked the secrets of the atom, and those secrets gave humanity the power to destroy itself.

Some of the greatest minds in history, the architects of this marvel of science, including the enigmatic genius J. Robert Oppenheimer who led the development of the mighty weapon, subsequently came to have some regrets about what they had unleashed on the world. In an interview two decades after the Trinity test, Oppenheimer recalled:

> We knew the world would not be the same. A few people laughed, a few people cried, most people were silent. I remembered the line from the Hindu scripture, the Bhagavad-Gita. Vishnu is trying to persuade the Prince that he should do his duty and to impress him takes on his multi-armed form and says, "Now, I am become Death, the destroyer of worlds." I suppose we all thought that, one way or another.

In their creation of the atomic bomb, the scientists of the Manhattan Project had demonstrated, more forcefully than ever had been done before, both the enlightening power of science to gain knowledge of the world and the horror that the scientific establishment can foist on humanity and nature.

If we are to understand the world in which we live and to bring about a sustainable and just society, we must grapple with both of these aspects of science: its power and its horror. From its foundation, the field of environmental sociology has taken a realist stance about environmental problems—they are indeed real, not just a socially constructed perception (see Lesson 1)—and thus has always had a commitment to learning from the natural sciences, which study the ecosystems and natural resources on which all societies depend. However, environmental sociologists have also always recognized the role that science, particularly in its contribution to technological development, has played in generating the modern environmental crisis (see Lesson 7). Thus, questions about the role of science in society have been central to the field of environmental sociology.

Most environmental sociologists would probably agree to a large extent that we must be simultaneously appreciative and thoughtfully questioning of science. If we are to understand the human interaction with the natural environment and to overcome the environmental problems we face, we must follow a fine line between two extremes: on the one hand, the rejection of science as a foundation for understanding the world and, on the other, the uncritical valorization of the scientific establishment. Here, I present an examination of the tension between these two extremes and discuss some of the ways environmental sociology has engaged the science question.

Before going any further, however, we must first answer the following question: What is "science"? There is no single widely accepted answer, which is in part due to the multifaceted meaning of the term. To help us gain some understanding of the topic, I will make a distinction between two different aspects of science. One I will call "the **logic of science**," and the other

I will call "the **establishment of science**." The basic argument I will make is that we need to understand, appreciate, and have a commitment to the former while being (constructively) critical of the latter.

By "the logic of science" I mean the philosophy of knowledge that underlies the scientific enterprise, informing its methods and theories. Science developed from the fusion of empirical and rational philosophies of knowledge, with particular emphasis on the former. Both of these philosophies can be traced to the ancient Greeks in the Western tradition (with parallels in other cultures), but their modern versions emerged in the 17th century. Francis Bacon (1561–1626) is often identified as a key figure who initiated the scientific revolution, with his argument that we should reject the long-established medieval practice of looking for truth in texts and, rather, seek knowledge from an examination of the natural world. This is the fundamental claim of **empiricism**: all true knowledge comes from our senses—sight, hearing, taste, touch, and smell—not from ungrounded speculation or divine revelation. Thus, perhaps the most central feature of a scientific approach to knowledge is that it relies on observation of the world of our experiences. Furthermore, it seeks explanations of the features of the empirical world grounded in conditions of the world itself, not in realms inaccessible to our senses, such as those invoked by mysticism and religion.

The scientific project also incorporated insights from **rationalism**, an intellectual tradition dating back to some of the greatest scholars of antiquity, such as Pythagoras and Plato, which was revitalized in the early modern era by a variety of philosophers including René Descartes (1596–1650). Descartes and other rationalists were interested in how knowledge could be gained without reliance on the senses since they considered the senses to be easily fooled. In a thought experiment, Descartes wondered what knowledge we could be certain of if our senses were systematically fooled by, for example, demons that wished to trick us. The modern version of this thought experiment is the proposal by some philosophers that we are living in a computer simulation, rather than in a real, material world, and all of our experiences are illusions stemming from computer code. The key question for the rationalist, then, is this: If we live in such a world where our senses cannot be relied on to give us accurate information, how can we have a sure foundation for knowledge?

Due to these types of concerns, rationalists prefer to base knowledge on what can be logically deduced from a parsimonious set of assumptions that is not based on sensory experience. This is best exemplified in the field of mathematics, where theorems are proven strictly by logical inference from a minimal number of axioms ("self-evident" propositions) without reliance on observational evidence. Rationalism is concerned with what the logical consequences are of a given set of propositions. In combining these two philosophies of knowledge, rationalism and empiricism, the logic of science can be described as an approach to gaining knowledge about the world based on the rational analysis of empirical evidence. Thus, empiricism grounds rationalism in the world of our senses, while rationalism tempers empiricism by teaching us to be skeptical of the reliability of the observational evidence available to us. Now, as I will discuss, this should not be taken to mean that scientific analysis in practice has always or even typically adhered to the strictures of rationalism and empiricism; but rational empiricism is at the core of science, at least in its ideal form.

All claims about the existence of environmental problems or an environmental crisis have embedded in them an assertion about the condition of an objective external world. If we are to understand this objective world, we need a methodological program that allows us to gain definite knowledge of it. The scientific philosophy outlined above provides the basis of a methodological program that can help us to understand the material world in which we live. Since efforts aimed at understanding the environmental crises of modernity and the role humans play in them are fundamentally concerned with the constituency of the natural world, the environmental social sciences cannot divorce themselves from the natural sciences. Following a scientific approach, if we want to have real knowledge of the natural environment, we must rely on empirical evidence about that environment, not ideological, spiritual, or other non-empirical arguments. For example, scientists recognized that human activity was leading to global climate change based on a large body of accumulating empirical evidence including rising concentrations of greenhouse gases in the atmosphere, increases in surface and ocean temperatures, retreat of glaciers around the world, sea level rise, and changes in the frequency of extreme weather events. Thus, scientists raised the alarm about climate change, despite it being inconvenient to acknowledge, because an overwhelming body of observational evidence indicate it is happening.

Now, it should be apparent to you that this discussion leaves out some very important issues. What does science have to tell us about ethical questions? After all, many of our most pressing concerns about the environment, as well as in other realms, are about what is right or wrong, not what is true or false. For example, the question of whether we *ought* to allow the killing of whales is at base a value question: Do whales (and other creatures for that matter) have moral worth? This is not the same as the questions of what the current population sizes are of various species of whales (or other creatures) and whether certain practices (for example, industrial whaling vessels prowling the world's oceans) are likely to drive whales to extinction. Indeed, some people even profess indifference to the extinction of many species. Considered in this light, it is clear that many of the hottest environmental debates are founded on both factual and ethical questions: (1) What are the effects of human activities on the natural environment? (2) Are the consequences of human activity good or bad, desirable or undesirable? The simple fact of the matter is that the logic of science can help us to address the first question but is mute with regard to the second. Thus, we see that there is an important scope condition to scientific inquiry. Scientific analysis can address questions of fact (i.e., empirical questions), but it can provide no particular guidance about questions of right and wrong (i.e., ethical questions). This is not to say that science does not raise serious ethical issues—a point to which I will return shortly.

While there is considerable virtue in the logic of science, when we turn to the "establishment of science" we find aspects that deserve our critical engagement. By the "establishment of science," I mean the actual practice of science: the social, economic, political, and cultural institutions which support it; the research centers (universities, transnational corporations, and national laboratories) where scientists work; and of course the scientists themselves. Whereas the logic of science is a philosophy of knowledge, the establishment of science is an actual socially situated set of institutions. Thus, the establishment of science must be assessed by examining how it really operates in society and what its consequences have been for nature and humanity, not by recourse to abstract philosophical reasoning. Since science is pursued by humans, it is intrinsically a social phenomenon and thus cannot be seen as a free-floating institution disembodied from other human endeavors. Although the scientific community does support the ideal of objectivity, in practice scientists are not free of the biases and prejudices; social, cultural, and economic pressures; psychological quirks; and emotional states common to all humans. Science has never been carried out on an ethereal plane, where cool, clear minds pluck unsullied truth from nature. Thus, scientific findings and theories may reflect to some degree the social milieu in which they were formed.

The scientific institutions of our time have their origins in the emergence of "**modernity**"—the period following the Renaissance in Europe, when feudalism was replaced by capitalism and industrialism, beginning roughly in the 17th century. Science through most of its history has been dominated by members of the social elite; and scientists have often sought to further the interests of those in power by engineering weapons of war, developing technologies aimed at aiding global economic imperialism, and accelerating the exploitation of natural resources and laborers for profit by capitalists (see Lesson 7). Thus, it is necessary to recognize that the modern scientific establishment from its start was not aimed simply at the goal of understanding the world in which we live but was intimately linked to existing power structures and typically focused on achieving ends dictated by the ruling class.

This link between the scientific establishment and those in power remains clear in the contemporary world. As highlighted at the beginning of this lesson, it is a matter of no small importance that so much of scientific effort has been directed at developing weapons. A very substantial share of the research that took place over the 20th century in physics, chemistry, and to a lesser extent biology—from work on rocketry and explosives to work on poison gases and deadly microbes—was done at the behest of, and with funding from, military interests. Furthermore, another substantial share of research effort is driven by raw financial interests, where corporations seek to increase profits by developing technologies of production and new products for the market, without particular regard for human well-being, environmental sustainability, or the lives of other creatures (see Lesson 4). For example, a considerable amount of experimentation on nonhuman animals is done merely to develop new consumer goods, such as cosmetics, that causes much animal suffering and does little to enhance human quality of life for the sole purpose of generating greater profits for corporations. Similarly, the development of genetically modified organisms (GMOs) is to a large extent driven by the desire of large corporations to increase profits since products stemming from genetic engineering (for example, GM crops, pharmaceuticals) may potentially have vast markets. In this, the corporations pushing such technologies do not have it in their interest to highlight the potential social and environmental costs associated with GMOs since the profits will flow to the corporations while the costs will be shared with society as a whole.

Science and scientists cannot be seen as disinterested parties seeking truth for its own sake. This is not to say that individual scientists are not typically honest and well-meaning. Furthermore, while it has often served the interests of the ruling class, the scientific community has also brought to light the impacts of societies on the natural environment, such as in its analyses of global warming, ozone depletion, and escalating rates of species extinction. However, it is necessary to recognize that the structure of the scientific establishment, particularly in its connections to the ruling class, cannot be relied on to consistently serve the interests of the mass of humanity or of the other creatures with which we share the Earth. There are, nonetheless, many scientists who pursue research in the public interest, such as studying the impacts to the environment and human health caused by industrial development. However, such "impact science," since it does not directly lead to profits, does not have the ready access to sources of funding that are available to researchers who do work that is helpful to corporations. Due to the nature of the scientific establishment, including the fact that scientific research often depends on funding from corporations and governments with their own interests, environmental sociologists and other scholars must continually engage in a critique of science. However, it is also necessary that in this critique we not lose sight of the importance of studying the natural and social world in a rational manner so that we can understand the processes that generate environmental and social crises.

The outright rejection of the logic and methods of science because of the environmental and social problems generated in the modern world by technology is fraught with danger. In fact, generating skepticism toward science at times has been a key tactic of powerful interests seeking to subvert environmental protection. Most notably, the fossil fuel industry has waged a tireless campaign to discredit the science demonstrating the crisis of human-generated climate change—where the scientific consensus is clear in its assertion that human activities are contributing to global warming—in much the same way that the tobacco industry sought to misrepresent scientific findings about the health effects of smoking (see Lessons 5 and 15). The assault on climate science and scientific research more generally is particularly severe under the presidency of Donald Trump, which (in a manner similar to practices during the George W. Bush administration) takes every opportunity to undermine global warming research and particularly the presentation of that research to the public. The Trump administration, like the Bush administration before it, works to cut funding for scientific research that highlights environmental problems, censor government scientists, and intimidate other scientists who conduct research and present findings that contradict the administration's political positions.

In light of these various considerations, environmental sociology has generally engaged the science question in a nuanced way. Environmental sociologists have examined how scientific claims about the environment are produced, contested, and presented to the public. Here, the main questions have been about how the environment is perceived by society and how some perceived conditions and changes in the environment come to be identified as "problems". These debates focus on the extent to which social (and scientific) perceptions of the environment are "socially constructed"—that is to say, perceptions are created in the social realm through discourse—rather than being reflections of the real external natural world.

As I have already mentioned, taking a strong social constructionist position undermines the entire field of environmental sociology because it in effect denies that there is an environment independent of human perception of it, or at least that we can have reliable knowledge of the natural world. However, milder forms of social constructionism have proved valuable in helping us to understand the social and political processes through which scientific and other claims are shaped and manipulated by social actors and how these social processes often can create public perceptions of the environment that are distinctly at variance with objective environmental conditions (see Lesson 1).

Researchers have focused on how the environmental movement and other social actors present information about the environment and make the case that human modifications of the environment are problematic. It is clear that environmental writers, such as Rachel Carson and Aldo Leopold, and the larger environmental movement, including national organizations such as the Sierra Club and grassroots environmentalists such as Earth First!, played key roles in increasing public awareness of the human effects on the environment, emphasizing some environmental conditions more than others (see Lesson 18). Thus, public environmental concern did not simply come from a diffuse and general public awareness of the environmental effects of modern societies but was generated by the concerted efforts of a variety of social actors. The environmental movement plays a key role in both disseminating and interpreting scientific knowledge about the ecological consequences of human actions and questioning the wisdom of such actions. Similarly, other social actors, such as conservative think tanks, have worked to deny the existence of environmental crises and to "deproblematize" human-generated environmental change (see Lesson 5). These actors frequently question whether environmentalists are correct in their identification of human effects on the environment and/or portray human-induced change as beneficial rather than detrimental.

In these types of debates, scientific claims are of central importance because they often serve as the starting point for the creation of socially salient ideas about what is happening in the environment, and the validity and interpretation of the science is highly contested. For example, as noted above, claims about global warming have been challenged by conservatives, particularly in the United States and Australia, despite the scientific consensus, with industry-funded anti-environmental groups claiming variously that humans are not affecting the environment or that global warming will in fact be good (or at least neutral) for societies. Similarly, the science of genetic engineering has been at the center of heated controversy over the development and use of GMOs, with various activist organizations questioning the safety of GMOs for human health and the environment and biotechnology firms and their allies denying the existence of any serious risks.

Recognizing the social influences on scientific findings is clearly important since research agendas are often determined by those with the resources to fund research rather than stemming from disinterested consideration of the intellectual merits of various topics. Although empirical evidence is a central part of answering questions about the natural world, data do not speak for themselves. Rather, what data are collected and how they are collected, analyzed, and interpreted are not independent of the social context of research. For example, timber companies are unlikely to fund research that demonstrates the detrimental environmental consequences of logging; and, unsurprisingly, scientists funded by timber interests are unlikely to design studies that highlight such consequences.

These issues are not limited to research done by corporations but also play out in universities and colleges, since many researchers who are not employed by corporations still receive funding from corporate sources. The influence of corporations on university research has become more intense as governments have cut funding to public institutions, increasingly pushing universities to seek private sources of funding. Furthermore, public universities, still being partially dependent on government support and concerned about cuts to their funding, are subject to political pressures from elected officials who are often sympathetic to corporate interests. For these reasons, a variety of scientists, from foresters to geneticists, even if scrupulous and fair-minded, are often limited in the type of research they can do and present. As noted earlier, it is too often the case that "impact science" receives less support than science serving the interests of industry. Thus, with good reason, many sociologists do not accept scientific findings uncritically and often take into consideration in their evaluation of factual assertions whose interests are served by various research programs.

In a similar manner, environmental sociology has analyzed the growing variety of technologically generated risks in modernity. Much of the debate in this area centers on the extent to which the "experts," primarily scientists, can be relied on to fairly assess the risks associated with new technologies. For example, who should decide whether or not to build nuclear power plants or allow the use of GMOs? Do scientists know better than laypeople whether or not the potential benefits of such technologies outweigh their potential costs? Although at first glance it may seem that scientists are the best candidates for making such decisions since they have specialized knowledge about the technologies to be considered, on further consideration the issue appears to be much more complex.

Since scientists depend on empirical evidence to make their assessments, when data are absent they do not necessarily have greater insight than laypeople. In the case of many technologies, such as the development of artificial intelligence and nanotechnologies, questions are often about the long-term consequences of large-scale use, and this cannot be assessed with high certainty for new technologies that have been tested over only limited time periods in a restricted number of settings. For example, scientists did not foresee the threat that chlorofluorocarbons represented to the ozone layer until after they came into widespread use. And, as I noted at the start of this lesson, there was considerable uncertainty about how large of an explosion the first atomic bomb would yield, despite the fact that it was studied by many of the greatest scientific minds in the world. (Did the scientists and military bureaucrats have the right to make the decision to conduct the Trinity test, despite the potential consequences for all of humanity and nature?) Scientific methods are good at assessing risk when there are sufficient data but have only limited potential to give reliable assessments in the absence of such data.

Since the potential costs and benefits of new technologies are not evenly distributed across society, issues of justice and fairness are central to risk assessment, and these are not entirely reducible to empirical questions. After all, in making calculations about risk by estimating the potential costs and benefits of new technologies, is an economic measure (such as dollars) the most appropriate, or should the life of humans and other creatures be assessed with a different metric? Clearly, there are ethical questions to be considered that will not yield to scientific analysis.

Furthermore, it is increasingly the case that scientists have financial stakes, beyond simply the funding of their research, in the technologies they advocate and thus commonly have a conflict of interest when asked to assess whether the benefits of new technologies are likely to outweigh the risks. For example, many geneticists hold patents for gene-based technologies and/or own shares of companies that stand to profit from biotechnology applications. Thus, the extent to which such scientists can be relied on for an objective evaluation of technological risks is quite dubious. Clearly, questions about how scientific knowledge should be applied and how decisions are made about which risks are worth taking are matters of no trivial importance. Environmental sociology, then, has studied how the public has sought to democratize science, as well as how the social elite has often sought to insulate decisions about technological applications and scientific ethics from public scrutiny. The work of environmental sociologists points to the importance of public advocacy for funding of impact science, rational discussion of scientific evidence, and democratization of decision-making in society.

I have touched on only some of the complex issues that environmental sociologists face in engaging science. There are three key points to take from this lesson. First, environmental sociologists, by necessity, generally take a realist stance toward environmental problems. That is to say, they recognize that concern for the environment is in substantial part due to real changes occurring in the natural world, not merely because of cultural changes in values, beliefs, and perceptions. Thus, environmental sociology is dependent on a scientific approach to understanding the human–environment interaction, where knowledge is sought through rational investigation of empirical evidence. Second, and existing in some degree of tension with the first point, environmental sociologists also recognize that social perceptions of the environment are affected by political, economic, and social processes, where those in power often manipulate, subvert, deny, or obfuscate scientific knowledge to further their own interests. Therefore, it is necessary to situate scientific knowledge in its social context. Third, environmental sociologists recognize that the effects of science on the environment have been double-edged. On the one hand, the logic of science has allowed for a growing understanding of the natural world and how humans have affected the biosphere. This rational knowledge allows for the recognition of environmental problems and an emerging understanding of what needs to be done to address them. On the other hand, science has given humans unprecedented power to manipulate nature, and this has contributed to a growing suite of technologies that generate new and greater threats to ecosystems and disrupt the metabolic exchange between society and the environment. Environmental sociology grapples with these many facets of science in an effort to understand society and nature. It is to be hoped that such understanding will help us to bring about a just and sustainable world.

SOURCES

Burningham, Kate. 1998. "A Noisy Road or Nosy Resident? A Demonstration of the Utility of Social Constructionism for Analysing Environmental Problems." *Sociological Review* 46 (3): 536–563.

Conner, Clifford D. 2005. *A People's History of Science: Miners, Midwives, and "Low Mechanicks."* New York: Nation Books.

Dunlap, Riley E. and Aaron McCright. 2015. "Challenging Climate Change: The Denial Countermovement." In *Climate Change and Society: Sociological Perspectives*, edited by R. E. Dunlap and R. J. Brulle, 300–332. New York: Oxford University Press.

Else, Jon H., dir. and prod. *The Day After Trinity*. 1980. Pyramid Films.

Gould, Stephen Jay. 2003. *The Hedgehog, the Fox, and the Magister's Pox: Mending the Gap Between Science and the Humanities*. New York: Harmony Books.

Levins, Richard and Richard C. Lewontin. 1985. *The Dialectical Biologist*. Cambridge, MA: Harvard University Press.

Merchant, Carolyn. 1980. *Death of Nature: Women, Ecology, and the Scientific Revolution*. San Francisco: Harper.

Mooney, Chris. 2005. *The Republican War on Science*. New York: Basic Books.

Oreskes, Naomi and Erik M. Conway. 2010. *Merchants of Doubt: How a Handful of Scientists Obscured the Truth on Issues from Tobacco Smoke to Global Warming*. London: Bloomsbury Press.

Rhodes, Richard. 1987. *The Making of the Atomic Bomb*. New York: Simon & Schuster.

Rosa, Eugene A. 1998. "Meta-Theoretical Foundations of Post-Normal Risk." *Journal of Risk Analysis* 1: 15–44.

Wootton, David. 2015. *The Invention of Science: A New History of the Scientific Revolution*. New York: Harper.

York, Richard and Brett Clark. 2010. "Critical Materialism: Science, Technology, and Environmental Sustainability." *Sociological Inquiry* 80 (3): 475–499.

7

Technological Change and the Environment

Kenneth A. Gould

Mushroom cloud/skull statue memorializing the site of the first controlled nuclear reaction, across from new nanotechnology facilities at the University of Chicago, Chicago, Illinois.

Post your photo on technological change and the environment to #TLEStechnology.

Photo by Ken Gould

One of the primary ways that human societies mediate their relationship with the natural world is through the development and use of technology. Societies use technology to overcome the obstacles to surviving and thriving that they perceive in nature and to modify the natural world in ways that meet certain human needs and desires. The social creation of new technologies transforms both societies and the natural world on which human societies depend. Therefore, in order for us to understand the dynamic relationship between social systems and ecosystems, we need to understand the role played by technology in shaping that relationship.

WHAT IS TECHNOLOGY?

So what is technology? In simplest terms, technology is how we make "stuff" and do "stuff." In order to make certain kinds of stuff and do certain kinds of stuff, we organize and reorganize social relations and nature. And technological change is most commonly produced by social actors and institutions. It doesn't fall from the sky, and it doesn't emerge in some predetermined path of linear progress. Specific social groups (corporations, governments, and other forms of social organization) make it their business to move technological change in specific directions and for specific purposes. For instance, take a look at the classroom when you go back to class to discuss this lesson. A classroom is, in part, a technology for making or doing stuff. In this case, the stuff to be made is educated people and the stuff to be done is education. The classroom is organized, created, and maintained by a social institution (your college). Manifest in your classroom are both social relations (the relationships between people) and relations between the social system and the ecosystem. Is your classroom organized with chairs in a circle or with all the seats facing a central point? The physical organization of the classroom (the technology of education, if you will) tells you much about the social relations within it as well as the social expectations. With seats in a circle, you expect to have to talk to others in the room quite a bit. With the chairs facing a central point, you expect to be spoken to and for you to speak much less, and then perhaps only to the person occupying the central point of focus (the lectern). In a circle, you expect social relations to be more egalitarian, with each participant playing a more equal role. With chairs facing a central point, you expect social relations to be more hierarchical and authoritarian, with a single power holder (your professor) commanding most of the attention.

What you can see by looking at the physical structure of your classroom is an indication of the social structure of the classroom. That is, the way that the technology of education (your classroom) is organized both reflects and determines social relations. The same is true of any technology for doing and making anything. The technology itself—a computer, a factory, a hog farm, an automobile, a smartphone, or a nuclear weapon—manifests specific social relations. Technology consists of both physical, tangible "things" and the social relations they imply. No technology is separable from its social relations, even though those relations are intangible and take a little more work to actually "see."

You will have missed the early part of your class thinking about the ways in which the physical parts of the technology of education reflect and determine the social relation parts of the technology of education instead of paying attention to what's being said. That's okay; you can get notes from the person next to you. Now think about the relationship to nature manifest in the classroom. What is all the stuff in the classroom made from? Your notebook is made from trees; your seat, made from plastic, made from oil; maybe some aluminum made from bauxite here and there. All of the physical things in your classroom have their origins in nature and have been transformed, through technologies (social relations and physical hardware), into something else to meet human goals.

You probably have electricity in your classroom too, to power lights, computers, projectors, and so forth. That means that your classroom is physically hardwired to some technology for transforming some natural element or process into electricity. Look at the electrical sockets in your classroom. You could follow the wires from those sockets all the way back to the cogenerator, power dam, coal-burning power plant, nuclear reactor, photovoltaic cells, or wind turbine that has been constructed to convert natural resources or processes to meet human goals (see Lesson 9). Perhaps the socket leads to a coal-fired power plant that burns coal mined in some region quite distant from your own. People there are busy transforming nature in their location in order to allow you to have lighting so you and your professor can produce education in your location. And that electricity is probably transmitted through copper wires, made somewhere off-campus, from copper mined in yet another distant community by still other people. In all likelihood, there aren't coal or copper mines on your campus. So your classroom and you are connected to other parts of the country and the world, using natural resources from distant ecosystems.

Your classroom, and any other technology you use or are a part of, connects you to a variety of relationships with the natural world, both immediate and far removed. And the technologies for converting natural resources into other stuff (electricity, books, seats, etc.) also connect you to other sets of social relations, with people you may never know or see, who mine coal and copper or work in factories producing wires or wood pulp for paper.

So technology is a series of entanglements with social systems and ecosystems, close and far, obvious and hidden. Your smartphone, your pen, your computer—all represent a series of relationships between you and others and between you and the natural world. Those relationships are not random. They reflect the social origins of the technologies, the goals of those who designed the technologies, the interests of those who require or request you to use the technologies, and the ways in which society has been organized to use and change nature.

TECHNOLOGICAL CHANGE

Social scientists who study technology and technological change have used a variety of schema to identify various phases or periods in the development of technology. You have probably heard some of these eras of specific technological applications described with terms such as "the bronze age" or "the iron age." Note that the materials used signify these eras of technology. Lewis Mumford, in his classic work *Technics and Civilization*, identified three distinct eras of modern technological development: "eotechnic," "paleotechnic," and "neotechnic." The eotechnic phase was typified by the use of wood as the primary material and the use of moving water and wind as the primary energy sources. The paleotechnic phase was typified by the use of iron as the primary material and the use of coal to generate steam as the primary energy source. The neotechnic phase, he argued, was typified by the use of steel as the primary material and the use of electricity. Here again, the elements of nature, modified through human intervention, are central to our categories of technological phase. The ways human societies use and transform nature are key to our understanding of what various technologies are.

We can categorize different technological eras in various ways by changes they produce in society and nature, both large and small. For our purposes here, let's look at two very large, very broad, and very transformative eras of technological change, both of which completely revolutionized the ways that human societies are organized and the ways that those societies relate to, modify, and rely on nature. These two periods of technological transition were so transformative of society and the natural world that they have been viewed by most as revolutionary: the agricultural revolution and the Industrial Revolution.

The Agricultural Revolution

The realization that by planting seeds of desirable plants, people could transform ecosystems to make them produce large volumes of preferred food crops radically changed the relationship between human societies and nature. Prior to the technology of agriculture, human societies were primarily organized for a hunting and gathering survival strategy. In order to get the food they required, groups of people collected the plants and other foods they found in nature. This meant that, as local plant and animal stocks were depleted, people had to migrate to other areas in search of food. They developed patterns of migration that followed the seasonal availability of food plants and the seasonal migration of other animals (which also followed seasonal patterns of the availability of food and water). The technology of agriculture changed all that, allowing humans to modify their local ecosystems to meet their food needs rather than modifying their societies (through migration) to meet local ecosystem conditions.

In a real sense, the power balance between environment and society was shifted toward greater human agency and greater ecosystem malleability. Humans cleared portions of local ecosystems of their naturally occurring plants, animals, and habitats and replaced them with increasingly vast fields of human-selected species of plants. This large-scale transformation of land from natural ecosystems to farm fields has continued ever since as prairies, savannas, and forests are cleared. Plants were selected for attributes most desired by humans (food and textiles), and that selection began to replace the process of natural selection in the evolution of certain species (see Lesson 12). A similar process occurred with the domestication of animals used for meat, dairy, and textiles. Animals were taken from the wild and raised and reproduced to serve human needs (see Lesson 13). Pastures were cleared, ecosystems transformed, and species gradually modified to serve human goals.

With settled agriculture, human populations could remain in a single location, modifying the environment to facilitate settlement. Settlement allowed for the building of permanent structures rather than the portable or disposable shelters logically necessary for societies of nomads. Settlement also allowed for the accumulation of material possessions. Keeping material possessions to a minimum makes good sense if you'll have to move them from place to place all the time (something that anyone who has ever moved quickly realizes). If you can plan to be in a locale indefinitely, you can begin to fill your permanent structures with "stuff," thus creating an incentive for the production of more material things. So, in a real sense, the technology of agriculture is what began the process of human societies constructing permanent houses and filling them with material possessions.

The successes of agriculture also led to the creation of what sociologists call a "**labor surplus**." Where soils were fertile and water was available, agriculture was very successful, and large quantities of food could be produced by fewer and fewer people. This process of increasing yields and decreasing demand for human labor has continued so that now, in countries like the United States, vast food surpluses are produced with a very small percentage of the population engaged in actual primary food production. But even very early in the process, fertile regions allowed for growing numbers of people to eat without themselves being engaged in food production. With large populations permanently settled in a single location without survival-oriented work to do (food collection or production), other activities and new ways of organizing people in more complex ways emerged. Along with permanent houses, permanent ritual sites, large-scale irrigation works to support agriculture, and other engineering projects requiring vast amounts of human labor were organized. Pyramids, temples, aqueducts, and astronomical observatories were constructed by harnessing surplus labor (often involuntarily). How the Egyptian pyramids were built is no mystery: The answer is agriculture. It is worth noting that much of this large-scale construction was organized to support agricultural success and expansion physically (irrigation works), to appeal to nature through religion for adequate rain and fertility (temples), and to track seasonal changes to determine appropriate planting and harvest schedules (astronomical observatories).

Supporting larger populations in one place required more complex social organization in governance and the production and distribution of a wider variety of goods and services. Labor surpluses also allowed for the creation of standing armies, and agricultural expansion increased the value of transforming and taking more land, especially in fertile areas. With hunting less important to survival, but conflict over access to arable land more important, the primary goal of weapons technology turned from killing other animals to killing humans. Agricultural societies gave rise to the first central state authorities, commanding standing armies and controlling access to land and the distribution of food. While we may think of ourselves as living in industrial or even postindustrial societies, it is easy to see that many features of both human social organizations and their relationship to ecosystems actually stem from the radical social system and ecosystem shifts that came with the technology of agriculture.

The Industrial Revolution

The discipline of sociology was initially developed by people attempting to understand the vast transformations of social organization that emerged in the 19th century with the rise of industrialization. While the great agricultural civilizations emerged primarily in Africa, Asia, and Latin America, the first great industrial civilizations emerged in Europe. European social analysts like Marx, Weber, and Durkheim established the scientific study of societies and social change in efforts to understand the new patterns of social relations generated by the emergence of industrial production. The Industrial Revolution produced the second great technological transformation of the relationship between social systems and ecosystems, although, as noted in the Introduction to this book, the ecosystemic aspect of change was not of particular interest to early sociologists. The industrialization of production generated a vast array of social changes, far too numerous to address at length here. Among these, however, it is worth noting the creation of new classes (such as those Marx termed the "proletariat," or industrial working class, and the "bourgeoisie," the capitalist class) and the formation of industrial cities (London being the first city to reach 1 million in population after the fall of Rome).

In terms of the society–environment relationship, industrialization ushered in societal dependence on enormous inputs of nonrenewable resources, particularly fossil fuels. Industrial civilization was, and remains, predicated on nearly limitless supplies of relatively cheap and portable nonrenewable energy inputs (see Lesson 9). It was the capacity to convert coal into steam, and thus energy, on an ever-increasing scale that gave industrial society its form and its trajectory. Our current society can be thought of as one designed specifically to thrive in, and to survive off of, endless increases in energy inputs. Those conditions appeared to be sustainable at the dawn of the industrial era, when the exhaustion of necessary resources appeared unlikely and the consequences of changing the chemical composition of the earth's atmosphere with carbon emissions were unknown. In the current era, it is the foreseeable end to increasing supplies of such energy (see Lesson 9), and the environmental impacts of using that energy (see Lesson 15), that are causing many to consider the need to wholly reorient the path of human society to what some are conceptualizing as a "post-fossil fuel society."

The technological changes that coalesced into the Industrial Revolution were intended primarily to vastly increase humans' ability to produce a growing range of synthetic products, from textiles to machines themselves. Just as the agricultural revolution made the large-scale production of food possible, the Industrial Revolution made the large-scale production of other goods possible. And just as agriculture required the expanding transformation of natural ecosystems into farm fields, industry required the expanding conversion of elements of ecosystems (trees, coal, metals, etc.) into natural resource inputs in the production of products. Of course, as industrial production expanded and new markets for new products were expanded to meet the increased supply, the pace and scale of the extraction of natural resources and their conversion to products increased, with two major results.

First, ecosystems and habitats, at first locally and later globally, were pillaged to meet the needs of industry for raw materials. We can think of these as ecosystem "withdrawals." These withdrawals would eventually lead to socially generated problems of natural resource depletion such as deforestation and oil scarcity. Second, the capacity of industry to produce on increasingly vast scales resulted in the world being increasingly full of social products and byproducts. The products, although useful for a time, eventually find their way into dumps, landfills, the oceans, and incinerators. The byproducts tend to be returned to ecosystems as industrial air-, water-, and land-based emissions. In addition, many of the products create byproducts themselves in the course of their use, such as cars producing air emissions, discarded batteries, and used motor oil. We can think of these socially created artificial elements injected by industrial societies back into ecosystems as ecological "additions." These new additions to nature would quickly give rise to problems of environmental pollution (such as pesticide toxicity and greenhouse gases). The Industrial Revolution is therefore most notable in terms of the social system–ecosystem interaction for increasing the social capacity for, and rate of, conversion of natural resources into products and byproducts. The result has been wholesale disruption of local and global ecosystems that natural scientists have only just begun to comprehend. After World War II, industrial production shifted to greater generation of single-use, disposable products, and products designed to become obsolete and need replacing quickly (see Lesson 2). Not only do we produce more stuff (like plastic water bottles and smartphones), but the time it takes for that stuff to complete its useful life and become waste has become shorter and shorter.

In giving rise to the modern city, the new industrial technologies also quickly gave rise to the familiar socioenvironmental problems that are part of urban landscapes: urban smog and resulting respiratory disease, the accumulation of trash and the difficulty of disposing of it in a safe and hygienic manner, the contamination of freshwater supplies and the threat of waterborne illness, and the social inequities in exposure to these urban environmental hazards (see Lesson 10). These environmental hazards were, and are, compounded with other key features of the urban social environment such as inadequate housing; congested infrastructure; and lack of healthcare, housing, employment, and justice. In addition, the urban environment cut off large portions of the human population from direct daily contact with natural environments, which had been a key fact of human existence since the dawn of the species. This disconnection from nature would lead many in "modern industrial society," including sociologists (see the Introduction to this book), to conclude that society was no longer dependent on nature and that the two could be thought of as separate concerns.

THE TECHNOLOGICAL TRAJECTORY

As you can see, both the revolutions in agricultural technology and industrial technology completely transformed the relationship between social systems and ecosystems. In the broadest sense, the greatest change that emerged from each was an enormous increase in the incentive and capacity to adjust natural systems to meet social needs rather than adjusting social systems to meet naturally occurring ecosystem realities. In this process, the human capacity for technological innovation, our ability to develop new techniques to transform the natural world, has been key. As social systems now come to realize the dramatic negative social implications of their vast transformation of ecosystems, it is important to ask: Where is our technological trajectory headed? Why? Who or what determines the path of technological innovation? And how might we choose a path of technological innovation that resolves some of the conflict between social systems and ecosystem?

Social Institutions and Technological Decision-Making

Social institutions pursuing specific social goals largely control the progress and direction of technological change. These institutions exert substantial control over the research and development process in numerous ways, including influence on educational institutions, research facilities, research and development funding, and the distribution of profits derived from outcomes. At each point of the research and development process, these social institutions are able to influence the agendas of scientists and engineers and, thus, the trajectory of technological innovation. There is no "runaway technology," as some environmentalists have argued. Nor is there a clear "natural evolution" of technological direction, as most might assume. The direction of scientific and technological research and development is a result of human intentionality and decision-making (see Lesson 6). As a result, the history and current direction of technological research and development reflect the power and the political and economic interests of the social institutions that control the process.

The main social institutions guiding the technological research and development agendas are universities, states, and corporations. Each of these institutions has specific interests, which are reflected in their agendas for scientific research and technological innovation and thus shape the social system–ecosystem interactions that the rest of the world inherits. Universities have historically been viewed as the institutions with the greatest dedication to the "objective" pursuit of scientific truths and as being somewhat independent of political and economic pressures. In universities, it was often the scientists and engineers who set the research and development agendas, and they were largely immune from the influence of the political and economic goals and rewards stemming from states and corporations. However, as the costs of research and development increased and public funding for universities declined, states and corporations gained greater influence over the agendas and goals of science and technology workers within universities. As a result, the interests of states and corporations ripple through the university system and reduce the capacity of these formerly more autonomous institutions to chart a distinct technological research and development direction.

Governments are the primary source of funding for basic scientific research. **Basic science** seeks to explain natural phenomena and forms the knowledge base that supports engineering. The knowledge base on which **applied science** will be built is thus influenced by the ways that state decision-makers prioritize certain paths of inquiry and distribute funding for it. The goals of states in funding basic science are fairly clear. First, states fund basic science and some applied research and development to enhance their military power. Since governments are the market for weapons systems, they have a vested interest in making sure that the creation of ever-more-powerful military technology is a major thrust of technological innovation. As a result, the pursuit of more effective military systems has become one of the dominant goals—if not *the* dominant goal—of the technology research and development agenda of our species. The enormous amount of funding offered by the state for military research and development directs the human technological trajectory toward destructive ends while sapping funding from quality of life–enhancing research along other paths of human inquiry (such as health, environmental protection and remediation, renewable energy, etc.). Since military technology is particularly environmentally destructive, energy-inefficient, and natural resource-intensive, it has a significant negative impact on the nature of social system interactions with ecosystems.

The other goal of states in sponsoring research and development is the pursuit of global "economic competitiveness." By using tax revenues to subsidize the research and development agendas of corporations based within their borders, states try to boost their gross domestic products. Increasing the economic power of the country increases the relative power of a state, giving it greater influence over the global arenas in which it competes with other states. Because of this, increasing the economic power of the state becomes a technological goal in its own right, along with increasing the military power of the state. And those two goals are intertwined in a military–industrial complex because the greater tax revenues gained through successful international economic competition make more funding available to support military research and development; and greater military power facilitates greater access to the global natural resources, **waste sinks**, markets, and labor pools needed for economic growth (see Lesson 3).

The interests of corporations in technological research and development are somewhat less complex than those of states. Corporations pursue technological innovation to enhance **profitability**. Corporations are the leading institutional source of funding for technological innovation and the primary employers of engineers. As a result, the goals of corporations have greater influence over the human technological trajectory than those of any other social institution. Corporations use the government subsidy of basic research as the basis for their applied research (see Lesson 6) that produces profit-enhancing products to be sold to states (military hardware), other corporations (including labor-replacing technologies), and individual consumers (consumer goods). Lines of research that will lead to products that may produce social or ecological benefits but do not promise to generate profits are not funded and not pursued. Corporate profitability is then, in some sense, the ultimate criterion for determining much of the human technological trajectory. Given that technology is such a big factor in shaping the relationship between social systems and ecosystems, we can see that corporate interests have come to be a major—if not *the* major—factor in determining how social systems and ecosystems will interact (see Lesson 5).

The goal of corporate profitability influences the direction of technological innovation in other ways. Corporate profitability sets much of the research agendas of scientists both within the firm and within the university. By sponsoring university research, corporations create a system of incentives and disincentives for the pursuit of various lines of scientific inquiry and engineering development. By providing the laboratories in which research and development are conducted, corporations control the scientific and engineering infrastructure of society. By offering shared profit incentives with educational institutions and university researchers, corporations influence the direction of higher education. The nature and structure of scientific and engineering education tend to reflect the social agendas of the institutions that fund it. Corporations have also been known to overtly and covertly squelch lines of scientific investigation that may threaten the goal of corporate profitability, as we have seen in research on the health effects of tobacco, the ecological threats from pesticides, the environmental impacts of acid rain, the health and ecological impacts of genetically modified organisms, and the contribution of carbon dioxide emissions to global climate change (see Lessons 5, 11, 15, and 16).

SCIENCE, TECHNOLOGICAL INNOVATION, AND POWER

The trajectory of technological innovation is greatly influenced by a relatively small number of decision-makers in governments and corporations who establish research priorities, provide research facilities, and determine the distribution of funding. The result is a global technological infrastructure, system, and direction that reflects the interests of a privileged few and pursues those interests despite the many obvious negative consequences for social system–ecosystem dynamics. The fact that the bulk of technological decisions are made in corporate boardrooms and opaque government institutions shields technological innovation agendas from democratic processes. Although the outcomes of research and development decisions often become obvious to the public at large, the decision-making processes that ultimately led to these outcomes are generally unavailable for public input and public influence. We all must live with the technological consequences in terms of the products that are and are not available, the technologies that do and do not exist, the employment opportunities that are created and destroyed, and the public health and ecological impacts that are generated or averted; but we are generally denied a role in determining those consequences.

For example, you may not even be aware that one of the leading areas of technological research and development investment right now is **nanotechnology**. Nanotechnology is the engineering of matter on an atomic and molecular scale to produce new materials and technologies with at least one dimension sized from 1 to 100 nanometers. Nanotechnology allows for the creation of a myriad of new materials not found in nature and the production of microscopic machines. Although you may not be aware that governments, transnational corporations, and universities are already heavily invested in nanotechnology, you may already have nanomaterials in your body. A wide range of cosmetics, sunblocks, and athletic wear includes nanoparticles, literally tiny particles of unknown (at least to us) materials. Nanoparticles can pass through your skin, enter your bloodstream, and cross the blood–brain barrier. We don't know what the health effects of nanoparticles are because there has been little investment in doing that research. The lucrative research in nanotechnology is in creating new nano products and getting them to market quickly. You might prefer for the research on the public health and environmental impacts of nanoparticles to have happened long before you started rubbing them into your skin. But since that is not profitable research, you would need a way to influence the research and development agenda before new products and processes are developed.

Democratic input into research agendas is quite limited. What often passes for democratic controls on technology are mechanisms for "public consultation" arranged after new technologies are created. These public consultations are often organized by the very institutions that sponsor technological research and whose interest is to gain public acceptance for the innovations. These public forums are designed primarily to reduce public fears, which are viewed by those who have a vested interest in technology as irrational (see Lesson 11). You have already been told that it is irrational to fear microwave radiation from smartphones and not to worry about the health effects of genetically modified organisms; you will soon be told not to fear the nanoparticles entering your body. Research on the social and ecological implications of technology is often highly politicized (see Lessons 6 and 14) and commonly intended to boost the chances for public acceptance of existing and new technologies. This makes it difficult for people to reach informed conclusions about the costs and benefits of technological change.

The Myth of "Progress"

Another factor that keeps the general public from participating in science and technology decision-making is the myth of "progress," a set of ideological constructs promoted by the institutions that control the research and development process. Most people tend to think that research takes a natural course determined by free inquiry and the evolution of ideas and that technologies are routed along a linear progression where one development automatically follows from another. That is, people are led to believe that there is in fact no institutional agency in the technological trajectory and that what little human agency exists is in the hands of individual experts pursuing either public good or private gain. The ideology of capitalism argues that the pursuit of private gain naturally leads to the common good. The combination of the myth of technological neutrality and the ideology of capitalist ethics produces complacency in regard to research and development on the part of the public. This complacency serves the interests of the institutions that do have agency in determining the societal technological path and the social system–ecosystem relations that go with it. People tend to ask, "What will they think of next?" rather than telling technology-producing institutions what they should be working on next. The myth of progress disables people from seeing that the technological path we are on is just one of an infinite number of possible technological paths; and that we, as a society, could choose something much different, and perhaps, much better.

While it is true that democratic citizenries could demand and exert greater influence over the research that states support, the ideological power of objective science (see Lesson 6), technological neutrality, and capitalist ethics keep this possibility from entering the public consciousness. Science and technology decision-making has, for the most part, been organized out of politics. The result is that powerful individuals and institutions are left to use the human technological capacity in pursuit of their own interests largely unchecked by the majority. In no other arena are the long-term consequences for human society and the environment as great and the political discussion so muted. Conflicts do emerge from time to time (on nuclear technology, genetic technology, etc.), but even then the political discourse largely revolves around a ban on the implementation of a specific technology rather than a quest for democratic control over the processes that generate technology. Should our social institutions invest in renewable energy research or military drones? Should science education promote genetic engineering or sustainable organic agriculture? Should engineers be working on more energy-efficient transportation infrastructure or the next iPhone upgrade? Should scientists spend more time and effort investigating the environmental and public health impacts of nanoparticles or developing new nanotechnology-based consumer products? If you knew that your cosmetics contained nanoparticles, whose health effects are unknown and unstudied, you might want some say in that decision. Rather than waiting passively to receive the next "big thing" from technology producers, perhaps we should be actively participating in deciding what "big things" they ought to start working on.

The Democratization of Technological Innovation

If we are to seriously pursue a more environmentally sound relationship between social systems and ecosystems, we may find it useful to make the technological innovation processes subject to democratic controls. The potential social and ecological impacts of technologies must be assessed by informed publics, under conditions in which citizens are empowered to determine the goals of research and development, the prioritization and funding of that research, and the manner in which technologies will be implemented or prohibited. This input needs to occur at the earliest stages of the innovation process, determining the purpose of basic lines of inquiry in order to use our scientific and technological capacity to maximize democratically determined social and environmental benefits. That would be a very different model than the one in place currently in which institutions produce and implement technologies without public input, and then the public must overtly object to negative social and ecological consequences once they appear (see Lessons 11 and 12). After-the-fact protests and control efforts in which the public expresses opposition to prior technological decisions are certainly less than optimal for democratic governance and the creation of a technological trajectory that serves social and environmental goals. A sustainable social system–ecosystem dynamic requires a new technological revolution, not just in what technologies are created but in how society organizes and directs the innovation process.

SOURCES

Beder, Sharon. 1997. *Global Spin: The Corporate Assault on Environmentalism.* White River Junction, VT: Chelsea Green.

Gedicks, Al. 2001. *Resource Rebels: Native Challenges to Mining and Oil Corporations.* Cambridge, MA: South End Press.

Gould, Kenneth A. 2006. "Promoting Sustainability." In *Public Sociologies Reader*, edited by Judith Blau and Keri E. Iyall Smith, 213–230. New York: Rowman & Littlefield.

Gould, Kenneth A. 2007. "The Ecological Costs of Militarization." *Peace Review* 19 (3): 331–334.

Gould, Kenneth A., David N. Pellow, and Allan Schnaiberg. 2008. *The Treadmill of Production: Injustice and Unsustainability in the Global Economy.* Boulder, CO: Paradigm.

Hess, David J. 2007. *Alternative Pathways in Science and Industry: Activism, Innovation, and the Environment in an Era of Globalization.* Cambridge, MA: MIT Press.

Konefal, Jason and Maki Hatanaka. 2019. *Twenty Lessons in the Sociology of Food and Agriculture.* New York: Oxford University Press.

Leguizamón, Amalia. 2020. *Seeds of Power: Environmental Injustice and Genetically Modified Soybeans in Argentina.* Durham, NC: Duke University Press.

Lukes, Steven. 1974. *Power: A Radical View.* London: Macmillan.

Maclurcan, Donald and Natalia Radywyl, eds. 2012. *Nanotechnology and Global Sustainability.* New York: CRC Press.

Mumford, Lewis. 1934. *Technics and Civilization.* New York: Harcourt Brace Jovanovich.

Noble, David F. 1977. *America by Design: Science, Technology, and the Rise of Corporate Capitalism.* New York: Alfred A. Knopf.

Nye, David E. 1996. *American Technological Sublime.* Cambridge, MA: MIT Press.

Schnaiberg, Allan. 1980. *The Environment: From Surplus to Scarcity.* New York: Oxford University Press.

White, Geoffrey, ed. 2000. *Campus Inc.* Albany, NY: Prometheus Books.

8

Population, Demography, and the Environment

Diane C. Bates

Strollers parked at Disneyworld, Orlando, Florida.

Post your photo on population, demography, and the environment to #TLESpopulation.

Photo by Ken Gould

The world's human population as of November 22, 2019, at 12:12 p.m. (EST) was 7,612,676,743, with more than one person added every 10 seconds. Social scientists have long debated how human population affects environmental quality; population growth is frequently cited as a leading cause of environmental degradation. Understanding human population dynamics goes well beyond merely counting the number of people in a location. For example, outmigration from rural areas changes how households use agricultural land and middle-class outmigration from urban areas can create an environment hostile to public health by leaving abandoned and vacant properties in poor communities. The age and class composition of a population predicts what sorts of environmental and health threats are likely to emerge. The stability and resources of a population affect its ability to respond to and recover from environmental threats.

Social theory on the relationship between population and the environment has historically focused exclusively on growth, but understanding how populations change over time is important for all students of the environment. Moreover, people experience population change at the local level rather than on the national scale more typical of what demographers and social theorists examine. For example, residents of the Northeastern rust belt may note how three decades of uneven population decline have left neighborhoods with vacant buildings, overgrown lots, and abandoned factories. On the other hand, residents of the suburban sunbelt cannot help but observe how more and more people keep moving into the area and converting open space into residential subdivisions, office parks, and shopping centers. This chapter ties together these local experiences with the larger study of the interaction between human populations and our environment. It first defines several key terms in understanding population dynamics and then proceeds to a discussion of the main controversies in population theory. It closes with a nuanced analysis of two case studies that highlight how demography informs our understanding of environmental migration and climate gentrification.

Population refers to the number of people living in a specific geographical area at a specific point in time. **Demography** is the discipline in the social sciences that studies the characteristics of human populations, including how they change. In the United States, the Census Bureau compiles the most comprehensive demographic data, including the decennial census and the annual American Community Survey. Census Bureau data represent the highest-quality demographic data available on a national scale and can be accessed freely at its website (www.census.gov). At the international level, the United Nations Statistics Division compiles census and other statistical information from member nations and publishes them annually in the *Demographic Yearbook* as well as making some of these data available on its website (unstats.un.org). Some of the most important demographic variables include population density, population growth rates, birth and death rates, and migration. **Population density** indicates the average number of people who live in a specified area unit, usually a square mile or square kilometer. **Population growth** measures changes in population over time by taking a population at one time and adding all the births and immigrants who arrive before a later time, while subtracting the deaths and emigrants. Rates are calculated by reporting the number of births/deaths/immigrants/emigrants for every 1,000 people in a given population. Although it does not distinguish between natural change (births and deaths) and migration, a crude population growth estimate can be calculated by dividing the population at a later time by the population at an earlier time. Likewise, simple population growth rates can be calculated by subtracting an earlier population from a later population, and then dividing by the earlier population.

In addition to counting the number of people in a population, demographers typically collect and publish data on other characteristics of populations, such as age and gender composition, consumption levels, and subpopulations, such as racial or ethnic groups. Unfortunately, the relationship between population change and environmental quality is not as straightforward or easy to define as demographic variables. Indeed, the relationship between human population growth and the environment has been the subject of social theory and social investigation for centuries.

MALTHUS, SOCIAL DARWINISM, AND MORAL CONTROL

Victorian-era social theorist Thomas Malthus famously proposed an inverse relationship between environmental quality and population growth. His *Essay on the Principle of Population* (first published in 1798) asserted that, without restraint, human population growth would eventually exceed the production of food, resulting in a massive crash in population. Specifically, he posited that human population growth increased exponentially; two people in generation 1 produced two children (generation 1 population = 2); each of those two people produced two children in generation 2 (population = $2 \times 2 = 4$); each one of those four people produced two children in generation 3 (population = $4 \times 2 = 8$); and so on. Based on his assessment of food production in Europe, Malthus reasoned that the production of food would increase only in an arithmetic or linear fashion, such that the increase between generations would be constant. Given these projections, Malthus warned that if humans did not control their own population growth, then a combination of war, disease, and especially famine would control population anyway. In part due to his own devout faith, Malthus believed that humans were unlike other animals in their capacity to exert moral control over their behavior. He therefore indicated that the most ethical course of action would be to limit human population growth, beginning with the working classes of European cities, whose lack of moral control (in his view) created large families that the poor could not feed on their own. This conclusion resonated with the era's Victorian elites in its emphasis on restraint of sexual impulses, moral condemnation of the poor, and opposition to charity designed to improve the situation of the poor, since feeding the poor would only prolong the inevitable misery and population crash.

Herbert Spencer, a founding theorist in sociology, echoed Malthus in his writings about the moral superiority of the elite, although his work also naturalized social hierarchy (Spencer [1864] 1972). According to Spencer, human society was evolutionary and progressed from less to more complexity. Spencer, like Malthus, believed that moral human individuals and groups demonstrate higher levels of progress and that these traits could be passed to the next generation. Over time, more evolved groups would come to dominate weaker groups; Spencer described this as the "survival of the fittest." In his view, the moral superiority of the European (and especially British) elite reflected its evolutionary position; and this subsequently explained and legitimated European geographical expansion and subjugation of African, Asian, and Native American human groups.

Malthus and Spencer both influenced the theory of Charles Darwin, who explained that plants, animals, and even humans evolved in a process of competition for survival. Darwin's *The Origin of Species* (published in 1859) asserted that environmental stressors gave a reproductive advantage to individuals and species that adapted best to them; more of their offspring would survive into the next generation. This reproductive advantage (that is, natural selection) will become more pronounced in subsequent generations such that entire species evolve to become progressively more suited to their environment. Darwin's evolutionary theory revolutionized scientific thought and eclipsed human exceptionalist arguments, including those advanced by Malthus. Ironically, Spencer's ideas were so well integrated into Darwinian theory that they are now sometimes referred to as "social Darwinism." **Social Darwinism**, like Malthusian theory, posits that the relationship between humans and their environment has a "natural" evolutionary course but that this course can be overcome through social action, particularly restraint on population growth among those groups considered less evolved. Sociologists have largely rejected both Malthusian theory and Social Darwinism as both racist and empirically indefensible, but their focus on birth rates and environmental change remain central to many contemporary theorists.

MODERNIZATION: THE DEMOGRAPHIC TRANSITION, THE GREEN REVOLUTION, AND NEO-MALTHUSIANISM

Following two world wars and the decline of the European global empires, Malthusian and social Darwinist thought reemerged in modernization theory, at least inasmuch as population policies assumed a connection between uncontrolled birth rates and food production. **Modernization theory** attempted to explain global inequality as a result of different levels of economic and cultural progress rather than as a set of innate, inherited, or moral characteristics. European domination could be explained because Africans, Asians, and Native Americans did not have the science, technology, or economic knowledge of Europeans. In a postcolonial context, European and North American knowledge would be shared with "less developed countries" in order to shepherd them into a more rationalized modernity. In terms of population dynamics, two particular elements of modernization theory stand out: the extension of modern agriculture known as the "green revolution" and the emphasis on birth control, particularly in order to achieve the so-called demographic transition. Modernization theory has been—like Malthusian ideas described above—widely criticized for its underlying biased assumption that the United States and other Western social and economic systems represent an ideal toward which other societies will eventually evolve (or fail to survive). Even so, this theory is echoed in environmental theories that rely on market-based and growth-oriented solutions, such as ecological modernization.

The **green revolution** refers to a series of technological innovations to the production of food crops that were designed to increase productivity; more food could support more people. In general, these technologies reflected the system of agriculture that had been most productive in North America, particularly systems that produced single crops (*monocropping*). The green revolution introduced and/or expanded the use of mechanized tools (for example, irrigation, tractors, threshers), chemical fertilizers, and chemical pesticides in all regions of the globe. Another central technology for the green revolution was the development and introduction of high-yield varieties (HYVs) of rice, corn (maize), wheat, and other staple crops. HYVs typically produced more edible grain, while allowing plants to grow faster in more marginal environments and better withstand the use of chemical fertilizers and pesticides. Agricultural scientists used advanced genetics and biotechnology to create HYV crops in international laboratories, such as the International Maize and Wheat Improvement Center in Mexico and the International Rice Research Institute in the Philippines. Green revolution technologies greatly increased food production worldwide; for example, world rice production more than tripled from 147 million metric tons in 1961 at the onset of the green revolution to over 728 million metric tons in 2018 (International Rice Research Institute 2019).

Unfortunately, the green revolution created additional and distinctly modern problems (see Lesson 12). Monocrop systems, especially HYVs, typically required higher levels of chemical input (fertilizers and pesticides) than traditional agriculture. Consequently, world fertilizer consumption grew faster than crop production: from 31 million tons in 1961 to over 267 million tons in 2018. Chemical additions to agricultural crops have since been linked to salinization and a decrease in biodiversity among beneficial species and in neighboring nonagricultural lands. The high water demands of mechanized, industrial agriculture have also led to an extension of irrigation systems that has significantly and negatively altered freshwater resources, most dramatically in central Asia's Aral Sea, which has lost more than half of its volume and geographical area since the 1960s. Green revolution technologies raised the cost of production substantially by requiring the purchase of HYV seeds (which were often infertile, so seeds had to be purchased each season), chemical inputs, farm machinery, and irrigated water. The increased cost of production meant that over the long term, the green revolution has favored larger and more capitalist producers over smaller ones, and small producers have been progressively squeezed out of production of basic grains. Moreover, HYVs are typically grown in fields of single crops at a scale appropriate for mechanized agriculture, as opposed to traditional agriculture, which was tended by human workers and contained a greater variety of plant species, including nonfood species used for livestock or fiber. These changes led to massive displacement of the rural labor force and nutritional deficiencies for many small farmers in countries as different as Mexico and India. Unable to compete in agriculture, many of these small producers and agricultural workers have relocated to cities, which have expanded spectacularly since the 1950s in all regions of the globe.

While the green revolution unquestionably increased food production (albeit with social and environmental costs), advocates of modernization also held that a modern society would have low birth and death rates and thus low population growth rates. A **demographic transition** would occur when low growth rates were achieved through controlled fertility and low death rates were achieved through modern healthcare and sanitation. According to this model, in premodern societies, birth and death rates were both high; but population growth remained small because the deaths more or less cancelled out the births. However, as sanitation, nutrition, and healthcare improved with modernization, life expectancies increased, and death rates declined (especially infant mortality rates). Because of the cultural lag following technological change, birth rates remain high and population growth increases dramatically. Only when family planning norms adjust downward to account for longer life expectancies and higher survival rates among children will population growth slow and stabilize, indicating that a demographic transition to a modern society has occurred.

The demographic transition model is based on the historical experience of European and North American societies but has been expanded to include Asian nations such as Japan, South Korea, and Taiwan. Less developed nations in Asia, Africa, and the Americas did see their death rates decline significantly in the postcolonial period, while their birth rates remained at traditionally high levels. Consequently, population growth in less developed regions of the world expanded dramatically in the latter half of the 20th century: Africa's population more than quadrupled in these 50 years, Latin America's more than tripled, while Asia's and Oceania's more than doubled (see Table 8-1). Even regions where the demographic transition had allegedly occurred increased their population, with North America nearly doubling its population and Europe adding a third of its population. Note, however, that these are raw population figures and do not distinguish between births and increases due to immigration, which accounts for significant proportions of the increases in both Western Europe and North America. Rates of growth have slowed in all regions, but total population continues to increase. Slowing growth is not expected to reverse global population growth for quite some time, and most analysts don't think this reverse will occur until the world population reaches somewhere between 9 and 12 billion.

Table 8–1 Population and Population Growth in Selected Regions, 1950–2015

	Population 1950 (millions)	Population 1980 (millions)	Population 2015 (millions)	Percent Change
Africa	250	483	1,182	473%
Asia	1,403	2,638	4,433	316%
Europe	547	693	743	136%
Latin America and the Caribbean	167	362	624	374%
North America	172	255	357	208%
Oceania	13	23	40	308%

Source: United Nations, Department of Economic and Social Affairs, Population Division (2019). World Population Prospects 2019; custom data acquired via website.

Population pyramids are often used to display the explosive population growth that occurs before a demographic transition. These graphs present national populations by age and sex (that is, the age and sex structures of the population) as a means for distinguishing between countries that have already made the demographic transition and those that have not. Figure 8-1

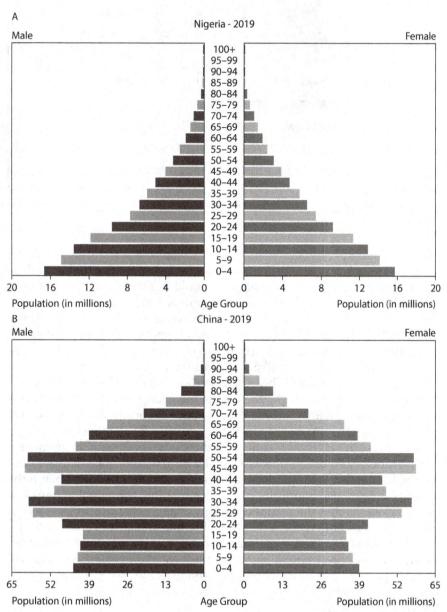

Figure 8-1 A–C Population pyramids for Nigeria **(A)**, China **(B)**, and Italy **(C)**
Source: US Census Bureau

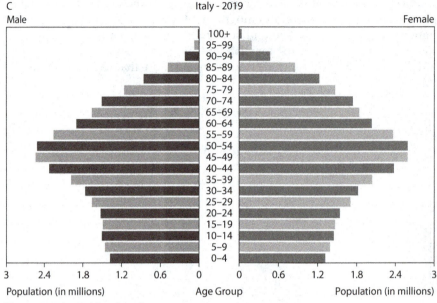

Figure 8-1 A–C *(Continued)*

depicts population pyramids for Nigeria, China, and Italy to highlight these different stages. Nigeria's population pyramid in 2019 looks like a pyramid, in which the largest categories of the population are children (0–14 years); this portends a future baby boom as these young people enter their prime childbearing years (15–29). In contrast, China's population pyramid displays a population evidently in the early stages of a demographic transition. The top half of this graph looks like a pyramid, with the largest proportion of people past their prime childbearing years (ages 45–55). However, the graph tapers in age categories below these ages, indicating that people are having fewer children, with a "echo boom" or "boomlet" from 25–35, likely the children of the larger cohort 20 years older. Notably this boomlet has not yet produced an echo of its own—although there is an increase in the number of zero-to-nine-year-olds, but this is a smaller echo than the one that preceded it—suggesting that young Chinese adults are controlling more of their fertility and/or delaying childbirth—both signs that the demographic transition has occurred. Finally, the pyramid for Italy exhibits characteristics of a population that has undergone a demographic transition, as evidenced by the relatively equal distribution among age categories. In fact, Italy's age structure reveals an aging population, with almost equal proportions of older and younger people—this is sometimes referred to as the "second demographic transition" whereby deaths outpace natural increase (births), and the population begins to shrink.

Because rates of growth remain highest in the poorest regions of the world, neo-Malthusian arguments emerged in the late 1960s calling for control of population and conservation of resources. Paul Ehrlich's *The Population Bomb* (1968) attempted to avoid the elitist trappings of Malthus by proposing an equation that measured environmental impact through a combination of population, affluence, and technology ($I = P \times A \times T$). Population (P) reflects the number of people, affluence (A) indicates the level of consumption by those people, and technology (T) reflects the type of technology used by those people. Environmental impact (I) thus varies not only by raw numbers of people but also by their consumption and waste patterns, sometimes now measured as their "**ecological footprint**," or the amount of land necessary to sustain consumption and absorb wastes. Based on higher consumption levels and use of more environmentally damaging technologies, the average North American individual is estimated to have over seven times the ecological impact of a Nigerian (see Table 8-2). Neo-Malthusians have also expanded on Malthus' attention to food supply to include references to the carrying capacity of a geographical unit (for example, an ecosystem, a nation, or the entire planet). The **carrying capacity** represents the total population of any given species (for example, humans) that can be supported in that geographical unit without permanently damaging the ecological systems that support that species. Damages come from extraction of resources from well as pollution added to that geographical unit. Neo-Malthusians generally predict that unless changes are made in terms of all components of the $I = P \times A \times T$ equation, the carrying capacity of the planet will be reached and famine, disease, war, and, at worst, complete global ecosystemic collapse will follow.

Responding to these concerns, population policy became an integral part of most nations' development plans. China has been widely criticized for its one-child policy for encouraging sex-selective abortions and female infanticide; but China's population growth rate has dropped significantly, from 1.9% annually in 1955 to 0.4% in 2018, despite the formal end of the one-child policy in 2015 (see Table 8-3; also review the age structure in Figure 8-1B). Unable to institute a policy like China's, India sent mobile sterilization teams into its rural areas to reduce its population growth rate, although these programs have also been criticized for sterilizing men and women based on quotas rather than the actual wishes of the people being sterilized. Funding from European and North American sources allowed for greater distribution of birth control and family planning technologies to developing countries in the 1960s and 1970s; but it came under increasing pressure from parties as

Table 8–2 Ecological Footprints (hectares [ha] per person) for selected countries

United States	8.1 ha
Italy	4.4 ha
China	3.6 ha
El Salvador	2.1 ha
Nigeria	1.1 ha

Source: Global Footprint Network (2019).

Table 8-3 Annual Population Growth Rates (percentages), 1955–2015 (selected countries)

	1955	1965	1975	1985	1995	2005	2015
China	1.9	2.1	2.2	1.4	1.1	0.7	0.5
India	2.0	2.3	2.2	2.1	1.9	1.6	1.2
Kenya	2.8	3.2	3.6	3.8	3.0	2.2	1.9
Mexico	2.7	3.1	3.2	2.2	1.9	1.3	1.2
United States	1.6	1.4	0.9	1.0	1.1	1.0	0.8
Italy	0.6	0.8	0.6	0.1	0.2	0.1	0.3

Source: United Nations Statistics Division (2019).

disparate as the Roman Catholic Church, the US government, and Muslim clerics, who argued against women's access to birth control and abortion. Even this debate could not stifle the excitement surrounding the United Nations Population and Development Conference in Cairo in 1994, where the links between controlling population growth and sustainable development were made explicit (see Lesson 20). In addition to their focus on population control, the UN's Decade of the Woman, from 1985 to 1995, highlighted women's education, economic security, and health as a means for reducing birth and infant mortality rates. Women in Development (WID) programs rely on the assumption that women who have opportunities outside of motherhood and who can depend on the survival of their children will have fewer children. Whether due to this global effort or to other changes in the global social system, population growth rates have slowed somewhat since the 1980s (see Table 8-3).

POPULATION AS A STRAW DOLL: MARX, FAMINE, AND XENOPHOBIA

Karl Marx called Malthus' 1798 *Essay* a "lampoon" that was popularized entirely because it legitimated the partisan interests of the English elite. Apart from this ideological component, Malthus was criticized by contemporaries and later social theorists for methodological weaknesses—notably his assumption of linear, arithmetic growth rates in food production, which apparently had no empirical foundation and was rendered inaccurate by the green revolution. Likewise, modernization theories involving food production and population dynamics have shown empirical and ideological weaknesses.

The main critiques of Malthusian, neo-Malthusian, and modernization theories about population growth point to the lack of discussion about the distribution of people and resources. A neo-Marxist critique of Malthus has been cogently and convincingly argued elsewhere by John Bellamy Foster. Foster has also drawn from Marx's work to call attention to the importance of population in terms of concentration in cities, where people have become dependent on industrial agriculture to produce food, and organic waste is disposed in landfills instead of returned to agriculture. The **"metabolic rift"** that has developed between human food production and waste has over-burdened rural natural systems by irrigation, fertilizer, and pesticide con-tamination and created pollution and health risks in urban areas (Lesson 2). Given the rural population displacement and urban growth associated with the green revolution, this metabolic rift has created massive pollution prob-lems in all regions of the world.

Critics also point to the lack of distributive concerns by neo-Malthusians. Responding directly to the assumptions of modernization theory, Amartya Sen's life work has sought to emphasize how the famines and poverty in places like sub-Saharan Africa and South Asia reflect the inhumane distri-bution of resources rather than any absolute shortage of food. Sen describes a world where the powerful use food as a weapon and famines reveal more about local and global inequalities than about food production. In contem-porary times, the persistent violence in the Sudan has forced hundreds of thousands (if not millions) of small farmers to abandon their agricultural land and flee to refugee camps. Stripped of their ability to produce their own food, these refugees rely on food aid shipments. However, the delivery of these shipments is controlled by warlords who demand loyalty from the refugees and camp personnel. Another powerful example of the politics of famine can be seen in Yemen, where the United Nations declared a famine in 2018, affecting 10 million people or more. The United Nations' World Food Programme claimed to have stored enough grain in its Red Sea port facilities to feed 3.7 million people for one month, but they were prevented from ac-cessing and distributing that grain for months due to "security concerns" by Houthi rebels. These examples demonstrate Sen's key concern that famines represent less of a shortage of food—or, as neo-Malthusians may suggest, population exceeding its ecological carrying capacity—than a manifestation of vast power differences between groups of people. When people interpret famines as examples of a population exceeding its carrying capacity, they ignore the human agents that cause famines and blame the victims for their own misery.

Apart from famines, local and global inequality directly determines how much food is available to people. A considerable portion of agricultural land worldwide is dedicated to export and luxury crops rather than basic food crops; often, these crops occupy the most productive agricultural land. I per-sonally have seen extensive tea plantations in Kenya, coconut plantations in northeast Brazil (see Figure 8-2), banana plantations in Guatemala, citrus plantations in Mexico, strawberry plantations in Florida, and artichoke plan-tations in California, while the workers on these plantations may suffer from basic health and malnutrition problems. Moreover, immense rangelands as well as oceans of grain (such as corn in the American Midwest and soy in the Brazilian south) feed cattle instead of humans (see Lesson 4). Only more affluent consumers include meats, especially beef, in their staple diets.

Figure 8-2 Coconut plantation in northeastern Brazil.
Source: Diane C. Bates

Since the 1980s, poorer nations have experienced strong economic pressure to continue to produce luxury and export crops as these represent some of the few means to generate hard currency used to repay national debts and eventually expand local markets, social services, and infrastructure. However, world trade has generally seen a decline in the value of agricultural exports relative to manufacturing and high-tech exports; countries that rely on agricultural production for foreign exchange (like Ecuador, which sells flowers and bananas) guarantee themselves a subordinate position in the global hierarchy.

A focus on population growth in the Global South may also reflect social fears in the Global North more than real population concerns. Increased immigration from the Global South to the Global North has contributed to xenophobic, ideological beliefs about population growth in poorer countries, particularly where immigrant newcomers are socially distant from natives, as with northern Africans in the Paris suburbs, Latin Americans in the US border states, South Asians in the north of England, and Asians in Australia. Workers in the Global South (agricultural and otherwise) are aware of the limits to advancement in their local economies and increasingly migrate to North America, Europe, East Asia, and the Middle East in search of better-paid work. This process of migration, in fact, has contributed greatly to the population growth rates in the Global North, where some countries (such as Germany and Italy) would register negative population growth rates were it not for immigration. Regardless of the relative size of these groups and the economic importance of immigrants in their host countries, many see the influx of newcomers as a population "problem" couched in environmental language as strain on local resources in receiving countries and an effect of "overpopulation" in sending countries. Nativism and xenophobia have bubbled up all over the Global North, making immigrants a vulnerable sub-population in environmental discussions, regardless of legal status. Sociologists Lisa Sun-Hee Park and David Naguib Pellow examine this process of scapegoating immigrants for environmental problems in detail in their case study of Aspen, Colorado. Wealthy Aspenites passed local ordinances against immigration from Latin America and designed to make it more difficult for low-income migrants to live in or near Aspen, with the logic that increased immigration threatened the regional environment. Without reflecting on how their own consumption of extravagant second homes and recreational skiing have much greater impacts on the environment, Aspenites were able to frame immigrants as the true threat to nature and to link this to national nativist narratives widespread among large North American environmental organizations, many of which were informed by neo-Malthusian ideas about population growth. While Aspen is an extreme example, without attention to the social complexity behind population dynamics indicated earlier in this section, local environmentalists risk reproducing elitist and xenophobic agendas.

ENVIRONMENTAL REFUGEES AND CLIMATE GENTRIFCATION: CASE STUDIES IN DEMOGRAPHY

Even as the slowing of birth rates in many countries may alleviate some concerns about global population growth, demographic change is increasingly a flashpoint in contemporary society and often a key element for understanding environmental controversies. This lesson will close with two examples of environmental controversies that can be best understood with attention to demographic processes. The first involves **environmental refugees** as a component of international migration, while the second explores "climate gentrification" of coastal areas affected by storms.

Environmental Refugees from Central America?

International migration is a feature of modern society, although it has provoked a rise in anti-immigrant sentiment in receiving countries around the globe. A fundamental question for environmental sociologists revolves around how much of this international migration can be attributed to environmental change. People who migrate due to underlying environmental problems are often called "environmental refugees," but this term lacks both legal meaning and analytic complexity. Some people responding to environmental change have a great deal of control over the timing and process of relocation, as well as the choice of destination, while others have very little control over the process of relocation.

In general, the more agency—the capacity to intentionally act—that people have in everyday life, the more agency they will exert over migration decisions. This capacity will be generally less for sudden disasters than for environmental change that unfolds over a longer period of time (Lesson 14). Agency is determined by intersectional social positions that vary dramatically according to local, national, and international stratification systems; but younger, relatively affluent, unencumbered, skilled workers who can draw on individual or group-held resources and social networks typically enjoy higher levels of agency in migration. Environmental migrants with relatively high levels of agency are difficult to distinguish from other types of migrants; and in the absence of an international legal definition of "environmental refugees," international environmental migrants are often treated as voluntary migrants, who are most frequently motivated to move by the prospect of improving their economic situation. It is particularly difficult to distinguish environmental from economic migrants for people facing long-term environmental decline in their place of origin, as those long-term declines often directly impact local economic opportunities; and so environmental migrants may—at the same time—also be economic migrants.

As a current example, consider the so-called Northern Triangle of Central America, comprised of the nations of Guatemala, El Salvador, and Honduras. El Salvador appears to be undergoing a demographic transition, with crude birth rates dropping for the last two decades and a growth rate of only 1.0 percent in 2018 (see Figure 8-3, panel A). Honduras, and especially

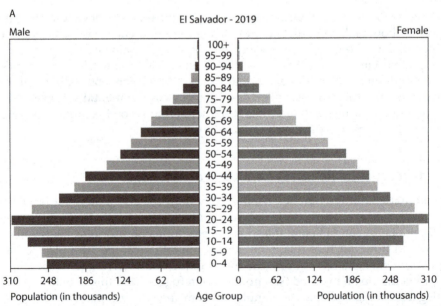

Figure 8-3 A–C Population pyramids for El Salvador **(A)**, Guatemala **(B)**, and Honduras **(C)**

Source: US Census Bureau

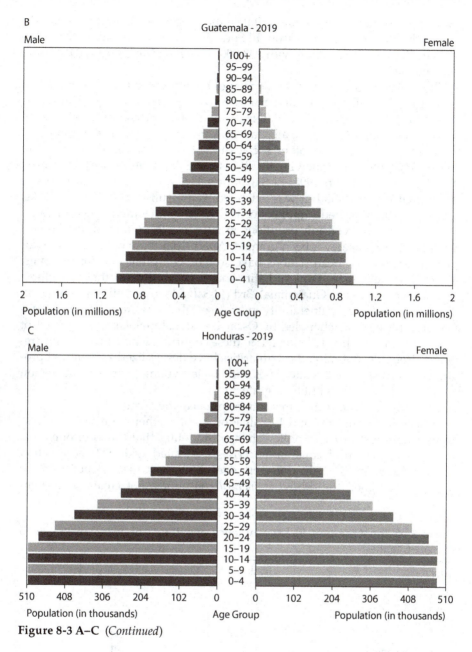

Figure 8-3 A–C (*Continued*)

Guatemala, continue to have growing populations, although these growth rates appear to be slowing, particularly in Honduras (Figure 8-3, panels B and C). Emigration from all three countries has increased in the past 10 years, primarily as a result of civil disruptions that have led to widespread feelings of social insecurity. Much of this emigration has led migrants from the

Northern Triangle to the United States: the Migration Policy Institute estimates that 188,000 migrants from El Salvador entered the United States between 2010 and 2017, along with 133,000 from Honduras and 128,000 from Guatemala.

But is this migration also a reflection of environmental change in Central America? Officially, the United States recognized environmental migrants from Central America through its Temporary Protection Status (TPS) program, which was created in 1990 to alleviate humanitarian concerns that can result from environmental and other social disruptions. Honduran migrants received TPS protection following the devastating floods and landslides caused by Hurricane Mitch in 1998; El Salvador's TPS was originally in response to its civil war in 1990 but was extended as a result of a 2001 earthquake. Guatemala has repeatedly applied for TPS designation—following hurricanes in 2005 and 2008, volcanic eruptions in 2010 and 2018, and an earthquake in 2012—but it has never been granted. Apart from these discrete events for which Central American nations have sought TPS protection for migrants, the CAF Development Bank of Latin America (2014) found that these three countries ranked 2nd (Guatemala), 3rd (El Salvador), and 4th (Honduras) in their climate change vulnerability index (see Table 8-4). According to a team of Costa Rican researchers led by Oscar David Calvo-Solano, the impact of climate change is already being felt in these countries, where increasingly frequent droughts and rainfall irregularities have destabilized agricultural production at least since the late 1990s and has left young people in this region with few other options but to migrate.

In 2018, the Trump Administration initiated the termination of the TPS programs for Honduras and El Salvador, among other countries. The Administration justified this policy change by noting that the environmental disruptions that the humanitarian crises associated with TPS designation for Honduras and El Salvador were over. Moreover, they argued that the TPS was designed to address *temporary* conditions, not create permanent

Table 8–4 Top Countries in Latin America and the Caribbean Vulnerable to Climate Change

Country	Rank	Climate Vulnerability Index Score
Haiti	1	0.58
Guatemala	2	0.75
El Salvador	3	0.79
Honduras	4	0.92
Dominican Republic	5	1.01
Nicaragua	6	1.19
Jamaica	7	1.50
Paraguay	8	1.58
Belize	9	2.25
Bolivia	10	2.48

Source: CAF Development Bank of Latin America (2014).

migration streams. This decision, along with chronic poverty and deepening civil destabilization, appears to have contributed to a rapid increase in Central American migration to the United States: official apprehensions on the Southwest border rose from 51,006 in October 2018 to 92,607 in March 2019, with more non-Mexicans (244,322) than Mexicans (155,452) apprehended at the US–Mexico border in 2018.

Are these environmental refugees? There is ample empirical evidence to indicate that the Central American agricultural economy has destabilized, and there is no doubt that the region has been hit by a number of very strong hurricanes and geological events. These have undoubtedly contributed to the growing number of people emigrating from the Northern Triangle. These countries also face high levels of civil violence and instability, which are undoubtedly exacerbated by internal migration also linked to environmental disruption. At the same time, available jobs, social ties, and the institutionalization of migration have contributed to increased migration to the United States from each of these countries over time. The intricate combination of environmental, economic, social, and institutional explanations for migration from Central America means that, in practice, "environmental refugees" may be virtually indistinguishable from other types of migrants. This is particularly salient in the Central American countries since the change in the environment to which migrants respond is linked to the declining agricultural sector. Apart from climate change, degraded land, low and unstable prices for agricultural commodities, and landlessness make rural occupations less attractive to young people, particularly when facing economic, political, or social disruptions in their home communities.

The case study of Central American environmental refugees illustrates the complexity of teasing out the causes of migration, particularly distinguishing between economic and environmental reasons why people migrate. Most will not meet the legal definition of political refugees (who must demonstrate a fear of persecution in their home countries) and will thus be subject to restrictions for voluntary, economically motivated immigrants by many receiving countries, including the United States. In such a way, environmental refugees are rendered invisible in larger understandings of global environmental change, even while depriving this vulnerable population from international protections afforded other types of refugees.

Climate Gentrification on the Jersey Shore?

This case study uses a local example to explore population change and how it interacts with environmental change to demonstrate how demographic analysis can be linked to local controversies regarding environmental justice. Environmental justice is explored in other lessons of this collection (Lesson 10 especially), but the analysis of environmental justice almost always has a demographic component because it is so often linked to which people live in which place. The environmental justice literature has clearly established that industrial zones contain more environmental contaminants, and that these same areas house poor communities, particularly those with concentrated communities of color. This literature also indicates that time order is not unidirectional. In some cases, industrial sites lower real estate values such that they attract low-income housing and the residents who have no other options in the housing market. In other cases, industrial facilities deliberately target poor communities of color because of their real or perceived limited social and political power to stop them. Environmental justice research thus must almost always begin with a demographic analysis of which social groups live in the affected community.

US cities have seen a renaissance in the last three decades, despite the "crash" in real estate early in the 21st century, that has led to a qualitative transformation of some urban neighborhoods. Much of this renaissance is called "gentrification," a politically loaded term used to describe local demographic change, when the new population is of a higher socioeconomic status (on average) that the residents who originally occupied the area. People who study neighborhood change use a variety of variables to measure the process of gentrification; but it is observed by using easily accessible measures such as income, education, race, and type of household. Gentrification is distinguished by an influx of wealthier, more educated, whiter residents who are more likely to live in smaller, often non-family households. As more affluent residents move into neighborhoods, property values and rents rise, making these neighborhoods less affordable for lower-income resident populations. Thus, gentrification is often associated with displacement of the original residents, who must search in other, less desirable neighborhoods for affordable housing.

Gentrification can be displayed with new mapping technologies, such as the Institute of Metropolitan Opportunity's national map of Low Income Displacement and Concentration that colors areas that have lost low-income residents (likely due to gentrification) and those that have gained low-income residents (that is, concentration of poverty). Regional maps are better able to demonstrate gentrification with more detail. For example, the City of Los Angeles' Index of Neighborhood Change (Figure 8-4) uses the following items to indicate neighborhood change: percentage change in proportion of high- versus low-income tax filers; percent change in adults with bachelor's degrees; percent change in white, non-Hispanic populations; percent change in median household income; percent change in median gross rent; and percent change in average household size determined with zip codes have gentrified since 2000. Their online map clearly identifies the gentrification in downtown neighborhoods, with gentrification radiating north and northeast. Similar gentrification maps—often online and interactive—exist for many cities around the United States.

While the gentrification literature has mainly focused on affordable housing and social justice in cities, there is a growing literature on connections between storm damage and gentrification. Pais and Elliot (2008) introduced the concept of a "recovery machine" whereby the destruction caused by major hurricanes empowered coalitions to promote demographic and

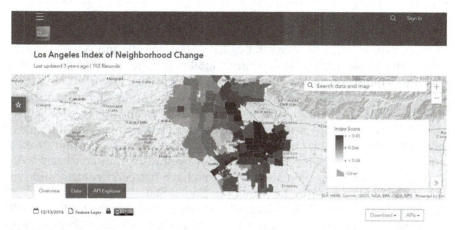

Figure 8-4
Source: © Copyright 2018 City of Los Angeles

economic growth in the wake of the destruction. Their study suggests that storms create an opportunity to foster new economic activity and attract new, more affluent residents in areas with valuable amenities like waterfront access. Recovery machines allow pro-growth advocates to capture the value of natural amenities, even while setting up the likelihood that future storms will be more expensive, which may also create more *social* costs because more affluent residents may have greater ability to mobilize public resources to subsidize future storm losses. This early research was recently confirmed in Fuseel et al.'s study of storms from 1980 to 2012 that found while storms had limited impact in US areas with low population growth, those areas that were growing rapidly before the hurricane could use storm recovery to hasten the transformation of desirable but risk-prone areas into more dense and more affluent residential areas. This change in who lives in high-growth recovery zones resembles what Keenan, Hill, and Gumber call **climate gentrification** in Miami-Dade County, where the additional costs of living near natural hazards (for example, meeting building codes, higher hazard insurance) prices previous residents out of living in areas that have already or could experience storm damage. Climate gentrification also refers to how more affluent people come to occupy places in potentially risky locations that have some protection against hazards, such as higher ground in flood-prone areas.

This process of climate gentrification can be seen on the Jersey Shore, following the damage associated with 2012's Superstorm Sandy (see Bates, 2016, for details about this storm's impact). This case study highlights three small census tracts in and around Asbury Park, New Jersey, in order to demonstrate the very local nature of demographic change. Census tracts are subdivisions within counties created for each decennial census that encompass about 4,000 people (1,600 housing units); this is the smallest geographic unit for which most recent Census and American Community Survey (ACS) data are available. The three census tracts studied here include two on the Asbury Park waterfront (hereafter called Asbury North and Asbury South, containing about half of Asbury Park's total population) and Ocean Grove, the adjacent, oceanfront neighborhood of Neptune Township. Between 2000 and 2010, all three of these census tracts showed signs of gentrification (see Table 8-5), but this was most evident in Ocean Grove. After Sandy, Asbury Park gentrified more rapidly. Somewhat unique to coastal regions, however, is the transition from occupied housing to seasonal (second) homes and the decline of year-round renters. This case study is thus consistent with other studies that demonstrate that storms have hastened gentrification in already growing coastal areas within the United States.

Separated by a small tidal lake, Ocean Grove and Asbury Park were all undergoing gentrification before Sandy hit. In 2000, all three census tracts contained residents whose incomes and home values were well below state averages, although Ocean Grove was better off (higher median income, higher proportion of owner-occupied houses, higher median value of owner-occupied houses) than either waterfront tract in Asbury Park (see Table 8-5). Even so, between 2000 and 2010, all three tracts got more affluent, with the greatest change being in the poorest of the three tracts. Median household income in Ocean Grove increased nearly 20 percent, while median incomes increased over 25 percent in Asbury North and over 40 percent Asbury South. The percentage of owner-occupied homes also increased in each census tract, but it more than doubled (from 6.8 percent to 13.9 percent) in Asbury South. Most tellingly, the value of owner-occupied homes skyrocketed—despite the

Table 8–5 Demographic Profile of Asbury Park Waterfront South and North and Ocean Grove, NJ

	Asbury Park – South			Asbury Park – North			Ocean Grove		
	2000	2010	2017	2000	2010	2017	2000	2010	2017
Total Population	5,430	4,149	4,684	3,458	3,466	2,969	4,263	3,622	2,943
Percent White	25.1	26.6	47.1	53.0	55.7	68.2	88.2	96.3	95.2
Med. Income (Household)	21,845	31,071	39,509	26,299	33,300	49,292	31,991	37,960	60,000
Md. Income as % of State Median	39.61	44.51	51.68	47.69	47.70	64.48	58.01	54.38	78.49
Percent Owner Occupied	6.8	13.9	11.7	14.4	17.2	18.3	42.9	47.7	50.2
Median Value Owner Occupied	127,100	381,700	462,800	84,500	390,000	339,700	149,200	380,300	482,400
Median Value as % of State Median	74.4	106.9	144.1	49.5	109.2	105.8	87.4	106.5	150.2

Source: US Census Bureau, Census 2000; 2010 Census; American Community Survey 2017 (5-year estimates).

national shock to the real estate market beginning in 2007. In Ocean Grove, median values more than doubled from $149,200 to $380,300; in Asbury South, median home values tripled from $127,100 to $381,700, and in Asbury North, median home values in 2010 were more than four and a half times higher than they were in 2000, rising from $84,500 to $390,000. While all three tracts had home values well below state averages in 2000, by the decade's end, all three exceeded the state median values.

Increasing property values is a telltale sign of gentrification, but it is accompanied by demographic changes in the people who occupy those homes. The people who were moving into Asbury Park and Ocean Grove were not just more affluent, but they were more likely to be white. In 2010, all three tracts had higher proportions of whites than they had in 2000, although Asbury South remained 73.4 percent non-white in 2010 and Asbury North remained 44.3 percent non-white, with very modest increases in white populations during the decade (1.5 percent and 2.7 percent in the South and North tracts, respectively). Having already started this time period with a predominantly white population (88.2 percent), Ocean Grove was almost exclusively white (96.3 percent) by 2010—in stark contrast with Neptune Township, whose white population decreased from 55.9 percent to 53.2 percent white from 2000 to 2010; and with New Jersey as a whole, whose white population dropped from 72.6 percent to 68.6 percent. Prior to Sandy, beachfront Ocean Grove became an increasingly segregated white community, when compared to both the municipality and state in which it was located. In contrast, even though the value of Asbury Park's real estate had increased, the racial composition of its population had not changed much in the decade before Sandy.

Did Sandy change the processes of gentrification that were already underway in Asbury Park and Ocean Grove? Asbury Park's oceanfront is a commercial boardwalk that continues into a downtown that reaches the northern shore of Wesley Lake, so relatively few homes in Asbury Park were affected by storm surge and flooding during Sandy. More damage was found in Ocean Grove, where homes line the beach and lake shore, and in Asbury North, where homes border Deal Lake. At least in part due to this storm damage, Ocean Grove and Asbury North had smaller populations and fewer housing units available in 2017 than in 2010, although in both tracts, homes were more likely to be owner-occupied in 2017 than they were in 2010. In Asbury South, new condominium and luxury apartments built after Sandy increased the number of available housing units, accounting for the decline in percentage of owner-occupied homes as well as the increase in population from 4,149 in 2010 to 4,684 in 2017 (a 13 percent increase). In sum, in the period after Sandy, there was less housing available in the areas where there was more storm exposure and more housing in areas that were protected from flooding, but this housing was considerably more expensive than it had been in 2010.

The combination of Sandy and gentrification not only affected the number of housing units, but it is also important to consider how housing units are used. Prior to 2010, both Asbury Park and Ocean Grove provided pre-dominantly affordable rental properties (again, see Table 8-5). The number and proportion of homes occupied by renters has steadily declined in all three tracts, even as gross rents have increased, as the stock of rental units transitioned from older, low-rent apartments into owner-occupied homes and new luxury apartments. The decline in available affordable rental prop-erties is aggravated by the fact that the number of seasonal housing units (summer homes) has *increased* in all three tracts—even in the two tracts where the number of units *decreased* after Sandy. Proportionately, this means that in Ocean Grove, 37 percent of all housing units were seasonal in 2017 (compared with 31 percent in 2010 and 29 percent in 2000), while Asbury's combined oceanfront tracts are now more than 17 percent seasonal, com-pared with 14 percent in 2010 and less than 7 percent in 2000. These second homes have removed nearly 2,000 units from the year-round market—almost certainly displacing lower-income residents.

Not surprisingly, the changes in housing have been accompanied by changes in the composition of the people who live in these communities after Sandy. Given that Ocean Grove was nearly exclusively white in 2010, it is not surprising to learn that it remains mostly white in 2017 (although marginally a little less white, dropping to 95.2 percent). Asbury Park, how-ever, has undergone a rapid demographic change, with Asbury North, just over half white in 2010 (55.7 percent), becoming more than two-thirds white (68.2 percent), and Asbury South changing from about a quarter white (26.6 percent) in 2010 to nearly half white (47.1 percent) in 2017. In short, while Asbury Park's oceanfront tracts had been an affordable and diverse area on the Jersey Shore before Sandy, by 2017, they were more expensive on average than other places in the state, and increasingly white.

But is this climate gentrification or is this just gentrification? As Fuseel and her colleagues found in other high growth regions that experienced major storms, demographic change seems to have intensified in this rapidly chang-ing region of the Shore, especially in Asbury Park. This conclusion is also supported in a comparison with other storm-damaged parts of the Shore that were not experiencing gentrification. For example, Point Pleasant Beach, just 10 miles south of Asbury Park, suffered substantially greater storm damage; but its population remained fairly constant between 2000 to 2017 in terms of racial composition, and the proportion of second homes there has barely increased.

There is also evidence of an active recovery machine actively seeking out public money to facilitate changes in Asbury Park that were happening anyway. For the region's growth coalition, Sandy provided a unique oppor-tunity to hasten urban transformations that were already underway and to tap into new public funding to do so. According to the NJ Sandy Transpar-ency Funds Tracker, the City of Asbury Park has received over $16 million in storm-related funds, while the much larger Neptune Township has received over $30 million. These are public funds that would not have been avail-able to these gentrifying communities if Sandy had not hit the Jersey Shore.

These funds help develop new facilities and a storm mitigation infrastructure that will protect the property and lives of increasingly affluent residents and second-home owners. These public and private investments will encourage further gentrification and will lead to increasing concentration of affluent whites and expensive property in oceanfront areas, while less affluent populations are pushed away from the coast.

CONCLUSION

Central American migrants and new residents of the Jersey Shore represents a tiny fraction of the world's growing human population, but sociologists must consider population dynamics and the demographic profiles of communities, whether considering environmental issues on a local, national, or global scale. How many people live in an area, their characteristics, and how that population changes in time determine how they interact with their environment. We don't yet understand the full implications of nearly 8 billion people for the global ecosystem; but with more people, rising levels of consumption, and more damaging technologies, global environmental problems such as climate change and atmospheric ozone thinning point toward more serious concerns for the future. Moreover, the uneven distribution of resources, ranging from food to stop famines to political power to compel remediation of contaminated sites or to mitigate against climate-related hazards, underscores the importance of understanding not just population growth but contextualized demography as an element in environmental sociology.

SOURCES

Bates, Diane C. 2016. *Superstorm Sandy: The Inevitable Destruction and Reconstruction of the Jersey Shore*. New Brunswick, NJ: Rutgers University Press.

CAF Development Bank of Latin America. 2014. *Vulnerability index to climate change in the Latin American and Caribbean Region*. Caracas: CAF. http://scioteca.caf.com/handle/123456789/509

Calvo-Solano, Oscar David, Luis Quesada-Hernández, Hugo Hidalgo, and Yosef Gotlieb. 2018. "Impact de las Sequías en el Sector Agropecuario del Corredor Seco Centroamericano." *Agronomía Mesoamericana* 29 (3): 695–709.

Darwin, Charles. (1859) 1909. *The Origin of Species*. New York: P. F. Collier and Son.

Ehrlich, Paul R. 1968. *The Population Bomb*. New York: Ballantine Books.

Food and Agricultural Organization of the United Nations (FAO). 2017. World Fertilizer Trends and Outlooks to 2020. Rome: FAO 2017. www.fao.org/3/a-i6895e.pdf

Foster, John Bellamy. 2002. *Ecology Against Capitalism*. New York: Monthly Review Press.

Foster, John Bellamy. 1999. "Marx's Theory of the Metabolic Rift: Classical Foundations for Environmental Sociology." *American Journal of Sociology* 105 (2): 366–405.

Fuseel, Elizabeth, Sara R. Curran, Matthew D. Dunbar, Michael A. Babb, Luanne Thompson, and Jacqueline Meijer-Irons. 2017. "Weather-Related Hazards and Population Change: A Study of Hurricanes and Tropical Storms in the United States, 1980-2012." *Annals of the American Academy of Political and Social Science* 669 (1): 146–167.

Global Footprint Network. 2019. "Footprint Calculator." Accessed June 15, 2019. https://www.footprintnetwork.org/resources/footprint-calculator/

International Rice Research Institute. 2019. World Rice Statistics Online Query Facility. Accessed February 27, 2019. (http://ricestat.irri.org:8080/wrsv3/entrypoint.htm).

Keenan, Jesse M., Thomas Hill, and Anurag Gumber. 2018. "Climate Gentrification: From Theory to Empiricism in Miami-Dade, Florida." *Environmental Research Letters* 13 (5). https://iopscience.iop.org/article/10.1088/1748-9326/aabb32

Malthus, T. R. 1914. *An Essay on Population*. New York: E. P. Dutton.

Marx, Karl. 1906. *Capital: A Critique of Political Economy*. New York: Modern Library.

Marx, Karl. 1865. "On Proudhon: Letter to J. B. Schweizer." Accessed February 27, 2020. https://www.marxists.org/archive/marx/works/1865/letters/65_01_24.htm

Pais, Jeremy F. and James R. Elliot. 2008. "Places as Recovery Machines: Vulnerability and Neighborhood Change after Major Hurricanes." *Social Forces* 86 (4): 1415–1453.

Park, Lisa Sun-Hee and David Naguib Pellow. 2011. *The Slums of Aspen: Immigrants Vs. the Environment in America's Eden*. New York: New York University Press.

Sen, Amartya. 1981. *Poverty and Famines: An Essay on Entitlement and Deprivation*. New York: Oxford University Press.

Spencer, Herbert. (1864) 1972. *On Social Evolution: Selected Writings*. Edited by J. D. Y. Peel. Chicago, IL: University of Chicago Press.

United Nations, Department of Economic and Social Affairs, Population Division. 2019. *World Population Prospects 2019*. Accessed June 20, 2019. https://population.un.org/wpp/Download/Standard/Population/

United Nations Statistics Division. 2019. "Demographic Yearbook System." Accessed June 18, 2019. https://unstats.un.org/unsd/demographic-social/products/dyb/

United States Census Bureau. 2019a. "International Data Base: Population Pyramids." Accessed March 5, 2020. https://www.census.gov/data-tools/demo/idb/informationGateway.php

United States Census Bureau. 2019b. "World Population Clock." Accessed March 5, 2020. https://www.census.gov/popclock/world

Vandermeer, John and Ivette Perfecto. 1995. *Breakfast of Biodiversity: The Truth About Rainforest Destruction*. Oakland, CA: Food First Books.

9

Energy, Society, and the Environment

Shannon Elizabeth Bell

The Flamingo hotel and casino on the Las Vegas Strip, Las Vegas, Nevada.
Post your photo on energy, society, and the environment to #TLESenergy
Photo by Ken Gould

> "The essential problem is not just that we are tapping the *wrong* energy sources (though we are), or that we are wasteful and inefficient (though we are), but that we are *overpowered*, and we are *overpowering* nature . . . The only reasonable path forward is to find ways to use *less* energy."
>
> —**Richard Heinberg**, *Energy: Overdevelopment and the Delusion of Endless Growth*, p. 3

What is energy? Energy is not something that we can easily describe or directly observe, but it is central to everything taking place in our natural world. Physicists define energy as "the ability to do work"; and owing to the tremendous technological innovations that our world has seen over the past two centuries (see Lesson 7), humankind has become increasingly successful at using the energy stored in fossil fuels, vegetation, wind, water, and sunlight to "do work" for us. However, many of the energy technologies we use have also come at very serious costs to our environment.

While a sociology of energy was recognized and described more than 35 years ago by Rosa, Machlis, and Keating (1988), it was not until the urgency of climate change became clear that energy became a topic of such critical importance to environmental sociologists: for energy production is the largest contributor to the generation of global warming-causing greenhouse gasses (see Lesson 15). Environmental sociologists ask questions both about how human behavior affects the environment and how the environment affects people and societies. Some questions we might ask about energy include: What are the social, environmental, and public health consequences of energy production? Which communities are most likely to bear the burden of pollution from energy production? Why do some communities protest pollution while others do not? What strategies do corporations involved in the energy sector use to acquire political power? How have some groups successfully fought for cleaner energy solutions in their communities? And what societal changes need to be made in order to reduce the amount of energy we use? As you continue to read, I encourage you to jot down other sociological questions that come to mind.

In this lesson, we will examine the interactions between energy, society, and the environment by first exploring global energy consumption patterns. Then, we will consider the major sources of energy and the social and environmental costs associated with these sources. Finally, we will contemplate the hope for change. A major goal of this chapter is to encourage reflection on the true costs associated with our energy consumption habits. As Butler and Wuerthner (2012) and others have argued, we do not simply have a fossil fuel problem; rather, we have an energy problem. We are an overpowered society, and if serious changes are not made to the energy consumption patterns of all sectors of society, including the industrial sector, transportation sector, residential sector, and commercial sector, we have no hope of halting this runaway train of climate change and environmental health devastation.

ENERGY CONSUMPTION PATTERNS

Over the past two centuries, worldwide energy consumption has risen at an alarming rate. Population growth certainly has a lot to do with this increase in energy consumption; the world's population is about seven times larger than it was right before the Industrial Revolution (see Lesson 8). However, as Butler and Wuerthner (2012) point out, we are not using seven times as much energy as we were 250 years ago—we are using *30 times* as much energy. Even within the past 30 years, the increase in energy use has been staggering:

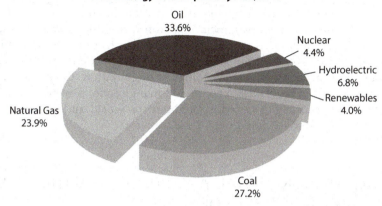

World Energy Consumption by Fuel, 2018

Oil
33.6%

Nuclear
4.4%

Hydroelectric
6.8%

Renewables
4.0%

Natural Gas
23.9%

Coal
27.2%

Figure 9-1

our world has gone from consuming 311 quadrillion BTU of energy in 1988 to 550 quadrillion BTU of energy in 2018 (BP, 2019).

As shown in Figure 9-1, of the energy that was consumed throughout the world in 2018, 84.7 percent was generated from fossil fuels, including oil (33.6 percent), coal (27.2 percent), and natural gas (23.9 percent).

In 2018, the United States consumed 91 quadrillion BTU of energy (BP, 2019), making it the second leading consumer of energy in the world, second only to China, which has more than four times the population of the United States. The United States has 4.3 percent of the world's population but consumes 17 percent of the total energy. Butler and Wuerthner (2012) estimate that on average, each person living in the United States uses the power of approximately 150 "energy slaves," meaning that if all the power that we use were supplied by human labor, it would require 150 people working around the clock every day in order to provide it. Take a moment to consider all of the ways that you use energy in your daily routine. As a student, you probably use a computer on a daily—possibly hourly—basis. Do you have a smartphone? How and where do you wash your clothes? Do you drive a car or ride a bus? Do you ever fly on an airplane to visit family or friends or to go on vacation? How do you keep your food cold? Do you cook your food? Do you turn lights on in your home when it is dark outside? Do you heat your home in the winter? Do you cool it with fans or air conditioning (or both) in the summer? Most Americans are consuming energy—and large amounts of it—throughout most (if not all) hours of the day.

It is also important to note, however, that the residential sector accounts for just 21 *percent* of the energy consumed in the United States. The other 79 percent is consumed by three other sectors: the industrial sector (about 32 percent, including manufacturing, mining, agriculture, and construction);

the transportation sector (about 28 percent, including trucks, planes, cars, buses, motorcycles, barges, ships, boats, and trains); and the commercial/ service sector (about 18 percent, including stores, shopping malls, hospitals, schools, hotels, warehouses, government buildings, restaurants, and offices; US Energy Information Administration [EIA] 2018). As energy production and consumption increase, so do ecological degradation, threats to public health, and losses in biodiversity. In the following sections, we will examine the major sources of energy used throughout the world and the social and environmental costs associated with these sources.

SOCIAL, ENVIRONMENTAL, AND PUBLIC HEALTH COSTS OF THE MAJOR SOURCES OF ENERGY

Oil (Petroleum)

As Butler and Wuerthner (2012) have noted, oil is "the lubricant of modern civilization." It is refined into many different products, such as gasoline, diesel fuel, heating oil, jet fuel, as well as asphalt and road oil. We are dependent on oil, not just for energy production, but also for many of the products we use on a daily basis, like plastics and various chemicals. About 34 percent of world energy consumption is from oil, and 61.5 percent of all the oil used throughout the world is in the transportation sector.

A little more than a decade ago, the media was awash with claims that we would soon reach "peak oil"—the year when the global rate of oil extraction will reach its highest point and then start to decline. However, concern over peak oil has all but disappeared from the media spotlight. Although oil supplies may have declined in conventional geological formations, industry has found new ways to access increasingly remote and what were at one time thought to be unretrievable sources of oil in tar sands, shale oil deposits, and tens of thousands of feet below the ocean floor. As the easy-to-reach oil reserves have become depleted, we have entered what Michael Klare calls "the era of extreme energy." The consequences of this quest for "extreme energy" include a tremendous amount of ecosystem destruction and an increased risk of environmental disasters like the BP *Deepwater Horizon* oil spill of 2010, during which an estimated 210 million gallons of oil gushed from a well on the ocean floor in the Gulf of Mexico and caused far-reaching devastation to sea life, wetlands, and coastal communities.

Whereas the United States has about 4.3 percent of the global population, it is responsible for 20 percent of the world's annual oil consumption. According to the EIA, about 92 percent of the energy used for transportation in the United States comes from oil. The electric car is touted as one major way to reduce our dependence on oil. But where does electricity come from? In the following sections, we will take a closer look at the primary sources of energy used to fuel the electric sector and examine the ecological and public health costs associated with these sources.

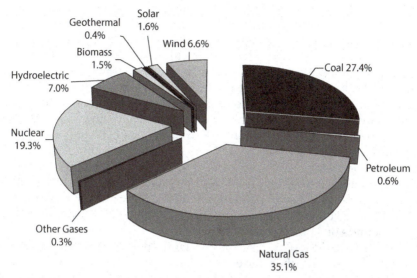

U.S. Net Electricity Generation, 2018

Figure 9-2

Electric Power in the United States

In terms of electricity consumption, the United States ranks number one in the world, at 3,844 billion kilowatt-hours consumed in 2017. Figure 9-2 shows the net electricity generated in the United States in 2018 by energy source. Natural gas provided 35.1 percent of the electricity produced in the United States, followed by coal (27.4 percent), and nuclear (19.3 percent). Renewable energy sources (including hydroelectric, wind, geothermal, biomass, and solar) accounted for 17.1 percent of electricity.

Coal

James Hansen (2012, 61), renowned climate scientist and former director of NASA's Goddard Institute for Space Studies, has called coal "the single greatest threat to civilization and all life on our planet." According to the International Energy Agency (IEA), in 2018 the generation of electricity from coal plants was responsible for 30 percent of energy-related global carbon dioxide emissions, making it the single largest emitter (IEA 2019). Although the demand for coal has declined in Europe and North America in recent years, it has continued to grow in China, India, and some other parts of South and Southeast Asia. This higher demand for coal in Asia has thus far outpaced declines in other parts of the world. In 2018, global demand for coal rose by 0.7 percent (IEA 2019). Coal continues to be the largest source of electricity globally and was the greatest contributor to the growth of energy-related carbon dioxide emissions in 2018.

Coal has a higher carbon content that other fossil fuels; thus, burning coal leads to the emission of more carbon dioxide per unit of electricity generated than any other fossil fuel. Further, the mining and processing of coal typically leads to the release of methane, which is trapped in natural deposits and is 28 to 36 times more potent a greenhouse gas than carbon dioxide over a 100-year time frame (and over a 20-year time frame, methane's heat-trapping ability is 86 times more powerful than carbon dioxide). Thus, coal is a leading (and growing) cause of global climate change. For this reason, James Hansen (2012, 62) asserts that "[a] moratorium on coal-fired power plants is by far the most important action that needs to be pursued" to help mitigate climate change.

In addition to the considerable role that burning coal plays in hastening climate change, it is also responsible for tremendous costs to public health. In 2014 alone, coal-fired power plants emitted 197,286 tons of particulate matter, 22,124 tons of volatile organic compounds (VOCs), 82,400 pounds of lead, 77,108 pounds of arsenic, 3.1 million tons of sulfur dioxide, and 1.5 million tons of nitrous oxides (Physicians for Social Responsibility 2018). According to a study by the EPA, the smokestacks of coal-fired power plants release 67 different toxic air pollutants, 55 of which are known neurotoxins that cause developmental damage to the brains and nervous systems of children and 24 of which are known, probable, or possible human carcinogens. In addition, coal-fired power plants are the largest source of mercury pollution in the nation; such plants emit more than 42 percent of all mercury air pollution (Physicians for Social Responsibility 2018). In December 2011, the EPA passed the Mercury and Air Toxics Standards, which set new federal limits on mercury emissions from existing and future coal-fired power plants. In the years since the new standards were passed, the amount of mercury emitted by coal plants has been reduced drastically. However, in December 2018, the Trump Administration's EPA Administrator, Andrew Wheeler (a former coal industry lobbyist), proposed a reversal of these new standards, claiming that the cost to industry was not worth the benefits to society. In fact, this is just one of many environmental regulations that the Trump Administration has rolled back or is in the process of rolling back since taking office. In June 2019, for instance, this administration also replaced the Obama-era Clean Power Plan—which aimed to reduce carbon dioxide emissions from existing coal and other fossil fuel power plants—with the much weaker Affordable Clean Energy rule. The new rule eliminated the carbon emission limits that the Clean Power Plan set for each state, thereby removing a major incentive to close older, high-emitting coal-fired power plants. In addition to increasing projected carbon dioxide emissions, it is estimated that by 2030, the increase in particulate matter, sulfur dioxide, and nitrogen oxides resulting from the rollback of the Clean Power Plan will lead to an additional 1,630 premature deaths, 120,000 asthma attacks, 140,000 missed school days, and 48,000 lost work days each year.

Does your college or university burn coal on campus? In 2009, more than 60 colleges and universities across the United States operated coal-fired boilers on site to generate heat, hot water, and, in some cases, electricity for the buildings on their campuses. Like many of the commercial coal-fired power plants in the United States, these smaller-scale plants are older facilities that have been **grandfathered** in under Clean Air Act regulations, which means that they are legally emitting large quantities of toxic pollutants that modern power plants are not permitted to release. The Sierra Club and Sierra Student Coalition's joint campaign, "Campuses Beyond Coal" (https://content.sierra-club.org/coal/campuses), has been working with communities and student environmental organizations across the country to retire coal-fired plants and replace them with cleaner energy solutions. Is there a student chapter of the Sierra Student Coalition at your college or university?

While the environmental and public health costs associated with burning coal are immense, the coal industry also causes great ecological and social harm before this fossil fuel is ever burned. Throughout the entire life cycle of coal—including mining, processing, washing, transportation, burning, and waste disposal—workers and local residents are imperiled by industry prac-tices (Bell 2013, 2016). Huge swaths of land are decimated by surface mines in coal-mining areas, leading to disastrous floods and ecosystem destruction. According to a 2009 Geographic Information System (GIS) analysis by Ross Geredien for the Natural Resources Defense Council, more than 1 million acres and 500 mountains in the Central Appalachian region of the United States have been destroyed by **mountaintop removal (MTR) mining**, which is a form of surface mining that blows mountain ranges apart to unearth thin seams of coal for extraction by enormous earth-moving machines called draglines. Public health researchers have conducted numerous studies about the health impacts of living close to MTR mining operations. These studies have found that communities near MTR sites suffer elevated rates of cancer, mortality from chronic cardiovascular disease, and birth defects. In addition, these communities experience greater poverty and mortality disparities and have a poorer health-related quality of life than non-MTR communities.

After coal is mined, it must be crushed and cleaned in processing plants to remove noncombustible materials (like shale, clay, or slate) and sulfur, which is a pollutant. Coal dust from these processing plants covers nearby towns, causing respiratory distress and asthma among local residents and making it impossible to enjoy the outdoors for any length of time. Toxic **slurry** from the "washing" of coal is stored in enormous open impoundments and in under-ground injection sites, sometimes leaching into the aquifer and contaminating well water with toxic metals and chemicals used in the coal-washing pro-cess. (See http://www.WVPhotovoice.org/Big-Coal-River-Problems.html for "photostories" created by women living in a community affected by coal-slurry contamination. These women were part of an eight-month Photovoice project that I conducted in five coal-mining communities).

After the coal is burned, the ash that is left behind, called **coal combustion waste** (CCW), must also be dealt with. CCW contains all of the heavy metals present in coal but in a more concentrated (toxic) form. CCW is most often stored as a liquid in impoundments next to the coal-fired power plants from which it came. These impoundments have been known to fail, like the coal ash disaster that occurred in December 2008 in Kingston, Tennessee, when a dike ruptured, releasing 1.1 billion gallons of toxic waste into the Emory River, contaminating the water and land. Another major coal ash disaster occurred in 2014 in North Carolina, when Duke Energy spilled 39,000 tons of coal ash and 27 million gallons of ash slurry into the Dan River. Although these two events received a great deal of media coverage because of their magnitude, there are also many small-scale CCW releases that happen regularly throughout the United States that are not reported in the news. In fact, a report of the Environmental Integrity Project found that of the 265 coal-fired power plants with monitoring data available, 242 (91 percent) had contaminated the groundwater with unsafe levels of one or more of the toxic pollutants present in coal ash. In 2015, the EPA enacted what is referred to as the "Coal Ash Rule," which was the first federal rule regulating the disposal of coal ash. The Coal Ash Rule limited the amount of wastewater that was allowed to be discharged into waterways, required groundwater monitoring at coal ash impoundments and landfills (and required that those data be made available to the public), and also required that all unlined coal ash disposal sites begin the process of closing in 2018. However, starting in 2018, the Trump Administration's EPA began the process of relaxing and delaying these regulations.

But what about clean coal? "Clean coal" is a term with no clear-cut definition. As Fitzgerald (2012) explains, the concept of "clean coal" first appeared in the 1980s to refer to technologies designed to reduce sulfur dioxide and nitrogen oxide that were implemented in coal-fired power plants built after the passage of the Clean Air Act. Then, in the 2000s, when concerns about climate change were on the rise, the phrase "clean coal" began to be used by industry groups to "brand" **carbon capture and sequestration (CCS)** technologies that were being developed to reduce carbon emissions. In CCS, carbon dioxide waste from power plants and other point sources is captured and then transported to an underground storage site, where it is deposited so it will not enter the atmosphere. Still others within the coal industry use "clean coal" to simply refer to any coal-burning technology that is in any way an improvement over previous technologies. As Goodell (2012, 149) asserts, "'Clean coal' is not an actual invention, a physical thing—it is an advertising slogan. Like 'fat-free doughnuts' or 'interest-free loans,' 'clean coal' is a phrase that embodies the faith that there is an easy answer for every hard question in America today."

Whether it's accurate to call it "clean coal" or not, the possibility that CCS could have a large impact on carbon dioxide emissions is widely contested, and there are numerous concerns about the safety of such technologies. While some small-scale CCS demonstrations have been enacted, even CCS proponents admit that we are likely at least 20 years away from mainstream use of these technologies. Moreover, according to a study out of the Massachusetts Institute of Technology, the efficiency that would be lost from implementing CCS would actually require that 27 percent *more* coal be burned in order to generate the same amount of electricity as a conventional coal plant.

Environmental justice activists (see Lesson 10) fighting irresponsible mining practices in Central Appalachia vehemently assert there can be "no such thing as clean coal." They argue that even if there were a way to sequester most of the carbon dioxide from coal-fired power plants, the coal extraction process, described above, causes so much pollution and harm to coal-mining communities that coal can never truly be "clean." As activist Lorelei Scarboro told me during our interview for my (2013) book, "I believe in 'carbon sequestration': it's *already* sequestered [in the ground], leave it there!"

Natural Gas

While coal-fired power plants have long been the dominant source of electricity globally, natural gas has become competitive with coal over the past decade, particularly in the United States, which has been dubbed the "Saudi Arabia of natural gas." While in 2006 natural gas plants generated just over 20 percent of the electricity produced in the country, in 2018, they produced more than 35 percent of the nation's electricity, surpassing coal, which produced about 27 percent. This growth in natural gas can be attributed to technological advances in gas extraction and a regulatory loophole (dubbed the "Halliburton Loophole") in the Energy Policy Act of 2005 that exempts the natural gas industry from a number of federal environmental laws, including the Safe Drinking Water Act, the Clean Air Act, and the Clean Water Act. These exemptions have made it possible for the industry to use a contentious technology known as **hydraulic fracturing,** or **"fracking,"** in combination with horizontal drilling, to access previously unrecoverable natural gas deposits trapped in shale formations that cover large portions of the United States. Hydraulic fracturing is also used to extract oil from shale formations.

Promoted as a "transition fuel" because of its lower carbon dioxide emissions than coal when burned, industry proponents often argue that natural gas can serve as a bridge between burning coal and generating electricity from renewable energy sources like wind and solar. The idea is that because burning natural gas is less carbon-intensive than coal, switching to natural gas now can mean lower carbon dioxide emissions in the short term while we continue to develop technologies to better harness and use renewable energy sources in the future. However, others argue that building infrastructure to increase our use of natural gas will likely hinder, not help, the transition to renewables. Because we are operating within a capitalist system, the sole purpose of which is to increase profits, companies that have invested in building new natural gas power plants, pipelines, and wells will have no incentive to cease their operations once the technologies for renewable energy advance enough for a true "transition" to occur. As an example, in 2017 alone, the Federal Energy Regulatory Commission (FERC) approved 2,739 miles of new natural gas pipelines in 26 states, which will add more than 30.8 billion cubic feet per day of natural gas pipeline capacity.

Many also believe the environmental benefits of using natural gas instead of coal are overstated; a number of scientists argue that hydraulic fracturing releases enough methane "to more than cancel out any green-house gas benefits" that come from burning natural gas rather than coal (Zehner 2012, 141). This assertion is supported by a recent study published in the *Proceedings of the National Academy of Sciences* by Scott M. Miller and colleagues, who found that the United States is actually emitting 50 percent more methane than previous EPA estimates suggest, and one of the major sources of this added methane is from the extraction and processing of natural gas. As was noted above, over a 100-year time frame, methane's heat-trapping ability is 28 to 36 times greater than carbon dioxide; and over a 20-year time frame, its heat-trapping ability is 86 times more powerful.

In 2016, the EPA enacted new regulations aimed at limiting the amount of methane that is released from oil and natural gas wells, storage facilities, and pipelines. These regulations required oil and gas companies to install technology that would detect methane leaks and to repair those leaks. However, the EPA under the Trump Administration has proposed rolling back those requirements. The Bureau of Land Management has also rolled back regulations limiting methane emissions from oil and gas drilling taking place on tribal and public lands. Many argue that, in addition to increasing methane emissions, the plentiful and cheap natural gas boom made possible by hydraulic fracturing comes at an incalculable cost to water resources and public health. Internationally recognized ecologist and writer Sandra Steingraber (2012, 153) has gone so far as to describe fracking as "the tornado on the horizon that is poised to wreck ongoing efforts to create green economies, local agriculture, investments in renewable energy, and the ability to ride your bike along country roads."

So, what exactly *is* hydraulic fracturing? As noted above, it is a technology used in conjunction with horizontal drilling to extract natural gas from shale formations. A vertical well is first drilled down to the shale layer, which is typically between 6,000 to 10,000 feet beneath the surface. Then, horizontal wells are drilled, extending up to two miles out from the vertical well. After the drilling, the fracturing phase begins. Once reinforced with concrete, explosions are set off in the horizontal well through the use of "perforating guns" in order to create small holes through the casing and concrete into the shale formation. The high-pressure injection of fluids is the next phase in the process. Millions of gallons of fresh water are mixed with a proppant (typically sand) and a proprietary concoction of chemicals. The liquid mixture is injected at an extremely high pressure into the well bore, creating a dense array of fractures in the surrounding rock. The chemicals in the "fracking fluid" serve various purposes: killing bacteria, preventing corrosion and the buildup of deposits in the pipes, and reducing friction so that the solution can travel farther. The proppant in the mixture acts to hold the fractures open once they are created. These induced fractures provide the necessary permeability for the natural gas to migrate out of the pore space of the rock and up through the well so it can then be captured and processed.

What happens to the millions of gallons of chemical-laden fracking fluid after the process is complete? First, it is important to note that not all of the fluid is actually recovered; wastewater retrieval rates can vary anywhere between 10 percent and 90 percent in a given well. Secondly, the fluid that returns to the surface (called "produced water" by the industry) brings with it naturally occurring toxic substances, including gasses, liquids, and solids, which are present in underground oil and gas deposits. Benzene is one such naturally occurring toxin that can be transported to the surface via the fracking fluid. Benzene is a deadly chemical that causes damage to the bone marrow and can also cause leukemia. The fracking process can also unearth naturally occurring radioactive materials—such as uranium, thorium, radium, and lead-210—as well as heavy metals and salts.

And then, of course, the wastewater also contains the vast array of chemical additives discussed above. In an effort to identify the possible public health ramifications of these fracking chemicals, Colborn and colleagues (2010) compiled a list of 632 different chemicals used in natural gas operations. Of these 632 chemicals, only 353 were identified by Chemical Abstract Services numbers (thus, these were the only ones they could research). The authors conducted a review of the literature on each of these chemicals to determine the potential health impacts of these substances. They found that 75 percent have effects on the liver, respiratory system, gastrointestinal system, skin, eyes, and other sensory organs. Over 50 percent of the chemicals in their study cause chronic and long-term damage to the nervous system, 40 percent cause damage to the immune system, 46 percent harm the cardiovascular system and blood, 40 percent cause kidney damage, and more than 25 percent can cause cancer and mutations. A total of 37 percent affect the endocrine system, which acts on a number of organ systems, including the reproductive system. Thus, many of the chemicals in the produced water are extremely harmful to human health (see Lesson 11).

Once the recoverable wastewater is removed from the well, it must go somewhere. While the industry has recently become better about recycling and reusing some of the wastewater for other wells, a large portion of this fluid is injected underground for "permanent" storage. As Horton (2012) found, there is increasing evidence that injecting wastewater underground is causing earthquakes in areas that have not historically experienced seismic activity. Furthermore, there are numerous accounts of surface water contamination from leaking on-site storage ponds or storage tanks, spills, or flood events. While industry denies the claims that wastewater could contaminate aquifers close to hydraulic fracturing sites, according to the EPA, increasing numbers of landowners have found toxic chemicals and other substances linked to natural gas extraction in their drinking water. As Bamberger and Oswald (2012) conclude, contaminated surface water can also enter the food chain through livestock, wildlife, and agricultural products that are consumed by humans.

Another risk associated with hydraulic fracturing is methane contamination of well water. In their study of 60 drinking-water wells in the Marcellus and Utica Shale regions of northeastern Pennsylvania and upstate New York, Osborn and colleagues (2011) found compelling evidence of methane contamination in drinking-water wells within 1 kilometer of "fracked" shale-gas wells. By analyzing the geochemistry of the methane found in the drinking-water wells and comparing it to the methane in the nearby shale-gas wells, the researchers determined that the carbon in the two methane sources had the same isotopic signature, leading them to conclude that the methane in the drinking-water wells did, in fact, migrate from the shale-gas wells. While the health effects of ingesting methane are not well understood, when mixed with air, the gas can become flammable and explosive. If you have seen the film *Gasland*, you may recall seeing a clip of tap water being lit on fire. Methane is such a potent gas that it can even make *water* flammable. In addition to its flammable properties, when it is released into a confined space, methane can lead to asphyxiation, due to the fact that it replaces oxygen in the air. Thus, methane contamination of drinking water supplies can pose dangerous risks to local residents.

Nuclear

Recently, the home page of the Nuclear Energy Institute, the main trade group for the nuclear industry, featured a photograph of a white, heterosexual, "nuclear" family happily holding hands in an open field beneath a big blue sky. The text accompanying the photo read, "NUCLEAR. Clean Air Energy." Nuclear energy is promoted as "green" and "clean" because it does not emit carbon dioxide while generating electricity. What nuclear proponents fail to mention is the fact that the waste from nuclear energy production includes radioactive toxins that remain *deadly* for tens of thousands of years, and that we have no permanent, or even semi-permanent, place to store this lethal waste. Right now in the United States, nuclear waste is stored on site at nuclear plants in chambers that were not designed for long-term storage. Furthermore, while nuclear reactors may not emit carbon dioxide, looking at the entire life cycle of nuclear energy reveals a different picture of the nuclear industry's carbon footprint. Mining uranium emits greenhouse gasses (both carbon dioxide and methane), and the construction of nuclear plants—built with large quantities of steel and concrete—produces tremendous amounts of carbon dioxide. Furthermore, as Stephanie Malin (2015) discusses in her book, *The Price of Nuclear Power: Uranium Communities and Environmental Justice*, there are numerous long-term public health consequences for communities close to uranium mines, including elevated rates of cancer, respiratory conditions, and reproductive disorders. When the externalities associated with nuclear energy production are accounted for, it is not accurate to dub this industry "green."

As shown in Figure 9–2, 19 percent of the electricity in the United States is generated from nuclear power plants. While a higher percentage of some other nations' energy portfolios is produced by nuclear (like France, where 75 percent of the electricity generated in 2012 was from nuclear power), the United States has more nuclear reactors and produces more electricity from nuclear plants than any other nation. There are currently 97 nuclear reactors operating in 59 power plants located in 29 states in the United States.

To produce electricity in a nuclear reactor, an isotope of either uranium or plutonium is split, which produces energy to heat water into steam, which then turns steam-driven turbine generators that create an electric current. While a tremendous amount of energy can be generated from a very small amount of fuel, the waste products of this process are radioactive and extremely poisonous. The 1979 Three Mile Island disaster (United States), the 1986 Chernobyl disaster (Ukraine), and the 2011 Fukushima Daiichi disaster (Japan) are all frightening reminders of the risks associated with nuclear energy production. In each of these events, a partial or complete meltdown of reactors caused radiation to be released into the air and water, producing varying degrees of illness and death among workers and residents in nearby areas.

The Fukushima Daiichi nuclear disaster poses an ongoing threat to Japan, and possibly the world. In March 2011, a 9.0 magnitude earthquake and resulting tsunami knocked out the Fukushima nuclear plant's power, causing the cooling system to fail, which led to the meltdown of three nuclear reactors. Decontamination of the plant and containment of the radioactivity have proven to be extremely difficult. In July 2013, more than two years after the disaster, it was discovered that radioactive water from the damaged reactors was leaking into the Pacific Ocean. The long-term effects and reach of this disaster will not be known for many years.

The effects of radiation exposure depend on the amount and type. Generally, the higher the amount of exposure, the sooner the effects will be seen, and the higher the likelihood of death. Radiation exposure causes DNA damage. This DNA damage can cause cell death, mutations, or cancer. Because radiation can affect genetic structure, that damage can be passed from generation to generation. As noted by Valerie Kuletz in her book, *The Tainted Desert: Environmental Ruin in the American West* this effect is evidenced in the higher rates of birth defects seen among northern Ukrainian children born after the 1986 Chernobyl accident.

Plant workers and emergency personnel who help in the aftermath of a meltdown typically experience the greatest exposure and may suffer from acute radiation sickness. According to Christodouleas and colleagues (2011), bone marrow, depression, severe gastrointestinal complications, and radiation dermatitis (burns) are among the major manifestations of radiation sickness. Furthermore, in areas surrounding a nuclear accident, nuclear reactor fallout may cause elevated long-term cancer risks as well as reproductive failure and, as previously mentioned, birth and genetic defects.

While nuclear meltdowns are disastrous events with long-term consequences for many people, they are relatively rare, given the number of nuclear plants around the world (about 450 of them). However, the risk of such events occurring may increase, given the fact that the United States at present has no permanent disposal site for nuclear waste. Yucca Mountain in Nevada was the proposed site for a long-term geologic repository for spent nuclear fuel; however, this plan was cancelled by the Obama administration in 2009. The Yucca Mountain site was abandoned in large part due to heavy opposition from the Shoshone Nation and the state of Nevada. With no permanent repository, spent nuclear fuel is currently housed in temporary storage facilities at the nuclear power plants where the waste is produced. Those storage sites won't last forever, though, and something will need to be done with all of the radioactive, lethal waste the nuclear industry has produced and will continue to produce into the foreseeable future.

SOCIAL, ENVIRONMENTAL, AND PUBLIC HEALTH COSTS OF RENEWABLE SOURCES OF ENERGY

As shown in Figures 9–1 and 9–2, just over 17 percent of the electricity in the United States is provided by renewable energy sources, including hydroelectric (7.0 percent), wind (6.6 percent), solar (1.6 percent), biomass (1.5 percent), and geothermal (0.4 percent). Does your university use any sources of renewable energy on campus? Student groups across the nation have been pushing their college and university administrators to make the transition to renewable forms of energy for heating and cooling their campuses. Ball State University in Muncie, Indiana, is one of the leaders in making this transition: in 2009, Ball State broke ground for the construction of the nation's largest ground-source, closed-loop district geothermal energy system; and in 2012, the system went live. Once it is fully operational, the system will replace the university's four aging coal-fired boilers with geothermal energy to heat and cool 45 buildings on the 731-acre campus (see https://www.bsu.edu/about/geothermal for more information about this exciting project).

As a whole, renewable energy sources tend to be better for the environment *and* better for public health. But can renewable energy save us? The short answer to this question is no, not if we do not find ways to reduce our society's overall demand for energy. In his study of the energy-use patterns of nations across the world over the past 50 years, Richard York (2012) found that the implementation of renewable energy production did *not* replace fossil-fuel use but rather increased the overall amount of energy consumed. The general pattern he found across the nations in his study was that for each unit of total energy use that came from non–fossil-fuel sources, less than one quarter of a unit of fossil-fuel energy use was displaced. This pattern was even more extreme in the case of electricity: For each unit of electricity that was generated by a non-fossil-fuel source, less than one-tenth of a unit of fossil-fuel-generated electricity was displaced.

Zehner (2012) also found similar results in his research. He terms this phenomenon the "**Energy Boomerang Effect**" and describes it thusly:

> Alternative-energy production expands energy supplies, placing downward pressure on prices, which spurs demand, entrenches energy-intensive modes of living, and finally brings us right back to where we started: high demand and so-called insufficient supply. In short, we create an energy boomerang—the harder we throw, the harder it will come back to hit us on the head. (172)

In other words, creating more energy creates more consumption.

A related phenomenon, which is associated with energy efficiency, is called the "**Jevons Paradox**." Increasing efficiency has the effect of making a resource less expensive to use, which then can actually cause an *increase* in the consumption of that resource (see Lesson 15). Thus, while energy efficiency can be an important aspect of decreasing energy use, in some cases it can actually have the opposite effect and increase energy consumption.

We must also be careful when looking at energy production data over time, as people often report these data in percentages. As demonstrated by York and Bell (2019), even as one energy source (such as solar or wind) comes to represent a larger *percentage* of the total energy that is produced over time—thereby reducing the percentage of total energy produced by fossil fuels over time—the actual *quantity* of fossil fuels may not decrease much (or may even continue to grow!) if the new energy sources have simply added to the amount of overall energy that is available for consumption.

In the remainder of this section, I will describe the main sources of renewable energy, including the benefits and drawbacks of each. While there are fewer environmental and public health problems associated with these energy sources (which is the reason for the shorter descriptions), there are still a number of hidden costs associated with renewable energy sources, particularly solar.

Solar

There is a tremendous amount of energy emitted from the sun. Environmentalists, such as the former president of the Earth Policy Institute, Lester Brown, often cite the statistic that the amount of solar energy striking the Earth every hour is equivalent to what it would take to power the world for an entire year. However, actually capturing this energy is another story. Based on calculations using the installed costs for existing solar projects in California, Zehner (2012, 9) notes that building enough solar panels to power the planet would cost about $1.4 quadrillion, which is about 100 times the GDP of the United States. Furthermore, "Mining, smelting, processing, shipping, and fabricating the panels and their associated hardware would yield about 149,100 megatons of CO_2." (Zehner 2012). As Zehner (2012) further argues, another hidden cost of solar involves the toxics associated with the construction and disposal of solar photovoltaics. The manufacturing process emits hexafluoroethane (C_2F_6), nitrogen trifluoride (NF_3), and sulfur hexafluoride (SF_6), which are all greenhouse gasses that are more than 10,000 times more potent than carbon dioxide.

As well as emitting extremely potent greenhouse gasses, solar photovoltaics are manufactured using highly toxic materials, and many of the manufacturing plants are in Global South nations where environmental and worker safety regulations are lacking. A solar panel has a usable lifespan of only about 30 years, and once that limit has been reached, it must be disposed of. As Mulvaney (2019) notes, many of the same toxic materials that are present in electronic waste (e-waste) are also present in solar panels, and some of the components are challenging to recycle. Toxic metals from solar panels dumped in landfills can leach into groundwater supplies, and incinerated solar panels can emit toxic substances into the air and waterways. A useful resource for consumers and institutional purchasers is the Silicon Valley Toxics Coalition, which is a non-profit organization that conducts research and advocacy "to promote human health and environmental justice in response to the rapid growth of the high-tech industry." This organization produces an annual Solar Scorecard (http://www.solarsscorecard.com/2018-19/) to help consumers compare solar manufacturers on a variety of environmental and social justice benchmarks, including worker safety, module toxicity, and end-of-life recycling.

Geothermal

While solar panels capture the energy from the sun that hits the Earth's surface, geothermal systems capture the heat from within the Earth's crust by pumping liquid through a series of underground tubes. As in the case of Ball State University, geothermal systems can be used to heat buildings and can also cool them by reversing the process and "sinking" heat into the ground. Smaller-scale geothermal systems constructed for heating and cooling buildings and individual houses can be much more energy efficient than traditional furnace and air conditioner systems. They do, however, require electricity to pump liquid through the buried tubes. Additionally, these types of systems require that there be a plot of land where the tubing can be buried. Thus, as Zehner (2012) reveals, household geothermal systems can be challenging in urban areas with dense housing, such as multiunit apartments and condominiums.

Larger-scale geothermal systems can also be used to produce electric power. Because geothermal is a constant source of energy, it is one of the few renewable energy sources that is considered a good substitute for coal. However, there are limited places where large-scale geothermal plants can be built and be economically viable. As Zehner (2012) points out, they need to be in locations where the Earth's crust is especially hot or where there are naturally occurring hot springs. Drilling deeper to construct engineered geothermal systems in other locations is possible, he notes, but there is a high risk of earthquakes associated with these systems.

Hydroelectricity and Megadams

While industrial-scale hydroelectricity production is a powerful renewable resource with low greenhouse gas emissions, it does have significant ecological and social costs. Habitat fragmentation, changes in flow rates and silt deposits, and loss of water quality are all problems associated with hydroelectric dams that can have serious consequences for vulnerable species. One example Butler and Wuerthner (2012) give is the network of dams constructed on the Columbia River in the Pacific Northwest. These dams impede the migration of wild salmon and have had far-reaching impacts on the health of this species and also on the Indigenous peoples whose diets have depended on salmon for centuries. As another example, dams on the Klamath River in California have also blocked critical salmon runs in the Klamath Tribe's ancestral lands, reducing the salmon population to "roughly four percent of their previous productivity" and leading the Karuk people to have experienced "one of the most dramatic and recent diet shifts of any people in North America" (Norgaard 2019, 4). These major dietary changes have had major negative health consequences for this Indigenous group, as evidenced by the fact that diabetes—a disease that was practically nonexistent a generation ago—is now affecting 21 percent of the Karuk people (Norgaard 2019). In addition to the effects on fish and other wildlife, dams have also been responsible for displacing millions of Indigenous peoples from their ancestral lands throughout the world. Furthermore, as gender scholar Yvonne Braun (2011) has demonstrated through her research in Lesotho, large-scale dam projects often deepen gender, race, and class inequalities on the local level.

Biomass

Referring to a number of different fuels, such as wood, energy crops, construction waste, animal waste, and garbage, biomass is yet another renewable form of energy that some have touted as a "green" solution. However, as with the other forms of energy, there are hidden costs. Biomass burning generates dangerous air pollution. Physician and medical groups have made statements against biomass incinerators, citing numerous health risks. For instance, the American Academy of Family Physicians states, "Current research . . . indicates that the burning of poultry litter and wood wastes . . . leads to increased risk of premature death and serious chronic illness" (Vick 2011, 4). The American Lung Association supports this sentiment, stating, "Burning biomass could lead to significant increases in emissions of nitrogen oxides, particulate matter and sulfur dioxide and have severe impacts on the health of children, older adults, and people with lung diseases" (Vick 2011, 5). Moreover, using agricultural land for growing crops that will be converted to biomass and biofuels (instead of using the land to grow food) threatens food security throughout the world.

Wind

Wind is arguably one of the most promising, and least harmful, renewable energy sources. However, wind technologies are, unfortunately, also heavily reliant on fossil fuels. As Zehner (2012, 42) states, "Wind is renewable.

Turbines are not." The unpredictability of wind is also a challenge. To maintain a continual supply of electricity, fossil-fuel plants have to be fired up to fill in the gaps in supply. Thus, it would be more accurate to think of wind as a "hybrid" energy source rather than one that is truly "renewable."

Critics of wind often cite the number of birds that are killed by wind turbines. However, the number of birds killed by wind turbines is actually quite small when compared to other causes of death. As Zehner (2012, 39) argues, the estimated 2.3 birds killed each year by one wind turbine (multiplied by 10,000 turbines, that is still only 23,000 birds a year) doesn't even come close to the 4 million birds that are killed from flying into communication towers each year or the "hundreds of millions" that are killed annually by house cats and *windows*!

THE HOPE FOR CHANGE

In the previous sections, I described many of the hidden and not-so-hidden environmental and public health costs of energy production across the major sources. However, I want to clarify that through presenting these costs, I am not implying that we should abandon the push to move toward renewable energy sources. Rather, what I am suggesting is that we also need to be spending a *significant* amount of effort to develop solutions that will *reduce* our overall use of energy. Our current rate of energy consumption is completely unsustainable (see Lesson 20). However, reducing energy consumption does not have to mean reducing our quality of life; to the contrary, it might actually improve it.

A great deal of research has established that high levels of energy use, and the associated contribution to carbon dioxide emissions, are *not* closely connected with societal well-being as measured by various objective social conditions, such as the mental and physical health of the general public. The **"Happy Planet Index" (HPI)**, developed by the New Economics Foundation, is one way of measuring the well-being of a nation's citizenry that stands as an alternative to the purely economic measure of GDP (see Lesson 20). The HPI calculates "happy life years" for nations using self-reported life satisfaction levels and life expectancy and dividing that value by the per capita ecological footprint of the nation. According to environmental sociologists Richard York, Christina Ergas, Eugene A. Rosa, and Thomas Dietz (2011), most of the nations with the highest HPI values are in Latin America, with Costa Rica scoring the highest on the HPI. At 114th out of 143 nations, the United States ranks quite low on the Index. As York and Bell (2014, 49) note, "there are quite a number of so-called 'less-developed countries' (LDCs) where people live long lives and report high levels of satisfaction, while having relatively small ecological footprints."

One example within the United States can be seen in the levels of satisfaction among different types of commuters. In a study of individuals in Portland, Oregon, who commuted using different forms of transit (biking, walking, car, and public transportation), Smith (2013) found that those who commuted to work via the "active modes" of biking and walking reported the highest levels of well-being, even after controlling for other factors such as distance of commute and income. Smith's study reveals an inverse relationship between the amount of energy consumed during one's daily commute and the level of happiness that person experiences with his or her commute.

While individual lifestyle changes can have some impacts on a society's energy consumption levels, given the fact that residential energy usage only accounts for 21 percent of energy that is consumed in the United States (and 37 percent of electricity consumed), larger systemic changes are necessary in order to significantly reduce overall energy consumption. In 2018, the commercial and industrial sectors together were responsible for 62 percent of the electricity consumed in the United States. Take one look at the Las Vegas "Strip" at night and it is quite obvious that commercial businesses waste a lot of energy—*a lot*. Thus, for any real reductions in energy consumption to occur, change needs to be implemented at a policy level with regulations imposed on the biggest polluters (see Lesson 3).

As much of the research presented in this lesson demonstrates, simply expanding the growth of renewable energy will not reduce our dependence on fossil fuels to the extent that is necessary to avert the worst consequences of climate change (see Lesson 15). Rather, what is needed "is an active suppression of fossil fuels" (York and Bell 2019, 43). A combination of policy approaches that focus on curbing the *supply* of fossil fuels will be far more effective than policies focused on curbing demand (Sinn 2012). One promising approach proposed by James Hansen and the Citizens' Climate Lobby is a carbon-fee-and-dividend system, which would collect a carbon fee where fossil fuels are extracted or at the port of entry where they are imported. All of the money collected from fossil fuel companies would then be distributed to the public in cash payments, helping to offset the increased costs of energy and other products on the consumer end. (For more information, see www.citizensclimatelobby.org.) This intervention could be made even more effective if limits were also set on the growth of the energy sector—what Robert E. King (2012) calls "capping the grid." As King suggests, through enacting what is essentially a moratorium on the growth of the energy sector, prices would increase due to scarcity, "ushering in the largest conservation and efficiency movement ever seen" (2012, 237). In order to protect lower income and vulnerable populations, a sliding rate scale could be implemented based on income, much in the same way that our income tax system works. What other ideas can you come up with to help suppress the supply of fossil fuels?

How Do We Get There?

One of the greatest barriers we face is shifting national and international energy policy debates away from asking, "How can we reduce our carbon footprint while still maintaining our overpowered lifestyles?" to the more important question of, "How can we reduce the overall amount of energy that is consumed?" In other words, there needs to be a transformation in the way we are framing how we think about our energy future.

As ordinary citizens, what can we do to contribute to this change in societal mindset? An important first step is to *talk about* this reality with friends, family, neighbors, classmates, and co-workers. Tell them about the environmental and public health consequences of our addiction to an ever-expanding energy supply. And then, importantly, discuss the many ways that quality of life can actually be *increased* by reducing our energy consumption patterns.

Taking it a step further, we can seek out environmental groups (see Lesson 16), such as the Post Carbon Institute (www.postcarbon.org), that are advocating for decreasing overall energy production and consumption rather than simply increasing the amount of renewable energy that is produced. Consider learning what you can do to participate in the Post Carbon Institute's advocacy actions and events. See if there is a Citizens' Climate Lobby chapter in your town (https://citizensclimatelobby.org/about-ccl/chapters/), and if there isn't one, start one! Write a letter to the editor of your local newspaper; organize a teach-in on your college campus; create a social media account to disseminate the facts about energy consumption and environmental destruction; or organize a lobby day at your state legislature. In all that you do, always remember to talk about possible solutions (some of which were discussed in this chapter).

One very important thing to remember is that, as Zehner (2012) discusses in his book *Green Illusions: The Dirty Secrets of Clean Energy and the Future of Environmentalism*, people are far more receptive to change if they do not feel that they will have to make major sacrifices. One of the most effective ways that you can advocate for instituting a cap on the energy grid is by identifying all of the quality-of-life *gains* that could be achieved by powering down our society. For instance, if we had limits on the amount of energy we could use in a given day, we would likely make different choices about what we do with our evenings. Instead of watching television to unwind after work or school, we might instead choose to play outside, garden, make art, ride our bikes, go for a run or a walk, cook, read for pleasure, or join a sports team. Furthermore, it is likely that far fewer of us would feel obligated to take our work home with us in the evenings, leaving more time for family, friends, and hobbies. We might also make different decisions about where and how we live. Rather than choosing to live in a suburban community with a 30-minute car commute to work every day, we might instead choose to live in a smaller home within biking, walking, or public transportation distance of work. And, as noted above, there is evidence that people who commute using these modes of transport enjoy their daily commutes significantly more than those who commute via single-passenger cars. In other words, powering down our lives would likely mean a happier, more socially integrated, and physically active existence.

SOURCES

Bamberger, Michelle, and Robert E. Oswald. 2012. "Impacts of Gas Drilling on Human and Animal Health." *New Solutions: A Journal of Environmental and Occupational Health Policy* 22 (1): 51–77.

Bell, Shannon Elizabeth. 2013. *Our Roots Run Deep As Ironweed: Appalachian Women and the Fight for Environmental Justice.* Chicago: University of Illinois Press.

Bell, Shannon Elizabeth. 2016. *Fighting King Coal: The Challenges to Micromobilization in Central Appalachia.* Cambridge, MA: MIT Press.

BP. 2019. *Statistical Review of World Energy.* Accessed July 1 2019. https://www.bp.com/en/global/corporate/energy-economics/statistical-review-of-world-energy.html

Braun, Yvonne A. 2011. "Left High and Dry: An Intersectional Analysis of Gender, Dams, and Development in Lesotho." *International Feminist Journal of Politics.* 13:2, 141–162.

Butler, Tom and George Wuerthner, eds. 2012. *Energy: Overdevelopment and the Delusion of Endless Growth.* Post Carbon Institute/Watershed Media.

Christodouleas, John P., Robert D. Forrest, Christopher G. Ainsley, Zelig Tochner, Stephen M. Hahn, and Eli Glatstein. 2011. "Short-Term and Long-Term Health Risks of Nuclear- Power-Plant Accidents." *New England Journal of Medicine* 364 (24): 2334–2341.

Colborn, Theo, Carol Kwiatkowski, Kim Schultz, and Mary Bachran. 2010. "Natural Gas Operations from a Public Health Perspective." *Human and Ecological Risk Assessment* 17: 1039–1056.

EIA. 2018. "How the United States Uses Energy." Accessed July 15, 2019. https://www.eia.gov/energyexplained/use-of-energy/.

EIA. 2019. "Monthly Energy Review." Table 7.2a. Electricity Net Generation: Total (All Sectors). Retrieved June 30, 2019, from https://www.eia.gov/totalenergy/data/browser/index.php?tbl=T07.02A#/?f=A&start=200001.

Fitzgerald, Jenrose. 2012. "The Messy Politics of 'Clean Coal': The Shaping of a Contested Term in Appalachia's Energy Debate." *Organization & Environment* 25 (4): 437–451.

Goodell, Jeff. 2012. "The False Promise of 'Clean' Coal." In *Energy: Overdevelopment and the Delusion of Endless Growth*, edited by Tom Butler and George Wuerthner, 149–150. Post Carbon Institute/Watershed Media.

Hansen, James. 2012. "Coal: The Greatest Threat to Civilization." In *Energy: Overdevelopment and the Delusion of Endless Growth*, edited by Tom Butler and George Wuerthner, 61-62. Post Carbon Institute/Watershed Media.

Horton, S. 2012. "Disposal of Hydrofracking Waste Fluid by Injection into Subsurface Aquifers Triggers Earthquake Swarm in Central Arkansas with Potential for Damaging Earthquake." *Seismological Research Letters* 83 (2): 250–260.

IEA (International Energy Agency). 2019. Global Energy and CO2 Status Report: Global Trends. Retrieved August 1, 2019 from https://www.iea.org/geco/.

King, Robert E. 2012. "Cap the Grid." In *Energy: Overdevelopment and the Delusion of Endless Growth*, edited by Tom Butler and George Wuerthner, 235–237. Post Carbon Institute/Watershed Media.

Korfmacher, Katrina Smith, Walter A. Jones, Samantha L. Malone, and Leon F. Vinci. 2013. "Public Health and High Volume Hydraulic Fracturing." *New Solutions: A Journal of Environmental and Occupational Health Policy* 23 (1): 13–31.

Malin, Stephanie. 2015. *The Price of Nuclear Power: Uranium Communities and Environmental Justice.* New Brunswick, NJ: Rutgers University Press.

MIT. 2007. "The Future of Coal." Cambridge, MA: MIT Press. Accessed May 2, 2013. http://web.mit.edu/coal/The_Future_of_Coal.pdf.

Miller, Scot M., Steven C. Wofsy, Anna M. Michalak, Eric A. Kort, Arlyn E. Andrews, Sebastien C. Biraud, Edward J. Dlugokencky, et al. 2013. "Anthropogenic Emissions of Methane in the United States." *Proceedings of the National Academy of Sciences* 110 (50). https://doi.org/10.1073/pnas.1314392110.

Mulvaney, Dustin. 2019. *Solar Power: Innovation, Sustainability, and Environmental Justice.* Berkeley: University of California Press.

Norgaard, Kari Marie. 2019. *Salmon and Acorns Feed Our People: Colonialism, Nature, and Social Action.* New Brunswick, NJ: Rutgers University Press.

Osborn, Stephen G., Avner Vengosh, Nathaniel R. Warner, and Robert B. Jackson. 2011. "Methane Contamination of Drinking Water Accompanying Gas-Well Drilling and Hydraulic Fracturing." *Proceedings of the National Academy of Sciences.* 108 (20) 8172–8176.

Physicians for Social Responsibility. 2018. "Coal and Air Pollution." https://www .ucsusa.org/clean-energy/coal-and-other-fossil-fuels/coal-air-pollution#bf-toc-0

Rosa, Eugene A. 1997. "Cross National Trends in Fossil Fuel Consumption, Societal Well-Being and Carbon Releases." In *Environmentally Significant Consumption: Research Directions,* edited by Paul C. Stern, Thomas Dietz, Vernon W. Ruttan, Robert H. Socolow, and James L. Sweeney, 100–109. Washington, DC: National Academy Press.

Rosa, Eugene A., G. E. Machlis, and K. M. Keating. 1988. "Energy and Society." *Annual Review of Sociology* 146:149–172.

Sinn, Hans-Werner. 2012. The Green Paradox: A Supply-Side Approach to Global Warming. Cambridge, MA: The MIT Press. Smith, Oliver. 2013. "Commute Well-Being among Bicycle, Transit, and Car Users in Portland, Oregon" (Poster). Transportation Research Board 92nd Annual Meeting, Washington, DC, January 14, 2013. Accessed March 3, 2020. http://web.pdx.edu/~jbroach/654/homework/Smith_2013.pdf http://bikeportland.org/wpcontent/uploads/2013/01/TRB_Osmith_55x44.pdf

Steingraber, Sandra. 2012. "The Whole Fracking Enchilada." In *Energy: Overdevelopment and the Delusion of Endless Growth,* edited by Tom Butler and George Wuerthner, 153–154. Post Carbon Institute/Watershed Media.

Vick, Therese. 2011. "Second Opinion: The Medical Profession Diagnoses Biomass Incineration." Blue Ridge Environmental Defense League. Accessed March 3, 2020. http://www.bredl.org/pdf3/SecondOpinion.pdf

Wilber, Tom. 2012. *Under the Surface: Fracking, Fortunes, and the Fate of the Marcellus Shale.* Ithaca, NY: Cornell University Press.

York, Richard. 2012. "Do Alternative Energy Sources Displace Fossil Fuels?" *Nature Climate Change* 2 (6): 441–443.

York, Richard, Christina Ergas, Eugene A. Rosa, and Thomas Dietz. 2011. "It's a Material World: Trends in Material Extraction in China, India, Indonesia, and Japan." *Nature and Culture* 6 (2): 103–122.

York, Richard and Shannon Elizabeth Bell. 2014. "Life Satisfaction Across Nations: The Effects of Women's Political Status and Public Priorities." *Social Science Research* 48:48–61.

York, Richard and Shannon Elizabeth Bell. 2019. "Energy Additions or Transitions? Why a Transition from Fossil Fuels Requires More than the Growth of Renewables." *Energy Research & Social Science* 51:40–43.

Zehner, Ozzie. 2012. *Green Illusions: The Dirty Secrets of Clean Energy and the Future of Environmentalism.* Lincoln: University of Nebraska Press.

Part 3

SOME SOCIAL CONSEQUENCES OF ENVIRONMENTAL DISRUPTION

10

Environmental Inequality and Environmental Justice

Michael Mascarenhas

Social movement organization relief center in the Lower Ninth Ward following Hurricane Katrina, New Orleans, Louisiana.

Post your photo on environmental inequality and environmental justice to #TLESjustice.

Photo by Ken Gould

In the spring of 2014, officials in the city of Flint, Michigan, switched the water supply from the Detroit Water and Sewerage Department (DWSD) to the Flint River in an apparent effort to save money for the indebted city. Community members in this majority black city immediately reported that their water changed color and had a strange odor. Some residents suffered from skin rashes and hair loss, others complained about back and muscle aches, and still others experienced gut bacteria problems and many caught the flu. The county health department refused to act, downplaying any danger, and a spokesperson for the Michigan Department of Environmental Quality coldly told the sick residents to "relax." We know now that due to government decisions, over 100,000 residents drank water that contained E. coli, cancer-causing trihalomethanes, and lead over a period of 18 months. One hundred thousand residents were poisoned, including 9,000 children, 200 confirmed cases of lead poisoning, and over 100 cases of Legionnaires disease from which at least 12 people died. Also, given that Legionnaires bacterium causes fever and other flu-like symptoms, the number of people adversely impacted by Flint's untreated water system could actually be much higher. It is now five years on as I write this lesson, and the residents in this majority black city still do not have access to safe drinking water and are still reeling from the cumulative and lasting impacts of this sickening event.

A Frontline investigation found the death toll from contaminated water to be 119, much higher than state health officials had acknowledged. Researchers also found a substantial decrease in fertility rates and a "horrifyingly large" increase (58 percent) in fetal death rates in Flint during the water switch (Grossman and Slusky 2017, 32). The advisory task force commissioned by the Office of then Governor Rick Snyder concluded that the lead poisoning of Flint residents was the result of government failure, intransigence, unpreparedness, delay, inaction, and environmental injustice. The report from the Michigan Civil Rights Commission went one step further: "was race a factor in the Flint Water Crisis?" Our answer is an unreserved and undeniable "yes" (Michigan Civil Rights Commission 2017, 6). In an article titled *A Question of Environmental Racism in Flint*, New York Times reporter John Eligon (2016) asked, "if Flint were rich and mostly white, would Michigan's state government have responded more quickly and aggressively to complaints about its lead-polluted water?" There was no mention of race in the 274 pages of emails released by Governor Snyder in January of 2016 on Flint's water crisis; but it is indisputable, the journal notes, that in Flint, the majority of residents are black and many are poor.

The Flint water crisis is far from the first case in which a community composed predominantly of people of color was disproportionately burdened by adverse drinking water. In 2001, the City of Washington, DC, water authority, then known as the "D.C. Water and Sewer Authority" (WASA) switched their treatment chemical from chlorine to chloramine. That created a chemical reaction that caused corrosion and allowed lead to leach from the city's older pipes into the water supply. In the District of Columbia, of an estimated 130,000 residences, approximately 23,000 (18 percent) had lead service pipes. Two-thirds of the 6,118 residences (4,075 homes) that WASA tested in the summer of 2003 had water that exceeded the lead limit of 15 parts per billion set by the EPA. The same testing revealed that 2,287 D.C. houses had lead levels exceeding 50 parts per billion, including 157 residences with more than 300 parts per billion. In the state of California, more than one million people don't have access to safe and affordable drinking water. An investigation published in June 2018 found at least six million Californians are served by water providers that have been in violation of state standards at some point since 2012 (Kasler, Reese, and Sabalow 2018). Today 11.6 percent of the US population are living without water security. A study conducted by Elizabeth Mack and Sarah Wrase at Michigan State University found that as much as 36 percent of the US population will not be able to afford their water bills in five years. The US Government and corporations have been poisoning Native American lands for decades, leading to obscene levels of water contamination in many Native American communities, and Native American bodies.

The history of American imperialism (See Lesson 3) is littered with **environmental injustice.** The Love Canal neighborhood in Niagara Falls, New York, was the home of Hooker Chemical before that company's property was sold for suburban development in the 1950s. The area was known to have puddles of oil and other chemicals in which children often played. In 1976, journalists reported that the community was suffering an unusual number of miscarriages, birth defects, and other health problems, and that toxic chemicals were present in the soil and water. Local authorities denied there was a problem, ignoring local activists' complaints of strange odors and documentation of residents' birth defects. Scientists too were divided, and studies were inconclusive about whether chemicals caused the reported illnesses. Only after two years of concerted public pressure by activists did President Jimmy Carter name Love Canal a federal health emergency and relocate the remaining 550 families to a safer environment. In both cases, we see how government, corporate interests (see Lessons 3 and 5), and the establishment of science (see Lesson 6) have the power to determine what knowledge is relevant and whose lives matter when interpreting social problems.

This lesson introduces the environmental justice framework as a theoretical and methodological approach to examining contemporary environmental inequity and injustice, such as the uneven ways in which pollution and other environmental hazards are distributed among particular social groups, communities, and regions (see also Lesson 14). The lesson pays close attention to the history of the environmental justice movement and debates within this burgeoning social science discipline. Lastly, this chapter lesson advances the notion of **critical environmental justice** as a framework to examine and theorize contemporary environmental inequity and justice.

HISTORY OF ENVIRONMENTAL JUSTICE

Over years of painstaking research and emotionally charged activism, environmental justice scholars have been able to link questions of social justice, equity, rights, and people's quality of life. Originally forged from a synthesis of the civil rights movements, antitoxic and waste campaigns (often referred to as NIMBY or not-in-my-back-yard), and environmentalism, environmental justice has focused on the class and racial inequalities of exposure to pollution. Rachel Carson's, *Silent Spring* (1962) has been described as a book that changed the world, drawing public attention to widespread chemical contamination. "For the first time in the history of the world," Carson (1962, 15) wrote, "every human being is now subjected to contact with dangerous chemicals, from the moment of conception until death." Other scholars followed Carson's lead, and beginning in the early 1970s, a substantial body of literature began to emerge in the United States documenting the existence of environmental inequalities among particular social groups—specifically minority, aboriginal, and poor communities.

In 1982, a major protest was staged in Warren County, North Carolina, over a Polychlorinated biphenyls (PCB) landfill in a majority African American town. Several hundred protesters (many of them high-profile civil rights activists) were arrested, and the issue of environmental justice was thrust into the national spotlight and onto the political agenda. One year after the Warren County protests, a study of several Southern states and found that a disproportionate number of landfills (about three out of every four) were located near predominantly minority communities. This regional study was followed in 1987 by a national study, Toxic Wastes and Race in the United States, by the United Church of Christ Commission on Racial Justice. This groundbreaking study found that race was the most significant factor in determining where waste facilities were located in the United States. Among other findings, the study revealed that three out of five African Americans and Latinx Americans lived in communities with one or more uncontrolled toxic waste sites, and 50 percent of Asian/Pacific Islander Americans and Native Americans lived in such communities. A follow-up study in 1994 concluded that this trend had worsened (Goldman and Fitton 1994). In 1990, sociologist Robert Bullard published his now-classic book *Dumping in Dixie: Race, Class, and Environmental Quality.* This was the first major study of **environmental racism** that linked hazardous facility siting with historical patterns of segregation in the South. This study was also one of the first to explore the social and psychological impacts of environmental racism on local populations and to analyze the response from local communities against these environmental threats.

In addition to the growing body of research, conferences, such as the Urban Environment Conference in New Orleans in 1983 and the University of Michigan Conference on Race and the Incidence of Environmental Hazards in 1990, brought together researchers from around the nation who were studying racial and socioeconomic disparities in the distribution of environmental contaminants. These conferences were attended by several leading "activist-scholars" who worked closely with community activists, and came together to present and debate their findings and implications. In the fall of 1991, the First National People of Color Environmental Leadership Summit took place in Washington, DC. US activists were joined by delegates from Canada, Central and South America, and the Marshall Islands. This landmark summit set in motion a process of redefining environmental issues and established a list of environmental justice principles. The scientific analyses and first hand accounts of activists presented at these and other conferences began to frame the toxics struggle in terms of power, class, and racial inequality.

Environmental justice activists and scholars present a broad concept of the environment in which we live, work, learn, and play. The environment from this perspective is not a people-free biophysical system but rather the ambient surroundings of everyday life activities and relationships linking people with their immediate environs. These include, but are not limited to, residential environments, working environments, and recreation environments. Turner and Wu (2002, 1) described the environment as encompassing "the air people breathe walking down a city or country street, the water drawn from their taps or wells, the chemicals a worker is exposed to in an industrial plant or strawberry field, and the forests people visit to hike, extract mushrooms, and engage in spiritual practice." This conception of the environment links labor and public health, recreation and housing, and culture and history. Furthermore, this understanding of the environment breaks the boundaries between nature and society, work environments and open spaces, and urban and rural places.

Environmental inequality (or environmental injustice), then, refers to a situation in which a specific group is disproportionately affected by negative environmental conditions brought on by unequal laws, regulations, and policies. A specific form of environmental inequality is the phenomenon of **environmental racism**, or the deliberate targeting of communities of color for toxic waste facilities, the official sanctioning of poisons and pollutants in minority communities, and the systematic exclusion of people of color from leadership roles in decisions regarding the production of environmental conditions that affect their lives and livelihoods.

THE STATE AND ENVIRONMENTAL JUSTICE

The proceedings of the aforementioned conferences were forwarded to the US EPA; and the Administrator, William Reilly, established the Environmental Equity Workgroup to review this growing body of evidence. In 1992, the EPA published its findings and recommendations in a report entitled *Environmental Equity: Reducing Risks for All Communities*. The 130-page report marked the first time in the environmental justice struggle that a government agency confirmed that racial minority and low-income communities bear a disproportionate environmental risk burden. Specifically, the report concluded that racial minority and low-income populations are disproportionately exposed to lead, selected air pollutants, hazardous waste facilities, contaminated fish tissue, and agricultural pesticides.

The EPA's report lent considerable legitimacy to environmental justice activists' claims, and corroborated the evidence of the earlier reports by the General Accounting Office and the United Church of Christ. The report also signaled a major commitment by a branch of the federal government, which put forth a comprehensive set of policy proposals to address these issues identified in the report. It led to the creation of an Office of Environmental

Justice in the EPA in 1992, as well as the National Environmental Justice Advisory Council (NEJAC). September 30, 2018, marked the 25th anniversary of the NEJAC, who through its 27-member committee has continued to provide advice and recommendations, in consultation with relevant stakeholders and communities, about issues and policy related to environmental justice. This commitment also inspired legislation in the United States that identified hazardous waste sites—commonly known as "Superfund sites"—and established a protocol for remediation.

In 1994, President Clinton issued Executive Order 12898, Federal Actions to Address Environmental Justice in Minority Populations and Low-Income Populations. The executive order directed the federal government to make environmental justice a part of the federal decision-making process. In addition, it focused attention on the health and environmental conditions in minority, tribal, and low-income communities with the goal of achieving environmental justice and fostering nondiscrimination in programs that substantially affect human health or the environment. The order required that

> each Federal agency shall make achieving environmental justice part of its mission by identifying and addressing, as appropriate, disproportionately high and adverse human health or environmental effects of its programs, policies, and activities on minority populations, and low-income populations.

This order was clearly aimed to rectify environmental problems that have disproportionately affected minority and low-income populations. The US EPA defines **environmental justice** as follows:

> [t]he fair treatment and meaningful involvement of all people regardless of race, color, national origin, or income with respect to the development, implementation, and enforcement of environmental laws, regulations, and policies.

However Congress never passed a bill to make Clinton's executive order law, effectively nullifying the order.

More than a quarter century has passed since the executive order, yet its effect on environmental justice programs such as Superfund is still rather ambiguous. Many policy, research, and advocacy groups attribute the lack of further environmental justice milestones and reforms to the eight years of President George W. Bush's administration. For example, Bush's budget for the fiscal year 2002 slashed overall spending for environmental and natural resources agencies by $2.3 billion, or 7.2 percent (Natural Resources Defense Council. 2015). This amounted to nearly a $500 million reduction from the EPA. The US environmental justice movement was largely stalled for the eight years of President George W. Bush's administration. Moreover, a Supreme Court ruling (*Alexander v. Sandoval*) in 2001 reversed earlier court interpretations of Title VI of the Civil Rights Act of 1964, which had previously allowed private parties to use the federal courts to enforce violations of federal agency regulations that had a disparate impact on people of color, regardless of intent. The Sandoval decision implied that those disproportionately impacted by federal agency regulations now had to prove intent for which no justification can be shown, effectively ending the EPA's ability to rely on Title VI for environmental justice.

President Barack Obama responsively acknowledged that pollution is distributed unequally in the United States, yet he was unable to strengthen existing environmental regulations or pass new laws stimulating environmental justice nationally. In fact, both the lead water crisis in Washington, DC, and Flint, MI occurred under the supervision of administrators he appointed to the EPA. The 2016 election of a real estate tycoon and reality TV host to president may be the ultimate challenge to the modern environmental justice movement. This president has openly maligned the EPA, saying "what they do is a disgrace." He has put forth budgets that would cut the EPA's budget by a third, or $2.6 billion. Perhaps more alarming is who Donald Trump appointed to lead the EPA: the former Attorney General of Oklahoma, Scott Pruitt. As Oklahoma's Attorney General, Pruitt became a leading advocate against what he referred to as "the EPA's activist agenda." As Oklahoma's Attorney General, Pruitt sued the EPA at least 14 times. In his campaigns for Oklahoma Attorney General, Pruitt received major corporate and employee campaign contributions from the fossil fuel industry of upwards of $250,000. Of course, industry supported Political Action Committees (PACs), would have dwarfed this "official" support (See Lessons 5 and 15). However, after a long list of controversies and multiple federal investigations over his spending habits, conflicts of interests, extreme secrecy, and management practices, Pruitt resigned as the agency's administrator. His replacement, Andrew Wheeler, was a former energy and natural resources lobbyist. As a lawyer, he represented the coal producer Murray Energy. He lobbied against the Obama administration's climate regulations for power plants and persuaded the Energy Department to subsidize coal plants with taxpayer dollars. It is fair to say that the fossil fuel industry now runs the nation's environmental protection apparatus.

In addition, since taking office, President Trump has made eliminating federal regulations a priority. The *New York Times* reported that his administration has rolled back 78 environmental regulations seen as overly burdensome to the fossil fuel industry, including major Obama-era policies aimed at fighting climate change (Poppvich, Albeck-Ripka, and Pierre-Louis 2018). Perhaps the most dangerous decision, in terms of threats to drinking water and ground water contamination, has been the EPA's proposal to weaken cleanup standards for per- and poly-fluoroalykl substances, a class of toxic chemicals more commonly known as PFAS. The repeal of environmental legislation and the reduction combined with major reductions in the budgets of federal, as well as state and local, environmental and natural resources agencies exacerbates and intensifies environmental inequality for people of color, Aboriginal peoples, the poor, and other historically marginalized groups because the ability to secure safe, healthy, and clean environs is increasingly connected to, and reinforced by, social inequality and social privilege.

THE STATE OF ENVIRONMENTAL JUSTICE

For many in this country and around the world, the environmental injustices that they face everyday has not improved; in fact it has worsened. For environmental justice scholars and activists, environmental problems are social problems; the two are often inseparable. This is, according to Andrew Szasz (1994), because "toxic victims are, typically, poor or working people of modest means. [Thus] their environmental problems are inseparable from their economic condition" (151). As Szasz clearly argued, integrated in demands for clean and healthy communities are larger assertions for "the restructuring of the current relationship between economy and society" (1994, 82). At a time when we are facing gross disparities in wealth, where three of the nation's billionaires have accumulated as much wealth as the bottom 50 percent of the entire US population, people are also facing deeply disproportionate environmental conditions. Race continues to be a predictor of where hazardous waste is located in the United States, and recent research suggests that those living near hazardous waste storage facilities are poorer than they were a decade ago, underscoring the double burden of ill health and economic insecurity.

In addition to the rising rate of inequality, we also need to revisit the role of the US nation-state as an institution that embraces and advances the institutional practices of imperialism, environmental racism, and ecological violence (see Lesson 3). The proposed rollbacks of the EPA and other environmental and natural resources regulatory agencies could have the largest favorable effect on the Defense Department as they use PFAS-related chemicals extensively. In her book, *The Tainted Desert: Environmental Ruin in the American West.* Valerie Kuletz observed that the majority of stockpiles and nuclear production facilities, as well as the dumping of uranium mining and milling, and other military waste repositories in the United States are located on *land-based* American Indian territory. Indigenous lands also represent a space, conveniently located on the margins of our spatial consciousness, to cheaply and inconspicuously dump the vast wastes of this phase of capitalist expansion. More recently, law enforcement officers in riot gear used a high-pressure water canon mounted atop an armored vehicle against hundreds of unarmed activists protesting against the Dakota Access Pipeline (see Lesson 3). The position of the Standing Rock Sioux Tribe is that the Dakota Access Pipeline violates Article II of the Fort Laramie Treaty, which guarantees the "undisturbed use and occupation" of reservation lands surrounding the proposed location of the pipeline. The Standing Rock Sioux also oppose the construction of the pipeline on the grounds that an oil spill would threaten their water supply and cultural resources. For those interested in learning more about this conflict, see https://americanindian. si.edu/nk360/plains-treaties/dapl.cshtml. In subzero temperatures, frozen water and a barrage of less-than-lethal weapons—including teargas, rubber bullets, and concussion grenades—were fired into the crowd, causing hypothermia, frostbite, and internal injuries in more than 300 unarmed protesters.

Native Americans and other protesters were detained and jailed for protecting their sovereign land rights. In colonized regions, Frantz Fanon wrote, the state "uses a language of pure violence. [It] does not alleviate oppression or mask domination." Instead, "the proximity and frequent, direct intervention by the police and military ensure the colonial are kept under close scrutiny; and contained by rifle butts and napalm" (Fanon 1963, 4).

The political project to systematically remove or substantially shrink public institutions, expand private property markets, and eliminate opportunities for democratic participation is referred to as **neoliberalism**. Particular neoliberal polices fly under the banner of "choice," "common sense," "austerity," and "let the market decide." As the water crises in Flint, Detroit, and other majority black and brown cities reveal, neoliberalism is increasingly tied to predatory and parasitic policies that target black and brown communities. This cultural shift can be seen in the numerous and sweeping amendments to virtually every law or statute that has dealt with environmental protection or natural resource management. Similarly, budgetary cutbacks of government agencies assures that industry seldom gets regulated for the public's best interest. And in an era when corporate rights take precedence over human rights, the beverage company Nestlé is permitted to extract millions of liters of water daily from Native American land while poor black cities like Flint and Detroit as well as numerous Native American and First Nations communities either drink poisoned water or have none at all. In the Western United States, water contamination has been a way of life for many tribes; 75 percent of abandoned uranium mines are on federal and Tribal lands; 40 percent of families on the Navajo Reservation, the largest Native American Reservation in the United States, lack running water at home. Native Americans argue that they've faced even worse water contamination than Flint, Michigan, for years and received far less media attention.

Indigenous peoples are increasingly becoming the target of the externalized social and environmental costs associated with neoliberal policy reform. This is because Indigenous peoples still maintain sovereignty over vast resource streams, many still held in common, such as water, oil, diamonds, and forests, to name only a few, which are desperately needed for this phase of capitalist expansion. This is still true in spite of a brutal history of colonialism that has devastated many Indigenous cultures and lands, leaving only a social and environmental skeleton of its previous wealth, knowledge, and culture. Neoliberalism, then, is a concerted effort by those in power to employ innovative techniques of government to disconnect, remove, and erase Indigenous peoples from their resources and land. The responsibility for this violence, asserts Mohawk political scientist Taiaiake Alfred (2005, 53) "begins and ends with the state, not the people who are challenging the inherent injustices perpetuated by the state." These injustices, environmental and human, Alderville First Nation writer, activist, and scholar Leanne Betasamosake Simpson wrote, call into question this system of settler colonialism, a system that is overwhelming, violent, normalized, and very, very dishonest.

POISON IN THE WATER

The tragedy that occurred in Flint is a complicated story. Its magnitude alone, namely, the poisoning of over 100,000 residents, has led many to ask how did so many people miss this? The water shutoffs that occurred in Detroit is also a complicated story. Moreover, it is difficult to keep them separate. One thing is for certain, the stories of lead poisoning in Flint and water shutoffs in Detroit cannot be explained by local corruption or people not wanting to pay their fair share, no matter how persuasive those narratives of meritocracy might be. Between 2014 and 2016, the DWSD shut off water in more than 80,000 homes and buildings in the city, amounting to more than 200,000 of the most vulnerable and disenfranchised Detroiters without water.

But shutoffs and poisoned water are the tip of the proverbial iceberg in what continues to ail and trouble Michigan's majority black urban communities. Poisoned water and water shutoffs were followed by government subterfuge, coverup, and an elaborate blame game. Local residents were characterized as helpless and somehow responsible for their hardship. In fact, when local Flint activist Melissa Mays spoke out against the efforts of outsider Marc Edwards, the latter's response was to launch a civil suit for $3 million against Mays and two others. The lawsuit was dismissed but left a chilling effect on those wanting to voice their concerns against outsiders' influence.

The human consequences of these water wars are hidden from most urban and suburbanites rooted in a condition of privileged white ignorance as they continue to have no idea what people of color go through in this country. Poisoned water and water shutoffs cleave families apart as some people relocate, seeking temporary relief and shelter elsewhere. Remaining families live in fear that welfare authorities might take their children from their homes for lack of water. Days are lost from working, and children miss school days, as families navigate new environs or try to figure out how to survive in these "forgotten places". Entire swaths of Detroit and Flint are left abandoned without water, leaving people unable to cook or clean, anxious about bathing or showering, and terrified to nurse their infant children. Living precariously from one bottled water to the next means facing a rising tide of personal despair and indignity, and having to ask for help and handouts from family, friends, and charity.

For many, mortgage foreclosures have led to homelessness as entire generations of accumulated black and brown wealth is forcibly taken, and homeowners are put out on the streets. Speaking during the public comment period at the third public hearing of the Michigan Civil Rights Commission on the Flint Water Crisis, Debra Taylor explains, "I'm here as a homeowner in Flint, I own two homes here. I am 61 years old. Both of the homes were a part of my retirement plan. Governor Snyder has shattered for what I have worked for decades. How many other thousands of homeowners here in Flint can sell a house right now? What is it worth? Have you looked at real estate?" Taylor continued, "The wealth of most black people has come with home ownership. 80% of the wealth in this country inherited." Taylor went on to describe how African Americans are "already 300 years behind" the wealth accumulation of white Americans. "So when you devalue property the way that this government has done," she concludes, you disproportionately devalue the wealth of African American homeowners (MDCR, 2017).

The harmful consequences of state decisions to take over local government and to switch Flint's water supply to the Flint River not only resulted in property damage and the eradication of black and brown wealth, but also killed and caused serious harm to people of color. Multiple and intersecting environmental injustices—health, family, economic, political—have occurred as a result of this neoliberal statecraft determined to force large-scale urban redevelopment and re-segregation on citizens in the name of fiscal responsibility and austerity. Yet, the true amount of systematic trauma that these communities have faced will never really be fully understood. They (state government and its backers) deliberately inflicted "conditions of life calculated to bring about physical destruction" (United Nations General Assembly 1948, 1) These actions, according the United Nations General Assembly, constitute **genocide**. They imposed measures intended to prevent births, and forcibly removed people of color from their communities. This is why people in Flint and Detroit also charge environmental genocide. Speaking at the third public hearing of the Michigan Civil Rights Commission on the Flint Water Crisis, Monica Lewis Patrick, CEO and cofounder of We the People Detroit, minced few words: "what I first want to declare is that we charge genocide. What we know is shutting off water is an act of war . . . and poisoning water is also an act of war. So having noted that, [and] we brought in the UN [United Nations]." In June of 2014, at the invitation of We the People of Detroit, three experts—the Special Rapporteur on adequate housing, Leilani Farha; the Special Rapporteur on extreme poverty and human rights, Philip Alston; and the Special Rapporteur on the human right to safe drinking water and sanitation, Catarina de Albuquerque—visited Detroit. What they saw was described as "an affront to human rights" (United Nations Human Rights Office of the High Commission 2014). "If these water disconnections disproportionately affect African-Americans," Farha asked, "they may be discriminatory," making the City of Detroit in violation of human rights treaties that the United States has ratified (UN News Centre 2014).

Water is critical in maintaining a safe home. You can't live in a house without it. If your gas or electric heating gets cut off you go cold. Put on a coat or blanket. If your cable is disconnected you stop watching television. But if your water gets cut off you can be evicted or you could have your children taken away. If your water is poisoned your house can be lethal. "In languages all over the world," sociologist Matthew Desmond (2017, 293) writes, "the word for 'home' encompasses not just shelter but warmth, safety, family— the womb." The home remains the primary basis of life, it is where meals are shared, quiet habits formed, dreams confessed, traditions created. Housing stability leads to employment stability. Housing instability can downgrade a child's health, ability to learn, capacity to cultivate peer groups, and sense of worth. In many ways, the home is *the* social determinant of health. All of this suffering is shameful; and in both the cases of Flint and Detroit, as in so many other harms done to people of color, it was also completely unnecessary. The decision to poison people and turn their water off was also a collective decision made by government officials and agency staff, those trusted with providing the public good, as well as those looking to make a quick buck or recuperate a loss. But all of this environmental devastation, suffering, and loss of life was easily rationalized because both Flint and Detroit are black cities.

CRITICAL ENVIRONMENTAL JUSTICE STUDIES

Traditional environmental justice scholarship has tended to focus on the measurement of environmental disproportionality (a landfill here, a toxic waste site there), substantiating environmental prejudice (abnormally high cancer rates or asthma rates in poor communities of color), and then advocating for better government policies. This substantial body of research has great merit, effectively forcing the hand of federal and state governments to write environmental justice laws and regulations. Business, too, has adopted a lexicon of environmental justice in their corporate image. The strategy, activists thought, was that if we could document on paper the ways in which environmental injustice takes place, policymakers would then use the information to minimize harmful impacts where minority and marginalized groups worked, lived, and played. The idea was that clearly documented environmental injustices would bring about less harm, less dispossession, less racism. However this assumption has proved problematic for two reasons.

The first problem has to do with the assumption that we all agree on what racism is and that its particular effects on groups of people and ways of life can be isolated and explained through some sort of statistical measurement. The second problem with this "catching it in the act" notion is that it assumes that disproportionality, dispossession, and racism are *accidents*, rather than being a strategic structure of **white supremacy** and settler colonialism. It is for this reason that the strategy of bringing about environmental justice via the state has proven to be largely ineffective because it ignores the role of government in producing unequal lives and segregated spaces as a fundamental axis of social organization. Cases like Flint and Detroit are examples of where the state was not only unable and unwilling to protect the health and wellbeing of particular social groups but was also willing to profit from their disproportionate treatment.

Critical environmental justice scholarship draws attention to racialized state violence, intersectional understanding, the role of white supremacy, and a system that marks certain populations for erasure. Critical environmental justice studies is a perspective intended to address a number of limitations and tensions associated with the more traditional environmental justice approach (Pellow 2016, 2018). First, critical environmental justice scholars question the degree to which scholars should place emphasis on one or more social categories of difference (e.g., race, class, gender, sexuality, species, etc.) versus a focus on multiple forms of inequality. In Flint, majority black and poor families weren't simply poisoned, they also missed school, work, and other commitments because they were poisoned. The value of Flint homes dramatically decreased after the water crisis, leaving many with underwater mortgages. The ongoing water problems have made it more difficult, if not impossible, to sell a house in Flint compared with other white suburbs. The Flint metro area had the highest rate of vacancy in the United States in February 2016 at 7.5 percent. The Flint water crisis separated families and divided communities. The environmental injustices in Flint go far beyond poisoned water; and traditional environmental justice analysis that measured race and exposure would miss the multiple and cumulative forms of inequality that resulted from the Flint water crisis.

Critical environmental justice studies also questions the extent to which scholars should focus on single-scale versus multi-scalar analyses of the causes, consequences, and possible resolutions of environmental justice struggles. Flint and Detroit are not the only predominantly black urban spaces where these anti-black polices are found. There has been lead poisoning of black communities in Washington, DC; Milwaukee; Chicago; New Orleans; and Denmark, South Carolina to name a few. Viewing Flint and Detroit as singular events overlooks the fact that this form of environmental racism is occurring in other majority black cities around the United States.

Critical environmental justice scholars also question the degree to which various forms of social inequality and power—including state power—are viewed as entrenched and embedded in society. The most recent report by the EPA's Inspector General seems to echo this concern, citing an utter lack of urgency on the part of state and federal authorities in the delayed response and prolonged crisis for nearly 100,000 residents (US EPA 2018). The Governor's own task force reported that the primary cause of this avoidable human-made crisis was the role played by the Michigan Department of Environmental Quality and the role of the state's Emergency Manager Law. Failing to understand the role of state government in creating the Flint water crisis would miss a major reason for its occurrence.

Furthermore, critical environmental justice studies examines "the largely unexamined question of the expendability of human and non-human populations facing socioecological threats from states, industries, and other political economic forces" (Pellow 2016, 223). "Look all over the country," a water activist told me, "anywhere where water and land are adjacent and poor people own it and control it, it is being seized, privatized, or commodified in some way." Water infrastructure, development, and pricing not only produces white privilege but also prioritizes white lives as well. Luscious golf courses, green lawns, and swimming pools in the city of Los Angeles ensure that over a million poor and mostly people of color do not have access to water in the state of California. And in California's Imperial and Central Valleys, water may flow to where food grows, but the people working in the fields and on the industrialized and factory farms cannot drink the water because it is unsafe. This happens all over the world. Lesson 19 outlines a water war in Bolivia that arose from the privatization of working peoples' water.

Lastly, this chapter would not be complete without also acknowledging who is doing the environmental justice work in our communities. It is mostly women of color who have inspired the grass roots, anti-racist, mobilization and environmental movement in Michigan; Detroit; Washington, DC; Bayview-Hunters Point, San Francisco; and other places of resistance around the globe (see Lesson 18). I am struck by the resilience and tenacity of these grass roots efforts that refuse to accept this new racial formation, while offering care in the absence of help. Women of color continue to be the catalysts behind major social movements both in the United States and across the globe. This is true in the case of Idle No More, Me Too, and Black Lives Matter, as it is with We the People of Detroit.

SOURCES

Alexander v. Sandoval, 532 U.S. 275 (2001)

Alfred, Taiaiake. 2005. *Wasáse: Indigenous Pathways of Action and Freedom*. Toronto, Ontario: University of Toronto Press.

Bullard, Robert D. (1990). *Dumping in Dixie: Race, Class and Environmental Quality*. Boulder: Westview Press.

Carson, Rachel. 1962. *Silent Spring*. Greenwich, CT: Fawcett Publications, Inc.

Clinton, W.J. (1994). *"Federal Actions To Address Environmental Justice in Minority Populations and Low-Income Populations"* Title 3 – The President Executive Order Order 12898 of February 11, 1994, *Federal Register* Vol. 59, No. 32, February 16.

Commission for Racial Justice. (1987). *Toxic Wastes and Race in the United States: A National Report on the Racial and Socioeconomic Characteristics of Communities with Hazardous Waste Sites*. New York, NY: United Church of Christ.

Desmond, Matthew. 2017. *Evicted: Poverty and Profit in the American City*. New York, NY: Broadway Books.

Eligon, John. 2016. "A Question of Environmental Racism in Flint." *The New York Times*, January 21, 2016, A1. https://www.nytimes.com/2016/01/22/us/a-question-of-environmental-racism-in-flint.html.

Fanon, Frantz. 1963. *The Wretched of the Earth*. New York, NY: Grove Press.

Feagin, Joe R. and Sean Elias. 2013. "Rethinking Racial Formation Theory: A Systemic Racism Critique." *Ethnic and Racial Studies* 36 (6): 931–960.

Flint Water Advisory Task Force. 2016. "Flint Water Advisory Task Force Final Report." Lansing, MI: Commissioned by the Office of Governor Rick Snyder, State of Michigan.

Grossman, Daniel S., & Slusky, David J. G. (2017). *The Effect of an Increase in Lead in the Water System on Fertility and Birth Outcomes: The Case of Flint, Michigan*. Econpapers. Retrieved from https://econpapers.repec.org/paper/kanwpaper/201703.htm

Goldman, B. and L. Fitton. 1994. Toxic Wastes and Race Revisited. Washington, DC: Center for Policy Alternatives.

Kasler, Dale, Phillip Reese, and Ryan Sabalow. 2018. "360,000 Californians have unsafe drinking water. Are you one of them?" The Sacramento Bee. https://www.sacbee.com/news/california/water-and-drought/article211474679.html#storylink=cpy.

Kuletz, Valerie. 1998. *The Tainted Desert: Environmental Ruin in the American West.* New York: Routledge.

Mack, Elizabeth A. and Sarah Wrase. 2017. "A Burgeoning Crisis? A Nationwide Assessment of the Geography of Water Affordability in the United States." *PLOS ONE* 12(4): 1–19.

Mascarenhas, M., T. R. Grattet and K. Tully. (forthcoming). Toxic Waste and Race in the 21st Century. An Enduring Social Problem *Environmental Sociology.*

Michigan Civil Rights Commission (MCRC). 2017. "The Flint Water Crisis: Systemic Racism Through the Lens of Flint." *Report of the Michigan Civil Rights Commission.* Michigan Civil Rights Commission.

Natural Resources Defense Council. 2015. "The Bush Record." *Natural Resources Defense Council.* Accessed March 17. http://www.nrdc.org/bushRecord/other_spending.asp.

O'Neil, Sandra George. 2007. "Superfund: Evaluating the Impact of Executive Order 12989." *Environmental Health Perspectives* 115: 1087–1093.

Omi, Michael and Howard Winant. 2015. *Racial Formation in the United States,* 3rd ed. New York: Routledge.

Pellow, David N. 2016. "Toward a Critical Environmental Justice Studies. Black Lives Matter as an Environmental Justice Challenge." *Du Bois Review: Social Science Research on Race,* 13(2): 1–16.

Pellow, David N. 2018. *What is Critical Environmental Justice?* Medford, MA: Polity Press.

Poppvich, Nadja, Livia Albeck-Ripka, and Kendra Pierre-Louis. 2018. "78 Environmental Rules on the Way Out Under Trump." *The New York Times,* December 28, 2018, Climate. https://www.nytimes.com/interactive/2017/10/05/climate/trump-environment-rules-reversed.html.

Ruble, Kayla, Jacob Carah, Abby Ellis, and Sarah Childress. 2018. "Flint Water Crisis Deaths Likely Surpass Official Toll." *Frontline,* July 24, 2018. https://www.pbs.org/wgbh/frontline/article/flint-water-crisis-deaths-likely-surpass-official-toll/.

Simpson, Leanne Betasamosake. 2017. *As We Have Always Done. Indigenous Freedom through Radical Resistance.* Minneapolis, MN: University of Minnesota Press.

Szasz, Andrew. 1994. *Ecopopulism: Toxic Waste and the Movement for Environmental Justice.* Minneapolis: University of Minnesota Press.

Taylor, Dorceta. 2014. "The State of Diversity in Environmental Organizations. Mainstream NGOs, Foundations, and Government Agencies." University of Michigan, School of Natural Resources & Environment, Ann Arbor, MI.

Turner, Robin Lanette and Diana Pei Wu. 2002. "Environmental Justice and Environmental Racism: An Annotated Bibliography and General Overview, Focusing on U.S. Literature, 1996–2002." *Berkeley Workshop on Environmental Politics, Institute of International Studies,* University of California, *Berkeley.*

United States Enivornmental Protection Agency (EPA). 1992. "Environmental Equity: Reducing Risk for All Communities." In *Volume 1: WorkGroup Report to the Administrator.* Washington, DC: United States Environmental Protection Agency.

United States Environmental Protection Agency (EPA). 2007. "Environmental Justice." August 3, 2007. http://www.epa.gov/compliance/environmentaljustice/.

United States Environmental Protection Agency (EPA). 2018. *Management Weaknesses Delayed Response to Flint Water Crisis*. Washington, DC: US Environmental Protection Agency, Office of the Inspector General.

US General Accounting Office (GAO) (1983). *Siting of Hazardous Waste Landfills and Their Correlation with Racial and Economic Status of Surrounding Communities*. Washington, DC: GAO.

UN News Centre. 2014. "Widespread Water Shut-offs in US City of Detroit Prompt Outcry from UN Rights Experts." United Nations. Accessed October 24th, 2017. http://www.un.org/apps/news/story.asp?NewsID=48129#.We9f2I7cGPh.

United Nations General Assembly. 1948. "Article II of the Convention on the Prevention and Punishment of the Crime of Genocide." *Approved by the United Nations General Assembly Resolution 260 A(III) of 9 December 1948*.

United Nations Human Rights Office of the High Commission. 2014. "Detroit: Disconnecting Water from People Who Cannot Pay - an Affront to Human Rights, say UN Experts." *United Nations*. Accessed May 29th, 2019. https://www.ohchr. org/EN/NewsEvents/Pages/DisplayNews.aspx?NewsID=14777&LangID=E.

Wilson Gilmore, Ruth. 2008. "Forgotten Places and the Seeds of Grassroots Planning." In *Engaging Contradictions. Theory, Politics, and Methods of Activist Scholarship*, edited by Charles R. Hale, 31–61. Berkeley: University of California Press.

Goldman, Benjamin, and Laura J. Fitton. 1994. Toxic Wastes and Race Revisited. Washington, DC: Center for Policy Alternatives.

Kasler, Dale, Phillip Reese, and Ryan Sabalow. 2018. "360,000 Californians have unsafe drinking water. Are you one of them?" *The Sacramento Bee*. https://www.sacbee. com/news/california/water-and-drought/article211474679.html#storylink=cpy.

U.S. Environmental Protection Agency. 2007. "Environmental Justice." *U.S. Environmental Protection Agency*. Access Date: August 3rd, 2007., accessed August 3rd, 2007. http:// www.epa.gov/compliance/environmentaljustice/.

11

Sociology of Environmental Health

Norah MacKendrick

Bus exhaust, Quito, Ecuador.

Post your photo on environmental health to #TLEShealth.

Photo by Tammy Lewis

When you think of toxic pollution, what comes to mind? A rusty metal toxic waste drum at the side of a river? A factory spewing noxious gases? But what about a plastic water bottle, a sofa, or a waterproof rain jacket? These seem like fairly benign objects, but when it comes to environmental health, everyday items like these are just as relevant as the smokestack or leaky toxic waste drum. They contain **environmental chemicals**, which are synthetic (human-made) compounds that migrate into the environment and living organisms, including humans. Some reside for a long time in our tissues, while others are excreted fairly quickly. Some of these compounds are known or suspected carcinogens (cancer causing), while others interfere with the development and function of our neurological and reproductive systems.

According to the Centers of Disease Control's (CDC) biomonitoring program, all Americans carry traces of environmental chemicals in their bodies. The CDC's most recent biomonitoring survey, published in early 2019, tested the blood, urine, and serum of a representative sample of Americans for 350 chemicals. Data like these from the CDC confirm that every person carries an internal chemical load, called a **chemical body burden.** This burden depends on where a person lives, their age, their occupation, diet, and lifestyle. Some of the compounds that comprise our body burden are byproducts of heavy industry (e.g., emissions from a petroleum processing facility or mercury from coal combustion), but some are used in the production of our food and consumer products.

Environmental chemicals enter the body through inhalation, ingestion, or absorption through the skin and are largely undetectable to the human senses. The chemical body burden forms without a person's knowledge. Think of it as the consequence of toxic trespass. Imagine if someone invited you to eat just a small amount of pesticide or inhale some dust with trace levels of flame retardants (chemicals designed to prevent an object from catching fire). You would likely refuse. But these compounds *are* entering your body whether you like it or not. For instance, if you started today with a shower, you've most likely been exposed to phthalates (a plasticizer that gives lotions and gels a smooth texture) and parabens (a preservative) in your soaps and shampoos. If you touched a smartphone or laptop, you've likely inhaled or ingested some flame retardants. If you ate something from a fast food restaurant, chances are you've ingested some of the perfluorinated compounds that were in the food container. If you applied makeup, you might have been exposed to trace amounts of triclosan (an antibacterial), asbestos, or lead.

The volume of environmental chemicals that enter your body on a daily basis is fairly small. In recent years, professional and scientific organizations representing endocrinologists, pediatricians, and obstetricians have issued position statements warning that even small exposures to these chemicals have significant, negative impacts on health over the life course—and consequences are more serious when they happen during fetal development, infancy, and early childhood. More and more studies link exposure to environmental pollutants to various forms of cancer, metabolic disorders, learning and behavioral disorders, and disorders of the reproductive system. And while overall human life expectancy has risen over the past century in the United States (although the opioid epidemic is thought to be responsible for a drop starting in 2016), we are seeing a higher incidence of neurodevelopmental disorders and some types of cancer, as well as declines in sperm counts. For instance, between 1997 and 2008, children diagnosed with developmental disabilities, such as learning disabilities, and attention deficit hyperactivity disorder (ADHD) increased by 15 percent. In Western Europe and the United States, sperm counts declined over 50 percent between 1973 and 2011. Thyroid cancer is on the rise globally, rising 7 percent between 1992 and 2009, with the highest incidence among women and an alarming increase in incidence among young people. Even though scientists and health professionals are aware of the link between chemical exposure and illness and disease, the regulatory system has been unable to keep harmful substances out of our food and consumer products. How is this possible?

The short answer is that these chemicals were produced at a time when scientists and doctors knew very little about their health impacts, and the structure of our economic and political systems has made it exceedingly difficult to convince regulators and industry that these compounds should be taken out of production. The consequence is that we, as individuals, are expected to protect ourselves from chemicals by buying eco-friendly products and certified organic foods (Lesson 2). Meanwhile, pollutants from that toxic waste drum and factory that you might have envisioned at the opening of this lesson remain real threats to communities located in highly polluted regions of the country. These communities struggle to have their local contamination recognized as an urgent threat warranting swift government action and assistance.

In this lesson, you'll learn how environmental health is sociological and get a brief introduction to the history of the environmental health movement. I'll cover how gender fits into the current alarm over chemical body burdens, and you'll learn how political ideology helps explain why there is so little regulatory action to slow down or stop environmental pollution. Before I begin, just a note about terminology. When I refer to women and men, I mean cisgender individuals whose biological bodies are male or female. The environmental health dynamics for transgender (particularly those undergoing medical treatment during transition) and intersex individuals is still not well studied or understood.

WHAT IS THE SOCIOLOGY OF ENVIRONMENTAL HEALTH?

Environmental health refers to the relationship between human health and environmental conditions, and it is determined by a number of factors including access to nature (including parks and forests) and exposure to pollution, overcrowding, and noise. Sociologists of environmental health are motivated by two central questions: First, what is the relationship between environmental conditions, social structures, individual behavior, and human health? Second, how and why do social institutions, groups and individuals respond to threats to their health that come from pollution or industrial development? To answer these questions, sociologists might search for information in historical archives, or work with large data sets that contain information explicating the relationship between environmental conditions and population health. Some sociologists study news media coverage of environmental problems or conduct interviews with groups or individuals to learn more about their behaviors and beliefs surrounding environmental health. Others study politics and lawmaking. Finally, some environmental health sociologists observe how scientific and medical knowledge is produced and subsequently used or rejected by individuals, groups, and lawmakers. Broadly, sociologists find that environmental health is a product of interrelationships between science and technology, human behavior, social institutions (including medicine and the family), and economic and political systems (such as capitalism and democracy).

Sociologists also recognize that environmental health is connected to gender, race, and class. In the United States, low-income and working-class communities, as well as black and Latinx communities, are far more likely than white, wealthy, and middle-class communities to be exposed to unacceptably high levels of air, soil, and water pollution. In New Jersey, where I teach, the cities of Camden and Newark experience high levels of air pollution from waste incinerators, freeways, and the shipping ports that handle the export and import of global consumer goods. In these cities, the neighborhoods exposed to the most air pollution are disproportionately black and Latinx. The white neighborhoods surrounding these cities do not experience this same localized air pollution. These issues are central to the concepts of environmental racism and environmental justice (see Lesson 10).

A person's occupation may also require regular contact with toxic chemicals (see Lesson 17). Coal miners, factory workers, firefighters, and nail salon technicians are just some of the workers that come into regular contact with toxic substances. Globally, less-developed countries contend with much higher levels of environmental contamination, often because toxic trash and banned pesticides are shipped from North America and Europe to these regions. In landfills outside of Bangkok, for example, workers pick through piles of e-waste made up of computers, printers, and cell phones that were discarded in North America and then shipped to Thailand by waste disposal companies. These workers are exposed to high levels of known toxins, such as lead and mercury. And in the northern and circumpolar regions of our planet, air and water currents deliver pollutants from southern areas where they become part of the local environment and accumulate up the food chain. Inuit and Indigenous people in the north have been advised by local public health officials to limit their consumption of traditional foods, like fish and marine mammals, as these organisms contain high levels of toxins, leaving residents to rely on expensive, processed, grocery store foods flown in from cities to the south.

Threats to environmental health do not represent a new or modern social problem. Social reformers in the mid- to late-1800s and early 1900s were also concerned about environmental health. Although they did not use this term, they spoke of the need to improve the living conditions for the urban poor. They raised awareness among elected officials of the dangers of smog from coal burning. They worked to end overcrowding in public housing and sought to determine the cause of infectious diseases like cholera and typhoid that arose from improper sanitation and the rudimentary infrastructure delivering drinking water to city dwellers. They also endeavored to teach middle- and working-class housewives to keep cleaner homes and prepare healthier family meals. At this time, **miasma theory** dominated, where the external environment was thought to be a key causal mechanism for illness and disease. But by the early 20th century, **germ theory** replaced miasma theory, and doctors and social reformers came to believe that pathogens (like bacteria and viruses) were a fundamental cause of illness and disease. This theory continues to underpin contemporary biomedicine, meaning that medical research and treatment protocols consider individual-level factors such as person's genetics, behavior, and lifestyle as the most important factors to address in preventing and treating disease. Biomedicine disregards the influence of socioeconomic and environmental conditions on individual health.

Although our scientific understanding of the **etiology** (or underlying cause) of disease has shifted dramatically over time, today's environmental health concerns are surprisingly similar to those of the late 1800s. We remain worried about air and water pollution, and we are bombarded with expert advice about healthy living and eating. Even so, the specific threats to environmental health we face today are different than in previous eras. Many environmental hazards originate from technological advances that took place after World War II when thousands of new chemical compounds went into production. These substances were vital for developing pesticides, building materials, and new consumer goods. Chemical innovation during this period fueled the rapid industrialization of agriculture (see Lesson 12), the growth of a consumer society, and growing urbanization. This innovation both fueled and was fueled by **industrial capitalism.** Industrial capitalism refers to an economic system built on the mass production of goods and sustained economic growth under a free market. As chemical technologies improved and new synthetic compounds were invented, most did not undergo thorough safety testing before being released onto the market, or into the air, water, and soil. It would take years before scientists could make lawmakers and corporations aware of how many of these compounds travel the globe without breaking down, and how easily they are absorbed by living things, including humans. Rachel Carson, the author of *Silent Spring* (1962), was one of the first scientists to alert the public, industry, and lawmakers about the potential for pesticides like DDT to build up in living organisms and disrupt their reproductive systems (Lesson 10). The US government banned DDT, but dismissed her warnings about risks of all synthetic pesticides.

In the United States, the agency charged with overseeing chemical safety is the EPA, and since the 1970s, it has abided by a regulatory framework of laws and rules that employ a **"proof of harm"** model. This means that the EPA will only restrict or ban a chemical if it determines that there is convincing evidence that the substance poses a threat to human health or the environment. Evidence might be called insufficient for many reasons: levels of exposure are too small to pose a threat to health; just because a compound causes cancer in laboratory animals, does not mean it will cause cancer in humans; more research is needed; a scientist is biased because of their ties to an advocacy group; or the study design is flawed. Moreover, the law asks the EPA to consider the impact on industry before it acts on a chemical of concern. So, the EPA is responsible for both judging the evidence *and* deciding whether acting on such evidence will place an unreasonable burden on the company producing or using a potentially harmful substance.

In the European Union (EU), the burden of proof is reversed. This model is based on the **precautionary principle**. The precautionary principle is an ideology that says that human health and environmental protection must be given priority during risk assessment. If an activity is suspected to be harmful to human health or the environment, the activity must be proven to be safe before it's given approval to go ahead. The EU, in other words, employs a **"proof of safety" model**. The precautionary principle is institutionalized in EU environmental and chemical regulation. Before a chemical substance is allowed onto the market, manufacturers must prove to EU regulators that this compound is safe for human health and the environment. In practice, the EU does not adhere perfectly to this model, and potentially harmful chemicals still find their way onto the market.

Even when supplied with strong evidence that a compound is harmful, the US government has been astonishingly reluctant to place limits on its production. One reason for this is the value of the chemical industry to the national and global economy. According to the American Chemistry Council—the main lobbying organization for the chemical industry—in 2018, US chemical exports totaled 140 billion dollars, which is 10 percent of total national exports. The regulatory system prioritizes economic growth and all other concerns are secondary—whether these are workers' rights, air quality, or public health. Communities or individuals who are negatively affected by chemical production must put up with it or organize to convince lawmakers to protect them. Chemical companies, in contrast, pay into lobbying organizations like the American Chemistry Council to influence law and policy so that their businesses and activities continue to grow. For instance, between 2005 and 2014—years when Congress and the EPA were revising the main act that regulates toxic substances (the Toxic Substances Control Act or TSCA)—the American Chemistry Council spent nearly 65 million dollars lobbying federal agencies to keep the law from instituting precautionary measures. Chemical companies like Bayer, Dow, and Dupont also employ their own toxicologists, lawyers, and public relations staff to produce evidence and arguments to lobby for the fewest government restrictions on their operations (Lesson 5).

In the context of environmental health, members of society argue over the question of how much burden the environment and human populations should reasonably bear as part of sustaining economic growth, and under what conditions government should intervene in economic activities to protect the environment and public health. Crucially, these questions are ideological ones that cannot be answered by finding a single truth or collecting better evidence. These questions ask societies to make normative judgments about how to balance economic growth with the public good. They ask us to think about what kind of environment we want, who is entitled to have their health protected from industrial activities, and who should pay for the costs of such activities. **Neoliberalism** is the dominant political ideology in the United States (see Lesson 2). A **political ideology** is a set of beliefs about how power should be distributed and government should be organized. Under neoliberalism, the market, rather than the state, addresses social problems. Consumer choice is maximized, and the costs of economic activity are absorbed by the environment and those with the least ability to make their power felt through the market.

COMMUNITY RESISTANCE

To fight for their rights in a polluted environment, groups have formed advocacy organizations and their own social movement (see Lesson 18) called the **environmental health movement**. A turning point for this movement was in 1978, at Love Canal, New York, when a group of concerned residents led by mother and community organizer Lois Gibbs, discovered that parts of their community, including the local public school, were built on an old toxic waste dump. Love Canal residents complained to local authorities about corroding toxic waste drums emerging from underground, a persistent chemical smell in the area, and an unusually high number of miscarriages, birth defects, and respiratory problems. Activists eventually got the attention of the national news media, prompting the federal government to relocate Love Canal residents. The federal government also created the federal **Superfund program** that is tasked with cleaning up toxic waste, and it still exists today.

The environmental health movement continues to be active at local, state, and national levels. It is concerned with a broad range of issues from toxic waste dumps, garbage incinerators and industrial chemical releases, and local air pollution to challenging the conventional understanding of disease etiology to recognize that environmental pollution may be responsible for "unexplained" or "contested" illnesses.

Sociologist Phil Brown and his colleagues write of the **dominant epidemiological paradigm** (DEP) that defines a disease, its etiology, and prescribes a treatment or solution. As part of the bedrock of biomedicine, the DEP looks to individual actions and behaviors as the primary cause of health and illness. Doctors are trained to look at lifestyle and family history as primary causes of disease, and they are not well equipped to detect or treat illnesses that are caused by environmental factors. In rare circumstances, if doctors detect a cluster of disease or illness in their patient population, they will pursue environmental explanations. This is what happened in 2015 when

Flint, Michigan pediatrician Dr. Mona Hana-Attisha discovered that rising blood lead levels in her patients (most of whom were infants and young children) corresponded with the city's switch to a new water source. Lead is a strong neurotoxin, and there is no safe level of exposure for infants and children. Hana-Attisha sounded the alarm, but even as a medical doctor, she experienced considerable blowback and skepticism from her supervisors and government officials. It was only after she went to the news media that her concerns were taken seriously, and the state of Michigan and city of Flint issued a warning about the water. Investigators discovered that officials knew that switching to a new water source could lead to a high risk of lead contamination for low-income black and Latinx neighborhoods, but they chose to go ahead with the plan, as the city was facing bankruptcy and the plan would save money. From a sociological perspective, Flint is a case of environmental racism under neoliberalism. The lives of low-income and black and Latinx individuals were devalued by governments seeking to save taxpayers money. The savings from the switch was ultimately paid for by the children and adults of Flint, costing them their long-term health and well-being (Lesson 10).

To challenge the DEP, residents of polluted towns and neighborhoods must advance a **public paradigm** to challenge existing scientific understandings of disease causation. The environmental causes of breast cancer movement is an example of a social movement that developed a public paradigm to draw attention to the relationship between exposure to environmental chemicals and breast cancer risk. When women living in Cape Cod, Massachusetts; Long Island, New York; and the San Francisco Bay area noticed that breast cancer rates were abnormally high in their communities, they wondered if environmental exposures might be responsible. They organized to increase public awareness of the environmental causes of breast cancer and advocate for the precautionary principle in the regulation of environmental chemicals. Members of the movement also sought to activate citizen-science alliances by participating in research projects and working with scientists to advocate for funding and studies that could illuminate the environmental causes of breast cancer.

Public paradigms and citizen-science alliances can emerge in the case of **contested illnesses**. Contested illnesses are diseases and disorders that prompt scientific disagreements and public debates about whether the illness has an environmental cause. One example of a contested illness is Gulf War-related illness. In 1991, veterans returned from the Persian Gulf complaining of joint pain, fatigue, headaches, memory loss, and dermatitis. Doctors and officials at the Department of Defense and Veterans Affairs chalked these symptoms up to stress, which was congruent with the DEP for war veterans. Many physicians and experts refused to believe that there could be a biophysical basis for these symptoms, questioning whether there was really any illness at all. But veterans reported being exposed to numerous environmental chemicals during deployment, such as pesticides, depleted uranium, nerve gas, and oil field smoke. They organized into various support and activist groups to speak out about their illness and demand medical treatment and care. Eventually, physicians, researchers, and government representatives began to recognize that Gulf War-related illnesses were caused by a complex constellation of factors, some of which were environmental and unrelated to the stress of combat and deployment.

What these examples show is that communities can come together to fight back against environmental pollution. They can forge alliances with scientists, doctors, and other activists to influence medical research and improve treatment protocols. They can introduce alternative paradigms of disease causation and set new policy agendas. But even in the context of resistance, contaminated communities shoulder the burden of proving harm. Activist groups must demonstrate that environmental factors are responsible for an illness cluster and supply convincing evidence that other possible causes (such as diet, lifestyle, family history, exposure to other toxic substances) are not the real culprit. This is an exceptionally high burden for most communities. Classic Hollywood films like *Erin Brockovich* (2000) and *A Civil Action* (1998) dramatically recreate real stories of communities that won their fight against polluters. These films capture exceptional cases. Not all communities get recognition from the biomedical community or political and judicial systems. Sometimes residents are told that their symptoms aren't real, or to move away if they believe the local environment is harming their health. They're told that addressing the cause of contamination is not feasible, as it will cost jobs, cause factories to shut down, and result in higher taxes. When industry and government fail to address environmental pollution, individuals and their families pay for the cost of pollution by means of a shorter lifespan, medical expenses to treat illnesses and disorders, expensive water filtration systems (if pollutants are in drinking water), and the stress of living in a contaminated environment.

GENDER AND ENVIRONMENTAL HEALTH

One distinctive feature of environmental health is how many women are involved directly or indirectly in environmental health organizing and activism. Women may be drawn to this issue because concern about health and well-being corresponds to **normative femininity**, that is, the dominant social standards that define ideal feminine appearance and behavior. Conversely, when women join or lead environmental health campaigns, they are less likely to have their activism called into question, as it seems "natural" for women to want to be involved in health-related issues. In communities of color, women's status as mothers is a respected marker of authority that legitimates their leadership role in community activism. Mothers in these communities often have to work together to protect their families from the health impacts arising from larger structures of social oppression and inequality.

Gender is relevant in another way, as a powerful social structure that shapes how environmental health research is conducted and the policy applications that come out of that research. That is, beliefs about gender are socially defined but influence the kinds of questions scientists ask about environmental health risks and the types of solutions promoted by public health authorities and experts. For instance, researchers know far more about the impact of environmental pollution on girls and women than they do about its impact on boys and men because female bodies have the capacity to gestate and produce breast milk. Society celebrates these biological capacities as the "gifts" of motherhood, but women in their reproductive years can expect to have their lifestyles and bodies come under intense scrutiny as part of preparing themselves for a healthy baby—whether they express an interest in becoming mothers or not. Pregnant women's bodies are highly surveilled, such that everything a pregnant woman touches or puts into her body is framed as a potential risk to her future child. Women trying to conceive and pregnant women encounter endless advice on how to have a toxic-free pregnancy. They are told to switch to organic food, use cosmetics sparingly, avoid conventional cleaning products (in addition to the usual advice of avoiding radiation, alcohol, raw fish and meat, and unpasteurized cheese). On the one hand, this advice reflects the fact that fetuses and infants are biologically connected to female bodies during gestation and breastfeeding. Biomonitoring of infant cord blood reveals that infants already contain traces of chemicals at birth, and biomonitoring of breastmilk shows trace levels of contaminants in mothers' milk. On the other hand, sperm is highly susceptible to toxic substances, and sperm are half of the reproductive "equation": one sperm, one egg. Likewise, the cells and tissues involved in producing sperm are thought to be highly sensitive to environmental chemicals—but the research on these effects is still rudimentary. Consequently, there is comparatively little advice about infant health and reproductive health for men. Nearly all advice is for women.

Gender is a social structure that defines the expected social roles and individual behaviors of men and women. These roles and behaviors define what men and women do and what is expected of them. What does this have to do with environmental health? First, gender ideologies define appearance standards for men and women, and these are typically stricter for women. Starting in preadolescence, girls begin using cosmetics and personal care products that promise to modify the appearance of their skin, hair, eyes, lips, and nails. These products are aggressively marketed to them, yet they contain hundreds of carcinogens and endocrine disruptors (chemicals that interfere with the body's hormonal systems) that are allowed under permissive chemical laws. Women and girls of color face beauty standards that encourage them to chemically straighten their hair and lighten their skin. The cosmetics necessary to achieve this look are some of the most toxic beauty products on the market, and they are marketed aggressively to women and girls of color. Unfortunately, mainstream cosmetic and personal care product companies have little incentive from regulators to use safer ingredients in their products.

Gender ideologies also define women as the natural caregivers within the family. Mothers, far more than fathers, are expected to manage family health and, accordingly, take charge of shopping, cooking, and caring for children's growth and development. These ideologies shape the expectations of what kinds of work women will do in the family. In heterosexual couples, women do most of the household shopping (including grocery shopping) and most of the food preparation. Men in heterosexual couples are expected to be *helpers*—that is, willing to lend a hand but not primarily responsible for organizing or initiating the everyday chores associated with raising a family. Accordingly, women in their reproductive years face social pressure to buy into the consumer culture of **precautionary consumption**. Precautionary consumption is a "better safe than sorry" orientation to shopping (Lesson 2). It involves reading product labels to identify potentially harmful chemicals, choosing certified organic foods over conventional foods, and learning what fruits and vegetables contain the lowest pesticide residues. Stores like Whole Foods Market and manufacturers of eco-friendly and certified organic foods and consumer products have capitalized on a regulatory system that does not carefully screen chemicals before they are allowed onto the market. Nontoxic and certified organic items were once difficult to find. They were available only at health food stores and food cooperatives. Now, many mainstream grocery stores carry them, although they continue to be harder to find in some rural areas. Most also command a price premium, making it difficult for low-income and even middle-class consumers to afford them.

Mothers feel a tremendous pressure to do precautionary consumption. They know that their bodies can transmit traces of environmental chemicals to their developing fetus or breastfeeding infant. Many are up to date on the latest health research showing that conventional sunscreen contains possible carcinogens, many brands of baby shampoo contain endocrine disruptors, and conventional apples are high in pesticide residues. If they cannot keep up with precautionary consumption because of the cost, time, and effort it requires, they feel guilty. In short, many mothers feel *individually* responsible for protecting their children from chemicals that are ubiquitous in the retail landscape and environment. Fathers, in contrast, do not feel this same responsibility to engage in precautionary consumption, largely because the culture of precautionary consumption reflects the larger cultural assumption that mothers are primarily responsible for producing healthy, well-adjusted children. Of course, the responsibility for protecting children from chemicals lies not just with mothers (or fathers) but with the government. And until the government acts to ban or restrict toxic substances in food and consumer products, mothers will continue to use precautionary consumption as the only option.

WHAT LIES AHEAD?

Looking ahead, there are a number of issues related to environmental health that will make the news over the next several years. First is the gradual dismantling of environmental regulation in the United States. In 2016, President

Obama signed into law a new TSCA that would introduce more rigorous safety assessments for new chemicals—meaning the EPA could flag harmful chemicals before allowing them to enter the market. However, in 2017, under the administration of President Donald J. Trump, the EPA chose to ignore this new rule and is fast-tracking chemical approvals. Moreover, EPA directors under Trump's administration publicly discounted the agency's own science that warns about the toxicity of a common agricultural pesticide called chlorpyrifos, and they have asked the agency to permit the use of this pesticide. Newly appointed upper management personnel within the EPA have extensive ties to the American Chemistry Council and petroleum industries and are expected to continue to erode the agency's role in upholding environmental laws and policies. From 2017 to 2019, the EPA announced rollbacks to over eighty environmental regulations that address emissions from energy production, air and water quality, and the management of toxic substances.

Another issue that will capture public attention is PFAS contamination across the country. PFAS refers to a family of about 5,000 chemicals and stands for per- and polyfluoroalkyl substances. They are considered "forever chemicals" because they take hundreds of years before they break down into simpler (and less toxic) compounds. That means once these substances are released into the environment, they might move around, but they don't disappear. PFAS are used for a lot of different things—from waterproof coatings that go into clothing and camping equipment, firefighting foams used on military bases, coatings for food containers like pizza boxes and hamburger wrappers, cosmetics, and nonstick cookware. Recently, people discovered that these chemicals are not just getting into our food and our bodies from our Teflon frying pans and eyeliner but also from our groundwater and soil via factories that produce them and industrial spaces that use high volumes of them (such as military bases and airports). The companies making PFAS have known for decades that their operations were polluting the environment, but they hid that information from the public. What is distinctive about this contamination is how it's happening all over the country and it's happening in rich and poor communities. In fact, researchers from Social Science Environmental Health Research Institute at Northeastern University and the advocacy organization Environmental Working Group have found PFAS in more than 1,500 water systems, affecting the drinking water of 19 million people across 43 states. It's only a matter of time before more contaminated water systems are discovered as communities begin to test their water for the presence of PFAS. Manufacturers of PFAS such as 3M, Dupont, and Chemours now face lawsuits and have been asked by states like New Jersey to clean up their mess. These companies argue that it's too difficult and too expensive to clean up entire water systems and insist that PFAS pose little health risk.

Widespread PFAS pollution will present a formidable challenge for local, state, and the federal government if companies won't cooperate with cleanup efforts. As you read about PFAS in your news and social media feeds, notice how various groups and individuals talk about risk and responsibility. Pay attention to arguments for more and better science and ask if scientific uncertainty is at the root of the problem or whether the problem is animated by ideological differences. Are public paradigms emerging that suggest PFAS are a serious health hazard?

REASONS FOR OPTIMISM

Reading this chapter may have left you feeling scared about your own exposure to chemicals or feeling pessimistic about the possibility for policy change. As someone who studies these issues, I share these concerns. A sociological perspective helps us understand the constellation of factors—political, economic, biomedical, social, and scientific—that shaped the situation we are in now. Seeing these patterns can help us identify places where change is happening or where change might be possible in the future. I remain optimistic that we will see real change that will positively impact environmental health. Some reasons follow.

First, this lesson has presented agencies such as the EPA as uniform organizations guided by singular agendas; this is an oversimplification for purpose of compressing a lot of information into one lesson. The EPA is a complex organization. There are people working inside the agency who are worried about how the EPA handles environmental health problems. They're doing what they can from their position within a large organization to affect change. Likewise, inside the National Institutes of Health is the National Institute for Environmental Health Sciences (NIEHS), a research and funding agency that supports toxicologists, biologists, and endocrinologists who are conducting new research into how to protect our environmental health. Their research will be incredibly important for setting new policy agendas and directions for social and political change.

Second, although the federal government has not banned very many toxic chemicals, some states are passing stronger environmental chemical laws. In 2019, Washington State passed a strong new rule regulating children's products that will force manufacturers to use safer ingredients. California and New York State banned chlorpyrifos. New York State also passed legislation making it mandatory for companies to list the ingredients in cleaning products and menstrual products. Up until now, makers of these commodities have been able to hide their ingredient lists. This new legislation will allow consumers to see which brands contain toxic substances and may encourage companies to phase out unsafe ingredients altogether as part of protecting the reputation of their brand.

Third, retailers are feeling the pressure from advocacy groups, states, and consumers. Stores like Target, Walmart, and Ikea have implemented purchasing policies that prioritize selling more nontoxic items and cutting back on the products that have toxic ingredients. These policies are an outcome of concerted advocacy group campaigns such as *Mind the Store*. These campaigns pressure retailers to change their purchasing priorities by replacing toxic products with safer ones. Big retailers can put pressure on manufacturers to make safer products. These kinds of programs are still fairly new, but they are something to watch. It's too early to say whether they will result in a safer retail landscape overall, or a more stratified one—where safe products are sold alongside traditional (and more toxic) products, thereby increasing consumer choice but not actually reducing the number of toxic commodities in the marketplace.

Finally, if the problem of chemical body burdens begins with chemical technologies, then why not ask chemists to evaluate the toxicity and endocrine disruption potential of their inventions? This is the objective of **green chemistry**. Green chemistry aims to invent new chemicals that are nontoxic, safe for the environment, and do not disrupt the endocrine system. Green chemists are working on renewable energy sources, new cosmetic products, food packaging materials, among other technological innovations.

CONCLUSION

The sociology of environmental health refers to the relationship between environmental conditions, social structures, individual behavior, and human health. Sociologists work to understand how individuals and communities respond to contamination. Although widespread environmental pollution can cause illness, traditional biomedicine does not recognize environmental conditions as primary determinants of individual health, making it exceedingly difficult for communities and individuals to have their environment-related illnesses recognized as legitimate health problems. Contaminated communities have to work hard to get proper recognition and treatment of their illnesses.

Sociologists also track how groups and individuals respond to evidence that environmental chemicals enter the human body. They point to the intersection of numerous economic and political factors, including the expansion of industrial capitalism, and the neoliberal political systems that have resulted in the widespread contamination of human bodies from objects that were once thought to be benign. The regulatory system in place in the United States assumes that a chemical is safe before it goes onto the market, meaning that most chemical substances in use today have never been properly tested for their effects on human health or the environment. To remove a substance from production, government requires extensive evidence of harm, and it must consider whether banning or restricting a chemical will have a negative impact on the chemical industry's bottom line.

In the absence of a strong regulatory system that ensures chemical safety and protects human health, individuals are on their own to determine if there are chemicals in their foods and consumer products. Women, by virtue of their physiology and caregiving role within the home, are expected to buy certified organic foods and nontoxic products for their children. Using a strategy called precautionary consumption, they invest considerable money, time, and energy into buying safer products. Meanwhile, communities, individuals, lawmakers, and doctors struggle to understand the extent and impact of widespread environmental contamination across the United States. The problem of PFAS is a contemporary issue just now rising to the surface of public awareness and will likely generate contentious debates about risk and responsibility in relation to human health and environmental protection.

Although there is plenty of reason to worry about environmental health, change is happening within some state governments and new fields of science and technology. In recent years, some states have passed new laws making it hard for companies to sell products with harmful chemicals within state lines, which may prompt manufacturers to remove these chemicals from products nationwide. Some retailers are changing their purchasing practices to limit the number of hazardous products on store shelves. Finally, green chemistry is a field poised to introduce new, safer chemical substances, meaning that the future of environmental health may get brighter.

SOURCES

Bard, Shannon Mala. 1999. "Global Transport of Anthropogenic Contaminants and the Consequences for the Arctic Marine Ecosystem." *Marine pollution bulletin*, 38 (5),: 356–379.

Bennett, D., Bellinger, D. C., Birnbaum, L. S., Bradman, A., Chen, A., Cory-Slechta, D. A., Engel, S. M., Fallin, M. D., Halladay, A., Hauser, R., et al. 2016. "Project TENDR: Targeting Environmental Neuro-Developmental Risks. The TENDR Consensus Statement." *Environmental Health Perspectives*, 124:A118–A122.

Brown, Phil., Zavestoski, Stephen, McCormick, Sabrina., Mayer, Brian, Morello-Frosch, Rachel, and Rebecca Gasior Altman. 2004. Embodied health movements: new approaches to social movements in health. *Sociology of Health & Illness*, 26 (1): 50–80.

Brown, Phil. 2007. *Toxic Exposures: Contested Illnesses and the Environmental Health Movement*. New York: Columbia University Press.

Bullard, Robert D. 1990. *Dumping in Dixie: Race, Class, and Environmental Quality*. Boulder, CO: Westview Press.

Carson, Rachel. 1962. *Silent Spring*. Boston: Houghton Mifflin.

Centers for Disease Control and Prevention. 2019. "Fourth Report on Human Exposure to Environmental Chemicals, Updated Tables, January 2019." Atlanta, GA: US Department of Health and Human Services, Centers for Disease Control and Prevention. https://www.cdc.gov/exposurereport/

Hanna-Attisha, Mona. 2018. *What the Eyes Don't See: A Story of Crisis, Resistance, and Hope in an American City*. New York: One World.

Krauss, Celene. 1993. "Women and Toxic Waste Protests: Race, Class and Gender as Resources of Resistance." *Qualitative Sociology*, 16 (3): 247–262.

Levine, Adeline. 1982. *Love Canal: Science, Politics, and People*. Lexington, MA: Lexington Books.

MacKendrick, Norah. 2018. *Better Safe Than Sorry: How Consumers Navigate Exposure to Everyday Toxics*. Oakland, CA: University of California Press.

McCormick, Sabrina, Phil Brown, and Stephen Zavestoski. 2003. "The Personal Is Scientific, the Scientific Is Political: The Public Paradigm of the Environmental Breast Cancer Movement." *Sociological Forum*, 18 (4): 545–576.

Pellow, David. N. 2007. *Resisting Global Toxics: Transnational Movements for Environmental Justice*. Cambridge: MIT Press.

Rosen, George. 2015. *A History of Public Health*. Baltimore: Johns Hopkins University Press.

Shamasunder, Bhavna, and Rachel Morello-Frosch Rachel. 2015. "Scientific Contestations over '"Toxic Trespass"': Health and Regulatory Implications of Chemical Biomonitoring." *Journal of Environmental Studies and Sciences*, 6 (3): 556–568. https://doi.org/doi:10.1007/s13412-015-0233-0

Szasz, Andrew. 1994. *Ecopopulism: Toxic Waste and the Movement for Environmental Justice*. Minneapolis: University of Minnesota Press.

Taylor, Dorceta E. 2000. "The Rise of the Environmental Justice Paradigm: Injustice Framing and the Social Construction of Environmental Discourses." *American Behavioral Scientist* 43 (4): 508–580.

12

Producing and Consuming Food
Justice and Sustainability in a Globalized World?

Jason Konefal and Maki Hatanaka

Saturday food market, Otavalo, Ecuador.

Post your photo on food and the environment to #TLESfood.

Photo by Ken Gould

E verybody eats! What we eat, where our food comes from, and how our food is produced all affect the environment. However, how many of you have *really* thought about the food that you consume every day? For example, how much do you know about the food you eat prior to its appearance on the shelves of your supermarket? Who produces it, how is it produced, and where? How has what we eat and how it is produced changed over time? To what extent are the production, distribution, and consumption of food sustainable and just?

This lesson addresses these questions using a sociological lens. The first part of this lesson examines the **conventional food and agriculture system**, which is where the vast majority of the world's food is produced. The second section provides an overview of the environmental degradation and social inequities produced by conventional food and agriculture. Next, **alternative**

food and agriculture and the possibilities for a more sustainable and just food and agriculture system are examined. Particular attention is paid to the use of **market-based approaches,** which have become the preferred strategy of many food and environmental movement organizations. In concluding, key questions regarding future potential relationships between food, agriculture, and the environment are presented.

CONVENTIONAL FOOD AND AGRICULTURE

A few generations ago, family farms were the norm in the United States. A huge variety of foods were grown locally. There was a minimum of processed foods. People purchased food from mom-and-pop stores and cooked meals from scratch. Today, the picture is very different. Very few people are farmers. Most food is not grown locally. Global transnational retailers, such as Walmart, have replaced mom-and-pop stores. Increasingly, food is standardized in that it is the same size, shape, color, and taste. There are many more processed foods than fresh foods. Increasingly, cooking is not necessary, as food comes already prepared. This section examines the current global, corporate, and industrial character of conventional food and agriculture, and how it came to be (see Lesson 13 for a discussion of hog production).

From Local to Global

Sociologist Philip McMichael (2009b) claims that in much of the world today, we have "**food from nowhere.**" What does this mean? First, for many people, it means that food just appears at their supermarket, or on their plate at the restaurant. This means that they have little knowledge of where the food they eat comes from, who produces it, or how it was produced. Second, it means that for wealthy people across the world, such things as geography, climate, and seasonality no longer matter in terms of what they eat. In other words, when most Americans go to the supermarket, they expect to find a vast array of food ranging from fresh produce, meat, and seafood to processed foods, regardless of where they live and the time of year. Lastly, it means that much of the food people eat is not produced anywhere near where it is consumed. For example, the lettuce in your salad may come from California, the tomatoes from Florida, your fish may be from China, and the fruit you eat for dessert may be from Mexico and Chile.

How have people in the Global North, and many urban centers in the Global South, come to have food from nowhere? Taking a world systems approach (see Lesson 2), **food regime theory** describes and theorizes the globalization of food (McMichael 2009a). It notes that the globalization of food and agriculture began during the end of European colonization (1870–1914). A key characteristic of colonization was supplying agricultural goods—such as sugar, tobacco, tea, coffee, and cocoa—to the core countries of Europe. Settler colonies, such as the United States, first became part of the world system as producers of wheat and meat, which were staples of the working class in Europe at the time. Following World War II, US policies of "dumping" (i.e., providing free or below-market-price goods) excess grains as food aid furthered the globalization of food and agriculture by making recipient countries dependent on imports of US grains. Most recently, with the implementation of neoliberal free trade policies, many (but not all) barriers to trade were weakened, allowing for the development of transnational agribusiness corporations that control much of food production, processing, and distribution globally.

Today, food and agriculture are truly globalized, with the Global South largely serving as a supermarket for the people of the Global North. Countries such as Brazil, Mexico, Chile, and Thailand are referred to as "new agricultural countries" and specialize in producing high-value, labor-intensive food for consumers across the world. This includes delicate fruits, such as grapes, but also increasingly a variety of processed foods produced by young "factory girls" on assembly lines. For example, Deborah Barndt's study chronicles the ways that tomato packing and processing, such as making ketchup, are increasingly characterized as women's work in Mexico due to women's *supposedly* obedient and submissive nature, nimble fingers, and cheaper wages. Hence, her research exemplifies the feminization of labor in much of the food processing industry.

From Family to Corporate

Who grows the food you eat? Who turns agricultural products into the foods at your table? Who sells you your food? For most people in the United States, and increasingly the rest of the world, the answer is corporations—and the trend is toward just a small handful of corporations. For example, ConAgra Foods advertises, "you'll find our food in 97 percent of America's homes." How did corporations, such as ConAgra Foods, come to control much of food and agriculture? And what does this mean for the kinds of food we eat, how, and by whom it is produced?

At the time of the United States' founding, approximately 90 percent of Americans were farmers. Today, less than 2 percent of Americans farm for a living, and only about 19 percent live in rural areas. While "family" farms still predominate, they are no longer the stereotypical pastoral family farm but increasingly large-scale businesses. Whereas not that long ago (early 1980s) a majority of US cropland farms were less than 600 acres, today the majority are over 1,100 acres, and many are five to ten times that size. In 2017, large-scale family farms (farm income of over one million) account for 39 percent of the entire value of US agricultural production. Similar trends are also found globally, especially in the Global South, where peasants have progressively lost access to land and natural resources. For example, rural populations decreased by approximately 25 percent from 1950 to 1997 globally and are projected to continue to decline through at least 2050. Not surprisingly, it is also during this time that there has been an explosion of urban slums across much of the Global South.

Alongside the decline in the number of farmers, the **corporatization of food and agriculture** has dramatically increased. In some instances, large corporations control farming itself, with the most notable examples being the transnational banana and pineapple companies, which own large amounts of land in Central America, Hawaii, and Asia. Today, more prominent is the corporatization of nearly all the other components of food and agriculture besides farming. In other words, large corporations have come to control agricultural inputs (e.g., seeds, fertilizers, and pesticides), processing (e.g., grain elevators and manufactured foods), and retail (e.g., supermarkets and restaurant chains). For example, it is estimated that in the United States, the CR4 (the percentage of the market controlled by the four largest firms) was 85 percent for beef processing, 66 percent for pork processing, and 51 percent for chicken processing in 2016. Globally, as of 2008, the CR4 was 54 percent for seeds in 2011 and 62 percent for agrochemicals in 2013 (Hendrickson, Howard, and Constance 2017). Figure 12–1 illustrates how Bayer, the largest seed company in the world, has expanded its control over the seed sector by buying up competitors, including Monsanto (the largest seed company at the time in 2016). This is generally referred to as **horizontal integration**, which is when a few firms control a particular sector or stage of production.

In addition to fewer corporations controlling each part of agriculture, increasingly it is also the same corporations controlling the different parts of food and agriculture. For example, Bayer produces and sells not only seeds but nearly all the inputs farmers need (see Figure 12–1). And if farmers buy one product from Bayer, they often have little choice but to also buy the associated products (e.g., pesticides and herbicides). Similarly, Cargill controls nearly the whole meat supply chain, as it is "one of the three major global traders of grain (the major ingredient in animal feed), the second largest animal feed producer, and one of the largest processors of hogs and beef" (Heffernan 2000, 69). Thus, much of food and agriculture has experienced not only significant horizontal integration but also **vertical integration**. Vertical integration is when a firm or set of firms controls multiple stages of production (e.g., inputs, production, and processing). The result is that today, food and agriculture are becoming more corporatized, oligopolistic, and vertically integrated in that just a handful of corporations control nearly every aspect of food, from seed to table.

From Natural to Industrial

We tend to think that food comes from farms. People also are likely to think that farming is based on natural processes. In other words, aided by humans, food is an outcome of nature. For many, food symbolizes nature's abundance and productivity. However, contrary to such assumptions, today much of food is produced through industrial processes. In fact, some even argue that much of agriculture has shifted from "**farms to factories**." What does it mean to say food and agriculture are industrialized? How did they become industrialized?

In short, industrialization means that agriculture relies less on nature and more on inputs. Hence, with some exceptions, such as organics, it is quite likely that your food was produced using significant amounts of chemicals and contains genetically modified ingredients. Growing food these days involves numerous technologies, including complex machinery and synthetic fertilizers to increase soil productivity, manufactured pesticides to control weeds and pests, and hybrid or genetic modifications of plants to improve productivity. One key innovation that has enabled the industrialization of agriculture was the ability to industrially produce nitrogen fertilizer. As a relatively affordable input, nitrogen minimized the need for integrated crop-livestock systems and crop rotations and has played an important role in making large-scale monocropping possible. According to the US Department of Agriculture (USDA), the use of nitrogen as a fertilizer has increased from 2,738,000 tons in 1960 to 13,295,000 tons in 2014. Similarly, the use of pesticides has also increased significantly. A 2014 USDA report (Fernandez-Cornejo et al. 2014) examines pesticide use in 21 crops and finds that pesticide use has increased in the United States from 196 million tons in 1960 to 516 million tons in 2008.

Genetic modification is one of the most transformative, and yet controversial, technological innovations in agriculture. In short, genetic modification is when the genes of a plant or animal are somehow altered, often through importing genes from other plants or animals. Plants have been genetically modified for a variety of reasons, but the most common is to make them more resistant to pests (for example, Bt corn) and resistant to pesticides (for example, Roundup Ready soybeans). Hence, the primary benefits have been making pest management easier for farmers. Proponents of genetically modified crops also claim that they have higher yields and lessen the use of chemical inputs. Thus, supporters of genetically modified crops argue that they are critical to feeding the growing global population and are good for the environment. They also claim that genetic modification offers the possibility for healthier food (for example, through modifying food to increase nutritional content) as well as greater adaption to environmental conditions (for instance, generating drought-tolerant varieties). Because the US government considers genetically modified varieties substantially equivalent to conventional plant varieties, it does not require that they be labeled, even though recent polls indicate that a majority of Americans would like these foods to be labeled.

The first genetically modified crop variety was approved in the United States in 1996, and today there are 197 varieties approved across 19 crops. The United States remains the leader in both the development of new genetically modified varieties and the amount of acreage planted with genetically modified crops. The most planted genetically modified crops are corn and soy. In the United States, 93 percent of all corn and 94 percent of soybeans were genetically modified in 2017. Consequently, in the United States, it is estimated that genetically modified ingredients are found in two-thirds of processed foods on supermarket shelves. Globally, approximately 189 million

Seed Industry Structure 1996 - 2018

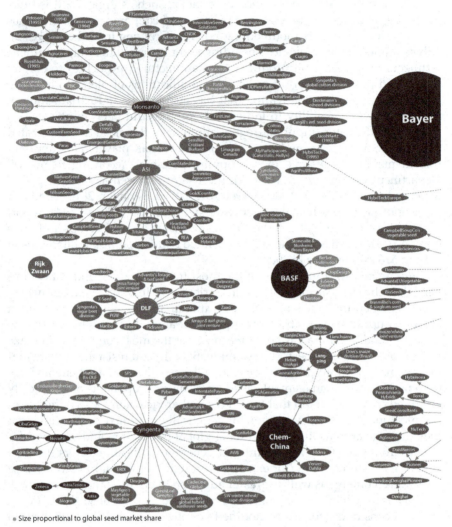

• Size proportional to global seed market share

Figure 12-1 Global Seed Industry Changes Since 2013.

Source: Phil Howard, Michigan State University. http://msu.edu/~howardp

hectares of genetically modified crops across 24 nations were planted in 2017. This is an increase of nearly 30 million hectares in only six years (ISAAA 2017). Furthermore, AquaAdvantage Salmon, the first genetically modified animal for human consumption, has been approved and the first batch is expected to be harvested in 2020 (see Clausen, Longo, and Clark 2019, for a discussion of this).

While the technological innovations for food and agriculture have largely originated and proliferated in the Global North, they have been increasingly

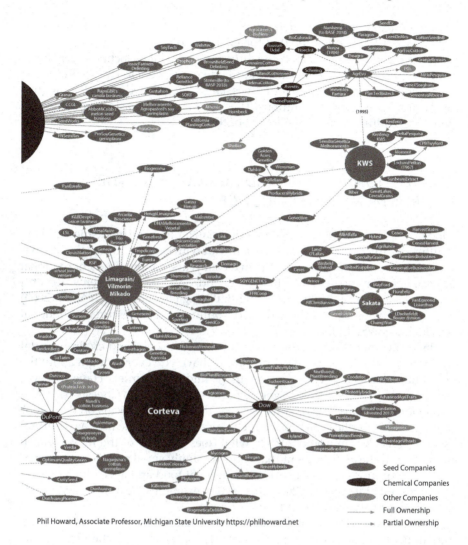

Phil Howard, Associate Professor, Michigan State University https://philhoward.net

Seed Companies
Chemical Companies
Other Companies
———▶ Full Ownership
----------▶ Partial Ownership

exported to, and have significantly restructured, agriculture in the Global South. Beginning in the 1950s and lasting until the 1970s, there were a series of public and philanthropic initiatives funded by the US government, private foundations, and development agencies (e.g., the World Bank) to export industrialized agricultural technologies and practices to the Global South (e.g., synthetic inputs, machinery, and management practices). This was known as the **green revolution**. Proponents of the green revolution argue that it increased yields and thus improved **food security** throughout much of the Global South. However, some critics contend that instead it has led to food insecurity, changes in diets and associated nutritional deficiencies, further dependence on the Global North and corporations for inputs, and a variety of negative environmental impacts. Currently, analysts such as food policy expert Raj Patel argue that the Global South is experiencing a second green revolution, which entails the diffusion of the latest technological innovations, most notably genetically modified crop varieties. The second green revolution is through private initiatives, largely controlled, as well as aggressively propagated, by corporations. The result is the increasing industrialization of agriculture across the Global South.

CONVENTIONAL FOOD AND AGRICULTURE, THE ENVIRONMENT, AND INJUSTICE

Globalization, corporatization, and industrialization have made food and agriculture highly productive and efficient, but with significant social and environmental costs (see also Lesson 13). In recent years, national and international assessments have concluded that food and agricultural systems are at a "crossroads" (Foresight 2011), "facing daunting challenges" (IAASTD 2009) and experiencing an "unprecedented confluence of pressures" (National Research Council 2010).

Have you ever taken a moment to consider the social and environmental implications of what you eat? For example, have you ever thought about the environmental costs of eating grapes in the middle of winter? Have you ever wondered how it is possible to get a Quarter-Pounder with Cheese, fries, and a soda for six dollars? Have you ever considered the chemicals on or in your food, and the implications of such chemicals for your health, agricultural workers, and the environment? Or, what does it mean for the food you eat, workers, and the environment that an increasingly small number of transnational corporations control nearly all aspects of food and agriculture? Using an environmental sociology lens, this section examines the high environmental and social costs of food and agriculture.

Perhaps most obvious are the effects that the industrialization of food and agriculture has had on the environment. The vast array of chemical inputs used in conventional agriculture pollutes ecosystems and water systems and affects wildlife. As noted earlier, nitrogen is a key component of industrial fertilizers. However, a considerable amount of nitrogen that farmers apply runs off farms and is a leading source of water pollution. In the United States, it is estimated that one-third of coastal rivers and bays face nitrogen pollution, with many having periodic dead zones (e.g., too much oxygen in the water for marine life to survive). Most notable is the annual dead zone where the Mississippi River (which drains the Midwest Corn Belt) enters into the Gulf of Mexico. In 2017, it was estimated by the National Oceanic and Atmospheric Administration to encompass 8,776 square miles, which is about the size of New Jersey. This is the largest ever! Pesticides contain a wide assortment of chemicals, including many potential carcinogens, and thus are also a significant source of pollution. At this time, Bayer is facing lawsuits from over 13,000 plaintiffs regarding links between Roundup Ready, one of the most widely used pesticides in the United States, and cancer. In addition to negative impacts on human health, pesticides have also been linked to declines in amphibians and are considered a potential cause of decline in pollinator species (e.g., bees and butterflies).

Food and agriculture are also significant contributors to global climate change. Globally, the production of food is responsible for 26 percent of greenhouse gas emissions. Do you know your **food footprint**? If not, visit the visit food calculator at the BBC News online and calculate the footprint of the foods you eat at https://www.bbc.com/news/science-environment-46459714. What you will find is the environmental impacts of food, particularly regarding greenhouse gases, varies considerably. Most notable is the difference between diets that include meat and vegetarian ones. Meat, aquaculture, eggs, and dairy contribute 56 to 58 percent of greenhouse gas emissions despite only providing 37 percent of the global population's protein and 18 percent of their calories. If we were to exclude these animal products from our diets, this would reduce agriculture's carbon footprint by approximately 49 percent (Poore and Nemecek 2018). And for those of you living in the United States, note per capita consumption of meat in America is about three times the global average! As a result, Americans have a very large food footprint.

Genetically engineered varieties of foods have also raised numerous environmental concerns. Some claim that scientists and corporations are "playing god" in that they are remaking nature. The problem, opponents argue, is that the consequences of such transformations are largely unknown. Specific concerns include biological pollution, the effects on animals, and the loss of biodiversity. Already, some of the environmental transformations are being seen in the advent of "superweeds" and "superpests." These weeds and pests have evolved to be resistant to the synthetic inputs designed to kill them and thus threaten to undermine the primary benefit of genetically modified varieties. Despite claims to the contrary, significant weed and pest resistance to Roundup Ready varieties of soybeans and their associated herbicide glyphosate are now documented. For example, while estimates vary, the Union for Concerned Scientists reported that 60 million acres were infested with superweeds in 2013.

Such examples illustrate one of the chief concerns regarding the sustainability of industrialized agriculture, namely, its treadmill character (see Lesson 2 for an overview of the "treadmill of production"). In short, efforts to increase productivity have led to the use of synthetic inputs and increasing dependence on them. However, while often increasing productivity, such inputs have often led to environmental degradation. The solution has been another round of technological fixes to "correct" the problems produced by the previous technological fixes. However, subsequent technological fixes have tended to generate new sets of environmental concerns, as illustrated by the emergence of superweeds. Ironically, the chief solution to superweeds being advanced by agribusiness is a return to the more toxic pesticides (such as 2,4-D, of which some versions contain dioxins), which genetically modified varieties were supposed to eliminate. At the same time, the increasing cost of inputs continually squeezes out more farmers and thus produces greater consolidation and corporatization of agriculture. Thus, congruent with the lessons on technology (6 and 7), technological innovations have been a mixed bag for the sustainability of food and agriculture.

The global character of conventional food and agriculture also has negative impacts on the environment. Most obvious is the energy withdrawals and pollution associated with the transportation of food and agriculture. However, more significant is the ways that the globalization of food and agriculture are affecting ecological limits. Congruent with world systems theory (see Lesson 2), a key characteristic of the globalization of food and agriculture is unequal ecological exchange. On the one hand, the globalization of food and agriculture displaces ecological limits for the Global North in that it is not constrained by domestic agriculture productivity. Put differently, if Americans had to rely only on domestic land and resources, current ways of producing and consuming food would not be possible. On the other hand, the globalization of food and agriculture shrinks ecological limits for many countries in the Global South, as significant portions of their land and resources (e.g., water) are being used to produce "cash crop" exports for the Global North.

As environmental justice scholars and activists have demonstrated, pollution and environmental degradation are not equally distributed across all people (see Lesson 10). Similar to other environmental issues, conventional food and agriculture is also characterized by significant inequality and injustice. While the chemicals used in conventional food and agriculture affect everyone who eats, farmworkers and neighboring communities are disproportionately affected. Not only is farm work among the lowest paid forms of work, it is also among the most dangerous. For example, pesticide-related illnesses continue to be a significant problem for farmworkers. People living in neighboring communities are also often subjected to pesticides through drift. Furthermore, in many instances, pollution from pesticides and the negative health effects are much greater in the Global South, where more toxic pesticides are often allowed (including ones banned in the United States and other industrialized countries) and regulations on residues and farmworker exposures are either weaker or less strictly enforced. In many instances, dangerous working conditions also extend to food processing, which in the Global South often resembles other forms of industrialized work, such as garment production (see the "factory girls" example in the "From Local to Global" section).

The globalization of conventional food and agriculture is partly based on "accumulation by dispossession," which is the privatization and commodification of formerly public resources or commons (McMichael 2012). Put differently, what were once largely public goods, such as land, water, and seeds, which nearly all people could access and use, are now increasingly private goods that people need to pay to use. This form of "development," in turn, affects land use patterns, often in ways that heighten environmental degradation (see Lesson 8). For example, having been removed from their historic lands by corporate-driven operations, peasants may seek new land and thus resettle to either more agriculturally marginal land or undeveloped land, such as rainforests in tropical countries. Or, more commonly, as the explosion of slums attests to, they tend to migrate to urban areas in search of work. The result has been the proliferation of shantytowns and a host of associated environmental, social, and health consequences. These include deforestation and increased susceptibility to natural disasters (for example, the 2010 Haiti earthquake), lack of access to clean water and sewage systems, elevated rates of infectious diseases, high rates of violence and crime, lack of job opportunities, and stigmatization. Genetic technologies have also introduced a new form of accumulation by dispossession in that seeds and genetics are increasingly becoming proprietary and thus no longer part of the global commons. Consequently, "saving seeds" is increasingly no longer possible for many farmers.

While the effects are not as dramatic, the corporatization of food and agriculture has also had negative impacts on communities in industrialized nations. Most notable is how the depopulation of farming in the United States has contributed to rural communities often accepting, and sometimes actively seeking, locally unwanted land uses (LULUs), such as landfills, power plants, and polluting factories, in order to spur economic development. Hence, as farming has become less of an engine of local economic development, rural communities have often been forced to choose between jobs or the environment.

Lastly, the globalization, corporatization, and industrialization of food and agriculture have simultaneously produced societies of abundance and scarcity, often within the same nation. The productivity and efficiency of agriculture, combined with the drive for profitability by corporations, has given rise to ever more processed foods. Compared to unprocessed produce and meat, processed foods tend to offer greater profitability and more opportunity for market differentiation. Consequently, new processed foods are continually showing up on supermarket shelves, and most have high levels of sugar, salt, fat, and cholesterol. Furthermore, those are the food products that the corporations tend to advertise the most. Marion Nestle (2013, 22) observes that "nearly 70% of food advertising is for convenience foods, candy and snacks, alcoholic beverages, soft drinks, and desserts, whereas just 2.2% is for fruits, vegetables, grains, or beans." One outcome of the proliferation of processed foods is a global obesity problem. In the United States, some argue that obesity is becoming an "epidemic."

At the same time, the proliferation of processed foods may also be contributing to hunger in the United States. Implicit hunger refers to micronutrient malnutrition caused not necessarily by a shortage of food but rather by access to unhealthy food. In 2015, 42.2 million Americans lived in households that were food insecure. This includes 13.1 million children (Myers 2019). The twin-notions of "**food desert**" and "**food swamp**" demonstrate the problem of implicit hunger in America. Food deserts are areas where people lack access to affordable fresh and nutritious foods, such as fruits and vegetables, while food swamps are places inundated with liquor stores, fast food chains, and convenience stores that tend to offer unhealthy food options (Myers 2019). Research indicates that food deserts and swamps tend to be found in poor and/or racial minority areas, and are the result of a combination of public policies (e.g., redlining and public transportation), corporate decision-making (e.g., store siting and development), and discriminatory actions (e.g., white flight). Given the lack of healthy eating options of many low-income and minority areas, as the *New York Times* notes, there is an "obesity-hunger paradox" in America in that "the hungriest people in the U.S. today, statistically speaking, may well be not sickly skinny, but excessively fat."

In addition to implicit hunger, there is also explicit hunger. Explicit hunger is when people do not have access to sufficient food. While explicit hunger continues to be a problem in the United States and other industrialized countries, it's a much more serious problem in the Global South. As of 2015, the United Nations Food and Agriculture Organization (FAO) estimated that approximately 795 million people globally were hungry, with the vast majority in the Global South (Myers 2019). Hunger in the Global South is usually explained in one of two ways. The first is simply that there is not enough food. Hence, solving hunger means producing more food, which means further industrializing agriculture. However, a second explanation contends that hunger is an outcome of an unjust world. Put differently, for many in the Global South, hunger is an outcome of a lack of access to food, mostly because people increasingly cannot afford it. Generally, food prices are outstripping increases in the incomes of people globally. For example, from 2005 to 2008, the World Bank reported that food prices increased 83 percent globally. This increase was an outcome of drought, which negatively affected production, but also changing diets (e.g., increased consumption of meat globally), financial speculation, and the conversion of agricultural products into biofuels, as opposed to food.

The increased production of crops for non-food purposes, such as biofuels, is a development that requires critical scrutiny. In the push to counter their dependencies on fossil fuels, much of the Global North is promoting the development of biofuels, which is fuel derived from agricultural crops. Often biofuels are promoted as a green alternative to fossil fuels, given that they are a renewable resource. Yet biofuels tend to be made from some of the crops that are the most energy- and chemical-intensive to produce and thus are among the most environmentally degrading. For example, in the United States, the majority of biofuels are made from corn, one of the crops requiring the most inputs. In fact, after feed, biofuels are the second most common use of corn. Of the 13,696 million bushels of corn produced in 2013, 10,500 million bushels (approximately 77 percent) went to feed and biofuels (US Department of Energy 2019). Even more problematic are the effects that biofuel production is having on hunger and **food sovereignty**. For example, large-scale land acquisitions by either other countries or investors have diverted land from food production to biofuel production in parts of the Global South. Hence, journalist George Monbiot (2012, 2) argues that

> Biofuels are the means by which governments in the rich world avoid hard choices. No one has to drive less or make a better car: everything remains the same except the source of fuel. The result is a competition between the world's richest and poorest consumers, a contest between overconsumption and survival.

As exemplified by the development of biofuels, today's globalized, corporatized, and industrialized food and agriculture system is characterized by substantial contradictions, unsustainability, and injustice.

ALTERNATIVE FOOD AND AGRICULTURE

In the last part of this lesson, we introduce some of the movements that strive to counter food safety and quality, environmental, and labor problems associated with the conventional food and agriculture system. These movements, generally referred to as "alternative food and agriculture movements," consist of a variety of stakeholders, including social and/or environmental movement organizations, farmers, consumers, and businesses. Broadly speaking, they share the view that the conventional food and agriculture system is unjust and unsustainable, as it prioritizes the maximization of corporate profits at the expense of food safety and quality, small farmers' livelihoods, cultural diversity, and ecological sustainability.

Alternative food and agriculture movements are characterized by significant diversity in terms of their scale, structure, and tactics. On the one hand, *La Via Campesina* (International Peasant's Movement) is a global grassroots movement that brings together millions of peasants, small- and medium-sized farmers, female farmers, landless people, Indigenous people, and agricultural workers. It strives to return food sovereignty—ranging from the right to use and manage lands, water, seeds, livestock, and biodiversity to the rights to know about how food is produced by whom and where—to producers and consumers. Local food movements, on the other hand, are community-based and thus localized and regionalized movements that promote the production and consumption of local food as a means to counter the conventional food and agriculture system. Initiatives such as farmers' markets and community-supported agriculture (CSA) are perhaps the most prominent parts of the local food movement. While quite diverse, alternative food and agriculture movements are tied together through their common goals—that is, the advancement of non-petroleum-dependent and sustainable food systems that are fair and just. Thus, they seek to develop a food system where producers and consumers have voice in the kinds of food produced and how it is produced.

Market-Driven Alternative Food and Agriculture

Of the wide variety of strategies being used by food movements today, market-based tactics have become one of the most prominent. This section addresses why this is the case. Specifically, it examines what market-based approaches are, how they work, and their potential to transform conventional food and agriculture. To begin, consider the following scenario: You go to a nearby supermarket to purchase some carrots. There are two options.

At first glance, the carrots look the same—same size, same shape, and same color. However, they are priced differently. One bag of carrots has the store-brand label and costs $2.10. Another bag has the USDA organic label, which means the carrots are produced without the use of synthetic inputs and genetically modified varieties, and costs $3.25. Which do you choose? Do you choose the store-brand carrots because they are less expensive, or do you choose the organic carrots because you think they are some combination of tastier, healthier, and better for the environment?

More likely than not you have experienced this scenario, if not with carrots then perhaps another kind of produce, or perhaps even a meat or dairy product. However, have you ever considered the following question: What are the implications of you, an individual consumer, choosing to purchase a particular product? Suppose you purchase the organic carrots. As these carrots were organically grown, this means that they were produced without the use of synthetically manufactured chemical inputs and genetically modified varieties. If you, and enough other consumers, purchase organic carrots, demand for such a product will go up. Greater demand will then lead to supermarkets carrying more organic products and, hence, more farmers growing organic carrots. Thus, through their purchasing practices, consumers can potentially shift food and agriculture toward more just and sustainable forms of production.

From the perspective of movement organizations, consumption is a key site where individuals can exercise their values and politics. This is what Michele Micheletti (2004, 114) termed "**political consumerism**," by which she meant "put[ting] your money where your mouth is." Thus, a key task of movement organizations is educating consumers as to the problems of conventional food and agriculture and the benefits of alternative forms of food and agriculture. Additionally, movement organizations (e.g., Greenpeace) seek to shift demand in the marketplace by pressuring large retailers or branded companies to make commitments to selling or sourcing only alternative products. Thus, Stewart Lockie (2002) describes market-based alternative food and agriculture movements as relying on the "the invisible mouth" (vis-à-vis the market being "the invisible hand"). In other words, movement organizations are using both actual and potential consumer demand as a tool to try to reform food and agriculture.

To distinguish alternative products from conventional products, movement organizations are increasingly relying on standards, certification, and labeling. Specifically, standards have been developed to define alternative production practices (e.g., environmentally sustainable and fair and safe labor conditions), certification is used to ensure that the product complies with the standards, and the product is labeled using a particular logo (e.g., fair trade and organic). In this way, consumers can distinguish alternative products from others on supermarket shelves. Today, alternative food and agriculture standards, certification, and labels are exploding. Prominent examples include organics (sustainable agriculture), Rainforest Alliance (sustainable agriculture and forestry), Marine Stewardship Council (sustainable fisheries), Aquaculture

Stewardship Council (sustainable aquaculture), fair trade (equity and justice in international trade), and nongenetically modified. Furthermore, market demand for alternative products is also rapidly growing. For example, according to the Organic Trade Association, the organic market in the United States has grown from $3.6 billion in 1997 to $43.3 billion in sales in 2015. Fair trade food products now encompass coffee, tea, cocoa, honey, bananas, pineapples, mangoes, grapes, nuts and oilseeds, beans and grains, and sugar, among others. Fair trade sales and the number of fair trade producer organizations and farmers all continue to grow. In 2016, there were 1,479,068 farmers in 73 countries that were certified by Fairtrade International (2018).

How do we interpret the growth in kinds and demand for alternative food and agriculture and assess the impacts of such growth in terms of the production of food? For example, do consumers, social movements, and producers have a greater say in food and agriculture? Is the conventional food and agriculture system becoming more sustainable and just, and/or is it gradually being replaced by a new model? While many proponents of market-based approaches answer "yes" to such questions, viewed through a sociological lens, the picture is more complex and contradictory.

A primary reason given for the proliferation of market-based approaches to social change is their congruence with contemporary neoliberalism. As Peter Taylor argues, in using market-based approaches, movement organizations are trying to be "in the market, but not of it." In other words, market forms of activism do not seek to constrain the market but rather use it to advance specific causes. Consequently, this means that market-based approaches do not challenge the structure and practices of markets; rather, they challenge the kinds of goods that are bought and sold. In fact, in many instances, movement organizations seek to cooperatively work with large corporations. The logic behind this is that given the tremendous influence that large corporations have, if social movements can make them into an ally, significant social change becomes more likely. For example, as Walmart sells more food than anyone else in the United States, getting it to sell and promote alternative products can have huge impacts. Through such efforts, activists hope to "mainstream" alternative products—that is, shift them from niche products consumed by only a small minority of people to everyday products used by the majority of people.

However, there is a burgeoning body of literature that questions if in using market-based approaches, alternative food and agriculture movements are being captured by the market. For example, Julie Guthman's study of organic agriculture illustrated how the organic movement was transformed from a largely local, small-scale movement aimed at countering industrialized agriculture to big business. In other words, as the demand for, and the profitability of, organic foods has increased, agribusiness has become heavily involved in the organic sector. In the United States, just two companies control roughly 80 percent of organic food distribution, and many of the leading corporations in the industrialized food system are also the largest organic companies. For example, General Mills owns the organic brand Cascadian Farms and Muir Glen, Dean's owns Horizon Organics, Coca-Cola owns

Odwalla, and Kellogg owns Kashi. Thus, critics of market-based approaches argue that they lead to a watering down or "conventionalization" of alternative food and agriculture. Put differently, as alternative food and agriculture becomes mainstreamed, its visions and principles often become diluted.

Another concern with market-based approaches to social change is their reliance on political consumerism. As noted above, while some see it as a powerful form of human agency, others are more doubtful. On the one hand, some critics point out that consumers tend to be disorganized and have fewer resources than corporations and thus are at a disadvantage in the marketplace. Others contend that consumption as a form of politics may lead to socially unjust outcomes. For example, at a coffee shop, will you pay $1 more to have fair trade coffee? What if the price gap is greater, perhaps $2 or $3 more? What is your threshold?

Obviously, not all consumers can afford to purchase alternative products. This raises questions as to who gets to participate in the movement, and what kinds of change can be achieved using market-based approaches. In *Shopping Our Way to Safety*, Andrew Szasz contended that political consumerism is deepening an already class-divided society in that those who can afford to are protecting themselves from risky and dangerous stuff, while the majority of people must suffice on the leftovers. Applied to food, this means that those who can afford to can eat fair trade, ethical, and organic food, while everyone else is stuck with the industrialized food from nowhere. Thus, from this perspective, political consumerism is understood as not changing society per se, but making sustainable, just, high-quality, and safe food into a private right.

Food Justice

Similar to what has occurred in US environmentalism where alternative movements, such as environmental justice and public health movements, have developed, a new wave of food activism has emerged around food justice and urban food production. This grassroots activism is undertaken by marginalized groups (e.g., poor, people of color and immigrants) and is focused on hunger, healthy food, and food sovereignty. For these movements, addressing these issues means also addressing political and economic inequalities, such as discriminatory policies. Hence, a key component of food justice activism is the right to self-determination, civic engagement, and community building.

Urban food production that takes unused land and turns it into productive greenspaces is one key strategy of food justice activists. For example, in Oakland, the organization Planting Justice builds and maintains community gardens in low income and racial minority neighborhoods. To fund these gardens, they have started several businesses, including a landscaping company, that employ mostly people of color and people who were previously incarcerated. In another instance, the International Rescue Committee has turned an abandoned urban plot in San Diego into a 2.3 acre community garden in which refugees grow a variety of crops, including ones from their home countries. As both of these examples illustrate, food justice activism is turning urban spaces into productive green spaces, providing healthy food to people who lack access to it, fostering civic engagement, and building community bonds. This approach represents another promising pathway to that of market-based approaches to build more sustainable and just food systems.

CONCLUSION

There is an old saying, "you are what you eat." If this is the case, what kind of person do you think you are? What kind of person would you like to be? What kind of person do you want your children and grandchildren to be in the future?

When we project the future of our food landscape, two scenarios are possible. The first is a continuation of the conventional food and agriculture system. In today's neoliberal world, similar to most other economic activities, transnational corporations largely control food and agriculture. Governments are captured by agribusiness and thus tend to implement business-friendly policies and regulations. Furthermore, agricultural science is increasingly privatized, with agribusiness corporations controlling much of research pertaining to food and agriculture. Hence, under such conditions, the increasing use of biotechnologies and chemical inputs, the lack of labeling of genetically modified foods, continued "fetishism" of the production of food (e.g., not knowing where food comes from and how it is produced), the proliferation of unhealthy foods, and lack of access to food are all likely to continue.

A second scenario would be a more sustainable, just, and healthy food and agriculture system. Thanks to alternative food and agriculture movements, such alternatives exist today, and questions about food, health, justice, and the environment have become public issues. Yet, alternative food and agriculture movements in the United States tend to be driven by middle- to upper-class white consumers who want healthier, more sustainable, and/or socially just food. Furthermore, the use of market-based approaches excludes a significant portion of the population who cannot afford to partake in political consumerism. Emerging today is another set of efforts to transform the food system, namely, food justice movements. Springing up in poor inner-city neighborhoods, in impoverished rural areas, and on Native American reservations, these grassroots movements are working to both get people access to healthy, sustainable, and culturally appropriate food and tackle inequalities and discrimination.

This lesson highlights that an increasing number of actors are making efforts, using a diverse array of approaches, to contest and change the conventional food and agriculture system. You can be part of such efforts! To do so you must understand that your food does not come from nowhere and what you eat tremendously affects people, the environment, and society. We end this lesson by providing a set of questions that need to be engaged if food and agriculture are to become sustainable and just:

- Can corporations coexist with a sustainable and just food and agriculture system? If yes, how?
- Do people need to change how they eat and what they eat?

- Does cooking need to be reinvigorated? If yes, how do we ensure people have time to cook?
- Can the US government be "freed" from agribusiness and used to develop more sustainable and just food and agriculture?
- Can public food and agricultural science be rejuvenated and can it be oriented to meet the needs of the public?

These are big questions. They are questions that sociology can help you think about. And they are questions that require collective action to do anything about.

SOURCES

Alkon, Alison. 2019. "Food and Justice." In *Twenty Lessons in the Sociology of Food and Agriculture*, edited by J. Konefal and M. Hatanaka, 351–366. New York: Oxford University Press.

Barndt, Deborah. 2008. "Whose 'Choice'? 'Flexible' Women Workers in the Tomato Food Chain." In *Food and Culture*, edited by C. M. Counihan and P. Van Esterik, 452–466. New York: Routledge.

Clausen, Rebecca, Stefano B. Longo, and Brett Clark. 2019. "From Ocean to Plate: Catching, Farming, and Eating Seafood." In *Twenty Lessons in the Sociology of Food and Agriculture*, edited by J. Konefal and M. Hatanaka, 165–180. New York: Oxford University Press.

ConAgra Foods. 2013. Homepage. Accessed April 1, 2013. http://www.conagrafoods.com/.

Dolnick, Sam. 2010. "The Obesity-Hunger Paradox." *New York Times*, March 12, 2010. Accessed March 30, 2013. http://www.nytimes.com/2010/03/14/nyregion/14hunger.html?src=me on.

FairTrade International. 2018. *Monitoring the Scope and Benefits of Fairtrade*, 9th ed. Bonn, Germany: Fairtrade International.

Fernandez-Cornejo, Jorge, Richard Nehring, Craig Osteen, Seth Wechsler, Andrew Martin, and Alex Vialou. 2014. *Pesticide Use in U.S. Agriculture: 21 Selected Crops, 1960-2008, EIB-124*. US Department of Agriculture, Economic Research Service.

Foresight. 2011. *The Future of Food and Farming: Challenges and Choices for Global Sustainability*. London: The Government Office for Science.

Guthman, Julie. 2004. *Agrarian Dreams: The Paradox of Organic Farming in California*. Berkeley: University of California Press.

Hendrickson, Mary, Philip H. Howard, and Douglas Constance. 2017. "Power, food, and Agriculture: Implications for Farmers, Consumers and Communities." *Social Science Research Network*. Accessed May 1, 2019. https://papers.ssrn.com/sol3/papers.cfm?abstract_id=3066005

Heffernan, William D. 2000. "Concentration of Ownership and Control in Agriculture." In *Hungry For Profit*, edited by F. Magdoff, J. B. Foster, and F. H. Buttel, 61–76. New York: Monthly Review Press.

Howard, Philip H. 2016. *Concentration and Power in the Food System: Who Controls What We Eat?* New York: Bloomsbury.

Howard, Philip. H. 2019. Homepage. Accessed May 1, 2019. https://philhoward.net/.

IAASTD. 2009. *Agriculture at a Crossroads: Synthesis Report*. Washington, DC: Island Press.

ISAAA. 2017. *Global Status of Commercialized Biotech/GM Crops in 2017: Biotech Crop Adoption Surges as Economic Benefits Accumulate in 22 Years*. ISAAA Brief No. 53. Ithaca, NY: ISAAA.

La Via Campesina. 2013. "Organisation: The International Peasant's Voice." Accessed March 28, 2013. http://viacampesina.org/en/.

Lockie, Stewart. 2002. "'The Invisible Mouth': Mobilizing 'the Consumer' in Food Production-Consumption Networks." *Sociologia Ruralis* 42 (4): 278–294.

McMichael, Philip. 2009a. "A Food Regime Genealogy." *The Journal of Peasant Studies* 36:139–169.

McMichael, Philip. 2009b. "The World Food Crisis in Historical Perspective." *Monthly Review* 61 (3): 32-47. https://monthlyreview.org/2009/07/01/the-world-food-crisis-in-historical-perspective/.

McMichael, Philip. 2012. *Development and Social Change: A Global Perspective*. Thousand Oaks, CA: Sage.

Micheletti, Michele. 2004. "'Put Your Money Where Your Mouth Is!' The Market as an Arena for Politics." In *Market Matters: Exploring Cultural Processes in the Global Marketplace*, edited by C. Garsten and M. Lindh de Montoya, 114–134. New York: Palgrave Macmillan.

Monbiot, George. 2012. "Must the Poor Go Hungry Just so the Rich Can Drive?" *The Guardian*, August 13, 2012. Accessed August 24, 2012. http://www.guardian.co.uk/commentisfree/2012/aug/13/poor-hungry-rich-drive-mo-farah-biofuels/print.

Myers, Justin Sean. 2019. "Food and Hunger." In *Twenty Lessons in the Sociology of Food and Agriculture*, edited by J. Konefal and M. Hatanaka, 223–238. New York: Oxford University Press.

National Research Council. 2010. *Toward Sustainable Agriculture Systems in the 21st Century*. Washington, DC: The National Academy Press.

Nestle, Marion. 2013. *Food Politics: How the Food Industry Influences Nutrition and Health*. Berkeley: University of California Press.

Patel, Raj. 2013. "The Long Green Revolution." *The Journal of Peasant Studies* 40:1–63.

Poore, Joseph and Thomas Nemecek. 2018. "Reducing Food's Environmental Impacts through Producers and Consumers." *Science* 360 (6392): 987–992.

Sbicca, Joshua. 2019. "Urban Food Production." In *Twenty Lessons in the Sociology of Food and Agriculture*, edited by J. Konefal and M. Hatanaka, 331–350. New York: Oxford University Press.

Szasz, Andrew. 2007. *Shopping Our Way to Safety: How We Changed from Protecting the Environment to Protecting Ourselves*. Minneapolis: University of Minnesota Press.

Taylor, P. 2005. "In the Market but Not of It: Fair Trade Coffee and Forest Stewardship Council Certification as Market-Based Social Change." *World Development* 33 (1): 129–147.

Union for Concerned Scientists. 2013. *Policy Brief: The Rise of Superweeds—And What to Do About It*. Cambridge, MA: Union for Concerned Scientists.

US Department of Energy. 2019. "Alternative Fuels Data Center." Accessed May 3, 2019. https://afdc.energy.gov/data/.

13

From Farms to Factories
The Social and Environmental Consequences of Industrial Swine Production in North Carolina

Adam Driscoll and Bob Edwards

Packaged pork and other meat products in supermarket grocery case, New York, New York.

Post your photo on farms to factories to #TLESfarms.

Photo by Ken Gould

From the Appalachian Mountains in the west to the beaches of the Outer Banks, North Carolina's natural beauty attracts millions of vacationers, retirees, and outdoor enthusiasts each year to enjoy its varied landscapes. The ecological diversity of rural eastern North Carolina's bountiful wetlands, rivers, estuaries, and sounds is no exception. Yet, over the past 35 years, these natural resources have come under increasing stress from pollution. When one thinks of industrial polluters, the images that readily come to mind are those of factories belching black smoke into the air or dumping unknown chemicals into a river; rarely is a farm one of the first associations. However, a 1998 Senate Agriculture Committee report estimated that the annual volume of livestock wastes—including pork, poultry, beef, and dairy—in the United

States constitutes the largest contributor to the pollution of America's waterways. In recent decades, the agriculture industry has been transformed by the replacement of family labor with advanced technologies. This **industrialization of agriculture** has changed the very nature of farming and replaced environmentally sustainable practices with ecologically destructive ones.

A case in point can be found in the North Carolina pork industry. The traditional pattern of numerous independent farmers raising hogs in small numbers, often to supplement their income from field crops like cotton, tobacco, corn, or soybeans, is all but extinct. Large, **vertically integrated** (the consolidation of multiple stages of production; see Lesson 12) corporations now own the pigs "from birth to bacon" and raise them using advanced, industrial techniques. Anecdotally this is borne out by the absence of pigs at county fairs in eastern North Carolina; showings and competitions among individual farmers and students have virtually disappeared. Gone as well are the benign environmental impacts of traditional pork production, replaced by ones that may best be described as corrosive. This lesson examines the North Carolina case to better understand these profound changes as well as their social and environmental impacts. Furthermore, the changes we describe that characterize North Carolina's hog industry are illustrative of ongoing trends in all animal production, including beef, poultry, and fish (see Lesson 12).

FROM FARMS TO FACTORIES

Between 1985 and 2000, the North Carolina pork industry changed fundamentally in several ways. First, and most obviously, the industry expanded dramatically in size. However, the fivefold increase in hog population (and wastes generated) rests on more subtle, but consequential, changes in the structure and technology of pork production. This section discusses the growth of the hog industry from 2 million to 10 million head and its concentration onto the coastal plain of eastern North Carolina. Second, we outline the industry restructuring that accompanied this period of dramatic expansion. Third, we describe the **confined animal feeding operation** (CAFO) technology typical of pork and other livestock production nationwide. Finally, we conclude by introducing our concept of "**externalities of scale**" as a tool for explaining how the above changes in the industry combined to transform it into one of the state's worst polluters.

Industry Expansion

Between 1982 and 1992, the North Carolina swine population doubled to reach about 4 million. Production had become **horizontally integrated** (the consolidation of firms occupying the same stage of production) and increasingly utilized capital-intensive CAFO technologies. These industry changes, along with active promotion by the state government, a massive new

processing facility, and the growing popularity of pork, set the stage for me-
teoric expansion to over 10 million hogs by 1997. Suddenly, North Carolina
had more pigs than people, with hogs outnumbering humans by 5 to 1 on
the coastal plain and by as much as 50 to 1 in individual counties. Pork surpassed poultry and tobacco as North Carolina's top agricultural commodity.
Yet, the number of farms raising hogs for market declined dramatically over
this same period, leaving the state with far fewer, but much larger, hog operations, as shown in Figure 13–1. Overall, these changes catapulted North
Carolina to the status of the United States' leading innovator in the expanding and rapidly globalizing pork market.

This explosion in the hog population was accompanied by a simultaneous
geographical implosion. In 1982, only one North Carolina county lacked commercial hog farms; by 1997, following the period of intensive growth, approximately
95 percent of all swine production had concentrated in the eastern counties of
the coastal plain, particularly in the southern portion of this region. The top 10
hog-producing counties in the southeastern region of the state accounted for a
full 77 percent of the state's hog population in 2006. Figure 13–2 provides an excellent visual representation of the industry's geographical concentration.

Industry Restructuring

The dramatic expansion of North Carolina's hog industry has been accompanied by equally profound changes in the structure of the industry's ownership. In short, 35-plus years ago, thousands of small farmers produced

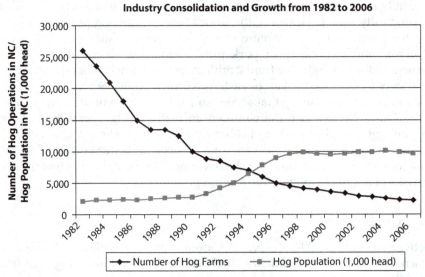

Figure 13-1 The North Carolina hog industry's consolidation and growth from 1982
to 2006.

Source: North Carolina Department of Agriculture

North Carolina's pork. They bought feed from local feedlots and sold pigs to a network of small slaughterhouses, which in turn sold butchered pork to meat wholesalers. Each step along the process consisted of numerous independent businesses. Today, the situation could hardly be more different. A single multinational corporation (previously Smithfield Foods, now WH Group) owns outright, or exerts contract control over, more than 90 percent of North Carolina's pork industry, from breeding to branded pork products for retail consumption worldwide. This and subsequent shifts have important implications for the consolidation of industry decision-making as well as for how the industry is regulated.

The first step of this industry restructuring came in the form of horizontal integration of hog production by corporate "integrators." These large firms replaced the traditional system of numerous independent farmers with one of corporate contract farming, where the integrators own the pigs and farmers are paid a set price for the weight the pigs gain while in their care. (This trend in North Carolina's hog industry mirrors the overall trend from family farms to corporate producers highlighted in Lesson 12). The practice of contract hog farming was introduced in 1973 by Wendell Murphy, a former feed mill owner who would go on to become the owner of Murphy Family Farms, Inc., North Carolina's largest and most influential corporate pork integrator. In 1997, Murphy graced the cover of Forbes magazine as America's "low-tech" billionaire. The success of Murphy Family Farms rested on the implementation of contract farming and the shift to CAFO-style production.

The contract system enables corporate integrators to determine the exact conditions under which hogs are raised. To meet processor requirements, integrators demand large herds raised with CAFO-style production technologies. This preference led to a "squeezing out" of smaller hog farms, where farmers who did not obtain a contract with a corporate integrator and shift to CAFO-style production could not sell their hogs and were driven out of business (hence the decline in the number of farmers raising hogs for market from over 25,000 to about 2,300). By about 1995, the process of horizontal integration was complete; and the few hog farmers whose businesses had survived were outsourced contractors, essentially renting their land, services, and CAFO to a corporate integrator.

The second step of the restructuring came with the vertical integration of hog production and processing by one multinational firm, Smithfield Foods of Virginia. By 1995, Smithfield was already the nation's largest pork processor and slaughtered over 95 percent of the hogs raised in North Carolina. In 1998, Smithfield was able to exploit a sustained downturn in pork prices (Figure 13–3) to reap windfall profits that were used to purchase North Carolina's largest corporate pork producers: Brown's of Carolina (1998), Carroll's Foods (1999), and finally Murphy Family Farms (2000). Vertical integration of domestic pork production and processing was good for Smithfield. In the first *quarter* of 2000, just after its acquisition of Murphy Family Farms, sales totaled $1.4 billion, with quarterly *after-tax* profits of $44.6 million, a 546 percent increase. Such profits were made possible in part because the

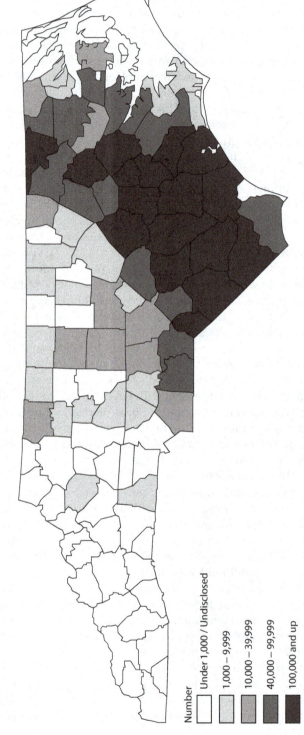

Number

Under 1,000 / Undisclosed

1,000 – 9,999

10,000 – 39,999

40,000 – 99,999

100,000 and up

Figure 13-2 Distribution of swine production in North Carolina by county.

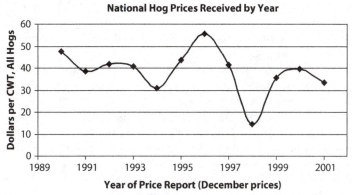

Figure 13-3 National hog prices for the month of December from 1990 to 2001.
Source: USDA National Agricultural Service

costs of waste disposal are paid by the human and ecological communities of eastern North Carolina.

Beginning in 1998, Smithfield used the profits from its fully integrated model to begin an aggressive campaign of global expansion. Over a 6-year period, it expanded into international markets by acquiring 11 domestic and foreign competitors, including Animex in Poland (1999), Mitchell's in Canada (2000), NORSON in Mexico (2000), AFG in China (2002), and SFGP in France (1999). This made Smithfield the world's largest pork producer and processor at the time. Yet, in a stunning reversal, Smithfield was purchased in 2013 by the Chinese firm WH Group, for $4.72 billion. At the time of the purchase it was the largest ever acquisition of a US company by a Chinese one. While the purchase did not substantially alter where Smithfield was selling their pork products, the purchase of a major US meat supplier by a foreign firm did raise concerns regarding US food sovereignty. This ties in directly to the processes outlined in Lesson 12.

Confined Animal Feeding Operations

Prior to the industry's explosive growth and restructuring, hog farming was conducted by numerous independent farmers raising hogs in small numbers on pasture or dirt lots. Farms specializing in hog production were rare, with most pigs being raised to supplement a farmer's income from field crops like corn, soybeans, or tobacco. Production techniques varied among traditional farmers, with hogs kept in different sorts of shelters with variable pastureland available to them. Similarly, feed consisted of a wide range of food sources, from on-farm scraps and crop byproducts to 100 percent off-farm purchased feed. Hog waste was frequently used as a natural fertilizer for restoring nutrients to fields that grew commercially viable crops on the same farm. The combination of small herd sizes and large accompanying fields led to this form of waste disposal producing no adverse environmental consequences.

Traditional hog farms of this type are all but extinct in North Carolina. Today, nearly all hogs are raised using CAFO technology. CAFOs are frequently dubbed "assembly-line swine" by their critics who want to emphasize that these operations more closely resemble industrial facilities than the traditional farms just described (see Lesson 12 for a discussion of this trend in agriculture as a whole). Swine CAFOs typically house 2,000 to 5,000 pigs in just a few large buildings, although larger operations exist that produce over a million head each year in a single facility. Contemporary production uses a three-stage process, with a different type of CAFO designed to accommodate each developmental stage. At the first stage of the process are "farrowing" operations, where breeding sows give birth to litters of pigs, which are raised there until weaning at about 15 pounds. "Wean to feeder" facilities are the second stage of the process. Once pigs at these facilities reach about 40 to 50 pounds, they are transferred to a "feeder to finish" facility. They remain at these finishing operations until reaching slaughter weight of about 250 pounds. All three stages combined, from birth to slaughter, take about five and a half months.

At all three stages, a swine CAFO consists of three essential parts: the hog house, the waste "lagoon," and the sprayfield. Hog houses are long, rectangular buildings with a center aisle and confinement pens along each side. Confinement pens vary in size depending on the stage of development of the pigs. In sow farms, pens typically consist of cramped "gestation crates" occupied by a single breeding sow. In later stages, the confinement pens are designed to accommodate a certain number of animals at the size they will be when they leave that CAFO for the next stage in the process. In other words, when 30 freshly weaned pigs of about 15 pounds each are first put in a confinement pen, they have room to maneuver and fill about one third of the pen. However, by the time they have grown to about 40 to 50 pounds and are ready to be moved to a finishing facility, their increased body mass has filled all the free space in the pen. Thus, on their last day at a given stage of the process, the pigs are so packed in that they cannot move or even lie down. This design is obviously efficient with floor space. It also enables operators to observe and tend to all pigs easily and in small numbers at a time.

Since the animals occupy the confinement pens around the clock, waste disposal is a critical issue. Hog house flooring is made of slats suspended over concrete subflooring. The spaces between each slat are sized so that animal hooves will not fit through them but urine and feces either falls between the slats or is pushed through as it is stepped on by the animals. Periodically, water is flushed along the subfloor to transport the swine excreta out of the hog house. This forms a liquid slurry of feces, urine, water, and anything else that falls through the slats. The slurry is then pumped into an adjacent waste lagoon.

Waste lagoons are open earthen pits 25 to 30 feet deep and several acres in surface area. Newer lagoons have a clay liner, but older lagoons are unlined pits dug directly into the coarse, sandy soil typical of the coastal plain. Swine waste remains in the lagoon to process anaerobically and evaporate. The evaporation of waste and its dispersion downwind is a key component of the lagoon–sprayfield waste disposal design. The intention is that the majority of the liquid portion of the swine waste will be dispersed into the atmosphere. The solid waste that remains behind is subject to anaerobic processing, wherein naturally occurring bacteria break the waste material down into its chemical components.

The other key feature of waste disposal practices is the sprayfield. Eventually, lagoons fill up from the mix of slurry and rainwater. As the lagoon level rises, its free board (the amount of space remaining in the lagoon before it overflows) decreases. When waste levels get too high, the slurry is pumped out of the lagoon and sprayed onto an adjacent field. While this system ostensibly mirrors the traditional practice of using hog waste as fertilizer, sprayfields do not grow crops with any market value. The grasses planted on sprayfields are chosen for their capacity to rapidly metabolize as much of the nitrogen and phosphorus in swine waste as possible. They can be thought of as giant, well-fertilized lawns with little to no commercial value. Sprayfields eliminate swine slurry in three ways. First, some of the waste evaporates during the spraying process. Second, some of it is metabolized into the grass. Third, the rest either soaks into the ground or leaves the sprayfield as runoff.

The last point to emphasize about CAFOs concerns their design and labor requirements. CAFOs are a capital-intensive technology, meaning they are heavily mechanized and automated and require little labor to operate (see Lesson 4). Animals enter a confinement barn pen when they arrive and typically remain in that pen until they move on to the next stage of the process. The dispensing of feed, water, and the various antibiotics and pesticides used to prevent disease among the herd is handled by the machinery. Similarly, the cleaning mechanisms described previously are entirely automated. Operators tend to the machinery but typically do not interact with the hogs unless a problem is observed. In fact, a recruiter for one of North Carolina's larger corporate integrators routinely sought to persuade farmers to construct a 3,000-head hog operation by describing it as a "housewife operation." He would explain that the farmer's wife could operate the entire CAFO during the middle of the day while the kids were at school. As described in Lesson 4 and by the treadmill of production theory (see Lesson 2), replacing human labor or making it more productive with capital-intensive technologies creates increased demands for fossil fuel energy and typically involves the use of artificial chemicals. It is only the use of copious amounts of inanimate energy that makes it possible for a single person to operate a hog CAFO by himself or herself. Similarly, the hogs can exist in such crowded conditions only through the use of a large number of synthetic chemicals to suppress disease and insect pests. CAFO technology may produce more pigs with less human labor, but it also creates a much higher environmental footprint for each pig raised in such a fashion.

Externalities of Scale

The industrialization and restructuring of the North Carolina hog indus-try has had tremendous consequences on how hog waste is managed and disposed. It is being produced at an unprecedented volume in a very small geographical area. Its composition is even radically different than the waste produced on traditional hog farms 35 years ago. These changes in the volume, concentration, and makeup of hog waste illustrate a concept we describe as "externalities of scale." This concept refers to a constellation of adverse, but not yet fully understood, economic, social, and environmental impacts found in large-scale pork production but largely absent in small-scale, traditional methods typical at the beginning of the period described here.

In traditional operations, hog herds that number in the low hundreds can be rotated over different pasturelands. The waste from the hogs contains little besides organic matter, and the fields are large enough to fully absorb the nutrients from the waste, which go on to fertilize future crops. With a low enough hog-to-land ratio, there is no pollution and you have a zero-discharge system. In concept, large-scale CAFOs use a similar system with their lagoons and sprayfields. However, full **bioremediation** is impossible for a CAFO with herd sizes in the thousands, as sufficient land is not avail-able. Hogs excrete much more waste than humans. Claims of exactly how much more vary depending on who is making the claims and their stake in the issue, but likely the amount is close to around four times as much. The reasons for this lie in a hog's growth rate. Consider that a market hog reaches a slaughter weight of 250 pounds at less than 6 months of age. A human who reaches 250 pounds at age 18 gains only 14 pounds a year. CAFO-raised pigs are gaining weight at a rate of 500 pounds per year. This tremendous growth rate requires a correspondingly tremendous rate of consumption and subse-quent excretion. Consequently, a small hog CAFO with 2,500 pigs is going to be producing the wastes of approximately 10,000 people each day. This volume is far greater than that which can be absorbed and incorporated in the surrounding fields.

When more hog waste is applied to a field than the soil can absorb (over-saturation), the extra waste washes off and into the local watershed. Even if the soil can absorb the physical waste, when more nutrients are added to the soil than the crops can utilize, the surplus nutrients leach out into the groundwater. At one point, three hog-producing counties in eastern North Carolina were generating more nitrogen than could be used by all of the crops in the entire state! The wastes and nutrients that leave the CAFOs go on to have negative impacts on surrounding communities' health, prosper-ity, well-being, and natural environment. Since the costs of this waste are being passed onto the public while the owners of the pigs realize most of the benefits, an externality is being created. Because the formation of this exter-nality is primarily due to the scale on which this process is being performed (excess waste is generated only by large-scale operations), we describe it as an "externality of scale."

Opponents of current CAFO and waste disposal practices often illustrate their concerns by suggesting that the 9 to 10 million hogs in eastern North Carolina represent the same excretory impact as 35 to 40 million people. Don Webb, a former hog farmer and founder of the Alliance for a Responsible Swine Industry, seldom misses the opportunity to portray the region as a giant cesspool, where the waste of 10 million hogs is simply laid on the land for nature to take its course. Others suggest that it is like four New York Cities moving to eastern North Carolina without the benefit of a single sewage treatment plant. Some critics emphasize that if 9 to 10 million humans lived in eastern North Carolina utilizing open-pit cesspools, it would be a public health crisis of epic proportions and a national embarrassment. Irreverent opponents joke about miracles of "immaculate excretion" when it comes to CAFO-raised swine. The bottom line is that waste is being produced on a scale far beyond that at which on-farm disposal is a feasible option. Moreover, it is important to note that this tremendous volume is not being spread evenly throughout the region. Instead, it is being concentrated onto less and less land, intensifying the runoff problem. In essence, the CAFO lagoon system stacks the waste into fewer and bigger piles.

Accompanying the differences in volume and concentration of hog wastes generated by CAFOs relative to traditional hog farms, the very composition of the wastes is radically altered by the CAFO system. In CAFOs, many things beside excrement can fall through the slats in the floor and get flushed along with the waste into the lagoons, including afterbirths, trampled and stillborn piglets, old batteries, broken bottles of insecticide, and antibiotic syringes. A more important component of CAFO hog waste, however, is excess antibiotics, vaccines, and insecticides. The extremely high concentration of hogs at high temperatures (often higher than 90°F) in close proximity to their own wastes creates the most unsanitary conditions imaginable. Most CAFOs depend on the subtherapeutic use of antibiotics as a substitute for disease control practices. Animals are routinely infused with antibiotics and vaccines and doused with insecticides (oxytetracycline, tulathromycin, ceftiofur, and tiamulin) in a preemptive attempt to combat the numerous pathogens that are festering in the relative filth of the hog barn. Whatever chemicals are not absorbed by the animals exit the barns as a component of the waste. The toxic quality of hog waste is most clearly exhibited in the color of the waste lagoons, where the interaction between the bacteria, blood, waste, and chemicals turns the liquid from a decent, healthy brown into various unnatural shades of pink.

"Externalities of scale" refers to all of the various ways that the social and environmental costs of large-scale, industrial forms of production may exceed those of more traditional methods. New production systems can be both technological, as with the shift to CAFOs, and structural, relating to how production is organized and how its costs and benefits are distributed. This second aspect of externalities of scale refers to how adverse social and environmental costs of production are often concentrated in socially and politically marginalized regions around the world, while most of the economic benefits of that production are channeled out of production zones to large corporations and their stockholders. In other words, the places and communities that most directly suffer the costs of production receive a much smaller share of its benefits (see Lesson 10). In the next two sections, we discuss the social and environmental costs of industrialized pork production on North Carolina's coastal plain.

SOCIAL IMPACTS

The radical expansion and industrialization of the North Carolina swine industry has had a wide range of far-reaching consequences. The externalities of scale created by this transformation are costs that extend into the realms of health, economics, and quality of life. This section describes these social costs, starting with the health risks created by this new style of hog production. Next, we discuss the impacts of hog CAFOs on the quality of life of members of surrounding communities. The third portion of this section deals with the economic impacts of this new model of agriculture. Finally, this section concludes with a discussion of the unequal distribution of these externalities among relatively impoverished communities with high percentages of residents of color.

The Health Risks of Exposure to Hog Wastes

A substantial body of research has established the adverse health impacts of exposure to concentrated hog wastes for swine confinement house workers. In poorly ventilated buildings, workers can be exposed to a number of hazards, including harmful levels of gases (methane, ammonia, hydrogen sulfide, and carbon monoxide), dust, infectious agents, and airborne bacteria. These hazards contribute to a wide range of respiratory disorders, from headaches and shortness of breath to hydrogen sulfide poisoning, bronchitis, atopic asthma, and acute organic dust toxic syndrome. There have been cases reported of workers dying from exposure to high concentrations of hydrogen sulfide gas or by falling into a waste lagoon. In one such instance, a worker performing repairs on a hog lagoon in Michigan was overcome by fumes from the lagoon and fell in. In an effort to rescue him, the worker's nephew, cousin, older brother, and father all separately jumped in. Like the initial victim, all four rescuers were overcome and killed by the toxic liquid and fumes.

More recent studies have examined health impacts among those living near swine CAFOs and have consistently found indications of adverse effects. Many studies have shown that the smell from swine CAFOs can be experienced by nearby residents as a sickening odor and a source of tension, depression, fatigue, and anger. Additionally, multiple studies have shown that residents living near hog CAFOs experience higher rates of respiratory, sinus, and nausea problems caused by the dust and gases being released.

Symptoms associated with proximity to a large-scale hog operation include, but are not limited to, burning eyes, runny nose, headache, cough, diarrhea, nausea and vomiting, dizziness, shortness of breath, and chest tightness. Moreover, the contamination of local drinking water, through lagoon leakage or sprayfield runoff, can allow pathogen transfer between pigs and people and lead to such human diseases as salmonellosis, giardiasis, chlamydia, meningitis, cryptosporidiosis, worms, and influenza. Additionally, waste lagoons have been linked to increased levels of nitrates in drinking water, which can cause methemoglobinemia, or "blue baby syndrome," a rare but potentially life-threatening condition for infants. Finally, a number of public health experts have expressed concerns over the linkage between hog CAFOs and H1N1, the swine flu. The pestilent conditions in these operations make them ideal breeding grounds for novel human diseases. These numerous health risks associated with swine CAFOs and the wastes they produce clearly demonstrate the need to treat them as a dangerous hazard.

Quality of Life

In addition to the direct health risks associated with proximity to a large-scale hog operation, there have been numerous findings of negative impacts of hog CAFOs on nearby residents' quality of life. Individuals living near lagoons or hog barns can find themselves virtually trapped in their own houses, unable to open windows or go outside and sit on the porch in nice weather. Clothes hung out to dry are said to come back in smelling of hog waste. While difficult to quantify, the impact of hog waste on individuals' quality of life certainly constitutes an important externality. Some hog CAFO neighbors have found themselves trapped in their homes in a different way. Research clearly indicates that the value of homes close to hog CAFOs is less than that of comparable homes farther away. Similarly, the value of existing homes declines significantly if a nearby farmer decides to construct a CAFO. Thus, some residents who wish to move away from a CAFO cannot do so because they are unable to sell their homes and cannot afford to continue to make payments on them while renting or buying another house elsewhere. These numerous quality of life issues formed the basis of 26 nuisance lawsuits that were filed against Smithfield by over 500 plaintiffs beginning in 2014. We discuss those lawsuits in greater detail below.

Economic Impacts

The North Carolina Pork Council has vigorously touted the industry as the economic backbone of eastern North Carolina. According to their claims, the North Carolina hog industry generates $6.7 billion in annual sales and supports 46,000 jobs. An economic input as large as this in an impoverished region is substantial and important. Yet, the "economic miracle" of the North Carolina pork industry comes with economic costs as well. First, no one disputes that the industry restructuring and conversion to CAFOs drove thousands of small farmers out of business and contributed to a wave of farm loss in North Carolina. Hog farmers who did not contract with corporate integrators were pushed out of the business entirely. The main mechanism for this came from slaughterhouse policies that would accept hogs only in lots of 1,000 or more. Independent producers, even those in co-ops of 40 or 50 farmers, could not amass 1,000 slaughter-ready hogs on the same day; only large corporate integrators could meet this demand. It is also worth challenging the claims of economic benefits with questions about how much of the money produced by the pork industry actually stays in the region. Due to the industry restructuring, the overwhelming majority of profits are realized by Smithfield Foods and its parent firm, WH Group, and their shareholders. The majority of the feed for the pigs is imported from the Midwest. Meanwhile, most of the jobs associated with this industry are found at the Bladen County slaughterhouse (remember that CAFOs are capital-intensive and require little in the way of labor), where wages are low and the work is hard and dangerous.

Additionally, while industry proponents may claim that the pork industry is the economic backbone of the region, the state's single largest industry currently is tourism. This industry depends on the perception of an uncontaminated environment. North Carolina has about 300 miles of coast along the Atlantic Ocean and another 3,000 or so miles of inland coast along its sounds and tidal river systems. All of these areas are popular vacation and recreation destinations. They are also attracting a substantial inflow of retirees. Neither vacationers nor retirees want to smell a swine CAFO. Nor do they want to wonder what's in the water. Prominent national media coverage of hog operations in North Carolina between 1995 and 1997, and then again following the massive flooding from Hurricane Floyd that inundated the region in 1999, and again in 2018 following Hurricane Florence, threaten to diminish the area's appeal as a vacation or retirement destination. In the 1990s, such fears motivated substantial segments of the state's business community to join with environmentalists in pushing for stricter regulation of the industry.

Environmental Injustice

Thus far we have discussed social, health, and economic impacts in general terms. However, the evidence is indisputable that these impacts have not been distributed evenly among the population of North Carolina, or even among residents of the eastern region. First, hog production, and thus any adverse impacts flowing from it, is concentrated in one region of the state. The region lies between Interstate 95 and the Atlantic coast and has been on the periphery, both economically and politically, throughout its history. Much of eastern North Carolina is socially isolated and has higher rates of poverty, a higher proportion of African American residents, and lower rates of homeownership and college graduation than other parts of the state. In many ways the region is a rural analog for what sociologist William Julius Wilson referred to as truly disadvantaged areas of concentrated poverty and social isolation (see Lesson 10).

Low-income, African American, and politically marginalized communities up and down the coastal plain complain that a disproportionate number of hog operations are locating in their communities, leaving them to suffer the consequences without sharing the benefits. At least five separate scientific studies have confirmed the accuracy of their claim of disproportionate exposure, finding that African Americans regardless of income and low-income residents regardless of race are significantly more likely to live close to a hog CAFO. As we discussed before, the presence of hog waste lagoons seriously diminishes both the health and the quality of life of those living nearby. Additionally, as they depress local property values, they further exacerbate the economic conditions of the low-income communities they are built in. Furthermore, a disproportionate amount of the farm loss associated with swine CAFOs is located within African American communities, as African American farmers are far less likely to receive contracts with corporate integrators. Overall, the trend in eastern North Carolina is that African American and low-income residents are more likely to suffer the adverse impacts of the swine CAFOs, while being systematically excluded from any of the associated benefits.

ENVIRONMENTAL IMPACTS

The Earth is a multifaceted ecosystem of systems within systems. Adverse impacts produced in one place diffuse globally, eventually affecting all places even if to a negligible degree. Nevertheless, the environmental damage caused by an industry's production will be most apparent in the specific places where that production is concentrated. Both the human and biotic communities living in zones of concentrated production will be more likely to pay the costs of environmental damage. This brings us again to our notion of "externalities of scale" and raises two interrelated questions about the environmental impacts of swine production: What kind of place is this zone of concentrated production ecologically? How well suited is it to tolerate the environmental stressors of hog CAFOs? This section explores and describes those costs, starting with a discussion on the unsuitability of eastern North Carolina for this particular mode of waste disposal. Following that is a description of the ways the lagoon system allows hog wastes to end up in the environment. Finally, this section concludes by discussing the impacts untreated hog waste can have on the ecosystems of eastern North Carolina.

Regional Vulnerability

Newcomers to the region are often overwhelmed by just how flat it is. The upper deck of the East Carolina University football stadium in Greenville may well be the highest point in the entire region. The Tar River in Greenville, 70 miles from the Atlantic Ocean, is no more than 50 feet above sea level when not in flood stage. This flat region, like other low-lying coastal zones, was once primarily swamps, or more accurately, wetlands. Colonial settlers in eastern North Carolina used enslaved laborers to dig a vast network of ditches throughout the region to drain the swamps so that they could be planted for agriculture. Without the network of drainage ditches, much of the region would still be underwater, or at least wetlands. Yet, this is the same region where the hog industry is concentrated. In this area the water table is close to the surface region-wide. By the time one digs 25 to 30 feet down to construct a waste lagoon, it is quite likely that the bottom of the lagoon will be very close to the water table, if not already in it.

Additionally, with the land so flat, the waterways move very slowly. When swine waste is applied to land already saturated from rain, it runs off into the system of drainage ditches that serve as direct transport into creeks and rivers. Nutrients like nitrogen and phosphorus run off and enter the slow-moving estuarine waterways. In other types of river systems in less-flat land, the rivers would quickly carry these pollutants downstream and eventually out to sea, transferring the environmental problem into an ocean "sink." Yet, in eastern North Carolina, the nutrients remain in the slow-moving creeks and rivers for days or weeks. Finally, the soils of eastern North Carolina are coarse and sandy, making them highly permeable to both liquid waste and small particulate matter. These geological features constitute a form of physical vulnerability (see Lesson 14) and make the region extremely ill-suited for the application of waste from 9 to 10 million hogs.

Nonpoint Source Pollution Still Pollutes

According to industry public relations statements, the lagoon-sprayfield system does not discharge hog wastes into waterways. Yet, as we describe in this section, substantial amounts of pollutants get into waterways from swine CAFOs. How can both statements be true? The answer lies in the important distinction between "point source" and "nonpoint source" pollution. **Point source polluters** are industrial facilities that are regulated under the federal Clean Water Act (CWA). These facilities must obtain a discharge permit from the US EPA, which regulates the type and amount of pollutants each facility is allowed to discharge. Municipal sewage treatment plants fall into this category. By contrast, **nonpoint source pollution** comes mainly from urban storm water and agricultural runoff. As the laws were understood prior to 2003, CAFOs qualified as point source polluters only if they had some distinct outlet (such as a ditch, drain, or culvert) through which wastes were entering waterways. Without such, by legal definition, they do not "discharge" pollutants and were not governed by the CWA. So when the industry claims that it does not discharge hog waste into waterways, all it is really saying is that hog CAFOs are nonpoint source polluters rather than point source dischargers. In truth, the waste lagoon-sprayfield system is consciously designed to transport pollutants off the farm through a variety of mechanisms.

The lagoon-sprayfield system is built to dispose of pollutants in swine waste through evaporation and subsequent condensation. For example, as much as 70 to 80 percent of the nitrogen in a lagoon evaporates and is carried downwind and dropped on nearby lands and waterways through atmospheric deposition. Thus, waste from hog CAFOs finds its way into the environment even when the lagoon-sprayfield system works just as designed. Yet, a significant amount of pollutants leave CAFOs routinely in ways not built into the design of the system. Swine waste enters underground aquifers and contaminates groundwater through leaking waste lagoons and the leaching of sprayfield waste. For example, a study by North Carolina State University showed that 38 percent of older, unlined, swine waste lagoons leached nitrogen compounds into the groundwater at "strong" or "very strong" levels, while a state testing program found that more than one-third of private wells near hog operations showed some contamination.

Contaminants from swine waste leave farms by runoff from sprayfields and waste lagoon leaks and occasionally by lagoon ruptures and discharges associated with flooding or very heavy rains. Any overapplication of hog waste to sprayfields, which often occurs shortly after, or even during, rain storms results in waste running off into local waterways. Lagoon ruptures, while not common, pose a serious threat to surface water. When the contents of a lagoon are not pumped onto sprayfields in a timely fashion, the lagoon can fill to the point of bursting. In a region where both northeasters and tropical storms are frequent, heavy rainfalls intensify the risk of lagoons rupturing and directly spilling millions of gallons of waste into the surrounding area. In 1995, heavy rains contributed to a series of lagoon failures, highlighted by a 22-million-gallon spill at Oceanview Farms, a 10,000-head operation in Onslow County. Spills of this type dump high volumes of pure hog waste directly into the region's waterways.

Hog waste lagoons are also vulnerable to hurricane-related flooding. As described, the flat topography of eastern North Carolina makes the region very vulnerable to extreme flooding following the intense rainfall that accompanies hurricanes. For example, both Hurricanes Floyd in 1999 and Florence in 2018 caused widespread flooding over a period of several weeks, with nearly every river basin in the region exceeding 100-year or even 500-year flood levels. In both cases, somewhere between 30 to 50 waste lagoons were underwater or filled beyond safe capacity. The amount of waste that entered waterways during this flooding is unknown but likely dwarfed isolated incidents like the Onslow County spill (see Lesson 14 for a broader discussion of the interaction between human systems, the built environment, and natural environments).

Clearly nonpoint polluters like swine CAFO's release substantial amounts of pollutants into surface and groundwater. One strategy thought to mitigate these impacts was to have CAFOs legally designated as point source polluters and brought under the regulations of the CWA. This played out in a series of lawsuits between the Waterkeeper Alliance and the National Pork Producers Council, which led to revisions of the CWA in 2003, 2008, and 2012. The final ruling at the national level designated all CAFOs as point source polluters. However, CAFO owners and operators were not required to apply for a permit, only to have one if they discharged waste. While this ruling grants the EPA the right to prosecute CAFOs that can be shown to have released wastes into waterways, it does not give the EPA any authority to monitor whether or not CAFOs are doing so. At the state level, a settlement by Smithfield in North Carolina included an agreement that all Smithfield-owned and contracted CAFOs would obtain CWA permits. However, to date, virtually none of them has done so. So the situation stands that any CAFO that is releasing wastes into eastern North Carolina's waterways is technically in violation of the law, but the burden of proof lies on those affected.

The Ecological Consequences of Hog Waste

We have described the vulnerability of eastern North Carolina's geography to water pollution and the various ways through which hog waste can find its way into the region's waterways. We now turn to the impacts of those hog wastes on the local ecology. It is important to note that the region in which these hog CAFOs are concentrated contains both the Cape Fear and Neuse river basins, the latter of which drains into the Pamlico Sound. The Pamlico Sound serves as a breeding ground for a number of anadromous fish species (fish that migrate to freshwater to spawn) found from Maine to Florida. Therefore, damage to the sound threatens the ecology of the entire North Atlantic.

The primary effect of hog waste on waterways is the "nutrient loading" that occurs in the local watershed. Simple nutrients play a crucial role in aquatic ecosystems, providing the basic building blocks of freshwater plankton and basic aquatic plants. However, when nutrients build up into excessive levels in the shallow, slow-moving waters, they create a state of **eutrophication** that promotes excessive plant growth and decay. This state can completely disrupt an ecosystem through the creation of algal blooms and oxygen depletion in the water, both of which can prove fatal to fish and plants that normally live in the waterways. While algae produce oxygen through photosynthesis during the day, they use it up through respiration during the night. Therefore, an overabundance of algae in the water can lower oxygen levels below that of what other species require to survive. Additionally, as the algae die off, they become food for bacteria, which multiply and use up available oxygen. So eutrophication can create an ecological breakdown by lowering oxygen levels below those required to support life. This damage is borne out by the numerous fish kills that occurred in eastern North Carolina during the 1990s, some of which totaled in the millions. Local residents tell stories of shorelines being completely covered with dead and rotting fish. At times, city employees in New Bern (a tourist town located along the Neuse River) had to remove dead fish from their boat ramp and picnic areas by the tons. These kills would be followed by periods in which the rivers seemed empty and lifeless.

In addition to the excess nutrients it contains, the pathogens found in hog waste can also severely disrupt aquatic ecosystems. Fecal bacteria and protozoans can disrupt a food system and, in sufficient quantities, can kill larger animals directly. In humans, these organisms can cause diseases involving flu-like symptoms such as nausea, vomiting, fever, and diarrhea. Bacteria can thrive on river bottoms for weeks after initial exposure. In one instance in 1994, a recreational lake in Duplin County with seven nearby hog farms was found to have a fecal coliform count (an indicator of fecal contamination) 60 times the allowable level for swimming. At such levels, the bacteria and pathogens contained in hog waste are a threat to the balance of any aquatic ecosystem.

POLITICS AND PROTEST

Thus far we have focused on changes to the pork industry and the social and environmental impacts of those changes. However, the transformation of North Carolina's hog industry from a sustainable small-scale system into the corporate-owned "swine factory" system we now have did not occur in a historical or political vacuum. A combination of events and individuals guided this shift and shaped the nature of the 20-year overhaul. This section describes and details that history, highlighting the roles of various stakeholders in both promoting and resisting the transformation of this industry.

Early Growth

To understand why the hog industry could grow so quickly in North Carolina, we need to return to the influence of Wendell Murphy. In addition to being the leading hog producer in the state, Murphy had been the college roommate of four-term Democratic governor James Hunt and served in the North Carolina General Assembly from 1982 to 1992. While in office, he passed legislative acts to promote pork production as an alternative to tobacco in economically distressed eastern North Carolina. These actions, widely referred to as "Murphy's Laws" by industry critics, included a bill that exempted large, CAFO-style hog operations from county-level zoning restrictions, an amendment that granted animal and poultry feeding operations immunity from North Carolina air and water standards, and a bill exempting the industry from selected state taxes and fees. Combined, this body of regulations was highly effective in promoting growth in the pork industry and shielding it from environmental regulation.

The Rise of Opposition

The transformation of pork production in North Carolina did not go unchallenged. A vigorous opposition to swine CAFOs in eastern North Carolina first surfaced in 1990–1991 with the formation of a number of grassroots organizations like the Alliance for a Responsible Swine Industry and Concerned Citizens of Tillery that "were tired of hogs stinking up their environment and decided to fight back." In 1993, Concerned Citizens of Tillery persuaded 42 North Carolina environmental and citizens' groups to form the Hog Roundtable. This unique coalition brought together grassroots, legal, and mainstream environmental organizations with the dual goals of protecting communities from the environmental health hazards associated with intensive hog operations as well as forging ties between environmental justice groups and mainstream environmental organizations (see Lessons 10 and 18). The Hog Roundtable further organized opposition to pork industry expansion and sought to put its social and environmental impacts on the public agenda.

Their efforts attracted serious press attention in 1995, when the *Raleigh News & Observer* published an investigative series entitled "Boss Hog: North Carolina's Pork Revolution." The series amplified and often substantiated the claims of industry critics who charged the pork industry with polluting the state's air and water, displacing traditional small farmers with integrated corporations, and using its political ties to state lawmakers to avoid economic and environmental regulations. The "Boss Hog" series touched off a firestorm of reaction from virtually every interest group in the state with a stake in the industry and went on to win a Pulitzer Prize for public service reporting. Further attracting attention to this industry, within months of the Boss Hog publication, heavy rains in eastern counties caused waste lagoons at seven hog facilities to burst. Over the next few weeks, over 40 million gallons of untreated swine feces and urine spilled into the streams and rivers of the coastal region. An estimated 10 to 15 million fish died as a result, and 364,000 acres of waterways were closed to commercial and recreational fishing.

A Partial Resolution and a Sustained Problem

Toward the end of 1995, North Carolina was at the center of growing national and regional debate and intensifying opposition to industrial hog operations. Then-Governor Hunt responded with a blue-ribbon commission to study agricultural waste. Public opposition, scientific study, and political debate over swine operations intensified; and by 1997, the politics of swine waste was the single largest and most contentious issue in North Carolina. Hog Roundtable groups mobilized public concerns over odor, water pollution, equity, and recreation into an effective lobby. Meanwhile, the North Carolina Pork Council responded with a statewide public relations media campaign, asserting that hog farms were the economic lifeblood of the state and claiming an unmatched record of environmental stewardship. After months of intense lobbying, the North Carolina General Assembly passed the Clean Water Responsibility Act (CWRA) in August 1997. The CWRA imposed increased regulatory controls over the industry to protect air and water quality as well as a 2-year moratorium on new and expanded hog operations. At the time, the passage of the CWRA was viewed as a tremendous victory for hog opponents.

While the CWRA halted industry growth, it did not eliminate public pressure for a long-term solution to the hog waste issue. With Smithfield Foods consolidating ownership of the North Carolina hog industry, it became the focal point of industry critiques and reform activities. It also created an opportunity for then-Attorney General Mike Easley to negotiate an agreement with only one party that would defuse a potent issue. In the Smithfield–Easley agreement of July 2000, Smithfield Foods agreed to provide $15 million over 10 years to fund research into alternative waste disposal technologies and to pay $50 million toward cleaning up abandoned waste lagoons and compliance monitoring. Additionally, Smithfield pledged to adopt the new technology on all company-owned farms within 3 years, if the technology were to prove economically feasible. In exchange for this, the state of North Carolina implicitly agreed to maintain the status quo until the research team made its recommendations. The agreement was widely hailed as a successful resolution that demonstrated the potential of public–private partnerships to solve environmental problems. Nevertheless, critics pointed out several flaws. First, Smithfield's profits were so great at the time that the agreement essentially required them to exchange 4 months' worth of profits for 10 years of being left alone to continue polluting as usual. Second, the agreement applied only to the 276 hog operations directly owned by Smithfield, not the other 2,000-plus operations in the state that contracted with Smithfield. Efforts by environmentalists to point out these flaws in the agreement gained little attention.

Following the passage of the CWRA and the Smithfield–Easley agreement, the hog issue largely dropped off the public radar until 2006, when the research that Smithfield funded through the Smithfield–Easley agreement produced a report that detailed five alternative technologies. However, none of them was deemed to be cost-effective by Smithfield Foods, and to date none has been implemented. Dissatisfaction with this outcome generated enough political pressure to make the moratorium of the CWRA permanent in 2007. Freezing the 1997 hog population in place did prevent the magnitude of environmental impacts from escalating, but the waste from a stable population of 9 to 10 million hogs sustains substantial adverse impacts year in and year out. So after 15 years of pushing for and then supporting the moratorium, North Carolina's environmental community reversed its stance and now opposes the moratorium in favor of a permanent ban on lagoon and sprayfield disposal technologies.

In 2014, local residents began filing a series of twenty-six nuisance lawsuits against Murphy-Brown and its parent company, Smithfield foods. These lawsuits alleged that the practices of the swine industry had adversely impacted their health and quality of life. As Smithfield owns the animals being raised in the CAFOs and sets the protocols for how the animals are raised, the plaintiffs did not include any of the farmers who own the CAFOs in their lawsuits. The first four of these lawsuits were decided in 2018, and

Smithfield was found guilty in all four. The first three cases resulted in almost $550 million in damages awarded to the plaintiffs, although a North Carolina damages cap law reduced that amount to approximately $98 million. In the fourth case, while the jury found Smithfield Foods guilty, the plaintiffs were only awarded a relatively low compensatory damage award. Smithfield has pledged to appeal the four verdicts and decried these lawsuits as attacks on agriculture, but with 22 more cases awaiting trial, Smithfield and its Chinese parent company may be facing substantial losses in both the economic sector as well as the court of public opinion.

CONCLUSIONS

This lesson has described how the industrialization of hog production in North Carolina has created a host of "externalities of scale" that were absent in traditional hog farming. These externalities include health risks, farm loss, reduced quality of life, and environmental degradation. Currently, this situation remains unresolved, with the waste from the production and slaughter of 10 million hogs still concentrated in an ecologically fragile region that contains a disproportionate number of poor and minority residents. Massive fish kills on the lower Neuse River in the falls of 2009 and 2012 (both within the range of 15 to 50 million dead fish) provide excellent testimony as to the environmental damage that continues to this day. Smithfield Foods and its parent company, WH Group, are still realizing incredible profits on the backs of eastern North Carolina's residents and ecosystems.

Furthermore, the lessons that can be drawn from CAFO-style pork production can easily be extended to apply to nearly all types of industrial protein production. Poultry, fish, shellfish, dairy, and beef are all currently being raised in a similar fashion. With this form of factory agriculture becoming the norm across the meat production industry, the issues and concerns raised about pork production in North Carolina have general implications up and down the global supply chain (see Lesson 12). Wherever animals are being raised in an industrial fashion, corporate profits are being accumulated at the expense of local communities and their physical environments.

SOURCES

Edwards, Bob, and Anthony E. Ladd. 2000. "Environmental Justice, Swine Production and Farm Loss in North Carolina." *Sociological Spectrum* 20: 263–290.

Fennel, Bettie. 1991. "Group Says Hog Farms Plain Stink." *Sunday Star-News* (December 1): 1B 4B.

Fine, Ken, and Erica Hellerstein. 2017. "Hogwashed." Indy Week, July 12. https://indyweek.com/news

Furuseth, Owen. 1997. "Restructuring of Hog Farming in NC: Explosion and Implosion." *Professional Geographer* 49: 391–403.

Juska, Arunas, and Bob Edwards. 2004. "Refusing the Trojan Pig: The Trans-Atlantic Coalition Corporate Pork Production in Poland." In *Coalitions Across Borders: Transnational Protest and the Neoliberal Order*, edited by Joe Bandy and Jackie Smith, 187–207. Lanham, MD: Rowman & Littlefield.

Ladd, Anthony, and Bob Edwards. 2002. "Corporate Swine, Capitalist Pigs: A Decade of Environmental Injustice in North Carolina." *Social Justice* 29 (3): 26–46.

North Carolina Department of Environment and Natural Resources. 1999. "Framework for the Conversion of Anaerobic Swine Waste Lagoons and Sprayfields." Office of the Governor, Raleigh, NC.

Smithfield. 2007. "About Smithfield." Accessed March 5, 2007. http://www.smithfield.com/about/index.php

Stith, Pat, Joby Warrick, and Melanie Sill. 1995. "Boss Hog: North Carolina's Pork Revolution." *News and Observer*, February 19–26, 1A–16A.

Wilson, William Julius. 1990. *The Truly Disadvantaged: The Inner City, the Underclass, and Public Policy*. Chicago, IL: University of Chicago Press.

Wing, Steve, Dana Cole, and Gary Grant. 2000. "Environmental Injustice in North Carolina's Hog Industry." *Environmental Health Perspectives* 108: 225–231.

14

Understanding Disaster Vulnerability
Floods and Hurricanes

Nicole Youngman

Remains of a home on Barbuda after the eye of category 5 hurricane Irma passed through Codrington, Antigua and Barbuda.

Post your photo on disaster vulnerability and the environment to #TLESdisaster.

Photo by Ken Gould

Environmental and disaster sociologists have long noted that our increasingly complex human social structures and technologies have created more complicated disasters that put greater numbers of people at risk, positing that the degree of exposure to these risks might become a more powerful source of social inequalities than social class or race. Decades ago, social theorist Charles Perrow pointed out that given enough time, things will inevitably go wrong in multifaceted systems like nuclear power plants, which create the potential for radioactive releases due to human error, technological failures, or extreme seismic and weather events. The Fukushima Daiichi disaster of 2011 proved to be a case in point when a coastal nuclear power plant in Japan experienced multiple meltdowns after being struck by an earthquake and the tsunami that followed.

Although these kinds of technological disasters seem to have clearly anthropogenic (human) causes, we tend to think of "natural disasters" like floods and hurricanes as extreme events that have their origins solely in the workings of the Earth's physical systems. But even though different kinds of disasters may have different *triggers*, which may or may not be the direct result of human activities, they are all caused by *interactions* among three overlapping systems: human social and cultural systems, the built environment, and the preexisting natural environments in which they are embedded. The impacts of all disasters, from tornado touchdowns to nuclear meltdowns, are directly related to how and where human societies organize themselves. As Kai Erikson noted in his study of the horrific Buffalo Creek flood, disasters always create **community** (rather than simply individual) **trauma** where long-established human connections among community members are wrenched apart. Some residents of disaster-prone areas are exposed to higher ongoing risks than others, however, making them much more **vulnerable** to extreme losses of life or property.

Several hurricanes that have struck the United States in recent years have clearly demonstrated how a myriad of human and nonhuman factors can come together to produce profoundly traumatic events. Hurricanes bring several dangers as they move ashore, including extremely high winds, storm surge (the ocean water picked up and pushed inland by the storm's winds and low pressure), inland flooding from heavy rainfall, and tornadoes. Each storm is very different. A relatively small storm might have category 5 winds over 155 miles an hour with a narrow impact and very little rainfall, while a larger or more slow-moving storm with much lower winds might be equally deadly due to the flooding it creates.

Recent storms have caused catastrophic flooding in heavily populated areas in the United States. Hurricane Katrina, the costliest hurricane in American history and by far the most deadly in over a century, was a strong category 3 storm that struck the Mississippi and southeast Louisiana coasts on August 29, 2005, killing over 1,700 people and engulfing 80 percent of New Orleans. It also inundated nearly all of St. Bernard and Plaquemines parishes (counties) to the city's south and east, and largely obliterated the Mississippi Gulf Coast. Hurricane Harvey, the second costliest hurricane ever to strike the United States, was a category 4 storm that moved over Southeast Texas during the last week of August 2017, flooding about a third of Houston. Its rainfall totals were truly mind-boggling—the highest ever recorded for a tropical cyclone in the United States—reaching over three feet throughout a large section of the metro Houston area and as high as 60 inches in some places. Additionally, Harvey's storm surge reached up to 10 feet high in some areas along coast. The storm produced over 50 recorded tornadoes and killed at least 68 people.

Superstorm Sandy, which began as an Atlantic hurricane, devastated the New Jersey and New York City coastal areas on October 29, 2012. While Sandy was technically no longer a hurricane as it came ashore, its impact was still severe, with over 140 lives lost in the United States and Canada, plus about 70 people killed in the Caribbean. Factors beyond wind speed turned Sandy into a monster: its enormous diameter of over 800 miles, its unusual late-season track up the Eastern Seaboard, and its merger with northern winter weather systems (a phenomenon that led then-FEMA [Federal Emergency Management Agency] director Craig Fugate to quip on NBC's *Today Show* that he hadn't "been around long enough to see a hurricane forecast with a snow advisory in it"). The unusual nature of the storm produced unprecedented flood impacts along the New York/New Jersey coastline, with storm surges of over nine feet on top of normal high tides in some locations. The storm washed away homes and rental properties throughout the area's low-lying coastal communities and knocked out much of New York City's transportation and electrical infrastructure, flooding subways and tunnels and creating massive blackouts across Manhattan and the surrounding areas.

Other recent hurricanes have created cataclysmic impacts even without any direct hits on large cities at landfall. Hurricane Florence's impact was in some ways similar to Harvey's. It came ashore in North Carolina on September 14, 2018, as a strong category 1 storm. Although its winds had dropped dramatically before it made landfall, Florence was a slow-moving storm whose rain bands often trained over the same areas for long periods of time, producing up to three feet of rain in some areas. Towns throughout the Carolinas and the Southeast, particularly near the coast, experienced deadly, record-high flash flooding. As with previous hurricanes in the Carolinas, the hog and poultry industries were especially hard hit; livestock deaths were massive, and animal waste from hundreds of gigantic flooded "hog lagoons" once again inundated the surrounding areas, creating an extraordinary ecological and public health menace (see Driscoll and Edwards's discussion of the hog industry in lesson 13).

Hurricane Maria tore across the island of Puerto Rico on September 20, 2017, wiping out electricity, water, and phone services to nearly the entire territory for several months, and in some areas even longer. The storm's death toll has been a huge source of controversy, with estimates ranging from an initial official government estimate of a few dozen to more comprehensive studies demonstrating that a few thousand people died both from the storm's initial impact and from residents' inability to access health care during the aftermath. The storm is the third most costly in American history, with the Trump administration's disaster relief effort receiving heavy criticism worldwide for its lack of efficiency and responsiveness to the human suffering created by the nearly category-5 storm.

Another major hurricane, Hurricane Michael, was retroactively upgraded to Category 5 status months after it came ashore near Mexico Beach, Florida, on October 10, 2018. While in some ways Michael was a more typical coastal hurricane than the others discussed here, the damage it left behind to small coastal towns, the Panama City area, and the surrounding forested area was far beyond what one might expect from an "ordinary" hurricane. Responsible for at least 74 deaths, Michael created enough debris to nearly bankrupt Mexico Beach and other nearby towns as they anxiously awaited appropriations of federal aid dollars for assistance with cleanup and rebuilding. The storm also destroyed around 500 million trees, creating both an increased danger of massive wildfires and a heightened risk of rainfall-induced flooding.

THINKING ABOUT VULNERABILITY

Flood vulnerability is rising worldwide for a variety of reasons, including higher levels of urbanization and industrialization, rapid population growth and development along coastlines and river valleys, and sea-level rises induced by climate change. Disaster sociologists distinguish between **physical vulnerability** and **social vulnerability**, which have different but overlapping causes and consequences. Physical vulnerability generally refers to one's geographical location; different parts of the world, of course, are more prone to various kinds of natural disasters than others. More specific locations matter, too: living downstream or next to a dam or levee that might break, on a hillside prone to slide in heavy rains, or in a poorly constructed dwelling increases one's risk of experiencing a catastrophe. This type of physical vulnerability is sometimes referred to as "unsafe conditions." Social vulnerability refers to preexisting conditions, rooted in social inequalities, that affect potential disaster victims' ability to escape, survive, and/or "bounce back" from a disaster: race, class, gender, age, disability, health status, and so forth. Physical and social vulnerability are frequently intertwined in complex ways and can exist at the individual, household, or community level.

All of the hurricanes discussed above can provide us with clear examples of how physical and social vulnerability overlap. In some ways, physical vulnerability in New Orleans cuts across racial and class lines. The city has both white/upper-class and minority/low-income neighborhoods that flooded catastrophically in Katrina due to their lack of elevation and/or proximity to drainage or shipping canals. Meanwhile, other well-to-do and poorer neighborhoods alike escaped flooding because they were built on higher ground in older sections of the city. This does not, however, mean that all of the city's flooded communities are equally vulnerable to disasters overall. Because residents in wealthier communities generally have considerably more financial resources and human capital at their disposal, they are much more likely to be able to eventually return and rebuild if they so desire or to "start over" elsewhere if they prefer. This is not to say that the recovery process is not difficult at best for all hurricane victims; lengthy, exhausting struggles with insurance companies and government disaster assistance programs, for instance, abound throughout all affected areas. But even so, wealthier victims are more likely to have had sufficient insurance in the first place, to have well-paying jobs to return to and high-quality schools and daycare available, and to have the skills and social networks necessary to negotiate the piles of paperwork and extensive new regulations that flourish in a post-disaster environment.

Race and social class also played important roles in Hurricane Sandy's impact. As the storm approached, New York's working-class, service-sector workers stayed at their jobs so that others with more means could stock up on supplies and prepare to keep their families safe. Hotel workers remained on site to look after wealthy evacuees who had checked in to take refuge away from the beaches. After the storm passed, much of the nation's media outlets focused their attention on the blow to New York City's infrastructure, particularly the widespread power outages and the flooded subway system. While experts from the Corps of Engineers worked to pump out the city's highway and subway tunnels—an effort sometimes compared to their work to de-water New Orleans in 2005—storm survivors away from the wealthy sections of Manhattan in the more modest communities of the Rockaways and Staten Island struggled to call attention to their desperate need for help after the storm wiped out their neighborhoods.

Public housing residents were hit especially hard, with 402 buildings comprising 35,000 housing units damaged by the storm. Authorities debated demolishing complexes near the river that already had a history of flooding and replacing the sites with mixed-income housing or green space that could be allowed to flood periodically, giving rise to heated debates about safety versus gentrification as displaced residents struggled to apply for FEMA housing vouchers and find somewhere to go. Additionally, New Yorkers who were black were more likely to live in areas that flooded, as were lower-income Latinos. In the Houston area, too, blacks, Hispanics, and lower-income households were more likely to live in census tracts that experienced flooding from Hurricane Harvey than were non-Hispanic whites and households with higher incomes. And in Puerto Rico, the island's status as an unincorporated territory of the United States and its colonial history played a major role in the high levels of poverty and lack of functional infrastructure its residents had to cope with even before Hurricane Maria hit.

Gender issues, too, play an important role in determining disaster vulnerability. While our society is considerably less patriarchal (male-dominated) than it has been in the past, women of all races and social classes still tend to find themselves dealing with considerably heavier childcare, elder care, and housework responsibilities than men. For single mothers, this is obviously a huge burden; but even married women with jobs and incomes comparable to those of their spouses often find themselves in this position due to cultural norms that still consider such activities "women's work." In the aftermath of a disaster, these "traditional gender roles" tend to be exacerbated, even for couples that have tried to create more egalitarian relationships. With buildings and infrastructures heavily damaged and many residents unable to return, schools and daycare centers may be unable to reopen for months after the disaster or may close permanently. Traumatized children, who may have lost their homes and belongings and/or had family members die, often "act out" in ways that can be difficult for their caregivers to predict or cope with. Widespread damage to businesses and office buildings can create long commutes for those relatively lucky residents who are able to go back to work when their jobs are forced to relocate to more distant locations.

With no outside help caring for children or elderly family members, many women end up staying home to tackle these responsibilities full-time while their male partners (who usually earn more than they do, even if both had worked outside the home previously) put in extraordinarily long hours commuting to work. Both single- and two-parent families may find themselves unable to return home at all without childcare available since the situation makes it impossible for mothers to go back to work, and many families rely on women's incomes to survive economically. Women also tend to find themselves with the primary responsibilities of applying for disaster aid—which often involves standing in long lines for many hours, with young children in tow—and dealing with the contractors who arrive to repair their homes, some of whom turn out to be con artists who take victims' money and promptly disappear. The stresses of dealing with these kinds of situations on an everyday basis can lead to significant marital and other family problems, particularly when men and women are facing different kinds of stresses and may have different coping strategies (for example, talking about them vs. "being strong" and "bottling up" emotions), making communication difficult.

Interestingly, however, there are some situations where being male might actually lead to *higher* disaster vulnerability, largely due to faulty decision-making processes. Generally speaking, men in our culture are heavily socialized to be tough, strong, and fearless, and as a result they are more likely to engage in risky behaviors than women are. This dynamic can prove deadly during floods, where most drownings occur when drivers misjudge their chances of safely navigating flooded roadways. Men are more likely to ignore warnings or miscalculate water depth and attempt to drive through, sometimes with tragic consequences. This was the case during Hurricane Harvey, where 70 percent of the deaths were men, and the vast majority of those were people who drowned, most often in their vehicles. During Hurricane Florence, too, the majority of people who drowned in their cars were older men.

Hurricane evacuations also provide examples of different kinds of physical and social vulnerability. For low-income residents, the physical vulnerability of living in a disaster-prone location is frequently compounded by the physical inability to leave when disaster threatens. Pre-Katrina research in the New Orleans area had clearly demonstrated that at least 100,000 residents did not have cars and thus would be unable to leave in advance of a major hurricane. This problem became all too obvious when tens of thousands of New Orleans residents, almost all of them African American, fled to the Superdome and the Convention Center downtown before, during, and immediately after Katrina made landfall, remaining stranded in the blistering heat for days with little or no food, water, or sanitation. The preexisting social vulnerabilities these victims faced led directly to extreme physical vulnerability, making them exponentially more likely to become trapped (and perhaps die) in the storm or its chaotic aftermath. A similar dynamic unfolded in New York, complicated by the height and density of much of the city's housing. In more heavily urbanized areas, many thousands of low-income, disabled, and/or elderly people who were unable or unwilling to evacuate found themselves trapped in high-rise buildings with no power—and no elevators. National Guard troops and masses of volunteers working with the emerging "Occupy Sandy" movement combed the buildings for weeks trying to locate people in need of food, water, and medical supplies.

Not everyone who fails to evacuate in advance of a hurricane stays behind for simple lack of transportation. Figuring out when and whether to go, even when told by authorities that leaving would be the best option, can be very tricky; and on islands like Puerto Rico that have high poverty levels and no hope of getting away from the storm completely, there may be nowhere safe to go. Gas, meals, and hotels while on the road can be very expensive, especially for those whose incomes are marginal. Employers and schools may be reluctant to close down until the very last minute, prolonging the decision-making process for those who are dependent on them. Traveling with children (and pets) is difficult and stressful under normal circumstances; spending hour after hour in traffic that barely moves is much worse. Not all cars are reliable, and even vehicles in good condition can break down in the stop-and-go circumstances of evacuating in rugged terrain or 90-degree weather, leaving their occupants potentially stranded and in an even more dangerous situation while the storm approaches. And to make things worse, since it is impossible to predict exactly where the eye wall of a hurricane will hit more than several hours in advance, some evacuations turn out to have been unnecessary, resulting in wasted time, money, and stress for many thousands of people. It is hardly surprising, then, that many coastal residents are extremely reluctant to put themselves through such an ordeal and may choose to risk the storm instead.

Failure to truly understand one's physical vulnerability—or a stubborn refusal to accept it—can also lead to a failure to evacuate. Paradoxically, both a lack of experience with hurricanes and considerable experience "riding them out" can give coastal residents a false sense of security, leading them to underestimate the true danger of a major storm. In rapidly growing coastal areas, newer residents who have no experience with hurricanes and therefore no idea what to expect when a warning is issued may assume that the risk is manageable if they stay home. But even longtime residents, who often have been through many smaller storms (or only the edges of bigger ones) with little more than power outages and downed trees to deal with, can easily arrive at the faulty conclusion that they can get through any hurricane with only a few inconveniences. For New Yorkers, Hurricane Irene's near miss the year before Sandy hit led many residents to believe that the media were overhyping Sandy's potential impact just as they felt the media had falsely predicted doomsday with Hurricane Irene. This understandable frustration with the media's tendency to overdramatize any large storm led many residents to brush off mandatory evacuation orders as nonsensical exaggerations, leaving an exasperated Governor Chris Christie of New Jersey to fume that waterfront and flood-zone residents who refused to go were being "stupid and selfish" by forcing emergency workers to risk their lives to rescue them when they became trapped by rising waters.

Those who have made it safely through truly horrendous storms are also likely to assume (not entirely irrationally) that since they and/or their homes survived the worst that nature could dish out, they can weather any subsequent storms. Some Mississippi residents who got through Hurricane Camille in 1969, for instance—a category 5 storm with 200 mph winds and a 28-foot surge—failed to evacuate for Katrina, mistakenly assuming that no storm could possibly be any worse than what they had already experienced. A long period of time between hurricane "hits" can play a role in development and evacuation decisions too. Coastal communities tend to develop "**hurricane amnesia**" when memories of the last terrible storm fade, which encourages a push for more "economic growth" in their region, increasing the area's long-term physical vulnerability as more businesses, residents, and tourists move in. When Hurricane Sandy struck, the Northeast had not seen a severe hurricane in many decades, encouraging many residents to comfortably assume that the storm "wouldn't really be that bad" or that their neighborhoods—many of which were recently built and had never been hit by a major hurricane—weren't in any real danger of serious flooding.

Finally, it is important to note that more than 60 percent of the people who drowned in Hurricane Katrina were over 61 years of age. Hurricanes Sandy, Harvey, and Maria all followed similar patterns. Though Sandy's death toll was a fraction of Katrina's, nearly half the people who perished were 65 and older. Of the fatalities from Hurricane Harvey, 29 percent were among people in that age group, and Puerto Rico saw a 27 percent higher death rate among elderly residents following the storm, particularly in nursing homes and emergency facilities. While many of these victims drowned, inability to access health care, falls, hypothermia, fires, and carbon monoxide poisoning from generators also caused fatalities among older residents. Deaths in the 1995 Chicago heat wave, too, followed a similar pattern: most of the people who died were low-income, elderly men who had weak social ties and no resources to get out of their cramped, un-air-conditioned apartments, even temporarily.

These statistics demonstrate another way in which physical and social vulnerability can overlap. For older people, the evacuation process can be frightening and difficult enough that "riding it out" seems like a comparatively smaller risk. While the prospect of a long road trip—perhaps to an unknown destination for an undetermined amount of time—may seem manageable or even a bit exciting for those who are younger and healthy and have some financial resources to fall back on, the elderly frequently live on fixed incomes and often must deal with a variety of health and mobility problems: poor hearing or eyesight, difficulty walking, arthritis pain, and so forth. They are also likely to require medication for severe conditions such as heart problems, high blood pressure, or diabetes and thus depend heavily on remaining close to their own familiar doctors and pharmacists. These difficulties can make traveling any distance unpleasant at best and dangerous at worst.

STRUCTURAL AND INFRASTRUCTURAL MITIGATION: DECREASING OR INCREASING VULNERABILITY?

Communities at risk for disasters have three basic options for trying to mitigate (lessen or prevent) their impacts: **structural mitigation, infrastructural mitigation**, and **nonstructural mitigation**. Structural mitigation generally refers to strategies in coastal areas and river floodplains that emphasize large engineering "megaprojects" to stop flooding and erosion, such as levees, floodwalls, groins, bank stabilization, and beach renourishment. Infrastructures are those things that physically tie a community together, including the drinking water, sewerage and drainage systems, roads and bridges, phone and Internet lines and towers, and power and gas lines. Infrastructural mitigation strategies, then, are efforts to make these systems more resilient to high winds, floodwaters, or seismic activity. Stronger building codes, too, are sometimes considered infrastructural mitigation. Nonstructural mitigation generally focuses more on keeping people (and property) out of harm's way in the first place: stricter zoning laws that prohibit or severely restrict building in some parts of a floodplain or coastal area, for instance, or restoring wetlands that absorb floodwaters and storm surges. In extreme cases, this can mean moving entire communities to higher ground, which some small Midwestern towns chose to do after the enormous Mississippi River flood of 1993. Flood and other disaster insurance, too, can be considered nonstructural mitigation.

Infrastructural mitigation tends to be one of the first things emergency management officials and government agencies try to improve after a disaster strikes (or nearly strikes), in an effort to quickly and effectively reduce their community's vulnerability. Communications systems, in particular, are obviously crucial during search and rescue operations and all too frequently fail completely or prove to be incompatible among different agencies under extreme conditions. Post-disaster **mitigation** planning, then, frequently focuses on finding new ways to ensure that police, firefighters, and other "first responders" can continue to communicate with one another despite widespread devastation.

New Orleans' experience with improved evacuation routes is an interesting case of infrastructural mitigation that was, eventually, highly effective. In a strange way, the city was actually very lucky to have gone through a couple of "near misses" before being inundated by Katrina. The city is surrounded by water, limiting the routes available to evacuees to just a few main highways. Places where these evacuation routes bottlenecked badly during evacuations for Hurricane Georges in 1998 and Hurricane Ivan in 2004 led to significant improvements in Louisiana's "contraflow" system, an idea first implemented in Georgia and South Carolina during Hurricane Floyd in 1999. Contraflow allows traffic to travel "the wrong way" on interstate highways during emergencies, doubling the roadways' capacity. When implemented in Louisiana, it allowed a much more effective evacuation for Katrina than might otherwise have occurred. While the plan was not perfect and traffic was still very slow, it was an enormous improvement over previous efforts, and several hundred thousand New Orleans-area residents (as well as many others in even higher-risk areas to the south) were able to leave before the storm made landfall. It is, of course, important to note that this approach was only "successful" for those who had the means to leave on their own and did nothing to help those without reliable transportation.

Various municipalities' experience with the contraflow plans highlights three concerns that disaster researchers have been expressing for decades regarding mitigation efforts. First, at-risk communities tend to rely almost entirely on structural and infrastructural mitigation techniques, at the expense of nonstructural strategies (such as restoring adjacent wetlands or moving people out of an area's most flood-prone locations) that have the potential to be far more effective over the long term. Second, these mitigation efforts tend to be "event-driven" rather than "threat-driven," meaning that they are designed and implemented *after* a disaster strikes rather than as a result of a careful risk analysis beforehand. Finally, structural and infrastructural techniques do not protect all members of a community equally. All these tendencies actually serve to increase rather than decrease communities' long-term disaster risks, but persuading governments, businesses, industries, and residents to place more emphasis on nonstructural mitigation methods is difficult for several reasons.

Residents and business interests that have been traumatized by a major flood or hurricane understandably want their community back the way it was as soon as possible. City **growth machines**—coalitions of municipal government officials, prominent business interests, and the local media organizations that support their efforts—must work to encourage (re)investment in their area by somehow overcoming the negative images and impressions of their community as destroyed and chaotic in order to restore confidence in its ability to rebound from the disaster and "get back to normal." Disaster victims tend to pressure their elected officials at all levels of government to find a way to "fix" their disaster vulnerability problem, to "do something, now!!" to ensure that such an event never happens again—but without forcing the community to make any drastic land-use changes. If ideas for long-term mitigation conflict with the community's immediate goals of getting the surrounding natural systems back under control, allowing residents to rebuild their homes, and returning to the normal routine of encouraging growth and development, they will almost always be rejected out of hand.

Not surprisingly, then, the post-disaster mitigation solutions that communities decide on usually involve more (or improved) flood control structures (structural mitigation), along with better evacuation routes and stronger building codes (infrastructural mitigation). Rezoning hazardous areas and moving human development away from them altogether (nonstructural mitigation), which would allow floodwaters to come and go in mostly unoccupied areas and thus provide better long-term risk reduction, are rarely considered seriously. Instead, at-risk communities repeatedly try to remove the dynamic, shifting aspects of the natural hydrological systems in which they are embedded and somehow make the land and water hold still indefinitely so that the area can continue to be developed. This approach ensures that as much land as possible will remain open to profitable (re)development, rather than being turned into less immediately beneficial spillways, "natural" beaches, or "green space." Ironically, communities hit by floods or hurricanes often find themselves in the midst of a building boom as the real estate industry works not only to rebuild what was destroyed but also to purchase and redevelop land that had once been vacant or built with small single-family homes, turning it into high-rise hotels and condominiums.

In decades past, these efforts to "conquer nature" were considered a noble cause that served to benefit the entire community. Experience has shown, however, that constructing elaborate structural flood mitigation systems frequently backfires. Such systems tend to create a vicious cycle that encourages more and more development in disaster-prone areas, which then needs increasingly higher levels of "protection," which then encourages still more development. Levees and seawalls give communities a false sense of security, something tangible that can make residents feel safe (and does, in fact, provide safety in smaller flood events) until they create an even bigger disaster when a flood too large for them to contain eventually occurs. Exceptionally large floods are actually more dangerous with levees than they would have been without, creating huge surges of rising water that wipe out everything in their path when the levees finally break, giving victims little or no warning or time to escape.

FLOOD INSURANCE: ENCOURAGING RISKY BEHAVIOR

Disaster researchers have heavily criticized the National Flood Insurance Program (NFIP) for increasing flood risks nationwide. Created in 1968, the program was intended to help people living in flood- and hurricane-prone areas recover from catastrophic floods, but unfortunately it has had a number of unintended consequences. When Hurricane Betsy hit New Orleans in 1965, one of the most salient political issues during the relief and recovery effort was the fact that the vast majority of victims' losses had been uninsured because homeowners' insurance did not (and still does not) cover flood losses. The NFIP was supposed to help ameliorate this problem by providing low-cost, subsidized flood insurance to those who were already living in coastal areas and flood plains, while discouraging further development in such risky areas. Municipalities had to choose whether or not to join the program, which would then make insurance available to residents with the requirement that local governments adopt land-use policies that would not increase the number of residents and businesses in high-risk areas.

This provision of the NFIP, however, has been poorly enforced since its inception. While the program has in fact provided much-needed relief to homeowners who lost everything in floods—particularly for lower-income families living in floodplains because they simply cannot afford to move to higher ground—it has also inadvertently encouraged growth and development in low-lying and coastal areas by making insurance available in places that had previously been uninsurable and allowing repeat claims for properties that flood frequently. Economists refer to this phenomenon as a "**moral hazard**"—a change in peoples' risk-taking behavior brought about by the availability of insurance. While insurance is technically a kind of non-structural mitigation, the problems created by the NFIP are very similar to those created by levees: helping to diminish risk in the short term, while actually making things worse in the long term.

The existence of a federal flood insurance program has also exacerbated disaster victims' already difficult task of applying for settlements from their homeowners' insurance companies. After a major hurricane, when insurance companies face many thousands of claims for the same event, it is to their benefit to award each homeowner as little as possible in order to keep their total payout lower. Because homeowners' insurance will pay for only wind damage, while the NFIP covers only flood damage, property owners with both kinds of policies frequently find themselves facing the rather surreal process of dealing with appraisers whose job it is to determine what percentage of their home was damaged and what percentage of that damage was due strictly to wind or to the storm surge. Given that hurricanes bring both, this distinction can be somewhat nonsensical in ordinary terms, but homeowners' insurance companies have a vested interest in declaring that most of the damage they survey is from water rather than wind, while appraisers from the NFIP may be making the opposite assertion.

The catastrophic damages of the 2005 hurricane season—which along with Hurricane Katrina included Hurricanes Rita, Wilma, and a score of others—left the NFIP deeply in debt to the tune of $19 billion. Superstorm Sandy raised the NFIP's debt to around $25 billion, forcing the program to borrow money from the US Treasury that it was unable to repay. In the summer of 2012, months before Hurricane Sandy, Congress passed the Biggert-Waters Act, which was intended to make the NFIP more financially stable by ending most flood insurance subsidies to people living in risky areas. The bill noted that increasingly catastrophic coastal flooding events were bankrupting the system, and aimed to raise flood insurance rates drastically on those properties that are built too low in a flood zone, with the intention of reaching "actuarial rates"—that is, rates that reflect the actual risk these locations face—in five years.

However, the gigantic rate increases that Biggert-Waters mandated sometimes led to policies costing tens of thousands of dollars a year, which could have potentially decimated coastal communities from New York to Texas by making residents' homes impossible to afford. This would have been particularly devastating for lower-income areas and historically Native American and African American coastal communities whose ancestors have lived in their regions for hundreds or even thousands of years. Political backlash against Biggert-Waters led to the passage of the Homeowner Flood Insurance Affordability Act in 2014, heavily watering down the prior legislation and giving homeowners some relief, but leaving the NFIP with no way to mitigate its ever-growing debt burden. The NFIP itself was supposed to have been reauthorized in 2017, but at this writing, Congress has repeatedly refused to do so, passing only short-term extensions for a few months or even a couple of weeks rather than properly updating the legislation and passing it for the usual five-year period. These brief reprieves have proven problematic for the housing market, as potential homebuyers who are required by their mortgage lenders to take out flood insurance policies may be unable to do so if the program lapses.

Insurance companies and city planners are also starting to take sea-level rise and the likelihood of more frequent severe storms into account when assessing flood risks. While determining whether a single storm is directly linked to **climate change** is difficult, the increased number of catastrophic hurricanes in the early years of the 21st century is consistent with scientists' predictions that warming seas worldwide will lead to the formation of more and stronger tropical systems, which are basically meteorological "heat engines" that feed off warm ocean temperatures. A deadly combination of steady sea-level rising resulting from global ice melts, changes in Arctic wind patterns that can steer storms toward the Northeast more frequently, and thermal expansion of ocean waters is slowly eating away at coastlines in Louisiana, New England, and everywhere in between. Louisiana's coastal wetlands are disappearing at a particularly alarming rate, forcing entire communities to retreat to higher ground as their small towns disappear into the Gulf of Mexico.

DECREASING VULNERABILITY?

Finding viable solutions to the complicated, intertwined realities of flood and hurricane vulnerability is extremely difficult. Improved evacuation planning and more sensible and equitable insurance policies are certainly important but do very little to tackle the underlying issues of **disaster resiliency and sustainability**—enabling communities to "bounce back" quickly from an extreme natural event with a minimum of damage and losses over the long term. Instead, these approaches continue to rely on a philosophy that could perhaps be characterized as "run like hell, then come back and fix it if you can." The inequalities built into our social system, however, simply do not give all potential disaster victims an equal ability to run away, or to come back and fix the damage to their lives and property after the initial danger has passed. Stricter building codes, including elevation requirements, are certainly a step in the right direction; but they tend to be fought by real estate interests and become watered down or unenforced by state and local governments, to the point of being almost meaningless, and are frequently prohibitively expensive for residents to implement without considerable financial assistance.

Both the New Orleans and New York areas have considered taking structural mitigation efforts a giant step further by building giant storm surge gates across vulnerable bays and inlets, particularly those that are highly prone to funneling such a surge straight into highly developed areas. Such gates would provide another layer of protection for vulnerable communities and would ideally function in a manner similar to the Netherlands' Delta Works, which was constructed after a catastrophic storm coming out of the North Sea killed nearly 2,000 people in 1953. Such gates are extremely controversial, however. They would be extraordinarily expensive, have the potential to create unacceptable environmental impacts, and might merely serve to redirect storm surges to coastal areas adjacent to the area being targeted for protection.

Switching to a heavier reliance on nonstructural mitigation is problematic as well, both from a political and a social justice standpoint. Disaster relief in the United States has been increasingly federalized over the last several decades and focuses largely on upholding the institution of private property. While homeowners may be eligible for a variety of loans and grants after disasters, there are few programs aimed at helping renters or public housing residents move back home, find new permanent housing, and get back on their feet. Structural mitigation, too, is largely aimed at protecting (and sometimes even creating) private property, and communities are likely to choose those structures that take up the least amount of space (that is, levees over "green space" and floodwalls over levees) in order to allow as much development as possible. Property rights organizations are prone to fight any government attempts to restrict what owners can do with their property but still insist that owners' investments should be protected with massive projects built at taxpayers' expense, even if they are along a beach or in a floodplain.

Government buyouts of extremely vulnerable homes and businesses that have been destroyed by a catastrophic storm or have suffered repeated flood losses are often proposed after catastrophic storms or floods. Theoretically, such "managed retreat" programs would be funded through disaster-recovery monies and would allow private property to be turned into "green space" such as public parks or restored wetlands, removing people from harm's way and creating flood-relief buffer zones that could help absorb high waters. These programs are extremely difficult to implement on a large scale, however, particularly since property owner participation is voluntary, and most flood victims wish to stay in their own communities rather than moving elsewhere. Successful buyout programs are not unheard of, though: one such effort in North Dakota purchased private property from several hundred homeowners after the Red River flooded in 1997, resulting in a drastic drop in property losses when the river flooded again in 2006.

It is important to understand that not all resistance to this sort of nonstructural mitigation planning comes from wealthy property owners who wish to maintain their vacation homes. Full-time coastal residents who do decide to let the state buy their property often find the process extremely lengthy, confusing, and frustrating. Offers may not be extended to all homeowners who are interested, particularly if their surrounding neighbors do not wish to sell; and people in lower-income neighborhoods are more likely to be pressured into selling out when government agencies want to buy as many homes as possible with the money they have available. Additionally, low- or modest-income residents often fear—not illogically—that attempts to rebuild their towns or cities with radically different "footprints" after a severe flood are merely thinly disguised "land grabs" aimed at taking over and destroying their public housing projects or long-established neighborhoods, turning them into city-owned parks or privately developed, highly profitable condominium complexes. Increasing emphasis on nonstructural mitigation after a catastrophe involves determining who will and will not be allowed to have their neighborhoods back, which raises difficult questions of equity, justice, and fair compensation.

While large natural disasters do provide opportunities for communities and disaster relief agencies to learn from their mistakes and improve their planning, response, and long-term mitigation techniques, they also serve to exacerbate rather than "even out" the preexisting social inequalities in devastated regions. While severe floods and hurricanes do in fact have a heavy impact on all kinds of people across the socioeconomic spectrum, they are far from being "great equalizers" that place everyone (perhaps literally) in the same boat. Finding ways to tackle centuries of discrimination and risky land-use decisions is considerably more difficult than improving communications technologies or contraflow plans, but it is essential for truly diminishing overall disaster vulnerability.

SOURCES

Bates, Diane. 2016. *Superstorm Sandy: The Inevitable Destruction and Reconstruction of the Jersey Shore*. New Brunswick, NJ: Rutgers University Press.

Beck, Ulrich. 1992. *Risk Society: Towards a New Modernity*. London: Sage.

Chakraborty, Jayajit, Timothy W. Collins, and Sara E. Grineski. 2019. "Exploring the Environmental Justice Implications of Hurricane Harvey Flooding in Greater Houston, Texas." *American Journal of Public Health* 109 (2) (February): 244–250.

Collins, Jason. 2008. "Evaluation of Contraflow Lanes for Hurricane Evacuation." PhD diss., Department of Civil and Environmental Engineering, University of South Florida, Tampa. https://scholarcommons.usf.edu/cgi/viewcontent.cgi?referer=https://www.google.com/&httpsredir=1&article=1183&context=etd

Colten, Craig E. 2005. *An Unnatural Metropolis: Wrestling New Orleans from Nature*. Baton Rouge: Louisiana State University Press.

Craig, Robin Kundis. 2018. "Harvey, Irma, and the NFIP: Did the 2017 Hurricane Season Matter to Flood Insurance Reauthorization?" *University of Arkansas at Little Rock Law Review* 40 (4) (Summer): 481–513.

Crisp, Elizabeth. 2019. "NFIP Reauthorization Makes It into Disaster Aid Deal Reached Before Congress' Week-long Recess." *The Advocate*, May 23, 2019. Baton Rouge. https://www.theadvocate.com/baton_rouge/news/politics/article_ed6ba570-7d69-11e9-914a-e71e62292185.html

Cutter, Susan L., and Christopher T. Emrich. 2006. "Moral Hazard, Social Catastrophe: The Changing Face of Vulnerability Along the Hurricane Coasts." *Annals of the American Academy of Political and Social Science* 604:102–112.

Erikson, Kai T. 1976. *Everything in Its Path: Destruction of Community in the Buffalo Creek Flood*. New York: Touchstone.

Erikson, Kai T. 1994. *A New Species of Trouble: The Human Experience of Modern Disasters*. New York: W.W. Norton & Co.

Eshelman, Robert S. 2012. "Experts Warn of Lost Chances to Storm-Proof NYC After HurricaneSandy."*ScientificAmerican.*Dec.4.https://www.scientificamerican.com/article/experts-warn-of-lost-chances-to-storm-proof-nyc-after-hurricane-sandy/

Extension Disaster Education Network. "Flood Premiums Rising Dramatically." https://eden.lsu.edu/educate/resources/floods-and-flooding-archived-eden-topic-page/?tab=menu-flood-premiums-rising-dramatically

Faber, Jacob William. 2015. "Superstorm Sandy and the Demographics of Flood Risk in New York City." *Human Ecology* 43:363–378.

Godschalk, David R., David J. Brower, and Timothy Beatley. 1989. *Catastrophic Coastal Storms: Hazard Mitigation and Development Management*. Durham: Duke University Press.

Haas, Edward F. 1990. "Victor H. Schiro, Hurricane Betsy, and the 'Forgiveness Bill.'" *Gulf Coast Historical Review* 6 (1): 66–90.

Jonkman, Sebastiaan N., Maartje Godfroy, Antonia Sebastian, and Bas Kolen. 2018. "Brief communication: Loss of life due to Hurricane Harvey." *Natural Hazards and Earth System Sciences* 18:1073–1078.

Jonkman, Sebastiaan N., and Ilan Kelman. 2005. "An Analysis of the Causes and Circumstances of Flood Disaster Deaths." *Disasters* 29 (1): 75–97.

Jonkman, Sebastiaan N., Bob Maaskant, Ezra Boyd, and Marc Lloyd Levitan. 2009. "Loss of Life Caused by the Flooding of New Orleans After Hurricane Katrina: Analysis of the Relationship Between Flood Characteristics and Mortality." *Risk Analysis* 29 (5): 676–698.

Harball, Elizabeth. 2013. "Arctic Melting Stacked Weather Deck in Favor of Superstorm Sandy." *Scientific American*. March 15. https://www.scientificamerican.com/article/arctic-melting-stacked-weather-deck-in-favor-of-superstorm-sandy/

Kirby, Andrew, ed. 1990. *Nothing to Fear: Risks and Hazards in American Society*. Tucson: University of Arizona Press.

Knafo, Saki, and Lisa Shapiro. 2012. "Staten Island's Hurricane Sandy Damage Sheds Light on Complicated Political Battle." *Huffington Post*, December 6, 2012. http://www.huffingtonpost.com/2012/12/06/staten-island-hurricane-sandy_n_2245523.html

Koh, Elizabeth. 2019. "Hurricane Michael Debris Hasn't Been Cleared: Why That Really Matters Now." *Tampa Bay Times*, June 6, 2012. https://www.tampabay.com/florida-politics/buzz/2019/06/06/hurricane-michael-debris-hasnt-been-cleared-why-that-really-matters-now/

Logan, John R., and Harvey L. Molotch. 1987. *Urban Fortunes: The Political Economy of Place*. Berkeley: University of California Press.

Logan, John R., Rachel Bridges Whaley, and Kyle Crower. 1999. "The Character and Consequences of Growth Regimes: An Assessment of Twenty Years of Research." In *The Urban Growth Machine: Critical Perspectives Two Decades Later*, edited by Andrew E. G. Jonas and David Wilson, 73–94. Albany: State University of New York Press.

McQuaid, John, and Mark Schleifstein. 2006. *Path of Destruction: The Devastation of New Orleans and the Coming Age of Superstorms*. New York: Little, Brown, and Company.

Mileti, Dennis S., et al. 1999. *Disasters by Design: A Reassessment of Natural Hazards in the United States*. Washington, DC: Joseph Henry Press.

Montano, Samantha and Amanda Savitt. 2018. "The Cost of Flood Is a Price Worth Paying." *Citylab*, August 1, 2018. https://www.citylab.com/environment/2018/08/the-cost-of-flood-insurance-is-a-price-worth-paying/566363/

Murphy, Raymond. 2004. "Disaster or Sustainability: The Dance of Human Agents with Nature's Actants." *Canadian Review of Sociology and Anthropology* 41 (3): 249–266.

NBC News. 2012. "FEMA Chief: Inland Damage is a Real Concern." Oct. 28. https://www.nbcnews.com/nightly-news/video/fema-chief-inland-damage-is-a-real-concern-44481092000

New York Times. 2012. "Hurricane Sandy: Covering the Storm." October 28, 2012. http://www.nytimes.com/interactive/2012/10/28/nyregion/hurricane-sandy.html

New York Times. 2017. "Hurricane Sandy's Death Toll." November 17, 2017. http://www.nytimes.com/interactive/2012/11/17/nyregion/hurricane-sandy-map.html

New York Times. 2013. "Rebuilding the Coastline, but at What Cost?" May 19, 2013. http://mwr.nytimes.com/2013/05/19/nyregion/rebuilding-the-coastline-but-at-what-cost.html?from=nyregion

Peacock, Walter Gillis, Betty Hearn Morrow, and Hugh Gladwin. 1997. *Hurricane Andrew: Ethnicity, Gender, and the Sociology of Disasters*. London: Routledge.

Perrow, Charles. 1999. *Normal Accidents: Living with High-Risk Technologies*. Princeton, NJ: Princeton University Press.

Platt, Rutherford H. 1999. *Disasters and Democracy: The Politics of Extreme Natural Events*. Washington, DC: Island Press.

Rodrıguez-Dıaz, Carlos E. 2018. "Maria in Puerto Rico: Natural Disaster in a Colonial Archipelago." *American Journal of Public Health* 108 (1): 30–31.

Santos-Lozada, Alexis R. 2018. "In Puerto Rico, Counting Deaths and Making Deaths Count." *Health Affairs* 37 (4) (April): 520–521.

Schwartz, Ariel. 2012. "How Can New York Prepare for the Next Hurricane Sandy?" *Scientific American*. Nov. 5. https://seagrant.sunysb.edu/media/sandy12/ScientificAmerican-Sandy110512.pdf

Siders, A. R. 2018. "Government-funded Buyouts after Disasters Are Slow and Inequitable—Here's How That Could Change." *The Conversation*. October 19, 2018. http://theconversation.com/government-funded-buyouts-after-disasters-are-slow-and-inequitable-heres-how-that-could-change-103817

Steinberg, Ted. 2000. *Acts of God: The Unnatural History of Natural Disaster in America*. Oxford, UK: Oxford University Press.

Stewart, Stacy R. and Robbie Berg. 2019. "National Hurricane Center Tropical Cyclone Report: Hurricane Florence." May 30, 2019. National Atmospheric and Oceanic Administration (NOAA). https://www.nhc.noaa.gov/data/tcr/AL062018_Florence.pdf

The Wave. 2013. "Read This! Special Editorial." https://www.rockawave.com/pageview/viewer/2013-03-29#page=0

Van Heerden, Ivor. 2006. *The Storm: What Went Wrong and Why During Hurricane Katrina—The Inside Story from One Louisiana Scientist*. New York: Viking.

Wisner, Ben, , Piers Blaikie, Terry Cannon, and Ian Davis. 2005. *At Risk: Natural Hazards, People's Vulnerability, and Disasters*. London: Routledge.

15

Climate Change

Laura McKinney

Lake Shore Drive threatened as increased precipitation raises Great Lakes water levels faster than sea level rise, Chicago, Illinois.

Post your photo on climate change to #TLESclimate.

Photo by Ken Gould

Global climate change is perhaps the most daunting ecological crisis facing all of humanity. The virtual scientific consensus on the anthropogenic (human-caused) basis of climate change indicts our reliance on carbon-intensive industrial production practices (see Lesson 7), nonrenewable energy sources (see Lesson 9), and industrialized agriculture (see Lesson 12), among other dynamics, as altering the life-sustaining balance of atmospheric gases we depend on to protect us from the sun. In the absence of drastic and prolonged action, emissions of a broad range of greenhouse gases (GHGs) are predicted to result in a change of 2 degrees Celsius by 2050, with dire consequences for all species, including humankind. Recent reports from the Intergovernmental Panel on Climate Change (IPCC) warns that without aggressive action, we will begin to experience catastrophic effects as early as 2040. Left entirely unchecked, current emissions rates are predicted to lead to warming in excess of 4 degrees Celsius, with abysmal ramifications for the planet's capacity to support human populations. Disruptions to food chains, frequent floods, extended droughts, intense hurricanes, severe wildfires, and the disappearance of entire communities due to sea level rise are just a few examples of the consequences that accompany climate change, many of which we have begun to experience and all of which will surely worsen. Even in the "best-case" scenario, warming of 2 degrees Celsius will have profound impacts on humanity, and staying below the 2 degrees threshold requires major departures from current trends in development, production, and consumption that infiltrate nearly every facet of life.

As you read through this lesson, I ask you to consider a few questions: How often do you think about climate change? Do you worry about the consequences for you and your loved ones? Do you think governmental, institutional, individual, or international efforts (or any combination) to reduce emissions are fruitful avenues to address the root causes of climate change? To what degree does concern for climate change shape your lifestyle choices? Do you bike, take public transportation, cut down on meat consumption, avoid plastics, or reduce air travel to curtail emissions? What are the challenges or barriers to doing so? Do you participate in social movements to bring attention to this problem? Have you joined divestment campaigns to cut university ties to the fossil fuel industry? How concerned are you about the future in the face of changing climates? How does the information you possess about climate change shape your hopes and dreams for the future? How heavily do environmental concerns weigh into your support for political candidates or other community-based efforts to confront the drivers of climate change? Do you feel climate change has been unfairly foisted on your generation by those who precede you?

It is likely that most of you have thought quite a bit about the questions posed above; perhaps some of you ponder these questions nearly every day in some form. If so, you are in good company, as the extraordinary efforts of climate activist Greta Thunberg spurred youth from more than 100 countries around the globe to skip class and take to the streets to demand action on climate change. The climate strikes and Thunberg's pleas to those in power to take action now are stark displays of alarm and awareness; your generation and those that follow will be forced to reckon with the damage to the atmosphere that is causing climate change and its effects on biodiversity, food production, and vulnerability to disasters, just to name a few. For many, this knowledge brings feelings of anxiety, uncertainty, fear, doubt, and even indignant outrage at the unfairness of it all. To be sure, your life course will occur under circumstances that older generations are privileged not to have encountered or factored in when making major life decisions, as your ability to live and thrive is under assault given our current trajectory toward global warming and all that it entails.

The purpose of this lesson is to provide an overview of a sociological approach to understanding climate change dynamics. You will find baseline information on the causes and consequences of climate change and how incorporation of a sociological imagination adds to our understanding of these topics. Applying the arsenal of sociological theories to the topic of climate change requires rigorous attention to the inequalities surrounding its causes and effects, which include disparities at the global, national, and local levels. The lesson ends with a discussion of current efforts to address and deny climate change, the political landscapes that serve as backdrops to both, and possibilities for future alternatives.

CAUSES AND CONSEQUENCES OF CLIMATE CHANGE

Scientists discovered in the 19th century that certain gases in the air trap heat that would otherwise escape into space. Carbon dioxide was identified as a key player, and further research confirmed the warming potential of additional gases, including methane and nitrous oxide. The greenhouse effect is the term used to refer to this process. As early as 1896, scientists predicted global warming would result as humans released carbon dioxide into the atmosphere. Currently, the presence of carbon dioxide in the atmosphere is about 43 percent greater than pre-industrial levels, and global warming trends track at about the rate scientists predicted it would. Despite scientific consensus, those who profit from the current system engage in myriad politically motivated efforts to deny, obfuscate, and derail widespread acceptance of knowledge about the scientific evidence substantiating global warming and the role of industrial processes in exacerbating it (see Lesson 6). Efforts range from campaigns to discredit the scientific basis of climate change and questioning the "natural" rhythms of changing climates to the more outrageous—for instance, President Trump has gone so far as to allege a worldwide hoax concocted by scientists to fool the public. The absurdity of his and other equally outlandish assertions has caused some oil and gas companies to distance themselves publicly, though they continue to finance misinformation campaigns and politicians who espouse climate denial. Similar to the tobacco industry's interest in denying linkages between cigarettes and cancer, oil and gas industry titans invest heavily to manage public discourse and thwart citizen outrage regarding the existence and causes of climate change. Unfortunately, efforts to undermine the legitimacy of climate science have gained traction among some segments of the population, particularly in areas with historical reliance on jobs in oil, gas, and coal production.

Scientists overwhelmingly agree that we are in big trouble. The Intergovernmental Panel on Climate Change (IPCC) is an arm of the United Nations that convenes climate experts from around the world to provide governments and policymakers with objective, scientific assessments of the risks and impacts of climate change. The 2018 IPCC report paints a dire portrait of the immediacy and severity of climate change consequences, concluding that effectively addressing this crisis requires transformations at a scope and scale that have "no documented historic precedent." Similarly, the US Global Change Research Program (USGCRP) is charged with delivering a thorough examination of the effects of climate change in the United States to Congress. The Fourth National Climate Assessment was released in 2018 to fulfill this mandate. The report, which is developed, reviewed, and approved by the National Oceanic and Atmospheric Administration (NOAA) and a Federal Steering Committee of representatives from USGCRP agencies in collaboration with over 300 experts, echoes the conclusions reached by the IPCC. Taken together, these warnings are the starkest to date in detailing the economic and humanitarian crises caused by global warming. Water scarcity, torrential downpours, severe heat waves, unrelenting wildfires, agricultural disruptions, and coastal flooding are just a few of the life-threatening consequences identified by these agencies. In as little as two to three decades, scientists agree we will encounter dismal effects with greater frequency and magnitude, including the occurrence of disasters (floods, droughts, wildfires, hurricanes) and abnormal weather patterns (intense heat waves, heavier rainstorms) that pose grave risks to human survival. Climate change has resulted in the loss of coral reefs (with mass die-off expected as soon as 2040) and the loss of other fragile habitats, posing major threats to biodiversity. According to the International Union for Conservation of Nature (IUCN), more than 27 percent of all assessed species (i.e., more than 26,500 species) are threatened with extinction, a trend that is expected to worsen as climate change intensifies. Experts also agree sea level rise will accelerate, and many believe a rise of 15–20 feet is inevitable, which will be catastrophic for coastal communities and low-lying nations.

One effective ecological check against emissions is carbon sequestration via photosynthesis, as we all know that plants and trees absorb carbon dioxide and return to us clean oxygen. However, the **carbon sequestration** capacities of existing forestlands are unable to keep up with global emissions rates. Moreover, the appropriation of forestland for corporate uses— such as converting the Amazon to grazing land to meet American demands for cheap beef—is an unfortunate and commonplace scenario that further undermines our capacity for carbon uptake. Another example that has garnered mainstream attention is the conversion of rainforests in the Philippines to palm oil plantations that eliminates their sequestration potential, which brings unfavorable environmental consequences for biodiversity and water resources as well as negative social impacts including the displacement of rural and Indigenous farmers and the virtual annihilation of their livelihoods. It is worth noting that the clearing of land taking place in the Amazon and elsewhere parallels development strategies undertaken by the United States and other settler regimes decades ago, which is often used by countries to justify their current deforestation trends in the name of development (see Lesson 20).

While climate science has rapidly formalized into a burgeoning area of scientific inquiry, leading publications continue to be focused more on the physical and biological properties of earth systems than on inequities in human well-being and developmental differences between, within, and across nations. There is widespread agreement that confronting climate change requires comprehensive assessments of interactions among economic, social, and environmental systems and their intersection with structural arrangements that confer power and privilege for some, but exploitation and oppression for others. Our current challenge is to understand the complex inequalities surrounding global environmental change. In doing so, it is imperative that climate change be understood in the context of a globalized and increasingly globalizing world. Sociology is helpful in this regard given its emphasis on the broader social forces in which **sustainability** dynamics are thoroughly embedded.

THEORETICAL APPROACHES TO ENVIRONMENTAL IMPACT

Spurred by growing awareness of ecological constraints, sociologists have increasingly begun to incorporate environmental concerns. Social responses to environmental threats, such as banning the use of DDT, and growing recognition of the delicate balance of flows between nature and society prompted sociologists to focus on the environment. The subfield of environmental sociology is a rapidly growing area within the discipline, a trend that is near certain to continue. Climate change has solidified the importance of sociological examinations of ecological crises as we work to understand the large-scale, structural forces driving global warming. In fact, the American Sociological Association recently convened a task force to produce an edited volume on global climate change. Sociological theories and methods have earned sure footing in scientific approaches to understanding the causes and effects of climate change, as well as informing strategies to mitigate those trends, to which we now turn.

HUMAN ECOLOGY: IPAT, POET, AND ECOLOGICAL MODERNIZATION THEORY

At its origins, human ecology emerged as a central approach to understanding nature—society interactions within environmental sociology. The IPAT formula represents a chief contribution of the human ecology framework that posits environmental impacts (I) are the multiplicative function of population (P), affluence (A), and technology (T). Rooted in Malthusian concerns that (geometric) population growth would outpace (arithmetic) gains in agricultural production (see Lesson 8), leading to population "checks," such as war, famine, and disease, the IPAT framework captures the variations of environmental impacts emanating from people, their consumption demands, and advances in technology. Empirical examinations have tied population and/or affluence to deforestation, carbon dioxide emissions, and methane emissions, all critical drivers of climate change. An important lesson emerging from these studies is that the effect of population size and growth is only meaningful when considered in tandem with affluence and consumption.

The POET model is a closely related perspective that identifies interdependencies among population (P), social organization (O), and technology (T), while maintaining that all three are key causes of environmental problems (E), as well as bring consequences of one another and of the environment itself. POET's holistic approach provides a useful framework for examining societal-environmental interactions. The introduction of the "O" term for organization is particularly important in any effort to understand environmental dynamics. A newer human ecology approach to environmental impact articulated additional insights about the importance of culture and social change. These "new human ecologists" maintained the Dominant Western Worldview (DWW) of the Human Exceptionalist Paradigm (HEP) was being supplanted by the New Ecological Paradigm (NEP), which was a greening of values (see Lesson 1). This rational awareness of the interdependence of humans and nature is viewed as an important mechanism for reversing the harmful impacts of population, affluence, and technology.

Ecological modernization theory (EMT) relatedly suggests that the process of development has the potential to improve the environment (see Lesson 2). EMT posits that with modernization, individuals and citizen groups become increasingly "green" in orientation, with positive effects on the environment. However, EMT has been heavily critiqued for flimsy statistical evidence and failure to situate domestic environmental impacts within the global context of international trade networks. The "Netherlands Fallacy" is a useful tool to illustrate this weakness; it refers to the erroneous conclusion that some nations that appear to be modernizing ecologically are actually shifting negative environmental impacts around the globe.

EMT also focuses on technological innovation and state intervention as plausible strategies for escaping environmental crises. With regards to the former, ecological efficiency is believed to emerge as technological advances reduce harmful environmental practices. However, a substantial amount of empirical research fails to support this belief. As the Jevon's Paradox warns (see Lesson 9), energy efficiency tends to increase production and consumption, resulting in more natural resource withdrawals, not less. As for the latter, state intervention is questioned as a viable strategy for addressing environmental threats given the global nature of material flows. Global trade networks enable affluent nations to enact pro-environmental state policies while maintaining high rates of consumption by exporting dirty environmental production. Moreover, economic globalization might encourage a "race to the bottom" among poor nations competing for foreign investors, whereby deregulation is deployed as a tactic to attract multi-national corporations to operate in their jurisdictions. The rollback or removal of safety, labor, and environmental regulations is a major incentive for moving the most environmentally damaging production activities to disadvantaged locales (see Lessons 2 and 4). Thus, the efficacy of state intervention as a means to check climate change must be vetted vis-à-vis the global context of transnational networks of production and exchange.

World-polity perspectives similarly emphasize that countries tend to conform to worldwide norms as they become incorporated into the global system, with related tendencies to develop environmental regulations, ministries, and subsequent environmental reforms. According to this approach, integration into world society stimulates national participation in environmentally focused intergovernmental organizations (IGOs), nongovernmental organizations (NGOs), and international treaties that promote environmental concern and the institutionalization of an "environmental regime," which fosters favorable environmental advances. The degree to which these reforms are actually undertaken, monitored, and enforced is, however, open to question. Environmentalism may be symbolic in that many states offer only a superficial compliance with sound environmental policies due to either the cost of monitoring and enforcement or the power of corporate interests. It is further unclear whether reforms, if implemented, are effective. Also, environmental values to the contrary, efforts to infuse the logic of **neoliberalism** globally (see Lesson 6) may be an overwhelming and opposing force shaping the economic and environmental activities of all actors in the world system.

Political-Economic Approaches

The political-economic tradition encompasses world systems theory, treadmill of production (TOP), and metabolic rift (see Lesson 2). These approaches are bundled because they share many basic assumptions. World systems theory and ecologically unequal exchange perspectives outline the ways in which vast power and wealth differentials influence domestic modernization via the allocation of economic activities, with companion impacts on environmental conditions. For instance, wealthy, powerful nations tend to specialize in highly profitable sectors, such as banking and financial services, that have few negative impacts on the local environment. Alternatively, poor, less powerful nations tend to specialize in extraction, mining, manufacturing, and industrial activities with substantial negative impacts on their immediate environment including deforestation, habitat destruction, and toxic air and water pollution.

The allocation of primary (extraction, mining, agriculture) and secondary (industrial, manufacturing) sector production to non-core nations via **offshoring** and outsourcing allows core nations to maintain high rates of consumption and relatively in-tact environments (see Lesson 3). Non-core nations siphon raw materials and engage in dirty industrial production for export to core nations, leaving behind marred landscapes and legacies of pollution and toxicity far removed from the point of demand. These global processes exacerbate ecosystem destruction in peripheral and semiperipheral areas, with major implications for their short-term and long-term sustainability, including vulnerability to climate change. For instance, a recent analysis of more than 4,000 climate-related disasters shows that poor nations experience far higher rates of mortality and homelessness in the wake of climate-related events than do wealthy nations.

Core nations tend to evidence specialization in service sector and high-technology industries (e.g., aerospace engineering), while offshoring the bulk of industrial and manufacturing production processes—and their negative environmental impacts. Intensification of environmental degradation accompanies this shift in production, resulting in land destruction, air pollution, and water contamination in non-core locales. The waste and toxic byproducts generated at points of production, transfer, and consumption as well as the disruption to natural ecosystems and depletion of precious resources required to meet core countries' consumption demands wreaks havoc on the environment. This is consequential because ecological destruction is tightly connected to climate change adversities, as declines in the quality of the environment erodes natural barriers to disasters (such as wetlands that temper hurricanes) and is directly linked to their occurrence (such as deforestation triggering landslides or extended droughts sparking wildfires).

World system theorists join TOP and metabolic rift adherents in arguing that the logic of capitalism requires continuous, intensive, and extensive exploitation (destruction) of nature that can never be realigned to be "green" in orientation. TOP theorists focus on the role of energy and chemical intensive technologies in creating greater demand for natural resources, increasing waste streams and chemical toxicity (see Lessons 2 and 7). The production treadmill, run by treadmill elites, plays a major role in increasing environmental destruction. A particularly instructive insight of the approach is that the movement of US capital abroad has reduced ecological withdrawals and waste additions to some degree within the United States but has exacerbated environmental disruptions in the countries to which the capital and waste have been transferred. The capitalist treadmill thus instigates environmental adversities around the world.

Metabolic rift theorists adopt the classical arguments of Marx, especially regarding his concern of "the problem of soil fertility within capitalist agriculture," the primary ecological crisis of his day, as well as his treatment of deforestation and urban pollution (see Lesson 2). Metabolic rift theorists assert the production and consumption trends inherent to the system of capital accumulation depend on the continuous overexploitation of natural resources and disruption of ecological metabolic processes. In the context of climate change, the "rift" can be seen in the excess waste (emissions) created at a rate faster than ecosystems can absorb them, disrupting the natural cycle of carbon in the biosphere. Due to the unequal power/dependency relations in the world system, much of the environmental degradation resulting from current modes of production, accumulation, and consumption are concentrated in less-developed countries. Empirical examinations confirm these expectations for deforestation (see Table 15-1), biodiversity loss, and the accumulation and transfer of hazardous waste in non-core locales.

One exception to this trend is carbon dioxide emissions, which tend to be concentrated in high- and middle-income countries (see Figure 15-1), due to the global organization of production outlined above. Specifically, the rates at which carbon dioxide gases are emitted as byproducts of core production and consumption trends cause an abundance of greenhouse gas emissions

Table 15-1 Forest land (in squares miles) by income group, 1990–2015

Countries	1990	1995	2000	2005	2010	2015	% Chg.[1]	Avg. Annual % Chg.
High income	10,316,559	10,348,342	10,380,127	10,382,188	10,385,224	10,427,004	1.07	0.07
Middle income	26,326,758	26,058,347	25,789,940	25,679,163	25,629,429	25,720,292	−2.30	−0.15
Low income	171,440,460	4,123,115	4,004,630	3,893,490	3,778,510	3,752,960	−97.81	−6.52

[1] Negative numbers indicate deforestation; positive numbers indicate reforestation.

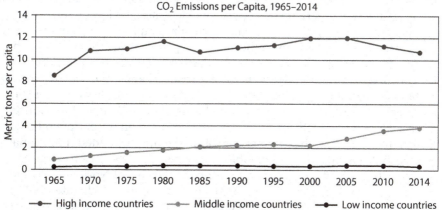

Figure 15-1 CO_2 Emissions (metric tons) per Capita across income groups, 1965–2014.

within developed nations, making this a chief form of "first world" environmental degradation. It is notable that although the highest rates of carbon dioxide emissions are concentrated in developed nations, the consequences affect people, species, and ecosystems globally. Disruption to natural metabolic processes, increased toxicity and waste streams stemming from advances in technology and industrialized production (see Lesson 7), and the quest for endless growth and capital accumulation are intrinsic aspects of the system of capital emphasized by metabolic rift, TOP, and world system perspectives that lead these theorists to conclude our current economic system is fundamentally at odds with sustainability.

The treadmill of destruction is a complementary theoretical approach largely inspired by TOP theory but with specific focus on the effect of militarism. Similar to the TOP framework, the treadmill of destruction emphasizes the role of treadmill elites in determining social, political, and economic responses to environmental problems. Treadmill of destruction adds to this the impacts of the military, highlighting the large withdrawals of natural resources and increased toxicity resulting from military institutions and activities (see Lessons 3 and 7). Maintaining military apparatuses around the world result in vast consumption of nonrenewable energy and other resources. With regards to climate change, war and military machines rely heavily on fossil fuels, with obvious implications for increasing CO_2 emissions. It is also the case that the military is often used to secure access to oil, which is another direct link to climate change dynamics.

CLIMATE CHANGE, GLOBAL INEQUALITY, AND ENVIRONMENTAL JUSTICE

Global warming dynamics are especially critical considerations for social and environmental justice perspectives (see Lesson 10), as those who contribute the least to climate change are subject to disproportionate concentrations of its adverse effects. **Climate justice** advocates increasingly view climate change as a general human rights issue with particular emphasis on its intersection with race, gender, class, and other existing power inequalities. Across nations, climate change is characterized by severe inequalities in contributions to, benefits from, and consequences of climate change, particularly across global North/South divisions. While the Global North (or Core countries) has greatly contributed to and benefitted from climate change, it remains the least scathed from its effects. Whereas the Global South (or peripheral counties), in relative terms, has neither contributed to nor benefitted from climate change, but remains most vulnerable to its consequences. This has led many to assert that wealthy, developed countries of the Global North (e.g., United States, Canada, Western Europe, Australia) owe a great "climate debt" to inhabitants of poor nations in the Global South (e.g., South America, Southeast Asia, Africa) for the social, economic, and ecological crises wrought by climate change. Even though China and India are major CO_2 emitters now, the majority of the CO_2 in the atmosphere today was emitted by the United States and Western Europe in the 19th and 20th centuries.

The global hierarchy of nations figures heavily into the poor performance of international efforts to address climate change. Low-lying nations, such as Bangladesh and the Maldives, have a strong urgency to halt human activities causing climate change that threaten their very existence but lack, in relative terms, the political sway to mobilize swift action. The relative stagnation, questionable effectiveness, and reluctance or outright refusal by some nations to participate in international agreements (e.g., Rio Earth Summit in 1992; Kyoto Protocol in 1997; Conference of Parties (COP) held annually since 1995) seeking global cooperation to reduce emissions are indicative of the vast power and wealth differentials across nations. For example, the George W. Bush administration's refusal to ratify the Kyoto protocol because it was "too costly" was a slap in the face to developing nations. How could the most affluent nation in the world not afford to implement sound environmental policies to address the climate crisis? This is especially insidious given that the United States alone emitted 50 percent more greenhouse gas emissions in the 20th century than all developing countries combined. The 2009 COP in Copenhagen was another exceptionally contentious assembly. Amidst mounting pressure to pay for the climate problem they created, an elite group of wealthy nations that are members of the Organization for Economic Co-operation and Development (OECD) promised to provide $100 billion annually (1/7 of the US military budget) by 2020 to help developing nations cope with climate change. In the absence of standardized accounting methodologies, OECD nations could decide what would count as part of their commitment. Follow up reports from the OECD to document progress on upholding their pledge have been heavily critiqued for lack of transparency, flawed estimates, and exaggeration if not blatant falsehoods. Disputes surrounding the accounting procedures remain a point of contention for developing countries as they await the funding they were promised and continue to dispute OECD claims of those promises being fulfilled.

There are multiple ways that climate change disproportionately burdens middle- and low-income nations. The economic impacts are predicted to be more drastic due to their geographic clustering around the equator (making them more vulnerable to heatwaves) coupled with their reliance on agriculture and natural resource extraction, both of which are profoundly impacted by erratic weather events. Health risks (see Lessons 10 and 11) are also amplified among low-income populations residing in low latitudes given the high prevalence and greater vulnerability to climate-sensitive diseases such as malaria. Less-developed and developing nations characteristically lack the capacity to prepare for and respond to various environmental hazards. Individuals in these nations are more vulnerable to disasters, which is especially worrisome considering the forecasted increase in severity and frequency of disaster events as a result of climate change. Their capacity to minimize pre-disaster risks and optimize post-disaster recovery is compromised by several factors such as inefficient evacuation strategies, exacerbated bouts of political and economic instability, institutional failures, and general lack of provisions for assistance and aid. Malnutrition is another central concern, as climate change threatens to propel millions into chronic states of food insecurity due to food shortages and food price shocks.

There is a wide body of research connecting warming temperatures to various forms of violence ranging from armed conflict and organized crime to self-inflicted and interpersonal violence. In addition to the direct impacts on mortality, collective violence impairs access to critical health resources including sanitation, medical care, health supplies, safe food, and clean water. Yet again, individuals in low-income nations in low latitudes are most vulnerable to temperature increases, and there is mounting evidence that charts the correspondence of spikes in violence with rising temps. Moreover, these nations are the least prepared in economic and political terms to combat insurgent forces, military coups, or state-led violence. Left unchecked, violent uprisings are expected to become more commonplace as the effects of climate change continue to intensify. Indeed, climate change is indicted as a key factor contributing to the civil war in Syria that has claimed nearly a half million lives, injured nearly 2 million people, displaced almost 7 million individuals, and created nearly 5 million refugees since 2011. The severe drought that plagued Syria from 2006 to 2010 triggered massive migrations to urban centers and food price shocks that exacerbated poverty and social unrest.

Low-income nations also face greater threats to population stability as they are ill-equipped of the political and economic resources needed to manage climate-related crises. They tend to have greater rates of displacement resulting from extreme weather events. Reliance on weather-dependent livelihood systems like farming, herding, or fishing intensifies pressure to relocate as changes in weather patterns adversely impact the sustainability of their subsistence strategies. The interaction of climate stressors with conflict may prompt substantial movements of people as population shifts compound civil unrest. Long-term deterioration in the habitability of locales could spark massive migrations as heat waves, rising sea levels, desertification, and diminishing freshwater aquifers impede local and regional ecosystems' ability to support human populations.

CLIMATE CHANGE, GENDER, AND INTERSECTIONALITY

As demonstrated previously, there are vast differences across nations regarding their ability to cope with climate change. Within nations, similar disparities exist. Individuals who occupy positions of power and privilege are less vulnerable to climate change adversities, whereas poor people will be hit first and hardest. Those at the fringes of society who depend on the environment in the course of their daily lives to fetch food, fuel, fiber, and other resources are among the most vulnerable to changing climates. Individuals engaged in subsistence agriculture and livelihoods dependent on natural resource inputs are especially susceptible to climatic changes that threaten their ability to provide for themselves and their households. Indeed, poor, rural, Indigenous women are particularly hard hit, as their daily tasks of gathering resources for the household are profoundly complicated by climate change dynamics.

An **intersectionality** framework is a helpful lens for understanding differences in vulnerability to climate change. Intersectional approaches eschew the tendency to focus on singular forms of social difference by emphasizing the complexity of interlocking systems of oppression, including (but not limited to) race, gender, class, sexuality, ethnicity, nationality, indigeneity, (dis)ability, religion, species, and rural/urban as well as Global South/North divides. Although intersectionality scholarship did not focus on human-environmental relations at its inception, the approach has been increasingly incorporated into socioecological theories. By examining how numerous axes of difference influence each other, intersectional approaches seek to understand the complex ways in which systems of inequality and privilege "intersect" in individuals' lives to create different vulnerabilities, opportunities, and outcomes to the same political, economic, and environmental circumstances.

Ecofeminism (see Lesson 2) is one such framework that employs an intersectional lens to illuminate the ways in which women are uniquely positioned in society as an acute sufferer of—and potential savior from—ecological destruction. Ecofeminist scholars assert the structure and logic of the world economic regime is such that large portions of costs associated with production are absorbed by both women and the environment, resulting in their interconnected domination and exploitation. Ecofeminists utilize an intersectional approach to understand the ways in which individuals experience and interact with the environment, as shaped by the constellation of inequities across racial, gender, class, and colonial divides as well as unequal development trajectories at the local, national, and global levels. This diverse body of work illustrates how social location, privilege, and disadvantage intersect to create very different effects on and experiences of the natural environment within society.

Reduced availability in the quantity and quality of natural resources complicates women's lives in numerous ways, with the worst disadvantages concentrated along predictable lines of colonial, racial, class, wealth, and power divides. As women seek to perform tasks of securing inputs for the household, declines in environmental quality present a growing challenge encountered in their daily lives. Women in poor nations are primarily responsible for subsistence farming; consequently, environmental problems, such as soil infertility and water contamination, impair their ability to provide food for themselves and the household. Women must walk further to find clean water when local sources are contaminated or compromised; they have to hoe longer or further from the home when soils are depleted. The sheer physical taxation of increasingly onerous pursuits for resources imposes direct burdens to women's health. Further, the tendency of women to "eat last" increases health risks posed by declines in the quality and quantity of available food, amplifying malnutrition and susceptibility to disease among women. Circumstances such as these impede women's ability to nurture the health and well-being of children and the elderly—responsibilities disproportionately assumed by women. For these reasons, the effects extend beyond women's lives with ripple effects on household and community well-being.

The amount of time and effort allocated to fulfilling subsistence tasks escalates when local environments are degraded, impinging on women's ability to seek formal employment outside the household that would otherwise boost their financial stability. The prolonged search for resources also diverts women's time away from educational pursuits that are powerful avenues for advancing their overall status and autonomy. Women are further disadvantaged by ecological degradation insofar as their ability to earn money by engaging in cottage industries is imperiled. The dwindling availability of resources used in handicrafts poses challenges to women who rely on these activities for income. With deeply limited options regarding paid work among women in disadvantaged locales, the additional constriction imposed by resource scarcity exacerbates their already precarious positions in the labor force.

Ecofeminist scholars equally emphasize the ways in which these dynamics make women especially well-suited to advance sustainability and climate resilience. Ecofeminist perspectives offer that women, when afforded positions of power in society, tend to promote environmental stewardship. To the degree that women are granted formal access to and control over economic resources, their ability to address environmental crises, including those related to climate change, is enhanced. For instance, women with access to credit can use funds to protect against disasters, such as structural improvements to homes that can withstand heavy wind and better tolerate downpours.

Political empowerment across gender lines is another key avenue for improving the environment. There is accumulating evidence of beneficial associations between female representation in governing bodies and positive environmental outcomes. Scholars demonstrate that CO_2 emissions are lower in nations where women have higher political status, and that nations with greater female representation in governing bodies have lower climate footprints. Collectively, these results indicate that when women have political power, environmental conditions improve. Thirty percent representation by women is often cited as a critical mass or the point at which women gain power to influence policy. Unfortunately, less than one-quarter of national parliaments meet this target at present, including the United States (the 116th congress was 23.7 percent women). This gap is meaningful because excluding women from decision-making processes does not bode well for altering policies to curtail climate change. Thus, increasing political participation and representation among women represents a critical pathway for climate resilience.

RESPONSES TO CLIMATE CHANGE

In line with the logic outlined above, ecofeminist scholars assert gender equality is a necessary step for effectively addressing environmental crises such as climate change. Showing particular disdain for techno-scientific solutions to environmental crises, ecofeminist frameworks unmask the political and economic motivations that stall progress toward climate resilience. For example, the tendency for the climate crisis to be cast as a "population problem" unfairly places blame on female-sexed bodies residing in poor nations while failing to address the disproportionately greater contributions to emissions stemming from capitalist production, Western patterns of consumption, and global corporate practices. Thus, an ecofeminist reading of population concerns uncovers the ways in which efforts to control women's bodies maintain the current global order by deflecting attention away from the true culprits of environmental harm. Others in this tradition reveal that market-based solutions to environmental problems often exacerbate existing inequalities and introduce new hazards. To illustrate, carbon trading schemes that apply market logic to the global atmosphere by treating it as a tradeable commodity are cast as eco-imperialist concoctions that reinforce the global economic order and worsen worldwide gaps of inequality. As such, ecofeminists believe it is both unreasonable and impractical to have faith in efforts by global elites to improve ecological sustainability and climate resilience.

In a similar vein, TOP theorists assert that the capitalist system is predicated on constantly expanding production and consumption, which generates ever-increasing rates of pollution, waste, and demands on natural resources (see Lesson 2). Profit-seeking capitalists try to grow their bottom line by replacing human labor with machines, with obvious implications for unemployment (see Lesson 4). Labor movements and politicians support economic growth, enticed by the promise of new jobs and increased tax revenues, respectively. Those in positions of social, political, and economic power push for policies that encourage economic growth that exacerbate labor displacement and environmental disruptions. The cyclical nature of economic growth leading to social problems that are then "addressed" by expanding production and consumption that creates even more social problems illustrates the "treadmill" connotation.

Metabolic rift perspectives note the disruption of natural metabolic processes resulting from expansionary tendencies inherent to the system of capital. With regards to climate change, the clearing of forests and burning of fossil fuels are key actions that disrupt the carbon cycle. In line with TOP, metabolic rift theorists view the drive for endless accumulation as a stable feature of the global system of capital accumulation that is distinctly at odds with addressing climate change. World systems theory and ecologically unequal exchange theory share these misgivings by emphasizing the global flows of materials unfairly disadvantage non-core nations and the people in them. For these camps, the only viable solution to environmental problems including climate change is a fundamental transition away from the political-economic system currently in place. For them, abandoning a system that prioritizes profits over people and environmental stewardship is an absolute requirement for climate resilience.

In contrast, ecological modernization theories posit that it is possible to work within the current system to instill sound environmental policies and related shifts in production to address climate change (see Lesson 2). State environmentalism, corporate "greening," and cultural values that promote environmentally friendly lifestyles are seen as promising avenues to bring about meaningful change. Critics of such proposals remain unconvinced that state, organizational, and individual-level solutions are viable remedies to what they believe is a systemic problem (a classic "square peg, round hole" scenario). Nonetheless, ecological modernization beliefs most closely characterize current initiatives by international organizations, nations, and institutions to address climate change, but there are many tactical hurdles to implementation, to which we now turn.

In 2015, 196 nations banded together under the Paris Agreement to limit global temperature rise to below 2 degrees Celsius above pre-industrial limits. In a collective effort to instill a pathway toward sustainability (see Lesson 20), countries participating in the Agreement set nationally determined contributions that outline plans for reducing emissions. Despite its fundamental importance, President Trump announced his intentions to withdraw from the Paris Climate Agreement (although he cannot formally do so until November of 2020) shortly after taking office. In response, major corporations voiced their dissatisfaction while several state and local governments reiterated their allegiance to complying with emission reductions outlined in the accords. However, scientists and climate justice advocates note that strict adherence to the Paris Agreement by all participants will still fall short of the transformative policies and practices necessary to chart a course for staying below the 2 degrees Celsius threshold. Thus, mitigating, slowing, halting, and even reversing the industrial practices causing climate change warrant decisive and momentous action if we are to meet stated goals. However, doing so is fraught with powerful political pushback.

There are many ways in which people in positions of power and privilege seek to undermine belief in climate change (see Lesson 5). The Koch brothers, fossil fuel industry billionaires, have spent over $127 million dollars financing more than 90 groups that attack climate change science and upward of $38 million on lobbying efforts to kill climate legislation. Funding conservative think tanks, advocacy groups, and political operatives, such as the Heritage Foundation and Cato Institute, are significant avenues for advancing climate denial (see Lesson 5). Prior to the 2016 election, the Heritage Foundation assembled a database of 3,000 names of trusted conservatives and supplied this list to Trump as he began appointing staff for various governmental vacancies; individuals from the database landed jobs in just about every government agency. When Trump was elected, Heritage convened a transition team to vet ambassadors, diplomats, and cabinet secretaries to make sure they are "change agents"—a key aspect of which is climate change denial. Trump also nominated the CEO of ExxonMobil to become the US Secretary of State.

Conservatives have gone so far as to try and criminalize climate science, as was the case when Virginia's Attorney General Cuccinelli targeted Michael Mann, a respected scientist whose research confirms the rapid warming of the earth. Cuccinelli alleged Mann was guilty of criminal fraud for using taxpayer's money to conduct his research; Mann was ultimately cleared of any wrongdoing. Media mogul Rupert Murdoch (founder of the transnational corporation that owns Fox News, the Wall Street Journal, and hundreds of media outlets globally) is another key player in the climate-misinformation campaign. Fox News routinely casts climate change as nonexistent, based on hype, hysteria, and uncertainty. Trump fuels the misinformation machine with his cries of "fake news" and related political discourse campaigns to discredit what he deems as "liberal" media outlets, such as the *Washington Post* and *New York Times* that routinely report on the scientific consensus in forecasting multiple humanitarian crises presented by climate change. As covered in Lesson 5, global media conglomerates control information in self-interested ways that limit the democratization of knowledge about climate change.

At the other end of the political spectrum we see an emerging class of politicians who demand action on climate change. The "Green New Deal" spearheaded by Representative Alexandria Ocasio-Cortez is an exemplary effort to mitigate climate change, address income inequality, and transition to a more sustainable energy regime. Despite some initial setbacks, the ambitious proposal has received widespread attention and seems to be gaining support across citizen groups. Attacked by conservatives as naïve and sophomoric, the stimulus program has thus far failed to garner the degree of favor needed from Democratic party heavyweights and career politicians to enact such ambitious legislation.

Other national, regional, and local responses to curtail carbon dioxide emissions are emerging to grapple with the alarming rates at which greenhouse gases are emitted. The European Union adopted a cap-and-trade system that sets ceiling limits on emissions while permitting companies to buy and sell carbon permits. However, because carbon prices in Europe remain low, the initiative has had negligible effects on overall emissions. China has been experimenting with similar cap-and-trade systems with plans to roll out a nationwide initiative in 2020 that, if successful, will be the largest program for carbon pricing in the world. In Britain, emissions are falling steeply due, in part, to the introduction of a carbon tax in 2013, which prompted the rapid switch of utilities away from coal-based power. Canada is in the process of instituting bold carbon taxing schemes to meet Prime Minister Trudeau's stated goal of reducing emissions to 30 percent below 2005 levels by 2030. Conservatives have vowed to repeal the tax should they gain control of Canadian governance.

Within the United States, the congressional gridlock on climate policy has prompted some action at the state level. For example, the Regional Greenhouse Gas Initiative is comprised of nine states in the Northeast (Connecticut,

Delaware, Maine, Maryland, Massachusetts, New Hampshire, New York, Rhode Island, and Vermont; at the time of this writing, Virginia and New Jersey are entertaining prospects for joining the coalition) seeking to reduce power sector emissions. The cooperative effort issues CO_2 allowances, with additional pollution permits auctioned to power plants. Despite uncertainty regarding its effect on emissions, participating states have used money from permit purchases to invest in clean energy. California enacted a more extensive cap-and-trade program that reaches beyond power plants to include manufacturers and refineries, among other polluters. Major emissions cuts have come from other state policies, such as efficiency standards for buildings and targets for transitioning to renewable energy.

Elsewhere in the United States, aggressive steps are being taken to reclaim profits from the energy sector to pay for the destruction and loss of natural ecosystems that buffer communities from climate-related threats. In Louisiana, local coalitions have catalyzed efforts to hold the oil and gas industry accountable for damages to wetlands caused by practices to extract and transport energy. Reckless demolition of fragile marshlands from dredging canals, drilling wells, and installing pipelines that connect wells to processing facilities is accelerating subsidence—the loss of land (see Lesson 14). Quite simply, the southeastern coast of Louisiana is disappearing due to violent destruction. Each hour, the state loses about a football field's worth of land.

Wetlands loss has catastrophic implications, as they are the state's first and strongest defense against hurricanes. In response, local activists in concert with the regional levee board leveled "the most ambitious environmental lawsuit ever" against 97 oil and gas companies in 2017, alleging gross industry negligence and failure to implement mandated guidelines for restoration. The energy companies targeted by the lawsuit (including ExxonMobil, BP, and Koch industries, among others) galvanized a powerful alliance of lobbying and political persuasion to derail the litigation. Ultimately, the energy industry emerged victorious—the board's lawsuit was dismissed in district court, refused by the court of appeals, and that denial was upheld by the Supreme Court. The stronghold by energy barons over legal procedure and political process was shown once again. At the time of this writing, seven Southern parishes in Louisiana have filed suit against a dozen corporate defendants seeking payment for damages to wetlands from the companies that profited mightily from their destruction. The success of their effort remains to be seen, but history suggests, at minimum, it will be a hard-fought battle.

CONCLUDING REMARKS

The sociological approaches to environmental impact treated in this lesson are rooted in classical theorizations of social development and change as articulated by Durkheim, Weber, and Marx (or the "Dead White Men"). Tracing these perspectives to their theoretical origins has major implications for how you think social change occurs and what actions are best suited to achieve specific goals. For instance, do you think government interventions, regulations, and policies are ideal avenues for creating a "kinder, gentler, greener" capitalism? Or, do you believe change starts from below with shifts in individuals' attitudes that lead to the institutionalization of environmental concern? Or, do you remain convinced that a new political-economic system is necessary to address climate change?

Durkheimian models (closely tied to human ecology and EMT) offer that the process of development presents possibilities for advancing climate resilience via the greening of corporate practices, state interventions, and individual values, in tandem with increases in efficiency, technological advances, and pro-environmental policies (see Lesson 2). Environmental reform and state environmentalism are theorized to be a "luxury" of the more economically and technologically advanced countries of the world. EMT suggests that political institutions and economic actors globally will eventually see the value of engaging in environmentally friendly practices and will push for stronger environmental laws and enforcement. The central thesis of EMT is that environmental problems can be solved through modernizing existing social, political, and economic institutions—that is, going further into the process of development. Critics of this approach question the ecological implications of promoting a Western model of development, noting that the global attainment of wealth at levels currently witnessed in the United States would have catastrophic environmental consequences. Others cast suspicion on the efficacy of state regulations and policies, arguing uncertain enforcement and monitoring of pro-environmental interventions make them merely symbolic.

For Weber, the (macro, structural) process of modernization is a historical trend of increased rationality in all spheres of life. As societies modernize, rational actors organize society and its institutions to maximize predictability, calculability, and efficiency. For Weber, this is an inescapable condition of modernity. Applied to the global scale, kindred theories (e.g., world-polity) identify cultural shifts toward rationality as the primary mode by which global environmentalism is achieved. As individuals and institutions embrace rationality as an organizing concept, and insofar as environmentalism is deemed rational, the cultural diffusion of pro-environmental norms is predicted to occur across nations engaged in the world society. Thus, environmentally friendly norms developed in advanced nations of the Global North may be adopted by hierarchically weaker nations in the Global South.

Similar to Durkheimian perspectives, critics of the Weberian model cast doubt on the efficacy of environmental ministries and participation in environmental treaties to bring actual improvements to the environment. A Weberian approach to social change prioritizes cultural embrace of environmental concern as the primary avenue by which sound environmental practices become institutionalized. However, the degree to which evidence of an environmental regime serves as an effective check against rising emissions remains to be seen. Weber is the ultimate pessimist in predicting the process of rationalization will ultimately lead to the "irrationality of rationality" whereby we become obsessed with the means (i.e., process) and lose sight of the ends (i.e., product) we seek to achieve. To illustrate, obsessing over the adoption of environmental treaties and protocols is meaningless if strict enforcement and careful monitoring of progress to reach stated goals remain elusive, which is a predicament for current initiatives to mitigate climate change discussed earlier. For Weber, as life becomes more calculating, it ultimately leaves us trapped in an iron cage of rationality that will remain this way "until the last ton of fossil fuel is burnt," (Foster and Holleman, 2012).

Marxist approaches and their recent iterations (world systems theory, metabolic rift, TOP) see no potential for aligning the system of capital with climate resilience. The inherent growth maxims that seek to spread capitalism to every nook and cranny around the world, commoditizing labor and natural resources to further the goal of endless capital accumulation, are viewed as diametrically at odds with ecological sustainability. Accordingly, for Marxist adherents, the only way to resolve the climate crisis is by transitioning away from the current political-economic system. For Marx, capitalism precedes utopia; gains in production brought about from the capitalist era arm us with the material advances necessary to transition to a just system that prioritizes the egalitarian distribution of resources. The 99 percent and Occupy movements share many ideological principles with Marxist beliefs that the history of civilization is a history of class struggle. Indeed, Marx theorizes the unsustainability of the capitalist system "sows the seeds of its own destruction" via the overexploitation of land that disrupts natural metabolic processes and the overexploitation of labor that leads to the emergence of a class consciousness. This shared consciousness is theorized to unite the proletariat (working class) in a revolution from below to overthrow the capitalist system, supplanting it with a new economic regime.

Critiques of this model argue Marx's predictions of a revolution have proved wrong. Others disagree with the basic premise that capitalism cannot be reoriented to align with principles of sustainability. Still others doubt the viability of reorganizing society in such profound ways without an existing blueprint for doing so, though there have been some efforts to provide concrete suggestions for possible alternatives to capitalism. There is also speculation about the ability of organized action to be strong enough to overcome such a powerful, firmly entrenched global system of capital accumulation. Finally, as some point out, most people find it easier to imagine the end of the planet than the end of capitalism.

Clearly, the orientation you adopt has deep implications for how you think society is best positioned to alleviate climate change. Taken together with the examples of recent responses to address—and efforts to deny—climate change treated in this lesson provides an opportunity to vet your philosophical leanings against existing strategies to implement meaningful change. There is also a certain amount of unpredictability associated with any vision of the future, which makes the choice even murkier. Ultimately, though, it is your generation that will confront climate change or be forced to live with the catastrophic consequences. Theories from Durkheim, Weber, and Marx and their modern iterations provide several scenarios for applying sociological concepts and models of social change to imagine possible ways forward. Armed with this sociological backdrop, it is now up to you to decide: What path will you choose? This is a major decision rife with implications for how to invest your efforts, so take your time in making the decision, but do not wait too long because it is your future at stake.

SOURCES

Alter, Charlotte, Suyin Haynes and Justin Worland. 2019. "TIME 2019 Person of the Year: Greta Thunberg." Accessed March 3, 2020 https://time.com/person-of-the-year-2019-greta-thunberg/

Arrhenius, Svante. 1896. "On the Influence of Carbonic Acid in the Air upon the Temperature of the Ground." *Philosophical Magazine and Journal of Science* 41 (5): 237–276. Accessed March 15, 2019. https://www.rsc.org/images/Arrhenius1896_tcm18-173546.pdf

Buckingham, Susan. 2010. "Call in the Women." *Nature* 468 (7323): 502.

Clark, Brett and Richard York. 2005. "Carbon Metabolism: Global Capitalism, Climate Change, and the Biospheric Rift." *Theory and Society* 34 (4): 391–428.

Dietz, Thomas and Eugene A. Rosa. 1994. "Rethinking the Environmental Impacts of Population, Affluence and Technology." *Human Ecology Review* 1 (1): 277–300.

Dunlap, Riley E. and Robert J. Brulle, eds. 2015. *Climate Change and Society: Sociological Perspectives*. New York, NY: Oxford University Press.

Ergas, Christina and Richard York. 2012. "Women's Status and Carbon Dioxide Emissions: A Quantitative Cross-National Analysis." *Social Science Research* 41 (4): 965–976.

Foster, John Bellamy. 1999. "Marx's Theory of Metabolic Rift: Classical Foundations for Environmental Sociology." *American Journal of Sociology* 105 (2): 366–405.

Foster, John Bellamy, Brett Clark, and Richard York. 2010. *The Ecological Rift: Capitalism's War on the Earth*. New York: Monthly Review Press.

Foster, John Bellamy, and Hannah Holleman. 2012. "Weber and the Environment: Classical Foundations for a Postexemptionalist Sociology." *American Journal of Sociology* 117 (6): 1625–1673.

Gaard, Greta. 2017. *Critical Ecofeminism*. New York: Lexington Books.

Gould, Kenneth A., David N. Pellow, and Allan Schnaiberg. 2015. *Treadmill of Production: Injustice and Unsustainability in the Global Economy*. New York: Routledge.

Hooks, Gregory, and Chad L. Smith. 2004. "The Treadmill of Destruction: National Sacrifice Areas and Native Americans." *American Sociological Review* 69 (4): 558–575.

Intergovernmental Panel on Climate Change (IPCC). 2018. "2018: Summary for Policymakers." In *Global warming of 1.5°C. An IPCC Special Report on the impacts of global warming of 1.5°C above pre-industrial levels and related global greenhouse gas emission pathways, in the context of strengthening the global response to the threat of climate change, sustainable development, and efforts to eradicate poverty* edited by V. Masson-Delmotte, P. Zhai, H. O. Pörtner, D. Roberts, J. Skea, P. R. Shukla, A. Pirani, et al. Geneva, Switzerland: World Meteorological Organization.

Levy, Barry S., Victor W. Sidel, and Jonathan A. Patz. 2017. "Climate Change and Collective Violence." *Annual Review of Public Health* 38 (2017): 241–257.

Magdoff, Fred and John Bellamy Foster. 2011. *What Every Environmentalist Needs to Know About Capitalism: A Citizen's Guide to Capitalism and the Environment*. New York: Monthly Review Press.

McKinney, Laura. 2014. "Gender, Democracy, Development, and Overshoot: A Cross-National Analysis." *Population and Environment* 36 (2): 193–218.

McKinney, Laura A. and Gregory M. Fulkerson. 2015. "Gender Equality and Climate Justice: A Cross-National Analysis." *Social Justice Research* 28 (3): 293–317.

Mies, Maria and Vandana Shiva. 1993. *Ecofeminism*. New York: Zed Books.

Mol, Arthur P. J. 1995. *The Refinement of Production: Ecological Modernization Theory and the Chemical Industry*. Utrecht: International Books.

Resurrección, Bernadette P. 2013. "Persistent Women and Environment Linkages in Climate Change and Sustainable Development Agendas." *Women's Studies International Forum* 40: 33–43.

Roberts, J. Timmons and Bradley C. Parks. 2007. *A Climate of Injustice: Global Inequality, North-South Politics, and Climate Policy*. Cambridge, MA: MIT Press.

Rocheleau, Dianne, Barbara Thomas-Slayter, and Esther Wangari. 1996. *Feminist Political Ecology: Global Issues and Local Experiences*. New York: Routledge.

Schnaiberg, Allan and Kenneth A. Gould. 1994. *Environment and Society: The Enduring Conflict*. New York: St. Martin's Press.

Terry, Geraldine. 2009. "No Climate Justice Without Gender Justice: An Overview of the Issues." *Gender & Development* 17 (1): 5–18.

Wallerstein, Immanuel M. 2004. *World-Systems Analysis: An Introduction*. Durham, NC: Duke University Press.

Wright, Christopher and Daniel Nyberg. 2015. *Climate Change, Capitalism, and Corporations: Processes of Creative Self-Destruction*. Cambridge, UK: Cambridge University Press.

York, Richard and Eugene A. Rosa. 2003. "Key Challenges to Ecological Modernization Theory: Institutional Efficacy, Case Study Evidence, Units of Analysis, and the Pace of Eco-Efficiency." *Organization & Environment* 16 (3): 273–288.

York, Richard, Eugene Rosa, and Thomas Dietz. 2003. "A Rift in Modernity? Assessing the Anthropogenic Sources of Global Climate Change with the STIRPAT Model." *International Journal of Sociology and Social Policy* 23 (10): 31–51.

Part 4

SOME SOCIAL RESPONSES TO ENVIRONMENTAL DISRUPTION

Normalizing the Unthinkable
Climate Denial and Everyday Life

Kari Marie Norgaard

Workers fill plastic bags with sargassum seaweed that has been burying Caribbean beaches since 2011 as the sea warmed and currents shifted due to climate change, Quintana Roo, Mexico.

Post your photo on climate denial to #TLESdenial

Photo by Ken Gould

In early January of 2019, the National Oceanic and Atmospheric Administration (NOAA) announced that 2018 marks the 42nd consecutive year in which global land and ocean temperatures were above the 20th century average. Nine of the 10 warmest years since 1880 have occurred since 2005, with the last five years (2014–2018) ranking as the five warmest years on record. Furthermore, NOAA reported that the highest ever reported figures for global land and ocean temperatures keep being broken, with new record highs set in 2005, 2010, 2014, 2015, and 2016. This should come as no surprise: for over three decades, natural and physical scientists have provided increasingly clear and dire assessments of how climate change is altering the biophysical world around which human social systems are organized. I took an entire course on climate change as an undergraduate student in 1990, just two years after James Hansen's congressional testimony on the seriousness of climate change made the front page of the *New York Times* in 1988. Recently, new temperature records have been coupled with extreme weather events such as Hurricane Maria, which hit Puerto Rico; devastating wildfires in California; and over a dozen billion-dollar climate related disasters in the United States in 2018 alone.

Yet despite these heat records, extreme weather events, and urgent warnings from the scientific community, climate change has remained a proverbial "elephant in the room." Climate scientists may have identified global warming as the most important issue of our time, but for urban dwellers in the rich and powerful Northern countries, climate change is still mostly seen as "no more than background noise." A photo of golfers continuing to casually play with the enormous Eagle Creek wildfire blazing in the background went viral on the internet and came to epitomize this mindset. Even after Hurricane Katrina hit, the March 2006 Gallup headline read, "Americans Still Not Highly Concerned About Global Warming." Gallup Organization first included climate change as a standard issue in its surveys in 2014. The category of climate change did not even make it onto the list of the Pew Research Center's annual January survey of national domestic priorities for the Government and Congress until 2007, some 19 years after the first front-page story in the *New York Times*! An effective climate skeptic movement has convinced a vocal percentage of the population that climate change is a hoax. Despite that, the majority of people are not outright skeptics—as of March 2019, 66 percent of Americans do understand that it is caused by human activity.

While "apathy" in the United States is particularly notable, this gap between the severity of the problem and its lack of public salience is visible in most Western nations. Indeed, no nation has a base of public citizens that are sufficiently socially and politically involved to effect the level of social and political engagement that predictions of climate science warrant. Instead we are confronted with a series of paradoxes: as scientific evidence for climate change pours in, public urgency and even interest in the issue fails to correspond. As events from California wildfires to Hurricane Maria to pine bark beetle infestations in Colorado and melting permafrost in Alaska reveal, changing climatic conditions are increasingly jeopardizing state economic resources, exacerbating social inequalities, altering community structures, and generating new patterns of economic and social conflict (see Lesson 14). How is it possible that such major threats to social infrastructure public safety and human health fail to mobilize public response? What explains the misfit between scientific information, unfolding events and public response? Are people just uninformed of the facts? Are they inherently greedy and self-interested? These are the questions that chart the course of my work, which concerns not the outright rejection of climate science by so-called climate skeptics but the more pervasive and everyday problem of how and why people who say they are concerned about climate change manage to ignore it in their everyday lives? For without the mobilization of the broader public, it is difficult for the necessary large scale political, economic, and social changes to take place.

For nearly 20 years the main explanation for the public's silence from the scientific community has been that the public just doesn't understand the seriousness of what is unfolding—in other words, that lack of information is the limiting factor in public nonresponse. The thinking has been that "if people only knew the facts," they would act differently. Psychological and "science communication" studies emphasized the complexity of climate science, while sociologists described political economic corruption as reasons people do not adequately understand what is at stake. Researchers have described the problem of "faulty mental models," lamented the confusion between global warming and ozone depletion, investigated the role of media framing, and described how understanding global warming requires a complex grasp of scientific knowledge in many fields.

For example, psychologists Graeme Halford and Peter Sheehan (1991) wrote, "With better mental models and more appropriate analogies for global change issues, it is likely that more people, including more opinion leaders, will make the decision to implement some positive coping action of a precautionary nature" (606).

On the sociological side, scholars have identified the fossil fuel industry's influence on government policy, the tactics of climate skeptic campaigns, how corporate control of media limits and molds available information about global warming, and even the "normal" distortion of climate science through the "balance as bias phenomenon" in journalism (Boykoff 2011). Many scholars have now traced the process of how the fossil fuel industry and conservative think tanks have challenged the scientific consensus on climate change by "manufacturing uncertainty," altering government documents, and launching political attacks on key climate scientists (Brulle 2016). The climate skeptic movement has been mostly organized from the United States. Corporate associations including the US Chamber of Commerce and the American Petroleum Institute together with conservative think tanks including the Heartland Institute, the CATO Institute, and the Marshall Institute, have played key roles in this process (see Lesson 5). Interestingly, according to research by McCright and Dunlap (2011a), acceptance of climate change also varies by gender and race, with conservative white men being more likely than other Americans to subscribe to "denialist views."

The climate skeptic movement in particular has played a powerful role in the distortion of public understanding of climate change just in the past 10 years. Note that explanations for public nonresponse that highlight corporate media and climate skeptic campaigns also implicitly direct our attention to a lack of information as the biggest barrier to engagement, though for different reasons. While all these explanations matter, corporate media control has hardly kept all information from public view. Certainly there are cases when the public may either lack information or be outright misinformed, but are these issues the main limiting factor behind greater public interest, concern, or political participation? Clearly knowledge is necessary to generate public response, but is knowledge sufficient? As has been pointed out decades ago, only two simple facts are essential to understanding climate change: Global warming is the result of an increase in the concentration of carbon dioxide in the earth's atmosphere; and the single most important source of carbon dioxide is the combustion of fossil fuels, most notably coal and oil. So how can it be that people around the world fail to understand these basic facts? And while such "information deficit" explanations are indispensable, they do not account for the behavior of two-thirds of the US public who know about global warming and express concern, yet still fail to take any action: the latest Gallup poll (March 2019) indicates 66 percent understand climate science, while 45 percent "worry about it a great deal." While there have been many surveys and public opinion polls on climate change, there have been almost no in-depth, qualitative or ethnographic studies of how people actually experience climate change. I arrived in Norway with a concern about global warming and an intention to conduct research on how the environmentally progressive Norwegians made sense of it. Norway was not only a place I had spent significant time growing up in, but also a nation I admired for its strong environmental and humanitarian values. Plus, the Norwegians have substantial wealth, which can be an asset, at least in making technological changes. Since the time I first lived in Norway as a teenager, I had been fascinated by the extent of progressive environmental policy and awareness there. Now I returned with my comparative sociological lens to ask questions that at the time could not be addressed in my own country, the United States. Indeed, at the time, the United States was the only country in the world where, thanks to extensive countercampaigns by the oil industry, one-quarter of the population still questioned whether global warming was actually occurring—now that figure has actually increased to about one-third (see above referenced climate poll). If any nation can find the ability to respond, it must be in a place such as this, where the population is educated and environmentally engaged. Furthermore, changes in the arctic are more pronounced than in lower latitudes. That winter and spring of 2001, I spent a lot of time attending public meetings, reading the newspapers, talking with people on the street, and generally watching and listening to what was going on. I conducted 46 interviews with a range of community members. As it happened, there was unusually warm weather during the 10 months I spent in the community of "Bygdaby." November brought severe flooding. The first snowfall did not come until late January, some two months later than usual. By then, the winter was recorded as

Norway's second warmest in the past 130 years. The local ski area opened in late December only with the aid of 100 percent artificial snow, a completely unprecedented event with measurable economic impacts on hotels, shops, taxi drivers, and others in the area. The local lake failed to freeze sufficiently to allow for ice fishing. Small talk commonly included references to "unusual weather" and to "climate change," accompanied by a shaking of heads.

It was not just the weather that was unusual that winter. As a sociologist, I was perplexed by the behavior of the people as well. Despite the clear social and economic impacts on the community, there was no social action in response to the warm weather. Nobody wrote letters to the local paper, brought the issue up in one of the many public forums that took place that winter, made attempts to plan for the local effects of climate change, put pressure on local and national leaders to develop long-term climate plans or short-term economic relief, decreased their automobile use, or even engaged their neighbors and political leaders in discussions about what climate change might mean for their region.

People could have reacted differently to that strange winter. The shortened ski season affected everyone in the community. In the words of one taxi driver, "It makes a difference if we move from five months of winter tourism to only three. It affects all of us, you know, not just those up on the mountain. It affects the hotels, the shops in town, us taxi drivers, we notice it too." Why didn't this awareness translate into social action? Throughout modern history, people have used a variety of strategies to draw attention to problems in their communities, such as staging marches and boycotts and writing letters to newspaper editors and political leaders. What might people have done differently? Community members could have done any number of things to express a sense of concern, from raising the issue in one of the many local political meetings to writing letters in the newspaper, developing plans for how their community might respond, or, at the very least, talking with one another about what climate change might mean for their community in the next 10 to 20 years.

Indeed, in other parts of the world that same year I lived in this community, reactions to climate change *were* different. Severe flooding in England that November was linked to climate change by at least some of the affected residents. People from affected communities in England traveled to the climate talks at The Hague to protest government policies. Since that time, several cities in the United States have taken action against the federal government over global warming. And although one cannot tie weather events per se to climate change, the fact that increased hurricane intensity is one clear outcome of climate change has led residents in Mississippi who are now homeless as a result of Hurricane Katrina to file a lawsuit against oil companies for their role in climate change. The residents of this town could have taken similar actions, rallying around the problem of the lack of snow and its economic and cultural impacts. But they did not.

"WE DON'T REALLY WANT TO KNOW"

That season I spent in this small town in rural Norway, global warming was frequently mentioned, and people in the community seemed to be both informed and concerned about it. Yet at the same time, I noticed that it was an uncomfortable issue. People were aware that climate change could radically alter life within the next decades, yet they did not go about their days wondering what life would be like for their children, whether farming practices would change, or whether their grandchildren would be able to ski on real snow. They spent their days thinking about more local, manageable topics. Vigdis, a college-age student, told me that she was afraid of global warming but that it didn't enter her everyday life:

> I often get afraid, like—it goes very much up and down, then, with how much I think about it. But if I sit myself down and think about it, it could actually happen, I thought about how if this here continues we could come to have no difference between winter and spring and summer, like—and lots of stuff about the ice that is melting and that there will be flooding, like, and that is depressing, the way I see it.

In the words of one person who held his hands in front of his eyes as he spoke, "people want to protect themselves a bit." Other community members in Norway described this sense of knowing and not knowing, of having information but not thinking about it in their everyday lives. As one young woman told me, "In the everyday I don't think so much about it, but I know that environmental protection is very important." As a topic that was troubling, it was an issue that many people preferred to avoid. Thus, community members describe climate change as an issue that they have to "sit themselves down and think about," "don't think about in the everyday," "but that in-between is discouraging and an emotional weight." Since members of the community did know about global warming but did not integrate this knowledge into everyday life, they experienced what Robert Lifton (1982) calls the *absurdity of the double life*, a phrase I adapt in coining the term *double reality*. In one reality was the collectively constructed sense of normal everyday life. In the other reality existed the troubling knowledge of increasing automobile use, polar ice caps melting, and the predictions for future weather scenarios. In the words of Kjersti, a teacher at the local agricultural school in her early thirties, "We live in one way and we think in another. We learn to think in parallel. It's a skill, an art of living."

What was happening in that community, and indeed what we can all observe in the public silence on climate change in United States and other industrialized nations, was not a rejection of information per se but the failure to integrate this knowledge into everyday life or transform it into social action. British sociologist Stanley Cohen calls this **implicatory denial:** "the facts of children starving to death in Somalia, mass rape of women in Bosnia, a massacre in East Timor, homeless people in our streets are recognized, but are not seen as psychologically disturbing or as carrying a moral imperative to act. . . . Unlike literal or interpretive denial, knowledge itself is not at issue, but doing the 'right' thing with the knowledge" (2011, 9).

THREE DISTURBING EMOTIONS

Both my research in Norway and follow-up work in the United States describes how for many people thinking seriously about climate change evokes a series of troubling emotions. There is *fear about a future* with more heat waves, droughts, and increased storm intensity. There is *fear that our present political and economic structures* are unable to effectively respond. And for many there is *guilt* since Americans are among the main contributors to global climate emissions, and Norwegians' high standard of living comes directly from their oil income. Finally, many people described a sense of not knowing what to do. Ultimately, sufficiently reducing global climate emissions is beyond the level of individual action. But neither national nor international efforts have been successful. Awareness of this generates for many a feeling of *helplessness*. Younger people, especially in the United States, have suggested that anger is a fourth emotion that should be considered. This emotion can as often be one that motivates action rather than retreat— Swedish youth activist Greta Thunberg mobilizes this emotion for example.

How we respond to disturbing information is a complex process. Individuals may block out certain information in order to maintain coherent meaning systems (e.g., cognitive dissonance), desirable emotional states, a sense of self-efficacy, and to follow **norms of attention, norms of emotion**, and **norms of conversation**. The denial metaphor of the elephant in the room is useful because it reminds us that ignoring a serious problem is not easy to do. Ignoring the obvious—tip toeing around the elephant without letting on that one sees it—can be a lot of work. In her work on apathy in the United States, sociologist Nina Eliasoph (1998) observes, "We often assume that political activism requires an explanation, while inactivity is the normal state of affairs. But it can be as difficult to ignore a problem as to try to solve it, to curtail feelings of empathy as to extend them. . . . If there is no exit from the political world then political silence must be as active and colorful as a bright summer shadow" (1998, 6). How did people manage to outwardly ignore what was happening in the community? Did they manage to ignore it inwardly as well?

Eviatar Zerubavel (2006) argues that society organizes patterns of perception, memory, and organizational aspects of thinking. In other words, what people pay attention to, think about, remember, and more are in large part a matter of what we have been socialized to notice, think about, and remember. These things are also a function of what people around us are paying attention to, thinking about, and remembering. These cultural norms are in turn attuned to specific political economic relations. Governments and media outlets shape the collective thought process through direct censorship, of course; but much more often this happens through the process of framing stories, distraction, public rituals, and other seemingly more benign techniques. My own work has examined this. Thus, alongside the serious threat to democracy posed by capital's control of the production and dissemination of knowledge (e.g., the fact that increased corporate control of media limits and molds available information about global warming, and corporate-funded research centers generate conflicting knowledge) is another phenomenon that reinforces public nonresponse: how people cope with the information that *does* become available (Lesson 5). Overt and more readily identifiable processes such as manipulation and control of information set the stage for the less visible (and to date less studied) process of socially organized denial that I describe here.

The concept of denial is generally considered the domain of psychology. But the information individuals find disturbing, and the mechanisms they employ to protect themselves from such information, may also be analyzed within the context of both social interaction and the broader political economy. Social context itself can be a significant part of what makes it difficult to respond to climate change. Sociologists remind us that notions of what is normal to think and talk about are not given but are socially structured. Although individual people experience the disturbing emotions of fear, guilt, and helplessness, the act of denial is not individual; rather, it is something that people do together as a community. Again, I draw on the work of sociologist Eviatar Zerubavel (2006), who coined the term "**socially organized denial.**" It is by paying simultaneous attention to individual responses and social context that we can begin to analyze people's reactions to global warming in reference to the larger political economy. Drawing next from my ethnographic data from Norway, I will describe how people use a variety of methods for normalizing or minimizing disturbing information, what can be called "strategies of denial."

Community members *collectively* held information about global warming at arm's length by participating in cultural norms of attention, emotion, and conversation, and by using a series of cultural narratives to deflect disturbing information and normalize a particular version of reality in which "everything was fine." For example, they tried not to think too far into the future, tried to avoid scaring one another or "being too negative," and often emphasized how "Norway is such a small country anyway" and "at least we're not as bad as the Americans." I have since done comparative work in the United States, where many of the feelings about climate change, as well as tactics of normalizing it, are similar to what I found in Norway—except that the "bad guys" in the United States are the climate skeptics and the Chinese.

CULTURAL DENIAL

People in the community managed to keep climate change at a distance from their safe everyday lives by following established cultural norms about what to pay attention to, feel, and talk and think about in different contexts.

I categorized these as "cultural denial." From the perspective of sociology of cognition, people learn to think through socialization into different "thought communities." At the same time as they feel "just like everyday life," these culturally prescribed norms of attention reflect a particularly insidious form of social control. While outright coercion is a serious matter, it is also more easily recognized, identified, and, in (so-called) democratic societies, condemned. As Cohen notes, "Without being told what to think about (or what not to think about), and without being punished for 'knowing' the wrong things, societies arrive at unwritten agreements about what can be publically [sic] remembered and acknowledged" (2011, 10–11). For example, to avoid emotions of guilt, fear, and helplessness, people in the Norwegian community I studied changed the topic of conversations, told jokes, tried not to think about climate change, and kept the concept off the agenda of political meetings. When disturbing ideas about climate change entered the conversation, people used a series of cultural narratives to deflect those ideas and to normalize a particular version of reality in which the scary problem of climate change was not occurring.

Thus, information about climate change disappeared into daily life for reasons that were more culturally diffuse. For example, simply upholding norms of attention with respect to space made the lack of snow and warm temperatures seem less significant (depoliticized in part because connections to unusual weather events elsewhere were not made), while following norms of attention with respect to time encouraged community members to not think too far ahead into the future, hence minimizing the extent to which the implications of immediate events are forecasted. Cultural norms of emotion limited the extent to which community members could bring strong feelings they privately held regarding climate change into the public political process, which in turn served to reinforce the sense that everything was fine.

INTERPRETIVE DENIAL: COMBATING GLOBAL WARMING BY INCREASING CARBON DIOXIDE

A second, more explicit, example of socially organized denial happened through narrative interpretation. Community members used a variety of social narratives, some produced by the national government, to deflect responsibility for and legitimate Norwegian climate and petroleum policy. I observed three types of narratives: **selective interpretation, perspectival selectivity**, and **claims to virtue**. According to Rosenberg (1991, 135), in the case of selective interpretation, to the extent that they are able, "people tend to assign those meanings to events that will produce the desired emotions." In this case, community members had a set of "stock stories" about who they were. By portraying Norwegians as close to nature, egalitarian, simple, and humble, these narratives of national identity served to counter the criticism and doubt Norwegians face with regard to climate and petroleum policies. Notions of "Mythic Norway" were portrayed in official government images and drawn on by advertisers and everyday people in the town. References to Norwegians as humanitarian and egalitarian were common in the national press, and we bought "Norwegian Mountain Bread" complete with an image of a person skiing in the mountains on 400-year-old ski equipment at our local store.

People also normalized information about global warming using what Rosenberg calls perspectival selectivity: "the angle of vision that one brings to bear on certain events" (1991, 134). For example, people may manage unpleasant emotions by searching for and repeatedly telling stories of others who are worse off than they are. Three narratives in this category—"Amerika as a Tension Point," "We Have Suffered," and "Norway Is a Little Land"—served to minimize Norwegian responsibility for the problem of global warming by pointing to the larger impact of the United States on carbon dioxide emissions, stressing that Norway has been a relatively poor nation until quite recently, and emphasizing the nation's small population size. For example, multiple newspaper articles in the national papers that winter and spring mentioned that the United States emits 25 percent of total greenhouse gas emissions while accounting for only 4 percent of the global population. While obviously the United States must be held accountable for its emissions, framing the figure in terms of total emissions and population makes the difference between the United States and "little Norway" appear greatest—a factor of 140 as compared to a factor of 2. When looking at per capita emissions in each country, the contrasts are not so large. Perspectival selectivity was used to create what social psychologists Susan Opotow and Leah Weiss (2000) call "denial of self-involvement." These narratives are discussed in more detail in the book that I published based on this research called *Living in Denial: Climate Change, Emotions and Everyday Life* (Norgaard, 2011).

A third interpretive strategy is in the vein of what historical psychologist Robert J. Lifton calls "claim to virtue" (1982). He coined the phrase to describe how the Nazi doctors in concentration camps who gave Jews lethal injections interpreted their genocidal actions in terms of compassion. From the doctor's perspective, their acts were compassionate because, by killing people who were ill (or who might become ill), they were able to prevent the spread of disease in the camps. Through the claim that unjust acts are actually working toward the opposite end as they appear to (in the case of the doctors, saving the Jews rather than killing them), these actions are made acceptable. Two such claims to virtue were in use that winter back in 2001 with respect to climate change. Although the Norwegian government spoke urgently of the need to reduce emissions of climate gases, they were at the time involved in two projects that do exactly the opposite: building two new natural gas facilities and expanding the petroleum sector by increasing oil development. Both actions have been justified by switching the focus from national targets and measures (as specified under the Kyoto Protocol and Paris Climate Accords) to emphasizing climate change as an *international* problem and attempting to meet Norwegian climate commitments by *trading* climate gas emissions rather than reducing actual output.

"GAS PLANTS ARE BETTER THAN COAL"

Beginning in the early 1990s, the Norwegian government in combination with oil and gas companies began presenting a series of justifications for the development of new natural gas facilities: as natural gas produced less carbon dioxide than coal, Norway could sell this excess energy to other nations and actually be helping overall global emissions (see Lesson 9). Thus, although the government acknowledges that Norway's emissions of climate gases must decrease, it has used a claim to virtue to argue that the building of two new natural gas plants, thereby *increasing* Norway's contribution to climate gases, was actually helping to solve the problem of global warming. However, as Norwegian researchers Hovden and Lindseth (2004) pointed out, "While it is claimed that these would be offset by reductions elsewhere, this does not change the fact that emissions from Norwegian gas-based power would increase the CO_2 emission reductions that Norway would have to complete in order to fulfill its international obligations" (63).

"INCREASING PRODUCTION OF NORWEGIAN OIL WILL HELP THE CLIMATE"

A second example, the justification for increasing national oil production, follows a similar pattern. Norway had increased production of oil and gas threefold in the preceding 10 years, dropped its plan of a national carbon dioxide emissions stabilization target, and shifted from a focus on national strategies (mandated under the Kyoto Protocol and Paris Climate Accords) to a focus on international efforts. Within the new international perspective, the government has argued that "since Norwegian petroleum products are not the dirtiest in the international market, Norwegian oil and gas production is good climate policy internationally" (Hovden and Lindseth 2004, 64). Hovden and Lindseth describe how

> Miljkosok, an environmental cooperative forum consisting of the petroleum industry, the government and various interest groups and organizations, produced a report in 1996 that in effect, concluded that Norwegian oil production was environmentally benign. The arguments were a) that a cut in Norwegian production would increase the price of oil on the world market, which would make coal more competitive, and, most importantly, b) that as Norwegian petroleum production has fewer emissions per unit of oil produced, it was environmentally preferable to the oil produced by other countries.

The unavoidable conclusion was that Norway should increase its Continental Shelf activity, as this would, in sum, be beneficial with respect to the global emissions of CO_2 and NO_x. (2004, 63)

Thus, by shifting attention from the national level (on which Norway is retreating from the Kyoto Protocol and other earlier reduction goals) to the international (in which Norway produces "cleaner" oil than other nations), the Norwegian government claims that increasing oil production is the best thing it can do for the global climate, even though these activities increase carbon dioxide emissions and are in direct opposition to their agreement under the Kyoto Protocol and Paris Climate Accords!

The interpretive strategies of selective interpretation, perspectival selectivity, and claims to virtue worked together to reinforce one another. For example, selective interpretation and perspectival selectivity gave a background picture of Norwegian environmentalism and innocence, whereas claims to virtue were linked to particular contested climate and petroleum activities such as the expansion of oil and gas production or plans of carbon trading.

CONCLUSION

The view from this one town in Norway portrays global warming as an issue about which people cared and had considerable information, but one about which they didn't really want to know and in some sense didn't know *how* to know. I have traced the three disturbing emotions of guilt, fear of the future, and helplessness, as well as how people normalized the idea of climate change in order to avoid these emotions. I describe how people changed the topic of conversations, told jokes, tried not to think about it, and kept the concept off the agenda of political meetings—all by following the "rules" of normal behavior. Weaving these pieces together, I follow an arc of power that moves from the micro level of emotions to the meso level of culture to the macro level of political economy and back again. According to my data both from Norway and from the United States, thinking about global warming is difficult for community members because it raises troubling feelings, feelings that go against a series of cultural norms. And these norms are in turn embedded in the particular social context and economic circumstances in which people live. Thus, in contrast to psychological and survey research that studies human perceptions of climate change on an individual level, I locate these emotional and psychological experiences in both *cultural* and *political-economic* contexts. As a result of this emphasis on cultural, economic, and social contexts, my approach shifts from an "information deficit" model, in which the public fails to respond because of a lack of information, to a "social organization of denial" model, in which the public on a collective level actively resists available information. As a result, what happened in this one town, and indeed what we can all observe in the public silence on climate change in the United States and elsewhere, was not a rejection of information per se but the failure to *integrate this knowledge* into everyday life or transform it into social action.

One implication of socially organized denial of climate change is that as individuals, we must struggle to imagine the reality of our current situation. In writing on the threat of global nuclear war, a problem that now seems infinitely more manageable than climate change, Lifton (1982) described many of the same difficulties we face in coming to terms with climate change (see also Lifton 2017). He wrote of our "fragmented awareness," how "we have no experience with a narrative of potential extinction," and how therefore we "cling to a desperate conventionality." He pointed out that the emotion of fear inhibits our ability to break through "illusions" to "awareness." And at stake in our "struggle for awareness" is the fact that "the degree of numbing of everyday life necessary for individual comfort is at odds with the degree of tension, or even anxiety that must accompany the nuclear awareness necessary for collective survival." He noted that with the appearance of nuclear weapons, imagining the reality of our situation became "uniquely difficult, and at the same time, a prerequisite for survival" (Lifton 1982, 117, 108, 5).

Can such socially organized denial be overcome? And if so, how? With socially organized denial, the question becomes not how better to educate and inform the public but the circumstances under which people are able to move beyond a sense of helplessness, guilt, or fear of the future and take actions that are in their collective, long-term, survival interest. Climate change requires large-scale reduction of emissions, but our current political economic structure is intimately embedded in our petroleum-based economy (see Lessons 7 and 9). We need democratic engagement and response, yet individuals retreat out of a sense of helplessness. Part of what makes people feel helpless at present is an assessment of this very serious problem in a context where nobody else is acting, an assessment that political actions are socially unacceptable or politically unfeasible, and a sense that larger international efforts are even more unlikely. How can we escape this circular pattern? Must we go into the streets? Probably a lot more people do need to march with signs down the main streets of every town in the United States, Norway, and around the world in order to break the cycle of invisibility regarding climate change (see Lessons 18 and 19). But for those with different instincts, there are many other things that can and must be done to make climate change visible and to show each other and our political leaders that we demand action, as Greta Thunberg has modeled.

If socially organized climate denial is a cycle held in place by individual fear and silence, complicit cultural norms, and a state logic based on fossil fuel extraction and economic profit at any politically acceptable cost, then this cycle can be interrupted at multiple points. In any political struggle there are infinite key strategic possibilities. In our present times of rapid social change, such strategic moments will continue to emerge, and we can be ready for them. More generally, individuals can get involved in the many ongoing local, regional, and national political efforts. Social theorists like Hannah Arendt (1958) remind us of the importance of power from below: even talking about climate change with family and friends is an important way to break the present cultural silence. We need to be able to see the relationships between human actions and their impacts on earth's biophysical system—call it an *ecological imagination*. And we need to be able to see the relationships within society that make up this environmentally damaging social structure. This second form of seeing is essentially what C. W. Mills (1959) calls a *sociological imagination*—a central concept in the field of sociology. Having conversations with one another is a key part to making this problem visible. And although they are not enough in isolation, becoming involved in local efforts to make climate change visible in one's community, to plan for coming changes in water supplies and energy use, and to reduce emissions at the county and regional levels that are based on existing community ties and sense of place and identity may provide a key for breaking through climate denial from the ground up. There is already a global movement building for communities to uncover how climate change is manifesting in their local contexts. Local political renewal cannot be enough on its own, but it may be the important next step for individuals in breaking through the absurdity of the double life and for renewing democratic process. As people participate in thinking about what is happening in their own place and how they will respond, they will begin to see why the facts of climate change matter to them and to develop a sociological imagination at the same time as they reconnect the rifts in time and space that have constructed climate change as a distant issue. Working together may over time create the supportive community that is a necessary (though not sufficient) condition for people to face large fears about the future and engage in large-scale social change. Other worthwhile actions to take include gaining inspiration by learning about all the things that people are already doing and joining into those efforts. People who are involved in taking action on climate change feel more hopeful, find more meaning in their lives, and feel less isolated. Facing climate change will not be easy, but it is worth trying.

SOURCES

Arendt, Hannah. 1958. *The Human Condition*. Chicago: University of Chicago Press

Brulle, Robert J. 2016. "The Climate Lobby: A Sectoral Analysis of Lobbying Spending on Climate Change in the USA, 2000 to 2016." *Climatic Change* 149 (3–4): 289–303.

Boykoff, Maxwell. 2011. *Who Speaks for the Climate? Making Sense of Media Reporting on Climate Change*. Cambridge, UK: Cambridge University Press.

Carmichael, J. T. and R. J. Brulle. 2018. "Media Use and Climate Change Concern." *International Journal of Media & Cultural Politics* 14 (2), 243–253.

Cohen, Stanley. 2011. *States of Denial: Knowing about Atrocities and Suffering*. Cambridge, MA: Polity Press.

Dunlap, Riley E. and Peter J. Jacques. 2013. "Climate Change Denial Books and Conservative Think Tanks: Exploring the Connection." *American Behavioral Scientist* 57 (6): 699–731.

Eliasoph, Nina. 1998. *Avoiding Politics: How Americans Produce Apathy in Everyday Life*. Cambridge, UK: Cambridge University Press.

Halford, Graeme and Peter Sheehan. 1991. "Human Responses to Environmental Changes." *International Journal of Psychology* 269 (5): 599–611.

Hochschild, Arlie Russel. 1983. *The Managed Heart: Commercialization of Human Feeling.* Berkeley: University of California Press.

Hovden, Eivind and Gard Lindseth. 2004. "Discourses in Norwegian Climate Policy: National Action or Thinking Globally?" *Political Studies* 52 (1): 63–81.

Jacques, Peter. 2009. *Environmental Skepticism Ecology, Power and Public Life.* Burlington, VT: Ashgate.

Jacques, Peter, Riley Dunlap, and Mark Freeman. 2008. "The Organization of Denial: Conservative Think Tanks and Environmental Skepticism." *Environmental Politics* 17 (3): 349–385.

Koehler, Derek J. 2016. "Can Journalistic 'False Balance' Distort Public Perception of Consensus in Expert Opinion?" *Journal of Experimental Psychology: Applied* 22 (1): 24.

Lifton, Robert. 1982. *Indefensible Weapons: The Political and Psychological Case Against Nuclearism.* New York: Basic Books.

Lifton, Robert Jay. *The Climate Swerve: Reflections on Mind, Hope, and Survival.* The New Press, 2017.

Mann, Michael. 2012. *The Hockey Stick and the Climate Wars: Dispatches from the Front Lines.* New York: Columbia University Press.

McCright, Aaron M. and Riley E. Dunlap. 2010. "Anti-reflexivity: The American Conservative Movement's Success in Undermining Climate Science and Policy." *Theory, Culture & Society* 27 (2–3): 100–133.

McCright, Aaron M., and Riley E. Dunlap. 2011a. "Cool Dudes: The Denial of Climate Change Among Conservative White Males in the United States." *Global Environmental Change* 21 (4): 1163–1172.

McCright, Aaron M., and Riley E. Dunlap. 2011b. "The Politicization of Climate Change: Political Polarization in the American Public's Views of Global Warming." *Sociological Quarterly* 52: 155–194.

Mills, C. W. 1959. The sociological imagination. Oxford: Oxford University Press.

NOAA. 2019. "Global Climate Report—Annual 2019." https://www.ncdc.noaa.gov/sotc/global/201913

Norgaard, Kari Marie. 2011. *Living in Denial: Climate Change, Emotions and Everyday Life.* Cambridge, MA: MIT Press.

Opotow, Susan, and Leah Weiss. 2000. "New Ways of Thinking about Environmentalism: Denial and the Process of Moral Exclusion in Environmental Conflict." *Journal of Social Issues* 56 (3): 475–490.

Oreskes, Naomi and Erik Conway. 2010. *Merchants of Doubt: How a Handful of Scientists Obscured the Truth on Issues from Tobacco Smoke to Global Warming.* New York: Bloomsbury Press.

Rosenberg, Morris. 1991. "Self-Processes and Emotional Experiences." In *The Self-Society Dynamic: Cognition, Emotion and Action*, edited by Judith Howard and Peter Callero, 123–142. Cambridge, UK: Cambridge University Press.

Sutton, Barbara, and Kari Marie Norgaard. 2013. "Cultures of Denial: Avoiding Knowledge of State Violations of Human Rights Violations in Argentina and the United States." *Sociological Forum* 28 (3): 495–524.

Weber, Elke, and Paul Stern. 2011. "Public Understanding of Climate Change in the United States." *American Psychologist* 66 (4): 315–328.

Zerubavel, Eviatar. 2006. *The Elephant in the Room: Silence and Denial in Everyday Life.* New York: Oxford University Press.

17

Labor and the Environment

Brian K. Obach

Abandoned Bethlehem Steel mill, Bethlehem, Pennsylvania.
Post your photo on labor and the environment to #TLESlabor.
Photo by Ken Gould

Imagine that you have worked in a lumber mill in a rural area in the Pacific Northwest for the last 15 years. Your father worked in the timber industry, as did his father before him. The timber industry is the primary economic engine in your area. Tourism has been growing, and the wilderness enthusiasts who come to town have also helped to bolster the economy through their spending on lodging, supplies, and services. But the jobs associated with serving these visitors do not pay very well, and the mill remains the main employer. However, timber sector jobs have been disappearing in recent years. Several mills elsewhere in the region have shut down, and your mill has laid off several workers. So far, you've been able to keep your job, but unemployment is high, and there is much fear and concern among the mill workers about their job situation.

The company says that the industry is being harmed by environmental groups that charge that logging is destroying the habitat of an endangered owl. The mill owners say that measures being promoted by "big-city environmentalists" would "lock up" a good deal of forest land that the industry depends on. Lawsuits filed by some environmental groups have already delayed logging on some parcels, and the company claims that this is what led to the recent layoffs. Along with your last paycheck, the company included a request that everyone write to their congressional representatives to oppose any new logging restrictions. Many of your fellow workers have already done so, and talk about these "damn environmentalists who want to destroy our jobs" is common throughout the community.

What do you think you would do in this situation? How do you think you would feel about environmentalists and the need for forest protection?

People form opinions and take political action on the basis of many different factors. As sociologists, we recognize that people have different interests and are exposed to different ideas and influences depending on their *social position*—that is, their economic class, the region they live in, their age, their race, their gender, their education, and other important facets of their lives. Unless you are returning to school, as a college student you are probably fairly young, you are already relatively well educated, you might have a part-time job or work over the summer in the service sector; and, while you may not necessarily be well off now, your education level will likely place you in a job that does not involve manual labor and that will provide you with a relatively decent income in the future. On the basis of your social position and the influences to which you are exposed within that location, your views on many issues are likely to be different from those of a middle-aged career mill worker.

Research demonstrates that, as with most issues, views on environmental protection vary depending on one's social position. Thus, to understand (and to shape) our environmental future, it is important that we examine what influences people's attitudes regarding the need for environmental protection. If people are in a position that leads them to deny the existence of real environmental problems, we need to understand why and to consider ways that would help to unite people to confront environmental changes that threaten human well-being. One's employment situation can be an important aspect of shaping one's views on environmental issues.

If you were the mill worker described above, you might view the need for forest protection with some skepticism. Logging restrictions would pose a potential threat not only to the basic economic interests of you and your family but to your whole way of life and the community in which you live. If the mill were to shut down, you would find yourself out of work, your community would likely deteriorate without its primary economic engine, and you would be cut off from some of the cultural traditions that extend back in your family for generations. In addition, your employer, who not only signs your paychecks but whom you probably consider to be knowledgeable about the industry, is telling you that environmentalists are responsible for this threat. Many of your friends and coworkers share the view that environmentalists are a problem. And what's more, these environmentalists are outsiders whom you do not know and do not necessarily trust. You know that logging has been carried out in your area for decades, even by members of your own family, and there have not been environmental problems before. What would these environmental activists, lawyers, and lobbyists based in Washington, DC, or other big cities know about the forest that they probably never even visited in the first place? It is likely that if you were in that mill worker's social location, you would be suspicious about these environmental claims and possibly even hostile to environmental advocates and the cause that appears to threaten your livelihood.

This is not to suggest that every person in such a position is going to react to this situation in exactly the same way. Human beings are extremely complex, and while we know that social position *influences* the beliefs and behaviors that people develop, that position does not *determine* the opinions and attitudes of every individual. Nonetheless, as sociologists, we are able to detect patterns that help us to understand how one's social position influences behavior and attitudes.

It is clear that one's employment situation and the associated influences can affect the way one views issues, including that of environmental protection. Examining the relationship between labor and the environment will help us to answer important questions: Will environmental measures harm the economic condition of workers? Or might a failure to act to protect the environment harm some industries and destroy jobs? Who will be most affected by environmental measures and in what way? How will employment concerns shape workers' perspectives on environmental protection? How will such concerns shape their political behavior? Are there ways to effectively address both environmental concerns and the economic interests of working people? What is the role of government, of labor unions, of employers, and of environmental organizations in this process? Our future as a society will depend on what policies we develop to address environmental issues. Those policies will be shaped, in part, by mobilized segments of the public, people whose views about the need for environmental protection are in turn shaped by their employment situation. Thus, it is crucial that we seek to understand the relationship between work and the environment.

ENVIRONMENTAL PROTECTION AND JOBS

Workers have obvious reasons to be concerned about environmental measures if they pose a direct threat to their jobs. But in reality, environmental regulations threaten very few jobs and, in many cases, actually *add* to employment. Overall, environmental protection measures have generated millions of jobs. Globally, over 10 million people are employed in the renewable energy industry alone. In 2011, the Labor Department reported that 2.6

percent of the US labor force was employed in areas providing green products and services. More recent estimates indicate that almost 10 percent of jobs in the United States are already part of the "green economy" and that this employment sector is growing rapidly. These workers are employed doing things such as manufacturing electric vehicles, building wind turbines, growing organic foods, recycling waste, or designing energy-efficient homes. Environmental protection also creates and sustains jobs in other sectors. Ecotourism has grown dramatically in recent decades; and in many regions, where attractive environmental features have been preserved, communities have prospered by selling services to tourists (see Lesson 20). Thousands more are employed as researchers, educators, lawyers, and policymakers in positions related to environmental protection. Given environmental imperatives and international measures being taken to address them, nations that have taken the lead in promoting environmentally sound, energy-efficient practices are likely to thrive economically relative to those that fail to act (see Lesson 9). Thus, environmental protection measures are having a dramatic, positive impact on employment.

It is also important to keep in mind that a failure to act to protect the environment will have devastating economic consequences. We have seen cases of this historically. For example, manufacturing industries grew dramatically along the Hudson River in New York State during the early to mid-20th century. However, the pollution that these factories released into the river, including many toxic substances, ultimately decimated the fishing industry, which was an important part of the regional economy. Thousands of workers lost their jobs as a result, and the fishing industry never fully recovered. We now face this danger on a much broader scale. If unchecked, climate change will have enormous economic repercussions. Extreme weather events and sea level rise will displace millions of workers and cause billions of dollars in damage to businesses, costs that we are already witnessing.

On balance, environmental protection measures and the growth in green industries are of huge economic benefit, generating millions of jobs. Yet in some rare instances, particular jobs may be threatened by environmental policies. These factors are never as significant as other major influences on employment, such as trade policy, corporate restructuring, technological change, and the general ups and downs of the business cycle characteristic of capitalist economies (see Lessons 4 and 7). As Schnaiberg describes in Lesson 4, the basic structure of the capitalist system drives owners to replace human labor with new technologies, making employment security a constant concern for workers. The small impact of environmental regulation relative to technological change is not surprising given that environmental protection costs typically make up less than 2 percent of a firm's expenditures. Yet environmental compliance can still cost jobs in some instances. One economic analysis indicated that roughly 3,000 jobs are lost annually in the United States due to environmental regulation. This represents a tiny fraction of jobs lost nationally on a yearly basis. In fact, already more workers lose their jobs as a result of "natural" disasters than they do from measures taken to protect the environment, a disparity that will only grow as climate change advances.

Despite the fact that job loss due to environmental protection is very small and that far more jobs are created by environmental measures to offset those losses, any job loss represents serious hardship for the affected workers. Such workers stand to lose something immediately tangible and fundamentally important to them, unlike the more abstract interests of workers who will be employed at some point in the future as a result of environmental protection measures. Workers who perceive policies as directly threatening to their current jobs are more likely to organize politically to fight such policies relative to the far larger numbers who would benefit in the long term. Perhaps more significantly, the very idea that there is a trade-off between jobs and environmental protection is a powerful rhetorical tool that some have used to argue against environmental measures (see Lesson 4). Thus, it is important to understand the relationship between jobs and the environment—not just to safeguard workers, but also to understand how the issue is used politically to shape environmental policy.

Who, if anyone, actually stands to lose their job as a result of environmental protection? Some early studies found that environmental measures have contributed to job loss in the metal, chemical, and paper industries, but environmental economist Eban Goodstein found that workers in the extractive industries have borne the brunt of the job loss. For example, his research indicates that the Clean Air Act resulted in the loss of about 10,000 coal-mining jobs in the 10 years following the passage of that legislation. He found that a similar number of timber industry workers lost their jobs following the implementation of measures designed to protect the endangered northern spotted owl in the Pacific Northwest, the basis for the scenario introduced at the beginning of this lesson.

It is worth noting that these job losses have primarily affected male, blue-collar workers, a population that has already seen their standard of living threatened by other economic forces, in particular, technological change and economic globalization. Employers have introduced labor-saving technologies like robots that have displaced millions of workers in manufacturing industries (see Lesson 7). And the outsourcing of manufacturing jobs to low-wage regions overseas has also resulted in significant job loss and downward wage pressure for blue-collar workers (see Lesson 4). In fact, many timber industry jobs were lost when business owners started exporting raw logs for processing in low-wage countries in Asia and then reimporting the finished lumber back to the United States. These factors have resulted in significant job loss and wage depression for blue-collar, primarily male workers. While their anger may be misplaced to some degree, this economic vulnerability makes this group particularly susceptible to claims that environmental regulation poses a threat to their livelihood.

"JOBS VERSUS THE ENVIRONMENT" CONFLICTS

Even though the number of workers negatively affected is very small, the "jobs versus the environment" issue commands a great deal of public attention, and it can have a significant impact on environmental policy. The "timber wars" of the 1980s and 1990s took on special significance for political candidates seeking to capitalize on voters' general economic insecurity. While running for president in 1992, Republican candidate George Bush Sr. claimed that if his more environmentally sympathetic opponents were elected, "we'll be up to our neck in owls and outta work for every American."

This tactic was used heavily during Donald Trump's campaign for the presidency in 2016. He routinely claimed that environmental regulation would eliminate jobs and ruin the economy. He went so far as to deny climate science and to call for the rollback of measures designed to prevent climate change, purportedly in order to save jobs in the declining coal industry. He donned a hard hat and posed with mineworkers waving signs proclaiming that "Trump Digs Coal."

Coal-mining employment has certainly declined in recent years, making the coal industry workers feel particularly defensive and insecure. But coal's decline as an industry has much more to do with technology and shifts in the energy market than environmental measures. Massive mountain top removal machines operated by a few people can extract coal at a far faster pace than can an army of workers with picks deep in an underground mine (see Lesson 9). While coal once employed over 800,000 people early in the 20th century, there are only about 50,000 in the entire industry today. This historical decrease in employment is largely due to technological displacement, but coal's more recent declines can be attributed to the development of the natural gas industry. New "fracking" technology in that sector has allowed for the easy extraction of natural gas, which now offers a much cheaper fuel source than coal. Today, even industry leaders acknowledge that coal will never again employ the numbers it had in the past, regardless of environmental policy. Yet, to workers who have suffered, the promise of a bright future can be appealing in spite of the facts. And political strategists have found that blaming environmental regulation is a very effective tool for mobilizing these discontented voters.

This characterization of the relationship between jobs and the environment can be contrasted with those presented by progressive Democrats who have called for a "Green New Deal" designed to create jobs by reemploying workers in industries that will help to address climate change. This is modeled after the New Deal policies that were implemented during the Great Depression of the 1930s in order to rebuild the ailing economy. Back then, public funds were directed toward such things as building the national highway system in order to generate employment and set the stage for economic growth. The Green New Deal is designed to create jobs by directing funds toward industries and public projects that reduce greenhouse gas emissions such as renewable energy and public transportation. Thus, in contrast to the trade-off characterization, this approach sees economic development and increased employment as *directly tied* to environmental protection measures.

These contrasting environmental and economic policies are reflective of more fundamental ideological differences regarding the role of government and markets. Traditionally, liberals tend to see a broader constructive role for government in addressing social problems like the lack of affordable healthcare, poverty, and access to education. They support more public funding for things like schools and colleges, health care, social welfare programs, and childcare. They also see a more active role for government in environmental protection and through the regulation of business generally. Thus liberal-leaning thinkers tend to focus on the positive relationship between environmental protection and jobs. They believe that polluting industries can be reformed and that "clean industries" can be nurtured through proper governmental policy intervention, yielding environmentally sound, sustainable employment. Without this intervention, liberals tend to believe that businesses will focus exclusively on short-term profit for their shareholders, sacrificing the environment and undermining the well-being of working people.

In contrast, conservatives tend to believe that any government intervention in the economy, be it restrictions on international trade, taxes, minimum wage laws, public healthcare, or regulations, including environmental regulation, harms free market functioning and causes a loss of jobs and prosperity. They believe that beyond some fundamental necessary functions of government, such as policing and national defense, the market will work best when left alone. They claim that when politicians get involved in regulating the market, efficiency suffers, profits decline, businesses shut down, and workers get laid off. Those who hold this perspective often refer to "job-killing environmental regulations."

While elected officials are the most visible figures voicing these contrasting perspectives, and it is they who actually make policy, it is important to bear in mind that political candidates take positions that will most effectively mobilize their base of support. Environmental organizations more commonly support Democratic candidates who, in turn, tend to take somewhat stronger positions in favor of environmental protection. But perhaps more influential are the business interests that back candidates running for office. Some businesses, such as the renewable energy industry, stand to gain financially from environmental protection measures, so they often back candidates who support such efforts. Many others, such as the very powerful fossil fuel and energy industries, seek to protect profits by blocking environmental measures, thus avoiding the costs of complying with such regulations.

Business interests who see costs associated with environmental compliance will often carry out publicity campaigns and fund research purporting to show that regulations will harm their industry and cost jobs (see Lesson 5). For example, when President Obama instituted rules that would limit toxic mercury emissions from power plants, a coal industry organization issued a report claiming that the measure would result in the loss of 1.44 million jobs.

The job loss claims made by employers in relation to environmental measures are often wildly exaggerated. As discussed earlier, negative job impacts from environmental measures are very rare and very small. Business owners oppose regulation primarily because they want to protect their profits and avoid the cost of complying with such rules. It would be difficult for them to rally public opposition to environmental measures in order to protect industry profits, so instead they frame the issue in terms of job loss. Some refer to this strategy of enlisting workers in the fight against regulation as **job blackmail**. Just as the timber business operator in the opening scenario encouraged company employees to contact their elected officials, employers often seek to mobilize workers by shifting the focus away from environmental protection and directing it toward alleged economic impacts. Employers will claim that burdensome regulations will drive them out of business or force them to relocate to countries that do not have strict environmental protections, thus stoking fears among insecure workers.

In addition to fostering job loss concerns, employers may also take advantage of the cultural differences that exist between blue-collar workers and the middle-class professionals who often fund or make up the active membership base of many large environmental organizations. In *Coalitions Across the Class Divide*, Fred Rose argues that due to their different education and work experiences, middle-class professionals have different understandings about the natural environment, about work, and about the value of scientific expertise relative to direct experience. These differences in **class culture** can be used to heighten fears about unfamiliar outsiders who threaten the workers' way of life. Industry owners and candidates for office seeking to win support from rural voters may characterize environmentalists as out-of-touch urban elites who are more concerned about birds and bugs than about the basic well-being of working class people. Even proven scientific findings can be characterized as the work of liberal university scientists and government bureaucrats who are inventing threats just to make themselves seem important. The situation is made worse when environmental advocates are insensitive to workers' concerns or when they harbor stereotypes about ignorant blue-collar workers who don't understand what is really good for them. These cultural differences by themselves can result in suspicion that inhibits the pursuit of mutually beneficial approaches to environmental problems. But this cultural gap is particularly difficult to overcome when employers or politicians exploit these differences to foster divisions involving environmental issues and their job implications.

THE ROLE OF LABOR UNIONS IN ENVIRONMENTAL CONFLICT

As sociologists, we know that we can learn a great deal about people by examining the conditions under which they live, and clearly one's employment situation is a very significant aspect of one's life. After all, for most people, it is through their labor that they earn their livelihood. It is also what many of us spend much of our lives doing. As a college student, you may already be working at a part-time or full-time job. But even if you are not currently employed, enrollment in college is probably tied to your aspirations for future employment. Because it is so central to our lives, sociologists, from the founding of the discipline, have placed a great deal of attention on economic institutions. The classical theorists each focused on aspects of the economy, from Emile Durkheim's analysis of the division of labor to Max Weber's research on the origins of capitalism to Karl Marx's detailed examination of class. Marx in particular was attuned to the conflicts that emerge around economic issues and the power that some groups have relative to others; thus, the general branch of theory emerging from his work is sometimes referred to as **conflict theory** (see Lesson 2).

We could apply conflict theory to understand how business owners exercise power to advance their interests within the economy, interests that, in at least some instances, facilitate ecological degradation. This power can be seen on the macro level, in terms of influence over the political and economic systems and control of the mass media, down to the micro-level control that an individual supervisor can exercise over an employee. Business owners have power in that they can choose to outsource jobs overseas or to other parts of the country, thus dramatically affecting the lives of hundreds or even thousands of workers left jobless (see Lesson 4). They can also influence government policy through lobbying and campaign support, shaping the laws that govern every member of society. At the micro level, they can use their power and influence at the workplace to pressure individual workers into opposing environmental measures that may threaten profitability.

Those who own the means of production certainly have a great advantage when seeking to influence government action, such as environmental policy. But in some cases, other workplace actors can play an important role in influencing individual workers and even, at times, in influencing larger policies and the general distribution of power within society. The organizations that play this role are **labor unions**.

Capitalist economies tend to foster organization among workers to counter the imbalance of power within a system based on the private ownership of the means of production. Most individual workers, because they lack assets of their own off which they can live, are forced to sell their labor to those who own the means of production. These capitalists employ workers to produce goods or provide services so that they can obtain profit by selling goods and services on the market at a rate higher than that which it cost them to have the goods produced. One way in which capitalists can increase profits is by minimizing labor costs—that is, by paying workers as little as is necessary (see Lesson 4).

Workers usually understand their lack of power as individuals within this situation. After all, a single worker is rarely of great value to any large enterprise; and, in any case, within market economies, there is always a pool of additional unemployed workers for the owner to draw from if any single worker needs to be replaced. Consider what would happen to you if you went to your employer and demanded a raise or more vacation time. If you persisted after your boss rejected your appeal, you would probably be fired and replaced by someone who is unemployed and more desperate for work. While individual workers lack power relative to their employers, at times workers recognize that if they were to join together and act collectively, they would be better positioned to challenge their employer and to demand better treatment. Workers, and disadvantaged people generally, have done this in one way or another throughout history. In the context of the workplace in capitalist economies, this usually takes the form of labor unions.

By forming unions, workers pledge to act together as a unit to counterbalance the advantage of the employer. While the employer can carry on unharmed without any single employee, if all the workers were to walk off the job simultaneously—that is, if they were to strike—this would impose significant costs on the business owner. Of course, employers still have a great advantage because, unlike the workers, they have the wealth necessary to secure their own survival (not to mention their very significant influence over other institutions such as the political system, the police, and the military). However, at least under some circumstances, employers may find it to be in their interest to make concessions to workers in the face of a strike or other workplace disruption rather than escalate the conflict or risk further delays in production.

Because conflicts between workers and owners are so common, most countries have developed **labor relations systems** to manage these relationships. Governments create a set of rules to moderate how the conflict between employers and workers will occur. The system of labor relations varies a great deal from nation to nation: some create rules that reinforce the advantage that owners have, and others go to great lengths to level the playing field between owners and workers. In some countries, such as Vietnam, independent unions are illegal, and workers are allowed to organize only through unions closely tied to the ruling political party, which controls the government. In others, such as Colombia, unions are not prohibited, but they have few enforceable rights, which leaves them vulnerable to violent repression by employers or their agents. Other nations, such as Sweden and Germany, have labor relations systems in which unions are afforded a number of legal protections that enable them to operate almost as equals with employers in making important decisions about issues such as workplace organization and compensation levels.

It is difficult for many in the United States to even imagine a system in which workers have a major role in running the company, like they do in places like Germany. In the United States, unions have few protections. Laws are designed and enforced in ways that make it fairly easy for employers to impose their terms on unions or to prevent workers from forming unions altogether. Despite this inequality, this system worked reasonably well for American workers through the 1960s. The period of great economic growth and prosperity that followed World War II allowed business owners to accommodate US unions while still profiting immensely. Unionized workers were able to command decent wages, and this spilled over, benefitting even workers who were not in unions. If your ancestors were working in the United States during the 1950s, chances are they were in a union. More than one in three workers were union members at that time. It was a result of this effort to distribute the wealth generated during this period that the middle class was built in the United States. It is not surprising that today, with unions in decline, we see growing economic inequality and the shrinking of the middle class.

The most significant decline in unions can be traced back to the 1970s, when the United States was hit by a major recession. At that time of declining prosperity, employers sought to protect profits by taking advantage of weak labor protections to challenge unions and drive down wages. Since then, a number of political and economic developments have furthered organized labor's decline in the United States. As described above in relation to the coal industry, new technologies allowed employers to automate many of the tasks previously performed by workers, thus eliminating jobs and reducing union numbers (see Lesson 4).

Economic globalization has also weakened unions and provided employers with greater leverage in the labor relations system. Starting in the 1980s, many large corporations pressed political leaders to enter into **free trade agreements** with other nations. This enabled businesses to shift production around the world in search of low wages, weak regulations, or other conditions that would allow for increased profitability. Many businesses, especially those in manufacturing industries, have moved operations overseas. If you look at your clothes or your cell phone or television, there's a good chance that these goods were not manufactured in the United States. But even those companies that have not actually moved operations can use the threat of relocation to extract concessions from their workers. This further diminished labor's bargaining power within a labor relations system that afforded them few real protections to begin with.

As a result of these factors and an aggressive anti-union assault by employers, the United States has seen its rate of unionization decline precipitously from roughly 35 percent of the workforce in 1955 to about 10 percent today. The decline has been most severe in the manufacturing sector, labor's traditional stronghold, but workers in other sectors are also under attack. Conservative elected officials have undertaken efforts to weaken unions representing public sector workers such as teachers, bus drivers, and fire-fighters. Private service sector employment is the largest employment sector of the US economy today. The service sector includes most jobs where workers are employed providing a service as opposed to manufacturing a product. Workers in retail stores, healthcare facilities, hotels, and restaurants are all service sector workers. This employment sector was never extensively unionized, although some of these workers, like those in the fast food industry, are seeking to organize unions today. However, as it stands, with low unionization in the service sector, together with the decline of unionized manufacturing employment and attacks on public sector unions, the US labor movement is among the weakest of all of the economically developed democracies.

Despite their current weakness, unions have a potentially very significant role to play in relation to environmental policy. Unions help to synthesize workers' concerns and enable individuals to act collectively to advance their interests; and clearly, workers, like all people, have an interest in a safe and healthy environment. In fact, survey research indicates that union members report stronger support for environmental measures than the average worker. Unions could serve as vehicles for advancing these sentiments, and sometimes they have. Yet their position on environmental issues is complicated and inconsistent. In some instances, unions have mobilized workers to promote environmental protection; yet in other cases, they have sided with employers to oppose environmental measures.

Some of this positioning has to do with the particular industry in which the union members are based. For those workers who face real potential threats to jobs, it is easy to see why their union might oppose certain environmental regulation. For example, the United Mine Workers have opposed a number of air pollution measures that they perceived would harm their industry and contribute to job loss. A recent environmental issue that has divided the labor movement is the construction of the Keystone XL Pipeline, a major pipeline project that would bring tar sands from Canada down to Texas for refining into fuel. Union leaders in the construction industry saw the project as a promising job creator. Environmentalists, on the other hand, have opposed the project both because of the risks of ecologically damaging spills and, more generally, because the pipeline infrastructure will encourage continued use of dirty fossil fuels and draw us further away from developing renewable energy sources. When the project was halted by the Obama Administration on environmental grounds, one construction union leader denounced environmental opponents as "job killers" out to "destroy the lives of working men and women." However, other unions, such as the Communication Workers of America and the United Auto Workers, sided with environmentalists, recognizing that all workers have a stake in environmental protection.

The different positions taken by these unions can in part be attributed to the different interests that workers have in the issue. Autoworkers and those in the communication industry did not stand to gain jobs from the project; they chose instead to fight for the environmental interests of their members. But there are other factors that shape union behavior more broadly.

In general, the US labor relations system channels unions into focusing on specific job-related issues, most significantly wages and benefits. As a result, union members come to view their union primarily as an organization that will protect their interests *at work*, especially in terms of the pay they receive. Some union leaders also come to see their role in that light. Union members don't often think of their union as a means to protect their broader interests in the political sphere. But the fact is that unions are one of the primary vehicles for protecting the interests of working people, even on issues that extend well beyond the workplace. Unions have championed causes like public education, Social Security, and access to healthcare through their political efforts.

As the primary political voice for working people, unions could also play a significant role in efforts to advance environmental legislation. But because the labor relations system encourages unions to focus on specific job-related matters, many union leaders have been reluctant to promote an environmental agenda. In addition, when an issue arises that allegedly creates a trade-off between jobs and environmental protection, unions may focus on the jobs issue instead of the more general interests of their members, including a safe and healthy environment.

So despite the fact that environmental sentiments may be strong among union members, their unions rarely involve themselves with such issues, especially when environmental measures may threaten their own economic interests or those of other union workers. Thus, for the most part, labor's political priorities have focused on job protection and economic expansion, policies that tend to threaten the environment through unchecked material consumption (see Lesson 4).

Despite the general channeling effect that the American labor relations system has had in terms of focusing unions on narrow economic interests, unions have at times played a significant role in some important environmental legislation. For example, unions were early supporters of clean water and clean air legislation. The American Federation of Labor-Congress of Industrial Organizations (AFL-CIO), the main labor federation representing almost all unions at the time, endorsed the creation of a wilderness preservation system as early as 1960, years before the rise of the modern environmental movement. They argued that working people should have access to nature for recreational purposes and for spiritual renewal, not just elites who could afford to buy land for their own use.

One area where labor has been particularly active historically is that of environmental health and safety (see Lesson 11). Health and safety issues have always been on labor's agenda, although this has never been given the same attention as wages and benefits. But because unions seek to protect workers' health, this creates fertile ground for cooperation with some in the environmental community (see Lessons 10 and 18). Historically, unions were supportive of environmental groups that took industrial pollution as their focus. This environmental health movement emerged from a different social context than that of the wilderness advocates who also began to mobilize in the late 19th and early 20th centuries. While early conservationists and preservationists tended to be elites seeking to protect resources for industrial or recreational uses, environmental health advocates were rooted in working-class urban areas where working people and their families were being subjected to the toxic effluents from industrial production (see Lesson 18).

This link between environmentalism and worker health has, to this day, provided an opportunity for unions and environmental advocates to come together. After all, the toxic materials that can threaten workers' health inside the plant are the very ones that threaten the outside community and the natural environment when they leave the plant. Business owners are often reluctant to provide proper safety measures for workers in the workplace, and they typically oppose regulations that would control pollution; both represent expenses for owners that can cut into profits. Thus, fighting business owners to control exposure to toxic materials is an endeavor that can unite workers and environmentalists. This came to the fore in the 1980s when unions and environmentalists united against their common political adversary, President Ronald Reagan, who sought to roll back all manner of government regulation. They worked closely together to advance the regulation of hazardous materials.

LABOR AND THE ENVIRONMENT TODAY

Given the basic structure of our economic and political institutions, there are always likely to be some tensions, real or perceived, between labor and the environment. When workers are unorganized, they are particularly vulnerable to job loss claims from employers who seek to mobilize them against environmental measures. Nonunionized workers do not have an organization that can conduct research and challenge false claims about the threat of environmental regulation. This can leave workers vulnerable to manipulation by employers seeking to protect profits and opportunistic politicians who want to win votes by claiming that environmentalists are the ones threatening jobs. And even when workers are organized, when unions cling to a narrow agenda of economic self-interest and job protection, they can compound the problem by siding with employers against environmental advocates. But unions are increasingly expanding their agendas to include issues of broader concern to workers, including environmental protection, and they are more open to cooperation with other progressive groups like environmental organizations.

In part this newfound willingness among union leaders to join with other movements can be interpreted as an act of necessity. Unions have lost so much of their power that they recognize the need for support from others to advance their goals, and, by necessity, that entails offering reciprocal support for other causes.

From labor's perspective, these alliances must still be strategically assessed in terms of whether they stand to advance core economic goals. After all, the basic structure of the labor relations system remains in place, and workers still expect that their union will primarily act to advance their work-related interests. Thus, unions, and for that matter environmental organizations, are still constrained in the extent to which they can fully support one another's goals when there is not a direct link to the primary mission of their own organizations. But there is a growing willingness on the part of both labor and environmental advocates to seek those opportunities for cooperation. This shift can be tied to the larger economic trends that have affected both movements.

One major economic trend that threatens the interests of both workers and environmentalists is **trade liberalization** (a trade policy that is part of a broader "neoliberal" political perspective). As mentioned earlier, businesses have pressed for the elimination of government restrictions on international trade. Historically, governments have regulated trade and taxed the importation of goods to protect domestic industries, to raise funds, or to prevent the sale of goods considered unsafe or otherwise harmful to consumers. Proponents of trade liberalization, including many large corporations with operations spread across several countries, argue that restrictions on trade or overseas investment inhibit the efficiency of the free market, thus driving down profits and increasing the costs of goods. Yet, as noted earlier, employers have used loosened trade rules as a means to weaken unions and drive down wages. The prospect of moving operations overseas and throwing everyone out of work is a potent threat that has placed workers at a severe disadvantage. But the ability to move operations not only allows employers to seek lower-wage workers, it also allows them to escape from environmental regulations. Free trade allows polluting businesses to seek locations where there is little or no environmental regulation, thus decreasing production costs and increasing profits. For this reason, trade liberalization is viewed skeptically by both workers and environmentalists.

Opposition to trade liberalization is an important force in bringing workers and environmentalists together. Unrestricted trade greatly diminishes the ability of workers and environmentalists to improve conditions domestically, as all nations become caught up in a "race to the bottom" as they seek to entice private investment through lower wages and weaker regulation. In the early 1990s, unions and many environmental groups joined forces in an unsuccessful bid to stop the North American Free Trade Agreement (NAFTA), a trade treaty between the United States, Canada, and Mexico. Perhaps the most dramatic instance of mutual effort in this area came during the 1999 protests against the **World Trade Organization** (WTO) in Seattle, Washington. There, tens of thousands of unionists and environmental advocates, among others, came together to speak out against the neoliberal policies being advanced through the WTO. More recently, unions and environmentalists joined to oppose the Trans-Pacific Partnership (TPP), a proposed trade agreement among twelve countries in the Pacific Rim. Like most such agreements, it contained provisions to protect business interests but lacked protections for workers and the environment.

Despite occasional disagreements, usually involving the building trades unions, in general, unions and environmentalists are becoming more creative about finding ways to cooperate and to identify common ground. Issues of health and safety have continued to serve as an area of intermovement cooperation. New organizations have sprung up in recent decades, following in the footsteps of the public health organizations that addressed environmental concerns during the early industrial period. Organizations have formed to fight the environmental and health effects resulting from the use of poisonous chemicals in manufacturing and agriculture. Environmental justice organizations, composed primarily of working-class people of color, have formed to fight against environmental health threats that disproportionately plague their communities (see Lesson 10). These organizations typically develop out of local struggles against immediate environmental health threats. While still generally considered to be part of the broader environmental movement, their members tend to have more in common culturally and economically with blue-collar union workers than they do with the more commonly middle- and upper-class members of conservation and preservation organizations.

Even the larger professional environmental groups have in many cases integrated health and social justice issues into their agendas, creating openings for cooperation with unions. For example, in Los Angeles, the Natural Resources Defense Council and the Sierra Club, two large national environmental groups, joined forces with the Teamsters union and the International Longshore and Warehouse Union to reduce truck pollution and improve conditions for truck drivers in the port area of the city.

Labor–environmental alliance-building efforts, even when initially based on calculated self-interest, open the door to further cooperation. Many cases provide evidence to show that instrumental cooperation of this sort can grow into a true merging of interests. As unionists get to know and work with environmental advocates, stereotypes about insensitive elitists or deluded "tree huggers" begin to fall away, and they come to recognize that environmentalists are sincere people concerned about real threats to the environment and to human well-being. Similarly, environmentalists who work with labor advocates come to understand that unionists are not selfish or ignorant "hardhats" but people who are trying desperately to protect the basic economic security that many workers feel is slipping away. As this mutual understanding grows, both unions and environmental organizations are more likely to integrate all of these concerns into their advocacy agendas.

LABOR AND THE ENVIRONMENT TOMORROW?

At this historical juncture, advocates for both workers and the environment face tremendous challenges. Although the environmental movement has been successful at raising awareness about threats to the environment, efforts to actually stave off environmental crises have not made sufficient progress. National environmental policies and global treaties designed to address important issues such as climate change, species loss, and forest preservation have failed to fundamentally alter the historical trajectory of ongoing ecological degradation. Workers are also losing ground. Economic inequality is growing globally and within most nations. Economic globalization has undermined the ability of both unions and environmentalists to hold accountable increasingly mobile corporate actors. Unions themselves have been decimated as employers exploit weak labor protections to undermine existing unions and prevent new ones from forming. Thus, on both the ecological and economic fronts, many conclude that the prospects for rapid, significant changes are poor. But these meager hopes are greatly diminished when workers and environmental advocates engage in conflict with one another. Both have a stake in challenging the private interests that seek to exploit workers and the environment. Although their positions within existing political and economic institutions can, on some occasions, place them at odds on the basis of certain narrowly defined interests, an alliance between these movements or a new movement that embodies their respective goals represents perhaps the greatest hope of achieving a world that is both ecologically sustainable and socially just.

How this will play out in the years to come is an open question. Bold environmental policy proposals designed to address the growing ecological crisis, such as the Green New Deal, continue to get mixed reviews from union leaders. Environmentalists have in many instances improved their approach by incorporating worker protections into environmental measures in the event that some economic sectors are harmed by new policies. The Green New Deal is specifically designed to generate jobs and improve working conditions all while restructuring the economy around more sustainable practices. "Just transition" provisions are included that would aid the small percentage of workers who may be harmed as polluting industries are phased out.

In a sign of growing enlightenment around environmental issues, some unions, such as the Service Employees International Union, have rallied behind the Green New Deal. But it has been met with skepticism from others. The leader of the laborers unions, one associated with construction work, has been very critical of the proposal, claiming that jobs will be lost and expressing doubt that support for displaced workers will be sufficient to protect them from economic harm. Conservative political leaders and their allies in the media have played up these concerns in an effort to drum up support from working-class voters for more environmental rollbacks. By denying the scope of the ecological crisis and offering the prospect that technological breakthroughs will be sufficient to stave off disaster, these powers offer an unrealistic but optimistic vision for desperate workers, one that also has appeal for some union leaders. In the meantime, we are witnessing an accelerating ecological crisis, all without any real relief for struggling workers. At best, workers in polluting industries may continue in their jobs for a few more years before ecological crisis and the associated economic repercussions make such industries unviable.

Yet, a different trajectory is imaginable. Unions could play an important role in educating workers about the need to address the ecological crisis. They could ally with environmental advocates to champion government policies that call for investment in the creation of good jobs that also advance environmental protection. Let's return to the hypothetical scenario with which we began, only now you are the child of the mill worker, and workers and environmentalists have united to reform labor and environmental policy. Your mother, who by now has lost her job at the mill, is currently enrolled in an accounting program at a nearby college where her tuition is being paid by a federal program that has also extended her old mill salary while she is retrained. She hopes to get a job with a computer software firm that recently moved to the area, attracted by the high quality of life in the region, which can be attributed, at least in part, to strong environmental protection measures. Other former mill workers have taken jobs at a new artificial wood manufacturing facility that uses recycled plastics and paper milk cartons to make a highly durable wood substitute. This facility was developed through a federal program that brought together environmental technology investors with the Paper, Allied-Industrial, Chemical and Energy International Union. These unionized workers now earn more than they had at the former mill. You are working at a camping supply store during the summer, serving the growing tourist population, but you are going away to college in the fall to study history and business. You plan to return to your community after graduation to open a bed-and-breakfast with an adjoining historical education center that focuses on the history of the timber industry.

Consider how you might feel about environmental protection policies from this vantage point. Such policies no longer represent a threat given the position in which you are now situated. On the contrary, your economic success depends on strong environmental protection. As in the original scenario, your views are going to be shaped by your social position, and a significant aspect of that is your labor force status and associated economic prospects. But institutional and policy changes have greatly altered the constraints and opportunities presented to you, and this is likely to affect your attitude about environmental protection, perhaps in ways that would lead to still more environmental policy improvements.

The need to drastically change the way that society interrelates with the rest of the natural environment is imperative. But existing institutional arrangements in many cases perpetuate ecologically destructive practices. The distribution of power in our society and the conditions under which people live and work create a confluence of forces that inhibit desperately needed changes. Our role as sociologists is to seek to understand how these institutional arrangements operate and, more importantly, to identify ways to re-shape those institutions so that we can create a socially just and ecologically sustainable society. Examining how work life can be made compatible with such goals is a central part of that mission.

SOURCES

Bureau of Labor Statistics. "Green Jobs." http://www.bls.gov/green/home.htm

Cummings, Scott L. 2018. *Blue and Green: The Drive for Justice at America's Port*. Cambridge, MA: MIT Press

Dewey, Scott. 1998. "Working for the Environment: Organized Labor and the Origins of Environmentalism in the United States: 1948–1970." *Environmental History* 1:45–63.

Dreiling, Michael. 1998. "From Margin to Center: Environmental Justice and Social Unionism as Sites for Intermovement Solidarity." *Race, Class and Gender* 6 (1): 51–69.

Foster, John Bellamy. 1993. "The Limits of Environmentalism Without Class: Lessons from the Ancient Forest Struggle of the Pacific Northwest." *Capitalism, Nature and Socialism* 4 (1): 1–18.

Goodstein, Eban. 1999. *The Trade-off Myth: Fact and Fiction about Jobs and the Environment*. Washington, DC: Island Press.

Gottlieb, Robert. 2001. *Environmentalism Unbound*. Cambridge, MA: MIT Press.

Gottlieb, Robert. 1993. *Forcing the Spring*. Washington, DC: Island Press.

Gould, Kenneth, Tammy Lewis, and J. Timmons Roberts. 2004. "Blue–Green Coalitions: Constraints and Possibilities in the Post 9–11 Political Environment." *Journal of World-System Research* 10 (1): 90–116.

Kazis, Richard and Richard Grossman. 1991. *Fear at Work*. Philadelphia, PA: New Society Publishers.

Mayer, Brian. 2009. *Blue-Green Coalitions: Fighting for Safe Workplaces and Healthy Communities*. Ithaca, NY: ILR Press.

Obach, Brian K. 2004a. *Labor and the Environmental Movement: The Quest for Common Ground*. Cambridge, MA: MIT Press.

Obach, Brian K. 2004b. "New Labor: Slowing the Treadmill of Production?" *Organization and Environment* 17 (3): 337–354.

Rose, Fred. 2000. *Coalitions across the Class Divide*. Ithaca, NY: Cornell University Press.

18

Environmental Social Movements

Jill Lindsey Harrison

Protesters arrive to hear Greta Thunberg speak at a Global Climate Strike event prior to the United Nations' first Youth Climate Summit on September 21, 2019, New York, NY.

Post your photo on US environmental movements to #TLESmovements.

Photo by Ken Gould

In August 2018, Swedish teenager Greta Thunberg went on strike from school and sat outside the Swedish parliament with a sign and leaflets that called for the government to take swifter action to address climate change. Her protests have inspired youth around the world. Angry and worried about climate change and its irrevocable harms to people, other animals, and ecosystems, students have taken time off from class in order to publicly and collectively pressure governments to pass policies that will reduce climate change. Their actions have turned into a movement, often called Fridays for the Future and youth climate strikes. The movement is gaining momentum—an unprecedented four million people participated in climate strikes in September 2019. Have you ever participated in a climate strike?

Previous lessons in this book highlight major environmental problems and key structural factors that contribute to them. For centuries, various actors have fought against these environmental harms. When people organize collectively to enact or resist change, such as in the youth climate strikes, we refer to them as a **social movement**. Through joining forces into a social movement, people are able to accomplish things that individuals on their own cannot. Environmental social movements play a crucial role in changing human-environment relationships.

This lesson provides an overview of major environmental social movements in the United States. After first describing how sociologists study these movements, I describe the most prominent environmental movements in the United States: Native Americans' struggles for land rights and sovereignty, resource conservationism, wilderness preservationism, reform environmentalism, deep ecology, ecofeminism, and environmental justice. For each, I describe the major issues and concerns motivating people to act, identify key actors and their primary practices, and address critiques that other actors have raised about these practices. Environmental movements in the Global South are covered in Lesson 19.

There are many synergies among the movements I discuss. Yet, as I will show, there are also some significant tensions among them. There are also tensions between environmental movements and other social movements, community members, and labor (see Lessons 17 and 19). These tensions are important to understand because they highlight how some movements neglect certain social groups and can actually harm them. In many cases, this prompts the formation of other social movements that attend to the needs of those marginalized by previous instances of collective action. Attending to the tensions allows us to deliberate how environmental movements can be reformed to better serve all people and species—to pursue both environmental protection and justice. This lesson introduces you to the range of environmental social movements, some organizations within each, and the challenges they face. My goals are to help you understand the world and also learn how you can participate in a social movement that supports causes that are important to you.

RESEARCHING SOCIAL MOVEMENTS

Just as social movement scholars have done in other contexts, environmental sociologists have sought to *describe* environmental social movements by asking, What kinds of changes have environmental movements pursued? Which practices do they use? What are the consequences of movements' priorities? Whose interests do they serve best? Sociologists also *explain* those patterns by asking, Which political economic factors (such as industry pressure), cultural forces (such as social norms), and other social structures shape environmental movement priorities, practices, and impacts? How have those structures changed over time? As is the case for other groups and for individuals, social movement organizations have *agency*—that is, they choose their priorities and practices. However, they operate within *structures* that are not of their own choosing—contexts that constrain what they do and can accomplish, such as policies, technology, the economy, and social norms.

Many environmental sociologists study movement **discursive frames** (or narratives) and their implications. Social movements' abilities to achieve their goals depend in part on how well they frame issues in terms that make sense to the public and policymakers. Framing refers to the language that actors use to present issues. To examine how movements frame environmental problems, scholars identify movement organizations, which issues they identify as problematic, which actors they cast as responsible for causing and remedying those problems, which mechanisms of change they deem appropriate, the arguments they use for all of these, and how these narratives change over time and vary among actors. Some scholars employ critical discourse analysis, which sees language as not simply reflecting the world around us but as actively establishing the power relations in society. Any given discourse can challenge the (highly unequal and unsustainable) status quo—or reinforce it and make it seem reasonable. Social movement scholars examine competing discourses and identify which become widespread, even taken for granted as fact, and why. For example, scholars have documented how social movements and other actors in recent years have tended to frame environmental and other social problems as things that should be solved through the market, imploring the public to "vote with their dollars" by buying more sustainable products such as organic food. These scholars show that framing social change in this way draws public attention away from pressuring the government to enact and enforce strong environmental policies. Scholars research social movement discourses by systematically collecting, categorizing, and analyzing social movement actors' claims. These data include organizations' written materials, such as websites, reports, press releases, and signs at protests, as well as social movement members' spoken claims. Scholars collect these data by interviewing participants and observing movement websites, meetings, rallies, and other events, sometimes as active participants in the movement. To explain these narratives' patterns and trends, they situate movement practices within the broader political economic and cultural contexts within which they operate.

Environmental sociologists also study the **political opportunity structures** that constrain and/or enable social movements—the changing power of movement organizations relative to other actors and institutions shaping politics. Notably, many scholars have explained that environmental social movement organizations' efforts are hindered by industry and other countermovement actors' abilities to control government agencies, elected officials, and public opinion. Environmental organizations press for environmental regulations that would restrict environmentally harmful but profitable industry practices. Industry and the political elites protecting industries' interests generally oppose such regulatory controls. Sociologists detail the practices through which such actors fight to undermine environmental movement organizations. For instance, polluting industries exercise their control over the state by selecting and financially supporting business-friendly political candidates who will weaken environmental laws, getting politicians to appoint corporate polluters to administer environmental agencies in ways that counter movement goals, lobbying against social movement proposals, and producing junk science that discredits movement arguments and policy proposals. Sociologists conduct such research by systemically reviewing and documenting countermovement actors' practices, and identifying their implications in terms of policy, regulation, movement responses, media framings, public opinion, public behaviors, and more.

Scholars have shown that these efforts have effectively undermined environmental movements in recent decades. Antiregulatory political elites have successfully rolled back many environmental regulations, cut the budgets of environmental regulatory agencies, and lobbied against proposals for new environmental regulations. These reforms are consistent with the concept of **neoliberalism**—the belief that society is served best by minimal government constraint on industry practices (see Lesson 10). Advocates of neoliberalism argue that if society finds certain practices to be undesirable, people can voluntarily address them, such as through purchasing more sustainable products. The rollback of environmental regulations has been characterized as the *neoliberalization* of environmental regulation. Additionally, as Shannon Bell, Stephanie Malin, and others have demonstrated, efforts to combat hazardous industrial development are undermined by countermovements that support those industries and argue that they will bring jobs and other amenities. The political opportunity structure for environmental movements became increasingly difficult under the Trump administration, which has rolled back environmental regulations and approved environmentally destructive projects to an unprecedented degree.

Other scholars taking a **resource mobilization** approach study the ways in which funding and other resources shape social movement outcomes. All social movements need resources to do their work, and social movement scholars have shown that economic resources help determine a social movement's ability to achieve its goals. In turn, movement accomplishments often end up reflecting the practices and priorities of the most well-funded movement actors. Robert Brulle has documented the funding differences among environmental social movements by examining the income and expenses nonprofit environmental organizations report to the Internal Revenue Service (IRS) and identified the consequences of these patterns. As I will discuss in more detail below, some environmental social movements receive much more funding than others, and this creates an uneven playing field in which some are much more able than others to accomplish their goals.

NATIVE AMERICANS' STRUGGLES FOR LAND RIGHTS AND SOVEREIGNTY

Since the early days of European settlement in what is now known as the United States, Native people have organized and fought for their rights to land and other natural resources. "Native" refers to people who lived in an area prior to European conquest; this term is used interchangeably with "Indigenous" and

"Native American." Today, the US federal government formally recognizes over 500 Native tribes. Although diverse and culturally distinct, they share a long history of oppression and collective struggle for sovereignty.

Native American people have been subjected to a devastating array of harms. Settlers have appropriated Native land and natural resources; forcibly removed Indigenous people to reservations; destroyed plant and animal populations central to Native people's identities and cultures; used Native lands for hazardous weapons testing, mining, and waste storage; forced Native people to assimilate into settler society; misrepresented Indigenous ideas and experiences in historical narrative, education, and everyday discourse; and otherwise continually violated tribal sovereignty. Indigenous people within the United States are still subjected to these various forms of appropriation, exploitation, and erasure (Lesson 3). Scholars use the term **settler colonialism** to characterize the current state of affairs in the United States; the term refers to the occupation and appropriation of Native lands that continues through the present day through political structures and cultural practices that harm Indigenous people. Kari Norgaard, Ron Reed, and J. M. Bacon (2018) explain that characterizing the contemporary United States as a settler colonial state appropriately foregrounds the *ongoing* appropriation of Native lands: "According to the settler-colonial frame, North American colonialism is not limited to the overt genocide or forced assimilation of the past but rather is enacted through state institutional structures and cultural practices that continue to impoverish communities and erode sovereignty today" (Norgaard et al. 2018, 99). They use the term "colonial ecological violence" to highlight the environmental and profoundly destructive consequences of these dynamics, which disrupt Indigenous cultures, communities, conceptions of personhood, and physical and mental health.

Dina Gilio-Whitaker, Winona LaDuke, Jace Weaver, and others have shown that many Native people collectively organize to reclaim and defend their rights to lands and other natural resources and, in turn, their sovereignty and ways of life. Scholars have studied various Indigenous social movements, documenting the practices they use, the structures shaping their efforts, their intersections with other social movements, and the retaliation they have often encountered. For instance, Native groups protested the Dakota Access Pipeline from being built near the Standing Rock Indian Reservation in North Dakota, as the pipeline would threaten their water resources and destroy sacred sites. Students and other non-Native people traveled to Standing Rock to protest in solidarity with the Native groups. Additionally, Native American farmers sued the US Department of Agriculture for discriminating against Native American farmers in implementing the USDA Farm Loan Program, in violation of Title VI of the 1964 Civil Rights Act, reaching a $760 million settlement. Today, various Indigenous groups strive to protect access to traditional subsistence foods, including wild rice, berries, and salmon.

Zoltán Grossman and Dina Gilio-Whitaker have drawn attention to the fact that, in some cases, white communities have joined Indigenous groups to fight against fossil fuel pipelines and uranium milling and mining, for cleanup of hazardous waste, for sustainable management of fisheries, and more. Several prominent organizations fighting for Native American natural resource rights are the Indigenous Environmental Network, the Seventh Generation Fund for Indigenous Peoples, and Honor the Earth. These networks help the movement's hundreds of small organizations consolidate resources and engage in unified political action.

RESOURCE CONSERVATIONISM

In the mid-to-late 1800s, a movement emerged within settler colonial society to more sustainably manage the use of natural resources. **Resource conservationism** emerged out of conflicts among actors vying for use of natural resources and concern that common, unregulated practices were destroying those natural resources faster than they could reproduce and regrow. These concerns related to timber, rangeland grazing, fishing, hunting wild game, and use of rivers for irrigating farming.

Organizations like the American Conservation League, American Conservation Association, American Forestry Association, and the Boone and Crockett Club pressed the government to use scientific, technical knowledge to actively manage the use of certain natural resources. They emphasized that this would maximize their availability over time, increase efficiency of extraction, and reduce waste. To these advocates, "conservation" meant government planning for orderly sustained yield management to maximize profitability. They saw the environment as a source of resources for meeting human needs—and thus perceived both the nonuse and the overuse of natural resources as "wasteful."

Resource conservationists successfully advocated for the development of national policies and federal agencies designed to orderly manage natural resources to maximize their profitable use over many years while preventing the resource base from degrading. Today, resource conservation is the leading principle guiding many government agencies in the United States, including the US Forest Service, the Bureau of Reclamation, and the Fish and Wildlife Service. These agencies regulate the harvest of timber from forests, the building of dams that supply water during dry times, the construction of canals and aqueducts that move water to farms and cities in dry areas, the issuance of hunting permits, and the allocation of permits for mining valuable oil, gas, and minerals. These agencies strive to maximize the profitable extraction of resources and curtail the problems associated with such practices (such as runoff from clear-cutting forests). They are generally tasked with abiding by the utilitarian principle of only imposing restrictions on resource use when the aggregated financial benefits of doing so outweigh the associated costs.

Current leading resource conservationist organizations include the Society of American Foresters, American Forests, Scenic America, Ducks Unlimited, Trout Unlimited, and the National Wildlife Federation. As their names indicate, most tend to focus on the management of a specific subset of natural resources. Resource conservationist organizations comprise a significant environmental movement in the United States, measured in terms of the funding they receive and their numerical representation among environmental organizations (Brulle 2000).

Although resource conservationism has valuably helped curtail many destructive practices, important concerns have been raised about this movement. Notably, resource conservationist policies, government agencies, and regulations that have improved the efficiency and longevity of resource extraction have not benefitted all people equally. Louis Warren has shown that wildlife game laws were promoted by urban elites who sought to restrict the hunting practices of immigrants and Indigenous people. Nor do resource conservation policies and practices ensure that those resources will be available in perpetuity—rather, they benefit (some) people today but often do not protect the needs of future generations. Additionally, through maximizing the profitable extraction of certain natural resources, resource conservationism has disregarded ecological relationships among species in natural settings, the role of natural settings as habitats for non-target species, and other intrinsic values of protecting spaces from highly disruptive forms of resource extraction. Forests are more than trees—they are important to Indigenous people and serve as habitat for owls, mice, and other wild animals. Indeed, Indigenous organizations and, as we will see below, wilderness preservationist and environmental justice movements, have organized in part to challenge these limitations of resource conservationism.

WILDERNESS PRESERVATIONISM

By the late 1800s, many people felt concerned about the ways in which the westward expansion of European settlement across the United States was leading to the disappearance of "wild" lands. Many urban elites sought to protect these nonurban areas and the animals within them from settlement and industrial development. **Wilderness preservationism** describes efforts to protect entire wild spaces undisturbed by human action. Its promoters have emphasized that wilderness has intrinsic value above and beyond the market value of specific resources within it. As such, they directly challenged resource conservationists for treating the environment as a collection of resources to be exploited for generating wealth. Wilderness preservationists saw nature as important for human beings' physical and spiritual well-being. They argued that spending time in nature—especially areas deemed exceptionally beautiful—helped rejuvenate people and serve as a respite from urban life's overcrowding, crime, pollution, illness, poverty, social unrest, and perceived immorality.

Numerous organizations were formed to advocate for preserving wilderness areas, including the Sierra Club, which was founded in 1892. These organizations sought to protect wild spaces as unaffected as possible by human influence. Due to their advocacy, the US government established National Parks to protect wild areas relatively free of industrial development and other human action. Yellowstone National Park, established in 1872, was the first, and Yosemite National Park was founded in 1890. The National Park Service was established by law in 1916 to manage these areas.

Today, the National Park System (NPS) covers over 85 million acres across the United States (NPS 2019a). In recent years, National Parks received over 300 million visitors annually, who spend time hiking, camping, climbing, and watching wildlife (NPS 2019b). Wilderness preservationist organizations continually work to defend these spaces from industries and political elites who try to open wilderness areas to oil and gas development, mining, and other lucrative and extractive activities. The evisceration of wilderness protections has been especially pronounced under the Trump Administration, which has shrunk the size of wildlife refuges and National Monuments held as sacred by Native American tribes, opened those lands to oil and gas development, and repealed regulations that had prevented mining companies from dumping their wastes into rivers. Notwithstanding these challenges, wilderness preservationism is a leading US environmental movement, measured in terms of number of organizations and funding (Brulle 2000). Today, leading preservationist organizations include the Nature Conservancy, the Sierra Club, and the National Audubon Society. The Nature Conservancy is the top of these, receiving three times as much income than any other organization and using its funding to purchase tracts of land and protect them from development.

Scholars have raised serious concerns about some key preservationist discourses and practices. William Cronon and others have argued that the movement's preoccupation with wilderness leaves unaddressed and casts as less important the environmental problems in the urban and suburban spaces we inhabit. As I discuss below, this concern ultimately fueled both reform environmentalism and the environmental justice movement.

Additionally, scholars have questioned preservationists' definition of "wilderness" as spaces undisturbed by humans (excepting, of course, wilderness enthusiasts who hike and camp within them). Preservationist calls to "preserve" wilderness inspired policies criminalizing rural people's traditional hunting, fishing, foraging, and timber-cutting practices and removed Indigenous peoples from lands they had long utilized and held sacred, as Karl Jacoby, Carolyn Merchant, Mark David Spence, and other critical environmental historians have shown. The forced removal of Native Americans for the establishment of parks and other wilderness spaces has been legitimized by popular ways of speaking and writing about parks that frame them as untouched, "pristine," discovered by white settlers, devoid of human inhabitants, and preserved due to the efforts of white visionaries. For instance, although environmental history texts attribute wilderness preservation to white charismatic preservationists like John Muir, scholars have recently shown that his ideas were inspired in part by writers of color. For instance, Dorceta Taylor illustrates how Phyllis Wheatley, a former slave who gained her freedom in 1773 and went on to became a published poet, wrote a century before Muir about the spiritually rejuvenating virtues of nature and influenced Muir, Ralph Waldo Emerson, Henry David Thoreau, and other romantic environmentalist writers. Rebecca Solnit also shows how museums reinforce this whitening of wilderness by designing exhibits that characterize Native Americans as extinct, rather than as people who still live and fight for rights to lands from which they were unjustly expelled. Additionally, Carolyn Finney and Dorceta Taylor show that racial norms and popular narratives have constructed wilderness (as with beaches, trails, and suburbs) as "white spaces" that are unwelcoming to people of color and obscure the rich and varied relationships people of color have had with the environment—including their key roles in preserving wilderness spaces.

REFORM ENVIRONMENTALISM

For nearly 150 years, organizations have also pressed government to reform industrial production practices and urban development to curb their environmental harms and assaults on public health. This type of mobilization can be characterized as **reform environmentalism**.

In the late 18th and early 19th centuries, a sanitary reform movement emerged out of concern about the hazards of urban life, including crowding, crime, garbage, air pollution, poverty, disease, and workplace hazards. These reformers, often working with labor unions, identified disease clusters among workers and residents and attributed some of them to environmental hazards such as sewage and toxic industrial chemicals (see also Lessons 11 and 17). Led by scientists and engineers, they sought to address some of these problems through treating sick individuals and reducing people's exposure to hazards, including through education and neighborhood cleanup campaigns. Some also sought to curb the production of hazards that cause disease, such as through establishing water quality standards, instituting water treatment systems, and pressing for legislation that would reduce industrial emissions.

Reform environmentalists gained unprecedented momentum in the latter half of the 20th century, fueled by the social unrest of the civil rights and antiwar movements in the 1960s and 1970s, as well as by large-scale industrial accidents, such as those at Three Mile Island and Chernobyl nuclear power plants. In the 1960s and 1970s, reform environmentalist organizations used grassroots education and organizing to build a broad base of popular support for environmental laws and government agencies to enforce them, including through organizing the first Earth Day in 1970. Its organizations help raise public concern about the risks posed to human health by air pollution, nuclear energy and weapons, petrochemical facilities, oil and gas extraction and transport, and the proliferation of hazardous pesticides and other chemicals in food, consumer products, and the environment broadly.

In recent decades, reform environmentalist organizations pursuing stronger laws and enforcement have relied less on grassroots mobilization and more on lobbying for stronger laws, litigation to force corporations and government agencies to comply with existing law, and technical environmental assessments to support those efforts. Accordingly, these organizations' staff are largely professionals formally trained in law, science, and engineering. At the same time, reform environmentalist organizations also increasingly pursue environmental change through encouraging individuals to adopt "greener" lifestyles, such as through recycling, reducing fossil fuel use, and purchasing more sustainable consumer products like reusable water bottles, organic food, and electric vehicles. Reform environmentalist organizations have also used boycotts and other techniques to publicly shame corporations into adopting more sustainable practices.

Much of the current work of reform environmentalism is focused on climate change mitigation and adaptation. The massive climate marches in 2017 and student protests against climate change in 2019 across the country illustrate the continued vibrancy of this movement. Measured in terms of funding and number of organizations, reform environmentalism is the largest environmental movement in the United States (Brulle 2000). Its leading organizations include the National Resources Defense Council, Environmental Defense Fund, Sierra Club Legal Defense, and Greenpeace. Out of all US environmental movements, resource conservationism, wilderness preservationism, and reform environmentalism together receive the overwhelming majority of funding today, have the largest and most widely recognized organizations, and have arguably had the greatest influence over policy, regulation, and public understandings of the environment. As such, these three together are often characterized as the **mainstream environmental movement**.

The reform environmental movement successfully advocated for the development and passage of key environmental laws. At the federal level, these include the Clean Air Act, the Clean Water Act, and the National Environmental Policy Act. Their efforts also lead to the establishment of the US Environmental Protection Agency in 1970, as well as the development of a highly complex and technical system of regulations that guide agencies in enforcing environmental law. More recently, reform environmentalists have successfully pushed the US government to sign on to some international environmental agreements. These include the Montreal Protocol on Substances that Deplete the Ozone Layer and the United Nations Paris Agreement on Climate Change (although in 2017, the Trump administration announced its intention to withdraw the United States from the latter). The laws, regulations, government institutions, and international agreements reform environmentalists have helped secure are widely credited with having reduced aggregate levels of air and water pollution in the United States.

Although reform environmentalism has produced indisputably valuable environmental improvements, it has also been subject to important criticisms. Notably, its gains have disproportionately benefitted middle-class and relatively wealthy white communities. The movement has tended to disregard the fact that environmental harms are clustered in working-class, racially marginalized, and Indigenous communities, which are dispropor- tionately vulnerable to the effects of exposure to those hazards. As I will show in the next section, these inequalities and oversights fueled the rise of the environmental justice movement (see also Lesson 10).

Additionally, scholars and activists have shown that common narratives used by environmentalists can be problematic. For instance, environmental- ists often make universalizing claims that "humanity" and "society" cause environmental degradation. Such narratives imply that all people are equally destructive. Notably, as J. M. Bacon (2019) has noted, they erase Native American communities' history, knowledge, land ethics, and practices that differ significantly from those of settler society.

Scholars have also raised critical concerns about reform environmental- ists' increasing propensity to pursue environmental improvements through non-regulatory means, such as pressuring polluters to voluntarily improve their practices and urging individuals to adopt more sustainable lifestyles. Reform environmentalists increasingly use such mechanisms of change in part because neoliberalization has made the pursuit of environmental regu- lations feel impossible. However, such privatized and individualized strate- gies of change absolve the state of its responsibility to protect environmental quality and render environmental protections a luxury limited to the rela- tively wealthy.

DEEP ECOLOGY

In the 1970s and early 1980s, some environmental groups felt increasingly frustrated with reform environmentalism for being too focused on human needs and too compromising in its approach. As Rik Scarce (2006) and David Pellow (2014) have shown, what has been characterized as the **deep ecology** movement has challenged the anthropocentric nature of other US environ- mental movements, arguing that nonhuman life has intrinsic value and should not be subordinated to human needs. Deep ecologists have advocated for restoring intact natural systems and defending the rights of nonhuman animal populations and other aspects of nonhuman nature. Deep ecologists assert that corporations and the state create and perpetuate violence against humans and the environment through privatizing land and nonhuman animals, destroying ecosystems, and creating inequalities among people. That is, modern, industrial society and capitalism are inherently destruc- tive, and thus the existing system cannot be simply reformed. Accordingly, they argue that societies must reduce the size of their population, with some calling for regulatory controls on the number of children per family while others advocating for achieving this through fertility education and provi- sion of birth control. Deep ecologists also argue that societies must restrict industrialization and economic growth and, ultimately, to replace industrial society with something entirely different.

Deep ecologist organizations have also criticized reform environmentalist organizations for being hierarchically organized and abandoning grassroots decision-making. Instead, they advocate using consensus-based, deliberative decision-making. They have challenged other environmentalists' tendency to compromise with governments and destructive industry. Instead, deep ecologist organizations tend to use confrontational, militant direct action against corporations and governments, such as disabling logging equipment and earthmoving vehicles, breaking into company offices, and using video footage and other measures to illuminate and protest their targets' destructive practices. Key deep ecologist organizations include Earth First! and the Earth Liberation Front. They also include Extinction Rebellion, a new network of British activists that has been using peaceful direct action—including blocking major roads and intersections, chaining themselves to factories and other buildings, and organizing large public marches—to pressure elected officials to formally acknowledge the severity of the climate crisis and implement measures to redress climate change. Compared to those in the mainstream environmental movement, deep ecology organizations tend to receive very little funding (Brulle 2000).

Organizations fighting to protect wilderness areas have often been criticized as undermining the livelihoods and cultural traditions of rural people, many of whom work in resource-extractive industries. (See Lesson 17.) Another primary critique leveraged against deep ecology writers and organizations is that framing population growth as a leading cause of ecological degradation has inspired policy prescriptions blaming women and families in the global south for environmental destruction. David Pellow (2014) has argued that the patriarchal and nativist elements of deep ecology organizations' narratives and practices reflect oppressive ideas and relations within broader society and stem in part from the fact that these organizations are comprised largely of white, middle-class men. He shows how they are striving to overcome some of these limitations, including through building alliances with grassroots organizations representing marginalized communities and acknowledging the links between environmental destruction and oppression within human societies.

ECOFEMINISM

Ecofeminism, also called ecological feminism, is a highly diverse intellectual movement that emerged in the 1960s and 1970s. Ecofeminists use analysis of gender and other social relations to help explain human-environment relationships, asserting that environmental degradation is linked to patriarchy, white supremacy, and other forms of domination. As Greta Gaard has argued, ecofeminism's "basic premise is that the ideology which authorizes oppressions such as those based on race, class, gender, sexuality, physical abilities, and species is the same ideology which sanctions the oppression of nature" (Gaard 1993, 1; cited in Pellow 2014, 15). Ecofeminists argue that environmental harm stems from certain societies' treatment of both nature and certain social groups, such as women, as property and as things to be controlled. They have criticized reform environmentalists and deep ecologists for not adequately acknowledging and challenging the connections between environmental harm and various forms of human oppression.

Ecofeminists thus argue that environmental sustainability requires confronting all relationships of domination, with regard to nature, gender, race, class, sexuality, indigeneity, and other hierarchies that privilege some people over others. Although ecofeminist organizations are a relatively small and underfunded portion of the broader environmental movement (Brulle 2000), ecofeminist principles manifest in environmental social movement organizations in a variety of ways. For instance, some organizations, such as the Women's Environment and Development Organization, challenge economic development programs that do not adequately honor the role of household labor in economic production, and they advocate for such programs to help empower women. Many grassroots environmental organizations are led by women who fight both against environmental harms and for greater control over decision-making.

Ecofeminists have played important roles in highlighting the interconnections between environmental degradation and cultural oppression. That said, some have been criticized as being *essentialist*—by portraying women as inherently, biologically more connected with nature than men are. Such generalizations reinforce gendered stereotypes, reify the male/female gender binary, and obscure significant differences between groups of women.

ENVIRONMENTAL JUSTICE

Although US environmentalism has played an important role in reducing many environmental hazards, these gains have not manifested equally. Some communities are overburdened with pollution, hazardous facilities, dilapidated infrastructure, and other environmental harms. Community-based organizations around the country have protested the hazards within their neighborhoods, condemning the fact that environmental problems are not distributed randomly or evenly but instead are disproportionately clustered in working-class, racially marginalized, and Native American communities. As Robert Bullard (1990) and many other scholars have shown, the **environmental justice** (EJ) movement (see Lesson 10) refers to this broad network of organizations working on a wide range of issues—from fighting toxics in low-income communities of color to supporting Native American struggles for land rights and sovereignty. The EJ movement stands apart from other environmental movements by framing environmental harm as being not only a technical problem but also a social justice issue. Scholars have helped substantiate and investigate EJ activists' concerns and convictions. Hundreds of studies have shown that these environmental inequalities are serious, that they persist over time, and that they contribute to racial and socioeconomic disparities in health and educational attainment.

Many EJ activists are personally harmed by environmental hazards, and they draw connections between them and patterns of illness and discrimination they have observed in their families, workplaces, schools, and neighborhoods. They are angry at polluters for exploiting their communities and at government agencies and mainstream environmental organizations for ignoring their concerns and conditions. They have formed hundreds of community-based EJ organizations across the United States and work in alliance with scientists, attorneys, and other supporters. Part of a long history of struggle against racist oppression in the United States, such activism gained momentum during the civil rights movement and coalesced as the EJ movement in the 1980s.

Scholars have analyzed EJ activism fighting a wide range of problems harming low-income, racially marginalized communities, including the siting of waste dumps in poor black communities in the US South, mountaintop removal coal mining harming poor rural communities in Appalachia, agricultural pesticides poisoning immigrant farmworkers who are largely from Mexico and Central America, the lack of affordable and nutritious food in low-income communities, the construction of oil and gas pipelines that threaten Native American communities' drinking water and destroy sacred sites, and climate change killing and displacing the earth's most vulnerable people. EJ organizations fight to both reduce these harms and to secure parks, gardens, sidewalks, social services, public transportation, access to healthy and affordable food, green jobs, and water and land rights for local farmers. A few longstanding EJ organizations include WE ACT for Environmental Justice, Alternatives for Community and Environment, Communities for a Better Environment, the Environmental Health Coalition, Greenaction for Health and Environmental Justice, UPROSE, and the Center for Race, Poverty, and the Environment.

EJ activist organizations are largely grassroots and, compared to mainstream environmental organizations, receive very little funding (Brulle 2000). Some have formed regional EJ networks and other EJ coalitions to more effectively share resources and shape state and federal policy. These include the California Environmental Justice Alliance, the New York City Environmental Justice Alliance, the Indigenous Environmental Network, the People's Climate Movement, the National Black EJ Network, and the Climate Justice Alliance. Importantly, the 1991 First National People of Color Environmental Leadership Summit, where participants adopted 17 "Principles of Environmental Justice," helped the budding EJ movement gain coherence and identity (Principles 1991). Numerous subsequent EJ conferences have further helped EJ advocates build alliances with each other and their supporters in academia, government, and elsewhere.

Although the EJ movement is very diverse and only loosely networked, EJ organizations share several tenets that have cohered them as a movement. They push for stronger regulatory and policy restrictions on environmental hazards, for government agencies to prioritize environmental improvements in communities facing the greatest cumulative environmental impacts, and for agencies to reduce environmental inequality among communities. They emphasize that communities bearing the greatest burdens of environmental harm should have greater influence over decision-making within government agencies as well as environmental organizations. Additionally, they argue that environmental regulatory decisions be made according to the **precautionary principle**, which asserts that when evidence indicates that hazards pose serious risks of harm, government agencies must reduce those hazards without waiting for full scientific certainty (see Lesson 11). The EJ movement has pursued these principles through fighting specific environmental harms in communities, reforming local planning processes, and pushing for EJ reforms to the ways government agencies do their work.

Luke Cole and Sheila Foster (2001) demonstrate that EJ activists have been strongly influenced by the civil rights movement, the labor movement, grassroots antitoxics activism, and struggles for Native American sovereignty; and that EJ activists' use of marches, protests, and other direct action reflects the tactics of these "tributary" movements. As much as EJ activists can be understood as part of the broader US environmental movement, they are also deeply critical of the fact that major US environmental organizations focus on protection of endangered species, wilderness areas, and other environmental concerns of the relatively wealthy; ignore the environmental knowledge of and environmental harms borne disproportionately by working-class, racially marginalized, and Native American communities; increasingly rely on market-based measures that render environmental protections available only to those with the financial resources to buy their way out of hazardous spaces and employment; and pursue urban greening efforts that lead to gentrification, displacing working-class residents. EJ organizations have also criticized mainstream environmental organizations for seeking policies that cause harm to Native people. For example, environmental organizations have fought against Indigenous organizations over hunting, fishing, and gathering rights, and in the process have discredited Native groups' rights and practices. Dorceta Taylor (2014) and other scholars have argued that such problems in mainstream environmentalism stem in part from the fact that the leadership of leading environmental organizations is almost exclusively white and male.

In innumerable marginalized communities, EJ organizations have helped pressure industry and the state to reduce environmental hazards and otherwise build more thriving, just, and sustainable communities. Due to pressure from EJ advocates, the US EPA created an Office of Environmental Justice in 1993; and in 1994, President Clinton signed an Executive Order on Environmental Justice that directs federal agencies to reform their practices according to EJ principles. State and federal government agencies have started to adopt EJ policies and reforms—although David Konisky (2015) and I (Harrison 2019) demonstrate agencies' EJ efforts still fall far short of EJ movement principles. EJ gained further traction in the policy arena in early 2019 when US Senator Ed Markey (D-MA) and US Representative Alexandria Ocasio-Cortez (D-NY) introduced their Green New Deal. The Green New Deal's call to aggressively reduce climate pollution and transform the energy sector gained widespread political attention. Just as importantly, it calls for protecting those most affected by climate change and other environmental harms: low-income communities, Indigenous communities, and communities of color. The Green New Deal has subsequently been endorsed and elaborated by many other elected leaders.

Some scholars have noted that the EJ movement's accomplishments have been limited in part by aspects of the movement itself. For instance, David Pellow (2018) has argued that the EJ movement is too reformist—that its pursuit of regulatory and policy reforms risks reinforcing the legitimacy of the state structures that help produce environmental inequalities in the first place.

CONCLUSION

In this lesson, I reviewed leading US environmental movements: Native American struggles for land rights and sovereignty, resource conservationism, wilderness preservationism, reform environmentalism, deep ecology, ecofeminism, and environmental justice.

These movements have much in common. Notably, they have played important roles in raising public awareness about environmental issues and shifting the framing about them from private issues to social problems—to issues that deserve collective attention and government response. In so doing, these movements have pushed actors in private industry and government to take important steps toward protecting natural resources, spaces, and public health.

At the same time, they all face serious challenges. For instance, because all US environmental movements seek to curtail the ecologically destructive practices of landowners, corporations, governments, and other actors who benefit from the status quo, all face hostility and resistance from those actors and the political elites who protect their interests. In recent years, as antiregulatory elites have risen in power, their attacks on environmentalism have escalated.

Additionally, all environmental movements struggle to gain adequate resources to do their work. Indeed, causes related to the environment and animals together received only 3 percent of all charitable giving in 2017 (Giving USA 2018). That said, US environmental movements do not all face this struggle equally. Of the movements described in this chapter, resource conservationism, wilderness preservationism, and reform environmentalism have together received the overwhelming majority of funding for environmental advocacy (Brulle 2000). In turn, this helps explain why they have been disproportionately able to shape policy change and public opinion and are regarded as "mainstream" environmentalism.

Although US environmental movements share much in common, there are also significant tensions among them. Each challenges some aspects of previous social movements and broader society. Attending to these tensions and conflicts helps illuminate the shortcomings of prior forms of activism and indicates what more needs to be done. These tensions are numerous; I will note two to illustrate how significant they are and thus how imperative it is that we engage with them. First, most US environmental movements have been fairly reformist, focusing mostly on addressing environmental problems through technological change and policy reforms that tinker with the existing capitalist economic system. Deep ecologists reject this approach, instead explicitly identifying capitalism and industrialization as the roots of environmental harm and arguing for a complete transformation of the political economic system and protecting nature from destructive human society.

Second, Native American environmental movements and the EJ movement challenge other environmental movements for being elitist—for largely representing and protecting the interests of the middle class and relatively wealthy, and for ignoring the environmental circumstances of working-class, racially marginalized, and Indigenous communities. They contest mainstream environmentalism's propensity to measure environmental progress in aggregated terms that ignore the breadth and depth of environmental inequality. Additionally, they criticize mainstream environmentalists' tendency to frame environmental problems in strictly technical terms; instead, Native American environmental organizations and EJ organizations show that environmental problems stem also from colonial and racist oppression. Accordingly, they argue that a truly just environmental movement will need to take seriously and grapple with oppression and domination rather than dismissing them as separate from the environmental cause. Scholars of environmental social movements can aid this task by continuing to evaluate movements not only in terms of ecological measures but also in terms of social justice. To be sure, those working to transition our current system to one that is both more sustainable and just find that these objectives can be hard to reconcile. Yet doing so is essential for environmental movements to be relevant in the highly unequal world in which we live.

SOURCES

Bacon, J. M. 2019. "Settler Colonialism as Eco-Social Structure and the Production of Colonial Ecological Violence." *Environmental Sociology* 5 (1): 59–69.

Bell, Shannon. 2016. *Fighting King Coal: The Challenges to Micromobilization in Central Appalachia*. Cambridge, MA: MIT Press.

Brulle, Robert J. 2000. *Agency, Democracy, and Nature: U.S. Environmental Movements from a Critical Theory Perspective*. Cambridge, MA: MIT Press.

Bullard, Robert D. 1990. *Dumping in Dixie: Race, Class, and Environmental Quality.* Boulder, CO: Westview Press.

Cole, Luke and Sheila Foster. 2001. *From the Ground Up: Environmental Racism and the Rise of the Environmental Justice Movement.* New York: NYU Press.

Cronon, William. 1998. "The Trouble with Wilderness, or, Getting Back to the Wrong Nature." In *The Great New Wilderness Debate,* edited by J. Baird Callicott and Michael P. Nelson, 471–499. Athens: University of Georgia Press.

Finney, Caroline. 2014. *Black Faces, White Spaces: Reimagining the Relationship of African Americans to the Great Outdoors.* Chapel Hill: University of North Carolina Press.

Gaard, Greta. 1993. "Living Interconnections with Animals and Nature." In *Ecofeminism: Women, Animals, and Nature,* edited by Greta Gaard, 1–12. Philadelphia: Temple University Press.

Gilio-Whitaker, Dina. 2019. *As Long as Grass Grows: The Indigenous Fight for Environmental Justice, from Colonization to Standing Rock.* Boston: Beacon Press.

Giving USA. 2018. "See the Numbers—Giving USA 2018 Infographic." Accessed June 5, 2019. https://givingusa.org/wp-content/uploads/2018/06/GUSA-2018-Infographic-FINAL.png

Grossman, Zoltán. 2017. *Unlikely Alliances: Native Nations and White Communities Join to Defend Rural Lands.* Seattle: University of Washington Press.

Harrison, Jill Lindsey. 2019. *From the Inside Out: The Fight for Environmental Justice within Government Agencies.* Cambridge, MA: MIT Press.

Jacoby, Karl. 2003. *Crimes against Nature: Squatters, Poachers, Thieves, and the Hidden History of American Conservation.* Berkeley: University of California Press.

Konisky, David M., ed. 2015. *Failed Promises: Evaluating the Federal Government's Response to Environmental Justice.* Cambridge, MA: MIT Press.

LaDuke, Winona. 1999. *All Our Relations: Native Struggles for Land and Life.* Cambridge, MA: South End Press.

Malin, Stephanie. 2015. *The Price of Nuclear Power: Uranium Communities and Environmental Justice.* New Brunswick, NJ: Rutgers University Press.

Merchant, Carolyn. 2003. "Shades of Darkness: Race and Environmental History." *Environmental History* 8 (3): 380–394.

NPS. 2019a. "National Park System." Accessed May 23, 2019. https://www.nps.gov/aboutus/national-park-system.htm

NPS. 2019b. "Visitation Numbers." Accessed May 23, 2019. https://www.nps.gov/aboutus/visitation-numbers.htm

Norgaard, Kari Marie. 2019. *Salmon and Acorns Feed Our People: Colonialism, Nature and Social Action.* New Brunswick, NJ: Rutgers University Press.

Norgaard, Kari Marie, Ron Reed, and J. M. Bacon. 2018. "How Environmental Decline Restructures Indigenous Gender Practices: What Happens to Karuk Masculinity When There Are No Fish?" *Sociology of Race and Ethnicity* 4 (1): 98–113.

Pellow, David Naguib. 2014. *Total Liberation: The Power and Promise of Animal Rights and the Radical Earth Movement.* Minneapolis: University of Minnesota Press.

Pellow, David Naguib. 2018. *What Is Critical Environmental Justice?* Medford, MA: Polity Press.

Pezzullo, Phaedra C., and Ronald Sandler, eds. 2007. *Environmental Justice and Environmentalism: The Social Justice Challenge to the Environmental Movement.* Cambridge, MA: MIT Press.

Principles. 1991. "Principles of Environmental Justice." *First National People of Color Environmental Leadership Summit.* Accessed June 12, 2019. http://www.ejnet.org/ej/principles.html. Accessed June 12

Scarce, Rik. 2006. *Eco-Warriors: Understanding the Radical Environmental Movement*. Walnut Creek, CA: Left Coast Press.

Solnit, Rebecca. 2014. *Savage Dreams: A Journey into the Landscape Wars of the American West*. Berkeley: University of California Press.

Spence, Mark David. 2000. *Dispossessing the Wilderness: Indian Removal and the Making of the National Parks*. Oxford: Oxford University Press.

Taylor, Dorceta. 2014. *The State of Diversity in Environmental Organizations*. Ann Arbor: University of Michigan. July 2014. Accessed June 12, 2019. http://vaipl.org/wp-content/uploads/2014/10/ExecutiveSummary-Diverse-Green.pdf

Taylor, Dorceta. 2016. *The Rise of the American Conservation Movement: Power, Privilege, and Environmental Protection*. Durham, NC: Duke University Press.

Warren, Louis S. 1999. *The Hunter's Game: Poachers and Conservationists in Twentieth-Century America*. New Haven, CT: Yale University Press.

Weaver, Jace, ed. 1996. *Defending Mother Earth: Native American Perspectives on Environmental Justice*. Maryknoll, NY: Orbis Books.

19

Environmental Movements in the Global South

Tammy L. Lewis

Protesting against the introduction of genetically modified corn, Porto Alegre, Brazil.

Post your photo on environmental movements in the global south to #TLESGlobalSouth.

Photo by Ken Gould

The term "environmentalist" means different things to different people. In North America, someone who recycles and buys "green" products might call themselves an environmentalist, as might someone who is concerned with the environmental effects of overpopulation, while another environmentalist argues that capitalism is the root of climate change. In the North American tradition, environmentalism has been strongly associated with membership in environmental organizations, such as the Sierra Club and the Nature Conservancy. Environmentalists in the Global South (lower-income countries of Latin America, Africa, and parts of Asia) also cover a broad range of beliefs and practices and do not fit neatly into one single box. In the Global South, there is less emphasis on membership in environmental organizations as defining an "environmentalist." While there are many overlapping concerns between environmentalists of the North and South, I begin by outlining some fundamental differences between environmentalists and environmental movements in the Global North and in the Global South.

DIFFERENCES BETWEEN ENVIRONMENTALISM IN THE GLOBAL NORTH AND IN THE GLOBAL SOUTH

In *Environmentalism: A Global History*, Ramachandra Guha asked readers to consider the differences between the "ecology of affluence" and "**environmentalism of the poor**." Guha, and others writing from the perspective of the Global South, argued that there is a strong environmentalism in the Third World (now called the "Global South") that looks different from the environmental movement in the United States and other nations in the Global North (including Canada, Japan, Australia, and countries in Western Europe).

The first and most visible difference is simply in organizational structure and tactics. The US movement is considered "professionalized" in that it is made up of formal organizations, with paid leaders and staffs, large budgets, lobbying arms, and extensive fundraising mechanisms. These **professionalized environmental organizations** differ from **collective action groups**, which use volunteer labor, have small to no budgets, and organize people to engage in direct action to preserve their local means of subsistence (the "environment").

The organizational differences are actually a result of different origins. Many Southern struggles are struggles in defense of economic livelihood. They arise from threats to people's economic survival. For instance, local "environmental" opposition forms when local economic resources are threatened. One of the most popular examples of this is the rubber tappers' movement in Brazil from the 1980s. The rubber tappers extracted rubber from trees in a sustainable manner to earn a living. When the rubber trees were threatened by cattle ranchers who wanted to clear the forests for ranching, the rubber tappers' union resisted the ranchers and fought for control of the land they had long used to make a living. They resisted environmental change because it threatened their economic well-being. Whether we classify this as an "economic" movement or an "environmental" movement is an interesting question. Guha (2000) asked us to consider the relationship between "environmental" issues and livelihood struggles in general:

Commercial forestry, oil drilling, and large dams all damage the environment, but they also, and to their victims more painfully, constitute a threat to rural livelihoods: by depriving tribals of fuelwood and small game, by destroying the crops of farmers, or by submerging wholesale the lands and homes of villagers who have the misfortune to be placed in their path. The opposition to these interventions is thus as much a defense of livelihood as an "environmental" movement in the narrow sense of the term. (105)

These types of struggles contrast with popular campaigns of environmental groups in the Global North that call on members to "Save the Whales" (or elephants, or pandas, etc.). Many Northern campaigns solicit urban dwellers to contribute to causes that are disconnected from their immediate surroundings or their lived experiences.

This leads to the third big difference in environmentalism of the North and South: the understanding of how humans fit into nature. Guha argued that a major difference between environmentalism in the Global South and that in the Global North has been the South's view that the environmental struggle is inseparable from the struggle for social justice. Humans and nature are part of an interconnected and interdependent web. The **nature–society dichotomy** that is prevalent in Western thought is not as widespread in other cultures. Therefore, movements in some other societies see humans as part of the environment, and thus the struggle for human rights is integrated into a movement to preserve the environment. When working to save the environment, these groups see that they are working to save themselves.

Mainstream environmentalism in North America was founded with the idea of preserving nature for nature's sake (what we now call "wilderness preservation") and for the good of humanity (see Lesson 18). John Muir, the first president of the Sierra Club (1892), argued for protecting undeveloped and undisturbed habitats, like national parks, so that the public could visit these areas for spiritual uplift and to enjoy recreational activities. (As is elaborated in Lesson 18, during the establishment of US national parks, the park service removed Indigenous peoples from the land. Historically the lands were not uninhabited nor undisturbed.) Later, US conservationists such as Gifford Pinchot (the chief of the US Division of Forestry, 1898) would argue that we needed to conserve lands for future development and the "wise use" of resources (though still not viewing humans as "in" nature).

US environmentalism is often stereotyped as an **"elitist" movement**. This stereotype has some validity if we look only to the history of land preservation and conservation. Muir, Pinchot, and others advocating for land protection were elite, well-educated, white men. However, if we expand our historical lens and take a broader view of environmentalism in the early part of the 1900s, we see that there were movements in US cities, often led by women, who were fighting for adequate sanitation and appropriate trash disposal. While they are not commonly thought of as part of the US "environmental" history, they can be thought of as part of a movement for public health, and today we might call them "urban environmentalists." In the United States, stereotypes of elitism in the environmental movement have also changed with the growth of the environmental justice movement (see Lesson 10). The environmental justice movement draws its constituents from a range of groups, including the working class and racial and ethnic minorities. Today, we have environmentalism within both wealthy and poor nations challenging the conventional wisdom that environmentalism is simply an elite movement.

Just as the charges of "elite" environmentalism are largely false in the United States, they are also false across the globe. Though affluence creates opportunities to participate in the movement, concern about the environment is not limited to elites. In fact, there are high degrees of concern about the environment in both the North and South; in some cases, there is more concern in the Global South. Not only "elite" (rich) nations are environmentalist. In the 1990s, Steven R. Brechin and Willett Kempton (1994) analyzed responses to public opinion data from around the world that show that richer nations do not have a higher level of environmental concern than poorer nations. In fact, in many cases, the opposite is true. For example, 77 percent of Mexicans surveyed perceive air pollution to be a serious problem, and 81 percent perceive species loss as "very serious." By contrast, in the United States, the figures are 60 and 50 percent, respectively. In their analysis, they showed that individuals in wealthier nations are more willing to pay more for environmental protection. However, people in poorer nations are more willing to pay in time (a resource more available than money for many in these nations) than were the respondents in richer nations. Riley Dunlap and Richard York (2008) followed up on these results with international survey data through to 2001 and confirmed that citizens' concern for environmentalism does not depend on affluence. In sum, survey data from multiple surveys and multiple years suggest that environmental concern is not just a concern for the rich; the concern is global.

CONTEXT FOR UNDERSTANDING THE DYNAMICS BETWEEN THE GLOBAL NORTH AND THE GLOBAL SOUTH

A little background in the sociology of development is useful for understanding why social movements in the Global South are different from those in the Global North. There are entire classes on this, and I recommend that you take them to more fully understand the complexity and history of what I explain here in a brief few paragraphs. I borrow from the framework outlined in Philip McMichael's (2016) book, *Development and Social Change*. The long history of economic development of the world has involved interactions among actors from different regions of the world. McMichael discusses these in terms of the projects of colonialism, developmentalism (1940s to 1970s), and globalization (1980s to 2000s). In each of these "projects," the main goals of political and economic actors are to get access to and control of natural resources. In this project, there are winners and losers. The inequality among nations that exists today has been built on the history of conflicts among groups over natural resources. Political and economic actors who have gained power and influence exert it over others to maintain and increase their power and influence, which generates an increasing gap between rich and poor. As you might expect, these conditions create conflicts; actors in less powerful regions generate social movements to resist powerful actors' influence over them.

During Western European colonialism, royal powers coupled with companies to explore foreign lands for resources. The territories of the Indigenous peoples of Africa, North and South America, and much of Asia were forcibly occupied by European powers who usurped their natural resources. This formed the basis of unequal exchange between Europe and the Global South, which served to enrich the actors of Europe at the expense of the peoples of Africa, Asia, and Latin America. In some cases, Europeans overwhelmed local populations and established settler regimes like the United States, Canada, Australia, and New Zealand. World systems theory, laid out in Lesson 2, explicates how the ongoing and unequal relationships between "core" (European) and "periphery" regions of the world exacerbate global inequality over time. As Lesson 3 shows, governments also create inequalities within nations through a process of colonizing marginalized groups, including Indigenous peoples in the United States. States/governments take advantage of native peoples to extract resources, as we will see below in the example of the Chipko. An important takeaway from the understanding of the colonial period is that long-standing unequal relationships that originated around the control of natural resources persist to this day.

In the developmental and globalization projects, the Global North sought to promote "development" of the Global South. One of the means by which this occurred was by lending money for large-scale infrastructure and industrial development projects like giant hydropower dams that could "modernize" poorer countries and help them move from being "traditional" to "modern" by way of industrial economic development. Loans were made by "international financial institutions," such as the World Bank. This did not work out as planned for many reasons. For instance, the projects did not deliver the expected outcomes, and the terms of the loans were unfavorable to the borrowing countries, sinking them further into poverty. There was a global "debt crisis" in which borrowing countries of the Global South could not pay back their debt. Another international financial institution—the International Monetary Fund (IMF)—stepped in to renegotiate loans. In doing so, they created loan conditions (formally called structural adjustment policies) that stated how governments could and could not spend funds. As this was an era of neoliberalism in which the dominant ideology was that private corporations were more effective at producing positive economic outcomes than the government, the IMF required that governments cut social programs, including education, healthcare, and environmental protection. They conditioned loans on the privatization of formerly publicly supplied services like water systems and power grids. There was global resistance to this loan conditionality. The example of the water wars in Cochabamba below fits into this context.

Finally, we must think about the consequences of economic globalization. As this brief section suggests, there has been trade among different regions of the world for centuries. In the last half century, however, this has sped up exponentially. For consumers in the Global North, economic globalization is part of our daily social reality. We wake up, drink South American coffee, pull on sneakers from Asia, and fuel our cars with African gas. Our consumption ties us to the resource use in these far-off places (see Lesson 7). We are linked to other individuals and nations through the global commodity chain. As such, we should be asking, How was the environment affected by the growth of this coffee? Is it "fair trade"? How were the workers treated who made these sneakers? Are they unionized? Who benefits from the extraction of the gas? Is it a transnational corporation or the people who live on the land where it is extracted? Keep this history of economic development in mind when reading about three cases of environmental movements from the Global South that are highlighted in the next sections.

GRASSROOTS CASES FROM INDIA, NIGERIA, AND BOLIVIA

Three brief examples from three different continents will illustrate how environmental actions (variously called "movements," "campaigns," and "environmentalisms") in the Global South are intertwined with livelihood struggles and how they are closely tied to attempts to promote social justice. There are numerous examples to draw from; I have selected one case each from Asia (the Chipko movement in India), Africa (the Movement for the Survival of the Ogoni People in Nigeria), and Latin America (the "water war" in Bolivia). While reading about these cases, keep in mind the environmental justice struggles going on in the United States. Think about the struggles of native peoples within the United States and Canada to defend their territories against fossil-fuel infrastructures, such as the resistance at Standing Rock. Some of these struggles take place in industrial workplaces and others take place where people live, especially in working-class and minority communities (see Lessons 10 and 17). So, while we make a distinction between environmentalism of the rich and environmentalism of the poor, these are not just differences between rich and poor nations, for there is also diversity of movement types within nations. The three cases that I present are well-known, often-referenced, historically important cases.

Asia: The Chipko Movement in India

The Chipko Movement began in 1973 and is perhaps the first internationally recognized "ecology" movement from a developing country. It became well known because of its use of direct action and due to the participation of women in the struggle.

After years of coping with flooding and the need to travel long distances for fuel wood, problems caused by deforestation and soil erosion, peasants in the Himalayan village of Mandal decided to put a stop to logging in the state-owned forests around their village. The village activists, many of whom were women, literally placed their bodies between the loggers and the trees. The loggers stopped; they did not cut the trees. This practice spread to other areas—the Reni forests and other parts of the region. It was not a centralized movement; rather, disparate communities replicated the protest. Numerous slogans were repeated throughout the countryside, including the famous "What do the forests bear? Soil, water and pure air."

Though "chipko" literally means "to cling," the movement was popularized as the movement of "tree huggers." The action was within the Gandhian tradition of nonviolent direct action, and it was directed at the state. Because of women's participation, this movement has also been considered a feminist movement. However, in a thorough historical examination of the movement, Guha (1989) argued that in many ways, the Chipko Movement was neither an environmental movement nor a feminist movement. Instead, he contended, it was simply a peasant movement against state attempts to control village life; in this case, to control their means of survival (the environment). Regardless of how we label Chipko, its interpretation as an "environmental," "feminist," and "peasant" movement serves to further demonstrate how Southern environmental movements represent a more integrated understanding of social justice and the relationship between social systems and ecosystems.

Chipko is just one of many cases from the vast continent of Asia; many others could be highlighted. For instance, J. Peter Brosius has written extensively about the struggles of the Penan (an Indigenous group), who reside on the island of Borneo in Malaysia. Their efforts to preserve the Sarawak rain forest was transformed into an international campaign for Indigenous rights. In Asia, damming rivers for hydroelectric power has been a controversial issue, especially where it has caused the displacement of people. In India, the Sardar Sarovar Dam on the Narmada River has drawn international attention, as has the damming of the Yangtze River by the Three Gorges Dam in China. China's rapid industrial development has exacerbated air and water pollution in cities and associated environmental health problems.

Africa: The Ogoni Resistance in Nigeria

The Chipko Movement was essentially a battle between the people and the state. The Movement for the Survival of the Ogoni People (MOSOP) focused its attention on a transnational corporation (TNC): the Royal Dutch Shell Corporation. However, this was not simply a people-versus-TNC battle; in this showdown, the state played a complicating role because the military government sided with Shell. Why was that? Simple: in Nigeria, 80 percent of the state's revenues come from oil exports.

Shell had been drilling in the oil-rich regions of Nigeria since 1958. When they started, the people were promised "development." However, years and years passed and the promises were not delivered. In Ogoniland, half a million Indigenous Ogoni lived in poverty and ecological devastation. Their villages were crossed by pipelines and surrounded by open gas flares. Oil spills polluted land and water, hurting fishing and farming. According to the *Ecologist* magazine (Rowell 1995), "From 1982 to 1992, 1.6 million gallons of oil were spilled from Shell's Nigerian fields in 27 separate incidents." The Ogoni were promised clean water, schools, and healthcare; but after over 30 years of drilling, they were much worse off. Both Shell and the Nigerian government benefited from the extraction within the Ogoni territories; the local Ogoni paid the costs.

MOSOP was founded in 1990 by author and outspoken Ogoni Ken Saro-Wiwa and others to oppose the environmental destruction created by Shell's oil production and because Shell did not compensate the Ogoni as it said it would. MOSOP attempted to bring international attention to the mess that Shell made on their lands. They demanded compensation and wanted Ogoni control of their environment. MOSOP was not just an environmental organization; it worked, and still works, for democracy, to protect the practices of the Ogoni, and for social and economic development. MOSOP called for an international boycott of Shell. Greenpeace and Amnesty International became involved in the case.

The military government did not like the problems that MOSOP was causing for Shell and for its revenues. The state used its power to quell resistance. There were violent conflicts in the region, with the police repressing demonstrations and torturing activists. In January 1993, the Year of Indigenous Peoples project brought 300,000 people to the region in protest. That same month, Shell withdrew its staff from the area. The Nigerian government sent security forces to dispel dissent and make the area safe for Shell. They continued to torture, detain, and kill Ogoni activists.

In 1995, Ken Saro-Wiwa and eight other activists were arrested. The government claimed that they had murdered Ogoni leaders. International observers did not believe they committed these crimes and called the military tribunal that found them guilty "unjust." In the end, the Nigerian government hung Ken Saro-Wiwa and the eight activists. This brought more international attention to Nigeria and turned Ken Saro-Wiwa into a martyr.

Sadly, this case from Africa highlights the deadly course that fighting for environmental and human rights can take. The MOSOP case was exacerbated by the Nigerian government's entrenchment with Shell. The people wanted schools and hospitals; the TNC and state wanted profit. The state ruled by force to silence protest and ensure its revenues. Most believe that the Nigerian military and Shell worked hand in hand to ensure this. Though the state in Africa has a reputation for corruption, this rather blatant case of the state's reliance on growth for its own capital accumulation is simply the grossest manifestation of what happens when capital accumulation outweighs a state's need for political legitimacy. Also, lest we think that violent repression of environmental activists happens only somewhere else, I recommend the 1996 book by Andrew Rowell, *Green Backlash*, which highlights attacks against environmentalists fighting the growth coalition in many nations, including the United States. One example is Judy Bari, the Earth First! and labor activist whose car was bombed in 1990. Less dramatic, but also telling are the denunciations of environmental leaders who threaten economic business as usual. Some examples that also illustrate a gendered approach to this include the American chemical industry's attacks on Rachel Carson in the late 1960s when she warned of the dangers of the chemical DDT. A modern example includes Donald Trump's sarcastic tweets and Fox news's mocking commentary directed at Greta Thunberg, a teenager who has led a charge aimed at politicians to take action to halt climate change.

Latin America: The "Water War" in Cochabamba, Bolivia

The final case study came to conclusion in 2000 and is heralded as a success for the people against the transnational giants of **neoliberalism**. I also discuss it because it illustrates an urban movement that intertwines environmentalism with radical democracy; and I expect that as more and more of the Global South moves to urban areas, these areas will be the sites of future environmentalisms.

Cochabamba, with a population of over 600,000, is the third largest city in Bolivia. Due to pressure from international financial institutions like the World Bank, the government of Bolivia began privatizing what had formerly been public resources. While the laws that started the trend dated back to the mid-1980s, the issue came to the fore in 1999/2000 when the state attempted to privatize water in Cochabamba. This was required by the International Development Bank as part of the conditions of a loan. At the time, half of Cochabambans were connected to a central water system, and the rest used community water systems organized by neighborhood groups and nongovernmental organizations (NGOs). The government changed the laws so that the latter forms of water acquisition would be illegal. Instead, a company, Aguas del Tunari, a subsidiary of Bechtel, a TNC based in San Francisco, would run the water system.

The people protested. They saw access to water as a fundamental human right, and the common good was being sold so that a corporation would benefit. People refused to pay. Neighborhoods were organized. Demonstrations were held. Oscar Olivera, a union organizer in the shoe factory, and others formed the Coordinadora (the Coalition in Defense of Water and Life). The Cochabambans were not willing to give up the right to decide how their natural resources would be used, bought, and sold. In the end, through multiple mass demonstrations, the people won and retained the right to access their water. This also reinvigorated Bolivian conceptions of democracy. Olivera (2004, 20) explains:

> What is happening more and more today is that *democracy is becoming confused with elections*. At one time democracy—at least to us—meant participation in the distribution of wealth; collective decision-making on issues that affect us all; and pressure and mobilization in order to influence state

policies. Now the only acceptable meaning of "democracy" seems to be *competition in the electoral market*. (italics in original)

One outcome of this movement was that in 2005, Bolivia elected its first ever Indigenous president, Evo Morales, who was part of the "water war." This movement, like the others discussed, is not just an environmental movement; it is about social justice, the environment, and the nature of globalization.

Latin America is rich with such cases of resistance. For example, the Indigenous people of Ecuador's Amazon region took Texaco to court in New York for environmental damage. In a global economy, our everyday actions, like filling our gas tanks, link us to environmental and social consequences elsewhere. The globalization of the economy also makes it more and more likely that actors in the Global South will fight agents in the Global North. In this David-and-Goliath fight, Cochabamba shows us that David can sometimes win.

CONSEQUENCES OF GLOBALIZATION OF OTHER INSTITUTIONS FOR THE ENVIRONMENT

From these examples, it might make sense to conclude simply that globalization (particularly economic) is bad for the environment. In the Bolivian and Nigerian cases, local populations responded to threats from TNCs that were aided in their quest for natural resources by national governments (**growth coalitions**). However, other aspects of globalization have been positive for the environment. For example, most organizations have been "greened" to some degree: states, international NGOs, intergovernmental organizations, and international financial institutions. In general, we are living in a historical era in which "the environment," as a concern, is taken seriously. This environmental moment does not show signs of ending anytime soon.

Take the following examples as evidence that the environment is an enduring concern. Over the past century, states around the globe have increasingly become more "green." A few ways this has been measured has been in the number of national environmental ministries, national laws requiring environmental impact statements, and national parks worldwide. At the international level, the number of NGOs and international governmental organizations dedicated to the environment continues to grow, year after year. International financial institutions, such as the World Bank, have enacted environmental standards for their lending programs. United Nations (UN) conferences on the theme of the environment have created an international forum for environmentalism to be discussed globally. In 1972, the UN Conference on the Human Environment was held in Stockholm, Sweden. This was followed 20 years later by the UN Conference on Environment and Development (popularly termed the "Earth Summit") held in Rio de Janeiro, Brazil. In 2002, this was followed by the World Summit on Sustainable

Development in Johannesburg, South Africa; and in 2012, the UN Conference on Sustainable Development (also known as Rio + 20), was again held in Rio. These conferences sometimes lead to important actions. For instance, at the Earth Summit, the United Nations Framework Convention on Climate change was adopted. It has been ratified by 196 nations, which constitute the "parties" to the convention. The framework acknowledges the existence of anthropogenic (human-induced) climate change. The Conference of the Parties (COP) is the decision-making group that works on combatting climate change. Each year the COP meets. The 21st meeting—the COP21—was held in Paris in 2015. A "Paris Agreement" was signed, and nations, including the United States and China, pledged to reduce greenhouse gasses. Despite this progress, in 2019 President Trump declared his intention to withdraw from the agreement.

There is a complicated relationship, then, between Southern environmentalism and globalization. For the environment, globalization is a double-edged sword. On the one hand, there is resistance to TNCs, the economic agents of globalization. On the other hand, people in the Global South are often aided by institutions that have been greened by globalization, such as international governmental organizations. In this sense, the idea of a "local" movement really does not make much sense. There are groups that are focused on specific geographical areas, but they are connected to the "global" world. Earlier, I mentioned the rubber tappers of Brazil and their struggle against local ranchers. This was a fight among Brazilians for the most part, but it drew on the "globalization of environmentalism."

The case of the rubber tappers is chronicled in at least two films, one a documentary and the second a dramatization (*The Killing of Chico Mendes* and *The Burning Season*). To make a long and very interesting story short, essentially what happened was that there was a conflict between rubber tappers and cattle ranchers in the Acre province of Brazil. Chico Mendes was a union organizer for the rubber tappers (*seringueros*). In the 1970s, he began organizing rubber tappers in Brazil against the cattle ranchers who were clearing lands for pasture. There were violent confrontations between the two groups. This local battle went international when the World Bank and the Inter-American Development Bank (IADB) approved loans to build a road that would essentially open up the land for more clearing. Locals were not consulted in the process. Mendes worked with NGOs in the United States, notably the Environmental Defense Fund, and eventually came to Washington, DC, to convince the US Senate that it should not support the IADB loan. The Senate withdrew its support, the IADB suspended its loan payments, and the road was stopped. Mendes and the rubber tappers short-circuited the Brazilian government to halt its road development plans. Eventually, the government, the *seringueros*, and the ranchers came to an agreement to create an "extractive reserve"—that is, an area like a national park that the rubber tappers could use to tap rubber yet maintain as a forest (this fits into a "sustainable development" scheme, as discussed in Lesson 20). This innovative idea joined the interests of local people's livelihoods with the larger "environmental" interests of the "global" environmental community. As with other Southern campaigns, we could ask whether the rubber tappers were really environmentalists or whether they were framing their interests creatively to best appeal to the shifts in international thinking regarding the environment. If they had framed this battle as one of human rights or workers' rights, it may not have succeeded at this time in history. Unfortunately, this story does not have a happy ending. Mendes went on to help other communities facing similar battles. In 1988, he was shot and killed by cattle ranchers. In some areas of Brazil, he is considered a hero. In 1989, the Brazilian government agreed to protect 50 million more acres in extractive reserves. This case shows how "local" environmental groups were able to gain support from global environmental actors to win (or at least make some gains) locally.

In my own work, I have looked at the consequences of transnational co-operation involving conservation movements with a focus on Latin America. In Ecuador, international NGOs have had a positive effect on conservation. Ecuadorian conservationists tell me that the Ecuadorian government has protected additional areas because of actions taken by transnational environmentalists and that without these actors' interventions, Ecuadorian forests would be worse off. In the 1980s, international NGOs created a funding mechanism for conservation called a "debt-for-nature swap." In a swap, conservation groups negotiate with banks on behalf of Southern nations so that instead of states making their full loan payments, a fraction of their payment is channeled within their country to pay for conservation and to fund conservation organizations. A number of swaps took place in Ecuador, which kept funds in the country that were earmarked for environmental activities and were tremendously important for conservation. In Ecuador, international conservationists helped protect a large percentage of land. They also helped found and fund environmental organizations. These were the upsides; the downside was that it created competition among Ecuadorian environmental groups for resources that were distributed by agents from the Global North. The competition among organizations for resources persists in Ecuador today and hinders the cooperation of Ecuadorian conservationists. Again, the "globalization of environmentalism" has had some complicated outcomes. While there are more groups working for the environment in Ecuador, they are not working together.

Another twist is that the organizations that were created by the influx of funds are professionalized organizations and their practices are more similar to NGOs in the Global North than to the grassroots resistance organizations described in the case studies. Environmental groups have been founded by international interaction throughout the Global South. In general, early environmentalism in these regions fit the patterns of livelihood struggles described in the case studies. Over time, however, as organizations sought international support, their forms became more institutionalized. In an analysis of the origins of environmental groups around the world, Wesley Longhofer and Evan Shofer (2010) noted that in the "industrialized west"

(Global North in the terms of this lesson), the average date of founding for environmental groups was 1958. In South and Central America, the average date was 1983. What this suggests is that while grassroots environmental campaigns, without official organizational status, or perhaps under the auspices of other groups like labor unions, existed prior to 1983, what happened in the 1980s and later is that organized, professional groups came into being.

RESISTANCE TO ECOLOGICAL IMPERIALISM

When international NGOs work in Ecuador to protect lands for the "good of humankind," what does this mean for locals? For sovereignty in Ecuador? Whose needs are being met? What if Japan wanted to buy a chunk of the Pacific Northwest to protect it? How would people in Oregon respond? Who controls the environment and decisions regarding its use?

Transnational environmentalism has been criticized by some from the South as a form of "**ecoimperialism.**" This critique parallels criticisms of colonialism and development. "Development" was intended to change "backward/traditional" societies into "modern" societies; however, much official development has led to greater inequality between the Global North and the Global South, and many nations that started out "poor" are now poorer and further in debt and have less control over their choices. The critique of transnational environmentalism is that organizations "helping" with environmental issues are creating the same problem. By becoming involved in the Global South, actors from the Global North are attempting to exert control over foreign environments. For example, Arturo Escobar (1998) looked at what he called the "dominant biodiversity discourse" that comes from the West and suggested that there are multiple ways that other actors understand biodiversity. He argued that international conservation projects based on the Western, "global" conception of biodiversity (which he called the "resource management dominant view") are just one way of understanding, and that locals have alternative conceptions of the nature–culture relationship. In the current formulation, the "globalization of the environment" has opened doors to funding flows between the North and South. This makes more and more possibilities for the North to "manage" the South.

Along this same line, Akhil Gupta (1998, 306) argued that "In contrast to the humanistic pronouncement of 'sharing one world,' made mostly by leaders and activists from the North, is the view of representatives of poor countries that the environment is a crucial arena where conflict between the haves and have-nots manifests itself." There have been specific instances of local groups in the Global South resisting the North's environmentalism. Back again to Ecuador: In 1995, frustrated, angry fishermen from the Galápagos Islands took their machetes and rounded up researchers from the Charles Darwin Research Station and held them hostage for 4 days. Why? The government limited fishing in the area on the basis of the Northern environmental scientists' assessment. The fishermen's access to fish, and thus their economic survival, was limited by Northern recommendations to limit withdrawals. This conflict in the Galápagos, between the local economy and international environmental protection, has been ongoing. This conflict, like ones dealing with sustainable development, highlights conflicts between the Global North and the Global South in which the North focuses on the environment at the expense of development and vice versa (see also Lesson 20).

Some interesting changes have been taking place with regard to "alternative development" and the environment, especially in Latin America. In Ecuador, Rafael Correa was elected president in 2006 and took office in 2007. *Alianza PAIS*, the political party that Correa founded, promised to create a new 21st-century socialism. Under President Correa, there was a referendum to elect a constituent assembly that would rewrite the constitution. The new constitution included constitutional rights for nature. Nature has "the right to exist, persist, maintain and regenerate its vital cycles, structure, functions and its processes in evolution," and the government is required to protect such rights. This was the first time nature has ever had these rights, anywhere. Bolivia adopted a similar change to its constitution in 2011. The Ecuadorian constitution also included language, written in Spanish and Kichwa (one of the dominant Indigenous languages spoken in the country), expressing the right to "*buen vivir*," and "*sumak kawsay*"—a right to living well. Many suggest that these changes create openings for Ecuadorians (and others) to create an alternative development model that incorporates nature rather than simply extracting it for human use. The Pachamama Alliance, an organization that works with Indigenous peoples in the Amazon and is based in San Francisco (with a sister foundation in Ecuador), summarizes aspects of the Indigenous conception of *sumak kawsay*:

> Sumak kawsay values people over profit. It is also a new way of viewing "developing nations" because it expresses a relationship with nature and surroundings that epitomizes the opposite of profit and commodification. A key piece is how development is defined: it calls for a decreased emphasis on economic and product development, and an increased focus on human development—not in population, but an enrichment of core values, spirituality, ethics, and a deepening of our own connection with pachamama [mother earth]. (The Pachamama Alliance, 2012)

These views of development and nature are at odds with the dominant worldview of the Global North.

One of the concrete proposals that came out of President Correa's administration, which was influenced by *sumak kawsay*, was a proposal that attempted to address global warming and lead the world to a "post-fossil fuel society." President Correa presented his ITT-Yasuní Initiative at the UN in 2007. The basic plan was that the state would not grant oil concessions in the ITT oil corridor that runs through Yasuní National Park if the international community could compensate Ecuador for half of the revenue that it would have earned over a 10-year period (in other words, asking for $3.6 billion in environmental donations in lieu of $7.2 billion in oil export profits). The argument was that the plan would protect one of the most biodiverse places on earth AND reduce greenhouse gas emissions AND protect Indigenous people living on those lands AND slow climate change. Environmental organizations formed to promote the project and solicit funding. Sadly, the initiative failed. But, Ecuador generated an alternative that caught the world's eye. Even though Ecuador was not able to "keep the oil in the soil," the proposal marked a stark contrast to the days when the Ecuadorian state allowed Texaco to drill and create environmental devastation and endanger Indigenous peoples' livelihoods in the Amazon. There is now an international movement to "Keep it in the Ground," including groups from around the world like Fossil Free USA, which helps college students organize fossil fuel divestment movements.

CONCLUSION

The Chipko, Ogoni, and Cochabambans are just three historical examples of global struggles for the environment and social justice. Around the world today, activists are resisting mining, the clear-cutting of rain forests to make way for palm plantations, and the construction of dams, among other activities. Increasingly, the globalization of communication has allowed ideologically similar actors in the Global North and Global South to network and work together to fight their battles. Ironically, economic globalization simultaneously creates both environmental problems and the technical means for people to mobilize around problems. Grassroots groups around the world can now connect through networks focused on issues including mangrove protection, food sovereignty, and keeping the oil in the soil. Transnational activists have also organized to address climate change, with simultaneous climate marches around the world in 2014 and 2019.

Grassroots environmentalism in the Global South is more akin to environmental justice struggles in North America than to the professionalized movement industry represented by mainstream groups like the Sierra Club and the Environmental Defense Fund. Over time, however, the Global South's environmental movement has become more professionalized along the lines of environmental organizations in the Global North, and it is creating two different forms of organizations in the Global South: (1) grassroots-based direct action activists and (2) professionalized environmental groups who work from their offices.

Environmental movements in the Global South must attend to the concerns of those who are poor and want economic development and those who are poor and suffering from the negative effects of economic development. In many cases in the South, there have been outright attacks against environmentalism, as in the case of attacks and killings of activists working for the U'wa and Ogoni as well as Chico Mendes, since environmentalism often comes into conflict with states' and TNCs' interests. Economic globalization is one of the biggest foes of the environment in the Global South and represents an issue that is bigger than what most single-campaign organizations can focus on. When I ask environmentalists in Latin America if they've been successful, they respond, "Yes, we've slowed environmental degradation, but as long as we continue on this economic development path, the environment is bound for destruction." Some alternative models, such as that presented by Ecuador, suggest that alternative forms of "development" and "good living" may be possible.

SOURCES

Brechin, Steven R. and Willett Kempton. 1994. "Global Environmentalism: A Challenge to the Postmaterialism Thesis?" *Social Science Quarterly* 75:245–269.

Brosius, J. Peter. 2001. "Local Knowledge, Global Claims: On the Significance of Indigenous Ecologies in Sarawak, East Malaysia." In *Indigenous Traditions and Ecology*, edited by J. Grim and L. Sullivan, 125–157. Cambridge, MA: Harvard University Press and Center for the Study of World Religions.

Collinson, Helen, ed. 1996. *Green Guerrillas: Environmental Conflicts and Initiatives in Latin America and the Caribbean*. London: Latin American Bureau.

Dunlap, Riley E. and Richard York. 2008. "The Globalization of Environmental Concern and the Limits of the Postmaterialist Values Explanation: Evidence from Four Multinational Surveys." *The Sociological Quarterly* 49:529–563.

Escobar, Arturo. 1995. *Encountering Development: The Making and Unmaking of the Third World*. Princeton, NJ: Princeton University Press.

Escobar, Arturo. 1998. "Whose Knowledge, Whose Nature? Biodiversity, Conservation, and the Political Ecology of Social Movements." *Journal of Political Ecology* 5:53–82.

Escobar, Arturo. 2011. "Sustainability: Design for the Pluriverse." *Development* 54 (2): 137–140.

Gedicks, Al. 2001. *Resource Rebels: Native Challenges to Mining and Oil Corporations*. Boston, MA: South End Press.

Guha, Ramachandra. 1989. *The Unquiet Woods: Ecological Change and Peasant Resistance in the Himalaya*. Berkeley, CA: University of California Press.

Guha, Ramachandra. 2000. *Environmentalism: A Global History*. New York: Longman.

Guha, Ramachandra and Juan Martinez-Alier. 1997. *Varieties of Environmentalism: Essays North and South*. London: Earthscan.

Gupta, Akhil. 1998. *Postcolonial Development: Agriculture in the Making of Modern India*. Durham, NC: Duke University Press.

Keck, Margaret E. and Kathryn Sikkink. 1998. *Activists Beyond Borders: Advocacy Networks in International Politics*. Ithaca, NY: Cornell University Press.

Lewis, Tammy L. 2016. *Ecuador's Environmental Revolutions: Ecoimperialists, Ecodependents, and Ecoresisters*. Cambridge, MA: The MIT Press.

Longhofer, Wesley and Evan Shofer. 2010. "National and Global Origins of Environmental Associations." *American Sociological Review* 75 (4): 505–533.

McMichael, Philip. 2016. *Development and Social Change: A Global Perspective*. 6th ed. Thousand Oaks, CA: SAGE.

364 / TWENTY LESSONS IN ENVIRONMENTAL SOCIOLOGY

North, Anna 2019. "Attacks on Greta Thunberg Expose the Stigma Autistic Girls Face." *Vox*, September 24, 2019. https://www.vox.com/identities/2019/9/24/20881837/greta-thunberg-michael-knowles-laura-ingraham-trump

Olivera, Oscar. 2004. *¡Cochabamba! Water War in Bolivia*. Cambridge, MA: South End Press.

Pellow, David N. 2007. *Resisting Global Toxics: Transnational Movements for Environmental Justice*. Cambridge, MA: The MIT Press.

Rowell, Andrew. 1995. "Oil, Shell and Nigeria." *Ecologist* 25 (6): 210–213.

Rowell, Andrew. 1996. *Green Backlash: A Global Subversion of the Environmental Movement*. New York: Routledge.

Smith, Jackie. 2008. *Social Movements for Global Democracy*. Baltimore: The Johns Hopkins University Press.

Taylor, Bron Raymond, ed. 1995. *Ecological Resistance Movements: The Global Emergence of Radical and Popular Environmentalism*. Albany: State University of New York Press.

Taylor, Dorceta E. 2009. *The Environment and the People in American Cities, 1600s–1900s*. Durham, NC: Duke University Press.

The Pachamama Alliance. 2012. "Sumak Kawsay: Ancient Teachings of Indigenous Peoples." Accessed 4 January 2014. http://www.pachamama.org/sumak-kawsay

20

The Paradoxes of Sustainable Development
Focus on Ecotourism

Kenneth A. Gould and Tammy L. Lewis

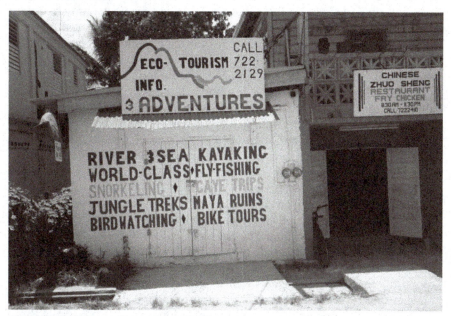

Ecotourism business, Punta Gorda, Belize.

Post your photo on the sustainable development to #TLESecotourism

Photo by Ken Gould

WHAT IS SUSTAINABLE DEVELOPMENT?

When we ask our classes "What is **sustainable development**?," they usually respond, confidently, along the following lines: "It's development that doesn't deplete natural resources." Ok. We push this a bit. We follow with, "What is development?" They respond this time, pausing: "Making things better?" Ok. We press on. What should be sustained? The environment? The economy? Human welfare? What should be developed? Who should be developed? Is development growth? And so on. The answers become murkier, and what sounded so nice and neat at first begins to unravel upon deeper scrutiny.

The most commonly used definition of sustainable development is from a 1987 report by the World Commission on Environment and Development titled *Our Common Future*. In the report, the term is defined as "development that meets the needs of the present without compromising the ability of future generations to meet their own needs." The term gained popularity at the 1992 Earth Summit (officially titled the United Nations Conference on Environment and Development). At the Earth Summit, heads of state of 178 nations met to address both the "environment problem" and the "development problem." Tensions between the relative priorities of countries in the Global North and those in the Global South were a key feature of the discussions. Many Southern nations viewed alleviation of the crushing poverty in the Global South and the growing economic inequalities between the Global North and Global South as central issues. In contrast, many Northern nations viewed habitat protection (particularly rainforests) as central, with Southern poverty secondary and North–South inequality largely peripheral. In that context, the concept of sustainable development was appealing since it presumed that **economic growth** and environmental protection could be reconciled. Northern and Southern economies could grow, and **biodiverse** habitats could be saved. The priorities of both the Global North and the Global South could be addressed in a "win–win" scenario of improving material standards of living and increasing environmental protection. Up until that point, many viewed "environment" and "development" as adversaries. Sustainable development opened up new avenues to discuss alternative ways to protect the environment and "develop" societies.

While the definition from *Our Common Future* has the greatest recognition, a range of definitions have emerged since that time. The common thread among these definitions is what *Our Common Future* identifies as the three main, but not equal, goals of sustainable development: (1) economic growth, (2) environmental protection, and (3) social equity. Different interest groups highlight different goals. For example, industrialists focus on economic concerns, environmentalists on environmental protection, and some governments and nongovernmental organizations (NGOs), especially those concerned with poverty alleviation, on **social equity**. Another term, "**just sustainability**," has since been developed to emphasize the social pillar of sustainability, which is often left out of practical applications of sustainable development. Julian Agyeman, Robert Bullard, and Bob Evans (2003) define just sustainability as "the need to ensure a better quality of life for all, now and into the future, in a just and equitable manner, whilst living within the limits of supporting ecosystems."

The ideas embodied in the term "sustainable development" were not entirely new in 1987. The concept of sustainable development draws on environmental discourses from the 1970s and 1980s, such as limits to growth, appropriate and intermediate technology, soft energy paths, and ecodevelopment. For instance, the limits-to-growth debate was centered on a study produced by the Club of Rome in 1972 titled *The Limits to Growth*. The study presented evidence that severe biophysical constraints would impinge on the economic growth and development of societies. It predicted ecological collapse if current growth trends continued in population, industry, and resource use. The study generated tremendous debate and critique about the quantity of remaining, exploitable resources and what could be accomplished with technology. In addition, the limits-to-growth idea became politically unpopular in the Global South: governments from poorer nations did not believe it was fair that they limit their economic growth in order to protect the global environment for the benefit of wealthier countries in the Global North, which had already depleted substantial resources for the benefit of their own economic growth. This was a precursor to debates over issues such as global warming in which rich and poor nations have divergent views regarding which countries should take the biggest steps toward lowering their emissions of greenhouse gasses. Sustainable development tried to bypass the idea of limits by postulating the possibility of growth within existing environmental constraints.

From the 1970s to the present, a remarkable change has occurred in a common understanding of the relationship between "environment" and "economic development." While the limits-to-growth debate asked whether environmental protection and continued economic growth are compatible, the mainstream sustainable development language assumes that the two are complementary and instead focuses on how sustainable development can be achieved. The sustainable development discourse does not assume that there are fixed limits; it is pro-growth and pro-technology. *Our Common Future* clearly states

> The concept of sustainable development does imply limits—not absolute limits but limitations imposed by the present state of technology and social organizations on environmental resources and by the ability of the biosphere to absorb the effects of human activities. But technology and social organization can both be managed and improved to make way for a new era of economic growth.

International aid agencies, such as the United States Agency for International Development (USAID), and international financial institutions (IFIs), such as the World Bank, adopted the sustainable development framework for the design of their programs. The emergence of the concept also coincided with the reframing of problems as "global problems." No longer was it enough to "think globally, act locally." In an era of sustainable development and globalization, the new interpretation of environmental problems suggested that we must "think globally, act globally."

A range of critics have attacked sustainable development. A leading criticism points to the lack of clarity in the meaning of the term. What should be "sustained"? The economy? The environment? Human welfare? What should be "developed"? Does development mean productive growth, which is typically measured by growth of **gross national product** (GNP)? Does it refer to environmental growth, such as an increase in environmental resources? Does it refer to growth in human welfare, including better health and working conditions? Similarly, when the "sustainable development" definition refers to "needs," whose needs are these? The definition of "needs" in the Global South contrasts sharply with the concept of "needs" in the Global North, which tends to expand into consumer "wants."

How much socioeconomic inequality is sustainable? What type of objective criteria could be constructed to determine if we are moving toward or away from sustainable development?

In part due to the lack of consensus of meaning, critics argue that being in favor of sustainable development comes commitment free. Bruce Rich (1994) (former World Bank employee and Environmental Defense Fund senior attorney) notes, "Sustainable development is a mother-and-apple-pie formulation that everyone can agree on; there are no reports of any politician or international bureaucrat proclaiming his or her support for unsustainable development." The "sustainability" tag is used to describe so many desirable institutions that it has lost meaning. Who could argue against sustainable cities? Sustainable agriculture? Sustainable tourism? As such, there has been widespread adoption of the term. The next section highlights how the corporations and the policy world have adopted the term.

THREE MANIFESTATIONS OF SUSTAINABLE DEVELOPMENT

Corporate

Many corporations embrace aspects of sustainable development. Business leaders making up the World Business Council for Sustainable Development (WBCSD), including Germany's Volkswagen, Japan's Mitsubishi, Brazil's Aracruz Cellulose, and the United States' 3M, see themselves as part of the solution to the global environmental crisis. BASF, Bayer, Dow-Dupont, and General Electric are also members of the WBCSD. Those companies are also among the 10 worst air polluters on earth, as indicated in the 2017 "Toxic 100" list. Corporations have created a number of voluntary agreements, such as the CERES (Coalition for Environmentally Responsible Economies) principles. Corporate signers pledge to participate in voluntary environmental reporting and ongoing environmental improvements. Businesses such as American Airlines, Coca-Cola, General Motors, and Nike have signed the CERES principles. Associating with such voluntary principles provides positive public relations benefits without requiring dramatic shifts in actual corporate behavior, and signals that there is little need for government intervention. Another example is the International Organization for Standardization's ISO 14000 framework. It is a way for industries to measure and evaluate their corporate environmental programs' movement toward sustainable business development.

An example of a corporation ostensibly attempting to follow sustainable development principles is 3M (Minnesota Mining and Manufacturing). 3M produces a number of consumer products, including tape. 3M was an early initiator of voluntary environmental actions through its Pollution Prevention Policy (3P). According to 3M's literature, "3P was established because it is more environmentally effective, technically sound and economical than conventional pollution standards." The company tries to prevent pollution at the source rather than by managing its wastes. They view this as a way to save treatment and disposal costs and reduce environmental impacts. 3M has four strategies to do this: product reformulation, process modification, equipment redesign, and recycling/reuse of waste. An example of 3P was the redesign of a resin spray booth that cost $45,000 to implement and saves $125,000 a year in resin incineration disposal. 3M has saved money, reduced pollutants, and won awards since implementing its strategies. In 2015, 3M established its "2025 sustainability goals," which include reducing water use by 10 percent, improving energy efficiency by 30 percent, and reducing greenhouse gas emissions to 50 percent of its 2002 baseline. Its stated ideal is to move toward zero emissions. This is also the goal of "industrial ecology" and "ecological modernization."

Ecological modernization approaches (see Lesson 2) fit into this line of reasoning. Theorists in this tradition argue that there is a material environmental problem that can be improved through industrial production that is cleaner, more efficient, and more profitable. Leading proponents of this theory Arthur Mol and Gert Spaargaren (2000, 36) stated, "More production and consumption in economic terms (GNP, purchase power, employment) does not have to imply more environmental devastation (pollution, energy use, loss of biodiversity)." Simply put, they believe green capitalism-based sustainable development is possible.

Policy

For countries in the Global North, such as the United States, incorporating sustainable development into policies has led to refocusing the activities of their aid agencies (such as the USAID). USAID supports many environment and development projects in the Global South, such as pollution prevention programs in India and Chile, biodiversity protection in Madagascar and Peru, and the training of energy professionals in Ecuador and Nigeria. USAID believes that poverty can be eliminated by economic growth (rather than redistribution) and that environmental quality will then improve. Other nations in the Global North, such as Canada, have also incorporated sustainable development into their aid agencies. **International financial institutions**, such as the World Bank, have also "greened" their image, and their activities now have emphases on the environment. For example, the World Bank is partnered with the United Nations' Environment Program and the United Nations' Development Program to administer the Global Environment Facility, which transfers funds to the Global South for environmental programs.

If sustainable development is a goal, there is also the question of how we know if we're getting closer. While GNP per capita tells us about economic growth, it doesn't really explain anything about the environment or equity or quality of life. A number of measures have been proposed to examine sustainable development. These include the Happy Planet Index (HPI), which takes into account ecological footprints and "happy life years," and the Genuine Progress Indicator (GPI). The GPI is used to compare actual levels of economic activity with sustainable levels of activity. It takes into account additional costs, such as costs of environmental restoration, to traditional income statistics. While higher consumption levels lead to traditionally "better" economic statistics, the GPI accounts for the environment-degrading effects of consumption, such as the negative effects of vehicle use and eating vegetables out of season. Using this measure, many development schemes are accounted for as net losses rather than gains because the environmental costs are calculated as outweighing the economic benefits.

In 2015, the United Nations adopted the Sustainable Development goals to be attained by the year 2030. These are non-binding goals that nations are encouraged to follow. They include the following broad set of objectives:

GOAL 1: No Poverty

GOAL 2: Zero Hunger

GOAL 3: Good Health and Well-being

GOAL 4: Quality Education

GOAL 5: Gender Equality

GOAL 6: Clean Water and Sanitation

GOAL 7: Affordable and Clean Energy

GOAL 8: Decent Work and Economic Growth

GOAL 9: Industry, Innovation and Infrastructure

GOAL 10: Reduced Inequality

GOAL 11: Sustainable Cities and Communities

GOAL 12: Responsible Consumption and Production

GOAL 13: Climate Action

GOAL 14: Life Below Water

GOAL 15: Life on Land

GOAL 16: Peace and Justice Strong Institutions

GOAL 17: Partnerships to achieve the Goal

Actions toward these goals are carried out at the national level, and updates to progress can be accessed at the United Nations' website.

Critiques

A structural approach to sustainable development offers a radical critique, examining the degree to which the mechanisms of sustainable development serve to reproduce global inequality. In particular, the critique focuses on three linkages between the Global North and the Global South: trade, aid, and debt. Critics of sustainable development argue that the unequal relationship between the Global North and the Global South during the post-World War II "developmentalist" period is reproduced in the sustainable development paradigm; thus, it is simply old wine in new bottles. In this view, the sustainable development concept emerged to avoid addressing difficult conflicts between the environment and economic growth, the Global North and Global South, the rich and poor; and unless those conflicts are addressed, neither long-term environmental protection nor poverty alleviation will be achieved. Such critics do not believe that sustainable development offers a real alternative to old practices that serve those in power at the expense of the "have-nots" and the environment. Instead, they see sustainable development as currently practiced as a ploy to co-opt demands for more effective efforts to protect the environment and address poverty and inequality.

Theorists writing in the critical structural tradition, such as Allan Schnaiberg and Kenneth Gould on the "treadmill of production," James O'Connor on the "second contradiction of capitalism," and John Bellamy Foster on "ecological Marxism," would disagree with the basic premise of sustainable development by arguing that it is within capitalist logic to maximize profit at the expense of the environment (see Lesson 2). Thus, any action, voluntary or not, that would limit profit making would be ultimately impossible for corporations to pursue as the need to remain competitive outstrips any desire to be better environmental citizens. Economic logic will always win over ecological and social logics as long as free markets dominate. They argue that limiting pro-environmental and pro-equity actions to those efforts that can also be profitable will not be sufficient to reverse the trends toward greater environmental degradation and social inequality. From that perspective, the very logic of the global economy demands ever-increasing levels of ecological withdrawals and additions in order to sustain itself. The conclusion is that only dramatic changes to the structure of the global economy, the goals that drive it, and the distribution of what it produces (both goods and bads) could bring us to a socially and ecologically sustainable relationship between social systems and ecosystems.

Frederick Buttel (1998) argued a middle ground, taking us back to a policy perspective. He suggested that efficiency in the use of resources and in the minimization of waste could be a means for capitalists to reduce costs and increase profits and that this could be especially true if policies penalize resource destruction and pollution and reward more environmentally benign behaviors. However, he also questioned whether capitalism can be sustainable, in the line of argumentation taken by theorists in the "treadmill of production" tradition.

To provide a look at real-world efforts to achieve sustainable development, we turn to the example of ecotourism. Ecotourism has been promoted as a means of simultaneously achieving economic growth and environmental protection, while alleviating rural poverty in the Global South. Ecotourism therefore offers us a good opportunity to explore the application of the sustainable development concept in action.

ECOTOURISM: A POTENTIAL MODEL FOR SUSTAINABLE DEVELOPMENT?

Ecotourism has been heralded as a model for sustainable development. International aid agencies, national governments, NGOs, the United Nations, and Indigenous groups have promoted ecotourism as a means to protect land and important biological diversity while at the same time providing long-term social and economic benefits through sustained resource use. Ecotourism and "wildlife tourism" have the potential to be big moneymakers: tourism is one of the fastest-growing industries in the world, according to the World Tourism Organization. For instance, in the United States, according to University of Utah's Outdoor Recreation, Education, & Tourism Lab, there has been an increase in visits to US national parks from 266 million visitors in 2003 to almost 331 million visitors in 2017, an increase of 24 percent. Tourism is also listed in three of the UN's Sustainable Development Goals, and the UN's World Tourism Organization actively promotes the sustainable development of tourism.

Like "sustainable development," the concept of "ecotourism" is full of hidden conflicts and contradictions. Where ecotourism is promoted as a vehicle of sustainable development, we find paradox. Just as sustainability has been employed in many different ways and to many different ends, ecotourism been used to label a wide variety of seemingly contradictory rural development forms. In some cases, ecotourism has been used to indicate a type of ecologically low-impact tourism development. But ecologically low-impact tourism could include touring San Francisco on $40 per day, which is an activity not commonly understood as ecotourism. In other cases, ecotourism has been used to refer to the touring of relatively intact natural ecosystems. However, this could include touring Amazonia on $2,000 per day, which could easily be a high-impact form of traditional luxury tourism. A more precise application of the ecotourism concept might apply to ecologically low-impact touring of relatively intact natural ecosystems, but that would include a remarkably small set of the phenomena to which the term has commonly been applied. Ecotourism is then a socially contested term used to define, legitimate, promote, and constrain a wide variety of nature-based tourism development schemes.

Perhaps we could gain greater clarity through reference to sustainable development, defining ecotourism as a form of nature-based tourism that contributes to sustainable rural development. The analysis of transnational ecotourism as a form of sustainable development is therefore a way for us to tease out the implications of the wide variety of applications of both the ecotourism and sustainability concepts and one that requires us to explore the connections between transnational processes, national development trajectories, regional political economies, and local efforts to provide a reliable economic base for rural communities as well as local control over decision-making.

The remainder of this lesson explores ecotourism in Belize to illustrate the complexities of sustainable development. We examine Belize's ecotourism industry because it has taken a conscious effort to enact ecotourism. Between the 1970s and the 1990s, tourism was second only to sugar production as Belize's primary source of foreign exchange and its fastest-growing industry. As a result of ecotourism's importance, the government of Belize placed increased emphasis on environmental protection, making commitments to use tourism to protect rather than destroy the environment. By the end of the 1990s, tourism surpassed export agriculture as the primary source of foreign exchange; and by 2011, tourism-related activity represented one third of Belize's total national economy. In the 1960s, 11,000 foreigners visited annually; and that figure rose to 64,000 by 1980, 190,000 by 1990, and 225,000 by 1993. In 2015, Belize hosted 341,125 overnight tourists and 957,975 day visitors. According to the World Bank, tourism employs 28 percent of the working population and remains the country's largest source of foreign exchange. Belize is not a "beachy" country, so tourists come to visit rainforests, wetlands, mangrove coasts, and coral reefs to view both nature and archeological sites. Ecotourism accommodations range from small rustic lodges built with local materials traditionally used by the Maya to luxury jungle resorts with pools, bars, private cabanas, and landscaped gardens. What's the reality of ecotourism development in one small country? We briefly examine some of the paradoxes of ecotourism, which highlight that to achieve sustainable development—that is, maximizing economic growth, social equity, and environmental protection—there are inevitably trade-offs among the three systems.

ECOTOURISM AND NATIONAL DEVELOPMENT IN BELIZE

One of the key impacts of globalization on the nation of Belize has been its rapid entrance into the transnational ecotourism market. The Belizean government has made a policy commitment to environmental stewardship to prevent the degradation of coral reefs, wetlands, and rainforests, and in Patty Pattullo's terms, to utilize tourism "to protect the environment rather than destroy it and so contribute to sustainable development" (1996, 117). However, such a government commitment may prove to be unsustainable in the face of growing transnational pressures to open its rich natural resource base to **transnational corporations** (TNCs) and to repay a mounting international debt. Belize's resources are attractive to tourists but also to TNCs as exportable raw materials. If ecotourism can't provide the income the country needs to support its citizens and pay its debts, resource exports will.

The social sustainability of Belize's nature tourism development trajectory will depend on its ability to provide a reliable economic base that rural communities can depend on. The ecological sustainability of Belize's nature tourism path will depend on its ability to offer sufficient economic incentive for the government and landowners to forego more ecologically destructive economic alternatives, as well as the willingness of those social actors to keep the scale and nature of tourism facilities within ecological limits.

RAINFOREST TOURISM IN THE ORANGE WALK DISTRICT: CHAN CHICH LODGE

Belize's western rainforests are sparsely penetrated, inhabited, and developed. The Orange Walk District in northwest Belize is the center of the nation's sugar industry. In the far west of Orange Walk, cane fields give way to tropical forest, allowing for the development of nature tourism. Within a few kilometers of the Guatemalan border, the Chan Chich Lodge offers a unique luxury rainforest experience. Chan Chich is a private reserve originally owned by the nation's largest private landowner (who died in 2010). He was a seventh-generation "white" Belizean and the wealthiest person in the nation. His initial plan for his Orange Walk estate was to clear the rainforest and develop the land as an enormous citrus grove. Part of his land was already in orange production when his expansion plans inspired a "save the rainforest" campaign. Widespread national outrage at the sale of the major part of his 700,000 acres (over 12 percent of the nation) to two Houston-based investors and Coca-Cola Foods for under US$9 per acre created major political obstacles to this agroexport scheme. Seizing ecological resistance as an opportunity, he embarked on an "ecotourism" initiative, developing part of the private rainforest for nature consumers while selling off only a portion for agricultural development. His Chan Chich Lodge was featured on a Discovery Channel special soon after opening in 1989 and immediately became one of the premier jungle lodges in the nation.

Chan Chich Lodge is the one of the most expensive rainforest tourism destinations in the country, with visits during high season ranging from $500 to $1,000 per day. It is located in dense jungle amid numerous unexcavated archeological sites. It is also located within what amounts to the private "nation within a nation" of the owners. Access to Chan Chich is through a private airport, the second largest airport in Belize. The airport is located in the privately owned town of Gallon Jug, where tourists are met by luxury tour buses that take them to the lodge on a private paved road. After crossing the private suspension bridge, tourists enter the ancient Mayan plaza, which now hosts the lodge building, pool, bar, hot tub, and 12 luxurious private cabanas amid carefully landscaped gardens. Chan Chich attracts wealthy Northerners searching for a rainforest experience within a bubble of Western amenities. In addition to an extensive network of trails, the lodge offers horseback riding out of private stables, canoeing on the private Laguna Verde, air-conditioned bus tours of the owners' agroexport enterprise, and international cuisine provided by its American chef. The lodge is managed by an American expatriate couple whose American expatriate relative serves as bartender. The rest of the staff is Belizean, drawn primarily from the sugarcane fields of the Orange Walk District. The lodge grounds are elaborately landscaped and require constant maintenance to keep the jungle from reclaiming the site. Belizean workers are endlessly on hand and knee, pulling weeds and trimming flowering plants.

The quality of the rainforest experience offered at Chan Chich is truly remarkable, with numerous species of rare fauna wandering through the plaza. A 10-minute walk into the jungle over Mayan ruins offers glimpses of the local wildlife for which most tourists come to the rainforest. The constant raking of the elaborately marked trail system by the Belizean staff provides relatively risk-free access to an ecosystem hosting numerous deadly snakes. Most of the amenities provided in the lodge and cabanas are purchased in Miami, and in-room water coolers offer the owners' own brand of bottled water. Electricity lines follow the private road from Gallon Jug, and most food supplies are brought in from outside of the estate. Roof thatching is from local materials, and the tropical hardwood for construction comes from the jungle clearing of the agroexport operation, cut at the owner's commercial sawmill.

In contrast to the multistory homes of the American expatriate senior staff, the Belizean tourism workers live with their families in two well-hidden compounds, one of which is immediately adjacent to the lodge's open-burn dump. The housing, electricity, and water are provided to the staff for free. As most regional employment outside of the estate is in the sugarcane fields that dominate the Orange Walk District economy, jobs at Chan Chich are quite attractive. Cane field work is long, hard, and dangerous. In contrast, a Chan Chich waitress will earn roughly double the wages of an agricultural worker for a 9-hour workday. While the bulk of employment is in kitchen staff and grounds maintenance, the three skilled guide jobs offer better wages and slightly more autonomy. But even for the guides, the work is often unfulfilling: 10-hour days, 6 days a week filled with raking miles of trails is boring work, with actual tour guiding offering brief moments of respite. There is substantial resentment of the American expatriate management and the impossibility of advancement beyond guide work. This is despite the fact that the local environmental knowledge of the guides is truly astounding. The Belizean workers are aggressively supervised by the vigilant Americans. The master–servant relationship between the "white" managers and mestizo and Mayan workers sets the tone for the deference that Northern elites expect from local workers.

The long-abandoned town of Gallon Jug to which tourists arrive was rebuilt by the estate owner to serve his plantation operations and includes one of his three homes, which sits atop a landscaped hill overlooking the town. The remoteness of this frontier agroexport operation has produced a classic company town, where agricultural workers live in company housing, shop in the company store, and have no local alternative employment options. The nearest non-estate-owned town is over 30 miles away, so agricultural and tourism wages are immediately recirculated into the owners' private economy.

In terms of ecological protection, the lodge has served to provide fairly high returns to the landowners from an intact rain forest. It has managed to keep the scale modest by keeping the cost to nature consumers high, thus limiting the clientele to the top of the global stratification system. However, the origins of the lodge and its primary role were not income generation but rather legitimation of the owner's status as a dominant economic actor in the nation. Providing a private nature preserve offers political cover for forest-clearing development schemes. However, private preserves exist at the whim of the landowners and therefore offer no guarantee of long-term protection. Unless national protest can pressure the Belizean state to intervene, the land base of this preserve may be put to whatever use the landowner desires. The fact that the lodge is an adjunct to forest-clearing agribusiness and represents the primary route of capital penetration into otherwise "pristine" rainforest indicates that rather than providing sustainable development for rural populations, Chan Chich provides the primary source of local ecological disruption where little or no rural population previously existed in recent history. However, it does provide the only economic counterweight to more ecologically destructive agroexport and resource extraction schemes.

In terms of social sustainability, the relationship between American managers and Belizean staff is problematic. The enormous control leveraged on workers in this isolated jungle outpost, the impossibility of locally owned tourism development, and the limited opportunities for occupational advancement provide similar relations of production as seen in a traditional plantation economy. As the workers are brought in from the non-rainforest areas of the Orange Walk District to populate company towns, it is impossible to speak of sustaining Indigenous rural communities. Local populations have no decision-making authority over local ecosystem uses. In addition, although Chan Chich does provide jobs for a number of families, the limited employment capacity of this single facility is inadequate to provide for a fully sustainable local economic base.

FOREST TOURISM IN "THE CAYO": MOUNTAIN PINE RIDGE AND GAÏA RIVERLODGE

The Cayo District is Belize's western mountain frontier, known for its dense jungle, rugged mountains, sparse population, and lack of economic development. Within "the Cayo," the Mountain Pine Ridge is an ecologically unique region. The state-designated Mountain Pine Ridge Preserve protects the largest expanse of pine savanna ecosystem in Belize (although not from the invasive pine beetle that has ravaged the forests in recent years). Entrance to the preserve is through a single dirt logging road with access controlled at a gated government checkpoint operated by the Forestry Department. Access into and within the Mountain Pine Ridge Preserve is by logging roads, and little additional transportation infrastructure had been constructed to facilitate tourism until quite recently.

The forests of Mountain Pine Ridge have been selectively logged since the 1930s, and the state still sells logging concessions within the preserve (much like a national forest in the United States). The logging is an export-oriented operation, with unprocessed logs and lumber cut at small local sawmills shipped to the United Kingdom, Japan, and the United States. Most of the logging operations are Belizean-owned. Although select logging allows for fairly rapid regrowth of the forest, the necessity of firebreaks, logging roads, and wet weather skidding produces significant erosion problems. The preserve includes spectacular wild rivers with numerous undeveloped falls, caverns, and mountain peaks. The elevation provides a mild climate, while the surrounding geography allows for quick access to tropical rainforest at lower elevations with some of the densest jungle in all of Belize.

Nature tourism facilities in the Pine Ridge rely on access to small and large parcels of state-owned land within the Cayo, including Caracol (the largest Mayan archeological site in the world) and Chiquibul National Park (a premier expanse of ecologically rich jungle habitat). Daily tours to these and other state-owned natural wonders provide the primary attraction for tourists, and the fees for these guided day trips serve as a primary source of revenue for small local tourism operators and nature guides. The land within the preserve is a mix of private and public land, as much of the private land was not nationalized at the time of "preserve" designation. Most of the private inholdings are foreign-owned, the majority of those landowners being Americans.

There are four major nature tourism lodges within the preserve. Three of these are foreign-owned and were built quickly with large initial capital investments. The Gaïa Riverlodge, the only Belizean-owned major lodge within the preserve, has been built slowly over the years with comparatively meager capital investments. It was originally named the Five Sisters Lodge after a local ecosystem feature, the magnificent Five Sisters waterfalls that it sits adjacent to. The name was recently changed to Gaïa Riverlodge, a term that has no local significance but that appeals to global ecotourists. The lodge began with a mestizo and creole family's purchase of 10 acres of land in 1991 that included the Five Sisters waterfalls and the land immediately above it on the banks of Privassion Creek. The owner and his family began constructing a small lodge building and four cabanas from local materials traditionally used by the Mayan inhabitants of the region, including palm frond thatching for which the government collected royalties for extraction from the preserve. The lodge opened in 1995 and has been slowly expanded with reinvestment of profits generated from the initial four cabanas. Gaïa Riverlodge's 15 cabanas and a lodge building together can host as many as 50 guests in peak season.

In the early years of operation, the lodge had no electricity and relied on propane tanks and kerosene lamps. Eventually, a small hydroelectric dam was constructed above the falls to provide a local renewable and independent power source. Food for the lodge is purchased in nearby San Ignacio. Fresh water is provided through rainwater collection tanks. "Gray water" is treated on site, and sewage is fed into an in-ground septic tank, which is pumped out and transferred to the district landfill. Covering only 10 acres, this family-owned lodge is the smallest of the four private lodge inholdings within the 300-square-mile preserve.

In addition to family labor, the Gaïa Riverlodge employs as many as 25 people in season and 19 people off season. As the lodge is rarely full off season, much of the May-through-October work is in maintenance and construction. The numerous lodges in the Cayo compete for trained personnel, keeping wages relatively high and demonstrating the economic advantage of competitive over monopolistic tourism development for rural populations. Compared to local logging and agricultural employment, tourism jobs at Gaïa Riverlodge still provide poor wages but good benefits and security for those fortunate enough to be a part of the year-round staff. An experienced guide still earns substantially less than a successful family farm might earn in the region. However, many local residents prefer tourism work, as it is viewed as more skilled and more rewarding and it provides the possibility of upward social mobility within the industry. Much of the Gaïa staff has experienced upward mobility, with some moving from waiter positions through guide work to high-level managerial positions. Loggers earn more money, but the work is difficult, dangerous, and insecure. For year-round staff, off-season employment is rotated on a 1-week-on, 1-week-off basis, which keeps the staff employed year-round but only part time. This arrangement helps to mitigate the problem of seasonality in employment, which is a common obstacle to the social sustainability of ecotourism.

The lodge provides housing and food for its employees, as is the norm for remote tourist facilities. Most employees are from San Ignacio, the largest town nearest the preserve, and most of the wages are spent in San Ignacio, contributing to the local economy. A smaller share of the wages is spent in San Antonio, a small village just outside of the preserve entrance. Local lodge operators view logging as the primary threat to their nature tourism investments and pressed the government for greater restrictions on logging as the disruption of forest ecosystems, erosion, fires, siltation, and degradation of scenic views reduce the quality of the nature tourism experience. Their concern is that nature consumers may choose to avoid working landscapes in favor of wilderness areas, as the global competition to attract rainforest tourists has largely become a war of authenticity among tropical nations. The irony here is that logging provided the transportation infrastructure that made nature tourism possible in the Mountain Pine Ridge, and now the local tourism industry that logging inadvertently facilitated has become the primary force opposing the continuation of the logging industry. If logging is displaced by tourism, tourism will have to expand in order to provide enough employment to sustain local populations. That expansion of nature tourism would in turn present ecological threats of its own.

The government of Belize, in league with nature tourism investors, would like to create an elaborate network of jungle lodges in the Cayo using the Mayan ruins as focal points for development (a model pioneered by Chan Chich Lodge) as part of the five-nation regional tourism initiative known as "La Ruta Maya." Such a system of lodges and trails would penetrate remote parts of Mayan country in the least developed region of Belize. Nature tourism development would then emerge as the primary threat to undeveloped jungle ecosystems as well as the subsistence economy of the Maya who inhabit them. The extension of roads, funded by World Bank loans, into remote jungle areas to make nature tourism possible simultaneously makes agricultural and logging development feasible by putting them closer to potential export markets, thus encouraging forest clearing. Such a development would therefore require the state to confer protected park and preserve status on additional parcels of jungle to protect its investment in nature tourism.

Although the state wants to expand ecotourism revenues, it also wants to expand revenues from natural resource extraction. In June 2005, oil was discovered in Belize. Drilling began in 2006. While oil extraction offers the possibility of increasing revenues (US$380 million was generated between 2005 and 2012) to a deeply indebted state, and providing economic expansion in a country with a 60 percent poverty rate, it also threatens the protected lands and marine reserves that form the basis of Belize's ecotourism economy. While the onshore oil concessions have been rapidly developed, the offshore concessions resulted in significant environmental protest. On April 18, 2013, the Belizean court invalidated the offshore oil concessions, citing a lack of environmental review, and effectively banned offshore oil development. The threat of oil development on the largest barrier reef in the Western hemisphere caused significant political mobilization. A petition drive drew enough support to trigger the nation's first "people's referendum," which attracted more than 10 percent of the eligible voting population of Belize. The referendum vote supported an offshore drilling ban. The long-term investment of the private sector in ecotourism, combined with the development of a significant domestic network of environmental organizations (see Lesson 19) combined to generate resistance to the shift toward extraction (especially in the barrier reef, which formed the early basis for the emergence of an ecotourism economy). The Belize Coalition To Save Our National Heritage (formed in response to the April 2010 Deepwater Horizon spill in the Gulf of Mexico) drew together over 40 domestic and international NGOs in support, representing every corner of the country. Clearly, the generalized threat to the reef from an offshore drilling accident has played out differently from the more localized, site-specific threat from onshore oil fields where drilling continues. Where onshore oil development poses mostly local trade-offs between extraction and ecotourism development, the threat of a major offshore oil spill that could undermine the entire reef-related ecotourism economy led Belizeans to choose environmentally protective ecotourism over potentially destructive extractive development.

THE PARADOXES AND TRADE-OFFS OF ECOTOURISM

The specifics regarding the case of Belize allow us to highlight some of the inherent questions of both ecotourism and sustainable development and to highlight some of the questions that serious attempts at sustainable development must address. For instance, who benefits? Whose economic growth is maximized? Which social groups make decisions about development? Do locals benefit? Does the state? How are benefits distributed? What's protected? At what cost? Recall that sustainable development, and ecotourism as an example of it, attempts to maximize economic, social, and ecological systems. Can ecotourism, as a form of sustainable development, really provide for sustained economic growth, sustained social equity, and sustained environmental protection?

We begin by highlighting the economic system and examining local employment. The cases demonstrate conflicts regarding who gets the best jobs as well as trade-offs between more employment and less environmental protection.

One of the best jobs in Belizean ecotourism is tour guide. In Belize, the state has developed a system of certification and regulation of nature tourism guides. With the assistance of a loan from the Inter-American Development Bank, the state contracted with Northern academic and private sector tourism consultants to design a system to guarantee the quality and ability of tour guides. Through the Belize Tourism Board, the state established a series of mandatory courses leading to legal certification of nature tourism guides. Tour guides are required to pay a license fee in order to be legally employed in the industry. The licenses are available only to those who have completed the required courses. A steep fine has been established for those found engaged in guide work without appropriate certification and licensing.

This program of tour guide standardization and control has a big impact on who remains in guide work and who is likely to enter guide work in the future. A key limiting factor is literacy and access to formal education. Belize is a nation where five different languages are spoken. Those with limited English reading and writing skills are less likely to pursue the required formal course work and to pass those courses if they try. The program therefore excludes many guides with extensive local environmental knowledge in favor of those with solid literacy but perhaps little local knowledge. In the rainforests of western Belize, literacy rates are lower, but knowledge of rain forest ecology is obviously higher. The value of that Indigenous knowledge has been decreased, while the value of formal academic skills has been increased. As the program has been implemented, fewer rainforest dwellers have been employed as guides at the same time that more formally trained guides from coastal Belize now explain rainforest ecology to nature consumers. If a goal of nature tourism as sustainable development is to provide a way for Indigenous environmental knowledge to be parlayed into a source of livelihood for local populations, such changes in the structure of the nature guide industry move away from sustainable development.

The number of people employed and "economically sustained" through ecotourism is often in direct relationship to the amount of environmental degradation caused by the enterprise. In other words, in terms of the scale of specific ecotourism development schemes, smaller-scale operations often employ fewer people and have fewer negative environmental impacts. The experience of Chan Chich Lodge shows that relatively small-scale operations can increase their employment capacity by providing more tourist amenities (pools, gardens, stables, etc.), but each of these comes at greater ecological costs. The concept of scale therefore relates not only to the size of the facility in terms of the number of tourists accommodated but also to the number of built amenities and the level of luxury in which each individual nature consumer is accommodated. Larger-scale operations are likely to provide more jobs, even though the increases are likely to be greatest at the lowest level of employment (waiters, maids, grounds maintenance workers) rather than the higher levels (chefs, managers, accountants, guides, bartenders). However, those increases in the number of tourists or levels of luxury in order to boost the social sustainability of the enterprise clearly decrease the ecological sustainability of the enterprise in terms of level of natural resource demands and waste production.

This process can be seen at Gaïa Riverlodge in the Cayo, where expanding occupancy requires additional clearing of riverine slopes, and the construction of additional amenities (a new bar at the base of Five Sisters falls) reduces the undisturbed quality of the local environment. As facilities expand and resource inputs and waste outputs increase, gains on the social side of sustainability become trade-offs with the ecological side. Without a careful and conscious balance, ecotourism development begins the slide into traditional tourism development, where ecologically low-impact tourism is abandoned in favor of ecologically higher-impact tourism of decreasingly intact ecosystems. While these kinds of changes in the ecological impact of nature tourism may not threaten local environments to the extent that all but the most discriminating nature consumers abandon the destination, the changes do mean that such a rural development scheme can decreasingly be defined as sustainable. As ecotourism becomes traditional tourism in a natural setting, social sustainability may increase (in terms of jobs) but ecological sustainability is lost, except in the relativistic sense that such development may still be more environmentally protective than resource extraction and export agriculture. The problems of maintaining appropriate scale, keeping ecological impacts minimal, and providing sufficient local employment while effectively competing with other potential uses of local ecosystems, notably resource extraction, lead us to the next paradox of ecotourism.

What is sustained by ecotourism? How does the environment fare? What are the costs to the ecosystem? There are numerous ways that the environmental system is affected by ecotourism.

Although the "eco" in ecotourism often implies that tourism may be ecologically benign, even low-impact tourism brings new sets of ecological withdrawals and additions to intact ecosystems. Low-impact is not no-impact, and even the most responsible ecotourism operators must recognize that nature would be less disturbed without their operations in remote and ecologically sensitive parts of the globe. Hence, ecotourism development in untouched and unthreatened ecosystems is, in and of itself, an ecologically disruptive force. Such unnecessary intrusions on nature, however mild, may be justified on the grounds that the exposure of nature consumers to these natural treasures increases their awareness of and dedication to the urgent need for environmental protection. As a consciousness-raising tool, low-impact ecotourism may inspire more general environmental protection than local environmental destruction. Nevertheless, at the local level, ecotourism does represent a primary, and perhaps the singular, ecological threat to "wild" nature in many parts of the world. That is, low-impact ecotourism connects ecosystems to the global economy. In areas with no human populations or hosting Indigenous subsistence-oriented economies, this can only bring ecological and/or social threat.

As noted, infrastructure expansion is one of the most obvious ways that ecotourism disturbs the environmental system. Ecotourism needs roads, dwellings, toilets, and more. Local roads are necessary to take tourists to remote regions. Typically, ecotourism either follows existing roads, which were built for extractive industries, or requires that new roads be built. In the case of the Mountain Pine Ridge, ecotourism occurs alongside logging, and access to ecotourism lodges is ironically facilitated by the extractive industry. Ecotourism generates value from sustaining resources in place (scenic ecosystems) rather than removing elements of the ecosystem and sending them to distant markets. Here, ecotourism competes with extraction for policy protection from the Belizean government. By following a logging path, the state can generate short-term revenue for itself, private capital investors, and local populations. The ecotourism path generates less revenue, though ideally over a longer period of time. States that need to increase immediate capital flows for debt repayment are unlikely to prioritize more sustainable tourism development over less sustainable extraction development. This means that international debt is likely to cause governments to prioritize less sustainable fast moneymaking schemes over more sustainable options (see Lesson 19). Private landowners may have similar fast-money priorities as well. Recall that Chan Chich was created only in response to public outrage that the land would be sold for export-oriented development.

When ecotourism emerges independently of extractive industries, new roads may need to be built. Here, ecotourism is aimed at bringing economic development to remote regions with intact ecosystems that have yet to be integrated into the global economy. Then, new transportation infrastructure becomes the first requirement of ecotourism development. Even if infrastructure is intended to facilitate ecologically low-impact tourism rather than traditional luxury tourism, the new roads (and airports) constructed by states, funded by IFIs, and promoted by private investors will represent the primary vectors of capital penetration into intact ecosystems. Ecotourism then becomes the vehicle of environmental disruption in otherwise undisturbed ecosystems, making it more difficult to view ecotourism as environmentally protective. This new infrastructure will make other potentially less sustainable economic activities (such as logging, mining, or agriculture) viable in previously inaccessible locations.

Finally, who decides? Who controls the process? What is the social system in which decisions and processes are developed? In Belize, two groups play key important roles: ecotourists and the government.

The ecotourist plays a large role in who decides. Like the definition of ecotourism, the definition of what constitutes an ecotourist varies widely. Nature tourists run the gamut from those using extensively modified nature (ski slopes, golf courses, etc.) to those using relatively undisturbed nature (all-terrain vehicle enthusiasts, jet skiers, etc.). Ecologically low-impact nature tourists tend to prefer lower-impact activities (hiking, canoeing, etc.) in relatively undisturbed nature. For this subgroup of nature consumers, the extent of the negative environmental impact of their nature-consuming activities is largely dependent on their proximity to the nature tourism destination and the total cost of their activity. The greater the distance they must travel to access ecotourism and the more money they spend to engage in ecotourism, the greater their negative impact on the global environment. Most ecotourism locations in the Global South are dependent on transnational ecotourists. These long-distance ecotourists may have the greatest negative environmental impacts despite their intention of engaging in ecologically low-impact forms of touring intact ecosystems and the value that they place on environmental protection. Despite their environmental awareness and concern, their global ecotourism endeavors require enormous levels of ecological withdrawal and addition.

What are the origins of the capital ecotourists' need to tour? The paradox is that this need is likely generated from ecologically destructive economic activities and investments in such activities. The surplus wealth that allows for the emergence of a group of relatively affluent Northern ecotourists who can be globally mobile is largely generated from the destruction of other ecosystems in other places, where other local populations pay the environmental, health, and cultural costs of production. Thus, even low-impact, environmentally conscious nature consumers seek to experience and protect some ecosystems by indirectly destroying other ecosystems, unless they fund their leisure travel from ecologically sustainable enterprises and investments.

The analysis brings us back to the paradox of transportation, but here at the global level. Transnational ecotourism requires vast expenditures of finite energy resources for inessential activities. Most transnational travel is fueled by high-altitude combustion of nonrenewable fossil fuels in jet aircraft. Any human activity that depends on the increased use of nonrenewable resources for a completely nonessential luxury activity accessible to only a small minority at the top of the world's wealth stratification pyramid can hardly be considered a form of sustainable development. Transnational ecotourism may promote relatively sustainable development in a specific ecologically threatened location but clearly cannot be considered ecologically sustainable as a global enterprise. If we accept the premise that air travel itself is a significant threat to sustainability in terms of ecological withdrawals (fossil fuel depletion) and ecological additions (greenhouse gases, ozone layer destruction), then the booming transnational tourism industry and even its ecologically conscious subindustry, ecotourism, represent more of a threat to, than a promise of, a more sustainable global development path. For the most part, low-impact ecotourism requires that nature consumers think globally but tour locally.

Where ecotourism utilizes public lands protected by the state in parks, preserves, and refuges, the sustainability of ecotourism is dependent on national development policy and orientation. That orientation will determine the extent to which public lands are managed in ways that are compatible with ecotourism and long-term ecological protection. As long as the state is dependent on ecotourism, public lands will be managed in ways that allow for that, even where other economic enterprises are permitted. Where ecotourism primarily uses privately owned land, the survival of ecotourism is wholly dependent on the economic choices of private landowners. In general, national development trajectories are less subject to rapid reorientation than private investment decisions, which may respond more immediately to shorter-term market opportunities.

The primary threats to state development orientation in terms of environmental protection and long-term management of public lands that is consistent with ecotourism development are the transnationally generated pressures originating from the IFIs. **Structural adjustment** policies promote the opening of national resource pools for TNCs in the interest of rapid national revenue generation to facilitate debt repayment. Debt crises and consequent structural adjustment policies therefore make national governments more likely to respond like private landowners to opportunities for quick profit and less likely to prioritize long-term sustainable development goals (see Lesson 19). Free trade reduces the authority of nations to set their own development priorities and agendas and undermines environmental protection initiatives necessary to promote sustainable ecotourism development. Ecotourism based on private land is primarily threatened by more lucrative short-term profit opportunities (as in the case of Chan Chich). Ecotourism based on public lands in nations with a large economic stake in tourism revenues is primarily threatened by the pressures of the IFIs to convert sustainable public land uses to rapid liquidation as a condition of further loans, entrance into free-trade blocs, or loan interest payment plans. The IFIs thus encourage states to prioritize short-term gain over long-term social and ecological goals. The IFIs have encouraged Belize to increase investments in agroexport production and extraction as a means by which to "stabilize" the national economy. However, agricultural and natural resource exports are subject to wide annual fluctuations in world market prices and have not historically been a source of economic stability for Southern nations. And agroexport and extraction are the primary threats to ecotourism development. Within the context of the global political economy, ecotourism based on the use of public protected lands probably has a greater chance of long-term social and ecological sustainability.

Sustainable development must ultimately be rooted in the relationship between specific human populations and specific ecosystems located in specific places. However, the main socioeconomic and political forces determining the relationships between human populations and natural systems are transnational and distinctly placeless. The TNCs and IFIs that increasingly determine the trajectory of natural resource utilization often operate with little regard for the specificities of places or the communities that inhabit them. Theoretically, ecotourism development can be designed and implemented in ways that meet both the ecological and social requirements of sustainable development in specific places. However, such local development does not occur within a macrostructural vacuum. In Belize, the impacts of the global political economy can be seen from the broad state reorientation toward unsustainable agroexport expansion down to the restructuring and redistribution of ecotourism guide employment. Therefore, if we are serious about pursuing sustainable development, we need to fully consider what is necessary to create the sociopolitical space in which communities may chart a sustainable development course in any specific place.

ALTERNATIVES TO DEVELOPMENT

As you've now seen in both the global-level conflicts between the Global North and the Global South at the United Nations Conference on Environment and Development and the national- and local-level paradoxes involved in establishing ecotourism-based development, determining the appropriate balance and acceptable trade-offs between meeting human social and economic needs and protecting the environment from which those needs must be met is complicated. It is also clear that natural science can offer us guidance toward sustainable development in terms of what impacts ecosystems can bear but can't offer us much direction in terms of determining how socioeconomic trade-offs could or should be negotiated. Environmental sociologists can provide analyses of what, how, and why various social needs, goals, and groups compete or coalesce around different ways of operationalizing the sustainable development concept.

Some analysts argue that traditional "development," including "sustainable development," have failed and that the limits of growth have been reached; thus, we need to reimagine and recreate a new social world. Rather than see this negatively, some, including Arturo Escobar (2015, 461), see the potential for new perspectives as "a beacon of hope." Alternative visions support environmental protection, social justice and economic vitality (not necessarily growth), and something more: something like the "good life," some happiness, some community, some connection, conviviality, some quality of life, something to live for. These ideas are akin to *buen vivir* discussed in

Lesson 19 and suggest that human potential and well-being does not simply boil down to economics and material gain. Instead of wanting more, more, more, there is also a reorientation toward enoughness and sufficiency. A concept that encapsulates these and is gaining in popularity is "degrowth," in which the "developed" nations downscale production and consumption to improve human well-being, ecological conditions, and social equity.

Ultimately, truly ecologically and socially sustainable development can be achieved only by making some tough collective decisions about what will be sustained and for whom and how social and ecological costs and benefits will be distributed. Such collective decisions are political; therefore, sustainable development is political. While sustainable development as a concept may have emerged as an effort to make an end run around conflicts between the economy, the environment, and distribution, sustainable development as a genuine enterprise will likely require that those conflicts be addressed directly. And it is the resolution of those conflicts that will prove to be the truly difficult work.

SOURCES

Agyeman, Julian, Robert D. Bullard, and Bob Evans. 2003. *Just Sustainabilities: Development in an Unequal World*. Cambridge, MA: The MIT Press.

Buttel, Frederick. 1998. "Some Observations on States, World Orders, and the Politics of Sustainability." *Organization and Environment* 11 (3): 261–286.

Escobar, Arturo. 2015. "Degrowth, Postdevelopment, and Transitions: A Preliminary Conversation." *Sustainability Science*. 10, 451–462.

Gould, Kenneth A. 1999. "Tactical Tourism: A Comparative Analysis of Rainforest Tourism in Ecuador and Belize." *Organization and Environment* 12 (3): 245–262.

Gould, Kenneth A. 2017. "Ecotourism Under Pressure: The Political Economy of Oil Extraction and Cruise Ship Tourism Threats to Sustainable Development in Belize." *Environmental Sociology* 3 (3):237–247.

Humphrey, Craig R., Tammy L. Lewis, and Frederick H. Buttel. 2002. *Environment, Energy, and Society: A New Synthesis*. Belmont, CA: Wadsworth.

Joyner, Leah, Qwynne Lackey, and Kelly Bricker. 2018. Ecotourism Outlook 2018. Outdoor Recreation, Education, & Tourism Lab, University of Utah. Accessed November 25, 2019. https://ttra.com/wp-content/uploads/2018/11/Ecotourism-Outlook-2018.pdf

Klein, Naomi. 2014. *This Changes Everything: Capitalism vs. the Climate*. New York: Simon & Schuster.

Kothari, Ashish, Federico Demaria, and Alberto Acosta. 2014. "Buen Vivir, Degrowth and Ecological Swaraj: Alternatives to sustainable development and the Green Economy." *Development* 57 (3–4): 362–375.

Lewis, Tammy L. 2016. *Ecuador's Environmental Revolutions: Ecoimperialists, Ecodependents, and Ecoresisters*. Cambridge, MA: The MIT Press.

McMichael, Philip. 2016. *Development and Social Change: A Global Perspective*. 6th ed. Thousand Oaks, CA: Sage Publications.

Meadows, Donella H., Dennis L. Meadows, Jorgen Randers, and William Behrens III. 1972. *The Limits to Growth*. New York: Universe Books.

Mol, Arthur P. J. and Gert Spaargaren. 2000. "Ecological Modernisation Theory in Debate: A Review." *Environmental Politics* 9 (1): 17–49.

Pattullo, Patty. 1996. *Last Resorts: The Cost of Tourism in the Caribbean.* Kingston, Jamaica: Ian Randle Publishers.

Rich, Bruce. 1994. *Mortgaging the Earth: World Bank, Environmental Improverishment and the Crisis of Development.* New York: Earthscan.

Sutherland, Anne. 1998. *The Making of Belize: Globalization in the Margins.* Westport, CT: Bergin and Garvey.

United Nations. Sustainable Development Goals. 2015 https://sustainabledevelopment.un.org

World Commission on Environment and Development. 1987. *Our Common Future.* Oxford, UK: Oxford University Press.

Conclusion: Unanswered Questions and the Future of Environmental Sociology

Kenneth A. Gould and Tammy L. Lewis

Throughout the preceding 20 lessons in environmental sociology, some inter-linking themes emerged that coincide with the four parts of the book. These themes summarize what environmental sociology is and what we defini-tively know:

1. Historically, sociologists have separated social and ecological systems; however, environmental sociologists have sought to integrate these systems both theoretically and empirically.

2. Environmental problems are the result of human social organization, and as such, their solutions are not simply technical but require chang-ing human social organization.

3. The negative effects of environmental problems are not equally distrib-uted; less socially powerful groups suffer more than others.

4. There are varied responses to environmental changes; those that at-tempt to alter human social organization have a tall task and face resistance. There is no single or simple answer to solving environmen-tal problems.

The preceding lessons in this book presented you with a broad overview of the kinds of questions environmental sociologists ask and the kinds of analyses they construct. Clearly, this book could not present *all* of the questions environmental sociologists have asked or *all* of the analyses they have constructed. But even if it could, it would still not include all of the questions environmental sociologists *could* or *should* ask or all of the anal-yses they *could* or *should* construct. And we do not pretend to be able to envision and list all of those here. What we can do with the few pages that remain is to suggest some of the questions that we believe most need to be addressed by environmental sociologists in the near future and to sug-gest the kinds of analyses that we see as most pressing for environmental sociologists to construct.

THE CITIZEN QUESTIONS—NO EASY ANSWERS

Throughout many semesters of teaching environmental sociology, students have confronted each other and us with the following question: What should we do to solve environmental problems? The lessons in this collection demonstrate how environmental problems are created by social arrangements and how the features of those social arrangements shape our collective responses to (or failures to respond to) environmental problems.

What can be done to address environmental problems? What can we do? How do we create social change? Where do we start? At what level should change be directed? Do we need to work simultaneously at changing individuals' opinions and actions and institutions' organization and practices? How do we begin to create a sustainable world?

The analysis inevitably leads to questions of our goals. What do we want? What's the desired end? What alternatives are available? How do we get outside the box? As sociologists, we understand that what seems "natural" and taken for granted is socially constructed and, thus, socially changeable. We encourage our students to reconstruct and envision new social arrangements. Some of their constructions and ours are utopian. However, given that students now also understand that power relationships are part of what keeps environmental problems problematic, we can also think about how we can make pragmatic (not just hopeful) steps toward these utopias. We can analyze various strategies. Should we form a green army that storms capitalist headquarters? Work to elect leaders who prioritize environmental and social issues? Join labor movements? Become teachers? Move to the woods?

In the 2005 book *The Logic of Sufficiency*, Thomas Princen posed the following set of questions:

> What if modern society put a priority on the material security of its citizens and the ecological integrity of its resource base? What if it took ecological constraint as a given, not a hindrance but a source of long-term economic security? How would it organize itself, structure its industry, shape its consumption?

How we proceed will depend on what we value. We ask our students to define "the good life," "development," and what they want for their futures. Despite being bombarded with media messages, advertisements, and a dominant social paradigm of "more is better," our students (and hopefully you, too) now question these basic social assumptions. A higher gross national product per capita is typically not part of student responses to questions about their visions of their futures. We hope you are also thinking about quality of life, not just quantity of stuff.

It would be nice if we could close this book by offering you "50 simple things" you could do to bring the social system–ecosystem interaction into better balance. Of course, by now you are familiar enough with the sociological perspective on environmental problems to understand that we think the solutions are not simple, nor do they rest solely on the changed behavior of individuals. More important than changing individuals is changing the relationships among them.

While it is nice to think that changing social institutions and social processes in ways that are more protective of the environment will ultimately be good for everyone, the lessons that have preceded this one illustrate that with social change, the distribution of social and environmental costs and benefits can be, and often is, quite uneven. How the costs and benefits of pro-environmental changes are distributed is likely to have a substantial impact on who supports those changes and who opposes them.

A SOCIOLOGICAL ENVIRONMENTAL IMAGINATION

In looking to solutions to environmental problems, C. Wright Mills's classic 1959 piece on **"the sociological imagination"** in the book by the same name and the chapter titled "The Promise" presents a still-useful analysis. Mills differentiated between "personal troubles" and "public issues." Personal troubles are within the scope of the individual and may be addressed by private strategies. However, what many of us experience as our own problem may also be shared by many other people. When this is the case, what seems to be very personal is actually what Mills called a public issue; however, we often fail to see it in this way. For example, say that you live in the city and suffer from asthma. You may consider yourself sickly and do what you need to do to manage your condition. This is a logical private strategy to solving your problem. However, if you step back and look at other people who live on your block, you might notice that a lot of people on your block have asthma. If this is the case, your personal problem is actually a public issue. The cause of public issues is not an individual defect; it is related to how we have organized society. Thus, your asthma may have little to do with your personal genetic makeup but instead, it may have a lot to do with the polluting industries in your neighborhood. Public issues such as this can only be fully addressed by changing how we organize such things. The nature of social organization creates public issues, which in turn affect many individuals. Public issues must be addressed by public strategies. Individuals can change their "selves" but alone cannot change those institutions that create public issues and, thus, affect their lives. Public issues must be addressed collectively.

Environmental problems are "public issues," and as such, their solutions cannot be found in individual behavioral changes alone. The solutions to environmental problems will be found in changing social institutions and processes. One thing that we hope the preceding lessons have made clear is that environmental problems are not simply the result of greedy corporate executives, ill-informed consumers, or careless workers, whose bad individual behavior can be adjusted with better environmental (and perhaps moral) education. While we agree that greed, consumption, and work all play a part in the imbalance between social systems and ecosystems, the problems stem from the way these behaviors are woven into our existing social structures, norms, and roles. From a sociological perspective, it makes little sense to try to "fix" individuals if the roles they play and the decisions they make in regard to the environment are largely generated externally, from the social order they participate in.

Changing that social order to address environmental problems will be one of the great collective public issue challenges of our era. How, then, shall we proceed?

BACK TO THE CLASSICS

We know that our productive system and the ecological system are linked: increased production creates increased environmental additions and withdrawals that lead to environmental problems; these environmental problems restrict further production. In his classic 1980 book *The Environment: From Surplus to Scarcity*, Allan Schnaiberg termed the tension between productive expansion and ecological limits the "socioenvironmental dialectic." He asked how the tension between the two can be reconciled.

Schnaiberg identified three ways the dialectic has been synthesized historically: (1) the **economic synthesis**, (2) the **managed scarcity synthesis**, and (3) the **ecological synthesis**. These come about by the choices of social-political actors engaged in the treadmill of production. For each of these syntheses, he considered what would happen with production, the environment, and social inequality. Let's look at what he projected.

The *economic synthesis* continues with production expansion and accelerates the treadmill of production (see Lesson 2). The result is increased ecological additions and withdrawals, as well as increased inequality, in part due to the use of high-energy technology and the displacement of workers (see Lesson 4). Politically, a great effort is required to deal with social welfare issues. Schnaiberg argued that under this scenario, the social future will play out as "the rich rob the poor."

The *managed scarcity synthesis* involves reducing or altering production to some extent to protect aspects of the environment, largely through mild forms of state intervention. Socially, the protection costs are unevenly distributed, with the poor taking most of the burden (see Lesson 10). This constitutes "business as usual," at least in the United States.

The third synthesis, the *ecological synthesis*, reconciles the social and the ecological systems by decreasing both production and inequality. Here, we use Schnaiberg's words:

> If the ecological synthesis could be achieved, it would be the most durable of the three. Production organization, once set around the biospheric capacities and flows, would require only small adjustments over time to maintain a sustained material production. . . . No eternal social peace is guaranteed by such a

synthesis, though. Changes over time in the social and political structure could lead to increased pressures for production expansion. Capital accumulation could grow within certain groups, leading to constituencies favoring either managed scarcity or economic synthesis. . . . The ecological synthesis is the most difficult to anticipate because it represents a major departure from managed scarcity. . . . The transition from managed scarcity to ecological synthesis is likely to be a long and painful one, if it does take place. (1980, 426)

Powerful growth coalitions and treadmill actors make this path socially and politically difficult (see Lessons 3 and 5). They will resist both ecological limits to production and more equitable social distribution of costs and benefits.

How do we create changes? How do we move toward an ecological synthesis? How can we change production to change the ecological and social systems? Schnaiberg argued that it would be tough to do this industry by industry or through the whole economy without causing social problems. A possible route is through state intervention. Again, in Schnaiberg's words

The task is a monumental technical and political one. We must first estimate a biospherically and geopolitically feasible, sustainable production level for the society. And then we must decide how to allocate the production options and the fruits of such production. (431)

Schnaiberg laid out "a socio-environmental program" with seven elements designed to shift us away from high-energy, low-labor styles of production to low-capital, high-labor forms. For example, it calls for taxation of new fixed capital (to shift to low capital) and employment tax credits (to encourage labor intensity). These goals are reformist in that they can take place within our current capitalist political-economic system. However, it is likely that those who benefit most from the current conditions will resist them.

Another alternative—socialist restructuring—has potential in that social welfare is treated seriously in socialist systems; however, historically, Schnaiberg argued, there has been variability with regard to how socialist approaches have interacted with the environment. Historically, many socialist societies have prioritized social welfare over environmental protection. In other words, socialism, on its own, is not the answer to reaching an ecological synthesis.

In the end, Schnaiberg's analysis of the treadmill of production suggests that the most fruitful path forward is in the formation of coalitions among social groups. He concluded his (1980) book by arguing as follows:

The treadmill of political capitalism was not built overnight, nor will it disappear in the short term. Sustained efforts at consciousness-raising, commitment to political conflict and the development of coordination between environmentalist and social equity movements may serve to take it apart, strut by strut. (440)

Interestingly, another important early thinker in environmental sociology, Frederick H. Buttel, arrived at a similar conclusion in laying out alternative environmental futures. In one of his last publications (2003), Buttel assessed four basic mechanisms of environmental improvement: (1) environmental activism/movements, (2) state environmental regulation, (3) ecological modernization, and (4) international environmental governance. (He also assessed green consumerism but largely dismissed it as a major source of reform.) He was concerned with understanding which is the most promising way forward for a "more socially secure and environmentally friendly arrangement."

> When all is said and done, the pressures for an environmentally problematic business as usual [Schnaiberg's managed scarcity synthesis] . . . have become so strong that citizen environmental mobilization is now the ultimate guarantor that public responsibility is taken to ensure environmental protection. (336)

He saw environmental movements and activism as the foundation of reform. Fundamental to this are the coalitions that have been formed between environmental organizations and other groups. Some of these include coalitions with the immigrant rights movement, the labor movement, the sustainable agriculture movement, the consumer movement, the anti-biotechnology movement, the genetic resources conservation movement, the antiracism movement, the slow food movement, and the human rights movement.

In sum, both of these founding thinkers in environmental sociology came to the conclusion that there need to be coalitions of social movement organizations that come together to work both for ecological rationality and social equity. In other words, things will not get better "naturally." If we want to see a more fair and ecologically sound world, we must work collectively to make it happen.

A FUTURE FOR ENVIRONMENTAL SOCIOLOGY?

Environmental sociology has sought to integrate the natural environment into sociological analysis. What environmental sociology needs to do now is to take that integration and extend it into all aspects of sociology as a whole. Environmental sociology has largely remained a subdiscipline unto itself. The result has been that little of our analysis of the interplay between social systems and ecosystems has been infused into the other subdisciplines of sociology. If environmental problems are going to be solved in ways that enhance the general well-being of people, the relationship between social systems and ecosystems has to be an important consideration in analyses of the nature of work and labor, social institutions, science and technology, social movements, cities and communities, and so forth. That is, the promise of environmental sociology to fully integrate the relationship between human society and the natural world into the ways in which we think about what society is and how our goals for society can be achieved has yet to be fully realized. The ultimate goal for environmental sociology ought to be that there will no longer be such a thing as "environmental" sociology. Instead, sociology, the study of society, will, by definition, be fully inclusive of the ways that societies are shaped by and reshape the natural world.

Within such an environmentalized sociology, the study of labor and work would, by definition, include consideration of the environmental health of workers, the ways in which labor participates (or fails to) in natural resource decisions, the impacts of the distribution of remuneration from labor on the natural world, and the ways in which workplaces and the organization of work enhance or degrade environmental quality. The same would largely be true of the sociological study of institutions, culture, race, gender, law, religion, and so forth. Environmental sociology will be successful when it becomes unthinkable to attempt to analyze aspects of social life without consideration of, or reference to, the natural world that, ultimately, provides the context in which social life happens. To be a sociologist would then require an environmental analytical lens as part of the larger sociological lens. Without the relationship between social systems and ecosystems in the equation, the sociological imagination is only partial and ultimately flawed.

LOOKING SOUTH

We find some hope for a more fully environmentalized vision of sociology in the scholars and scholarship of the Global South. As you read in Lesson 19, most Southern environmental movements and activists do not view environmental problems and development problems separately but rather as a cohesive matrix of production and distribution issues. Such a Southern view resonates with the approaches suggested by Allan Schnaiberg and Frederick Buttel. Therefore, one path for the social organization of environmental sociologists we see as promising is greater intellectual exchange with scholars in the Global South.

As we noted in the Introduction to this book, because of the way that sociologists have organized themselves professionally, there has been only limited organized intellectual exchange between US-based environmental sociologists and our colleagues in other countries. There has been a concerted effort to foster greater interaction between US and European environmental sociologists, and those exchanges have invigorated the subfield. Given that most of the environment, and most of society, is encompassed in the geographical and social space often referred to as the "Global South" and that the tendency in the South is to take a more holistic view of environment and development, we believe that a concerted and sustained effort at fostering similar intellectual exchange between Northern and Southern environmental sociologists is crucial to the future of the subfield. In other words, environmental sociologists need to consciously organize to change their patterns of social relationships too.

SOURCES

Buttel, Frederick. 2003. "Environmental Sociology and the Explanation of Environmental Reform." *Organization & Environment* 16:306–344.

Catton, William R., and Riley E. Dunlap. 1978. "Environmental Sociology: A New Paradigm." *American Sociologist* 13:41–49.

Guha, Ramachandra. 2000. *Environmentalism: A Global History*. New York: Longman.

Guha, Ramachandra and Juan Martinez-Alier. 1997. *Varieties of Environmentalism: Essays North and South*. London: Earthscan.

Keck, Margaret E. and Kathryn Sikkink. 1998. *Activists Beyond Borders: Advocacy Networks in International Politics*. Ithaca, NY: Cornell University Press.

Mills, C. Wright. 1959. *The Sociological Imagination*. New York: Grove Press.

Princen, Thomas. 2005. *The Logic of Sufficiency*. Cambridge, MA: MIT Press.

Schnaiberg, Allan. 1980. *The Environment: From Surplus to Scarcity*. New York: Oxford University Press.

Index/Glossary

climate gentrification: The process whereby affluent individuals and house-holds replace less affluent households in areas destroyed or threatened by climate-related events (such as hurricanes) or replace less affluent residents in those areas vulnerable to climate change that have some form of protection from likely hazards (such as high ground in a flood-prone area)., 151–155, 152t

climate justice: The view that climate change is a general human rights issue characterized by severe inequalities in contributions to, benefits from, and consequences of climate change. Nations in the Global South have neither contributed to, nor benefitted from, climate change, but re-main most vulnerable to its adversities; whereas nations in the Global North have greatly contributed to and benefitted from climate change, but remain the least scathed from its effects., 280

coal combustion waste (CCW): The ash that is left behind after coal is burned in coal-fired power plants. CCW contains all of the heavy metals present in coal but in a more concentrated (toxic) form. CCW is typically stored in liquid form in impoundments next to the power plants from which it came., 163–164

collective action groups: A group of people banded together to engage in direct action to preserve their local means of subsistence ("the environment"); their actions are voluntary and uncompensated; their efforts are often contrasted with "professionalized environmental organizations.", 349

commodity chains: A concept indicating that the production of goods or commodities forms a series of links with nodes situated in different locations, often in different countries. An example would be parts of an auto-mobile being produced in different countries and assembled in another., 31, 32, 53, 353

community trauma: Collective pain brought about as a result of the loss of deep communal ties, established social networks, and beloved neighborhoods or landscapes in a disaster., 255

Moreover, women are more concerned about, affected by, and motivated to act against environmental degradation compared to men. Taking a social constructivist approach, ecofeminists offering women's relatively greater concern for the environment stems from the cultural contexts and norms that positions them as care-givers, subsistence providers, and collectors of resources for the house-hold. Given their deep connection of women to the environment makes them especially well-suited to advance sustainability goals. As a social movement frame, ecofeminists believe that solutions to environmental problems must incorporate feminist perspectives., 29, 48–52, 54, 283–285, 340–341

Ecofeminism (Mies & Shiva), 49

ecoimperialism: The imposition of environmental ideas and practices de-rived from dominant societies on subordinated populations, especially with respect to assumptions about the universality of Western definitions and objectives in the management of environmental resources. See also environmental imperialism., 285, 360–362

ecological colonialism, 50

ecological externalities: The environmental costs of producing a good or service that are absorbed by individuals, institutions, or societies as a whole but not included as costs of production by the producing firm. The costs of pollution from a production process may include increased health costs to exposed individuals; remediation costs borne by taxpayers through the work of local, state, or federal environmental agencies; or lost recreational enjoyment of ecosystems. In pursuit of increased profitability, firms tend to oppose environmental regulations and standards that aim to make them internalize pollution costs in their economic calculus through safer waste disposal, waste treatment, or waste reduction., 81

ecological footprint: A metaphor for the amount of land necessary to sustain consumption and absorb wastes for an individual (or group or nation)., 19, 31, 32, 141, 141*t*, 174

ecological Marxism: A theoretical tradition based on Karl Marx's description and critique of capitalism. It emphasizes the contradictions of the system (e.g., class inequality) and the crises they create. It highlights the contra-dictions between the capitalist means of production and the environment., 29, 40–43, 53, 371

ecological modernization theory (EMT): A theory based on the principle that cap-italism possesses the institutional capacity to reverse existing environmental destruction and that it can become environmentally sustainable. The theory proposes modernization through the employment of green or environmentally sustainable technologies.

    applications of, 29, 31
    on climate change, 286
    corporations in, 31–33
    critiques of, 53–54, 289
    on environmental impact, 276–277
    industrialization in, 32
    on sustainable development, 369

ecological synthesis: A relationship between society and the environment in which demands for production expansion are routinely subordinated to environmental limits and the necessity of sustaining the ecological systems and processes. Under such a regime, demands for the alleviation of material deprivation are met primarily through redistribution., 392–393

ecological violence: The disruption or destruction of ecosystems in whole or in part, whether intentional or otherwise. This can occur in an instant or over a long period of time in what Rob Nixon calls "slow violence.", 59, 64, 71, 188, 333

ecology
    of affluence, 349
    deep, 339–341, 345
    hog waste and impact on, 248–249
    industrial, 369
    intellectual history of, 3–4
    theories of environmental impact in, 276–280
ecology movement, 5–6

economic Darwinism: A theory that proposes that only the fittest individuals or organizations will prosper in a competitive economic environment. Representing socially constructed economic structures as natural processes, this theory views economic "winners" (firms or individuals) as inherently more "fit" than economic "losers," and so justifies out-comes as natural and thus morally acceptable., 77

economic globalization: The ways in which economic activity is integrated on a planetary scale. While there has been some amount of transnational economic exchange for centuries, in recent decades, levels of trade and investment across national borders have increased dramatically.

economic growth: Increase in the amount of goods and services produced over time; often measured at the national level by gross domestic product (GDP).

economic synthesis: A relationship between society and the environment in which environmental concerns are routinely subordinated to demands for production expansion and economic growth. Under such a regime, both ecological disorganization and inequality continually increase., 392

ecosystems: A complex set of relationships between living organisms and the nonliving components of their environment. Ecosystem communities are linked together through energy flows and nutrient cycles.

ecotourism: A form of tourism in which "nature" is a major draw for the tourist and in which some effort is made to minimize the negative environmental impacts from tourism activities. Ecotourism is marketed toward those concerned about the environment and is often presented as a means to enjoy and preserve natural areas, although such claims are sometimes suspect., 371–385

elitist movement: A movement made up of individuals from powerful social groups;

genocide: The term is often narrowly associated with the Holocaust. But it is worth noting that the United Nations Convention on the Prevention and Punishment of the Crime of Genocide, which was adopted on December 9th, 1948, and written on the heels of Nazi Germany, was not simply about the Holocaust. In 1948, the United Nations General Assembly de-fined genocide as "any of the following acts committed with intent to destroy, in whole or in part, a national, ethnic, racial, or religious group as such, killing members of the group, causing serious bodily or mental harm to members of the group, deliberately inflicting on the group conditions of life calculated to bring about its physical destruction in whole or in part, imposing measures intended to prevent births within the group, and forcibly transferring children of the group to another group.", 191

germ theory: A dominant theory in Western biomedicine that identifies pathogens, such as bacteria and viruses, as a fundamental cause of illness and disease., 201

Global North: The Global North/Global South divide is largely measured by socioeconomic and political criteria. The Global North is generally considered to be the richer and more developed regions of the globe, whereas the Global South is generally considered to be the poorer and less developed regions of the globe. "Development" is generally measured by some combination of the following: GNP, education, access to basic human rights—including food, water, and shelter—life expectancy, and mortality rates. The Global North includes the United States, Canada, Western Europe, and Japan. The Global South comprises most of the countries in Africa, Latin America, and Asia.

trapped in shale formations to be released and captured. This technique uses huge quantities of fresh water and generates a large amount of toxic wastewater after the process is complete., 105, 165–168, 315

hydroelectricity, 172–173
HYV (high-yield variety) crops, 137

I

IADB (Inter-American Development Bank), 358, 380
IEA (International Energy Agency), 161
IFIs. *See* international financial institutions
illness. *See also* environmental health; public health; *specific conditions*
    from biomass burning, 173
    contested, 203–205
    etiology of, 201, 203
    germ theory and, 201
    from herbicides, 47
    from hog waste, 242–243
    from industrial pollutants, 49
    miasma theory and, 201
    from pesticides, 222
    from radiation exposure, 93, 169
    waterborne, 126
Imagined Communities: Reflections on the Origin and Spread of Nationalism (Anderson), 64
IMF (International Monetary Fund), 352
immigrant populations
    environmental refugees, 145–149
    exclusionary policies targeting, 64, 65
    language used in discussion of, 65
    as scapegoats for environmental problems, 145
    TPS program for, 148–149
    xenophobia in relation to, 144, 145
impact science, 114, 116, 117

imperialism: A system of foreign power in which another culture, people, and way of life penetrate, transform, and come to define a colonized society.

    defined, 66
    ecoimperialism, 285, 360–362
    economic, 113
    state practices of, 66–73, 183, 188

implicatory denial: A concept from Stanley Cohen (2011) indicating that events are acknowledged but are not seen as psychologically disturbing or as carrying a moral imperative to act. Unlike other forms of denial that Cohen has coined, knowledge is not at issue, but doing the "right" thing with the knowledge is., 300–301

implicit hunger, 223–224

implosion: The process of one social phenomenon collapsing, or contracting, into another—for example, the merging of the categories of being "at home" and "shopping.", 23

India
    Chipko Movement in, 353–354
    pollution prevention programs in, 369
    population control strategies in, 141
    Sardar Sarovar Dam in, 354
Indians. *See* Indigenous peoples
Indigenous Environmental Network, 71, 334, 342
Indigenous peoples
    dam construction and, 173
    Dawes Severalty Act and, 69–70
    doctrine of discovery and, 69
    ecological colonialism and, 50
    environmental health and, 200
    environmental movements by, 332–334, 345, 354
    pipeline construction and, 71, 188–189, 333
    reservation lands of, 70
    sovereignty of, 69, 71, 189, 333, 343
    toxic waste sites near, 184, 188
    water contamination among, 183, 189

industrial capitalism: An economic system built on the mass production of goods and sustained economic growth under a free market., 5, 35, 201, 210

industrial ecology, 369
industrialization
    of agriculture, 201, 216–220, 223, 233
    in classical sociology, 5
    deep ecology on, 340, 345
    in ecological modernization theory, 32
    of food production, 216–220, 223
    fossil fuels and, 125
    of hog industry, 233–234, 240, 242
    of production, 79, 125
    toxic waste generation due to, 63
    in world systems theory, 44, 45

industrialization of agriculture: The production of food and fiber in a rationalized system that relies on processes and strategies (including mechanization, large-scale production, high use of artificial inputs, and increased specialization of both labor

market-based approaches: The use of the market by social movement organizations to achieve their objectives.

metabolic rift: A Marxist term, popularized in environmental sociology by John Bellamy Foster, that describes the transfer of energy from the countryside to the cities when food produced in the former is sold in the latter. Soil nutrients decline in agricultural areas because they are transferred to cities, where they are disposed of as waste, creating pollution and health risk., 41–43, 53, 143, 278–280, 285

miasma theory: A theory from the 19th century that identified the external environment as a key causal mechanism for illness and disease. This theory was replaced by germ theory., 201

mitigation: The planning and implementation of strategies designed to lessen or eliminate potential disaster impacts.

modernity: The period in Western history beginning approximately in the 16th or 17th century, characterized by the rise of capitalism and the move away from medieval institutions.

modernization theory: A theory popular among US policymakers during the Cold War that explained global inequality as a result of different levels of economic and cultural progress rather than as a set of innate, inherited, or moral characteristics. Modernization was the theoretical

location. Also, the extent to which a person or com-munity has access to protective shelter during a disaster., 246, 257, 259–261

pigs. *See* hog industry
Pinchot, Gifford, 350
pipeline projects, 71, 188–189, 321, 333
Plan Colombia, 68

planned obsolescence: a design process in which the product is created to have an ar-tificially short lifespan to ensure that con-sumers will have to buy a new product in the future. Through utilizing this design process, companies increase demand for their newest products even through the older models are still functional., 37–38, 40

plantation agriculture, 143, 144*f*
Plato, 111

pluralism: A term that describes politics in a democracy as a process in which various stakeholders (e.g., trade unions, business groups, faith-based organizations, and activist organizations) engage in a compe-tition for access to state resources and gov-ernmental influence., 60, 66

POET model, 276

point source pollution: A form of pol-lution that has a single, distinct point of origin (i.e., a smokestack or drainpipe)., 246–248

political consumerism: The notion that what you buy can be political. Specifically, it is the idea that people can express their ethical and political values through their shopping choices., 46, 226, 228, 229

political ideology: A set of beliefs about how power should be distributed and gov-ernment should be organized., 199, 203

political opportunity structures: Structural factors that constrain and/or enable social movement organizations. The changing power of social movement organizations relative to other actors shaping politics., 331–332

Pollan, Michael, 79, 80
pollution. *See also* toxic waste
    air (*see* air pollution)
    cancer and, 43, 49
    chemical, 78

environmental inequality and, 62–63
exporting of, 45
health effects of, 43
from hog waste, 233, 246–248
insurance policies related to, 33
from manufacturing, 313
metabolic rift in creation of, 143
point vs. nonpoint source, 246–248
prevention strategies, 368–369
uneven distribution of, 187
water (*see* water pollution)
polychlorinated biphenyls (PCBs), 94, 184

population: The number of people living in a specific geographical area at a specific point in time., 133–155. *See also* population growth

    carrying capacity and, 141, 143
    case studies, 145–155
    climate change and, 282
    defined, 134
    in evolutionary theory, 135, 136
    of industrial cities, 125
    overpopulation, 145, 348
    relationship with environment,
        133–135, 155
    risk distribution across, 46, 47
    settlement patterns, 123–124
    wealth distribution across, 61
The Population Bomb (Ehrlich), 141

population density: The average number of people who live in a specified area unit, usually a square mile or square kilometer., 134

population growth: A measure of changes in population over time by taking a popu-lation at one time and adding all the births and immigrants who arrive before a later time, while subtracting the deaths and emigrants.

    calculation of, 134
    control strategies, 141–142
    deep ecology on, 339, 340
    defined, 134
    energy consumption and, 158
    in Global North/Global South, 144–145
    international comparisons, 138, 138*t*,
        142, 142*t*
    Malthus on, 135
    pyramids for display of, 139–140,
        139–140*f*, 146–147*f*
    relationship with environment, 133, 135
    sustainable development and, 142

vertical integration: A business strategy focused on consolidating multiple stages of a single commodity chain. Vertical integration is achieved when a firm or small set of firms controls all of the stages of production (e.g., inputs, production, processing, retailing)., 99, 216, 233, 235

vulnerable: Those groups and individuals particularly susceptible to harm.

W

waste sinks: An area or element of the environment that social institutions use to absorption human made waste., 128